D1559714

RESISTANCES AND INTERVENTIONS

RESISTANCES AND INTERVENTIONS

The Nature of Therapeutic Work

Robert Langs, M.D.

New York • Jason Aronson • London

Chapter 11 is based on "Interactional and Communicative Aspects of Resistance," which appeared in *Contemporary Psychoanalysis*, vol. 16, pp. 16–52 (1980).

Chapter 12 is based on three papers: "On the Formulation and Timing of Interventions," which appeared in the *Journal of the American Academy of Psychoanalysis*, vol. 7, pp. 477–498 (1979); "Interventions in the Bipersonal Field," which appeared in *Contemporary Psychoanalysis*, vol. 15, pp. 1–54 (1979); and "On the Formulation of an Interpretation," which appeared in *Contemporary Psychoanalysis*, vol. 16, pp. 460–478 (1980).

ISBN 87668-433-9

Library of Congress Catalog Number 80-69667

Manufactured in the United States of America.

To the memory of
Ralph Greenson

CLASSICAL PSYCHOANALYSIS AND ITS APPLICATIONS

A Series of Books
Edited by Robert Langs, M.D.

CONTENTS

x CONTENTS

PREFACE

The completion of the present volume is of considerable importance to myself personally, and, I hope, meaningful to my readers as well. It is the last of a series of four volumes on the fundamental dimensions of the therapeutic interaction and its techniques. Previously I examined the basics of attending to this interaction in *The Listening Process* (1978a), the ground rules, setting, and hold in *The Therapeutic Environment* (1979), and the realm of transference and countertransference in their broadest sense in *Interactions* (1980a).

In the course of this work, I have completed a transition which began as a shift from the usual classical psychoanalytic approach to one that I first termed adaptational-interactional, and which I now characterize as the *communicative* approach to classical psychotherapy and psychoanalysis. The present constellation of clinical precepts, theory, and specific techniques shares much with prevailing classical psychoanalysis, but it is to be distinguished from that eminent, however ill-defined, body of theory and technique in extremely important ways. It is these differences which I believe each therapist should personally experience, confront, and debate; hopefully, he will discover the distinctive aspects of communicative classical technique important to his own clinical work.

In an effort to broaden the implications of the communicative approach, and to make it as comprehensive as possible, I have developed in this volume a series of ideas regarding the object relationship between the patient and therapist. Focusing the listening process on this aspect of treatment helps to develop a systematic consideration of what I term the maturational mode of relatedness between the two participants to therapy, which has implications both for technique and the process of cure. The communicative approach to the therapeutic relationship is thereby broadened and its theoretical foundation expanded and solidified. The overall goal has been to demonstrate that the communicative approach is the means to the best possible therapy, and provides the wisest and most comprehensive perspective available on the therapeutic interaction.

I am aware that these are bold words, but I consider it necessary to state my challenge to current clinical practice as clearly as possible. In each of the three volumes which have preceded the present one, I have presented clinical data, a method of observation, and a series of conclusions and postulates in as specific a fashion as possible. In my study of the communicative interchange (Langs 1980a), I also carefully reviewed the pertinent psychoanalytic literature in order to specifically delineate the areas of agreement and disagreement between the classical and communicative positions. In the present work, I have extended these ideas as definitively as possible.

In introducing the present volume, I feel an obligation to clarify why I have turned to a study of resistances and intervening in this last volume on technique, rather than from the outset. I remember quite well a discussion with Ralph Greenson, the prime theoretician of psychoanalytic technique to whom this book is dedicated, in which he asked why my two-volume *Technique of Psychoanalytic Psychotherapy* (1973, 1974), did not, as his work had done, begin with resistances? After all, the acceptance of unconscious processes, of transference, and of the existence of resistances, are the fundamentals of psychoanalysis. Why postpone until the end a consideration of this subject so vital to actual clinical practice?

In approaching the present series—I think of the four volumes as constituting the *communicative series* on technique—I was quite mindful of Greenson's words. As I developed the listening process,

I thought often of how to relate it to the subject of resistances. And while it was possible to learn how to more carefully listen for expressions of resistance, somehow the need to fully delineate the nature of the listening process itself took all of my attention. I felt justified in this effort by believing that a more complete understanding of the listening and validating processes would enable me to better deal with the difficult subject of resistances once I confronted it.

I thought of turning immediately to that very subject; still, I found it impossible to do so, since I had not yet clearly established the nature of the therapeutic setting, its meanings and functions. Without a clear understanding of the therapeutic environment, it would be impossible to define the nature of the transactions which occurred within its confines, that is, the bipersonal field. Throughout my study of this environment and its alterations, I was mindful of problems of resistance. I touched upon the subject often, primarily by attempting to demonstrate ways in which deviations by patients in respect to the ideal therapeutic environment expressed some type of opposition to insightful therapeutic work, and how similar alterations in the framework served the counterresistances of the therapist. Still, it was not possible to afford more than passing attention to this crucial subject.

Again, when I turned the specifics of the therapeutic relationship and interaction, I fully expected to deal immediately with resistances since they are so intimately connected with these transactions. I found, however, that my attention was drawn instead to the nature of the unconscious and conscious communicative exchanges between patient and therapist—realities that are filled with direct and indirect, conscious and unconscious, implications. It became an all-absorbing task to identify the elements of these transactions, and to offer a conception of the patient's relationship with the therapist and the therapist's relationship with the patient in light of their communicative interchanges. While it was possible to identify disturbances in these exchanges, the specific investigation of resistances was once again postponed.

At last, having discovered how to listen in depth, having identified the ideal therapeutic environment, and having understood the communicative interaction, I find myself well prepared to deal with the subject of resistances. The study of obstacles to the therapeutic process also immediately introduced the problem of how therapists intervene, though this latter had drawn some attention in the earlier investigations of the therapeutic environment and interaction. Still, with the recognition that resistances stand high among the indications for interventions, the two dimensions of the therapeutic process could be readily explored together.

The earlier work had led to a sequence of insights which permitted the distinction between gross behavioral and communicative resistances. Many new perspectives on resistance emerged, especially those which could be understood in light of the communicative interaction through which the therapist's contributions to the patient's resistances was revealed. Similarly, having been compelled to intervene in respect to the management of the framework and to deal with the therapeutic interaction itself, we had already empirically tested a wide range of interventions and were moving toward the conclusions delineated in the present book: namely that silence, managements of the framework, and interpretations-reconstructions constitute, by and large, the only consistently useful and validated interventions offered by therapists and analysts alike. Beyond that, the communicative approach had cleared the way for a wide array of new insights into the intervention process and its techniques.

The format of the present volume is similar to its predecessors. Part I contains nine seminars in which, through case presentations based on process notes, we attempt to evolve a basic conception of resistances and the techniques they require, as well as to define how and when a therapist intervenes. I continue to be highly indebted to the participants of these seminars for their excellent presentations, and for their active and highly constructive discussions.

Part II contains three lengthy chapters. The first is an extended consideration of the classical psychoanalytic literature on resistances. The second offers an elaborate communicative study of this subject and the relevant techniques. The third is a comprehensive consideration of valid and invalid interventions, their formulation, their offer to the patient, and considerations of confirmation. I have, in addition, developed several appendices: one which summarizes the essentials of the listening process, others which concisely organize significant elements in respect to the nature of

resistances and in regard to the structure and function of interventions, and finally, a glossary of terms used in and defined by the
communicative approach.

I want again to express my deep gratitude to those who have
assisted me in this work: Sheila Gardner and Nancy Weisbard for
their secretarial assistance, John Simmons and Michael Farrin for
their conscientious and superb editorial efforts, and Jason Aronson
for his steadfast support. I am indebted also to the many classical
and other psychoanalysts whose insightful and conscientious efforts
form the foundation for the communicative approach.

The five years since the publication of *The Bipersonal Field*
(1976b) have been both exciting and stressful beyond anything I
ever imagined. The interpersonal-intrapsychic approach has provided us with a systematic means of mining the depths of the
therapeutic experience in ways never before available. It seems
inevitable that the excitement of fresh discovery and mastery will
lead us into new areas for exploration and insight. I can only hope
the reader will find clinically useful the new understanding which,
I believe, is delineated through the communicative investigation of
these two most important and challenging aspects of psychotherapeutic procedure: resistances and interventions. With an open mind,
relatively devoid of resistance, let us now move on.

Robert Langs, M.D.
November 1980
New York, New York

I believe it is no longer necessary for us to spend our lives defending or attacking Freud's major discoveries. Our task is to pursue further knowledge and be willing to modify and amplify what we have learned from him. To my mind that is in the true spirit of Freud—not in being an orthodox or classical or Kleinian Freudian—but in being a psychoanalyst.

Ralph Greenson
"The Origin and Fate of
New Ideas in Psychoanalysis"

Part I

Chapter One

THE NATURE OF RESISTANCES AND INTERVENTIONS

Langs: We come at long last to the final segment of the circular process through which our understanding of the therapeutic interaction and its techniques has and continues to be developed. We began with listening and then studied the therapeutic environment, and moved from there to the communicative interchange between patient and therapist. Now we will deal with resistances and interventions.

I am well aware of the intensity of the needs we have built up for this final segment of this course, and suspect that we shall all feel relieved once we have covered it. I will forgo further introductory comments and leave it to our therapist and patient to begin to shape this final part of our work.

Therapist: I would like to make a couple of introductory remarks. I consider myself a scientist and have therefore decided to present a tape recorded session rather than process notes. Based on our work with the therapeutic environment, I understand some of the issues this may raise. However, I believe there are some advantages to the use of a taped session, and also feel open to learning about the influence of recording on both the patient and myself.

I selected this tape totally at random; I don't know what's on it. I did go over the previous session and have written some fairly detailed process notes of that hour. I would like to outline this session and emphasize my interventions, then play about the final five minutes of the session and take things from there.

Langs: I admire the spirit with which you are approaching this presentation. Please go ahead as you wish.

Therapist: This is a twenty-six-year-old young man who presented himself to me about eight months prior to this session with symptoms which suggested a severe depressive episode. He had been working toward a Ph.D. at a university on the West Coast and could not handle the work. He dropped out and returned home in a crisis, suffering a severe depression.

I have been seeing him twice a week since that time. At this point—some eight months later—he was still in a rather severe depressive state. He was very isolated, not seeing anybody, having a lot of sleep difficulties, and was not working. Basically, he was a mess.

At the invitation of my supervisor, I began to tape record his sessions about five months ago. I told the patient that it was to serve as an aid to help my understanding of his case and that I would be using it for supervision—that I would be discussing it with one other person. He seemed intrigued and was actually pleased that someone else would be looking after things. Since then, there have been vague allusions both to the recording and to the supervision.

Discussant: Aren't you referring here to manifest references? Isn't it necessary also to think of both the supervision and the tape recording as important adaptive contexts, and to organize the patient's material as Type Two derivatives around such contexts?

Therapist: I agree. Much of this work took place before I began this course.

Langs: It is no coincidence that we begin with a comment on the basics of the listening process. As you will soon see—and hopefully have already seen in other respects—our method of listening has a major influence on our definition of resistances and on the ways in which we intervene.

Discussant: We also have here a major modification in the ideal therapeutic environment. As such, it seems to me we can expect important derivative communications from the patient in reaction to the deviations. I'm not clear whether the presence of the tape recorder for such a long time will blur or obliterate such derivatives, or whether, despite its long-standing presence, the patient will nonetheless still respond to it in significant ways.

Langs: I welcome attempts to anticipate or predict the material we will soon be hearing. However, while we inevitably will comment briefly on other issues, let's agree to concentrate on the areas of resistance and intervening.

Before entertaining further comments, however, I want to remind you of a presentation offered in *The Therapeutic Environment* (Langs 1979, chapters 11 and 12), in which a therapist alluded directly to the presence of a supervisor for the treatment situation. The consequences were traumatic and meaningful, and those of you who are interested might wish to review that material in this context.

Now, does anyone want to make a prediction with respect to resistances based on the presentation to this point?

Discussant: We already have a bit of the patient's response to the introduction of the tape recorder and the supervisor. On the surface, it sounds like he feels that therapy may be safer under these conditions. There seems to be an idea that therapy would be dangerous without a supervisor. Based on our previous seminars, this might imply that the patient feels safer when there is little chance of a therapeutic regression.

Discussant: I can see that point, and I am trying to think about how that will affect his resistances. I realize we haven't defined the term as yet, but I sense a contradiction. On the one hand, the patient might feel freer to talk, but, on the other, his material might have some meaning on a superficial level while lacking derivative significance.

Langs: Yes, we should define resistances as quickly as possible. I also want to point out that we have established a basic listening attitude: to enter each and every session without desire, memory, or understanding (Bion 1977, Langs 1978b). I therefore want to make it clear that the efforts at prediction which I encourage in this seminar are entirely for instructional purposes and should not be taken to reflect our approach to actual sessions. In my model of practice, the therapist enters the hour in a relatively blank state, but is quickly directed toward silent hypotheses, free-floating associations, a bit of theoretical thinking, specific recollections about a particular patient, and such, responding as much as possible to the patient's associations. In these seminars, I have stressed the more cognitive and predictive aspects of such work as a way of testing specific hypotheses and of showing how previously validated hypotheses can be used as principles allowing us to generate clinical predictions with a high degree of probability.

Though we will arrive at our clinical definition of resistance based on the material to be presented, we should perhaps adopt in the meantime a brief theoretical definition as a way of orienting ourselves. Who can help us?

Discussant: I am familiar with Greenson's definition (1967), which is to the effect that resistances include all obstacles within the patient to analytic or therapeutic work.

Langs: Yes, that is brief and to the point, and we owe a debt of gratitude to Greenson for having systematically studied the nature and function of resistances, as well as the analytic techniques required for their insightful resolution. There are remarkably few extended considerations of this subject, even though Freud, throughout his discussions of transference (e.g., 1905, 1912, 1914, 1915), emphasized that the analysis of resistances is a prime therapeutic task and the key to sound analytic work. Greenson fully agreed. He began his book on the technique of psychoanalysis with the single most thorough exploration of resistances available in the analytic literature. And to this day, we will find it a sound clinical principle that the analysis of resistances is at the heart of sound therapy and that resistances must be dealt with and resolved before any other type of therapeutic work can take place.

Discussant: We are predicting an intensification of resistances in this patient because of the presence of the tape recorder and supervisor. Aren't we saying that the therapist can be the cause of the patient's resistances? Also, don't we need a term for resistances in the therapist himself? Something like, counterresistances?

Langs: Yes, that's excellent. We are indeed formulating a silent hypothesis that a pair of related interventions by the therapist may well intensify resistances within the patient. These interventions may also represent a specific form of countertransference in the therapist which we could then term *counterresistance*. This we would define as any obstacle to therapy which exists within the therapist. In general, virtually every countertransference expression would constitute a form of counterresistance. There may be rare exceptions, but if so, we'll let the clinical material tell us about them.

Discussant: I must say that a concept as vague as "any obstacle to therapy" disturbs me. It sounds to me like there would be a strong judgmental factor operating, a great deal of uncertainty, and that much would depend upon your idea of how therapy should proceed.

Langs: Yes, that's quite true. The identification of resistances must rely upon the therapist's clinical judgment and his basic conception of the therapeutic process. It is therefore a very complicated matter. There have been some efforts to offer specific criteria, especially by Greenson (1967), who attempted to catalogue indications of resistance. I suggest that we attempt to generate our own conception and clinical definition before evaluating the literature. However, I do want to mention that it was Klauber (1968) who wrote quite specifically on the subjective factors within the therapist in evaluating the presence of resistance within the patient—an issue I myself later considered in some detail (Langs 1976b, 1980d).

Discussant: I am struck by the absence of total confidentiality. There, too, I sense a possible problem in respect to the identification of resistances. It will be safe for the patient to talk about some things, and unsafe to talk about others. How then will we be able to determine the existence of resistances?

Discussant: I wonder too if there won't be certain communications that are intended for the supervisor. And whether they would represent resistance or be meaningful per se?

Discussant: Can't we agree from the outset that resistances are meaningful? As I recall, this was Freud's position (1914). In fact, I am glad to have a chance to express my confusion as to how we can suggest that a patient is in a state of resistance and is obstructing his therapy, if at the same time there is meaning to what he is doing?

Langs: It's as if you have all stored up your questions regarding resistances and can't wait to raise them. Your concerns correspond with questions that have been raised by therapists and analysts since Freud first introduced the concept. They enable us to sense the confusion that surrounds the concept of resistance—meaningful obstacles to therapy, if you will—and the problem of establishing its clinical referents. They present us with some important clinical and theoretical tasks which I hope we will be able to accomplish. For that, we must delve into the clinical material.

Discussant: It seems to me that this supervisory arrangement might diminish the therapist in the eyes of the patient and could thereby lead to resistances. I would also expect the patient to feel threatened and angry on some level. I wonder too, in light of the therapist's introductory comments, whether the patient wouldn't feel that he's being experimented with, and on that basis become mistrustful and resistant.

Langs: Yes. In that it's likely to evoke what I have termed *iatrogenic paranoia*, the patient might well manifest intense opposition to both therapy and therapist.

Discussant: There is a patient I recently evaluated with two students in attendance. I then saw this person in therapy. After about five months, she revealed a fantasy that she had had at the time of the evaluation, to the effect that she was a laboratory animal being dissected by myself and these other people.

Langs: Yes, but remember that you are now reporting a *conscious* fantasy undoubtedly prompted by an immediate adaptive context. Its implications in respect to that context far outweigh the revelation related to the earlier experience, even though the latter is also, of course, quite meaningful.

Discussant: Won't the patient's reaction depend on how the therapist himself feels about tape recording? If the therapist sees it as a help rather than an intrusion, won't the patient be more accepting of it?

Langs: As I understand it, the therapist does feel that way in this situation. We'll soon see how the patient responds. In principle, you are touching upon the therapist's conscious feelings and intentions in introducing a modification in the ideal framework. While his attitude undoubtedly will have some influence upon the patient, I suspect we will find in this deviation many implications, largely unconscious, and that these will have a far more powerful influence.

Discussant: You seem to be saying that there are both conscious and unconscious intentions, and that the latter will more powerfully affect the patient. With regard to the subject of resistances, this would imply that we could expect to see a high level of resistance in this patient rather than a relatively low one.

Langs: Yes, though we will have to define our terms before making such appraisals.

Discussant: Isn't there also something voyeuristic, even devouring, in tape recording? It's as if the therapist takes the patient into himself forever, and plans to exhibit him to others. To me, these are unconscious implications, and they mostly speak for responsive resistances in the patient.

Discussant: I thought of that. I also thought that the tape recording makes the session a permanent incident that does not pass. There is a diminution of the separateness between patient and therapist, and the patient might well experience himself as always with the therapist. This could lead him to sidestep many issues and be resistant in that sense. He could also be quite gratified by the immortality involved, and by the sense of fusion with the therapist. These factors might well preclude important aspects of the therapeutic work, and would therefore contribute to additional resistances.

Langs: These are all excellent hypotheses and preliminary comments. They are characterizations of the unconscious implications of two activated adaptive contexts. They all require, as we know, Type Two derivative validation from the material we will be hearing. We need more clinical material in order to provide a more substantial basis for our discussion of resistances and for the development of our own clinical and theoretical definitions.

Permit me one brief comment before we get into the case presentation. I have used the term *adaptive context* extensively. With respect to the clinical meaning of this term, however, I have found that a degree of confusion persists among those who have read my work. In response, I want to propose two new synonyms for adaptive context, each designed to highlight certain main characteristics. The first is *adaptation-evoking context*, a synonym designed to stress that "adaptive" is used here to imply a psychologically meaningful stimulus from the object which evokes such responses in the subject. These contexts require or demand reaction and adaptation, and as you know, such responses constitute a major part of the *derivative complex*—the patient's unconscious and disguised reactions to an activated adaptive (adaptation-evoking) context.

The second synonym is *intervention context*. With this term I stress the clinical finding that, with few exceptions, the main adaptive contexts pertinent to the patient's neurosis are constituted by the therapist's interventions. This particular synonym requires that we always turn to the therapist's interventions in organizing the patient's derivative material, and will help us avoid taking the therapeutic context or indicators—a patient's lateness, absence, or some other stimulus from the patient himself—or outside stimuli as primary adaptive contexts. It will help us concentrate on an analysis of the implications of the therapist's interventions as the almost exclusive means through which we accord the patient's derivative responses their specific meaning.

Let's now turn to the presentation.

Therapist: I sense that you are telling me that there is something quite seductive about the tape recording of the sessions, and that it communicates a multiplicity of meanings, conscious and unconscious. Some therapists I have discussed this deviation with have experienced the tape recording as a barrier, protection. Others have seen it as a form of symbiotic fusion and even of homosexual gratification. But it seems to me that, in addition to generating resistances, each of these implications could stimulate important therapeutic work.

Langs: You seem primed by our previous clinical work to raise important issues well before the material will permit us a definitive answer. You are suggesting something I expected us to discover in the clinical material, and undoubtedly we have done so in earlier segments of this course. That is, you are indicating that modifications in the ideal framework probably—let's take this as a silent hypothesis—contribute to certain types of resistance in the patient which gratify aspects of his psychopathology and which may well preclude meaningful therapeutic work in these areas. At the same time, these deviations might well stimulate meaningful therapeutic work since they serve as intervention contexts likely to evoke Type A communications—meaningful representations of the adaptive context and a rich and coalescing derivative complex—that could permit effective therapeutic work in other areas. It remains for us to discover whether this second hypothesis accords with the facts, though we already have considerable evidence in its favor. We have found last (Langs 1979) that virtually all deviations contain an element of countertransference. This helps create a sector of misalliance and resistance. In addition to these damaging effects, however, the deviation—as well as any other countertransference expression from the therapist—is often evocative of meaningful and analyzable responses from the patient.

We are therefore hypothesizing that countertransference-based intervention contexts will tend to evoke mixed responses from the patient with respect to resistances: heightening obstacles to insightful therapeutic work in some spheres while promoting meaningful opportunities—i.e., a lessening of resistance—in other spheres. The key question, however, is this: Do the sectors of resistance actually interfere in some way with the effectiveness of the therapist's interpretations in the areas in which the patient is, for the moment, expressing himself meaningfully? Further, do deviations and other errors by the therapist evoke resistances within patients which disturb the basic therapeutic relationship and essential pursuit of insightful structural change?

For example, we already know that this patient entered treatment with a depressive disturbance. What we have said about the intervention context suggests that the tape recording could offer an artificial means to the patient for resolving important aspects of his sense of depression: it permits pathological fusion with the therapist and thereby bypasses important aspects of his separation anxieties. It may well be that this sort of defensiveness and gratification, and the related resistances, would preclude effective therapeutic work with respect to the latter symptom.

Our subject is enormously rich and evocative, and I can see that it is difficult for all of us—myself perhaps most of all—to hold off responding to even this first small bit of clinical data. I will therefore limit myself to just one further point. We are saying in effect that the therapist has an enormous influence on the patient's resistances, and that he can either promote them or help the patient reduce or eliminate them. Let that too stand as a silent hypothesis in need of specific validation, and let's now return to the clinical material.

Discussant: If I may first make one brief comment: I could see the tape recording as a kind of hypomanic or manic defense—a form of fusion. In that sense, you could certainly cure the patient's depression without ever subjecting it to analysis.

Langs: I fully recognize my responsibility in encouraging you all to develop silent hypotheses in anticipation of the clinical material. At a certain point, we must all resist further speculation, and turn to the clinical material itself. So, if I may, I would like to ask again that we hear your summary of the introductory session. We know full well that there are many additional potential implications of the tape recording and the supervisor, but let's now attempt to allow the material from the therapeutic interaction to direct our further formulations.

Therapist: With this introduction, I can't wait to tell you what happened. I would like to state that in general this patient has had the kind of split Dr. Langs has described as rather typical where modifications in the framework have occurred (1979). On the surface, the patient has been very happy about the recordings and has had a very positive attitude. However, as I think about the material in light of this initial discussion, I strongly suspect the presence of derivative communications with very negative implications.

In any case, on the surface, when the tape recorder breaks, he gets upset and asks where it is. He always wants to make sure that it is set properly for the session.

On the issue of fusion, in the hour prior to this session which I have summarized, that particular issue had arisen in a somewhat stilted way. I had been trying to make an interpretation as to why he broke down in graduate school. I suggested that it had to do basically with a feeling of fusion that he had with his father, and that it was based on his inability to leave his father behind him. His father is a concentration camp survivor. Basically, I had been telling the patient that he had a classic success phobia, and that he couldn't tolerate the success of finally getting his Ph.D. after his humble beginnings. I also suggested that he set himself up to fail because he couldn't tolerate being away from his father, and I pointed to the guilt he had in leaving him and in being more successful than this poor soul who is having all of these difficulties in his humble surroundings.

Langs: You have just now introduced us to the subject of interventions. Granted, we have none of the material on which you based your comments, but nonetheless you afford us an opportunity to develop some preliminary ideas in our second sphere of concern: interventions. Who will comment?

Discussant: This intervention seems to be an effort at interpretation. It sounds as if the therapist is attempting to bring something within the patient to consciousness.

Langs: I am delighted that you begin by touching on the formal classification of interventions. Who can identify the categories?

Discussant: There are questions, clarifications, confrontations, and interpretations.

Discussant: There are also reconstructions.

Langs: As you may know, it was Bibring (1954) who, in a discussion of the distinctions between psychoanalysis and psychoanalytic psychotherapy, offered the basic classification of interventions, one that is accepted by most therapists and analysts to this day. His categories, as I recall them, were suggestion, abreaction, manipulation, clarification, and interpretation. Under interpretation, I believe, he included reconstruction.

While Freud made ample use of all these techniques, he wrote relatively little about them. He did, of course, have a great deal to say about the interpretation of dreams (1900), and showed in his case histories (1905, 1909, 1918) a remarkable capacity for both interpretations and reconstructions, and a strong sense of a need for some type of validation from the patient. In addition, there are many scattered comments about the role of interpretation in analytic work (e.g., Freud 1912), and he wrote a specific paper on reconstruction (1937b).

Greenson (1967) and I (1973) both accepted the Bibring's categorization and elaborated from there. By now much of this should be familiar territory for you, and I will not review these readings here. Instead I hope to allow the therapist's interventions and the patient's responses, as they unfold in these clinical presentations, to direct us to revisions in our thinking about interventions.

In any case, the intervention at hand is as you noted, an effort at interpretation: an effort to make conscious for the patient something in regard to which he has previously been unconscious, be it contents such as fantasies or perceptions, or mechanisms and functions such as defensive operations and processes. For the moment we will simply establish the prevailing definition as a baseline, and maintain the expectation that our communicative approach will lead us to important revisions.

Who will offer brief definitions of the other basic interventions?

Discussant: Well, silence is easy—it's not intervening, not speaking. Of course, there can be nonverbal cues, such as body position, but it is basically the absence of an active intervention.

Discussant: Questions or queries involve asking the patient about something he or she has said, or for that matter about anything else the therapist might wish to raise. Clarifications are attempts to resolve confusions or uncertainties in the patient's material, or within the patient himself.

Discussant: Confrontations are efforts to call to the patient's direct attention something he has said or done, something that is readily experienced consciously once the therapist has called the patient's attention to it. We have already defined interpretations. Reconstructions, as I understand them, are attempts to establish incidents in the early childhood of the patient of significance to his neurosis.

Discussant: I believe that reconstructions can include efforts by the therapist to identify early childhood fantasies as well.

Langs: Yes, these are all well stated and can stand as basic definitions. We won't quibble over minor issues for the moment. I am quite pleased that you have a grasp of these basic concepts, since it means that you all have a good foundation on which to build.

Discussant: It seems to me we have left out managements of the framework, as well as other interventions you introduced to us earlier in the course.

Langs: Yes. You're beginning to anticipate me. In the classical psychoanalytic literature, management of the ground rules and therapeutic environment has not been specifically identified as a separate realm of intervening. It is known implicitly, but seldom examined specifically. I will say no more about this subject for the moment, but to simply establish two basic and overlapping categories of interventions: managements of the framework, and efforts geared toward the patient's eventual understanding and insight.

Discussant: In that connection, haven't we segregated a group of verbal and nonverbal interventions that are not designed for insight? I am thinking of manipulative interventions and offers of so-called support.

Langs: Yes, we might classify those as noninterpretive interventions, using the term very broadly to include all efforts not designed ultimately toward insight for the patient. I have tended to include such interventions along with deviations and errors in the management of the ground rules, but there is good reason to segregate them out. I will therefore accept your revised tripartite classification: (1) interventions geared toward understanding; (2) noninterpretive interventions; and (3) managements of the framework, such as the setting, arrangements, and the therapist's neutrality and anonymity.

That gives us a sound formal classification. Do we need anything more?

Discussant: From our prior discussions, it seems clear that we need some type of classification of the unconscious functions and meanings of the therapist's interventions. We need something that extends beyond the surface of his intentions.

Langs: Exactly. We need a classification of the unconscious communicative meanings and functions of all interventions. For us, that will be a prime task. It is relatively unexplored territory and there is no telling what we will discover.

Based on the material to this point, can anyone suggest, largely as a tentative silent hypothesis, some communicative functions of this particular intervention? Please be cautious, since we have very little data.

Discussant: It seems clear that the interpretation we're examining alludes to the patient's relationship with his father, and in no way takes into account the relationship between patient and therapist.

Langs: Yes, in terms of formal characteristics, the sphere within which a particular intervention is made—here, an interpretation—is quite important. There has been considerable debate in the analytic literature whether valid interpretations can be made with respect to the patient's relationship with figures outside of the analysis, or must instead always pertain to some aspect of the analytic relationship.

In brief, it was Strachey (1934) who coined the term "mutative interpretation" for interpretations alluding to some aspect of the ongoing interaction between patient and analyst. Strachey saw interpretations pertaining to outside relationships as preliminary and uncertain. More definitive, he felt, are those that involve immediate, activated wishes in the patient directed toward the analyst, as well as the defenses against such wishes. He pointed out that the analyst is in a position to know the state of only one person, himself, and that there are great risks in interpreting the patient's responses to others. In addition, he saw special value in resolving an activated wish-defense system which existed in the immediate therapeutic relationship and which had for the patient—and the analyst as well—a very special cathexis. Finally, he saw both insight and positive introjective identifications as the constructive consequences of such interpretations, and tended to stress modifications in the pathological aspects of the patient's superego effected by such positive introjects. Only a mutative interpretation could have such a dual effect.

The contrasting position has been most clearly stated by Brenner (1969, 1976). He has pointed out that unconscious fantasy constellations are expressed in the patient's relationships both outside analysis and with the analyst, and on that basis proposed that effective analytic work may be carried out in either sphere.

Without pursuing this particular debate further for the moment, the general principles of intervening in psychotherapy, in contrast to analysis, have been stated somewhat differently. In my own books on technique (1973, 1974) I spelled out what I believed to be the generally accepted position. I did so despite the rather overwhelming way in which my own clinical material indicated otherwise—a point that became evident to me only later. This line of thought, with which I believe you are all familiar, is that the interpretive work in psychotherapy is concentrated on material that pertains to outside relationships. In general, only when the so-called transference becomes a resistance or, more rarely, a possible source of important and selected insights, will an interpretation be based on reactions of the patient to the therapist.

The rationale for this approach is the belief that patients in psychotherapy either do not develop a so-called transference neurosis or, if such a neurosis does unfold, it is difficult to manage and interpret. The supposed danger of such efforts is uncontrolled regression. However, many therapists simply feel that the material from the patient in psychotherapy does not offer analyzable transference expressions.

If I may, I would like to take a little more time to characterize the position of many analysts and therapists with respect to psychotherapy. In this final segment, we are now in a position to more clearly recognize some of the ways in which the prevailing position differs from the one I have developed in this course, and, more important, to understand some of the reasons why. I think we can develop some important perspectives if we attempt to outline the prevailing position and compare it as we go along with some of the findings and concepts we have established and will be developing, and to test it again in the clinical material. Please understand: I have no wish to create straw men; instead I wish to state a viewpoint quite fairly, to show its essential foundation, and then to explore its strengths and weaknesses.

Toward the end of this course, I will distribute a paper in which I derive from the psychoanalytic literature the classical concept of resistance, its clinical and theoretical basis, and offer both an extended critique and a comparison with the communicative or interactional approach (see chapters 10 and 11). I will not make a similar effort to document my impressions of classical approaches to psychotherapy, since much of it is based on individual teaching, passing comments and papers, and only rarely on a systematic text. Oddly enough, we may take my own two-volume work, *The Technique of Psychoanalytic Psychotherapy* (1973, 1974), as such a standard, since it is probably the most widely used text in the field. So let this be Langs the classical communicative psychotherapist evaluating and criticizing Langs the classical Freudian psychotherapist.

As we already know, this ill-defined classical psychoanalytic approach to psychotherapy is based upon a *clinical* definition of transference primarily as *manifest* allusions to the therapist, or on minimally disguised references to obvious displacement figures (Langs 1980a). Even with this somewhat mistaken criterion of transference, there is strong evidence that the most meaningful expressions of the patient's neurosis arise in connection with his relationship with the therapist, and that they afford ample opportunity for effective interpretive work in that sphere. However, we have established here that transference is based on pathological *unconscious* fantasy constellations. We also know that nontransference is founded on valid unconscious perceptions, and that they too are a factor in neurosogenesis and in the expression of the patient's neurosis within the treatment situation, albeit in derivative form. On this basis, we have found that virtually every association and behavior from the patient has some implication for the therapeutic relationship, much of it expressed in derivatives. As a result, many of the patient's associations which pertain to outside relationships have their most cogent implications as *derivatives* of unconscious fantasies and perceptions pertinent to the therapeutic interaction. The patient expresses and works over his neurosis primarily in response to activated intervention-adaptive contexts within the therapeutic experience, and because of this the therapist who wishes to resolve such a neurosis through insight has no choice but to work interpretively within that sphere. This is familiar territory, though always open to renewed validation; allow me to move on to a few additional comments.

The general approach to psychotherapy is to intermix interpretive efforts with interventions such as questions, clarifications, confrontations, and a wide range of supposedly supportive and often manipulative measures, all of which are justified by a basic concept of psychotherapy which sees it as significantly different from, and not on a continuum with, psychoanalysis. Of course, validation through Type Two derivative responses—indirect confirmation in the generation of selected facts—is virtually absent in these clinical situations. Instead, the patient's *manifest* acceptance of such procedures and his direct responses to them are taken as justification—so much so that there is little room for contradiction or nonvalidation. In fact, negative responses are sometimes viewed entirely in terms of the patient's pathology, while positive reactions are considered a sign of the patient's health and good sense in accepting a particular intervention. There is such an overriding emphasis on the manifest content level of communication and relatedness in such work that the patient's derivative responses are virtually ignored. Similarly, the derivative meanings and latent contents and functions of the therapist's interventions are for the most part set aside.

Finally, with respect to the ground rules and framework, the basic classical approach is that a therapist may be far more loose or "flexible" in his application in psychotherapy than in psychoanalysis—though even there some degree of flexibility is in practice rather standard. Ground rules are readily modified in the name of the therapist's humanity and support of the patient, with virtually no consideration of the unconscious implications of such interventions for both patient and therapist.

Overall, we could characterize the classical approach to psychoanalytic psychotherapy as one in which a rather loose framework is established and the main effort is directed toward interpretive work—with the understanding that it will be relatively superficial and focused largely on relationships other than that with the therapist, and buttressed with a wide range of noninterpretive interventions.

I must conclude this characterization with a clear statement that I am not suggesting that psychoanalysis and psychoanalytic psychotherapy are identical treatment procedures. Nor am I saying that an identical therapeutic approach will be adopted for all patients regardless of diagnosis. Both psychotherapy and psychoanalysis are treatment procedures whose essential qualities are established by the therapist's explication of the ground rules and boundaries, and both profess to be designed to generate insightful and adaptive resolution to the patient's neurosis. Because of this, consciously and especially unconsciously, the patient in either treatment modality comes to expect and require a distinctive setting and a special way of managing the fundamental relationship with his therapist or analyst. The therapeutic process itself will also be comparable in the two settings, primarily because, given such a relationship and set of conditions, the patient will consistently express his neurosis in derivative form, primarily in response to the ongoing therapeutic interaction. Noninterpretive and deviant responses in either setting will characteristically generate non-validating cognitive reactions and negative introjects in the patient.

These days, psychoanalysis and psychotherapy are in practice distinguished by frequency of sessions far more than whether the patient is on the couch. I lack suffcent data for a definitive statement, but my supervisory and personal clinical experience indicates that psychotherapy can be carried out quite successfully on a once- or twice-weekly basis with a patient on the couch. It is my impression that the prejudices against use of the couch in psychotherapy derive from the poor techniques used in that setting, and from misunderstandings of the true implications of the patient's material.

Psychoanalysis is a more intensive experience than psychotherapy. As such, we would expect it to reach more deeply into the expressions of the patient's neurosis and its genetic basis. However, it seems obvious that frequency of sessions is but one variable among many which determine the depth and effectiveness of the treatment experience.

It is my impression that the effectiveness of psychotherapy two or three times a week, or even once a week, has been greatly under-estimated. In time, with the adoption of communicative under-standing and its therapeutic approach, we shoud be able to garner sufficient clinical data to establish the major differences in clinical outcome attendant on treatment in the two modalities. I have the impression that psychoanalysis can indeed produce more long-lasting adaptive and structural change within a patient than is possible with psychotherapy. On the other hand, I also believe that psychotherapy can effect significant structural changes in patients far deeper than those presently conceptualized by most therapists. Clearly, we have an area here that will be difficult to research and that requires considerable further study. (For additional comments, see chapter 12.)

As to which techniques we should adopt for patients with different clinical diagnosis, this is such a complex topic that for the moment I can make only a few preliminary comments. I am aware that I have not focused on this issue in this course. Instead I have attempted to emphasize broad and basic principles which can be applied in keeping with the material and therapeutic needs of each patient. I have attempted to develop a fundamental technique with sufficient elasticity to be applied to a wide spectrum of psychopathology. In particular, I have not made the assumption that patients with different diagnoses require different techniques, nor have I assumed that psychotic and schizophrenic patients require an approach varying in significant ways from that applied to the functional or symptomatic neurotic or the neurotic character disorder.

To introduce a few general remarks in the hope that we can specifically demonstrate some of these points with these last case presentations, I want to emphasize first that both neurotic and psychotic patients—to cite the extremes of the continuum—require a therapist able to establish and maintain a secure therapeutic environment and relationship. The literature reflects a powerful though unsubstantiated tendency to deviate in this respect with relatively disturbed patients, which is most unfortunate and entirely unsupported by the patient's derivative and even behavioral responses.

This view implies the adoption of a basically interpretive approach within the context of a secure framework with all patients. Differences—and they do exist—unfold in principle based entirely on the nature of the patient's communications to the therapist—his associations and behaviors. By definition, these are different in many areas in these two groups, even though there is some overlap. Thus, while maintaining an interpretive approach, the therapist will vary the timing of his interventions, address ego dysfunctions, and develop a distinctive sense of tact and delineation depending entirely upon the patient's therapeutic needs and the ways in which his illness is expressed.

In general, with a psychotic patient we would expect to have to do more work with his ego dysfunctions, though in principle almost entirely within an interpretive context. We would expect to deal with more primitive communications and more frequent and intensely disruptive impingements against the framework and therapeutic hold. And we would expect to be dealing with more regressed material and to offer interpretations which would vary depending on the available derivatives—sometimes moving toward deep interventions, genetic factors, and such, while at other times interpreting upward in a way that lessens the primitive qualities of the patient's own communicative expressions.

All you need do is follow the lead of your patient and he will unconsciously shape the nature of the therapy, though he will always require a certain unvarying basic approach. And that is the central sense of the communicative understanding in this respect: the existence of certain fundamentals beyond which the individual needs of each patient and the distinctive style of each therapist has ample room for full expression and satisfaction. And forgive me, but once again I must say that all of this has been derived empirically through the communicative approach, and that it entails no brief for rigidity as such; it merely reflects what virtually every patient asks of each and every therapist on some fundamental and derivative level.

Enough of general characterizations. Let's now return to this clinical material. As you may recall, the therapist has told us that he has been interpreting to the patient his fear of success, his need to remain fused with his father, and his guilt with respect to leaving him and being more successful than he. This is, of course, an effort at interpretation which pertains to an outside relationship— that between the patient and his father. And since it is a summary of a series of interventions carried out over several prior sessions, we will not be in a position to examine the extent to which the patient responded with Type Two derivative validation, and the degree to which he did not do so and attempted to direct the therapist elsewhere. However, there are two things we can do with this material to this point: first, we can offer an alternate interpretation based on the little that we already know about this patient, therapist, and therapeutic situation; and second, we can listen to the material from the sessions which we will be hearing in detail and attempt to ascertain the extent to which the patient's associations and behaviors support the therapist's interpretation, or point to either the alternate we will propose or to some other, for the moment unknown, possibility.

Who can help us develop an alternate hypothesis and silent intervention? Let's begin by reviewing the formal characteristics of this intervention, and by identifying its unconscious communicative functions.

Discussant: I think this is an attempt at interpretation, and that the therapist has tried to make the patient aware of reasons for his failure in school, as derived from his relationship with his father and from his inner conflicts and anxieties.

Langs: Yes, this is indeed an attempt at interpretation and as you imply, it is a form of genetic interpretation. The theoretical purpose would be to help the patient to become aware of factors within himself that are interfering with his finding success and his ability to leave home, and thereby producing a consequent state of depression.

As you can see, it's a very neat package. It sounds fine and it makes sense. And in reading the literature, you will find that frequently you are offered a summary of this kind, with just about this amount of clinical material. It's appealing and hard to argue with. Hopefully, we will later see the patient's specific responses to interpretations of this kind and we will have a chance to see where and why they fail to obtain Type Two derivative validation.

What are the communicative properties of this intervention, as far as we can tell?

Discussant: Well, based on this course to this point, any interpretation that pertains to the patient's relationship with an outside figure can be designed to take the patient away from his relationship with the therapist and from the therapeutic interaction.

Discussant: If we are free to speculate, I would suggest that the therapist could be offering this type of genetic interpretation as a means of escaping from something in the present that exists between himself and the patient.

Langs: Yes, these are the type of silent hypotheses we are likely to develop based on the communicative viewpoint. What then might be an alternative intervention?

Discussant: Do you mean interpretation or rectification of the framework?

Langs: Your question suggests to me that you already know the answer.

Discussant: What I had in mind was the fact that these sessions are being tape recorded. It seems to me that the first step here would be a rectification of the framework in the form of a cessation of all recordings.

Langs: Yes, that's excellent. You seem to be catching on quite well. Actually, the first intervention from this therapist of which we were informed was his introduction of the tape recorder and his telling the patient that his case was under supervision. The second intervention of which we have knowledge is, of course, the effort at interpretation. And it would be foolhardy to offer an alternate interpretation without securing the frame. However, let's be certain to remember that we will do so only at the behest of the patient's derivative communications, not unilaterally and abruptly. In this instance, the rectification as it pertains to the tape recorder would be obvious to the patient—he couldn't help but notice its absence—though it might also deserve verbal reinforcement by interpreting the derivatives through which the patient unconsciously directed the therapist to secure the setting.

In addition, this is the type of clinical situation in which I would strongly recommend cessation of supervision as well, something that the patient would have to be told directly in order for him to know that that particular aspect of the therapeutic environment has now been rectified and secured. And I can guarantee you that after those types of corrective efforts the patient would tell you far more, both consciously and through derivatives, about your tape recordings of the sessions and your presentation of his material to a supervisor, than you have heard from him to this point—more, perhaps, than you might dream exists.

The communicative approach has clearly established this basic principle of technique: *rectification* before, or at the very least, simultaneous with, *interpretation*. Framework before content; frame-related resistances before all other obstacles to therapy. Only within the confines of a sound therapeutic environment will the interpretive efforts of the therapist have their intended meanings and effects. An altered frame belies every otherwise genuine effort at interpreting. Consistently, such deviations give the lie to any other intended implication of the therapist's verbal-nonverbal, affective, spoken, and interpretive endeavors.

Now, who can offer us a possible interpretation that could accompany the rectification of this frame? We have very little data; but who can put it all together?

Discussant: I sense that there is something about the tape recorder, such as the way in which it affords the patient a pathological symbiosis, that might take precedence in intervening. This must come before, and then be tied to, the pathological symbiosis between the patient and his father.

Langs: You are quite close to it. It is fortunate that we attempted to formulate some of the implications of the tape recording and supervisor before hearing the therapist's effort at interpretation. That particular approach affords you a remarkable opportunity to discover the extent to which the therapist's interpretation of the influence of the patient's relationship with his father on his illness contains within it important elements of our formulation regarding the tape recording itself. It thereby contains within it in some disguised form the nature of the underlying and more chaotic truths within the therapeutic interaction. It offers the patient, then, a derivative lie-barrier system. I will have more to say about this type of conceptualization of interventions later on.

For the moment, let's recognize that we are in agreement that the alternative interpretation would involve the patient's relationship with the therapist. It would organize the implications of the patient's material, which the therapist interpreted in respect to the father, in terms of the ongoing therapeutic interaction, and in particular in respect to the unconscious implications of the prevailing deviations.

Discussant: If I may ask, why intervene around the relationship with the therapist? Isn't the patient's father the critical genetic figure for the moment? Granted, we do not know as yet about the contributions of his mother, but why not direct it to the source, so to speak?

Langs: Yes, that's an excellent question. It reflects the rationale by which many therapists justify interpreting material of this kind in terms of the immediate relationship with the father, tracing from there the earlier genetic components. Once again, logically, it seems to make sense to go right to the source. Some therapists would do just that. Others, especially if this were an analysis, might hear in the material aspects of what they might term a "father transference." They would interpret the material first in terms of displacements from the relationship with the therapist, and then directly in terms of the relationship with the father. There has been considerable confusion in this regard, a point that Leites (1977, 1979) has written about.

To resolve the confusion I will offer a principle, open to validation though it has been validated many times before. At this point, we are limited by the sparseness of clinical material so I will be brief. You will find, almost without exception, that the patient's primary emotional cathexis and investment, and the primary sphere within which he expresses and communicates about his neurosis, is his relationship with the therapist—from the moment of the first telephone call and perhaps even earlier. Material of the kind the therapist has heard is most meaningfully related to adaptive contexts which are based on the therapist's interventions, and their conscious and unconscious implications. These contexts possess for the patient genetic connections which reflect both distortions of the ties to the past and valid realizations of ways in which the therapist's behaviors do on some level repeat the pathogenic behaviors of past figures.

Because of this, you will find that only an interpretation which begins with the therapeutic interaction, and touches upon both unconscious perceptions and unconscious fantasies, and traces the genetic links from there, will receive Type Two derivative validation. If the therapist bypasses the nodal point within the therapeutic interaction for the patient's responses and material, he will be unconsciously perceived by the patient as denying his contribution to the patient's reactions. He will be seen also as trying to lay everything off onto the father. Such perceptions, since they are valid, will totally undermine the interpretive effort.

Incidentally, in this context I want to mention again that Gill (1979) has adopted a position to the effect that all interpretive work should begin with the here and now in the analytic interaction, with the actual contributions from the analyst, before tracing out the connections to past and present outside figures. However, his emphasis remains for the moment on the ways in which the actualities within the therapeutic interaction prompt transference responses, thereby focusing ultimately on distortion and pathology without affording sufficient attention to nondistortion and valid responses. In addition, he adheres to the clinical definition of transference which emphasizes its manifest and intermittent expressions, rather than its derivative and continuous representations.

This material and discussion also provides us with an excellent opportunity quite early in the final part of this course to expand our understanding of a dimension of therapy which I identified as one level of listening in the first part of this course (Langs 1978a)—the object relationship sphere (the other two levels entailing, of course, the cognitive realm and that of interactional mechanisms and processes).

As a level of listening and conceptualization, the object relationship dimension between the patient and therapist is, of course, of considerable importance. Until now, we have covered this aspect—though with little effort at systemization—by addressing role and image evocations, the sense of alliance and misalliance between patient and therapist, and the extent to which their relationship appears to be healthy and mature or pathological and constituted in a way likely to interfere with growth and insightful symptom resolution. More specifically, we have considered the degree to which the relationship appears to entail a healthy, growth-promoting symbiosis or a stultifying, infantilizing, pathological symbiosis inimical to growth and genuine insight.

It is important now to approach the object relationship sphere with a greater degree of systemization. I have been giving the subject considerable thought of late, especially since the distinction, first alluded to by Sandler (1976), between the object relations and interactional spheres has become quite distinct for me. Previously

I felt that these were relatively overlapping areas of conceptualization. While this may still be true, the differences now seem far more important to me than the similarities. This has led me to a more concentrated study of the object relationship between the patient and therapist. Incidentally, I must express my regret at Freud's choice of the term *object* for object relationship, since it dehumanizes the persons involved and can have a misleading mechanical influence on our thinking. My own preference would be to call this a personal relationship, and that quality is implied in all of my discussions—past, present, and future.

I believe we can develop a basic framework for out thinking in this area. Borrowing from both Bion (1977) and Searles (1979), I would suggest that there are four distinctive types of object relationship between individuals—including the patient and therapist. I would term the first *commensal*, in which some type of mature gratification filled with potential for growth and understanding is achieved by both participants at the expense of neither. The second I would term a *healthy symbiosis*, a holding and containing relationship in which one member of the dyad receives the major share of appropriate gratification (the *symbiotic receiver*), while the other member (the *symbiotic provider*) obtains a smaller amount of satisfaction and functions primarily to care and provide for the first participant. The third type would be a *pathological symbiosis* in which one member of the dyad obtains inappropriate, nonunderstanding and nongrowth-promoting satisfactions at the expense or behest of the other member, who usually obtains a smaller amount of such satisfactions. The fourth would be termed a *parasitic* relationship, one in which either member of the dyad endeavors to destroy, harm, or exploit the other member. Actually, to complete this categorization, we could include a fifth type of pairing: a mode of nonrelatedness which would best be termed *autistic*, in which one or both individuals are essentially withdrawn and noninteractive.

One of my initial concerns in this area was that it would be quite difficult to offer empirical criteria for each of these modes of relatedness. This has not, however, proven to be the case. Patients tend through derivatives to rather distinctively characterize the nature of their relationship with the therapist, and I believe that a consensus in regard to the prevailing mode of relatedness—and clearly, this mode may shift, and even be constituted by intermixtures though usually one type will predominate and should be identified—will be relatively easy to achieve. In addition, you will find that a consistent consideration of the type of object relationship between the patient and therapist will help to clarify the nature of the patient's resistances as well as the functions and implications of the therapist's interventions. It also provides a fresh perspective on the nature and management of the ground rules and boundaries of the therapeutic relationship, generating new evidence that it is this basic aspect of the therapeutic interaction—the frame—which is a prime determinant and influence upon all of the other dimensions of the treatment.

Returning now to this material, I would like to propose as a tentative formulation, open to validation, that a therapist who makes use of a tape recorder and supervisor has introduced a deviation from the ideal therapeutic environment through which he relates to the patient on a parasitic or pathological symbiotic level, attempting to obtain gratification from the patient which both depletes him and uses him to obtain inappropriate satisfactions.

In this regard, we may briefly define the therapist's appropriate satisfactions as those which derive from his establishment of a proper and secure therapeutic environment, from clearly delineating the ground rules and boundaries of the therapeutic situation and relationship. There is also the satisfaction of holding and containing the patient and his material, of being appropriately silent, and of interpreting to the patient when indicated. This leads to the further satisfaction of helping the patient to achieve insightful and growth-promoting symptom alleviation and of accomplishing the eventual termination of treatment and of the therapeutic relationship.

By definition, then, all other efforts at gratification on the part of the therapist are inappropriate and pathological. If they are designed, consciously or unconsciously to exploit and harm the patient, they would be considered parasitic. If instead they are designed with some helpful wish in mind, however inappropriate and unrealistic, and if in addition they offer the patient some type of pathological gratification, the relationship would be considered pathologically symbiotic. I believe that is the case here.

For his part, the patient should be seeking insightful resolution of his symptoms and an opportunity for growth, maturation, autonomy, and individuation. Healthy symbiosis is essential to eventual individuation, while pathological symbiosis interferes with that process, and with all of the other goals of treatment. In addition, the patient should be seeking the appropriate gratifications of being understood on a manifest and especially on a derivative level, obtaining appropriate interpretations and framework management responses, and having his material—pathological and otherwise, including his projective identifications—contained and metabolized by the therapist toward interpretation. Appropriate holding, so long as it is used by the patient as an opportunity for meaningful communication and ultimate understanding and individuation, is also a healthy satisfaction available to him in the therapeutic relationship. With this as our baseline, then, all other gratifications would have either parasitic or pathological symbiotic qualities, while virtual withdrawal would involve a form of autism. This implies, of course, that all efforts to obtain noninterpretive interventions and to generate deviations in the basic ground rules and boundaries involve parasitic or pathologically symbiotic modes of relatedness.

Discussant: From what you're saying, it seems to me that most psychotherapy, as it is now practiced, has parasitic and pathological symbiotic qualities.

Langs: I suspect you are quite right, though I would hold off any evaluation of current practices and of the literature until we have more clearly defined this area for ourselves. If we were to offer an immediate generalization, it would be to suggest that all deviations from the ideal ground rules and boundaries of therapy lead to the establishment of either a pathological symbiotic or parasitic mode of relatedness between the patient and therapist. This implies that under such conditions the only viable interpretations would have to pertain to this basically inappropriate form of relatedness and that all other so-called interpretive or noninterpretive work would be essentially ineffective in light of the type of relationship existing between the patient and therapist. It follows too that rectification of the deviation, carried out appropriately at the behest of the patient's material and with accompanying interpretations, is the essential means through which a healthy symbiosis or even commensal relationship can be established, and that it is only under these conditions of relatedness that sound interpretive work can take place.

Discussant: Does pathological symbiosis imply some type of inappropriate fusion or merger?

Langs: Yes, that's an excellent point. The study of object relationships suggests that there is a hierarchy of separation anxieties, some of them quite primitive, which are a motivating factor in the formation of pathological symbiotic ties which do indeed entail some mode of fusion or merger. Healthy symbiosis and movement toward individuation entails mobilization of these anxieties which can be very painful for both participants. On the other hand, deviations such as the tape recorder and supervisor can provide both patient and therapist with such a strong sense of fusion that the underlying separation anxieties are never truly activated, and individuation becomes impossible to achieve. The patient may also obtain some type of misalliance cure through the merger, though he would then require this mode of relatedness with others in his outside life to maintain his pathological equilibrium. In this light, by the way, the very common persecutory anxieties seen when therapists establish sound ground rules and boundaries, especially in separation-sensitive patients (though in all patients as well), are quite easily understood.

With this as our introduction, we will now pay more attention to the object relationship between the patient and therapist. The initial formulation is to the effect that the presence of the tape recorder and supervisor provides both participants, especially the therapist, with pathological symbiotic gratification, with an actual and psychological means of inappropriate merger, with a way of eliminating or minimizing separation anxieties, and with little opportunity for insight and individuation on the part of the patient. We will keep these formulations in mind as we hear further material.

Therapist: I will move now to the session prior to the one we will be hearing on the tape. I had been feeling somewhat uncomfortable about the interventions I had been throwing out at him. I felt there was a kind of artificial quality about the whole thing. We seemed to be dealing with the past and to be getting into a kind of rut about why this had happened to him. There was also a sense that we had to thrash it out and that he wanted to have a debate with me about the whole thing as a way of getting to the bottom of it. He is very bright.

We had been talking in the previous sessions about his guilt over leaving. He started to ask me if that was it? He wanted me to give him some references on the subject of guilt. He said, I am working on the guilt thing.

This reminds me that I had also told him that one of the reasons he had failed in his efforts to obtain a Ph.D. was that he had become confused about selecting his dissertation. He had two different subjects in mind, and knew nothing about either of them. He had made his choice just before he left the program.

Langs: I would take the patient's request for references on the subject of guilt as an initial validation of some of my comments regarding the object relationship between this patient and therapist. Here, the patient seeks an inappropriate piece of gratification through a modification of the ground rules through which he hopes to obtain a reading list from the therapist. In terms of the definitions I offered a moment ago, this would constitute a form of pathological symbiotic satisfaction (the therapist is not exploited or parasitized) and, in addition, it is a derivative communication which conveys what I believe to be the patient's own unconscious perception of the actual nature of the prevailing therapeutic relationship on both sides. We have here an essentially pathological rather than healthy symbiosis. Clearly the patient is satisfied for the moment with the relationship on this level and seeks to continue and extend it. Notice too that the references would provide the patient with a concrete form of merger with the therapist—obtaining a list, verbal or written, and therefore some part of the therapist—which would further set aside any basic sense of separateness or separation. By implication, then, both relative autonomy and individuation could not take place under these conditions.

Discussant: If we listen to this material along the me/not-me interface, it almost sounds as if the patient is saying that neither the therapist nor his supervisor knows what he is doing.

Discussant: About resistance, don't we consider intellectualizing to be a sign of resistance, and isn't the request for references to read also a manifestation of resistance?

Langs: Yes. In attempting to define resistances clinically, we are looking for anything that might interfere with the spontaneous flow of material and with the therapeutic work. We are prepared to discover that such obstacles are filled with meaning, but they do have a different quality from a sequence of communications which clearly facilitate an interpretive intervention or a rectification of the framework.

For the moment, you are pointing to the surface manifestations of resistance. You can immediately recognize that there is a subjective evaluation involved, and that there might be some disagreement among therapists as to when a patient is intellectualizing or expressing himself meaningfully though cleverly. And some therapists might even feel that the reading would facilitate rather than interfere with the therapeutic work—not adhering to the principle of spontaneous free associating. This touches upon one of the recurrent problems in identifying resistances: some are quite clear and generally agreed upon, such as a patient falling totally silent, while others depend not only on the therapist's conceptualization of therapy, but also on his understanding of the type of associations which facilitates the therapeutic work.

In practice, the concept that a patient is intellectualizing is meant to imply that the patient is talking about ideas, theories, possibilities, and such, and that he is doing so without the presence of instinctual drive derivatives and without any sign of emotionally meaningful conflict. Nonetheless, you might sense that it would be helpful if we had more specific criteria as to when the patient is communicating meaningfully and when he is not. And if meaning implies interpretable derivatives, it might now begin to dawn upon you that the communicative approach could do just that.

As I said, even the request for articles to read would be viewed by some therapists as a positive sign, as an indication that the patient wishes to understand himself and to function in a knowledgeable manner. For other therapists—and those who use the communicative approach would be among them—this would be seen as a further attempt at intellectualization, and as an effort to experience or deal with aspects of the patient's neurosis outside of the therapeutic interaction. It would also have a further meaning; can anyone suggest what it is?

Discussant: If we think of it as a deviation, it might be the patient's way of trying to bring to the therapist's attention the other breaks in this frame.

Langs: Excellent. In all likelihood, it is exactly that—an attempt through derivatives to call to the therapist's attention his own alterations in the framework—and, in addition, to say to the therapist: Look, if we're going to attempt to effect symptom alleviation through deviations, I would like to introduce a few of my own. If you have a supervisor, I would like to have a reading list.

This material also demonstrates an important aspect of the relationship between resistances and mode of relatedness. The request for the reading list would be understood by some therapists, quite correctly, as a form of resistance—it is an effort to bypass meaningful and especially derivative communications from the patient and interpretive responses by the therapist. This implies that the establishment of a parasitic or pathologically symbiotic mode of relatedness between the patient and therapist is essentially a form of resistance—resistant relationships, if you will. With this as a base, specific gross behavioral resistances often emerge in an effort to maintain and extend the pathological mode of relatedness.

Clearly, the search for pathological symbiotic and parasitic satisfactions will often entail major gross behavioral, and sometimes even communicative, resistances. The acceptance of a healthy symbiosis on both sides will lead to more meaningful material from the patient and therefore to a general diminution of resistances, both gross behavioral and communicative. On the other hand, because of the emergent separation and other anxieties which are aroused through the establishment of the boundaries and ground rules essential to a healthy symbiosis, certain types of gross behavioral and communicative resistances will emerge under these conditions as well. The essential difference is that, in the first situation, the resistances are an expression of the pathological symbiosis and will prove difficult to modify; while in the second situation, they are an inappropriate reaction to the offer by the therapist of a healthy symbiosis and often prove to be analyzable.

This material has additional implications for the subject of resistance. I would propose that this particular obstacle to therapy probably has two sources: the patient's use of intellectualizing defenses, and the therapist's modifications in the framework. Empirically, we will find that many resistances in patients derive significantly from the interventions and countertransferences of the therapist. I have proposed the term *interactional resistances* as a way of suggesting that they derive important inputs from both patient and therapist.

My impression is that virtually every resistance within the patient has some interactional quality, and that we are dealing with a typical continuum: at one end, there are those resistances which stem primarily from the intrapsychic tendencies of the patient, while at the other end lie those resistances that derive mainly from the countertransference of the therapist. Of course, there is no such entity as a purely intrapsychic or purely countertransference-based resistance; there is inevitably a minimum contribution from both participants to the resistances of the patient (and the counter-resistances of the therapist).

This leads me to alert you to a point that we will consider more carefully as we proceed. Resistances are related in some way to defenses. We will not assume for the moment that the two terms are identical, since there is already reason to believe that this is not at all the case. Also, we are learning that resistances are prompted by intervention-adaptive contexts, and that they are motivated responses. They have, as Greenson (1967) so clearly pointed out, their reasons, their sources, and their manifestations. But in stating that they are motivated defensive behaviors, we will not be content with the classical notion that restricts such motivating factors to those entirely within the patient, whether in terms of intrapsychic conflict, danger situations and disturbing affects, or disturbances in the regulation of self-esteem and the self-system. We will be open to motivational factors that derive through the patient's object relationships and his interactions with others—to externally-based motivating factors—in a manner not unlike that used by Sandler and Sandler (1978), and to some extent implied in the work of Kernberg (1975, 1976). For us, that means that both the therapist's valid interventions and his errors may generate repercussions which motivate the patient one way or another, doing so in terms of the nature of the intervention—the manifest and latent implications of the adaptive context—and the patient's own conscious and unconscious propensities. Both sources—primarily internal and primarily external motivating systems—are actually interactional products determined by factors within the patient and those with whom he is related, in actuality and within his mind and imagination—the latter, of course, constituting internal object relationships and fantasy-memory systems.

In all, then, I am proposing a concept of object relationships which takes into account both actual and fantasied interactions and representations, and need-evoking stimuli that are both internal and external to the patient—or therapist, when these concepts are used to understand his functioning and behaviors. Specifically, this implies that resistances may derive from either unconscious perception constellations or unconscious fantasy constellations, or any mixture of the two.

If you think about it, we should be prepared to find that critical resistances derive from threatening unconscious perceptions of the therapist, which make it all the more dangerous to communicate clearly to him or to work effectively toward therapeutic progress. Viewed in that way, we will soon have a far more sympathetic understanding of the patient's needs to resist the therapist, and not see such obstacles simply as some kind of unwanted disruption or even spite work. True, resistances may be part of an unconscious or conscious effort to harm the therapist or analyst—a point specified by Bird (1972)—but at other times, resistances may serve the safety not only of the patient, but of the therapist as well. As you can see, once we get into the clinical material, we discover many interesting issues.

Therapist: He was thinking about the question of his guilt. And he was also thinking about his decision to study two subjects in putting together his thesis. He had chosen a practical subject and a theoretical one, concentrating on political science and its underlying philosophy. This was opposed to his previous major, which had been in the area of anthropology.

In the session, he said that there were lots of reasons why he decided to go into political science and its philosophy. First, he had always felt somewhat insecure about his training in anthropology . . .

Discussant: At this point, I again hear, along the me/not-me interface, a possible introject of the therapist. In therapy with a trainee, especially with someone who tape records the sessions, the patient could be commenting upon the therapist's own insecurity, about his training, and even suggesting that he change his ways.

Langs: Yes. We will continue to monitor the material in that way until we have derived a specific formulation, and observed as well the patient's responses to additional adaptive contexts in the therapist's interventions.

Discussant: Is this patient being seen twice weekly?

Therapist: Yes.

Discussant: I thought of that when he mentioned two subjects, neither of which he knew very much about. I also saw your point, Dr. Langs, that the two subjects could also refer to the therapist and his supervisor.

With respect to resistances, it seems to me that the patient now seems to be getting into some meaningful material about the conditions under which he fell ill.

Discussant: But how do we know at this point that it will be meaningful? How do we know that he won't continue to intellectualize?

Langs: Yes, you can see that just because the patient is free associating and touching upon areas of seeming importance, there is no guarantee that resistances are relatively absent. In principle, we can expect another continuum. At one end are sequences in which resistances predominate and are so powerful that even their very nature cannot be determined; while at the other end are sequences in which interpretable meaning is quite evident and the islands of opposition absolutely minimal. We can expect too that even the most meaningful communication will serve on some level as a resistance against some other underlying expression.

In continuing to try to map out the area of study with respect to resistances and interventions, your discussion brings out another important point. I have already indicated that there is one group of resistances which are manifest, some of which are rather self-evident, and others of which would require a consensus. Let's establish our terminology by suggesting that blatant resistances be termed *gross behavioral resistances,* and that the more subtle resistances which take place in the context of a full flow of free associations be termed *communicative resistances.* In this way, we will soon be able to establish criteria for the presence of resistances, manifest or latent, and especially for those which fall into the communicative sphere. As a result of this schema, the debate we heard a moment ago could be easily resolved: if the patient's associations organize meaningfully on a communicative level we would say that there is a relative lack of resistance; in contrast, if they do not do so, we would postulate the presence of communicative resistances.

Discussant: Aren't you implying that the question must be decided in terms of whether the patient's material organizes meaningfully as derivatives around a specific adaptive context?

Langs: Yes, indeed. I am very much moving in that direction, though I cannot develop the point further as yet, since we do not know the specific adaptive contexts which transpired in the session prior to the one we are now hearing. Let's therefore be patient and continue to block out major issues in a broad way, waiting for additional material before we become more specific.

Therapist: Parenthetically, this patient did extremely well in anthropology and had received a grant for field work. He was well thought of by several professors at his university and seemed on his way to a successful career. He even wrote a chapter for a book with one of his professors.

Discussant: That too, along the me/not-me interface, could be a derivative related to the tape recorder and the presence of the supervisor.

Langs: Of course. Please continue to monitor this material in that way. For our main purpose, however, let's move on with this particular session.

Therapist: I simply wanted to point out that the patient had actually plagiarized about half of his work.

Discussant: I am struck by the reference here, in derivative form, to lie therapy.

Langs: And to the tape recording—its dishonest qualities and the implied misuse of the patient. The message appears to be that the therapist who tape records his sessions with his patient is incapable of doing his own work and needs to incorporate the patient in some type of total way in order to express himself. While we have yet to see the influence of the tape recordings on the extent to which the patient is resistant, and on its exact form, we can already sense that the recordings have helped to create a pathological symbiosis or parasitism between this patient and therapist, and has provided, as I said before, a concrete means of fusion between them. We will attend to the material for further data on this issue.

Therapist: He said that there were some real and concrete reasons why he decided to take up these new fields. He went on: I felt I needed to test myself to see if I could go into an area and start with a clean slate.

Discussant: I hear the comment about starting with a clean slate as a model of rectification, an unconscious directive to the therapist to clean up his act.

Langs: We can take that as a silent hypothesis. Let's see where it leads us in respect to resistances. What is your adaptive context here?

Discussant: The tape recording of the sessions and the presence of the supervisor.

Langs: And what would you say about the patient's state of resistance?

Discussant: Well, he is certainly free associating so there are no gross behavioral resistances, as you term them. I'm not sure about this material on a communicative level.

Langs: Can anyone help us?

Discussant: I would have to say that we are generating meaningful formulations. If the patient's material continues along this way, it seems to me that we would postulate a relative absence of resistance.

Langs: Yes, that's exactly the point. Based on our efforts with the *listening process* we are prepared to define communicative resistances. In essence, the ideal—i.e., resistance-free—communicative network is one in which the patient represents the adaptive context either manifestly in passing or through easily identified derivatives—disguised expressions which could be readily played back to the patient with the expectation that he would immediately recognize the represented context. With that as its nodal point, this ideal communicative network would include a set of meaningful and coalescible derivatives which provide unique implications to the patient's experience of the intervention context, doing so in terms of both unconscious perceptions and fantasies, and often by adding a variety of dynamic and genetic implications.

Finally, the indicators or therapeutic contexts—the representations of the patient's symptoms and of other sources of disturbance—are conveyed here quite directly or with a minimum degree of disguise. In sum, then, the relatively resistance-free communicative network contains a manifest indicator, a well represented adaptive context, and a varied and coalescing derivative complex. Such a communicative network readily facilitates, primarily through its derivatives, the therapist's use of interpretation and proper managements of the framework. From the communicative viewpoint, the patient is in a low state of resistance when his associations and behaviors facilitate sound interventions, while he is in a high state of resistance when this is not the case. As you can see, this particular definition of resistance is based on a number of underlying assumptions with respect to the nature of psychopathology and of the therapeutic process, and of the best means of enabling patients to insightfully resolve their symptoms.

On this basis, in the clinical situation it is possible for us to postulate the presence of resistances whenever there is a disturbance in any aspect of this communicative network. Major resistances would be postulated, for example, when there is no clear indicator or therapeutic context, or especially when an unreported indicator emerges in a later session, thereby revealing this repression.

As you would expect, the most significant form of resistance would entail the patient's failure to meaningfully allude to or represent the prevailing intervention context. Since the adaptive context is the fulcrum for all interpretations and managements of the framework, noncommunication in this area deals a serious blow to the therapist's capacity to intervene properly. Later on, we will see that his best resource at such times is either silence or the playback of selected derivatives organized around the known missing intervention context, especially when it involves a deviation in the fixed frame. And remember: interventions contexts ideally are represented directly (manifestly) and in passing, while it is the derivative network which may be well disguised and nonetheless meaningful.

Finally, the patient's resistances may attack the derivative complex, failing to produce coalescible derivatives, and showing a variety of forms of disturbance in this area. Thus, there may be an absence of dynamic implications or genetic links, or there may be a fragmentation of the derivative complex or a flattening to the point where it is repetitious and relatively empty.

It is my impression that communicative resistances operate quite unconsciously. In addition, as we soon will see, they may attack any one of these three major elements of the communicative network—the indicators, the adaptive-intervention context, or the derivative complex. Empirically, I have already observed many variations in this regard, and consider it an important area for future research.

If you are having any difficulty in following these conceptualizations, simply go back to the listening process and review its basic components. When each of the three elements of the communicative network is fully and meaningfully represented, we have a relative absence of resistance. As impairments appear in any of the elements of this network, we postulate the presence of resistances. Take your time and think about the model, and try to apply it to your own clinical work. In this course, now that we have established this basic framework, we will attempt to utilize it repeatedly with the material presented to us.

To do this for you as an illustration, using the material presented to us in this session to this point, we have accepted the tape recording of the session as the adaptive context—for the moment we'll leave aside the supervisor and other possible contexts from the prior hour. The essence of the material is that the patient is working over his guilt, talking about the guilt that he had in leaving his father, and asking the therapist for some references to read on the subject. There are allusions to feeling guilty over studying two subjects, and reasons for changing his acknowledged major area of study. He also mentions feeling insecure about his training in anthropology and the presence of concrete reasons to get into the new field. Finally, there is an allusion to getting into a new area and starting with a clean slate. All else involved parenthetical comments from the therapist derived from material of earlier sessions. Am I correct in this summary?

Therapist: Yes, you have it right. That's the essence of how the session began.

Langs: Well, based on this summary, who will help us to determine the extent to which the patient appears for the moment to be showing communicative resistances. Where would we begin?

Discussant: With the adaptive context.

Langs: Yes. What is the best representation of the intervention context* and how readily does it lend itself to interpretations to the patient?

Discussant: The reference to the two different areas of study could represent the therapist and the supervisor, or even the therapist and his tape recorder.

Langs: While that may not be the best representation of the adaptive context, what would you say about the degree of disguise

---

*Throughout this volume, the terms adaptive context, intervention context, and adaptation-evoking context will be used interchangeably. This stresses the finding that the therapist's interventions are the critical stimuli for the patient's most meaningful derivative responses.

involved? Is it a close and relatively clear derivative, or a distant and highly disguised one?

Discussant: I would have to say that it is highly disguised.

Langs: Yes, it is a very remote derivative of one of the prevailing adaptive contexts. As a result it would not especially lend itself to interpretations by the therapist. You will find that the clarity with which the adaptive context is represented is one of the most crucial determinants of whether a therapist is in a position to intervene.

Can anyone suggest another representation of the adaptive context?

Discussant: I heard something in the patient's request for some references on the subject of guilt. I would say that that is a fairly well disguised representation, but it does involve a deviation in the framework and an allusion to published material. Can we call it an intermediary representation?

Langs: Indeed we can. That is quite well stated. In this material, for the moment, the clearest representation of the adaptive context of the tape recordings and their unconscious implications is the patient's request for references on the subject of guilt. And that particular derivative lends itself to some extent to interpretation, though not easily. Thus, if one chose to intervene, it might be possible to say to the patient that he is asking you as his therapist to provide him with something outside of treatment, to modify the usual way in which they work together, and to do so by referring him to papers that have been made public in the field.

Remember, we intervene only as far as the patient's material permits. We do not make the leap to the tape recording until the patient does so. We playback his derivatives in a way that hints at additional meaning, adding as little as humanly possible to them.

In principle, then, I am suggesting that we do not bypass resistances; we work within their confines or interpret them. In the model intervention I just offered, I would be working within the limits imposed by the patient's resistances for the moment, rather than attempting to interpret their unconscious sources, functions, and implications. I would be accepting the presence of resistance in that the patient has indeed utilized defenses to disguise his allusion to the adaptive context, and I would be attempting through my playback to enable the patient himself to modify these defensive barriers.

In principle, I anticipate that we will discover that there are two basic approaches to resistances: their interpretation in light of the prevailing intervention context, and a playback of disguised representations designed to help the patient to modify the resistances themselves. Of course, there is also silently accepting resistances until they become interpretable or available for playback, and we should not make light of that particular response since you will find it to be an extremely common one—perhaps the most important intervention of all.

As you can see, I am implying that confrontations with resistances—perhaps the most often used of prevailing techniques in this area—are not an effective means of resolving their presence or of developing the material necessary for their interpretation. I expect to have ample opportunity to demonstrate the validity of that particular thesis as we go along.

For the moment, I do not want to add more in respect to technique. Instead, let's pursue our formulation that the best representation of one of the prevailing intervention contexts for this session has been moderately disguised. We therefore would propose that this is a sign of a moderate degree of communicative resistance in the area of representing the adaptive context. Such is our basic approach. Clearly, it involves the subjective judgments of the therapist, but in addition it offers specific criteria as guidelines. All we need do is to identify the prevailing adaptive contexts, and examine the patient's associations as derivative or direct communications which may represent these contexts. We then evaluate the extent of disguise, and decide on the degree of communicative resistance in that sector.

Next—and sometimes even before examining the representation of the intervention context—we examine the material for the presence of indicators. Who can help us in that regard?

Discussant: There is a reference to a sense of guilt. This implies some type of symptomatic response. However, it occurred to me that we had proposed earlier that the guilt might well be an introject from the therapist, or even an unconscious or derivative suggestion to the therapist that he should feel guilty for tape recording the sessions and exploiting the patient. Does this imply that indicators are like the motivational systems you described earlier for resistances—that they may arise primarily from sources within either the patient or therapist?

Langs: Yes, that is certainly the case. Many intervention contexts are also indicators in that they involve mismanagements of the framework and erroneous interventions, reflecting countertransferences and generating pathological introjects within the patient. As a result, they constitute indicators derived from the object relationship with, and introjections of, the therapist and have a major source within the therapeutic interaction. Of course, such indicators are processed by the patient and may create more or less of a disturbance, depending on the nature of the indicator-intervention context, and the patient's own inner mental world. In fact, all adaptive contexts serve to some extent as indicators, since a sound intervention will also stir up therapeutic needs in the patient.

Discussant: Doesn't this also imply that the tape recording of the session is an indicator?

Langs: Yes, that is exactly the point. With that in mind, how well represented is that particular indicator in this session?

Discussant: I would have to say that it is quite poorly represented, and that there is a high level of resistance in this respect.

Langs: Yes, and we will find that this is often the case when an indicator or therapeutic context is based on a deviation in the ideal framework or on a countertransference-based verbal intervention by the therapist.

We will explore this subject in considerable detail as we move along. For now, let's continue our model exercise. Examine now the patient's associations not so much in terms of manifest contents, but as derivative responses to the intervention context of the tape recording of the sessions. Who will help us evaluate the extent to which these derivatives are heavily or lightly disguised, and the degree to which they coalesce meaningfully and diversely around the prevailing adaptive context?

Discussant: I tried to figure out the reference to guilt. I ended up organizing it around the me/not-me interface, and my hypothesis corresponds to something you said a moment ago. It seems to me that the patient is saying that he is experiencing an unconscious perception and introject to the effect that the therapist feels guilty for tape recording the sessions; or he senses an absence of guilt and is unconsciously suggesting that the therapist should be feeling guilty when he is not. For me, that derivative relates to the adaptive context of the tape recording, but I would have to say that it is heavily disguised.

Langs: Yes, it is. In addition, you have selected a single isolated derivative, suggesting that you do not detect a coalescing network of disguised representations.

Discussant: Yes, I was having trouble organizing the balance of the material around the intervention context of the tape recordings. As I think further about it, the patient is saying something about making a change in his area of study. That could refer to the introduction of the tape recorder. The reference to feeling insecure about his training in anthropology could be an introjective identification of the therapist who undoubtedly felt insecure in having to tape record the sessions. So, I guess we have a somewhat coalescing derivative network here. I would say it is moderately disguised. I hope I haven't gone too far out on a limb.

Langs: In formulating silently, take risks, and then evaluate the extent to which you are responding idiosyncratically or based on poorly substantiated impressions, and the extent to which your thesis is justified by the material. See too whether subsequent associations extend and validate your initial impressions. In my opinion, you have very meaningfully developed this derivative complex, and I would agree fully with you that it is moderately disguised. This implies that in respect to that particular dimension of the patient's associations there are moderate resistances. In all, moderate to severe resistances prevail in the patient's representation of the indicators, the intervention context, and his expressions of the responsive derivative complex—the latter constituting the patient's responses to the *adaptation-evoking context.*

As you can well imagine, any combination is possible: heavily disguised adaptive contexts with clear derivative complexes, or directly represented complexes with either well-disguised or easily deciphered and readily coalescible derivative complexes. As far as I have been able to determine, defenses and resistances may be directed either at the representation of the adaptive context or at the expressions of the derivative complex, in that these are separate factors, however related.

As we proceed, we can collect further impressions. Our first sense is to the effect that this particular patient shows the same degree of moderate resistance with respect to the two basic elements of the communicative network: the adaptive context and the derivative complex. Even though the tape recording is both the adaptive context and indicator, we formulated a greater sense of resistance with regards its importance as a therapeutic context, in that the representations of the tape recording only minimally suggested a therapeutic need for intervention. In this respect, the allusion to guilt as it may apply to both an introject of the therapist and the disturbance within the patient is clearly the most directly represented indicator in the session, and it may on some level also be seen as the disguised representation of the patient's therapeutic needs derived from the introduction of the tape recordings.

In light of this extensive discussion of communicative resistances, it is well for us to remember once again that we have little or no evidence of gross behavioral resistances for the moment. The patient is free associating and talking about aspects of his life which seem meaningful. Here again, in this course we will initiate an empirical investigation as to the relationship between gross behavioral and communicative resistances. Theoretically, there are many possibilities. Certain gross behavioral resistances entail communicative resistances, such as silence. Other gross behavioral resistances may be accompanied by a meaningful communicative network.

On the basis of this discussion, I have begun to revise my impression of the level of resistance I would assign to this particular derivative complex. It is now my sense that we have here a situation in which we can put together a number of coalescible derivatives, which would suggest a relatively low level of resistance. On the other hand, each derivative is fairly well disguised, which would point to a moderate to strong level of resistance. Although the derivative complex is thus somewhat difficult to evaluate, I would have to conclude that there is a moderate level of resistance in this area.

This discussion points to the need for some kind of rough quantification regarding the strength of resistances. I would suggest that we scale the level of resistance from one to ten, and recognize that this particular rating will be the inverse of any rating we would make of the extent to which the derivative complex is meaningful and coalescible. Here, I would suggest a rating of five for the level of resistance, thereby suggesting that it is somewhere toward the middle of the scale.

To clarify this point, I would like to refer again to the allusions to starting with a clean slate, an excellent but quite disguised derivative designed to direct the therapist toward the rectification of the frame. There is also evidence of meaningful unconscious perceptions of the therapist—for example, a possible recognition of his sense of guilt and a disguised reference to his lack of expertise. We have also seen expressions of a sense of conflict which may exist either within the patient or within the therapist, and a disguised representation of a genetic link which connects the inadequacies within the patient's father to those perceived within the therapist. There may also be hints here of thoughts of leaving treatment—though they are once again conveyed through quite remote derivatives.

Remember too that these are simply the initial associations in this hour. You will soon discover that resistances tend to fluctuate within a given session, and from session to session. Because of this, I will soon stress the importance of silent waiting in dealing with many communicative resistances. In this particular hour, it may well be that the patient will spontaneously lessen his resistances, and that less disguised derivatives will emerge. For example, the

patient may offer a clearer representation of the intervention context—one that would facilitate both interpretation and rectification. On the other hand, because of the break in the frame, it would
not at all be surprising for the patient to maintain this particular
level of resistance, which would not permit any sound intervention
for the moment. It seems to me that the derivative complex is too
disguised to permit a playback, and that any other type of interpretive or noninterpretive intervention would introduce major countertransferences into the therapeutic field. In this context, I want to
mention that it is quite common, in the presence of a major break in
the framework, for patients to show this particular type of communicative resistance: poor representations of the indicators and
adaptive context, and a fragmented and moderately disguised
derivative complex. All too often, therapists ascribe some meaning
to such material divorced from the prevailing intervention contexts.
Interpretations offered on such a basis do not find Type Two
derivative validation, but as you would expect, such therapists tend
to accept manifest elaboration or direct agreement as confirmation
of their efforts. Were this not the case, these therapists would have
recognized long ago the ways in which the presence of third-party
payers such as insurance companies modify the communicative
properties of the bipersonal field and therapeutic interaction, and
tend to promote communicative resistances of this kind.

We will have much more to say in respect to fluctuations in the
level of resistance, shifts from one communicative style to another,
and matters of this kind. To offer but one initial impression, I have
observed that sessions in which the resistance level is high at the
beginning of an hour will tend to remain high throughout, while
those in which the resistance level is moderate to low will sometimes lessen further and permit meaningful interpretive and framework management interventions.

In a few moments we will take a brief intermission before continuing with the clinical material. Are there any questions with
respect to the concepts and ideas introduced so far?

Discussant: Some of us have been reviewing your book, *The
Listening Process* (Langs 1978a), and have been discussing again
many aspects of listening. It seems to me that today's discussion
bears out that among the most critical concepts in listening, that

related to derivatives is extremely important. I wanted to be sure we understood what you mean when you speak of the patient's derivatives or his derivative communications.

Langs: Yes, I too have become aware that these shorthand phrases are open to misunderstanding. The derivative concept is, indeed, quite crucial. In essence, we imply by the term *derivative expression* all those meanings, functions and implications contained within the manifest content of the patient's associations and in his direct behaviors which are not simply apparent on the surface, but which nonetheless exist in encoded form and can be detected through some sort of decoding procedure. This implies that the patient's manifest associations are, in part, a disguised expression of partially concealed meanings and such.

As you know, these underlying implications can be detected by engaging in direct inference making and thereby generating Type One derivatives. Or instead, you can use the prevailing adaptive contexts, and their conscious and unconscious implications, as organizers or decoding keys. In that way you will be led to ascertain particular disguised implications in the manifest material which are determined entirely by the organizing force of the adaptive context. And in actuality, it is our hypothesis, of course, that the intervention context itself is the adaptation-evoking stimulus for the patient's direct and especially indirect (derivative) responses as reflected in his associations and behaviors. And finally, it is this level of expression—derivative communication—which is the language of neuroses. It is the means of their expression, working over, and definition—both in terms of disguised fantasies and disguised perceptions. Derivative communication, then, involves both unconscious fantasy and unconscious perception constellations. It is another way of describing unconscious communication.

In the hope that this is clear, let's take a brief respite.

[*Intermission*]

Langs: Please continue.

Therapist: The patient went on to talk about this professor from his undergraduate days to whom he is very personally attached. He spoke again about how he feels very guilty for his plagiarism. He went on: The professor really liked me and I felt I needed to do it for him. I needed to prove myself for both myself and for him.

Langs: Concentrating on the issue of the level of resistance, who would care to comment? We will also entertain brief additional remarks.

Discussant: If we stay with the adaptive context of the tape recordings of the sessions, it seems to me that the patient is now talking about his homosexual attachment to the therapist, and his need to submit to the recordings on that basis, and as a means of proving himself and helping the therapist to prove himself as well.

Discussant: Doesn't the plagiarism introduce the concept of lie therapy? As I hear this material in the intervention context of the tape recordings, it seems to me that the patient is saying that he feels a need to lie under these conditions or that they constitute the conditions for lie therapy.

Langs: Yes, that's a very important point. The patient finds his own way of characterizing the treatment situation with a major modification in the framework as dishonest, as inappropriately exploiting him, and as a form of lie therapy. As you know, I worry considerably about the reaction among analysts and therapists to the concept of lie therapy. For about a year, I kept reconsidering the term. I tried substitutes such as barrier therapy, fiction therapy, and the like, and found that none of those terms served as the kind of critical selected fact that lie therapy was able to generate.

I did have the implicit support of the writings of Bion (1970), which was important to me, but which would hardly create tolerance or cool contemplation of the data among analysts and therapists in general. I was aware of the usual moral sense of the term, and the difficulties that many would experience in divorcing themselves from its moral overtones in order to recognize its critical nonmoral implications. I was also aware of a kind of silent taboo in learning about lies, since there is virtually no psychoanalytic literature on the subject. In the index of the *Standard Edition*, there is only a single reference to the subject in Freud's writings, and that involves children's lies. Quite recently, Weinshel (1979) has written about patients who lie to their analysts, stressing the genetic roots of such tendencies.

All these writings allude primarily to the conscious and deliberate lie, even the considerations by Bion (1970). Typically, they refer to patients, not at all to analysts or therapists, or to the therapeutic interaction. And in this situation, despite the patient's reference to a deliberate falsification and lie, my discussion, based on the concept of lie therapy generated by empirical observation, would center around the therapist's *unconscious* need for lie conditions. Still, it is a loaded term and I am indebted to patients who through their derivatives repeatedly reassure me that I have selected the right term and have spoken the truth about lies—if I may put it that way. The human need for the conscious and unconscious lie is enormous, and it is high time that analysts and therapists carefully examined this entire area as it applies to both their patients and themselves. It is critical in our pursuit of the truth to know the truth about lies, their nature and functions. They are an important dimension of life and of human functioning, especially when we consider both the conscious and unconscious lie, the deliberate and inadvertent lie, and the obvious as well as the well-disguised deception and falsification.

This clinical material serves as a remarkably lucid means of introducing the connection between lie therapy and the pathological symbiotic and parasitic modes of relatedness. In this situation, through a highly meaningful derivative communication the patient defines his relationship with the therapist as comparable to that between himself and his professor. In the latter situation, the mode of relatedness was unmistakably pathologically symbiotic, filled with apparent satisfactions of inappropriate needs on both sides.

I very much welcome the characterization of the unconscious homosexual qualities of this pathological symbiosis, since much of the writings on this subject tends to exclude instinctual drive considerations. My own use of pathological symbiosis implies inappropriate gratifications related not only directly to object relatedness itself, but also to both ego and superego functioning and to the realm of instinctual drive gratification. Pathological symbiosis implies inappropriate fusion, disruption of individuation, impaired ego functioning, and diminution of autonomy; and in addition to all of these, it indicates some type of pathological instinctual drive and superego satisfactions. Here, the homosexual qualities are striking, and the pathological symbiosis undoubtedly satisfied a wide range of unconscious homosexual fantasies and needs for both participants.

Pathological symbioses—please keep this in mind since it is so neglected elsewhere—may have phallic penetrating, orally and vaginally devouring, and other instinctual drive derivative meanings and functions. It is essential to include this aspect in your formulations since interpretive responses to the patient must address this level of expression if they are to be complete. It is also a means through which you are more likely to respond interpretively rather than manipulatively to the presence of this type of unhealthy symbiotic interaction.

It seems clear from this and other material that on an object relationship level, lie therapy entails either a pathologically symbiotic or parasitic mode of relatedness. In contrast, truth therapy implies the presence of a commensal or healthier symbiotic relationship. In these relationships, the therapist maintains the ground rules and boundaries and manages the framework toward its being secure, and responds essentially interpretively to the patient. For his part, the patient is either a Type A or Type C communicator, depending on the presence or absence of an activated and meaningful adaptive context within the therapeutic interaction.

As you can no doubt sense, on an object relationship level, lie therapies are constituted to effect some form of pathological symbiosis through the development of one or another lie-barrier systems. Some types of lie therapy are distinctly parasitic, especially when the lie-barrier systems of the patient and therapist tend to clash. It is no coincidence that the patient turns to a derivative communication which characterizes both the lie-barrier and pathological symbiotic qualities of his relationship to the therapist.

Discussant: There is another concept which I believe is supported in this material. The patient, talking about his use of the lie, an aspect of his own pathology, stated that he had to do this for his professor. In a sense, I hear the patient saying that both he and the therapist are operating as functional patients and that for the moment, there is no functional therapist in this treatment situation.

Langs: Yes, I am delighted that you developed that particular aspect of this material; I had planned to do so myself. To put this in general terms, the existence of a major break in the frame constitutes an expression of therapeutic need by the therapist, and often serves to place him in the role of functional patient. For the moment, it would seem to me that the material would support the thesis that the designated patient is functioning as both a functional patient and a functional therapist. The evidence for the former is the patient's allusion to the plagiarism, which is indeed a symptom. The patient's own therapeutic needs are also reflected in his submission to the professor-therapist, and in his seemingly inappropriate and pathological need to prove himself no matter how. On the other hand, his role as the functional therapist is reflected in the increasingly meaningful qualities of this derivative complex through which he seems to be offering a series of unconscious perceptions and unconscious interpretations to the therapist, ranging from the need to rectify the framework to the therapist's dishonest misuse of the patient and his actual or called-for guilt.

As for the level of communicative resistance at this jucture, who would make an estimate?

Discussant: It seems to me that the material is becoming even more meaningful. Could we rate the derivative complex at about level three or four in respect to resistances?

Langs: Yes. These are closer derivatives, still disguised but readily decipherable expressions of the patient's unconscious perceptions of the therapist and his own dynamic response to the alteration in the frame. But notice—and this is another point we will come back to again and again—that at the very moment when we would state that the patient is in only a moderate state of communicative resistance, he continues to utilize major intrapsychic defenses. Though the allusion to plagiarism suggests the lowering of resistances, with respect to the intervention context, in that it is a somewhat less distant derivative than the previous reference to the literature on guilt, it is still a moderately well defended representation, since it contains no links to treatment and little in the way of an unmistakable connection to the tape recordings.

In respect to the derivative complex, then, we can see a clear lowering of resistance, with a continuation of major intrapsychic defenses. For example, the patient displaces his unconscious perceptions of, and responses to, the therapist onto his professor. He also uses a defensive form of introjective identification to represent the therapist's dishonesty through the allusion to his own plagiarism. There is consequently evidence of the use of repression and possibly even denial—the latter depending on how aware the patient is of some of the implications of the tape recordings of his sessions.

It is therefore possible to quickly establish a distinction between resistances and defenses, despite the overlap in these two concepts. Greenson (1967) and other classical analysts have tended to define resistances as the patient's expression of defense in his relationship with the analyst, and to treat the two terms synonymously. Stone (1973), on the other hand, has suggested that the two need not entirely overlap, though his reasoning was quite different from my own (see chapter 10). For us, once we have defined communicative resistances, it is easy to see that there are important distinctions between intrapsychic defenses and resistances, and that a patient may be in a state of communicative expression with minimal resistance, while still utilizing major defenses. Here too there is a complex relationship and we will develop it further as the material in these presentations permits.

To summarize, in this last segment, the patient alludes to his unconscious attachment, pathological symbiosis and lie-barrier relationship, to the therapist. He does so through a derivative in the form of a displaced reference to his professor, and manages simultaneously to represent the therapist's pathologically symbiotic unconscious attachment to the patient. The clinical material supports an initial hypothesis that this pathological symbiosis has distinct underlying homosexual implications and gratifications, and that it also serves as a form of fusion designed to set aside significant separation anxieties on both sides of the therapeutic relationship.

There also is a further reference to guilt, which now becomes a repetitive theme. Its major implications remain to be seen. We can postulate guilt within the patient for participating in the tape recordings, and possibly for consciously or unconsciously lying to or deceiving the therapist under these conditions. We can also postulate unconsciously perceived guilt in the therapist for recording these sessions and presenting them to a supervisor—or, as we said before, an unconscious interpretation to the therapist that he is doing something dishonest for which he should feel guilty.

This guilt is also characteristic of an unconscious dimension of most pathological symbiotic relationships. It applies as well to parasitic interactions. It represents an underlying sense of guilt based on the pathological and inappropriate satisfactions involved in these particular modes of relatedness. The guilt-evoking aspects of pathological symbioses also tend to be overlooked, and they therefore deserve to be underscored since they are so clearly represented here.

Then there is the reference to plagiarism, to the lie therapy, which we have already discussed, and to some level of dishonesty in both patient and therapist. There are hints of the patient's unconscious perception of the seductive qualities of the tape recordings—the reference to the professor really liking him—as well as to the patient's own passive and submissive, probably homosexual, needs.

Finally, there is some type of need for proof and reassurance, a defense against weakness and possibly against castration anxiety. There is also a sense that the patient unconsciously recognizes this particular treatment situation as one in which there is a considerable degree of shared homosexual pathology, and that under these conditions, both he and the therapist are alike to some important and pathological degree. There is therefore the suggestion of some blunting of the important differential gradient between the patient and therapist, and as a result, little likelihood of positive introjective identification on the part of the former with the latter. This is implied too in our thought that under these conditions, both patient and therapist are expressing themselves as functional patients.

Discussant: I am puzzled by one thing—well, at least one thing for the moment. It seems to me that we had anticipated that with the introduction of the tape recordings the patient would become resistant. And yet, up to this point, the formulation is that there is only a small degree of communicative resistances, at least as far as the derivative complex is concerned. Certainly, there is more resistance in respect to the representation of the adaptive context. In any case, I had expected instead highly fragmented material and a high level of resistance.

Langs: If we were to approach the situation with total naivety, we might not know what to expect. Many therapists would believe that the tape recordings would have no effect on the level of the patient's resistances. Others would suggest that its presence would destroy the communicative properties of the bipersonal field and that there would be nothing but resistance.

Observation from the communicative vantage point shows that the patient goes through cycles: highly resistant for one or two sessions, then likely to work over in some meaningful way the disturbing deviation and adaptive context, only to become highly resistant again when the therapist fails to rectify the frame and interpret the material in light of the pertinent intervention context. It would be impossible to predict which point in these cycles we would find the patient when this presentation began. As far as I can tell, he seems to be working over in a meaningful fashion the adaptive context of the tape recording, though as you correctly indicated, his failure as yet to represent the adaptive context in a manner that facilitates interpretation creates a situation where that particular intervention, in its fullest form, would not be possible. Instead, we would have to resort to a variation on interpretation created for just these conditions, an effort in which you would play back selected derivatives, organizing them around the unmentioned adaptive contexts (see chapter 12). For the moment, I do not want to delve too deeply into interventions since I think we will find it far more constructive to have a full grasp of the subject of resistances before moving into the other central area for this part of the course.

One final point must be made, and it is quite critical although I cannot fully demonstrate it here since we do not know anything of the prior session. However, you will find that regardless of other existing intervention contexts, when faced with a major break in the framework, the patient's derivative material, if it is coalescible in a meaningful manner at all, will organize around the unconscious implications of the deviation and will not coalesce meaningfully around any other adaptive context. It is no coincidence that we are able to generate considerable meaning for this derivative complex in light of the adaptive context of the recordings. If we had discovered other issues in the treatment, such as an erroneous interpretation, we would find that the patient responds far less intensively on a derivative level to that particular adaptive context than he does to the break in the fixed frame in the form of the tape recordings and their consequences.

To state this as a general principle, open to subsequent validation: in the presence of a major break in the framework the patient's material will, from time to time, organize meaningfully as derivative responses to the particular alteration in the frame, in terms of both unconscious perceptions and unconscious fantasies. The consequences of this type of intervention context may entail either a high level of resistance or periods of low level resistance, depending on factors within the patient, therapist, and therapeutic interaction. Nonetheless, virtually no other invervention context will generate a meaningful derivative response in the patient under these conditions. Thus, in the presence of a major deviation in the fixed frame, there will be critical intrapsychic and interactional resistances in respect to all other adaptive contexts outside of the deviation at hand.

There are, of course, broader implications here. There may be sessions in which there are two or more major adaptive contexts, and the patient may show major communicative resistances in response to some of these contexts and relatively little resistance in response to others. Reactions to one context may serve to defend against reactions to another context. There is no single level of communicative resistance but a series of levels, each of which pertains to a specific intervention context. We should have ample opportunity to clarify this point when we hear further clinical material.

I trust that this clarifies your specific question regarding the effects of the tape recordings. Taping may lead to major communicative resistances in response to that particular adaptive context or it may not; but it will, as a rule, lead to major communicative resistances in the responses to all other contexts. That particular silent hypothesis should be open to validation in this particular presentation, since we expect to hear at least two sessions.

Again, we need more clinical data.

Therapist: He says again: There are reasons I did what I did. I was not simply trying to undermine myself or to have what happened occur for some deliberate reason.

Here, I believe he was responding to my intervention in the previous session in which I probably did imply that he was deliberately trying to undermine himself.

He went on: I had my reasons. How could what you said be true? I even stumbled into the whole post-graduate program in the first place. I didn't even have that much to do with it; my professor set it up for me. I kind of stumbled into this whole thing and it really wasn't my fault at all.

Discussant: Here too the patient represents himself as helpless and as the victim. In pathological symbiosis there is likely to be a sense of victim and victimizer. There is also a continued sense of homosexual surrender which we have seen to be an aspect of the pathological symbiosis between this patient and therapist.

Langs: No sequence of material in any session has definitive meaning without your specifying an adaptive context. We are at a point in the course where we must insist upon that particular nodal point. Type One derivative speculations are preliminary in nature and must be transformed into Type Two derivative formulations.

Discussant: I hadn't thought of it, but I was implying that these were continued derivative responses to submitting to having his sessions tape recorded.

Langs: Yes, we can then accept your hypothesis in some tentative manner, though these derivatives do tend to validate our early formulations regarding the patient's need for a pathological, passive homosexual relationship with the therapist. Often in a pathological symbiosis there is some sense of pressure, manipulation, domination, and on the other side, helplessness and submission. Note too how the patient here represents the manner in which pathological symbiotic relatedness is inimical to growth.

So, for the moment, we can take this material as offering tentative validation, and recognize that it is part of a meaningful derivative complex through which the patient is unconsciously attempting to respond to and understand both the therapist's need to record the sessions and his own need to agree. On an object relationship level, he is trying to explore and elaborate upon the pathological symbiosis, and perhaps unconsciously to provide the therapist—and possibly himself—an opportunity to reconsider, and even to modify, this pathological mode of relatedness.

I am also aware that the patient has not provided us with a dramatic bridge to therapy and that without it, all of these formulations are tentative silent hypotheses that have not as yet been validated through Type Two derivatives. Everything fits well, but such a sense of fit is only a very preliminary form of validation. We need something to convince even the most skeptical listener that the patient is indeed working over the adaptive context of the tape recording of his sessions.

Discussant: I can hear this material in another way, organizing it around the adaptive contexts of the supervisor and the tape recorder. In derivative form it may well be that the patient is attempting to excuse the therapist for introducing the tape recordings. He may see something very passive and latently homosexual about the therapist, something reflected in the way he acknowledged the presence of a supervisor and introduced the tape recordings.

Langs: Yes, you are now applying the me/not-me interface to this material, and generating valid tentative formulations. In a way, the more the material from the patient enables you to generate and validate silent formulations, the less likely he is in a state of communicative resistance. The presence of such resistances implies an experience within the therapist of great difficulty in organizing and conceptualizing the material. Here too you can see how subjective these evaluations are, and you can recognize the extent to which the therapist's capabilities to listen and formulate directly influence his evaluation of the level of resistance within the patient.

Therapist: As he was speaking, there was a stilted quality to what he was saying because he had repeated all of this several times over. It led me to begin to wonder what was really going on here.

Langs: Your comment is important. First, it may imply that, through derivatives of this kind, the patient has from time to time attempted to work over his unconscious perceptions and fantasies related to the tape recorder, failing to evoke from you valid interpretations, and certainly the necessary rectification, called for by the situation. However, there may be a second implication: the patient may be using drained and hollow material that is essentially devoid of meaning for the moment, despite our ability to organize it around the adaptive context of the tape recording. I must say that I think that this last possibility is quite unlikely. I think that the problem here is more likely to lie in your having heard this type material again and again without being able to identify the essential adaptive contexts which have evoked it in the past and present. Without an awareness of the contexts, you become bored and experience the patient in a state of resistance—a formulation we are unable to consensually validate and which may well be in error.

Therapist: Yes, that is my point: it all seemed hollow and empty to me, and I didn't see any connections to an adaptive context or to any other issue we were working with. I had made interventions of the kind I described earlier, and I felt that the patient was not picking up on them and that he was being resistant.

Langs: Here we have an example of how our respective conceptualizations of the therapeutic process and our use of the listening process influence our evaluation of the state of the patient's resistances. Your interventions involved outside relationships and manifest contents along with Type One derivatives, and they did not receive any type of validation even within the limited confines of that approach. You experienced the patient as repeating himself and could find no dynamic meaning for this material. Your concept of therapy was to the effect that interpretations related to outside relationships and genetic factors should produce some type of meaningful insight, and therefore evoke in the patient fresh sounding material. Repetitious associations do not meet that criterion and you therefore concluded that the patient was in a state of resistance.

With the communicative approach, we always begin with an immediate intervention context. From there, we address the patient's associations in terms of their *functional capacity*—their implications in light of the prevailing precipitants. There is no such thing as material *qua* material, and no way that we could evaluate the level of the patient's communicative resistances without identifying an adaptive context. Thus, the degree of familiarity of material is not a criterion of the state of resistance at all. The determination instead revolves around the extent to which the associations take on meaning in light of a context.

As a result of these distinctions, at the very moment where you formulate a high level of resistance, we, using the communicative approach, have formulated a low level for the derivative complex and a moderate level for the representation of the indicators and adaptive context. As a totality, there is a moderate degree of resistances here and the key issue remains whether the patient will represent the prevailing adaptive context in a form that lends itself to interpretation.

You will have a chance to read a paper in which I demonstrate, through a vignette offered by Greenson (see chapter 10), the differences between his evaluation of the patient's state of resistance as adopted from the usual classical psychoanalytic viewpoint and my own evaluation as derived from the communicative approach. As you will see, at certain points where Greenson formulates a high level of resistance, it is possible for us to identify an adaptive context which he has missed and to demonstrate that the patient is, instead, at a relatively low level of resistance vis-á-vis the missed intervention context. In principle, then, the determination of the level of communicative resistance relies on the therapist's capacity to identify the prevailing adaptive context for the patient, and to recognize and formulate derivative responses in terms of unconscious perception and fantasy constellations, and the related dynamic and genetic elements.

Therapist: The patient went on: I didn't even start with practical and theoretical political economics. I had thought about doing philosophy and religion instead. But so many people told me that it was a ridiculous thing to get into. They asked me what was I going to do with religion and ancient religions at that. So I changed my mind.

Here, he described in detail what it was like at the university where he had attempted to get his doctorate. We had gone through this about six times already. From day one, things were pretty rough but somehow they were okay. And then problems started and he had some legitimate difficulties because he had not fully prepared himself for that particular field with the kind of college courses that some of the other people in the graduate program had taken. And he went on to say that something had happened finally, and at first it just seemed to be his naivety and his feeling intimidated by his thesis advisors. But something did happen and he started to fold. He said, I started to fold and when I started to fold, the academic pressure got so much worse and I went into a panic.

He went on: The guilt, I've been thinking about the guilt some more. It was at that point that the guilt came in and the guilt weakened me. Suddenly I was deluged by feelings about the past and the guilt I felt about the plagiarism, for graduating with high honors when I really didn't deserve it, and for winning several awards and even a partial scholarship. And I knew I had beaten out a number of people who were my personal friends, people who wanted that scholarship. And I felt at the time, Now I am blowing it.

He also felt guilty for blowing it, and continued: So maybe the guilt is implicit. The guilt is important, but the guilt happened later and not before, and you were saying (referring to my first intervention, about twenty minutes into the session) that the guilt is the thing that got to me.

Langs: Before we clarify your intervention, who will comment on the level of resistance at this point?

Discussant: I see immediately that in order to do that, we must attempt to formulate the material around the prevailing adaptive contexts. I found that more difficult to do at this point, which I guess is a way of saying that I experienced the patient as becoming more resistant. For me, the material became scattered, even though I could see some connections to the adaptive context. There is something here about being under pressure and becoming panicky, and of course there's a lot more about guilt, though I did not find it especially illuminating. And then there is more about being dishonest and competitive. In a way, it now seems to me that even on a derivative level, organized around the adaptive context of the tape recordings, the patient is becoming repetitious. On that basis, I would conclude that his resistances have intensified.

Langs: Yes, that's an excellent appraisal. For the moment the basis for my statement is that your evaluation agrees with mine. That, of course, is but one rather weak and risky level of validation.

This brings up another important matter. Our comments imply that it is especially difficult to validate a formulation of a patient's level of resistance when we decide that it is quite high. When we believe that the resistance level is low it is likely that we will be able to interpret and thereby test that particular evaluation by observing the extent to which we obtain responsive Type Two derivative validation. But matters are different when the patient's level of communicative resistance is high. Certainly, it may be possible to put together an adaptive context and derivative complex which would illuminate the unconscious motives and functions of the resistance. In that instance, however, I would state that the communicative resistance level is high in some sectors, but low in respect to a particular adaptive context which illuminates the patient's other levels of resistance.

I can see by your puzzled faces that matters are now getting complicated. Let me backpedal a bit. At times, there may be a single and clear adaptive context, and as in this session, we may see that the patient at first generates a meaningful derivative complex, but fails to represent the adaptive context with sufficient clarity. As a result, we are unable to intervene. As we remain silent, the derivative complex may begin to fragment, to become repetitious and to become flat to the point where we believe that the patient has become more intensely resistant in both spheres (I will omit reference to indicators for the moment)—in respect to both the adaptive context and the derivative complex. At such a point, we do not have a clear enough representation of the adaptive context to offer the patient an interpretation of the unconscious basis and functions of his resistances. We have no choice but to be silent—an intervention that will, as I said, loom quite large in respect to work with communicative resistances. We allow the patient to work over and possibly work through his communicative resistances, doing so as we hold and contain both him and his associations, awaiting a moment at which it will be possible to either rectify the frame or offer a valid interpretation.

In the presence of a major deviation—tape recording sessions, filling out insurance forms, and the like—which has the qualities of a *vested interest deviation*, one in which the therapist has a very special investment, it is extremely characteristic for patients to show cycles in which they communicate at a low level of resistance (though usually without a clear representation of the adaptive context), only to become strongly resistant before presenting such a representation of the precipitant. Such patients seem to be moving toward meaningful communication, only to back away just before any type of interpretation is possible. Halpert (1972) offered two vignettes which have this particular characteristic, and there were several such situations in the presentations we heard while studying the therapeutic environment (Langs 1979).

Matters would have been different if the patient had suddenly referred in passing to the tape recording, or if he had offered a close and easily decipherable derivative of that context, such as some mention of a tape recording studio, of somebody who's making a record, of someone who takes notes. If this were to occur now, in light of the prevailing communicative resistances, it might be possible to point out to the patient that he was becoming repetitious and ruminative because of something that apparently related to the tape recording of his sessions, pointing to the exact derivative through which he represented that adaptive context. And it might be possible then to take matters even further, using the earlier derivative complex, which was so filled with meaning, to show the patient that he unconsciously perceives the therapist as dishonest, as misusing him, as something of a plagiarist like himself, as seductive—all this in the realm of nontransference. Carefully, the therapist eventually could also add that the introduction of the tape recording was facilitated by the patient's own needs to be loved, to submit, and to prove himself—the transference elements in evidence here for the moment. An intervention of this type would then constitute a transversal interpretation of the unconscious basis for and meanings of the communicative resistances, and would include both the unconscious perceptions and fantasies on which they are founded.

Again, I am well aware that there is a great deal to digest here. I have simply offered a model interpretation, and will do so repeatedly as we continue. In principle, I am saying that an interpretation begins with an *indicator*—a therapeutic context or sign of need for understanding within the patient. I will leave aside a classification of indicators for the moment, only noting that resistances and breaks in the frame are high-level indicators per se. Any error or deviation by the therapist generates a major need within the patient for a subsequent therapeutic response by the therapist. All along, we have been taking as the indicator for this session the presence of the tape recordings, and you will note that at times it is possible for the indicator and the adaptive context to be one and the same.

Wherever possible, we want to structure interpretations as efforts to understand the prevailing indicators, since these usually touch upon or convey the patient's neurosis in some way. We illuminate these indicators by identifying the prevailing adaptive context— and often the context itself has evoked or is identical with the indicator—by indicating its unconscious meanings and functions, and by demonstrating the patient's responses in terms of valid unconscious perceptions and distorted unconscious fantasies.

When the indicator involves communicative resistance, as exists in this part of the session, and when we have a represented adaptive context and a meaningful derivative complex that illuminates these communicative resistances, we are dealing with an interpretation of *relationship* (or interactional) *resistances*. Notice that I said *relationship* resistances rather than *transference* resistances, because at this point these particular resistances are a product of both transference and nontransference; they are interactional in the sense of deriving from the actualities of the therapist's interventions as well as from some measure of distortion within the patient. As you would expect, relationship resistances can either be primarily transference resistances or primarily nontransference resistances. In the presence of the tape recordings, we would have to suggest that we are dealing with a primarily nontransference resistance founded largely upon valid unconscious perceptions and introjects of the therapist. I expect that we will find that many resistances within patients have a similar structure.

Discussant: I was always uncertain of my evaluation of resistances in patients, and can see how the communicative approach offers some specific criteria. I can also recognize now that the evaluation of a high level of resistance is difficult to validate. Is there any way that it can be done?

Langs: For the moment, it seems to me that the only possibility is repeated appraisals. This would include fresh efforts to identify each and every possible currently active adaptive context, and endeavors to organize the patient's manifest associations as derivative material around these contexts, and in terms of the ways in which they represent the precipitants. Clearly, blind spots are difficult to overcome and the best that can be done is to make repeated applications of the listening process, and to begin each session without memory, desire, or understanding in order to permit a fresh evaluation of the level of communicative resistance.

Sometimes, the presence of gross behavioral resistances will prompt fresh evaluations, though you must be prepared to find the presence of either high or low levels of communicative resistance. In general, the latter should be taken as a possible indication of a major technical error, and this may include a failure to recognize a meaningful derivative network and to make an available interpretation. Finally, since the basic approach to uninterpretable, high-level communicative resistances is silence, it is possible to attempt to validate the use of silence by organizing the patient's derivative material as a response to that particular context.

In all, then, the appraisal that a patient is in a high-level state of communicative resistance must be examined freshly again and again, and should prompt the search for possible missed adaptive contexts and for possible countertransferences. As we have seen, the therapist's countertransferences will contribute to the level of the patient's resistances, a situation which calls for both rectification and interpretation. In addition, countertransferences may influence the evaluation of the level of the patient's resistances and to recognize this particular difficulty is far more arduous and requires extensive understanding not only of the listening process, but also of the therapist's own personal equation.

I must say that I hadn't expected to move so deeply into these issues in our first seminar. I have done so in part because I hope that you all came in today prepared to move into this area and that you each have a secure base from which to do so. I was also encouraged by your comments and questions, which show a good grasp of the concepts that we have covered earlier in this course. If it is a bit too heavy, simply accept these comments as preliminary. We have now touched upon so many fundamental issues I feel certain we will be reexaming each and every one of them. If I have given you a sense of the nature of gross behavioral and communicative resistances, and the ways in which the latter are identified, we have accomplished more than enough for this first hour.

Discussant: It's really been quite fascinating. Whatever vague concepts we had about resistance have been shaken up and perhaps even destroyed. I at least feel grateful that you have already introduced a substitute concept and model. I was wondering as you spoke of the patient's communicative resistances whether you aren't saying in some way that the patient has shifted from a Type A communicative mode to a Type C mode. If so, is the Type C mode by definition a highly resistant form of communication?

Langs: Yes, there is some degree of overlap in these conceptualizations. However, the situation is even more complex. There are different types of resistances in the Type A and Type C communicative fields. This material illustrates that point very clearly, so allow me to burden you with a bit more.

During the first part of the session, we had a relatively meaningful but well-disguised representation of the adaptive context, and eventually a highly meaningful derivative complex. In the adaptive context of the tape recordings, this suggested a Type A communicative response by the patient. There are ample derivatives, though there was no direct reference to the recordings. Under these conditions, we could postulate the presence of resistances and defenses, and see that they themselves were represented through derivatives in the material. These are *derivative resistances*, and the patient either ultimately resolves them himself to the point where the disguise lessens and interpretation is feasible, or he shifts into more opaque, *nonderivative resistances* which are characteristic for the Type C communicative mode.

To briefly illustrate how a resistance is communicated in derivative form by this patient, we may take the reference to plagiarism. On one level, this alludes to the patient's lie system and his own dishonesty. He is not representing his own genuine feelings and understanding; as it pertains to his associations in this session, this alludes to his avoidance of the tape recordings. In principle, the patient will represent in derivative form his own unconscious awareness of resistances, and often it is possible to allude to these representations when interpreting their presence.

Another example involves the patient alluding to his getting into a field such as religion where he could do nothing with it. As the patient begins to ruminate, he is indeed philosophizing and speculating in a way that is relatively devoid of meaning. This is a form of communicative resistance represented through that particular derivative.

It is important when listening to a patient's associations to observe when the material includes derivative allusions to the resistances which exist within the patient—and the therapist as well. Of course, in addition, the patient will represent the motives for his resistances, the sources within himself and in his unconscious perceptions of the therapist and in the therapist's behaviors, and the functions of the resistances and their form. All of this is important. In preparing to intervene, it is critical to make use of the patient's own derivative representations of his communicative resistances and their sources. As always, we allow the patient to put into us all we need for an intervention.

In essence, then, within the Type A communicative mode, resistances are represented in derivative form, and they exist within a communicative field in which the patient ultimately represents, relatively clearly, the pertinent adaptive contexts and offers a meaningful derivative complex that permits the interpretation of the resistance. The Type A mode therefore includes both derivative defenses and derivative resistances, which ultimately prove to be modifiable through interpretation.

In contrast, the Type C mode contains nonderivative defenses. These defenses are opaque; they are seldom represented in the patient's material, and they occur within a communicative field in which the patient either fails to meaningfully represent the adaptive context or to offer a coalesible and meaningful derivative complex. Such resistances either cannot be interpreted at all or can be interpreted only in a very minimal way. They cannot be approached without some effective representation of the adaptive context and without a sound interpretive effort. I no longer simply play back derivative representations of the Type C communicative mode, such as the patient talking about tanks, walls, and vaults, but always wait for an opportunity to interpret the presence of such nonderivative resistances around an immediately cogent adaptive context.

Here, the patient has shifted from a Type A defensive system to an intermediary system, with properties of both the Type A and Type C communicative modes. This latter material is not entirely opaque, since it does repeat a number of derivatives—such as those related to someone getting into difficulty and becoming panicky, to guilt, to dishonesty, and to harming others. As I review it, I would have to say that we are dealing here with a highly defensive form of Type A mode, derivative resistances, and not with a Type C mode at all. In a Type C field, the derivatives would be much more flat and empty. Nonetheless, this material has given me a chance to outline some additional concepts related to resistance, and, as I have said so often today, we will come back to this subject again as we move on.

Discussant: I wonder if this material does not reflect some kind of homosexual panic in response to being tape recorded.

Langs: There are many possible derivative implications here, as they apply to both the patient and the therapist. The material also can help us to give meaning to the allusion to becoming panicky a bit more clearly. Can anyone help us?

Discussant: There is some reference to the patient finding himself deteriorating and then becoming panicky. It is possible that this is how he viewed the therapist's decision to introduce the tape recordings and supervisor.

Langs: You are quite right. This could very well be how the patient experienced the introduction of that particular device. And notice too that he indicates that it only made matters worse, generated feelings of guilt, and that things deteriorated further from there.

This sequence has importance in that it enables me to demonstrate how this particular deviation was experienced unconsciously by the patient as virtually identical to aspects of his own earlier experiences as he became increasingly ill. He panicked, grasped at straws, and deteriorated; you, his therapist, panicked, grasped at straws as far as he was concerned, and deteriorated. Here, too, the patient suggests that he has reason to believe that you and he share each other's problems, and that in this repsect, you are both operating as functional patients.

Of course, all of this implies that under the conditions of tape recorded sessions, there is little likelihood that this patient will resolve his symptoms. If he were to do so, it would have to be because he mobilizes himself and his own resources in response to his disturbing perceptions of the therapist. For this patient, and to a large extent rightfully so, he and the therapist are alike, and neither has the internal resources to adaptively resolve his anxieties and inner disturbances—homosexual and otherwise. This is an important unconscious implication of the introduction of the tape recorder which emerges only in the patient's derivative communications, and not in his direct comments.

Discussant: I have some difficulty in following what you are now saying. I agree that the patient could be panicked by the impression that he and the therapist are somewhat alike in terms of sharing symptoms, and that this would be upsetting. And I think that we would be lying if we were to say that we ourselves never picked up a countertransference reaction from our therapist or analyst. But we are concentrating so much on the therapist and so little on the patient who, before he was ever in therapy, was prone to incorporating, taking in, fusing, plagiarizing, and panicking. And he was inclined to be submissive and passive. Why do we connect this all to his relationship with the therapist?

Langs: Please remember that I am talking about indications that a patient *unconsciously* has detected a contertransference problem in the therapist or analyst, not to a direct awareness. In addition, in repsonse to your main question—and by now it is a familiar one—the fact that we identify unconscious contributions to the patient's panic and to the material which pertains to that state in the therapist's behaviors and interventions does not imply that propensities within the patient and his genetic history are irrelevant. It is meant to indicate that the meaningful nodal point of the material from the patient derives from the adaptive contexts of the therapist's intervention, and that everything else radiates out from there.

Hopefully, you will have still another opportunity to discover for yourself the reasons for concentrating first on the adaptive context of the therapist's interventions, and for appending all else to that element of the continuous spiraling communicative interaction. It is here that I need still more material from the patient to once again validate this particular hypothesis. You remind me how frequently my attempt to develop a balanced picture, with the communicative interaction as the central organizing factor, has been misunderstood as if it intended to exclude the patient's tendencies or the influence of earlier relationships. Of course, this is not at all the case.

Discussant: I was concerned here with the distinction between empathy and intuition on the one hand, and projective identifications into the patient on the other. It is very easy for us as therapists to see our own problems in our patients, and to attempt to work through our own psychopathology in the therapeutic work with others.

For example, I think that most people do have a certain degree of success neurosis. I don't believe I have a success psychosis or anything like that, but it would be possible for me as the therapist of this patient to project into the therapeutic situation and into him my own success neurosis. And when you state that there is evidence that the patient and therapist share the same problems, I become concerned that the therapist may attribute to the patient his own problems rather than recognizing the distinctive difficulties of the individual he is treating.

Langs: There is some confusion here, and I will take a moment to clear it up. As I have tried to demonstrate, there is a subjective factor in every evaluation which a therapist makes, whether it relates to the nature of the patient's neurosis or to the presence of resistances. Of course, there is always a danger of projecting into the patient one's own problems, attributing to the patient difficulties which actually exist within the treating person. There are even dangers of projectively identifying one's own neurosis into the patient, doing so interactionally and actively to the point where the patient is forced to contain that neurosis and to metabolize it—or to be refractory if he wishes. For us, these should be familiar problems by now.

However, such difficulties should be distinguished from a formulation of material which suggests that among the unconscious implications of a therapist's intervention is a reflection of a type of neurosis or psychopathology that is in some ways comparable to the neurosis and psychopathology of the patient. Here, we are making this formulation as an observer of this therapeutic interaction. True, if you are the therapist and you make this evaluation, you must be very careful to check out any possibility of pathological projection or projective identification. However, I am basing these comments largely upon the patient's derivative communications, his unconscious perceptions and introjects of the therapist. There is always a danger of misreading such material, and we must certainly validate it silently with additional associations and ultimately with an interpretation which obtains Type Two derivative validation. I am simply suggesting that we keep in mind two rather distinct possibilites: the therapist attributing to or stirring up within the patient aspects of his own pathology, and the therapist behaving in ways which actually reflect pathology comparable to that of the patient. Both are countertransference-dominated situations, and each may evoke either a high level of resistance within the patient or powerful and meaningful derivative communications of low resistance valance.

Please continue.

Therapist: The patient said that he felt guilty because he felt he was blowing it. Here I said to him that I think that what happened was that the guilt he experienced consciously during this time was something that he was experiencing all along, and it just came out now.

Langs: We are near the end of today's seminar, and it is clear that there has been far too much to absorb. But it might be helpful to outline some initial points toward a basic introduction to interventions. How does the group feel?

Discussant: I think we would appreciate some introductory comments.

Langs: Well, let's establish three basic considerations in approaching an intervention: (1) its formal categorization; (2) its communicative structure; and (3) its conscious and unconscious meanings, functions, and implications. I have touched upon aspects of these categories earlier today. Let's develop them briefly again in response to this intervention. Who will offer a formal categorization?

Discussant: It's something like an interpretation again.

Discussant: I hear it more as a confrontation.

Langs: Actually, it is a cross between a confrontation and an interpretation, in that it calls to the patient's attention something that he is experiencing, but also suggests that the affect of guilt existed earlier, at a time when the patient was unaware of it. It is probably best termed a general interpretation.

As for its communicative structure, there are three key points: the indicator, the adaptive context, and the derivative complex. Who will comment?

Discussant: If I understand the concept of indicator, it seems to me that the therapist was attempting to deal with the patient's sense of guilt. That also seems connected to the patient's symptoms and difficulties.

Langs: Yes, there are, as I said, a hierarchy of indicators. Listing them in a general order of decreasing importance, there are first the therapist's errors, both breaks in the frame and interpretive; next, there are the patient's resistances, including his own breaks in the frame, as well as a variety of gross behavioral and communicative obstacles to treatment; and finally, there are the patient's symptoms and characterological disturbances, and problems which arise in his relationship with others. To those we should add the disturbing qualities of sound interventions. Each of these categories possesses a hierarchy of its own which must also be taken into account. For example, the appearance of suicidal or homicidal symptoms constitutes a far more powerful indicator than a fleeting experience of anxiety. Major breaks in the frame are more important than minor ones. And resistances which threaten the continuation of treatment have a greater valence than those which are minor and in all likelihood temporary.

In principle, each intervention, whether a rectification of the frame or interpretation, should deal first and foremost with the highest level of indicator before going to the lower levels. Further, it is quite important to recognize that our experience of therapeutic needs within the patient, and therefore our own inclination to intervene, should be determined by the intensity of these therapeutic contexts. I use this latter term to remind us that these sources of internal and external disturbance for the patient are second-order organizers of the patient's material—the prime organizer being, of course, intervention contexts.

It is also well to realize that often both the indicators and the communicative complex constitute adaptive and maladaptive responses to the prevailing adaptive contexts. Further, a complete interpretation should identify the nature of the intervention contexts and the implications of the derivative complex in a manner which clearly illuminates the unconscious meanings and functions of the major indicators in a particular hour. Thus, an interpretation deals with an activated expression of the patient's neurosis—an indicator—and attempts to help the patient to understand the unconscious basis for the disturbance, both in the present and genetically, in terms of an activated adaptive context and the patient's derivative responses—perception-introjects and fantasy-memories. In this way, each session has the potential for illuminating an activated segment of the patient's neurosis and may constitute a sort of minianalysis in and of itself. It is the accumulation of many such sessions which constitutes the totality of an effective and insightful psychotherapy or psychoanalysis.

As you may sense, there would be a question here in regard to the therapist's decision to intervene in respect to a patient's disturbed affect, rather than in response to the communicative resistances which we detected. In keeping with the hierarchy which I offered to you, the precept that we interpret resistances before content remains valid within the communicative approach.

What now of the communicative structure of this intervention?

Discussant: It does not deal with an adaptive context.

Langs: Exactly, and it reduces this rich and convoluted derivative network to the single element of the patient's allusion to guilt. It fails to utilize the multiplicity of derivatives communicated by the patient. We can therefore state that while it does allude to an indicator, though probably not the prime one for this hour, it does not refer to an adaptive context and makes virtually no use of the derivative complex.

Now, what about its conscious and unconscious communicative properties? It is here, of course, that we must examine the correctness of an intervention, its fit with the patient's material, and both the therapist's conscious intentions as well as his unconscious communications. Who will comment briefly?

Discussant: It seems to me that one of the first polarities has to do with whether the intervention deals with the therapeutic relationship or with an outside relationship. Here, the therapist touches upon an outside relationship and excludes the therapeutic interaction.

Discussant: He also denies the existence of the derivative complex, and of the adaptive context of the tape recording—or of any other context for that matter.

Discussant: It also addresses the patient's intrapsychic state, without any allusion to the therapist, and without any use of the me/not-me interface.

Langs: Actually, we could detail many communicative properties for this intervention. You are quite right that an important
dimension involves the extent to which a particular intervention
deals with the therapeutic relationship or fails to do so. This is
another way of saying, though only up to a point, we want to know
whether the intervention begins with an adaptive context.

In essence, this intervention is a relatively straightforward effort
to suggest to the patient that there has been guilt within himself for
a long time, of which he has been unaware until recently. It is quite
simplistic, and yet many therapists would accept this as a preliminary kind of interpretation designed to further the therapeutic
work. It is, however, an intervention that deals with the manifest
content of the patient's material, and to some small extent, a Type
One derivative inference—that the guilt has been present for a long
time. Actually, the patient himself virtually says just that.

It is common for therapists to justify interventions of this kind as
an initial interpretive effort, and to fail to realize that it engages
the patient on a manifest content level of relatedness with many of
the characteristics which we have already identified for this type of
interaction (Langs 1980a). It speaks for a large degree of denial in
respect to adaptive contexts from the therapist, implications of the
unconscious conscious communicative interaction, and the derivative communications of the patient contained in these associations
—especially their Type Two derivative meanings.

It is, as we know, quite important to evaluate the unconscious
communicative functions of an intervention, since these are critical
properties of the new adaptive context to which the patient will
now respond. For the moment, we are faced with an intervention
that pertains to outside relationships and to the surface of the
patient's material. Let's now listen to the patient's commentary on
such therapeutic work.

Discussant: I wondered if there isn't some effort at reconstruction
here?

Langs: That's an excellent point. As I indicated in my books
on technique (Langs 1973, 1974), there is a category of reconstruction which touches upon relatively recent events. And there is
indeed a rather superficial or simplistic attempt here to reconstruct

the presence of an affect of which the patient was unaware. Thank you for calling it to our attention.

Incidently, in categorizing interventions, you will find that I group interpretations and reconstructions together (see chapter 12).

Discussant: In light of the material which preceded this, it seemed to me that the therapist was telling the patient that he was in error, that the guilt existed for a long time and did not occur just recently. That quality of the intervention does not fit clearly into the categories you propose, though it might be subsumed under clarifications.

Discussant: It has a hostile and confronting quality as well.

Langs: Yes, there is an effort to correct the patient, far more than to utilize his material to shape the intervention. Interventions should be placed into the therapist by the patient, communicated as segments or islands of derivatives—information bits—which the therapist then simply puts together and properly synthesizes. This particular intervention lacks that important quality.

As for the hostile element, you will find that most confrontations and clarifications, especially when they contradict the patient, have an aggressive quality. Patients will often respond to that aspect of the intervention in rather powerful ways, though almost always through derivative expressions. However, if the confrontation is blatantly aggressive, you may get a directly hostile reaction.

I am quite impressed with how quickly so many basic clinical issues have arisen in our discussion of the material in this first seminar on resistances and interventions. Because the hour is late and we want to allow time to hear the patient's commentary on this particular intervention, I will respond only briefly to your remarks —largely as a way of introducing considerations regarding which we will afford considerable thought in the ensuing weeks.

It has become increasingly clear to me that there are many therapists who almost never utilize the patient's associations in terms of their derivative implications. Among those analysts who do attempt to work in this way, their efforts tend to be centered on translation derivatives—Type One derivatives—rather than on derivatives organized around intervention contexts in the form of Type Two derivatives. A therapist's mode of deriving derivative meaning from a patient's associations is an important determinant of the types of interventions he uses, and the type of therapy he practices.

In brief, the present classical model could be characterized as constituting a pursuit of derivatives directly available but seemingly latent to a particular manifest element. The search is for hidden associations which can be ferreted out through questions and confrontations. Such efforts are linear pursuits at clarification in the belief that the new information so revealed constitutes the expression of previously repressed or suppressed fantasies. Implicit here is also the belief that these fantasies emerge whole and bear a meaningful relationship to the patient's neurosis.

Without going into detail or offering clinical documentation for the moment, I will present the contrasting communicative approach. It is based mainly on the finding that the critical expressions of the patient's neurosis appear in the form of Type Two derivatives. This viewpoint proposes that the patient's neurosis is always expressed through disguise and derivatives, and is not revealed manifestly. But it has discovered that these derivatives appear as scattered bits of information which emerge as the patient shifts from one subject to another, always under the influence of the prevailing intervention context. Such expressions seldom appear directly or in whole cloth, but always require synthesis based on scattered communications whose derivative meanings are revealed in light of an activated adaptive context.

It follows, then, that the communicative therapist will make use of silence as his main means of facilitating the patient's expression of neurotically pertinent derivative communication. Of course, such silence implies holding and containing, and has a number of other implications. It is to be preferred, however, to efforts at confrontation and question which address the manifest content of the patient's association and which narrow the patient's associative range far more than the techniques used by the communicative therapist. Through his silence, this type of therapist permits the patient to shift from one manifest theme to another, and discovers that in the Type A communicative field, each of these manifest themes contains within it important and distinctive derivative responses which can be coalesced into a meaningful whole.

The communicative therapist has considerable faith in a patient's unconscious wish to express his neurosis and to communicate meaningfully. He permits the patient to express himself both meaningfully and through resistances, and allows the patient to place the fragments of meaning into the therapist which he can then interpret in light of a represented adaptive context simply by organizing the derivative implications of the material at hand. In this way, the patient leads the way entirely. There is no sense of pressure and no effort to force out the expression of hidden thoughts and fantasies. And of course, this permits time for contemplation and understanding by the therapist, who does so not only in terms of derivative expressions of unconscious fantasy constellations, but also in terms of unconscious perceptions.

There is more to be said, but now let's turn to the patient's response to this intervention.

Therapist: He agreed with me, and said, Yes, all that summer I knew that my credentials weren't so solid. I knew my background would kill; I knew that I wouldn't be able to write the papers. All of these things happened when I got to graduate school. I didn't deserve it; I didn't deserve to go there. Instead of dealing with these things rationally, I used these things to torment myself. I punished myself with my guilt and I froze myself in the depression.

Langs: The single most critical way of learning about valid and invalid interventions, and about the conscious and unconscious meanings and functions of what we express to the patient, is, of course, through their direct and especially indirect and derivative responses to our interventions. What does this commentary teach us?

Discussant: There is a sense of superficial confirmation, though I see no form of Type Two derivative validation. In fact, he eventually seems to intellectualize further about his sense of guilt, rather than providing us with something surprising or unique.

Discussant: As a commentary on the intervention, the patient says that his credentials are not solid, that his background would kill, and that he used these things to torment himself. As I hear it, this touches upon the hostile qualities of the therapist's intervention, and appears to be the patient's way of saying that it was not an especially solid intervention at all—if anything, it was rather destructive.

Langs: Yes, and the comment about his background creating an atmosphere in which he would be destroyed could well be an embedded derivative which alludes to the tape recorder, as it relates to the basic therapeutic environment and hold. As you know, direct agreement does not constitute psychoanalytic validation. We require instead Type Two derivative confirmation through some expression that serves as a selected fact. And I would agree that there is no evidence for such a communication in this material.

Instead, the patient says that interventions of this kind are poor and perhaps even false—here, I allude to the lie qualities of his background. They are destructive and interfere with expression and communication. They are used to torment and punish the patient, and to create a sense of depression within him. And along the me/not-me interface, they are seen as expressions of the therapist's hostility and of his own sense of depression, or as some effort to defend against that affect.

As you can see, there is no evidence of a positive introject here. In fact, the allusions to the patient himself are rather negative and pessimistic. And so, despite surface agreement and direct extension —much of it repetitious—this response lacks derivative cognitive confirmation, and interactionally lacks the emergence of the indications of a positive introjective identification with a well-functioning therapist.

As we have done throughout this course, we can now attempt to offer a general principle on the basis of this single experience, at this juncture as a silent hypothesis to be validated. I would suggest that virtually all confrontations and contradictory clarifications are experienced by patients as efforts to torment them and often as expressions of, and defenses against, depressive states within their therapists. They reflect poor credentials as a therapist, are essentially destructive, and interfere with the communicative properties of the bipersonal field. They are not rational in the sense that they are not the correct intervention called for by the material from the patient. On that basis, I would propose that we would discard confrontations and clarifications from our lexicon of interventions, and instead seek out more appropriate means of working with the patient. Naturally, I am making this type of proposal because this particular observation is supported by many others; still, I am not proposing it as the final word, but simply as a tentative precept to be reexamined as the clinical material permits.

Notice too that this patient shows strong depressive trends, and that he is likely to be pathologically gratified by the therapist's hostility, and to remain in therapy on that basis. This would apply whether the destructiveness is reflected in a verbal intervention or in a mismanagement of the framework. There is evidence here that the patient has a severe and pathological superego, that he is in some way plagued with guilt, and that he would readily submit to various levels of abuse by the therapist, however inadvertent, in an attempt to placate his superego.

How much more is there to this hour?

Therapist: I have a lot more, since this is a verbatim transcript.

Langs: Since time is short, could you now summarize the balance of the hour?

Therapist: Mainly, he got into this business about how he wasn't worthwhile, that he couldn't do the work in graduate school, and that it wasn't his fault. My next intervention was to the effect that he seemed to be trying to impress upon me his own helplessness with what happened before.

As an aside, I can see that once again I was working on a manifest content level and being somewhat critical. If I may, I would say that this is an attempt at confrontation which once again pertains to outside relationships, and bypasses the adaptive context of the deviations and of my last intervention. I can readily see that the patient would feel criticized and attacked by what I had said.

In the session, I went on and told him that he simply wasn't able to handle things then, and that he's having difficulty in handling things now, including understanding what I am saying.

Parenthetically, I must tell you that I am somewhat shocked at the quality of these interventions, now that I hear them in the perspective offered by this course. Here, too, I am working on the surface. I am contradicting the patient, and I am being very critical and harsh. I can even see a repetitive pattern in terms of some of the qualities of my interventions, and they are not very nice qualities at that.

Langs: Yes. It is certainly quite painful to realize such things in the course of a presentation, but nonetheless these are all interventions which you felt were necessary, and which you considered to be justified based on the patient's material. You can see at first hand how easy it is to set aside or to try to bypass resistances, and to fail to appreciate errors in intervening and reflections of significant, preponderant countertransferences in your work.

Therapist: Not surprisingly, the patient responded by saying that just thinking about all of his makes him very depressed, adding that he feels trapped and boxed in.

Langs: It may be painful for you as the therapist, but you are helping us to learn a great deal. Contradicting the patient, and clarifying his material in a hostile way, is often a means through which you projectively identify your own sense of depression, and your own tormenting superego, into the patient. Your interventions are in the Type B communicative mode, and appear to push the patient more toward lie systems than the truth system.

There is a quality of projection here, in that you are attributing to the patient something of your own difficulty in handling things in the present—however true this may be of him as well. In addition, there is a clear effort at interactional projection in that, as I said, you are berating and tormenting him in a manner that may well reflect your own inner sense of dissatisfaction and torment. The patient then feels cornered and overwhelmed by the projective identification, and is clearly having difficulty in metabolizing it. He becomes depressed both because of the depression you have placed into him, and because of his own tendencies and response. In that respect, it may well be that he is intensely angry, in addition to feeling victimized, and that his own anger evokes guilt and depression as well.

In principle, we must propose that hostile clarifications and confrontations are efforts by therapists to place into their patients aspects of their own feelings of depression and persecution, and of their own tormenting superego, as well as their own inner sense of badness. All this in addition to the more evident hostility and possible projections involved. As such, there is no possibility of generating insight or adaptive symptom alleviation.

Notice too that this type of intervention is offered without an adaptive context. The communicative approach, through which you continuously evaluate the unconscious implications of your interventions, tends to slow you down. It has an effect which modulates your impressions of your patients, and helps you to identify your own contributions to their symptoms, defenses, and other difficulties far more readily than otherwise. It provides you with a perspective through which you are better able to understand the true sources and functions of their defenses and resistances. Adaptive context listening, especially when applied to your own interventions, quickly leads you to eliminate virtually all noninterpretive interventions. The communicative approach provides you with a balanced sense of responsibility with respect to all disturbances within the participants to the bipersonal field.

Therapist: He goes on: I'm worried that I will go back to graduate school next year and fail. Here, I referred to our pending separation, and suggested that maybe what he is worried about is that he won't have me to bat around these problems with.

Parenthetically, I said this because it was evident that he wanted to engage me in an argument, and that he was going into all this stuff in order to do so.

He said, I have you, and you make it all appear as if I have a psychological mental problem rather than a deficiency in my intelligence, and it was my mental problem which caused my downfall. That's reassuring. They didn't do that for me at graduate school.

Langs: Any brief comments?

Discussant: It is hard now for me to determine the level of the patient's resistances. The therapist is intervening too often, and it is difficult to evaluate the communicative qualities of the patient's responses.

Langs: Yes, though in itself your comment suggests the possibility of a relatively high level of resistance. Actually, the patient responded to each intervention with meaningful derivatives that organize quite well around this sequence of adaptive contexts and their implications. However, in no case does he represent an adaptive context in a form that would lend itself to interpretation. This, by the way, is one commmon pattern of response to an erroneous, countertransference-based intervention: strong and co-alescing derivatives, in the absence of a clear representation of the adaptive context which makes the connection between the material and the intervention unmistakable.

I would therefore say that there is a relatively high level of communicative resistance here, much of it concentrated on the representation of the adaptive context of the therapist's interventions, and the background contexts of the tape recording and the presence of the supervisor. It would therefore be impossible to interpret this material to the patient, despite the presence of strong indicators in the form of erroneous interventions from the therapist. What then might be the main intervention here?

Discussant: It must have something to do with rectifying the frame, possibly correcting the error.

Langs: Yes, the main intervention is that of silence, and attempting to not repeat this particular type of erroneous intervention. In time, the patient's responsive resistances—which are, of course, an interactional product derived from both the therapist's errors and the patient's own defensive needs—would be modified by him to the point where meaningful communication might once again emerge, especially in a secured therapeutic space. As I said, an important intervention in dealing with resistances, especially if they have critical sources in the therapist's interventions, is that of silent correction and silent rectification. Not repeating an error stands high among the means with which we best deal with resistances in patients and counterresistances within ourselves as therapists.

Discussant: Are you implying here that some of this material organizes around the adaptive context of the therapist's verbal interventions? If so, does that contradict your thesis that this material would organize only around the basic deviation in the framework as represented by the tape recordings and supervisor?

Langs: Thank you for calling that point to our attention. Because our time is short, I did not attempt to show you how the patient's derivative responses in this part of the hour could also be organized meaningfully around the adaptive contexts of the tape recording and supervisor. I think that here you have a good example of condensation, and that the material takes on meaning in light of both sets of contexts: the erroneous verbal interventions and the deviations. Patients will often condense their repsonses to the therapist's errors and countertransferences in just this way.

To do this quickly, think back on a patient's feelings of depression, and the extent to which he feels trapped and boxed in. Certainly such feelings can be related to the adaptive context of the tape recording, through which the patient is indeed captured. As you may recall, we also postulated early in this discussion that the patient would see the tape recordings as a maniclike defense against depression on the part of the therapist, and this formulation can be related to the patient's feeling of depression in the hour. The fear of failure could also be related to the tape recording, as could the other derivatives.

Discussant: Can you say a brief word about why the patient feels reassured?

Langs: Yes. In the adaptive context of these erroneous interventions and of the deviations, a reasonable hypothesis would be that the therapist has expressed himself in powerful ways as the functional patient, and unconsciously, is perceived by the patient as suffering from major psychological problems. It is here that the principle of nefarious comparison might step in, and lead the patient to be reassured that his problems are not so awful in light of the difficulties being expressed by the therapist. In addition, there may have been some appeasement of this patient's superego through the punitive qualities of these confrontations, which could provide him with a temporary sense of relief.

Therapist: Well, he eventually got around to saying something about how much pressure he feels he is under right now in his life. I then said something about his ambivalence about doing well, and about allowing himself to be successful. He responded by saying that he may have conflicts about that, but he didn't see how it is related to his father. He said he was very confused.

Langs: Had you mentioned his father in your intervention?

Therapist: Yes, and he went on to say that he is confused, his brain is stuttering and his mind is stuttering. He feels a void.

Discussant: We are moving along very quickly now, but it seems to me that along the me/not-me interface, the patient is commenting on the inadequacy and emptiness of the therapist's interventions. The therapist's last comments seem to be an attempt at interpretation, with the usual characteristics of avoiding the therapeutic interaction and the adaptive contexts in his recent interventions. The patient sees this as a product of confusion. He also denies that it relates to his father, as if to imply that actually, it pertains to the therapist.

Langs: Yes. I suspect that you will all now hear many different interventions refuted by patients, much of it through derivatives. It will remain a challenge to find a valid intervention for this course so we may hear the difference in the patient's responses.

It seems to me that this material should suggest to us that interventions regarding outside relationships do not obtain Type Two derivative validation, and that they often generate highly destructive and negative introjects within the patient. The material also suggests that efforts at so-called interpretations which exclude adaptive contexts have similar effects.

Therapist: I would now like to simply play the last part of the tape of this session. From time to time, unfortunately, there is a blurring on the tape. Despite that, you will be able to sense what is going on since much of it comes through quite clearly.

Patient: At the moment, I'm not able to think that way, to see your point. I can't even see what you are talking about, but if I did, there would be a great light going off in my head and I'd jump in and write a paper about it in five minutes. I don't understand that at all. I mean, there is nothing to think about. Can you describe something or say something that might help? Perhaps it just won't register if you say it, I'm not sure. I mean, I can't think about this. I mean I can't allow myself to even try to think about this, because I don't think I will get anywhere with it, and I'll just be wasting my time.

Therapist: You might take a little lesson from it. Maybe in some ways you think an awful lot about things, and you try to be particularly intellectual and rational about things which may turn out to be actually beneath it all, quite irrational. And a way for you to deal with it, is for you to kind of plunge through it, and to try to reason with that area that has the guilt in it. But I think that maybe you might be inclined, particularly here, to try to think a little less and simply say whatever is on your mind.

Patient: I know I should try to do that. Perhaps then the material will be spontaneous.

Therapist: You came in today with a whole dialectic. Well prepared. And I think that that is a way you use to deal with it, to deal with certain anxieties that you have.

Patient: I am aware of this need to sort of organize things.

Therapist: I think this is particularly the case when you are very anxious about something. You take your reactions and try to fit everything together into a little package.

Patient: Yes. That is my style. I try to understand everything. When I have a problem, I feel it would somehow be resolved by thinking of doing something or just by thinking of it in a certain way. It seems that what you are saying is that this relates to the way I feel about my father and that it somehow influenced my academic problems. Or it may be fair to say that it's my evaluation that I have academic problems. It somehow becomes uncertain and irrational.

Langs: Well, I see that our almost time is up. In this last moment, would anybody like to comment on this material in light of our discussion today of resistances and interventions?

Discussant: This is only a small segment of the session, but I found it very intellectualized and empty. Off the top of my head, I sense a great deal of resistance.

Langs: In general, when we evaluate the level of resistance in that way, we are working as manifest content and Type One derivative therapists.

Discussant: Since this is the latter part of the session, and we have already heard the material which preceded it, it seems to me that we can refine matters just a bit further. In light of the adaptive contexts of the tape recording of the sessions, the presence of a supervisor, and the interventions made by the therapist in this hour, I would have to say that the patient, while showing no special evidence of gross behavioral resistances, is in a state of strong communicative resistances.

Discussant: To be fair, we would have to say that the therapist is showing strong counterresistances. These seem to be what you call interactional resistances within the patient. I am struck with the intellectualized qualities of both the therapist's interventions and the patient's associations. There is no effort here to intervene around an adaptive context.

Therapist: It's already proving especially disquieting to present this tape recorded material in this seminar. Somehow, this is a setting in which so many of our vulnerabilities and poor techniques seem certain to be exposed. In other seminars the instructors seemed to operate as we do, and they not only reinforce these obviously poor techniques, but provide us with direct support and even injunctions to make use of them. I realize now that in some way, the patient is excluded from all of that, especially when it comes to his derivative communications. And while this is all quite embarrassing, I am also learning an enormous amount.

Langs: I am glad that you appreciate the spirit in which the work in this seminar is carried out. Without pursuing that theme further—there is so little time—I would like to indicate my agreement with the assessment of this tape recorded material to the effect that it reflects major communicative resistances within both patient and therapist, each as interactional products. The highly intellectualized quality of these associations might well constitute, however, a form of gross behavioral resistance as well. Despite the fact that the patient is associating freely, he engages in a type of communication which would probably not illuminate any adaptive context whatsoever. Of course, it would remain for us to identify the specific activated context and to confirm this impression. And once that has been carried out, we could then evaluate the material for the level of communicative resistances.

In principle, when you discover upon reflection that you have intervened without allusion to instinctual drive derivatives, you should alert yourself to the likelihood that you are offering the patient an obsessive form of misalliance, and that you are also working with Type C, lie-barrier systems. A common corollary of the failure to work with Type Two derivatives is that of eliminating what are often compelling instinctual drive expressions when intervening. There is the use of generalities and of intellectualized terms such as dependency, self-image, and those which apply to a variety of concerns which, whatever their merits, serve functionally to remove the patient from intense, specific, instinctual drive-related conflicts, fantasies, and perceptions. This is a common failing in the interventions of many present-day therapists.

Discussant: It seems to me that tape recording sessions creates what you would call a lie-system bipersonal field. I also have the impression that the high level of communicative resistances we see in this material for the moment stems from both the therapist's way of intervening and from the presence of the tape recorder. For the moment, the patient seems, in strong measure because of the impact of the therapist's interventions, to be moving away from a meaningful working over from the major breaks in the framework of this therapeutic situation.

Langs: Your comments are quite perceptive. There does indeed appear to be a high level of communicative resistance here for the moment. I did hear an embedded derivative which seemed to represent the adaptive context of the tape recording of the sessions in the patient's allusion to writing a paper if he had any sense of insight. Nonetheless, it is a type of representation which does not readily afford an opportunity for intervening. Instead, it is a small clue to the underlying issues which are being sealed off for the moment through Type C barriers which are being generated by both patient and therapist.

As for the derivative complex, it is highly defensive and ruminative, and reflects a high level of resistance. You can see here what happens when a therapist responds to such a derivative network as if it were meaningful. Any attempt to interpret or confront the patient, as was done here for example, with some type of defense against anxiety which is unrelated to and in no way connected to the therapist, or to the prevailing resistances, will only promote an intellectualized, obsessive, and ruminative sector of misalliance.

Finally, you will notice that the therapist included a directive to the patient to free associate rather than to plan out and prepare in advance for his sessions. In so doing, he was attempting to deal with another gross behavioral resistance without making use of the patient's derivative communications as a basis for the content of his comment, and without any effort at interpretation.

For example, the likelihood that this particular resistance is an interactional product which relates strongly to the tape recording of the sessions is set entirely aside. The resistance is addressed on a manifest level, confronted, and the patient is directed to modify such obvious defensive efforts. There is no sense of critical unconscious determinants for this behavior—especially those involving instinctual drives—and above all, no indication of a realization that in some important way the therapist has contributed to its presence.

Notice too that the intervention used here can be described as a nonderivative lie or lie-barrier system. That is, it suggests that the patient has a particular way of dealing with his anxieties without specifying a specific adaptive context which has evoked these anxieties, and without applying the me/not-me interface in order to recognize that the patient's resistances are an unconscious version of the therapist's counterresistance—e.g., his efforts to deal with his own anxieties by tape recording the sessions. The intervention therefore obliterates rather than interprets the central unconscious dynamics of this therapeutic interaction—the most pertinent truths for the moment.

In light of the therapist's comments about the approach of other teachers and supervisors to the problems of resistance, you will find that the psychoanalytic literature reveals that most analysts view resistances in terms of their direct manifestations and will not infrequently employ directives as one aspect of their efforts to modify these perceived obstacles to the treatment process (see chapter 10). Many will, in addition, attempt to reach the patient's unconscious motives for a resistance, but will do so virtually entirely in terms of the patient's own intrapsychic conflicts without any sense of possible contributions from themselves as therapists or analysts.

This has been a most illuminating presentation. As I said, it was so enormously evocative that it led me to identify far more issues than I had hoped to cover in this first seminar, in respect to both resistances and intervening. Still, if it has given you a sense of the complexities of these two dimensions of the therapeutic process, and if it has helped to prompt a questioning attitude in both areas, it will provide us with a firm basis for subsequent extended and more specific discussions. Thank you.

Chapter Two

NONTRANSFERENCE AND TRANSFERENCE RESISTANCES

Therapist: I would like to finish the session I was presenting in the last seminar. From there, we can move into the next hour.

Patient: It's like there's a contradiction. Our relation, any relation, would seem to me to involve some sort of structural organization. That exists in any relation I can think of.

Therapist: But perhaps the dread that is bothering you and giving you some hell is not something in the past or even in the present, that you have an intellectual grasp of, nor is it something totally in your control.

Patient: Yes, I didn't even think of that. Are you saying that for me to try a path that would be counterproductive would be to . . .

Therapist: To package it.

Patient: Yes, to get in charge of it, to work it up nicely. I don't follow it entirely. I'm sorry. I sort of feel that way about what you said. I don't know if I was thinking of a way of establishing control and arranging for things to come out the way I want. I realize I can't. But I thought that when we come to this kind of point where we are supposed to discuss this kind of thing, I find I just can't produce what you want at all. I'm not capable of doing it.

Therapist: What do you think I want?

Langs: We are in the process of refining our understanding of both resistances and interventions. The therapist has now intervened three times. Let's pause and entertain some comments.

Discussant: This material brought back a good deal of the previous session which, as I remember it, had this strongly ruminative quality on both sides.

Discussant: The first intervention completed an idea for the patient. I was wondering how we would categorize it?

Langs: Let's remember that this is the end of the session, and that we heard most of it last week. The material from the patient continues to have a strong sense of both behavioral and communicative resistance. I will therefore say less about resistances than interventions for the moment, and will examine each of the therapist's three comments.

Remember too, we want to approach interventions by analyzing their properties and characteristics in terms of what I would now propose to be four categories:* (1) their formal definition, ranging from silences through interpretations-reconstructions; (2) the level of listening reflected in the interventions—manifest content, Type One derivative, and Type Two derivative; (3) the communicative definition—whether the interventions include the major indicators and the best representation of the adaptive context, and make full use of the derivative complex; and (4) the communicative properties, especially the unconscious implications in terms of the ongoing communicative interaction.

I believe you will find that this categorization is a bit different than the one I presented last week. It is based on further reflections about what we actually did in analyzing the interventions at that time, and on a sense of how we might more fully and clearly define

---

*An expanded and refined version of this evolving catalogue of the basic components of the intervention is presented in Appendix C.

and extend our efforts. We should remain open to the possibility of defining still more critical attributes.

Discussant: Do you intend to include in the category of formal definition both so-called supportive interventions and managements of the framework?

Langs: Yes, that's exactly where such considerations belong. For a while, and perhaps throughout the balance of this seminar, let's analyze the interventions presented to us in terms of these categories of attributes. (We will introduce other categories when it seems appropriate.) Would you remind us of your first comment?

Therapist: In effect, I had pointed out that there was some type of dread that was bothering him and giving him hell. And I suggested that it needn't be something in the past or even in the present, but that whatever it is, he's trying to get hold of it and place it under his control.

Discussant: I found the intervention confusing when we heard it on the tape recording, and I still find it that way now.

Langs: Yes, that would fall into the fourth realm, the communicative properties of the intervention. Who will identify its formal definition?

Discussant: It's either an attempt at interpretation or at confrontation. It is so vague that it is difficult to decide.

Langs: I would agree. Perhaps we need to state that any intervention may be well stated or confusing, clear or unclear. We'll get to that a bit later on. Nonetheless, it is possible to make a sound interpretation or a poor one. Still, in deciding, you will have to address some of its communicative properties.

Discussant: As for listening, it seems to deal with manifest contents and perhaps slightly with Type One derivatives.

Langs: Yes.

Discussant: I'll try its communicative definition. It lacks an adaptive context and makes virtually no use of a derivative complex.

Therapist: As we said last week, this intervention—as several others before—takes the patient away from the therapeutic interaction and places all of his difficulties inside of himself. I would agree that it is somewhat confusing; communicatively, I would have to believe that I am conveying my own sense of confusion to the patient.

Discussant: Even though it addresses the patient's anxiety, it has an intellectual quality. It offers an obsessive misalliance to the patient.

Langs: We are reaching the point where I need only provide you with a framework, and you can do the rest of the work on your own.

Here, all I need add or confirm is that this particular intervention places all of the disturbance within the bipersonal field in the patient; it can readily serve to deny the therapist's countertransferences and both his own sense of dread and defenses against it. We did not hear enough material to ascertain the extent to which the intervention is in keeping with what the patient has expressed or the degree to which the therapist has introduced his own thoughts and fantasies.

Let's pause and identify some subcategories. For the formal definition of an intervention, you already know the range: from silences to interpretation-reconstructions to noninterpretative efforts, and in addition, managements of the framework. We are all familiar with the three levels of listening, and only need to add that we could also indicate whether the intervention deals with the patient's cognitive material, with interactional mechanisms such as projective identification, or with the object relational sphere such as role- and image-evocations.

The three elements of the communicative definition are also familiar: the indicator, the adaptive context, and the derivative complex. Last week, I mentioned the major indicators: verbal and framework errors by the therapist; resistances in the patient; and disturbances which face the patient, internally as symptoms and externally as life crises. We will need more clinical material to further develop this categorization and clearly understand its clinical referents.

Finally, as for the communicative properties of an intervention, there seems to be a number of different possibilities. To identify some of those with which we have already worked: the degree of clarity or confusion; the inclusion of the therapeutic relationship and interaction; the full and sensitive use of the patient's material or the therapist's introduction of his own associations; and the extent to which the intervention reveals the therapist's psychopathology—countertransferences—or instead is in keeping with disturbances within the patient.

Each of these categories is quite complex in itself, and they tend to overlap. We could also include the extent to which the intervention is built on the patient's derivative rather than manifest communications, and whether it integrates disparate elements or reflects a different approach—for example, the reading of implied meanings, the addition by the therapist of material from other sessions, or even the introduction of his personal opinions. An intervention is comparatively affectively insightful and tactful or inappropriately hostile, seductive, premature, even tactless. We would also classify interventions with respect to whether the therapist unconsciously offers the patient pathological derivative defenses or Type C barriers, and in addition, the degree to which the intervention constitutes a pathological projective identification.

Communicatively, interventions can reflect the bias of the therapist or the material from the patient, and usually are intermixtures of each. Another important category is the extent to which they contain allusions to specific types of pathological contexts, such as instinctual drive expressions, ego defenses, and superego derivatives—the basic ingredients of neurosis formation and resistances. As you no doubt realize, the question of the extent to which an intervention arises from the impressions and fantasies of the therapist, as compared with a synthesis of information elements (derivative bits in terms of fantasies and perceptions), touches upon one determinant of how much an intervention reflects the therapist's countertransferences. Such countertransferences can be expressed in a wide range of errors with respect to intervening, and require classification in terms of the dimensions of interventions we are now developing.

As you can see, classifications of the communicative properties of an intervention are complicated and touch upon diverse, though often interrelated and overlapping, aspects of the intervening process. Toward the end of the course, I will distribute a listing of these various areas of subclassification (see Appendix C). As we proceed, you will undoubtedly discover important additional subcategories and add them to this list. It is this dimension of intervening which makes the evaluation of a particular comment or management of the framework quite complicated and sometimes rather difficult. Nonetheless, we have four major categories for evaluating the work of the therapist which will provide us with a valuable set of guidelines.

Let's now move on to the second intervention.

Discussant: I think you are referring to the therapist's completing the patient's sentence about trying to package his thoughts in some neat fashion. That intervention appears to be a clarification, and to address manifest contents.

Discussant: It deals neither with derivatives nor an adaptive context.

Discussant: The tricky part seems to lie in its communicative properties. For some reason, until I took this course, I virtually never thought about the unconscious implications of my interventions. Certainly, I was taught to take a look at possible reflections of countertransference, but that was a very vague concept. Usually, it came down to whether I became consciously aware of some difficulty in what I said.

Based on our work here, it seems to me that the communicative properties of an intervention are perhaps its most important aspect. In this case, I sense something that I do not recall in your categorization. It touches upon countertransference, but it seems to me that by finishing the patient's sentence, the therapist is unconsciously merging himself with the patient.

Langs: Your point is a good one. While I touched upon instinctual drive and superego gratifications for the therapist in countertransference-based interventions, I did not include some type of category related to maintaining a reasonable sense of separation of patient and therapist, both internally in terms of self- and object representations, and interactionally in terms of unconscious efforts to either fuse or merge on the one hand, or to generate inappropriate interpersonal barriers on the other.

You might also describe this category as involving the extent to which the therapist unconsciously attempts to gratify pathological symbiotic and even parasitic needs. This can be carried out, of course, not only by finishing a sentence for a patient, but also by intermingling the therapist's own thoughts and associations with those from the patient. The intervention could become parasitic and invasive at a point where the therapist offers more of his thoughts and ideas, feelings and such, than he derives from the material from the patient, to an extent where the patient himself is being exploited and even harmed.

This discussion leads me to comment further on the object relationship between the patient and the therapist, a subject we began to develop in some detail last week. We can see here that an intervention is, on one level, an expression of one of the four modes of object relatedness I defined in our last seminar—commensal, pathological symbiotic, appropriately symbiotic, or parasitic. Each mode of relatedness has conscious and unconscious aspects, and is an actuality which will have a greater impact upon the patient than the manifest contents of the therapist's interventions. This implies that the type of relatedness effected by an intervention will greatly influence the patient's understanding of the therapist's conscious and unconscious message, and his response to the total intervention. In principle, only interpretive interventions and managements directed toward securing the ground rules and boundaries of the therapeutic relationship can express, consciously and unconsciously, a therapist's wish for a commensal or healthy symbiotic relationship with his patient. All other interventions afford both participants pathological satisfactions, many of them related to instinctual drives and to fusion. They serve to constitute or extend either a pathological symbiosis or a parasitic type of interaction.

We should remember that not all interventions are designed by the therapist to fuse or merge with the patient in some type of symbiotic link, so to speak. The therapist may make a strikingly hostile intervention or so modify the ground rules and boundaries of the therapeutic relationship that the patient is pushed away and too great a separation and sense of barrier is created. Interventions of this kind may well represent autistic needs in the therapist, or efforts to parasitize the patient. Or they may constitute a form of hostile symbiosis which arouses intense separation anxieties and hostility within the patient, much as comparable destructive efforts on his part may arouse this type of reaction in the therapist. Paradoxically, such interventions may prematurely force the patient to develop some degree of autonomy and individuation from the therapist, though the underlying basis is uninsightful and infused with qualities derived from the pathological introjects of the therapist. This should serve as a reminder that all forms of pathological relatedness have gratifications as well as liabilities, a point which I attempted to establish in some detail when we discussed various types of lie-barrier therapy. I suspect that it is these pathological satisfactions, defenses, and sanctions which help to account for symptom alleviation in the course of many present-day therapeutic experiences.

What now of the third intervention, in which the therapist asks the patient what he thinks the therapist wants?

Discussant: That is a question and reflects listening on a manifest level. I don't think we mentioned that the prior intervention lacked an indicator, though the therapist may have been trying to deal with some type of defense or resistance by pointing out the patient's efforts to overorganize and categorize things. With this last question, there may have been some vague effort to deal with a resistance, though I could just as well suggest that the intervention did not deal with any particular indicator at all.

Therapist: Well, I thought perhaps that I could clarify the basis of his resistance in his trying to please me in some way.

Langs: We can accept that as the indicator: an effort to deal with a gross behavioral, and probably communicative, resistance.

Discussant: Once again there is no effort, however, to identify an adaptive context or derivative complex. Communicatively, the question could be experienced as provocative or hostile.

Langs: Yes, and it leads me to add another type of communicative property: the level of relatedness which the therapist, through his intervention, is attempting to establish with the patient. With each of these interventions, we have a strong sense that the therapist wishes this would be on a manifest content level. In time, you will develop a clearer picture of this constellation of relatedness. Other constellations of this kind are Type One derivative relatedness, which tends to be intermixed with that on a manifest content level, and Type Two derivative relatedness, which is quite distinctive.

Notice again that this particular question, even though it pertains to the therapist, takes the patient away from the unconscious communicative interaction, and from any prevailing adaptive context within the bipersonal field.

Discussant: Won't it serve as an invitation for defensiveness or rumination, and perhaps as a Type C barrier?

Langs: Yes, it may. It might also have qualities of a projective identification, in that the therapist may be responding to some sense of pressure from the patient by dumping that pressure back into its source. The intervention may also be ill-timed and defensive.

I hope that you can all see now that applying our four categories to a sequence of interventions from the therapist reveals a rather consistent pattern of work. Despite our observation that these three interventions had rather different formal definitions—confrontation-interpretation, clarification, and question—we found considerable communality in the level of listening, concentrated on manifest contents, and the communicative definition of each. They tended to only vaguely address an indicator, and to consistently fail to deal with either the representations of a prevailing adaptive context or a pertinent derivative complex.

On the whole, the communicative properties emphasized denial of contributions from the therapist, movement away from the therapeutic interaction, some degree of intellectualization and confusion, and—in considering the last two interventions—a fluctuation between an overinvolved sense of merging and a provocative effort at distancing and barrier formation by the therapist. In all, the effort is to develop a manifest content form of relatedness in which unconscious processes, and especially unconscious perceptions and introjects of the therapist, would be denied and obliterated.

By inference, we hope through our various categories to develop a lexicon of interventions which would not possess the failings identified here. By showing the various flaws and countertransference contributions in these interventions, soon we should be able to realize some properties of more valid efforts by the therapist. Hopefully, we will eventually come to a situation in which we have a chance to experience an essentially valid intervention, and investigate its consequences.

This last comment leads me to add a fifth category to the properties of an intervention. It is somewhat different from the other four. Can anyone suggest what I have omitted?

Discussant: From the drift of your comments, I was led to think of whether an intervention receives Type Two derivative validation.

Langs: Exactly. That particular property of an intervention actually involves the subsequent material from the patient, and I therefore set it aside in my earlier categorizations. However, it must remain as the hallmark of a sound effort by the therapist, and while not a direct property of how the therapist has expressed himself, it is important enough to be included in this classification.

We will now hear the patient's response to this last intervention. To this point, I think you would all agree that there is no indication whatsoever of Type Two derivative validation.

> *Patient*: I think you want some sort of spontaneity and that I should admit my weaknesses. It's like you're telling me that the only thing I'm going to do and see in this way has to do with distracting you. Do you think this is more than a distraction? That it is somehow much more connected up?
>
> *Therapist*: The only thing I would like for you to do now, and the only thing that it seems you could admit for now, has to do with what's happening here. You're kind of fighting a certain intellectual battle concerning something that I've said

about your father. Some feelings about your father and some feelings about your past.

Patient: I'm willing to discuss my father.

Therapist: I know you are. But I think it is difficult for you to do this on anything but an intellectual level at this point.

Patient: It seems to me that you're right, that I'm not capable of doing it, and I have a strange feeling that I never felt before. Are you sure you won't have a pretzel?

Therapist: He had come into the session with a bag of pretzels.

Discussant: Was he eating them during the session?

Therapist: No, he ate them on the train coming to the session. He offered me some at the beginning of the session and some as he left. Actually, this is the end of the hour.

Langs: Who will comment?

Discussant: We heard several more interventions. The first, as I recall, had to do with the therapist pointing out that the patient was fighting some kind of intellectual battle in respect to his feelings about his father, present and past. I heard that as a confrontation.

Langs: And with what did you feel the therapist was confronting the patient?

Discussant: That he was using some kind of intellectual defenses.

Langs: Yes, and we'll have something more to say about the content of the therapist's interventions in a moment. Perhaps that should be a sixth component of interventions: the content and purpose of an intervention, in which we would distinguish efforts to deal with resistances and defenses from efforts to gain insight into key dynamics, core conflicts, and major unconscious fantasy and perception constellations, with their genetic aspects. In making these distinctions, we should remain aware that the resistance/core-pathology continuums show considerable overlap in the middle

range, and that the interpretation of resistances and defenses consistently reveals unconscious fantasy and perception constellations,
and shades into therapeutic efforts pertinent to nonresistant clusters
of communication.

Along these lines, we might also distinguish genetic interpretations from those which deal primarily with currently activated
dynamics—though of course, ultimately, we hope to include an
understanding of both. We might also want to note whether the
intervention arose from an issue related to the therapeutic environment or framework, or from something in the patient's associations, with their verbal, nonverbal, and affective qualities. We might
want to identify responses to actions and behaviors of the patient as
well. Finally, to restate a category which I included under communicative properties, but which also would be relative to the
content or the purpose of an intervention: we would want to
distinguish those interventions which pertain to the therapeutic
relationship and interaction from those which pertain to the patient
as he interacts with and relates to figures outside of the therapeutic
situation.

As you can see, interventions are enormously complex entities.
Nonetheless, if we remain flexible while making use of the six
categories of attributes we have identified, it is possible to do a
fairly thorough job in evaluating the therapist's active efforts. It
soon becomes possible to identify the properties of a sound intervention as compared to those which are countertransference-based,
and beyond that, to become quite sensitive to the many otherwise
unconscious implications.

Here, there is an effort primarily to confront the patient with his
intellectual defenses and resistances—the two are, for the moment,
identical as far as the therapist is concerned. Before commenting
further on this intervention, who will complete our categorization
of its properties?

Discussant: It seemed to be a straightforward and clear intervention as I heard it. Certainly, it involves the patient and his father
and not the therapeutic interaction. It occurs to me also that we have
overlooked the fact that the therapist was telling the patient something he would like him to do for now, and that we might have

included in the formal definition of the intervention the presence of a directive.

Langs: Yes, that is an important realization. Anything else?

Discussant: I found the intervention a bit stern, as if the therapist were reprimanding the patient. It seemed to me that the patient took it that way when he responded that he was willing to discuss his father with the therapist.

Langs: And did you consider that response a form of validation?

Discussant: Not at all, at least in the psychoanalytic sense of Type Two derivative validation as you defined it here. I thought that the patient had become defensive because the therapist had been somewhat attacking.

Discussant: I also saw the intervention as an effort to maintain a manifest content-Type One derivative form of relatedness, and I saw the patient tending to comply.

Langs: As we proceed, we want to select clinical observations from which we can draw general hypotheses which we hope to validate through further clinical material. After all, we have been studying the therapist's interventions since we began this course, though with little effort at systematization. We have therefore been collecting impressions for some time, and we should attempt now to generate some specific technical principles—some rather firm hypotheses and clinical tenets.

For example, we want to begin to identify the types of interventions from the therapist which do not, as a rule, obtain Type Two derivative validation. We want to see if they do, indeed, also tend to generate negative introjective identifications by the patient with the therapist, and disruptive responses, rather than constructive and insightful growth-promoting reactions. While for some reason this idea may sound strange to you—I have not seen it stated in the literature—we certainly should be prepared to discard interventions which tend to be detrimental to the therapeutic process and the patient. By definition, such efforts must reflect the countertransferences of the therapist—his own pathological needs and tendencies. I believe that it is possible clinically to identify a number of interventions in current use which meet these criteria. In fact, it is my impression that we have already done this from time to time earlier in this course. At this point, we should attempt to synthesize and state specifically the fruits of these labors.

If we review the therapist's interventions throughout this session, we have already found that his noninterpretive comments—his questions, his clarifications, and now his confrontations—all met with nonvalidation and some degree of negative responsiveness. These interventions tended to ignore the prevailing intervention contexts and the available derivative responses from the patient—perceptions and fantasies. We saw that they tended to be used on a manifest content or Type One derivative level, rather than in terms of Type Two derivative communication. We also garnered evidence that they had properties of pathological projective identifications from the therapist, and often constituted the offer to the patient of Type C barriers. And remember, all of these generalizations applied despite the fact that, at times, the therapist attempted to deal with important indicators, such as the patient's resistances and defenses, though repeatedly this was done without any consideration of his own contribution to these obstacles and of the interactional nature of these phenomena.

These observations are very much in keeping with our findings in previous seminars. I will therefore offer a general proposition on the basis of this material which we can verify or modify as we go along: *The therapist's use of questions, clarifications, confrontations, and noninterpretive interventions reflect unconscious countertransference constellations and do not find validation in the patient's responses.* They are detrimental and disruptive to the therapeutic experience and process, do not serve the therapeutic needs of the patient, and should be excluded from our therapeutic armamentarium.

Now, some of you might wish to suggest that we have simply heard poor or erroneous applications of these interventions, and that we should not be too hasty in discarding them entirely. Of course, we will keep an open mind and see if we discover a valid instance of such work. I can only state that we have not found that to be the case up to this point in our work, and that this is in keeping with my experience as a therapist and analyst, and as a supervisor. In addition, my study of the literature also supports this position. Among experienced analysts, this group of interventions is often rationalized as a way of gaining access to the unconscious dimensions of resistances and core conflicts and fantasies. In actual practice, however, this is virtually never the case, even in their own illustrations. Such work is almost universally carried out in terms of manifest contents and Type One derivatives, and draws upon direct inferences from the patient's material. In contrast, the communicative technique calls for the derivation of meanings and functions as reflected in the material from the patient by organizing his manifest associations and behaviors around prevailing intervention contexts. As a result, the types of interventions used by a communicative therapist are different in important ways from those used by classical therapists.

Who will comment on the other interventions made by the therapist at the end of this session?

Discussant: I think his second intervention was a condensed repetition of the first.

Langs: And it was offered in the absence of Type Two derivative validation to the initial effort. In principle, do not repeat an intervention in a given hour—especially in the absence of confirmation from the patient. Notice too that the therapist's comment, to the effect that he knows that the patient is willing to discuss his father, is a self-revelation and a modification of anonymity. It is a noninterpretive intervention of a kind that could easily escape notice—at least on our part, though seldom on the part of the patient.

What about the therapist's final intervention? It's quite easy to fail to recognize that the therapist's refusal of the patient's offer of pretzels is an intervention.

Discussant: I was thinking about that. I wondered if this wasn't an impingement on the framework. It brought me back to the adaptive context of the tape recording of the sessions. For a moment, I sensed the presence of a Type Two derivative, perhaps to the effect,

along the me/not-me interface, that the therapist is swallowing up
the patient and gratifying himself through what the patient has to
offer. In the terms you have recently introduced, the patient seems to
be representing a type of relationship which I would have to characterize as either a pathological symbiosis or parasitism. Somehow, I
keep thinking of what happens to the pretzel when it is eaten, a point
which leads me to wonder if tape recording of sessions is not seen
by the patient as far more parasitic than symbiotic.

Langs: Excellent. You can see how easy it is to miss entirely
what turns out to be a most meaningful communication from the
patient when it takes the form of a manifest behavior. We often
overlook the derivative implications of such actions and fail to
develop their possible encoded implications in terms of an activated
intervention context—here, of course, the tape recording of the
sessions. You are quite correct, the presence and offer of the pretzels
actually provides us with Type Two derivative validations of a
number of silent hypotheses we developed last week in respect to
the unconscious implications of the tape recordings—itself an
important behavioral intervention of the therapist.

Taping is indeed an incorporative act, carried out at the expense
of the patient, and highly destructive to the therapeutic hold, to the
therapist's containing capacities, and to the basic sense of trust
necessary for a healthy symbiotic or commensal type of relationship. In this light, it is well to recognize that a sound therapeutic
alliance, manifestly and on a communicative level, implies one of
these two modes of relatedness, and cannot exist in the presence of
a pathologically symbiotic or parasitic interaction. We must therefore remember, in evaluating all interventions, to turn quickly to a
categorization of the type of relatedness expressed by each response
of the therapist—including his silences. Clearly, it is possible for a
therapist to permit a patient to obtain all types of parasitic and
pathologically symbiotic gratification by failing to respond interpretively to the available material. Pathological modes of relatedness may evolve through erroneous active interventions or through
inappropriate silences by the therapist. Then too an assessment of
the nature of the therapeutic relationship can be made only through
an understanding of the appropriate satisfactions for each partici-

pant to the therapeutic situation, and a full appraisal of an intervention in light of activated intervention contexts.

The reference to the pretzels, as a derivative representation of the tape recordings, clearly suggests parasitism, although the feeding qualities involved—clearly an inappropriate satisfaction for both patient and therapist in the treatment situation—may allude to a pathological symbiosis as well. As you know, many therapists would fail to recognize the implications of an offer of this kind, even take kindly to it, feeling they were sharing something with the patient. Seemingly minor inappropriate gratifications of this kind are sanctioned by many writers in the analytic literature. However, they overlook the extent to which exchanges of this kind, if accepted by the therapist, preclude a healthy mode of relatedness and interpretive therapeutic work. While erroneously viewed as preparatory to such efforts, in actuality they serve to reinforce the pathologically symbiotic and parasitic qualities of the therapeutic relationship. They can so modify the patient's anxieties and gratify his inappropriate instinctual drive and merger needs that all painful efforts to generate meaning and interpretation are set aside.

We see again the importance of the ground rules and boundaries of the therapeutic relationship and situation. Perhaps you can now fully accept the thesis that it is this dimension which forms the basis, as Bleger (1967) so cogently noted, for the healthy symbiosis necessary for sound therapeutic work. To extend this point, I would suggest that the therapist's management of these ground rules is the single most critical determinant for the type of therapeutic relationship he effects with the patient. It is in this realm that the choice between healthy or pathological symbiosis is made.

Unconsciously, patients tend to know this quite well, and you will find that those capable of tolerating a healthy symbiosis and the pursuit of truth therapy will accept the ideal ground rules and boundaries described earlier in this course. On the other hand, patients with intense and primitive separation anxieties, who dread autonomous functioning and individuation, attempt to have the therapist deviate in one or more ways, and will repeatedly challenge him in this sphere. These patients tend to respond to interpretive efforts and to managements of the framework directed toward securing its boundaries with striking Type Two derivative valida-

tion on the receptive side, but then they often shift immediately to
Type C barriers and obliterating mechanisms. Essentially, they
validate the therapist's interventions and then deny their own
insight and understanding, becoming filled with persecutory and
separation anxieties which prompt them to make renewed efforts at
merging. As a result, low resistance is usually followed by a high
level of defensiveness on both the gross behavioral and communicative levels.

You can see too that when it comes to a question of a ground
rule the therapist has no choice but to respond and to do so in a
nonneutral manner. He must decide whether to adhere to the
established boundaries and frame, or to permit and participate in a
deviation. On the object relationship level, then, he must choose
between a mainly healthy or pathological symbiosis.

In this situation, the therapist refused the pretzels. This is a
management of the ground rules and boundaries, and a noninterpretive intervention. It is an effort to establish a reasonable
boundary between himself and the patient, and to effect a sector of
healthy symbiotic, potentially Type Two derivative, relatedness.

On the other hand, if the therapist continued to relate to the
patient on the manifest content level, a pathological symbiosis
designed to seal off the underlying chaos would emerge through a
manifest content mode of relatedness. Patients often attempt to
modify the basic ground rules as a means of engaging the therapist
in this manner. The ideal response to such efforts is to first invoke
the fundamental rule of free association, and then to interpret the
therapeutic context of the patient's effort to modify the frame in
light of activated adaptive contexts to which the patient is responding—including the therapist's nonparticipation in the deviation
and those prior contexts which prompted the efforts to modify the
ground rules.

This reference to the manifest content and Type Two derivative
forms of relatedness leads me to now attempt to integrate our
earlier discussion of the three modes of relatedness between the
patient and therapist with our present discussion in terms of certain
basic object relationship satisfactions which lead to characterizations such as autistic, symbiotic, parasitic, and commensal. As you
may have already realized, the manifest content mode of relatedness
is always pathological, and may be autistic, pathologically symbi-

otic, or parasitic. The same applies to Type One derivative related-ness, while of course Type Two derivative relatedness is essential to healthy symbiosis and commensal relationships. This correlation indicates an intimate connection between the mode of communication between patients and therapists and the type of satisfaction or maturational relationship being effected by each participant.

Every effort by the patient to modify the ground rules and boundaries of the therapeutic relationship is in part a form of resistance designed to sidestep or obstruct the therapeutic process as it is geared toward interpretation and insight, as well as growth, autonomy, and individuation. Rather than laboring to associate and understand, the patient attempts to directly gratify himself and the therapist in ways designed to set aside the usual type of thera-peutic work. Empirical data is clear that this type of satisfaction is in no way a prelude to a more therapeutic approach; instead it leads to misalliance and arouses in the patient wishes to continue to obtain deviant gratification.

The therapist's actual intervention deals neither with the adaptive context nor the derivative complex. The offer of the pretzels, a rather close though somewhat disguised representation of the adaptive context of the tape recording of the sessions, and the material which preceded the offer seem to constitute a highly defended and therefore resistant derivative complex. It suggests that the patient prefers for the moment to maintain a mutually parasitic or pathologically symbiotic mode of relatedness with the therapist, and not provide him with a meaningful derivative com-plex through which these needs could be interpreted and modified.

As for the communicative properties of the therapist's interven-tion, his refusal of the pretzels is a statement which pertains to the therapeutic relationship and which creates some sense of inter-personal barrier. However, since it does not do so through an interpretive response, it does not provide the patient with a healthy sense of separateness, but only with an uncertain sense of distance. Further, we know nothing of validation from the patient since the offer was made at the end of the hour. We would tend to predict an absence of Type Two derivative confirmation.

As for the structure of the intervention, it is, as I said, an effort to deal with a resistance and a frame issue, and with the nature and type of therapeutic relationship, though it does so through a directive rather than an interpretation. As such, it may generate some measure of separation anxiety within the patient, though it could not be expected to modify the basic mode of relatedness which exits in this therapeutic dyad at this time.

In actual practice, the ideal intervention here would be an interpretation of the implications of this offer. Only an interpretive response can create both a sense of separateness and movement toward a healthy symbiosis. It is difficult for the moment to formulate a specific interpretive response since the entire session is no longer fresh in our minds. However, the therapist might have suggested that the patient seemed to be attempting to modify a basic aspect of their relationship in his offer of the pretzels. There are some striking qualities to this offer in that the patient wishes the therapist to take in and swallow something which belonged to the patient. Undoubtedly, this is not a coincidental communication, but in some way contains important and unrecognized implications. And this must be related as well to the patient's earlier comments about doing things badly, being inexperienced, needing too much help from others, feeling inordinately guilty, committing plagiarism, and submitting unnecessarily to his professor—to add those aspects of the derivative complex which I recall best from last week's seminar and which are pertinent to the unmentioned adaptive context of the tape recordings.

I would offer this intervention because of the therapist's break in the fixed frame through tape recording the sessions and the patient's effort to modify the frame through the offer of the pretzels. These are high-level indicators, and on a scale from one to ten, I would classify this as nine or ten. This means that we are postulating a very powerful need within the patient for interpretive and management interventions from the therapist.

In principle, as hopefully you now recognize, this particular intervention is a playback of derivatives in the absence of a directly mentioned or well-represented intervention context. It is a variation on interpretation-reconstruction which we would use primarily in the presence of a break in the fixed frame or an issue in that area. It should not be used randomly and is seldom successful when it refers to an unmentioned interpretive error by the therapist. It is an intervention which is easily abused and often used to rationalize the playback of manifest contents either in terms of surface implications or Type One derivative inferences, and there are even more random playbacks offered in the hope of generating an unforeseen response from the patient. Clearly, these latter applications are incorrect, and the intervention should be restricted to those situations in which there is a powerful intervention context, usually related to the ground rules, which powerfully organizes a group of meaningful derivative elements that lend themselves to this type of comment. And as a rule, it is best to begin the playback with the best representation of the adaptive context—the organizer—available in the material. Here, of course, this is the offer of the pretzels.

Such an intervention may include genetic referents in a manner similar to the way in which I included a genetic connection to the father in the model intervention I proposed a moment ago. Whatever the patient is dealing with in his relationship with his therapist apparently touches upon aspects of his relationship with his father, past and present. Since that is in the material, we would include it in our playback.

To further summarize, this particular intervention is designed to deal with an interactional resistance generated by both patient and therapist. It is primarily a nontransference (i.e., only secondarily transference-based) resistance, since the therapist must accept a major responsibility for its existence at this time. At the point where he no longer tape records the sessions, and the framework is otherwise secured, and there is a relative absence of countertransference inputs, an attempt by the patient to modify the ideal therapeutic environment in this way would be seen as an expression primarily of transference resistances rather than nontransference resistances.

I trust that you can see that what has been termed in the literature as transference resistances—obstacles to therapy which arise in connection with the patient's relationship with the therapist— have been recategorized through the communicative approach into nontransference and transference resistances. Together they can be termed relationship resistances.

We have a typical continuum here and the label we apply will depend upon the primary source of the resistance, with the provision that as long as the therapist is making a significant contribution, the patient's response will be seen to fall into the realm of nontransference. And under such conditions we will also be prepared for extensions into the transference sphere, though we would not expect to focus on those aspects until we have clearly understood, interpreted, and rectified the nontransference component.

Relationship resistances constitute the single most common source of obstacles to treatment. It may surprise you to learn that nontransference resistances are probably far more common than those derived from transference. In any case, both gross behavioral and communicative resistances may arise on the basis of nontransference and transference factors. In the former situation, the obstacle to treatment is based on an essentially valid unconscious perception and introject of some type of psychopathology and defensive need in the therapist. Thus, the patient may perceive something disturbing, conflictual, and threatening as reflected in the therapist's silences or interventions, and he responds by becoming disruptive and defensive. In other circumstances, the patient may incorporate a defense offered consciously or unconsciously by the therapist, and use it himself in a resistant manner. It is common for a therapist to evoke resistant reactions in his patients which are designed not only to protect the patient himself, but also to spare the therapist material and reactions he seems to be, and is, incapable of handling.

We have already seen in this course that nontransference resistances are extremely common. They correspond to what I have earlier termed interactional resistances, and the two terms are essentially synonymous. It is, of course, important to identify this type of resistance for many reasons, among which is that the therapist must not only interpret but also *rectify* his contributions to the patient's defensiveness. As we already know from our discussion of the ground rules and framework, and from our consideration of the therapeutic interaction, the therapist has two interrelated and yet distinctive tasks in the presence of a significant countertransference-based input: (1) self-analysis and the elimination to the greatest extent feasible of the expressions of the unconscious countertransference constellation; and (2) interpretation of the patient's total responses based entirely upon his behavioral and associative reactions.

In general, nontransference resistances are, on an object relationship level, responses to a therapist's effort to effect a pathological mode of relatedness with the patient. It is for this reason that rectification is essential, and is an actuality which expresses the therapist's willingness to establish a healthier mode of relatedness. As you can imagine, interpretation of nontransference resistances without concomitant rectification generates a self-contradictory and split image of the therapist: understanding what is going on on the one hand, but doing nothing to correct the situation and, therefore, in a sense failing to understand and preferring a pathological symbiosis. In contrast, rectification without interpretation conveys to the patient a wish to modify the mode of relatedness without an indication of a full appreciation of its pathological qualities and without a clear call, however indirectly, for a healthy type of interaction. Such a measure may at times prove helpful in the absence of a meaningful derivative network, and must serve as preliminary to interpretive work.

Transference resistances would be defined as those obstacles to treatment, behavioral and communicative, which derive primarily from the patient's own unconscious fantasy-memory constellations and psychopathology, as they detrimentally influence the therapeutic work and relationship. Within the therapeutic interaction, these arise in response to the therapist's noncountertransference-based and sound interventions, ranging from silences to valid interpretations and managements of the framework. Motivated by the threat of therapeutic regression, the dread of exposing the sick and even psychotic parts of his personality, and the envy and other paradoxical responses to the therapist's effective functioning, the patient may become resistant and obstruct the therapeutic effort. It is here that resistances based on superego pathology, disturbances in the self-system, conflicts derived from pathological instinctual drives, and the patient's own use of pathological defenses all contribute to the emergence of resistance. In a well-run psychotherapy or psychoanalysis, such resistances are quite common, while in a poorly run treatment situation, they are quite rare; nontransference resistances predominate instead.

It remains to be seen how often we will have a chance to study transference resistances as defined in the communicative approach. They are common in situations in which the therapist maintains a secure frame and a basically interpretive approach. Oddly enough, they are often difficult to interpret, since they tend to be accompanied by a highly resistant derivative network. Often, they must be responded to with silence and holding, and with tolerant waiting for those relatively rare moments when an interpretation is feasible. In a well-run therapy, such resistances are a major type of indicator for intervening, though they are all too rarely accompanied with an interpretable derivative network.

Nontransference resistances, then, emerge either as a reaction against a therapist's efforts to maintain a pathological mode of relatedness with the patient or, paradoxically, as an effort to perpetuate this type of relatedness. In contrast, transference resistances are, as a rule, defensive reactions evoked by separation anxieties caused by a therapist's offer of a healthy symbiotic mode of interaction. These resistances arise when the therapist is functioning well cognitively and in terms of relatedness. They are motivated by separation anxieties, fears of individuation, anxieties related to autonomy, as well as by the more familiar unconscious fantasy-memory constellations within the patient. Transference resistances are therefore designed to shift the therapist from a healthy to a pathological mode of relatedness, and can often be interpreted in such terms.

I do not want to get too far ahead of our present clinical material. In the main, this discussion has enabled me to help you clearly distinguish between the two ends of a new continuum: nontransference resistances at one end and transference resistances at the other. And as you no doubt realize, the resistances we have formulated to this point in the presentation at hand have largely fallen into the nontransference sphere. They will require both rectification and interpretation.

Two final points. First, I have again defined the hallmarks of an interpretation and wish to make that definition quite clear. An interpretation is an effort to help the patient to become conscious of contents and functions of which he is unaware. However, it has three specific properties: it begins with the prevailing indicators, identifies the major adaptive contexts, and helps the patient to understand the nature of his derivative responses. In essence, a derivative reaction to an adaptive context should provide an understanding of the unconscious basis of an indicator—resistance, symptom, or otherwise. In that way, each session becomes a kind of minianalysis, and the interpretive work accumulated over a series of sessions leads eventually to the completion of the therapeutic work.

Please be clear too that the derivative complex is the totality of the patient's available adaptive responses to a given context. It contains both unconscious fantasy and perception constellations, and includes all that is pertinent for the moment, both dynamically and genetically. This is a definition of interpretation which begins with the here and now—the conscious and unconscious communicative interaction between patient and therapist—and traces from there all meaningful activated implications, present and past.

My second point is this. As we know, the patient's material, however resistant, may also, through condensation, reveal aspects of his unconscious fantasy or perception constellations. In a Type A field, resistances are based on such constellations. However, in addition, the same material which reflects the resistance may also reveal aspects of the patient's core conflicts and dynamics. While maintaining the principle of dealing interpretively with resistances first, wherever feasible you should endeavor to include as much of the pertinent dynamics as possible. As you can see, an interpretation of the unconscious basis of a resistance will inevitably shade into such dynamic and genetic implications.

Once again, it has seemed necessary to develop extended comments about resistances. I have also now defined the essentials of sound intervening, and especially of the interpretive effort. For the moment, my main hope is that the distinction between nontransference and transference resistances will remain with you, as should the specific properties of an interpretation. Once again, we will most certainly review these concepts and demonstrate them clinically through subsequent material.

Discussant: Could you comment on the way in which the patient and therapist seemed to go back and forth toward the end of the session?

Langs: Yes, that is a rather noticeable quality of the therapeutic interaction in the closing moments of this hour. It is not uncommon in psychotherapeutic situations in which a wide range of noninterpretive interventions are utilized. The two recent volumes by the Blancks (1974, 1979), for example, contain many vignettes with exchanges of this kind.

As a rule, this type of interchange takes place on a manifest content level, and is designed as a resistance to underlying derivative communications. It serves as a means of acting in and therefore expresses both resistance and counterresistance. It is designed to gratify a variety of pathological impulses and defenses, and to preclude interpretive work related to Type Two derivative expressions.

By and large, this type of back and forth exchange takes place in the presence of rather intense, though often unconscious, hostile and seductive countertransferential needs within a therapist to control the patient, dominate him, and press home his point. They are also often countertransference-based responses to a patient's resistances and the hostile implications experienced by a therapist when a patient obstructs his therapeutic efforts and even negates them. It was Brian Bird (1972) who, after so many years of study by classical analysts, finally suggested that resistances within patients may constitute actual efforts to thwart or even harm the analyst.

This realization, which is self-evident from the communicative viewpoint, is extremely important. It helps us to understand that resistances are not simply matters of intrapsychic defense, but also have very important interactional implications. For example, resistances derive not only from introjects of the therapist, but may also be designed as destructive projective identifications into the therapist, and at times, as hostile and seductive acts. Obviously, all such implications should be taken in by the therapist, properly incorporated and metabolized, and responded to by means of an interpretation in keeping with the principles we have just developed. Any other response is countertransference-based and counterproductive—to use a term we often hear these days.

Therapist: There was a comment in this session—the one I just completed—in which the patient said he felt something like a slot machine. I can see that now as a representation of the tape recording of the sessions, and as another one of those embedded derivatives which would be easy to miss unless one were thinking of the adaptive context.

Discussant: The slot machine image also has a quality of being manipulated and being a victim.

Therapist: Yes, and the patient said in this hour, as he had said many times before, that it is often difficult for him to speak in the sessions. He would often liken a session to testifying before a jury—another association that takes on considerable meaning in light of the intervention contexts, including the presence of a supervisor.

I thought of the pretzels as some kind of bribe. In that way, I may have been getting in touch with some of the corrupt aspects of tape recording sessions. I realize that I failed to mention that that particular offer, a break in the frame, was the patient's first communication in the hour. I can see now how easy it is to overlook communications of that kind, and how they may be among the most important of the patient's behaviors and associations. As a derivative, it constitutes an effort to modify the basic framework and to offer me some inappropriate gratification. Had I been alert to these issues, I might have made use of its derivative implications in interpreting to the patient.

Langs: Yes, the recognition of critical intervention contexts, especially when they involve breaks in the fixed frame, often serves as a selected fact which provides new and integrated meaning to the patient's material. A slot machine allusion seems to have more parasitic than pathologically symbiotic qualities as a representation of the therapeutic relationship. It even has a certain nonhuman, and therefore possibly autistic, aspect. This suggests that the tape recordings may have been experienced by the patient as a means through which the therapist has dehumanized the therapeutic relationship and withdrawn into himself. Overall, the patient's representations of the maturational or satisfaction dimension of this therapeutic relationship speaks strongly toward pathological qualities, and seems to suggest a strikingly parasitic mode of relatedness in which the therapist is exploiting and misusing the patient far more than the other way around.

Discussant: I have always been taught to think of resistances as equivalent to defenses except that they appear within the context of therapy. And while we haven't much discussed the motives for resistance, I think that most of us are aware of the psychoanalytic theory that views defenses as protection against anxiety and danger situations, and as efforts to protect the psyche from disturbance. But I am beginning to wonder if there is any such thing as pure intrapsychic conflict. I suspect now, based on this course, that there is always an interaction between such anxiety and some kind of anxiety which arises on the basis of conscious and unconscious perceptions of others—out of object relationships. As I think about it, there can be considerable threat both intrapsychically and in our relationships with others, especially if the other person is unaware of how he is threatening us. To apply this to the concept of resistance, I gather that you are saying resistances may arise out of intrapsychic and interpersonal anxieties and threats.

Langs: Yes, that is a nice review of the subject, in keeping with our discussion last week. As you know, classical psychoanalysts have focused on the intrapsychic aspects of defense and resistance, to the relative neglect of the interpersonal or interactional aspects, which are only recently coming under consideration through the work of Sandler and Sandler (1978) and others.

Remember too that defense and resistance, on a communicative level, imply disguise and the use of derivative communication. If the derivative communication is understandable and interpretable in light of an adaptive context, we would be dealing with defenses but with a minimum degree of resistance. If on the other hand, the disguises are extreme or even totally obliterating—to the point of effecting an opaque Type C barrier—we are talking about both major defenses and major resistances.

And certainly, any error by the therapist or expression of his countertransferences, especially conveyed unconsciously and encroaching upon the boundaries of the therapeutic relationship, can generate a great deal of anxiety within the patient, and prompt both intense conflict and strong defensive effort. The situation becomes one in which the patient has a great need for the therapist and his help, and yet unconsciously perceives the therapist as dangerous, destructive, unhelpful. It becomes extremely risky and anxiety-provoking to directly confront the therapist or communicate openly to him, especially since the patient's associations are likely to cluster around the adaptive contexts of the countertransference-based interventions—an area of considerable threat for him. As a result, the patient will, as a rule, quite automatically and unconsciously resort to the use of defenses and resistances.

From this vantage point, we soon become quite sympathetic with the patient with respect to his defensive efforts, and understand their self-preservative aspects. We are also less inclined to confront resistances and attempt to blast them away because we know that first and foremost we must examine, identify, and rectify any contribution which we have made to the patient's defensiveness. We must do that long before we can help the patient to understand the true unconscious basis of a resistance, and thereby help to create both the insights and conditions of treatment under which defenses and resistances can be adaptively resolved. Changes of that kind, when based on sound interpretations and rectifications of the framework, should have a major impact on the patient's symptoms since, by and large, the same pathological defenses he applies to danger situations within the treatment relationship are applied to danger situations in his everyday life, and account in part for his characterological disturbances and symptomatic responses.

In this context, I want to emphasize that, as you may know, there are many defenses which are not pathological. Similarly, there are many resistances which, upon careful analysis, also turn out to be nonpathological and to reflect quite appropriate defensive efforts. Many nontransference resistances are well founded and sensible once clearly understood. After all, it is hardly inappropriate to protect yourself against overly aggressive or seductive therapists, or against a therapist who unconsciously is exploiting your for his own needs.

Technically, this implies that in evaluating a resistance, it is essential to trace its sources and motivations, seeking factors in both patient and therapist. Often, what appears to be a therapeutic resolution of a resistance based on some kind of insight is simply a modification in the patient's defensive armamentarium which takes place in response to a therapist's rectification of some type of countertransference-based expression. This enables me to stress again the importance of correcting countertransference influences for the resolution of gross behavioral and communicative resistances.

To cite an extreme example, a therapist who is making repeated errors may prompt in his patient a wish to terminate the therapy. Typically, most therapists would see this as a type of pathological resistance—after all, they could hardly conceive of anything healthy in a patient wanting to terminate with them. Nonetheless, careful examination of the therapeutic interaction may well indicate that the wish to terminate is a healthy and appropriate response, granted the extent to which the therapist is under the influence of unresolved preponderant countertransferences. In fact, the communicative approach indicates that while such a wish can readily be understood, far more puzzling and pathological is the finding that many patients will continue with such therapists and choose to remain in chaotic treatment situations. Still other patients will decide to leave therapy at the moment it is established that the therapist is highly competent, a capable interpreter, and able to secure a sound therapeutic setting. These seemingly paradoxical responses need far more clinical investigation.

Let's return to the session at hand.

Therapist: I would like to get through as much of this tape as possible. Unfortunately, it will not be possible for me to continue with this seminar because of another commitment. It therefore may not be possible for us to get through a single entire hour. I hope that this doesn't create problems.

Langs: We will keep these limitations in mind. It will certainly make it difficult for us to make meaningful predictions. In light of these limitations, let's continue to focus on establishing basic principles and concepts.

Patient: I have some very strong feelings about my father, although I don't see any connection with anything else. It would be difficult for me to admit that there wasn't a connection between these strong feelings and almost anything else that I get involved in. I think that that much is clear. Even in the very conflicted, the contradictory feelings about my dad, I think that there was a strong influence on what happened to me. Seeing that, I see something strange, although I can see how these feelings would do something like that. But I do think that there are times when I have discussed these feelings directly with my father, and I'm amazed at his stupidity. It is then that I wonder about the connection between my relationship with him and the rest of my life.

Discussant: As I listen to this material, applying the me/not-me interface, I wonder if the patient is talking about his own confusion or that of the therapist, and whether he is referring now to his father's stupidity or that of the therapist. I don't mean to be nasty, but we did hypothesize that the therapist was missing the main point of this patient's material as it relates to the tape recording of his session and the therapeutic relationship. I hear him saying that he has tried to discuss these problems with the therapist, probably through derivatives, and that he is amazed at the therapist's inability to hear and understand.

Langs: Implicitly, you have adopted two adaptive contexts: the tape recording of the sessions and the therapist's recent interventions. Through an introjective process and communication, the patient seems to be saying that both he and the therapist failed to see what is disturbing the patient and how things are connected, one to the other. In fact, through derivatives, the patient appears to be indicating the powerful extent to which his relationship with the therapist influences all of the rest of his life, including his relationship with his father.

Two questions: What then of the level of resistance here? And how would you formulate the patient's allusion to his father?

Discussant: In light of the formulations we have made, it seems to me that the derivative complex is moderately meaningful. There is some level of resistance, but it might be possible to manage an interpretation in this session.

Discussant: The same seems to apply to representations of the adaptive context. For me, the best representation was the reference to the slot machine, and while that is a very nice derivative, it is also fairly well disguised. I would have to say that the patient shows a moderate degree of resistance there too.

Langs: Yes. And what of the indicators?

Discussant: They would correspond to the adaptive context: the tape recording of the sessions and the therapist's erroneous interventions.

Langs: I find it useful not only to categorize indicators in terms of their nature, but to afford them a rating from one to ten, with one constituting a situation in which there appears to be virtually no indication for an intervention, while in contrast, at ten we would have a situation in which the therapist would make the best possible intervention available regardless of the nature of communicative resistances.

For example, at a point where a patient announces his wish to terminate treatment, he expresses a need for intervention that is virtually total. Under such circumstances, the presence of a meaningful communicative network offers some hope of interpretive resolution to the crisis, while the existence of strong communicative resistances bodes very badly for the outcome. Nonetheless, even in situations where you know that the patient absolutely requires an intervention from you, it is critical to be capable of sitting back and allowing the patient to first place into you the derivatives and representations you will need for your interpretive response. All too often under such conditions, in which powerful pathological projective identifications from the patient prevail, therapists tend to respond on manifest content and Type One derivative levels, very much to the detriment of the therapeutic process and with considerable loss of insight for the patient. Often these responses actually constitute projective counteridentifications—responsive pathological interactional projections—which reflect difficulties in metabolizing the patient's interactional pressures under these circumstances.

As you may remember from the first meeting, I suggested that we should also grade behavioral and communicative resistances on a scale from one to ten. I am well aware of the danger of becoming too mechanistic, but my point in offering such approximations is to provide you as therapists with fairly definite ways of deciding whether to intervene. This decision can be based on an interplay of the power of these three scales: the intensity of the indicators, the disruptive qualities of the gross behavioral resistances, and the intensity of the communicative resistances. The more intense the indicators, the greater the need in the patient for an intervention and the greater should be the therapist's responsive inclination. The same applies to the extent of the gross behavioral resistances, in that major disruptions, such as absence or threats to terminate, would in themselves constitute powerful indicators.

Matters are somewhat different and more complex when it comes to communicative resistances. On the one hand, the more intense their expression, the less likely will a communicative network afford intervention; and by and large, the greater the degree of communicative resistances, the less probable is it that you will intervene. On the other hand, their greater intensity makes more likely a need within the patient for an intervention and for understanding, even though the material does not facilitate such work for the moment.

Highly resistant communicative networks do not permit interpretive interventions which will obtain Type Two derivative validation. As a rule, they require silence from the therapist, holding and containing, until a more meaningful network emerges. The only alternative is to resort to a noninterpretive intervention which will be experienced by the patient—and rightfully so—as deriving from countertransferences and as reflecting some aspect of the therapist's psychopathology. It will not further insightful therapeutic work, but will tend to prove disruptive and increase the level of the patient's communicative, and sometimes, behavioral resistances.

In this connection, allow me to state again the importance of having *faith* in your patients: in their wish to communicate through derivatives, even when they appear for the moment to be highly resistant, and in their wish to insightfully resolve their psychopathology, even though they also have a contradictory wish to maintain their illness. You will find virtually without exception that levels of resistance fluctuate, and patients are quite capable of resolving communicative resistances spontaneously, quite on their own, especially when they are, in general, trying to use the Type A communicative mode. However, even with Type C patients, it is critical to maintain a holding and containing attitude, since to do otherwise is to generate pathological introjects and to foster the working over of your own communicated psychopathology rather than a more primary analysis of the difficulties within the patient.

The ideal situation for intervening, then, is the presence of a strong indicator and a low level of communicative resistances. The strong indicator suggests not only a therapeutic need within the patient, but a mental set in which insight and inevitable positive introjects will be accepted in deeply meaningful fashion. This occurs because they provide the patient with much needed adaptive resources in the face of a major disturbance which he is experiencing —be it primarily within the patient himself, the therapeutic relationship, or some outside relationship. This latter is, of course, always interpreted in light of a prevailing adaptive context within the therapeutic interaction. Strong indicators, then, are a sign of therapeutic need in the patient and tend to suggest a favorable climate for interpretive work.

In contrast, in the presence of weak indicators, the patient may be poorly motivated to incorporate and integrate what is otherwise a valid interpretation from the therapist. Under these circumstances, in response to a sound interpretation, the patient will often respond with some form of immediate Type Two derivative validation, only to prove refractory to any subsequent working through of the implications of the insights so derived. Of course, there are times when a valid interpretation in the presense of relatively weak indicators can nonetheless lead to major insights and working through. On the other hand, there are risks that under these conditions the patient will back off from the painful aspects of the interpretation and the threat of further therapeutic regression, because of a low level of anxiety or other type of disturbance.

In principle, then, the decision to intervene depends entirely upon the therapist's evaluation of the intensity of the indicators and the availability of an interpretable communicative network. The more intense the indicators and the lower the level of resistance, the more we approach the ideal circumstances for interpretation and managements of the frame.

Of course, much will depend on the therapist's clinical sensitivities, tact, sense of timing, and knowledge of the patient. No matter how much we are able to develop principles and categorize these dimensions of the therapeutic interaction, the personal equation of patient and therapist will always play a delicate and critical role. Those of you who are concerned with becoming overly mechanical or rigid because of efforts of this kind need not worry. As Fenichel stated (1941), therapists are always faced with the Scylla of too little in the way of organizing the patient's material and too much unprincipled and even arbitrary analytic work, and the Charybdis of too much organization and not enough affective and somewhat spontaneous effort. The ideal approach lies between the two extremes.

It seems to me that analysts have, in general, tended to work far too much without principles and basic tenets, and that they suffer from a lack of sound conceptualization and technical precepts. We are able to develop such precepts here, and to validate them through Type Two derivative confirmation. It is my hope that months or years of experience will enable these tenets to become a relatively automatic and unobtrusive aspect of the therapist's work. It can provide you with a secure foundation for the more human and directly responsive aspects of your efforts with your patients. Without such a foundation, too many clinical situations become quite chaotic and dominated by countertransferences. There need be nothing inappropriate or antiaffective about sound conceptualizations and technical principles for psychotherapy and psychoanalysis.

Discussant: Just to make the point, it seems likely to me that the reference to the patient's father is primarily nontransference-based. The patient seems to be saying that the therapist, in his stupidity and in his failure to connect things properly, is behaving in some way comparable to his father in the present as well as in the past.

Langs: Yes, that would constitute an essentially nontransference formulation, which could be incorporated into an intervention around either of the two adaptive contexts and indicators we have mentioned—the recording and the recent interventions. Much would depend on which of these contexts the patient most clearly represents either directly or through derivatives. In all likelihood, the recordings will continue to take precedence, however.

I should mention at this point that the ideal representation of an adaptive context is a reference *in passing* to that particular context. For example, if the patient were to make a passing comment about the tape recording in this hour, it would provide an excellent representation and nodal point for an interpretation. It is unlikely that the patient would allude directly, even in passing, to the therapist's noninterpretive and otherwise poor interventions, though he might, for example, mention being confused by someone at work whose comments don't make sense. A playback of that type of derivative could serve quite well as a basis for an interpretation of the patient's pertinent unconscious perceptions and their genetic links.

In evaluating the representation of the intervention context toward the offer of an interpretation, one of the most critical variables is the presence of a *link* to therapy or the therapist. Of course, a direct reference to the context always contains such a link. But in addition, many disguised representations can be drawn from the therapeutic situation rather than from experiences outside of treatment. The presence of such a link indicates a lower level of resistance than generally seen in its absence. It provides a connection to treatment which facilitates the organization of the derivative material around a pertinent intervention context.

I find it useful to distinguish the link to therapy from the more general *bridge* which the patient may provide at any point in the session. This term alludes to any nonspecific reference to the therapist or treatment situation, and will often appear in the latter part of an hour. It is often a sign of relatively low resistance, facilitating interpretation by affording the therapist an opportunity to connect all of the material in the session with the therapeutic interaction.

In situations in which there is a clear-cut and strong indicator, and a meaningful communicative network (a well represented adaptive context and coalescible set of derivatives), the timing of an interpretation is often determined by the appearance of a bridge back to therapy. Lacking such a bridge, you will usually find ample room for therapeutic creativity in picking up an especially apt derivative through which an interpretation can be introduced. Often, some other relatively undisguised, though indirect, representation of the adaptive context will serve. At other times, it is an especially compelling element of the derivative complex. It is here too that the therapist's sensitivities and capabilities in respect to listening and shaping interventions come into play. As De Racker (1961) so nicely stated it, allow the patient to feed you the intervention, to place it into you in fragmented form, to the point where all you need do is metabolize and synthesize the bits and pieces. Allow each intervention to be as much the patient's construction as your own, and in fact, far less your construction than that made unconsciously by the patient.

Once you have intervened, sit back and listen. Work over the possible unconscious implications of your intervention, and try especially to discover implications of which you were unaware as you spoke. Seek the segments of inevitable countertransference and their expression, and check the intervention for the possible influence of preponderant countertransference. Try to determine how accurate and valid the intervention now appears to be. Listen to the patient's material as a *commentary* on the intervention, filled first and foremost with valid unconscious perceptions, introjections, and understanding, and secondarily with relatively invalid and distorted reactions. Determine the extent to which you have obtained Type Two derivative validation, and in its absence begin to silently investigate the possible basis for this lack. Take nonconfirmation first as a valid commentary on your intervention, rather than as a sign of intrapsychic resistance. If you prefer, learn to think of nonvalidation as a form of nontransference resistance—valid defensiveness and nonconfirmation—before even considering the possibility of transference-based resistance. Remember that, in principle, the latter evaluation cannot be made secure unless there is some minimal initial sign of Type Two derivative validation. Sound interventions consistently obtain some small measure of this type of confirmation, after which the patient may indeed become resistant or instead (to state the other extreme), significantly modify his defenses, producing extensive and unique new material and insight. And of course, try not to become overinvested narcissistically in your intervention and its validity, but instead take a more humble approach, prepared to find at least some degree of error in every effort you make and a significant level of incorrect work from time to time.

One final point. In case it is not clear to you, my proposal earlier today to eliminate a wide variety of noninterpretive interventions leaves us with only three valid forms of intervening: (1) silence; (2) interpretations-reconstructions, or the playback of derivatives around a selected but unmentioned adaptive context, most usually in the form of a break in the fixed frame; and (3) the establishment and management of the therapeutic environment.

Please continue with the session.

Patient: But somehow, I'm not as fed up with my mother as I am with my dad. And yet, at other times, I'd do almost anything for him, at any time. I think that I have always had a problem with my dad. I think that I mentioned it to you. When I was in high school, I gave some speeches to very large audiences. There was a Veterans of Foreign Wars speech, and it was a competition. I wouldn't let my dad come to hear me speak because I felt that I couldn't perform.

Discussant: I notice that the therapist has become silent. And with that, I have experienced this material as considerably more meaningful than, for example, at the end of the previous session where the therapist kept intervening, and both he and the patient seemd to become more confused and disorganized. Could we take the observation, that the patient's material now begins to develop around coalescing derivatives and through a relatively clear representation of the adaptive context, as an indication that the therapist's silence was a valid intervention?

Langs: Your point is well taken. The therapist's use of silence is, indeed, validated by the appearance of new and meaningful material which proves a relatively clear representation of the adaptive context—the public speeches, of course—and a meaningful, coalescing derivative network.

Who will quickly apply the listening process to this material in order to help us ascertain the level of resistance?

Discussant: The adaptive context seemed very well represented when the patient mentioned speaking before audiences. It seems to me that the therapist could easily use that representation as a lead-in to an intervention organized around the derivative complex as it pertains to the tape recording of the sessions. There is also the patient's reference that he would do almost anything for his father at any time, that he's always had a problem with his father, and that he wouldn't let his father show up at his performances for fear that he wouldn't be able to perform. And there is the earlier reference to his father's stupidity and to missing out on how one thing influences another. The genetic elements, many of them nontransference in nature, are quite clear here.

Langs: Can anyone give additional meaning to the patient's comment about not wanting his father to come to hear his speeches?

Therapist: If I may, I hear that as what you have called a model of rectification. He is telling me that I shouldn't be tape recording the sessions, and that because I do, he is unable to perform. I suppose that implies that he is unable to communicate meaningfully to me, and that I am creating anxiety for him by what I am doing.

Langs: Yes. This is a good example of what I meant about allowing the patient's material to shape your interventions, including rectifications of the framework. In order to offer a model of what I believe would be a validated interpretation, allow me to integrate this discussion by proposing an intervention. In doing this, let me make clear that I probably would not have intervened at this point. This patient's level of resistances is lessening considerably as he moves along, much of it in response to the therapist's silence. There is every reason to believe that he will offer either a much-needed bridge to therapy or additional and meaningful derivatives pertinent to both the adaptive context itself and the derivative complex. I would therefore wait for such a bridge or for an especially clear derivative, and for the full development of a well integrated derivative complex. However, since our time is limited, and since this is a nice derivative which could well lead to an intervention if it were offered toward the end of this session, I will show you how I would integrate this material into an interpretation and rectification of the framework.

However, again before I do so, I want to emphasize one more point, in the hope that it might become unforgettable. Notice that it was *not* a precise interpretation—and certainly not a confrontation—which prompted this patient to lower his level of communicative resistances to the point where he has provided us with an interpretable communicative network. It was simply the therapist's use of silence, a tactic which also enabled him to not repeat his previous errors in intervening.

It is certainly true that this patient had expressed himself earlier at a level which approaches but did not reach the relatively low level of resistance we are now hearing. But it is my impression that he did so each time only when the therapist became silent for a while. I can assure you that you will find that in your own clinical work this often proves to be the case: many interludes of high-level resistance within the patient are based on interactional resistances which are largely nontransferential and which receive significant inputs from the therapist. At the point at which the therapist simply desists for a while from making these countertransference-based interventions, the patient begins unconsciously to develop a sense of hope. He feels safer to express himself, and he no longer has an immediate basis in his perceptions of the therapist to justify his defenses and resistances. And as a rule, especially in the presence of a major indicator such as the tape recording of the sessions —i.e., at moments when the patient is strongly motivated to resolve an issue within himself or in his relationship with the therapist which pertains to his symptoms and to the availability of a sound therapeutic space—the patient will, indeed, be inclined to express himself with material which reflects a relatively low level of communicative resistance. He will, of course, continue to make use of disguised and defended communications, but they will be far more easily deciphered than on those occasions where the therapist is intervening actively and erroneously.

It is observations such as these which have led me to conclude that silence—silent rectification and holding—is probably the single most important and effective intervention available to the therapist in the presence of resistances within the patient. This is the case especially when they are interactional and nontransference-based, though also when they are primarily intrapsychic and transference-based. Allow me to stress that I am speaking of appropriate silence at a time when any verbal intervention would constitute a countertransference-based error. This is an extremely common set of conditions, and the silence constitutes a reflection of the therapist's ability to manage his countertransferences and to desist from errors which are contributing to the patient's resistances. Empirical observation suggests that this measure, more than any active intervention, is the most important technical response to ongoing resistances which do not pose an immediate threat to the continuation of treatment. However, with certain gross behavioral resistances which threaten the continuation of the therapeutic situation and which reflect acute disruptions in the therapeutic alliance, it will be necessary, as a rule, in addition to rectifying any contribution from the therapist, to offer a sound interpretation or management response. This rule of silent holding applies as well to many transference-based resistances because patients tend, in their presence, to eventually produce a meaningful derivative network through which the unconscious implications of such resistances are revealed.

I think that therapists must learn to value the importance of their ability to create a stable and secure therapeutic environment, and to lessen their narcissistic investment in their interpretive skills. Interpretations are, of course, quite important at the right moment, but so is a therapist's ability to not interpret and to remain silent when indicated, especially when this is needed over many weeks and even months. It is my belief that our value system in regard to intervening is overly weighted in the direction of interpretive work. It is quite difficult for most therapists to maintain appropriate silence and to refrain from active interventions.

Let's now turn to my proposed intervention. I would begin with the most recent representation of the adaptive context, knowing that it also corresponds to the major indicators. I therefore might wish to say to the patient, You just mentioned speaking before audiences competitively. You alluded as well to experiencing anxieties under those conditions, and spoke of how the presence of your father interfered with your performing—of how you preferred that he not be there when you spoke. You also mentioned how you would do almost anything for him, and how he can be very stupid at times. You also spoke of not being able to properly connect one thing of meaning with another.

I have just proposed a *silent* intervention. It came off the top of my head, and now as I have experienced it, I can comment on it. In my own clincal work, I would also do this silently to myself, appraising whether the intervention should actually be offered to the patient, and the degree to which it would be possible for him to understand my implicit or explicit meaning.

As you may have noticed, it was not possible for me to connect either the representation of the adaptive context or the coalescing derivative complex to the therapeutic situation and interaction. I very much needed a bridge to therapy, and in its absence I proposed an intervention which could easily be experienced as intellectualized by the patient or as an attempt to deal with conflicts in his relationship with his father. In the actual session, having experienced this important deficit, I would have remained silent, waiting to see whether the patient would provide me with the missing connection to therapy. At that point, it would be easy for me to link my proposed intervention to the treatment situation and to his perceptions of me, and to suggest that they involve something related to speaking before large audiences—public exposure.

In the absence of a bridge to therapy, I would have two choices. First, I could remain silent in the hope that in the following hour, granted that I had not repeated my other errors, the patient might well be more inclined unconsciously to offer a more readily interpreted communicative network—i.e., that this would help him to decrease his communicative resistances on his own. My other choice would be to play back these derivatives around the unmentioned adaptive context of the tape recordings, shaping the material in light of the missing adaptive context. In this situation, since the omitted context is indeed a breach in the fixed framework, there is a strong likelihood that the patient would fill in this missing and critical component. To do this, it would be necessary to say that something has prompted the patient's reference to large audiences and competition, his thoughts about wishing his father would not be present when he performed, and references to stupidity and such—I would fill in with the additional derivatives. Alternatively, you might say that there seems to be more to the themes that are on the patient's mind, delineating them once again, including the representation of the adaptive context through the allusion to speeches, and continue on from there.

In principle, then, if the adaptive context is mentioned in passing or if there is some bridge to therapy, it is often possible to interpret to the patient. In the absence of the necessary bridge, it may prove feasible to play back selected derivatives as long as you are dealing with a major break in the frame. If instead you are dealing with interpretive errors and more subtle expressions of countertransference, it will prove best to remain silent and to endeavor to resolve the underlying countertransference constellations, in order not to repeat the error in some form. In situations where there is no bridge to therapy, no clear-cut representation of the adaptive context, and no meaningful derivative complex, you have no choice but to sit back, remain silent, and to continue to contain and metabolize the material from the patient.

Allow me to qualify these last comments. I have stated them definitively as the clearest principles available based on many clinical observations. However, I do want to indicate those areas which still concern me, and regarding which I feel the need for further clinical study. It is not that I have a better principle to propose for the moment; rather, I feel somewhat dissatisfied with the utility of the tools available to us, as defined from the communicative approach. It stems from a wish on my part that I could do more under the circumstances, despite finding that this is simply not possible.

Some of my dissatisfaction undoubtedly derives from remnants of the idealized image of the therapist and analyst which prevails in our field. As most of you know, the point of optimal satisfaction for a therapist arises when he is able to make a compelling interpretation which obtains Type Two derivative validation. As I mentioned, most therapists value their active interventions far more than their silences. With silence comes feelings of helplessness and even inadequacy, the fear that the patient will feel that the therapist does not understand him, and other forms of depression and anxiety. These are, however, countertransference-based responses which must be reduced to a signal level. Some of them are inevitable though manageable, while the remainder must be resolved and modified through self-analysis in order to work at optimal efficiency. Just as I have tried to show you that the management of the ground rules and framework is a much-neglected yet critical area of intervening, therapists must also learn to gain appropriate satisfaction in their ability to remain silent in the absence of interpretable material—a frequent occurrence in every psychotherapy and psychoanalysis.

It is my impression that the many threatening qualities of remaining silent helps to account for its devaluation in the eyes of most therapists. Fears of being overwhelmed, of passivity and even bodily harm, and on quite a different level, of losing the patient are all quite inappropriate in the context of a correct application of silence. There is a failure to understand the enormous therapeutic qualities and ego support which patients gain from a therapist's offer of a holding environment. In addition, the judicious use of silence also reflects the therapist's capacity to contain the patient's disturbing or empty communications and pathological projective identifications, and to manage his own inner mental world. This provides the patient with important positive introjective identifications which are also, in a general way, ego strengthening. In fact, I would suggest that, far more than any type of active intervention, including so-called supportive comments and manipulations, the therapist's use of silence when called for by the material is the single most important form of implicit support that he can offer to his patient. Unconsciously, patients are quite sensitive to the therapist's erroneous interventions and their implications, and experience such work in quite negative fashion.

You will find empirically that in the absence of an interpretable derivative network, any intervention attempted by the therapist receives a nonvalidating response, generates negative introjects, and is experienced as a reflection of the therapist's countertransferences. While we certainly know that such interludes may mobilize aspects of the patient's neurosis which might otherwise remain untapped, their negative elements consistently prove disruptive to the therapeutic process—whatever secondary gain may be derived through interpretations of the patient's unconscious perceptions of the therapist's errors.

The question remains, however, whether there is some type of intervention which can be made under these conditions. I refer to those situations where there may be a moderately strong or only relatively weak indicator, but the adaptive context is either not meaningfully represented or is represented with considerable disguise. If the adaptive context is more clearly represented, there is no meaningful derivative complex. Or finally, the intervention context is poorly represented and there is a meaningful derivative complex that cannot be interpreted to the patient in the absence of a clear expression of the precipitant. It is clear that confrontations have an adverse effect, and interpretations are not feasible. I would suggest that this is an important therapeutic dilemma. It may well turn out that continued silence and patience is the only possible intervention.

You must consistently reevaluate your silence in order to determine that it is indeed appropriate despite the patient's continued high level of communicative resistance. This occurs most frequently with the Type C patient, though it may occur over a period of several sessions with a Type A communicator. It is one of the most difficult situations you will experience when it comes to evaluating your clincial work. Type C patients wish the therapist to be confused, prefer to place nonmeaning and voids into him, and attempt unconsciously to frustrate and thwart his therapeutic efforts. There is often a strong underlying sense of envy of the therapist in the patient, and in many ways, such actual interactional efforts make it virtually impossible for the therapist to intervene interpretively.

Throughout this course, I have emphasized the defensive aspects of the Type C communicative style—the manner in which it reflects the development of relatively impervious barriers designed as falsifications which seal off underlying chaotic truths. While I have mentioned its interactional functions, this aspect of the Type C style comes to the fore when we more carefully consider the therapist's interventions. With a Type C patient, you will subjectively experience an extreme sense of frustration. Often, the patient begins to meaningfully represent the adaptive context or to develop a coalescing derivative complex, only to become highly defensive at the point where you begin to think you will be able to intervene interpretively. Further, because these patients do not provide you with an interpretable communicative network, you are often left with no active recourse but to remain silent. Interventions under these conditions are almot universally and accurately perceived by the patient as a reflection of your own hostility, frustration, and despair, and of your difficulties in containing nonmeaning within a therapeutic relationship in which nonrelatedness looms so large. It is easy to intervene noninterpretively, only to find that there is an absence of Type Two derivative validation and that instead, the patient will, sometimes directly and at other times through derivatives, almost gloat in his triumph over you. You become for the patient the weak and failing therapist, the sick one who is unable to tolerate this type of aggressiveness and sometimes subtle assault.

It is my impression that many of these patients actually require long periods of holding and containing to enable them to communicate meaningfully around prevailing intervention contexts. This is the case because of their very fragile and threatening inner mental worlds and psychotic cores, which they seal off behind their Type C barriers. It is also necessitated by their intense pathological, often quietly expressed, symbiotic needs.

From time to time, however, when a critical intervention context arises, often at their behest and because of an underlying therapeutic need—especially in the form of a break in the fixed frame—or when they have a need to work over some other issue which touches upon the therapeutic interaction, these patients will shift to the Type A communicative mode and permit a brief period of interpretive work. Type C patients are quite difficult to treat and to hold without making erroneous interventions, and require considerable therapeutic patience for long periods of time. They show a high level of communicative resistance, and pose a major problem with respect to whether there is benefit in continuing the treatment situation or deciding instead that their material should be used to help them approach a consideration of termination.

On the whole, it is my belief that this holding period is both vital and therapeutic for these patients, and that they are able to shore up the more healthy aspects of their Type C barriers under these conditions. They benefit considerably from the holding environment alone, even in the absence of interpretations over long periods of time.

In context, I want to stress that the realization of clinical problems of this kind could only arise through applications of the communicative approach. As you may know, one of the rewards which rises with the production of a selected fact is the recognition of, and challenge generated by, new questions and previously unrecognized difficulties.

Discussant: I heard something different in the derivative about not wishing his father to be there when he spoke. It suggested to me a message to the therapist that he should not share the sessions with his supervisor.

Langs: Yes. I hope that you can all experience this particular derivative as a model of rectifying the frame. They are always there when needed. Be patient and the patient will place all that you need for his cure into you; all you need to do is integrate the disparate elements into a meaningful whole.

> *Patient*: And the reason for not wanting my father there is that somehow I couldn't see myself doing something like that. I didn't want my dad there. It was as if it were sadder for me to realize that I didn't think I could exist with my father in the same room. It's sort of like, I think it is like not admitting your father to your bedroom when you're married. You just don't do it.

Langs: Our time grows short now, and it is clear that we will not be able to hear this session in its entirety. I therefore want to make an exception and ask you if you got around to interpreting this material in terms of the patient's reaction to the indicator and adaptive context of your tape recording the sessions. If so, it might be well for us to skip to that part of the hour. If not, it will matter little that we do not hear this session out to its end.

Therapist: As you would expect, I did not make such an intervention. I dealt with this material directly in terms of the patient's relationship with his father.

Langs: In that case let's introduce another element which we developed during the listening part of this course and which should come up again now that we are studying interventions. Let's begin to ask: To what extent does this material reflect aspects of the patient's core conflicts, the genetic sources of his difficulties, and his major pathological unconscious fantasy and perception constellations? In a related vein, we might also ask to what extent the underlying nature of, and unconscious motives for, this patient's resistances reflect his core pathology and its sources.

Remember that, in principle, both resistant and nonresistant material reflect underlying dynamics. Interludes with resistance will often tend to stress the defensive aspects of the patient's fantasy and perception constellations, while relatively nonresistant material might well reflect more of the instinctual drive aspects. The superego influence occurs in both situations, as does the genetic factor. And of course, virtually every type of anxiety and disturbing affect, and every type of self-disturbance, and intrapsychic and interpersonal conflict can be involved in resistant and relatively resistant-free material. Having stressed the dynamic and genetic aspects in our discussion of listening, I will develop them again in this part of the course only as the clinical material permits.

Who would like to evaluate the level of resistance in this material?

Discussant: I continue to sense a low level of resistance in respect to the derivative complex. The problem now seems to be that the patient has not represented the adaptive context in a form that will permit interpretation, and he has not provided the bridge to therapy which you said would facilitate an interpretive intervention.

Langs: Yes. The resistances have attacked the bridge to therapy and the representation of the adaptive context—the tape recordings— far more than the derivative complex. On the scale from one to ten, I would have to rate these resistances at about a level of six. Anything above a five would make it difficult for the therapist to invervene interpretively. Here, a playback might be feasible. The indicator is an eight or nine in that it is a major break in the fixed frame which requires rectification as soon as possible. There might be some reason to propose that the indicator belongs at a nine level, since the tape recording has existed for such a long time and since we should allow room to remain silent in this session if the patient does not provide a bridge to therapy or the therapist.

We also have an opportunity here to observe the structure of a resistance, in the form of derivatives of unconscious perceptions and fantasies as they exist within a patient who is expressing himself through the Type A communicative mode. It seems to me that using the communicative approach, it is relatively easy to identify gross behavioral and communicative resistances. We can therefore readily establish their presence within the patient and his material.

In addition, once you have developed a sensitivity to countertransferences and a capacity to detect expressions of unconscious countertransference constellations in your silences and interventions, it should be possible for you to identify the presence of technical errors and to make at least some effort toward rectifying their existence and influence, and understanding their underlying basis—doing so privately, of course. At the very least, you should be able to develop a capacity to recognize technical errors and not repeat them, at least in their original form. Unconscious countertransference constellations can crop up in other forms, so self-analysis is essential; still, some degree of rectification is feasible based on a grasp of the technical precepts we have developed.

More difficult to conceptualize and understand are the unconscious motives for a particular resistance constellation as they exist within the patient and in sources related to the therapeutic interaction—contributions from the therapist. In the presence of gross behavioral and communicative resistances, it is necessary to constantly ask yourself what the adaptive context is for these obstacles. What has precipitated the defensiveness? And having identified the context, what is the nature of the patient's derivative response? What are the qualities of his unconscious perceptions and what are the pertinent unconscious fantasies and memories? It is here, of course, that we introduce dynamics and genetics, psychosexual stages, conflicts, self- and object-representations, and everything else of dynamic pertinence to a neurosis.

There are two ways of understanding the resistance valence of a patient's material. One involves the extent to which the material is defensive; the other is the extent to which the implications of the patient's behaviors and associations can be understood, formulated, and interpreted. It is my impression that these two uses of the term resistance have not been generally distinguished in the literature.

The communicative definition of resistance is based mainly on the second set of criteria. It emphasizes the extent to which the patient's material is meaningful—whether it reveals defensive operations, core fantasies, unconscious perceptions. Material which illuminates the nature of the patient's defenses would be considered relatively nonresistant. And of course, such is the case at this point in this session.

To clarify the distinction between defense and resistance: material from the patient may meaningfully reflect his intrapsychic and interpersonally derived defenses in a way which reveals their nature, structure, motivations, and the underlying unconscious fantasy and perception constellations. At such interludes we have a situation in which the patient's defenses are in operation though resistances are at a low level. There is an available adaptive context, a meaningful derivative complex, clear indicators, and a full opportunity to interpret—here, primarily in terms of the patient's defensive armamentarium. At other times, however, the patient may be both defensive and resistant. During these interludes the defensiveness is evident but the material does not organize meaningfully around a represented adaptive context and interpretation is not feasible. At such times, silence and holding appears to be the only resource available.

In principle, the interpretation of a resistance is facilitated when a patient represents in his associations the resistance and the defenses involved. When it comes to a gross behavioral resistance, this is often through some passing comment by the patient on his absence, lateness, or silence. On rare occasion, in the presence of an interpretable communicative network, it has proven feasible to interpret the implications of a gross behavioral resistance—a major indicator—in the absence of a verbal representation when the resistance itself is in evidence during the session—the patient has been, for example, late or is silent. In general, it is to be greatly preferred that the patient himself has alluded to the resistance by some detail, or through some easily deciphered derivative.

The situation is somewhat different when it comes to communicative resistances. The patient is almost never aware of such resistances; they are quite unconscious. As you can readily see, gross behavioral resistances can be evident to both patient and therapist. Consequently, and also because therapists have tended to work on the manifest content and Type One derivative levels, almost all of the present literature on the subject is based on observations of gross behavioral resistances. Both Greenson (1967) and Stone (1973) have tried to address more subtle resistances, but based on the classical psychoanalytic approach, they were unable to do so with any degree of success and consistency (see chapter 10). In *The Therapeutic Interaction* I made a major attempt to formulate the presence of resistances in patients who appeared to be otherwise free associating and cooperative with the therapist or analyst. At the time, I was aware that such resistances did exist, though I too was at a loss as to how they could be consistently identified. I discussed them in terms of relatively subtle efforts at reenactment in the relationship with the analyst, relating the concept to Racker's (1957) idea of vicious circles created between patients and analysts, and to my own notion of the development of therapeutic misalliances (Langs 1975a). As I think about this effort now, I can see that I was attempting to describe situations in which patients wished not so much to understand the nature of their communications and neurosis, but to live out their illness with the analyst with relatively little interest in gaining insight and understanding. The idea was a distant forerunner of the Type C communicative style, and to some extent of the Type B mode as well. Even though I had already developed the concept of the adaptive context, I was still some distance from recognizing the nature of the ideal communicative network and developing a concept of resistance on that basis.

In the classical analytic literature, especially in the paper by Stone (1973), more subtle resistances are seen to be signaled by the absence of symptomatic change, hiatuses in the material, and other subtle manifestations, many of which can be detected only through an extended period of time. Stone also attempted to distinguish between defenses and resistances, viewing the former as essentially intrapsychic and the latter as more complex. These trends will be outlined in a paper which I will give to you toward the end of this course (see chapter 10).

You will virtually never have a situation where a patient directly refers to a communicative resistance, though theoretically it is possible and undoubtedly it occurs on rare occasions. Instead, it is one of two possibilities will prevail: (1) the patient fails to meaningfully represent the communicative resistance, or does so in a manner that does not lend itself to interpretation; (2) the patient represents the communicative resistance through a close derivative which readily facilitates an interpretive intervention. Since the interpretation of a resistance must begin with its manifestations, this particular determination—whether and how the patient represents the communicative resistance—is critical in the decision whether to intervene.

When the communicative resistance is represented meaningfully, you are in a position to examine the communicative network. As a rule, you will find that if the patient meaningfully represents the resistance indicator, he will also tend to meaningfully represent the adaptive context and generate a coalescible derivative complex. There are, of course, many Type C communicative patients who will not do so, but even among them, you will find that if the indicator is represented, the rest tend to follow. Incidentally, this does not hold for gross behavioral resistances; often the resistance will be represented directly or through an obvious derivative, but the additional material fails to clearly represent the adaptive context and provide a coalescible derivative complex.

So, in principle, when we have a communicative resistance represented in the material, we turn to the communicative network in order to ascertain the material available to us for interpretation. If the resistance level is low in that area, an interpretation is feasible.

To illustrate, this patient represents his own unconscious awareness of his communicative resistances by stating that under certain conditions—specifically, where his father was an observer and part of a larger audience—he was unable to perform, to speak. We have here a derivative representation of a communicative resistance, of a difficulty within the patient to express himself and do the therapeutic work when his sessions are being tape recorded in order to be presented to a supervisor.

In psychotherapy, as you now well know, nothing is simple. This particular derivative, along the me/not-me interface, is a representation of an introject of the therapist whom the patient experiences as having difficulty in carrying out his responsibilities under these same conditions. As a result, you have a single communication which condenses the patient's communicative resistances with the communicative counterresistances of the therapist. The latter refers to errors in intervening which generate communicative disturbances within the patient and the therapeutic interaction because of their countertransference elements.

This material, in fact, happens to offer an excellent opportunity for us to recognize that it is possible to identify gross behavioral and communicative counterresistances in therapists. In brief, gross behavioral counterresistances involve major lapses such as the therapist's failure to remember a session with a patient, lateness, or some other type of absence. The category could be extended to include clearly nonneutral and noninterpretive interventions, such as efforts to attack or to seduce the patient. Grossly muddled and confusing interventions and obvious failures to intervene are also forms of gross behavioral counterresistances.

Communicative counterresistances would have to include all of the direct and implicit mismanagements of the framework and erroneous spoken interventions. We have addressed this realm in many ways; it involves all of the obstacles for therapy generated by the expressions of the therapist's countertransferences in his attitudes, behaviors, and interventions with the patient.

To return now to the main theme, we have, as I said, a situation in which the patient has meaningfully represented his state of communicative resistance, in a general yet definitive manner. The next step is to evaluate his representation of the main adaptive context which accounts for the communicative resistance. Please be clear on this point: with the communicative approach, we do not simply confront the patient with the presence of a resistance, nor do we immediately connect it to isolated dynamics such as primal scene experiences and anxieties. Every communicative resistance bears a critical relationship to an activated adaptive context. If the context is infused with countertransferences, we are dealing with a nontransference type of resistance. If on the other hand, the context is based on an essentially valid intervention, we are dealing with a transference resistance.

An interpretation of a communicative resistance takes the form of all other types of interpretation. It begins with the best representation of the adaptive context because this is the context which is prompting or evoking the resistance, or, to turn it around, because the resistance is the patient's adaptive response to the conscious and unconscious communications contained in the immediate precipitant. I stress this point because the structure of the interpretation of a communicative resistance does not derive from some type of theoretical construct, but from clinical observations based on a full comprehension of the therapeutic interaction, including the manner in which factors within that interaction evoke resistant responses. As always, these primarily defensive operations are an interactional amalgam, deriving from propensities within the patient and the stimuli to which he is responding, which of course, includes the contributions from the therapist.

Any attempt to offer some type of understanding to the patient with respect to a resistance which does not include the pertinent adaptive context will constitute a form of manifest content or Type One derivative intervention, and consequently fall into the realm of lie-barrier therapy. It will serve primarily as a fiction about the patient's inner mental world designed to deny the influence on the patient of the therapeutic interaction and in particular, of the therapist himself. Often, it becomes a matter of blaming the patient and holding him totally accountable for disruptions to which both he and the therapist have contributed. In fact, every resistance is at least in part a response to an adaptive context within the therapeutic interaction, and can be properly formulated only in the light of that particular realization.

Discussant: As I understand it, Greenson (1967) distinguished transference resistances from other kinds of resistance, though I do not believe that he used the term nontransference resistance. I am confused, since it is my impression that many therapists think of the patient as resisting certain types of material which might have little to do with the therapist himself, though most would agree that those resistances evoked by a feeling or fantasy toward the therapist are especially important—at least in psychoanalysis. In the psychotherapeutic situation, it is not clear to me whether there is any consensus as to the type of resistances which are most common, or how they should be dealt with.

Langs: From the communicative viewpoint, every resistance unfolds in both psychotherapy and psychoanalysis out of the ongoing, spiraling, conscious and unconscious communicative interaction. This is a naturalistic observation, the truth of which has been validated many times but which is, upon reflection, not at all surprising. Now, it may well be that from a manifest content and Type One derivative viewpoint, a therapist might develop a concept of resistance which pertains to the patient's wish to suppress or avoid material of a certain kind—such as sexual or aggressive fantasies, or associations pertinent to a particular troublesome outside relationship. Such therapists would distinguish between transference resistances—using the term to allude to what I call relationship resistances, nontransference and transference—and resistances pertinent to other types of material and relationships.

My own distinction of transference and nontransference resistances applies entirely to the patient's relationship with the therapist, and separates those obstacles to therapy that derive primarily from the patient's pathology and distortions from those that stem from relatively valid unconscious perceptions and introjects of the therapist.

Discussant: But what of resistances that do not immediately pertain to the therapist and therapeutic interaction?

Langs: From the communicative viewpoint, avoidance of a particular type of material would be seen as a gross behavioral resistance. It is not a communicative resistance as defined here, since such avoidance may take place in a session in which a particular adaptive context is well represented and a meaningful derivative complex available—a gross behavioral resistance may occur, for example, in a situation of low communicative resistance, permitting some type of interpretation. At other times, this type of gross avoidance may take place in sessions in which there is no meaningful derivative network. The level of communicative resistance can only be determined by an evaluation of the state of that network. In addition, on an unconscious level, the need to avoid a particular type of material would always, to a greater or lesser extent, be linked to a particular adaptive context and to some aspect of the therapeutic interaction, despite the fact that on a manifest level no such connection seems evident.

Your comment has helped us to establish an additional category of gross behavioral resistances, and perhaps, as well, to see more clearly some of the basic differences between the usual classical psychoanalytic and communicative approach to these phenomena. I would like now to return to the clinical material.

The communicative resistance-indicator has been represented by the patient. As we already know, the same segment of material constitutes a representation of one of the prevailing sets of intervention context: the tape recording of the sessions and the presence of a supervisor. A second and relevant context, the noninterpretive and ruminative qualities of the therapist's interventions and his avoidance of the therapeutic interaction, is not as clearly represented. In this session, because of the importance of the break in the fixed framework, I would probably do little in the way of therapeutic work with that particular source of the patient's resistances, and for the moment I would concentrate on the adaptive contexts which are more clearly represented. Once those issues are resolved, there will be plenty of time to deal with the patient's reactions to the therapist's style of intervening.

So, we have a well represented communicative resistance and pair of adaptive contexts. What of the derivative complex? Well, we had established earlier that there was a good bit of meaning on several different levels. There is an allusion to the genetic link to the patient's father, which is to be formulated primarily in terms of a nontransference-based repetition by the therapist of aspects of the father's pathogenic behaviors. There is the patient's awareness on some level that he would submit to his father-therapist despite his anger and disillusionment, and despite their stupidity. There is the reference to public speaking, which I have already touched upon, and even a model of rectification: the patient could express himself better if the father were not present. While somewhat ambiguous, this allusion could be used to help the patient see that he is expressing his dissatisfaction with both the tape recording of the sessions and the presence of a supervisor, and that he is indeed indicating that he would do far better in their absence. There is also the patient's representation of his pathological symbiotic tie with his father based on his unwanted presence in the audience.

Finally, there is a derivative which condenses a clear model of rectification with hints of genetic implications and dynamics, primarily of a sexual nature. I refer of course to the patient's saying that speaking in front of his father is like admitting him into his bedroom if the patient was married, and that it just isn't done. Here, through a mixture of both heavily disguised and relatively transparent derivatives, the patient has conveyed many implications. The presence of the supervisor and tape recordings turns therapy into a marital partnership, and probably into some form of the primal scene—a sexual experience between patient and therapist to which the supervisor is the observer. It generates homosexual qualities to the therapeutic interaction and constitutes a failure to establish appropriate boundaries and privacy. It is a break in the framework which must be rectified.

As you can see, this is a rich and diverse derivative complex. It contains genetic elements, reflections of the patient's psychopathology, indications of the patient's unconscious perceptions of the therapist's psychopathology, a directive to rectify the frame, and an intense working-over of these fundamental flaws in the therapeutic environment. For the moment, although difficult to establish which is more central, both seem pertinent: the therapist's and the patient's unresolved homosexuality and exhibitionistic-voyeuristic needs. It seems likely that the two are intertwined, but as we already know, the therapist's contributions must be rectified and the patient's responses to them interpreted, before the patient's contributions—the realm of transference—can be worked through.

This derivative complex also contains a type of unconscious interpretation to the therapist, to the effect that he is tape recording the session because of his lack of knowledge, some type of competitive strivings, exhibitionistic and voyeuristic needs, and unresolved homosexual and primal scene-related conflicts and fantasies. At this level, this unconscious perception constellation and group of introjects are contributing powerfully to the patient's communicative resistance. This is, of course, the realm of nontransference resistance. In addition to interpreting the sources to the patient, it calls for rectification by stopping both the tape recordings and the supervision, as well as any other inclination to expose the patient inappropriately. Once these steps have been carried out, the material could be interpreted in terms of the patient's own homosexual and primal scene-related psychopathology—material likely to emerge within the adaptive context of the therapist's rectification of the framework and valid interpretation.

In intervening for now, all you would have to do is put together the elements and derivatives I have just identified. You might say to the patient that he seems to be talking about a difficulty in expressing himself, in communicating openly and freely. If there had been a bridge to therapy, you could immediately connect it to the treatment situation. If it did not appear, you would have to content yourself with a playback of derivatives.

Having established the representation of the communicative resistance, you could go on to say to the patient that the disturbance seems to have something to do with speaking in public, before audiences, and especially before an audience which includes his father or father figures. It has to do with issues of competition, stupidity, and submitting blindly to another person's needs. It also touches upon a situation which has the quality of admitting his father into the privacy of his marital bedroom. Whatever it is about, you are indicating unmistakably that something is being done that is inappropriate and that it should not take place.

Because of the nature of the patient's defenses, I probably would not at this point emphasize the primal scene and homosexual aspects of the situation. I would wait for more specific representations, but I would not feel that the job was completed until these derivatives had been identified and understood—again, in terms of both unconscious perceptions of the therapist and unconscious fantasies within the patient. I would also want to be sure eventually to link this material to present and earlier experiences with the father, and to establish in some way the sense that the patient felt that, through these deviations, the therapist was indeed repeating some aspect of his father's behavior which had contributed to his neurosis. It probably will be impossible for me to document it here, but I can assure you based on other experiences, that with an interpretive approach of this kind, the patient would soon connect all of this material to his symptoms and shed new light on their unconscious dynamics.

To synthesize, I have just provided a model of an interpretation of a communicative resistance. It began with a representation of that resistance, used the best derivative representation of the pertinent adaptive context, and spelled out the implications of the responsive derivative complex. I framed the intervention largely in nontransference terms because that particular element was clearly primary. I hinted at my readiness to rectify the framework, a decision which I would hope to make explicit before this hour ended. But I did so at the behest of the patient's derivative communications, not in some arbitrary fashion. I therefore followed a basic principle we established earlier: in dealing with nontransference communicative resistances, we must both rectify the therapist's contributions to that resistance as well as interpret the meanings and functions to the patient. At this juncture, this is an inter-actional resistance—a failure to communicate—with major inputs from the therapist.

This has been an extended discussion, but the basic principles are actually relatively simple, though effecting them in clinical practice requires considerable sensitivity. We begin always with communicative resistances, and adopt an essentially rectifying-interpretive approach. We adhere to the model of indicator-adaptive context-derivative complex, and use the latter two as a means of illuminating the unconscious implications of the former. We will have a chance to apply these principles with further clinical material. For the moment, unless there are questions, we should return to this presentation.

Discussant: I take it that you would apply the same principles to a behavioral resistance. If I follow you correctly, a behavioral resistance may occur along with a communicative resistance, or may not.

Langs: Yes, the principles remain the same: deal with resistances before other types of issues, and framework-related resistances top the hierarchy of indicators. Whether the resistance is gross behavioral or communicative, we adhere to the interpretive approach, shedding light on the unconscious implications and sources of the obstacle by identifying the adaptive context which has evoked it and the patient's derivative responses which show its meaning and functions for him at the moment. As always, we take these derivative responses as commentaries with truth before fiction, valid perception before fantasy-based distortion.

Discussant: Haven't we established in our study of the therapeutic environment that deviations of this kind tend to be linked by the patient with primal scene experiences? It seems rather evident that tape recording the sessions places the patient in a situation which repeats the primal scene constellation, whatever additional distortions it may evoke.

Langs: Yes, that point now seems quite clear. Let's continue a bit.

Patient: I want it that way, and it's sort of the same thing that I felt in the auditorium.

Langs: Unfortunately, our time is nearly up. We will all have to accept the frustration at not being able to hear this session to completion. It would have been interesting to see if the patient's derivatives became clearer, or if communicative resistances intensified when the therapist failed to intervene properly, and depression set in.

Therapist: In general, that last is actually what did take place.

Langs: Well, for the moment, the outcome of this hour is of no special consequences for us. Your presentation has provided us with an opportunity to further refine our understanding of both resistances and interventions. Thank you for having the courage to present tape recorded material, and for the illuminating and evocative qualities of your presentation.

I will close with one final comment. In our discussion today, it seems to me that I have resolved an inequity in my development of the listening process as compared to the intervening process. In respect to listening, I stressed representations of the adaptive context and the nature of the derivative complex, and afforded less attention to the therapeutic context or indicator. Now that we are addressing the question of resistances and interventions, we have given these indicators the full attention they deserve. In so doing, it became possible to clarify the relationships between indicators, adaptive contexts, and derivative complexes. I spoke to this point earlier, and now want to conclude with a final crystallization since it is somewhat new and extremely important.

Central, of course, is the intervention context, the precipitant for the patient's responses. In one direction, it generates indicators or therapeutic contexts—therapeutic needs that motivate the patient to communicate meaningfully, generating coalescible derivative networks. In the other direction, contexts evoke communicative responses, adaptive and maladaptive, which reveal the unconscious implications for the patient of the precipitant.

Overall, both indicators and derivative complexes are responses to adaptation-evoking contexts, each a bit different and with a distinctive set of implications—though there may also be overlap. They may derive from the object relationship with the therapist, as well as from internal needs and conflicts within the patient. They are usually reflections of disturbance, disequilibrium, and maladaptation. They are always interactional products. If I stress those therapeutic needs which stem from the errors of the therapist, I do so mainly because they have been neglected and because they are so prominent in these presentations. In a well run therapeutic situation, the balance will shift so that most indicators will derive from the internal conflicts and needs of the patient.

An adaptive context is the nodal point. It will excite a group of therapeutic needs and motivational systems, pathological and nonpathological, to which the patient responds with behaviors and associations that constitute an attempt to adapt to these inner disturbances. The indicators are a sign of the disturbance generated within the patient and his need for help, and the derivative complex is a further reflection of that disturbance as well as an expression of the patient's efforts to cope with the precipitant. The rule is that, in listening we begin with the patient's representations of the indicators, and move from there to the adaptive context and derivative complex; in intervening, we do much the same. In this way, both listening and intervening correspond; they are two versions of the same basic process.

I hope that each of you find this synthesis illuminating.

Chapter Three

THE STRUCTURE OF
INTERPRETATIONS

Langs: We begin today with a new presentation.

Therapist: I have decided to continue with a patient I presented earlier in this course (see Langs 1980 chapters 4, 5, and 6). In fact, I thought it would be interesting to pick up exactly where we left off. As you may recall, this is a woman in her mid-thirties who is obtaining an advanced degree in psychology and who is involved with a graduate student affiliated with this center. She's been divorced and was also recently in the midst of throwing an anniversary party for her parents and of talking about the issues that arose between herself and her sister in that regard.

This is the patient with whom I had to change offices, and she dreamed at the time of being in a different office with another arrangement of the chairs, to which she associated a question about whether I ever sat in the patient's chair and her wishes to know more about me.

In the session prior to the one I will present today, she had been speaking about the anniversary party and how her mother was able to see to it that she herself was well taken care of, while the patient felt inadequate. There was a great deal of talk about her current boyfriend's mother, who was a loud and seductive, had got involved with the cab driver who brought her to the anniversary party, and was approached by one of the patient's uncles.

I pointed out to the patient that she had left out her concern about her relationship with her sister which had come up in the previous hour. The patient responded that everything was fine with her, that her sister was embarrassed only when someone tried to kiss her. In fact, the patient felt that her sister had handled the situation better than she had, and spoke of how unattractive she had felt.

There was also some material about meeting her present boyfriend's old girlfriend, who had been a bit negative in her response to the patient. The patient also described writing a rather moving letter to her parents after the anniversary party. I asked her why she was having such difficulty in talking about these things; and the patient went on to describe how she had apologized in her letter and expressed her love for them. Her parents had called her and both of them had cried. I had commented that it is still difficult for the patient to reveal things to me, and that she shows a tendency to hold back and keep her distance, even in her relationship with me. It was on that note that the previous session had ended.

Langs: As I recall, we have already discussed this material in some detail. Since the discussion took place some time ago, I do not remember the specific issues we explored. I suspect, however, that we did not consider in any detail either of our current topics: resistances and interventions. In an effort to set the stage for the material we will now be hearing, who would like to comment briefly in these areas?

Discussant: It seems to me that the therapist attempted to confront the patient with a questionable type of gross behavioral resistance: holding back or avoiding certain subjects. I say questionable because it seems to me that the material could be very meaningful on a communicative level, despite the fact that the patient did not come back to the subject of her sister which concerned her so much in the previous hours. I wondered if the patient's relationship with the therapist, rather than her sister, wasn't really the subject of the previous hour, since we know that there was a dream about him. Without more material, it would be difficult to say.

Discussant: It seems to me that it would be impossible to determine the level of communicative resistance without knowing the adaptive context of the previous session.

Langs: Exactly. The best we could do with this type of material is to monitor it along the me/not-me interface for derivative commentaries on the therapeutic relationship and on broad qualities of the therapist's interventions. On that basis, the images are mixed: the material about the boyfriend's mother suggests some concern about the boundaries of the therapeutic relationship, some sense of seductiveness, and some degree of loss of control. There are also derivatives which suggest some type of comparison in which one person comes off far more favorably than the other; we are not in a position to locate these qualities in either the patient or the therapist.
What about the therapist's interventions?

Discussant: Each of his interventions appears to have been designed to deal with what the therapist had formulated as some type of surface resistance: avoidance of the material about the sister, difficulty in talking about the letter to her parents. Also, these interventions are mainly on a manifest content level and clearly avoid the therapeutic relationship and interaction.

Langs: Yes, I hope that you can all sense the somewhat arbitrary quality and underlying clinical judgments involved in these interventions. We are being a little loose in our discussion, however; you did not begin by identifying their formal nature.

Discussant: I think they were all confrontations

Langs: Yes, and they reflected, as you say, a manifest content level of listening. The indicator used by the therapist was a postulated surface resistance, but no effort was made to address either an adaptive context or a derivative complex. The comments dealt with material which pertained to outside relationships, though they focused on difficulties the patient was having in talking to the therapist about them. We saw no evidence of Type Two derivative validation. However, the patient did reveal some manifest thoughts and feelings she had apparently set to the side. While this would be taken as a confirmatory response by a manifest content therapist, a therapist who uses the communicative approach would not agree.

Discussant: I sensed a kind of controlling and hostile quality to these confrontations.

Langs: Yes. Confrontations almost always have such attributes. Notice also that it would be difficult to reach a consensus as to the level of the patient's gross behavioral resistances in this situation. Some therapists might agree with the present therapist, that the avoidance of allusions to the patient's sister in this particular hour constituted a resistance. Other therapists might postulate that this was no longer a source of concern to the patient, and feel that there was no inherent reason why such an omission should be seen as a form of resistance. Some therapists would find the patient's hesitancy in talking about a letter to her parents as quite understandable, and others would see it as an obstacle to a full appreciation of what the patient was trying to express.

It would be difficult to establish surface criteria for resistances based on an approach of this kind. As I hope you can see, the evaluations here have to do with the manifest content of the patient's associations, the surface of the material and evident omissions, the obvious signs of reluctance to communicate. With silence as the ultimate expression of surface resistance, therapists who adopt this approach tend to concentrate on gaps in the patient's material for signs of withholding.

Certainly, when the withholding or avoidance reaches major proportions, it should be considered as a form of behavioral resistance. Technically, however, we would not simply confront the patient with the manifestations of her gross resistance, but turn instead to the communicative network in an effort to understand its sources and underlying basis and functions. Only then would we be in a position to interpret the purpose and nature of such gross behavioral resistances.

Quite often, gross behavioral resistances are accompanied by communicative resistances. But this need not always be the case. It is therefore critical to extend your examination of the patient's material for resistances to the communicative level, and to recognize that relatively minor forms of gross behavioral resistance may be of little consequence or of considerable importance—depending in large part on the state of the patient's communicative expressions.

For example, the patient's avoidance of further mention of her sister may be meaningful both in light of her relationship with her sister, and her conscious and unconscious relationship with the therapist. If the interplay with the sister does not lend itself readily to derivative expressions of responses to adaptive contexts within the therapeutic interaction, avoiding such material and using other forms of manifest communication—here, for example, the material about the boyfriend's mother—would not be evaluated as a sign of an important resistance. The ultimate decision would depend on the level of communicative resistance, and unfortunately, as has already been pointed out, we cannot make that determination here without knowing the material of the previous hour. We can simply utilize this summary as a basis for establishing certain principles which can be more specifically elaborated as we proceed.

My emphasis for the moment is on the observation that manifest avoidance or shifts in the material cannot be seen as forms of resistance per se, since to do so is to operate on a manifest content level. Since neuroses are expressed through derivative communications, the critical level of resistance is in the communicative realm and has to do with the clarity of the representations of indicators and intervention contexts, and the meaningfulness and coalescibility of the derivative complex.

Can anyone relate this discussion to what I will now call the *developmental* or *maturational dimensions of relatedness*, which, as discussed earlier (chapter 1), involves autism, symbiosis, commensal interaction, and parasitism?

Discussant: It might be that the patient is saying that her object relationship needs are being poorly met. I wonder too whether the reference to the seductive future mother-in-law might not represent a sexualized form of pathological symbiosis.

Discussant: The therapist's interventions seem to parasitize the patient a bit, and at the very least to reflect a wish to establish with her some form of pathological symbiosis.

Langs: Yes, confrontations, and virtually all noninterpretive interventions, do indeed tend to have parasitic qualities, and at the very least attempt to engage the patient in some mode of pathological symbiosis. This mode of relatedness arises, as the patient suggests through her derivative communications, when one member of the therapeutic dyad feels inadequate, and experiences seductive or aggressive needs. It may be that this material also reflects, especially in the reference to the letter the patient wrote to her parents, an effort to propose to the therapist that they develop a more healthy form of symbiotic relatedness.

Now, let's get into the new session.

Therapist: The patient came into this hour very upset, and she grabbed for a tissue and started to cry. She told me that yesterday she had not gotten out of bed the whole day and she was depressed. It had begun two evenings ago.

Langs: Let's not miss it: there is an intervention here. Who can identify it?

Therapist: I didn't give her the tissue; she took it.

Langs: That's excellent. Many therapists would not consider the availability of tissues as an intervention. But nonetheless, it is just that. It is part of the therapeutic environment and constitutes an implicit intervention. How are we going to classify it?

Discussant: I would see the tissues as part of the framework. It seems to me that there is always a box of tissues in a psychiatrist's office.

Langs: Perhaps not always. In any case, let's attempt to apply our categorization of the attributes of interventions to this particular instance.

Discussant: Well, it's certainly not a form of interpretation. I guess it would have to be classified as some type of support. But then, too, the same would apply to making a chair available to the patient.

Langs: It is easy to sense your discomfort and skepticism in response to my effort to examine every possible intervention by the therapist. I know that it is easy to ridicule the communicative approach, in which we allow the patient's derivative commentaries to be the judge. But it has led us to question many accepted practices both in response to spoken interventions—with their verbal and nonverbal qualities—and managements of the framework. As therapists and scientists, we must not hesitate to examine every possible dimension of the therapeutic situation.

In that light, we might well question the decision by a therapist to make available to the patient a relatively comfortable chair to sit in, or a similarly comfortable couch to lie upon, as parts of the basic therapeutic environment. After all, this patient did dream about the chair; and while we utilized that material to discuss other issues, we might just as easily have applied it to the questions of the nature of the basic therapeutic environment. I suspect—though I cannot document it—that the patient's derivative commentaries would find the offer of a chair to sit in a necessary and appropriate part of the basic framework, and that the patient would find essentially no basis to view it as an expression of countertransference or as inappropriate to the basic therapeutic frame. I fully acknowledge that this is speculation, though perhaps we will have a fresh opportunity to examine that particular aspect of the treatment setting and validate my hypothesis.

For the moment, however, we are examining the therapist's decision to make available to his patients Kleenex-type tissues. On the face of it, this is not an essential part of the therapeutic setting. In addition, it carries with it a number of evident implications which we can identify. Through these, we can develop a series of silent hypotheses to be validated by the patient's material. Such is our methodology, and let's not hesitate to apply it wherever it might arise.

Discussant: Well, I would see this as a form of support and as reflecting a manifest content form of listening and relatedness. If we are taking it as a response to the patient's crying, the indicator is a symptom, but there is no use of an intervention context or derivative complex. You know, while some of this feels strange, it also makes a lot of sense to me. I experience us as setting aside shared blind spots, and there is a good feeling to it.

Langs: I am delighted that you can appreciate some of the more positive qualities of this type of approach. Who can help us with some of the possible unconscious communications conveyed by the tissues?

Discussant: I have always seen tissues as an expression of concern, of warm interest. Now I begin to wonder about some of the other possible meanings. There is something symbolic about the offer of a tissue, as if the therapist is permitting the patient to touch a part of himself.

Discussant: Isn't that a concrete gratification, rather than symbolic? Doesn't it imply, in light of our recent discussions, an inappropriate gratification of the patient, and to some degree of the therapist, so that it becomes part of a way of establishing a pathological symbiosis? Also, the tissues may imply that the patient is needy, not the therapist, and the patient is the sick one.

Discussant: It could be some type of directive: the patient is supposed to cry. And then the therapist will comfort her by giving her a tissue, directly and concretely gratifying and reassuring her. I can readily see this as a model of an infantilized, pathological symbiosis. I had never realized the possible implications of this kind of deviation in the ideal therapeutic environment.

Discussant: I thought of it as something like a security blanket or transitional object, providing the patient with a pathological form of merger with the therapist.

Langs: All you need do is open your minds to a consideration of possible unconscious implications of the availability of tissues. Many of them do indeed involve the offer of a pathological symbiosis, a thesis supported by the patient's report that she had stayed in bed the entire previous day. Infantilism and lack of individuation is clearly implied.

As you can see, in psychotherapy, even a seemingly innocuous item like a tissue may unconsciously convey to the patient a wish within the therapist for a pathological mode of relatedness. We are beginning to collect clinical data which indicates—and my own continued observations are quite compatible—that all modifications in the ground rules and boundaries of the therapeutic relationship and the ideal therapeutic setting and conditions, serve to establish either a pathologically symbiotic or parasitic mode of relatedness between the patient and therapist. In addition to their infantilizing qualities, the tissues unconsciously represent some aspect of the person of the therapist offered to the patient in a concrete manner—much of it has a quality of offering himself to the patient for incorporation. Tissues do indeed function as transitional objects, a point supported by the observation that many patients take them and put them into their pockets or purses, leaving the office with the tissue in their possession. Often, they are sad and depressed, struggling with intense and primitive separation anxieties, and they now have a piece of the therapist inside of them; they are in a position to achieve some degree of framework deviation cure.

Therapist: If I had run out and gotten another box of Kleenex, I could appreciate what you're saying. I've had patients who start to cry and they look at me and say, Why don't you have a box of tissues? Patients seem to expect it.

Langs: What does it imply when you don't have such tissues?

Therapist: That the patient will have to use his own resources. Okay. Now I begin to see your point.

Langs: Yes, the manifest level has to do with caring, and for this reason many therapists have mistakenly believed that such deviations reflect healthy wishes to nurture the patient in order to promote growth and individuation. However, they overlook the latent and derivative communications and needs expressed through such behaviors which entail infantilizing the patient, and not expecting him to have his own resources and a capacity to handle his emotional upset through whatever means necessary.

Further, as you may be able to now sense, if the patient's sense of upset is not handled through the offer of concrete gratification and a mode of relatedness that is pathologically symbiotic, he would have little choice but to attempt to cope on his own. Much of this would unfold through the expression of meaningful derivatives which would lend themselves to interpretive responses and eventual insight for the patient. In general, pathological relationship satisfactions alleviate the anxiety and conflicts which derive from and cause the patient's neurosis, and preclude efforts at insightful resolution and individuation. Clinical data shows unmistakably the gratifications of this kind undermine rather than promote meaningful therapeutic work.

Your comment also helps us to establish a criterion regarding the therapeutic setting: we certainly cannot expect the patient to have his own chair, though we can expect him to carry a handkerchief or some tissues. You've all heard the joke about "Have couch, will travel"; this would call for a variation: "Have chair, will be patient."

Incidentally, Sandler (1976), in his paper on role responsiveness within the analyst, offers a vignette in which he made it a practice to hand a woman patient in analysis a Kleenex each time she needed one. The analytic situation eventually became stalemated, and it was only when he realized the unconscious implications of handing the Kleenex to the patient and stopped doing so, that he then got the material from the patient that enabled them to resolve the impasse and to complete her analysis.

Discussant: Doesn't the Kleenex infantilize the patient, and isn't it seductive? In its own subtle way, it also modifies the boundaries between patient and therapist. It's as if the patient is touching the therapist, and the therapist is making himself available for that purpose.

Discussant: Is this session back in the therapist's regular office?

Therapist: Yes, the water leak and the change in the office had occurred in the previous hour. I hadn't mentioned it, but the dream about the change in the office had been reported in that session.

Discussant: The tears now have a different quality, in light of the leak in the therapist's office. They could have some dynamic meaning.

Discussant: Would you consider the patient's crying to be some type of indicator?

Langs: Yes, it is in some sense a symptom, an indication of depression. The same applies to the fact that she remained in bed the day before the session. We have here an indicator which is directly represented in the patient's material.

After our last discussion, I realized more clearly than before that a fully balanced picture of communicative resistances would point to each of the three focal areas in which the patient might apply his defenses: in representing the indicators, in representing the adaptive context, and in generating the derivative complex. I have not sufficiently emphasized the first of these, and wish to do so now.

In a sense, indicators are symptoms and signs of disturbance within the bipersonal field. If the therapist behaves in keeping with his countertransference, and therefore modifies the frame or intervenes incorrectly on a verbal level, he will generate a pathological introject within the patient which constitutes an indicator. If the patient himself is inappropriately resistant, experiences a symptom, or a disturbance in some outside relationship, all of this is funneled into some type of inner disturbance within the patient once again, and also constitutes another series of indicators. Indicators are therefore therapeutic contexts, expressions of need for help within the patient.

Especially with indicators which derive from the therapist's interventions, the patient may prove to be quite resistant—defensive—in representing the disturbance. Usually, when the problem lies within the patient, it is alluded to directly, often in passing, during the session. In fact, except for observations of disturbance in the patient's behaviors and expressions within a given hour, these direct allusions to symptoms and other problems would be virtually the only source available to the therapist for identifying symptomatic indicators within the patient. Occasionally, it might be possible for the therapist to infer an indicator from the flow and nature of the patient's associations, though this is fraught with difficulty.

In all, then, indicators within the patient may be perceived directly through the patient's behaviors in the session, and by inference from the nature and quality of the patient's associations. Indicators which derive from disturbances within the therapist may also be represented directly, though more often they will be represented indirectly through some type of disguise and subjected to some degree of defensive operation.

Therapist: In light of your discussion, it seems to me that the patient's decision to take the tissue would have to be seen as a response to some adaptive context in the previous hour.

Langs: Exactly. We have been addressing the intervention side of this behavior, in terms of your making the Kleenex available. From the side of the patient, it is a behavior with manifest and latent meaning. Can anyone relate this behavior to a known adaptive context?

Discussant: I can see as background context the usual lack of confidentiality—secretaries and supervisors and such, breaks in the boundaries in which the therapist participates.

Discussant: There is also the change in the office. The therapist was involved in some type of self-revelation and made a major change in the therapeutic environment.

Discussant: In a way, the therapist's interventions, which were critical but which avoided important contexts from within the therapeutic interaction, could have led the patient to experience him as relatively unavailable. By taking the Kleenex, she calls the therapist's attention to the therapeutic relationship and obtains some type of direct gratification.

Langs: These are all sound possibilities. We would especially look to breaks in the framework since this particular behavior impinges upon the usual boundaries and framework of the treatment situation and relationship. Mainly, I wanted to establish the possibility of derivative meaning to this behavior, so we no longer take things of this sort so casually or manifestly. Now let's hear what happened.

Therapist: She was saying that she's depressed, and tears started coming. She grabbed a Kleenex and told me that she got a card from Alan two evenings ago, the night she became depressed. Alan is her ex-husband.

Langs: Our interest is in resistances, but we can never entirely set aside the listening process and its applications. There was some skepticism about this discussion of the Kleenex. Does this first communication from the patient help to resolve some of the doubts you may have had?

Therapist: She got the tissues from me, and she got a card from Alan. Something concrete and apparently something disturbing. Something that bridged a gap since she is now divorced from Alan.

Langs: Yes. All it took was the patient's first association to reveal a series of unconscious implications in respect to your making the tissues available to her, and her taking them. You offer her a concrete form of contact, a way of undoing separation and loss, and something to hold onto. I would take this as a form of Type Two derivative validation, since the association serves as a rather meaningful selected fact which gives considerable meaning to the patient's behavior. That particular quality is a component of a low level of resistance—here, we see a derivative which constitutes a rather adaptive response to the intervention (adaptation-evoking) context of your making available the tissues.

Discussant: If the Kleenex is an error and in part an expression of countertransference, isn't it true that we must first rectify the situation and then interpret the patient's responses—or at least, do both relatively simultaneously?

Langs: Exactly. Along these lines, there are two conditions under which the therapist intervenes: those which contain an important element of countertransference and those which do not. And as we already know, the image of the therapist, the state of the bipersonal field, and the experiences of the patient are quite different for each of these conditions.

In the presence of countertransference, an intervention which is
accompanied by rectification provides the patient not only with insight, but also with a shifting introjective identification which
moves from having negative and disruptive qualities to having
positive and constructive attributes. Erroneous interventions always
provide the patient with inappropriate gratification, defenses, and
superego sanctions. Correct interventions are offered in the context
of appropriate and therapeutic frustration, reasonable boundaries
and limits, and as part of our essentially sound functioning.

Correct and erroneous interventions have different properties not
only in terms of their cognitive attributes and contents, but also in
terms of their unconscious implications, projected aspects, and
image of the therapist. There is a tendency to think of interventions
in terms of their verbal and cognitive attributes, and to overlook
the extensive ways in which they reflect the therapist's personality
and character structure, as well as his management capacities,
conflicts, fantasies and perceptions, and other positive capacities.

Of course, the more valid an intervention, the less personally
revealing it is with respect to the therapist, though clearly there is
no such entity as an intervention without some degree of unconscious and personal communication. The goal is to eliminate, as
much as possible, the idiosyncratic and countertransference elements. We covered much of this when we discussed the two basic
sequences in psychotherapy (Langs 1980a): one which begins with
a valid intervention from the therapist, and the other which begins
with a countertransference-dominated and erroneous intervention.

It is naive, and a way of constructing a lie-system, to think of
interventions solely in terms of their cognitive accuracy. We saw
that patients have distinctive communicative styles, only one of
which entails a wish to express one's self meaningfully and to
understand. Another basic style entails wishes to be rid of inner
tensions and contents without understanding—the Type B mode,
or more accurately, the Type B–C mode. Other patients prone to
projective identification utilize these mechanisms in the service of
understanding—patients we would label Type B–A. And there is
also the Type C patient who wishes not to understand by generating lie systems and lie-barriers designed to seal off truth, understanding, and meaningful relatedness.

It is now time to apply these distinctions to the therapist. It
behooves us also to add a seventh component of intervening (see

Appendix C): the communicative mode within which the intervention is offered. In keeping with recent refinements, we will classify
these as Type A, referring to therapists who are capable of managing
and maintaining a secure frame and of offering affectively meaningful cognitive interpretations which obtain Type Two derivative
validation. Next, there is the Type B–A therapist who offers sensitive and meaningful understanding to the patient, even though it is
intermixed with some degree of projective identification and dumping. This particular combination is theoretically possible, though
it implies the presence of only a minimal degree of interactional
projection and a maximal degree of insightful comment.

Far more common among Type B therapists would be the Type
B–C therapist who makes use of interactional projections into the
patient as a means of denying and sealing off underlying truths
within the therapeutic interaction and of disrupting meaningful
relatedness. Finally, we will have to recognize Type C therapists
whose interventions are unconsciously designed to seal off underlying chaotic truths rather than to identify, understand, and experience them. The interventions from these therapists are designed
to destroy understanding and relatedness, and to create falsifications, clichés, and lie barriers designed to seal off the most compelling truths within the therapeutic interaction.

You may recall that in a previous part of the course (Langs
1980a), I offered a classification of therapists along these lines, and
in addition, in a chapter entitled "Truth Therapy, Lie Therapy," I
attempted to delineate the *modus operandi* of these various types of
therapeutic efforts. As you can quickly realize, the Type A therapist
works consistently with representations of indicators and adaptive
contexts, and with meaningful derivative complexes, while the
Type C therapist works with only a portion of the meaningful
communicative network offered in derivative form by the patient,
or instead works on a manifest content or Type One derivative
level.

We will term this the communicative mode of an intervention,
and will include it in our classification from now on.

Discussant: I take it that you are implying that the offer of
Kleenex is something like a Type C mode intervention. I also seem
to remember that his patient will be facing a forced termination
and a loss of her therapist in a few months. That could be another

172 RESISTANCES AND INTERVENTIONS

background adaptive context for this intervention and her response. It certainly is in keeping with the first association which relates to her lost ex-husband.

Langs: Your points are well taken.

Discussant: As I hear you, you are saying that a sound interpretation has a particular form of gratification, and that its qualities are appropriate and nonpathological. An erroneous intervention, on the other hand, seems to contain pathological gratifications and may be directly gratifying without producing insight. Is this what you mean by a noninterpretive intervention?

Langs: There is some confusion on your part. A valid interpretation does indeed offer the patient a particular form of satisfaction and adaptive resource that would constitute a type of gratification which is quite healthy and appropriate to the therapeutic situation. On the other hand, an erroneous intervention constitutes an unconscious offer of pathological satisfactions, inappropriate defenses, and such—all maladaptive and inappropriate to the therapeutic effort.

Beyond that, there is a separate class of interventions in which the therapist attempts to directly gratify the patient, such as offering specific advice, providing Kleenex, and even offering a cup of tea. This is but one form of noninterpretive and erroneous interventions. They are what we have called manifestly supportive interventions. However, there are many other ways in which a therapist may inappropriately gratify a patient, including the use of an erroneous interpretation.

Remember, an interpretation is an effort to make conscious to the patient something of which he is unaware. This can be done incorrectly, be poorly timed, and stated in a way that is essentially invalid and through which the therapist projects all sorts of pathological contents and mechanisms into the patient. Such an intervention would constitute an interpretive error on an erroneous interpretation.

In sum, interventions may be classified as interpretive or noninterpretive. We are dealing here with all those efforts by the therapist which fall outside of the management of the ground rules or framework. I have had difficulty in selecting a single term for such work, since calling them either verbal interventions or efforts directed toward understanding is inaccurate. After all, managements of the framework often require verbal responses. And of course, the therapist may make a wide variety of comments which are not interpretive in nature or directed toward understanding.

Perhaps the term *nonframe comments* best fits the bill. This group of interventions, as I have already indicated, should be restricted to interpretations and reconstructions, and should be understood for all of their verbal and nonverbal qualities. With the communicative approach, then, we restrict such interventions to interpretation-reconstructions or the playback of selected derivatives around an unmentioned intervention context. All other nonframe comments fall into the noninterpretive sphere, and as a rule they are under considerable countertransference-based influence. They may traumatize the patient or pathologically gratify him. Only in dire emergencies are such interventions sometimes—but by no means always—necessary; and even then, in addition to their salutory effects (e.g., momentarily preventing an attempt at suicide), they will evoke in the patient all of the detrimental consequences of such responses. In all cases, then, it is best to restrict yourself to interpretive and framework management efforts wherever possible, and reserve for crises, those rare moments when all else fails (in all likelihood due to important countertransference-based contributions), noninterpretive interventions.

Allow me to add a comment or two regarding the interplay between interventions and developmental mode of relatedness. It should be clearly understood that a sound interpretation or framework management response conveys to the patient on an object relationship level, the therapist's wish for, and preparedness to engage in, a healthy symbiotic and eventually commensal relationship. It implies efforts to promote both relative autonomy and individuation in the patient, and expectations that he will work over the insights offered to him and utilize them toward modification of his neurosis and personal growth. You can sense some of the qualities of a healthy symbiosis in that, for example, an interpretation provides the patient with something he is unable to generate for himself, while pointing him toward symptom alleviation and the development of a full capability for dealing with his own anxieties and conflict. It reflects inherently an ability in the therapist to renounce pathological satisfactions.

These two interventions, along with appropriate silence, are the only means through which a healthy symbiosis can be effected by the therapist. They have distinct caring qualities, which account for the appropriate gratifications involved, while at the same time they imply some degree of separateness between the therapist and patient, and pressures toward individuation—mainly for the patient though secondarily for the therapist.

All other interventions involve inappropriate relationship (and drive) gratifications for both patient and therapist, and therefore entail pathological modes of relatedness. In general, you will find that the more manipulative, self-revealing, and noninterpretive interventions tend to be relatively more parasitic than erroneous efforts at interpretation, and that milder forms of deviant intervention tend to engage the patient in pathological symbioses. A perusal of present-day clinical literature will show you that many noninterpretive interventions are invoked in the name of support and as a foundation for helping the patient to achieve individuation and autonomy, while their unconscious implications are exactly the opposite: they infantilize the patient, interfere with autonomy and individuation, and pathologically gratify both participants to the treatment situation.

We have so much to cover in our discussion of resistances and interventions that it will be possible to extend our discussion of the developmental mode of relatedness only at selected moments. However, I do hope that this dimension of the therapeutic interaction is now considerably clearer to you. Please continue.

Therapist: She got a card from Alan. He sent her a birthday card, a belated birthday card. And in the card he tells her that he's engaged. He adds that soon he will be getting married.

Discussant: This material seems to organize well around the adaptive context of the pending forced termination.

Discussant: The marriage theme could also touch upon one meaning of using the therapist's Kleenex. She now gives that particular deviation a traumatic quality.

Therapist: She says that she got this card from him, and that it's a very painful card because he's telling her he's getting married.

She went on to elaborate about the card. He wrote that this was a very traumatic time for both of them. She didn't understand why he included her in the card. And she added that he has just bought a business in Canada, and that he will be moving there. After she read the card, she was upset and cried.

She went on to say, It all seemed so permanent. His getting married again. I think that I'm still in love with him. And Arnold— her present boyfriend—came home and she told him that she got the card. He saw that she was upset. She told him that she got the card from Alan, and that he was getting married, and that this upset her. And when she cried, he began to cry as well.

Langs: Who will comment on this material?

Discussant: I find it getting repetitious on the surface. I've been searching to identify which adaptive contexts it may relate to. When did this session take place?

Therapist: In January, soon after the New Year.

Discussant: Well, it may indeed pertain to the pending forced termination. But even so, the patient is adding little in the way of new derivatives. She introduces her present boyfriend and creates some kind of threesome. And there's something about the two of them crying together. But somehow I guess that that relates to the Kleenex and sharing something. My point is that, as I hear this material, it is not too easy to organize.

Langs: I would agree. We have identified the prevailing adaptive contexts and some of the present indicators. In your comments, you did not address the degree to which they have been represented. As for the indicators, we would now have to add the pending forced termination, which corresponds to an anticipated adaptive context. How does the patient represent that particular situation, and how would you estimate the level of resistance involved?

Discussant: It is represented in the patient's comments about the loss of her husband, his plan to marry and to move. The patient is indicating that this is quite depressing for her. Without a bridge to therapy, I would say that there is a moderate degree of resistance, in that it seems to me that the derivative is clear, but its connection to the pending forced termination is not.

Langs: Yes, that is quite well stated. It would not be possible for the moment to intervene without a clear-cut bridge to therapy, and without some additional derivatives. By implication, our earlier discussant was indicating that the derivative complex is not especially rich. There is, of course, the taking of the Kleenex from the therapist, and now the reference to the loss of her ex-husband. There is a sense of depression, but for the moment no specific unconscious fantasy and perception constellations emerge. We would have to conclude that there is a moderately high level of resistance here, and that it attacks all three elements of the communicative network: the indicators, the intervention context, the derivative complex.

What can be said about the sources of these resistances?

Discussant: They are clearly interactional in nature. We already know that the therapist has avoided allusions to the therapeutic interaction in his interventions, except to comment on the patient's manifest avoidance of certain topics. And in addition, it seems to me that his plan to terminate the therapy because he will have completed his training at this center would also prompt defensiveness and resistance in the patient.

Langs: Yes, for the moment, these are shared defenses, and to some extent, understandable efforts by the patient to protect herself from a greater sense of depression and loss. A therapist who behaves in a manner designed to satisfy his own needs when they are in conflict with the patient's therapeutic needs will consistently be viewed as selfish and dangerous, and will always evoke some element of resistance in the patient's responsive communications.

What about the therapist's intervention?

Therapist: I made no verbal intervention; I was silent.

Langs: Exactly. To what extent is the silence being validated by the patient?

Therapist: That is difficult to say. We seem to agree that there is a relatively high level of resistance here, and that might indicate that silence is not the appropriate intervention. However, it seems quite clear that it would not be possible to intervene interpretively at this time. The patient has offered me no opportunity to rectify the frame or to interpret her response to the prevailing adaptive contexts. I would therefore have no choice but to be silent, even though the material does not seem to be deepening.

Langs: Yes, it is well for you to experience the clinical dilemma involved. When there is a relatively high level of resistance, you must determine its sources, decide whether it arises because of your silence, and therefore because you have failed to appropriately intervene, or whether it derives instead from a Type C communicative style which is primarily the responsibility of the patient.

But there is another possibility, and it is in evidence here. The patient has obtained a momentary framework deviation cure, and this has undone in some small way her separation anxieties and sense of loss. On the basis of that relief, she is no longer motivated to communicate meaningfully. While it may surprise you, an action as seemingly subtle as taking a Kleenex from the therapist may greatly influence the resistances and communicative balance within the patient. As we have now seen, quite often, in the presence of unrectified modifications in the framework—especially those which afford the patient some degree of pathological relatedness, gratification, and defense, and some sense of deviation and pathological relatedness cure—the patient may shift to a Type C communicative mode and accept the stultifying pathological symbiosis offered by the therapist. It is here that the mode of developmental or maturational relatedness considerably influences the flow of the patient's material and the appearance of resistances. The greater the extent of pathological symbiotic gratification, the greater the likelihood of resistances, especially on a communicative level. On a gross behavioral level, the patient may accept the mode of relatedness at one moment, showing no resistance, while at another moment, often quite suddenly, become distinctly resistant on a manifest level. However, there is no doubt that many extended therapeutic situations are maintained without noticeable gross behavioral resistance on the part of the patient through an established pathological symbiosis between the two participants to the treatment situation, with little in the way of sound interpretive work or growth and true individuation.

In any case, these are the types of silent hypotheses you should entertain as you attempt to evaluate your use of silence. As an intervention, silence may be valid or not; it requires continual appraisal, both subjectively and through your evaluation of the material from the patient.

Therapist: It seems to me that we could develop some sort of classification of silences. You are saying that they could be valid or invalid. They can be a way of getting the patient to understand more about herself. They could be a way of frustrating the patient and of being hostile. My question is, how can you tell what your silence means?

Langs: I have already attempted to spell that out. Perhaps it has not come across clearly. With each intervention we make, including silence, we monitor the material from the patient as a commentary on the intervention, and in addition, evaluate our subjective responses to our own efforts. In addition, we keep reevaluating the material from the patient on a cognitive level in order to determine whether we have the elements for an intervention: a clearly represented indicator, a well represented adaptive context, and a meaningful derivative complex. Ultimately, these evaluations depend on your clinical knowledge and self-understanding.

Here, how would you formulate the patient's specific commentary on your continued silence?

Discussant: She could be saying that she appreciates the silence. She even seems to experience it as a form of togetherness, as represented in her crying along with her boyfriend. There seems to be an implication that she had received a painful message and that the boyfriend had been supportive, a derivative which could imply that the therapist's silence is far less painful than the things he has been saying.

Langs: Yes, it's important to monitor the patient's derivative communications for their implications, in addition to searching her associations for validation or its lack. Here, there are actually two possibilities: the patient could be experiencing the silence as some kind of assault and hurt, or she could be experiencing the silence as supportive and as a form of merger. The nature of the interventions and of the patient's associations seems to support the latter possibility far more than the former.

We must attempt to consider every derivative in this material along the me/not-me interface, and attempt to understand its implications as commentary on your intervention. For the moment, our cognitive appraisal that the material does not permit an active intervention, and the indications of a positive introject from the patient, lend support to the postulate that your silence is essentially valid, despite the absence of expanding material. Still, we will not rest at this point, but will continue to monitor this material for further commentaries and possibilities.

Discussant: I take it that you feel that the derivatives are insufficient to interpret the meaning of the patient having taken a tissue from the box made available by the therapist.

Langs: Yes. As you can see, the patient is just beginning to represent this particular indicator, referring to her tears earlier in the week. However, the crying probably alludes more to her depression than to her use of the tissue. The best representation of that particular indicator is probably the allusion to the post card, which indicates the patient has been upset by what was made available to her. As you may recall, her former husband had written that it was a very traumatic time for both of them. Oddly enough, the patient wondered why he had included her. I bring up this point because in the adaptive context of the pending forced termination, the patient seems to be attempting to say that the trauma is more disturbing for the therapist than for her. Whatever truth there is to that particular communication, we would nonetheless have strong reasons to hypothesize that it contains a major quota of denial as well.

As we saw in *The Therapeutic Environment*, when a break in the frame is seemingly minor or when it gratifies the patient directly, the patient will often not represent the deviation—which is, of course, the adaptive context—either directly or in a manner which fosters interpretive intervention. Under such conditions, lacking a workable communicative network, your best recourse is to remain silent, to avoid new error, and to quietly rectify the frame during or after the hour as the situation permits.

We have greatly underestimated the interventions of silence and rectification. The former, as I said, has many implications. For the moment, I would like to stress that valid silence implies not making or repeating an erroneous active intervention. It is without question one of the most important and salutary interventions available to the therapist. There is, as I believe we have seen, an enormous tendency within therapists to repeat their mistakes, to bypass sound efforts at validation or to apply them with almost blatant prejudice, and to continue to intervene with nonvalidated comments because of some inner conviction, however filled with unrecognized countertransferences, that a particular point must be made and understood by the patient.

Remaining silent in order not to make or repeat an error is no simple matter. Here, for example, in the presence of a poorly represented adaptive context related to the basic framework, it would be an error to intervene in respect to any other material without finding some way to link it to the implications of the deviation for the patient. In principle, in the presence of modifications in the framework, the patient's material will not coalesce meaningfully around any other issue. However, should there be some other pressing problem, especially if it pertains to some other aspect of the therapeutic relationship or setting, it might be possible for the patient to express herself meaningfully in respect to one context while sealing off another. It is important to be aware of such a situation, and to attempt to intervene in a way that interprets the meaning of the material in light of the well-represented context and derivative response, while hinting at the defensive component as well. More important, it is critical to not intervene with respect to secondary issues when the patient has become resistant in response to a framework deviation. Such interventions constitute reinforcement of the patient's own resistances and defenses, since they support the communicative avoidance of a basic framework issue.

Discussant: If the patient had mentioned the tissues, do you feel there are enough derivatives here to intervene?

Langs: Who will comment?

Discussant: It's early in the session. It seems to me that the Kleenex might well link up to the issue of the forced termination. I sense a need in this patient to concretely repair the loss of her former husband and her relationship with the therapist as well. I would feel more satisfied with an intervention if it covered both issues.

Langs: Yes, and please allow me to state this as a precept: if, as the session unfolds, we become aware of two critical adaptive contexts, it is advisable to delay intervening until both contexts have been represented and the patient has generated a meaningful derivative complex in respect to each. This permits time to observe whether the patient deals more clearly with one issue than the other, and to locate the focus of his resistances.

On the other hand, if there appears to be only one adaptive context, and it happens to relate to an indicator of high priority such as a framework issue—and as such, the indicator and adaptive context will often coincide—it is best to permit as full an unfolding of the derivative complex as possible. It is essential to develop a capacity to be silent in this sense, to permit the patient his expression, and to be able to keep in touch with the various derivatives conveyed in the material. Having listened for a while and garnered a coalescible derivative complex, you would intervene at one of three points: (1) when the patient offers a striking bridge back to therapy; (2) when the patient offers a dramatic derivative which helps to bring together the entire network (assuming that the adaptive context and indicators have been represented in a manner which links them to the therapy); or (3) when the material begins to flatten out—under which conditions your silence has been extended too long, and given a meaningful communicative network, it is well to intervene with any reasonable lead-in.

Discussant: How many derivatives does one wait for? Is it possible to interpret a reaction to an adaptive context based on a single derivative?

Langs: Theoretically, it may be possible. But I trust that it is clear by now that the more derivatives you have, the more varied their implications, the more complete the intervention will be. And as you may remember, the ideal derivative complex might contain some valid unconscious perceptions of the therapist, some dynamic distortions derived from the patient's own intrapsychic conflicts and pathological introjects, a bit of an unconscious interpretation to the therapist and sometimes to the patient himself, an expression of the most important genetic implications, and if need be, a strong model of rectification. Sometimes it is necessary to work with a few pieces at a time. However, I would strongly recommend the use of patience and delay, remaining silent in order to collect meaningful derivative material.

In principle, an interpretation is simply a reordering and synthesizing of separate elements of disguised derivatives around the implications of an activated adaptive context. The creativity in the interpretation lies in this synthesis and in the recognition of the implications of the derivative communications. It should not lie in your own associations and in blatant additions you make to the patient's material and its meanings. There is more than enough room for creativity and sensitivity in being able to understand and integrate whatever it is that the patient has expressed in disguised form.

As you know, there is a great narcissistic need within therapists to add their own ideas to the patient's material, just as they have strong tendencies to control, manipulate, and even to inappropriately gratify their patients. Reasonable discipline does not imply a lack of spontaneity, creativity, and sensitivity. Therapists have tended to devalue discipline, principles, and such, and have attempted to promulgate the notion that such efforts are inherently destructive to the treatment process. It is my impression that such attitudes are used to defend countertransference tendencies, and that therapists and analysts have been all too lax in this regard.

Discussant: I am beginning to have a clearer idea of what you mean by coalescible derivatives. I am also beginning to understand that there are degrees of disguise, and what you mean by close and distant derivatives.

Therapist: If I may, I would also like to say that this situation has helped me to see how important the representation of the adaptive context is to the question of whether it will be possible to intervene. If this patient does not represent the adaptive context of the tissue in a more evident form than receiving a post card from her former husband, I would find it extremely difficult to interpret this material as a reaction to the availability of a box of tissues. On the other hand, if she did happen to mention it in passing, I would now be comfortable enough to build an intervention around such an issue. The image of the patient crying together with her boyfriend, and of sharing problems with her former husband, could easily be tied to the availability of tissue. And I would agree with the discussant who suggested that eventually this material must be tied to the pending forced termination. I am beginning to see how interventions are shaped.

Discussant: If there are several adaptive contexts, can you make a judgment as to which of them is more important?

Langs: You must weigh the influence of your own clinical experience, which provides a hierarchy of general indicators—here, you are using the term adaptive context to coincide with indicator. You balance that assessment against qualities derived from the patient's material. Usually, there will be guides which indicate that the patient is being defensive in a particular area, though not always.

This is the kind of question which is best answered in light of specific clinical data. Often, the decision is not that difficult. For example, here, we have been discussing two indicators: the availability of tissue and the pending forced termination. It seems relatively easy to reach a consensus as to which is more important. I won't assume it; I'll ask. How many votes for the tissues? And how many votes for the forced termination? As expected, forced termination wins unanimously. Certainly, there are situations that are more difficult to decide. Learn to rely on your human sensitivities, general orders of importance, and careful attention to the patient's derivative communications.

Discussant: I would like to add a third indicator: the therapist's interventions in the previous session. This would include the change in the office and the restoration of the regular setting in this particular hour. But more important for my point are the therapist's verbal interventions in that hour which were somewhat critical and hurtful, not very interpretive, and directed away from the therapeutic interaction. It seems to me that the patient represents that particular indicator and adaptive context through the hurtful post card she has received from her former husband. To extend my comment in light of our discussion, it would be my evaluation that that particular representation does not lend itself to an interpretation from the therapist. There is no easy connection to therapy. I simply wanted to point out that there were at least three, rather than two, indicators.

Langs: Yes, your point is well taken. Typically, erroneous interventions—Grade Two deviations in the form of errors in interpreting—are represented by patients in a highly disguised manner. As I have said before, in response to such errors, the opportunity to interpret the patient's unconscious perceptions and introjects, and their extensions into fantasy and transference, are quite rare. Once again, the use of judicious silence and self-corrective measures designed to avoid a repetition of previous errors comes into play. And for the moment, the therapist has done exactly that, which accounts in part for the positive elements in the patient's associations. Still, the hurt from the previous session and the anticipated hurt of the forced termination are generating negative introjects. But the therapist's silence is valid and he is not actively hurtful for the moment. Through derivatives, the patient expresses her appreciation of these qualities to his silence.

Now, it seems likely that we might have some measure of disagreement on how to order these three indicators: the tissues, the prior intervention, and the pending forced termination. Any suggestions?

Discussant: The pending forced termination appears to be a major break in the frame, and I think it should take precedence. The erroneous interventions might come next since they lacked neutrality and were unconsciously self-revealing. I would put the tissues last because they have been around for a long time, and constitute a minor break in the frame.

Discussant: But shouldn't any clear break in the fixed frame come before erroneous interpretations?

Langs: Actually, we won't belabor the point. A case could be made either way. This tells us that there will be times when our evaluation of a particular pair of indicators may be equivocal. At such junctures, we would interpret the indicator which is most clearly represented and which generates the most meaningful derivative complex, and try to work on the second indicator only when possible. We would expect the patient herself to do so in a later session. In the meantime, we would be in a position to rectify the framework or the error even if we had not interpreted to the patient the qualities of her response.

I think certain principles of intervening have emerged rather clearly. We must first establish a hierarchy of indicators, and see if they correspond to prevailing adaptive contexts. If not, we then take a seond step and establish a hierarchy of contexts. Finally, we evaluate the derivative complex in order to determine which particular context it fits best. Avoided contexts have been subjected to defensive operations—resistance. If these contexts are especially critical, we would hold back until the material permitted an interpretation of the resistances involved. We would do so by identifying the best representation of the pertinent adaptive context and by organizing the derivative complex in terms of the extent to which it illuminates the unconscious basis for the patient's defensiveness. On the other hand, if an important adaptive context-indicator has been well represented, and if there exists a meaningful coalescible derivative complex, we would be comfortable in confining our interpretation to that particular sphere.

Discussant: Would you also accept in principle that recency deserves consideration? For example, you have often pointed out that we should deal with a relatively recent error before addressing one that is more remote.

Langs: Yes, immediacy is a critical variable. It is not uncommon for a therapist to organize material around a past error, while missing a mistake in the immediate session. In principle, we always work from the present to the past. Often, since errors tend to be repeated and to overlap, it is easy to make the mistake of dealing with a relatively obvious but remote transgression, while overlooking a current and perhaps more subtle lapse.

Discussant: While we're stating principles, would you agree that another can be suggested to the effect that indicators and contexts within the therapeutic interaction take precedence over those outside the treatment situation?

Langs: Empirically, that is quite correct. I should hope that by now you have seen sufficient clinical evidence to support that precept. The only question is whether contexts and indicators derived from outside relationships can ever be utilized meaningfully in offering the patient an interpretation, without including some link to the therapist and therapeutic interaction. The evidence we have reviewed in this course suggests that this is very rarely, if ever, the case.

I want also to make it clear that we have actually been in the process of formulating an important aspect of resistance. To collate our observations and crystallize their implications: communicative resistances involve intrapsychic and interactional defenses which interfere in the patient's production of an ideal communicative network—well-represented indicators and adaptive contexts, and a coalescing derivative complex. These resistances may be directed at any of the three elements of the derivative network—indicator, adaptive context, or derivative complex. But they may also be directed at the communicative constellation pertinent to one adaptive context while relatively absent in connection with a different, coexisting context. This implies that the patient is highly selective in applying his defenses, and that he may do so within limits which permit the understanding and interpretation of the consequent disguises and distortions, or that he may do so beyond such a point so that either or both interpretation and recognition are no longer feasible.

It occurs to me to coin two terms here: *resistant defenses* and *nonresistant defenses*. The former apply to those intrapsychic and interactional defenses which interfere with understanding and interpretation, while the latter refer to those defenses which do not have such an effect, but which instead allow for full comprehension and interpretation. Clearly, we have a typical continuum, with resistant defenses at one extreme and nonresistant defenses at the other. And of course, an evaluation of this kind depends greatly on the therapist's self-knowledge, understanding of the patient, and capacity for listening and validating.

Technically, since resistant defenses disrupt the communicative qualities of the patient's material to a significant degree, silence is by far the most common and appropriate intervention. With nonresistant defenses, interpretation would be used most often.

I hope these concepts are now relatively easy for you to understand, and that they will prove useful. Please continue.

Therapist: She talks about how Arnold had been crying, how he started to cry when he came home. And she says that she doesn't like the fact that he cries, and that he cries so easily.

Parenthetically, I think that material substantiates your point. It seems to me she's saying that I cry too easily and that I encourage her to cry too easily as well. It's as if she doesn't want my sympathy, at least not in that form.

Discussant: Isn't that almost a model of rectification—Don't join me in my tears, be a man—?

Langs: Yes, though be careful to recognize that you added the quality: Be a man. That may be what the patient is implying, but allow her to say it through some derivative.

Therapist: The next day Arnold went to work and she just didn't get out of bed. That was the day before this session.

Langs: How do you hear these associations as derivatives organized around our adaptive context?

Discussant: As we had said, or even predicted, the offer of the tissues renders the patient nonfunctional.

Discussant: At the very least, it invites her to stop functioning. There is also a sense of hurt and retreat in response to the pending marriage of her former husband, which we would have to connect with the pending forced termination.

Langs: You are implying that this is another meaningful derivative which pertains to at least two, and probably all three, of the activated adaptive contexts. The third is, of course, the nature of the therapist's recent interventions.

What other category—one that we have been discussing—could this material fit into?

Discussant: Isn't it also an indicator, a symptom?

Langs: Exactly. This is an indicator, expressed in the form of a symptom within the patient, which now is clearly distinctive from the prevailing adaptive contexts. In addition, our formulation indicates that this particular symptom is a response to at least one or two of the adaptive contexts within the therapeutic relationship: the pending forced termination and the nature of the therapist's recent interventions. It would be a bit extreme to suggest that because the therapist provides his patient with tissues, she easily retreats into bed. Still, I would not be surprised if this does play some small role, and it may be part of a superficially supportive attitude of the therapist which unconsciously serves to infantilize the patient. These derivatives fit so strongly around the adaptive context of the tissues and its implications, they suggest to me the likelihood that the tissues actually are but one representation of a more pervasive aspect of this treatment situation.

In discussing the timing of interventions, I have stressed the communicative qualities of the material, the extent to which they facilitate intervening. I have also suggested that the specific moment of interpretation or rectification depends mainly on the presence of a meaningful bridge to therapy. Last week, I discussed in more detail the interplay between the weighting of the indicators and the clarity of the derivative complex.

With this material, I want to make another point. Our ultimate goal is to help the patient resolve her symptoms in an insightful and constructive manner. While I have weighted the power of symptomatic responses in the patient lower on the general scale of indicators than the therapists's errors and the patient's breaks in the frame, I do not mean to imply that the report of symptoms should be taken lightly. By all means, the patient is describing a form of suffering and retreat, and the therapist should do everything possible to help her. However, in principle, this must be confined to interpreting and rectifying efforts, since anything else, while well meaning on the surface, would constitute on a latent and derivative level unconscious support of the patient's illness.

This implies that the allusion here to the patient's symptom expresses a strong therapeutic need on her part. The accumulated indicators would rank relatively high on the scale, around eight. I would hope to cover most of them in intervening, and would certainly want to include the tissues in this effort. If possible, I would also hint at the influence of the pending forced termination and the qualities of the therapist's recent interventions. But intervening would require a nonresistant representation of the adaptive context. We already know that we have here a meaningful and coalescible derivative complex. Clearly, the main resistances have attacked the representations of the adaptive context. This is especially true because the patient has now directly represented one important indicator for the hour. Our problem, then, lies in the lack of a bridge to therapy and in the absence of a specific representation of the intervention contexts which might also contain links to the treatment situation.

I hope that most of you are now thinking that this particular defense corresponds to the defenses used by the therapist. Whatever the patient's propensities, the therapist's interventions excluded the therapeutic interaction and helped to foster this particular resistance, its nature and its form. The therapist avoids their relationship, the patient follows. This is indeed a good example of an interactional resistance.

There is more. We have an opportunity to identify the model of interpretation which applies in the presence of a symptom reported by the patient. I trust you can all sense the importance of understanding how we work with symptoms in psychotherapy. With all the attention that I have paid to the framework and to errors by the therapist, you might mistakenly think that it is my contention that psychotherapy constitutes the analysis of deviations in the ground rules and the implications of the therapist's errors. Sometimes, because of the nature of the therapist's efforts, this proves to be the case. On the other hand, in the presence of a secure frame and relatively error-free therapy, symptomatic responses within the patient will be a far more frequent and major indicator than otherwise. Under these conditions, the relevant intervention context will tend to involve the valid interventions of the therapist, rather than his mistakes. Often, it involves efforts by the *patient* to alter the frame, and the therapist's valid endeavors to keep it secure and to interpret the patient's pressures to deviate.

The work in this last part of the course has led me to realize that a large portion of therapeutic work in any treatment experience will involve framework issues. There is no doubt that this is consistently the case with therapists who tend to deviate. Any intervention which fails to deal with the break in the frame involves lie therapy rather than truth therapy. However, even in treatment situations where the therapist is capable of establishing and maintaining a secure therapeutic environment, a high proportion of interventions will address the patient's efforts to break the frame—situations in which the therapist's maintenance of the framework is the main adaptation-evoking context. This further highlights the extent to which therapists and analysts have neglected the implications of management of the ground rules, and its importance in the therapeutic process. Even with respect to resistances, we are already discovering that many resistances and counterresistances take the gross behavioral form of efforts to modify the frame, and that in addition, breaks in the frame serve as an important form of resistances in patients. In the presence of a secure holding environment, a patient who experiences a need for an interpretation will unconsciously (or more rarely, consciously) create a frame issue to enable the therapist ultimately to satisfy that need. In addition, the secure frame may itself create anxieties and therapeutic needs in the patient.

Returning to this clinical material, and to the subject of symptoms, a patient may report emotional disturbances in the presence or absence of a secure frame and erroneous interventions by the therapist. The functional implications of these symptoms will depend on the state of the therapeutic environment and interaction. These indicators must always be understood in terms of the prevailing adaptive contexts.

In this particular situation, our silent hypothesis is that the therapist's recent interventions and the anticipation of a forced termination are contributing to the patient's symptomatic response. The patient also offers a manifest precipitant for this symptom in her outside life—the post card from her former husband. Typically these responses to the more obvious context are quite linear: she is upset and retreats to bed. There is no sense of the mediating effects of unconscious fantasy and perception constellations, and a complete lack of specific dynamics. The communication is direct rather than convoluted, and is essentially nonneurotic even though it involves an emotional reaction. On the other hand, the connections to the adaptive context within treatment have the sense of complexity which is the hallmark of neurotic expression.

As for the model interpretation, our goal would be to identify this particular indicator, link it to the two adaptive contexts within treatment, and show the patient's derivative responses to the context in terms of perceptions and fantasies. In principle, we would demonstrate to the patient that she has responded to these two contexts with a series of unconscious perceptions and fantasies on the one hand, and with her symptoms on the other; and further, that the unconscious meaning and functions of her symptoms are specifically represented psychologically in terms of the adaptive context-derivative complex constellation.

Please understand, I am not suggesting that I would offer such an interpretation at this point in the session. As I have already indicated, the patient's failure to represent the adaptive context with a link to treatment poses an almost insurmountable obstacle in this respect. I would be left only with the options of remaining silent or playing back derivatives around the two unmentioned adaptive contexts. Since one of them does relate to a modification in the fixed frame, it might be possible to obtain a validating response. However, since there has been no recent direct mention of this context, it is my belief that such an intervention would be too remote from the available material, and that it would fail to find confirmation. I would therefore opt at this point for silence, though I would intervene if any bridge to therapy appeared or if an interpretable representation of the adaptive context were to appear.

Let me propose a hypothetical interpretation as a model. Some of what I will say is not in the material, but I will use it in order to illustrate my point. I might say, you have been talking about the finality of the loss of your husband and have, in that connection, mentioned that something is troubling you about treatment, even though you are unable to define it.

Of course, I am adding the latter element, imagining that the patient had eventually made such a bridge to therapy, and I am doing so because having it is necessary to intervene in this session. A playback of derivatives around separation issues, as I said, is the best alternative, and it is my impression that it would be too remote from this material. However, if the patient were suffering greatly, I would offer such an intervention. Notice too, that I began my interpretation with the representation of the adaptive context—the loss of her husband. As a rule, we begin with either the context or the indicators before moving to the derivative complex.

I would go on: You are also still holding a tissue you took from the box on my desk. You went on to say that Arnold talks to you in a hostile and disruptive way. (Here too I am adding a derivative to hypothetically represent the adaptive context of the therapist's recent interventions.) You have said something (I would continue) about Alan's problems, about losing him, about his imposing his problems on you, and about the finality of the sense of loss. You've also commented upon Arnold's crying too easily, and how it disturbs you. If we put all of this together with your unhappiness about treatment and my making tissues available to you, it would appear that there is some problem pending that has something to do with a final separation of sorts. You seem to be suggesting that it is more my problem than yours, that it is hurtful, that it is being avoided, and that this avoidance—yours and mine—is expressed in your decision to stay in bed yesterday. You are also saying that, in some way, the offer of tissues is a way of my crying with you and treating you as weak and incapable of functioning. It seems to be experienced by you as a means of encouraging your retreat. Arnold's nastiness also seems to be connected to me in some way. That, too, you view as his problem much more than yours. It upsets you and also prompts you to withdraw. In all, some kind of nastiness from me, some threat of final separation, and the offer of tissues has led you to feel upset, depressed, and to withdraw.

In trying out this particular intervention, I am quite dissatisfied with the available material, and especially with the derivative complex and the representations of the major adaptive contexts. It was necessary for me to make up two representations of the contexts to even offer the intervention. In addition, the derivatives as they pertain to the major context of the pending forced termination seem quite weak and difficult to work with. It may well be that one of you could shape them far better than I have, but I experience them as well disguised. They did not seem to lend themselves readily to the interpretation I was trying to develop.

This intervention can only serve as a model. It is the type of silent intervention I often make to myself as I listen to material from a patient—though I do not usually add elements of my own. In so doing, I experience the qualities of the intervention and try to evaluate the extent to which the patient would understand or be confused by it, and I attempt to determine its relative richness and cogency or flatness and awkwardness. If I experience the silent intervention as relatively ineffectual, it is quite likely that I will not offer it to the patient. On the other hand, if I experience the silent intervention as rich and deeply meaningful, it is highly likely that I will present it to the patient—especially if the patient's subsequent associations add to its richness and validate my thinking.

As a model, I hope you are able to follow how I identified the representations of the prevailing adaptive contexts, organized the derivatives meaningfully as transversal communications around these contexts, attending to both perceptions and fantasies, and then linked each element to the patient's symptomatic response. I included an implicit acknowledgment of my own contribution to the patient's symptoms. I avoided confessions and self-revelations, and attempted to use only the material the patient had generated in the hour, with allowances for the derivatives I simply made up for this exercise. Take that as a model interpretation related to a symptom, and try to apply it in your own therapeutic work.

Finally, I hope that you can see in her allusion to how they both cried that on an object relationship level, the patient may well be complaining in this derivative way of the helplessness of both she and the therapist, and their inability to effect anything other than a pathological symbiotic mode of relatedness. However, and this point is to be stressed, it is only through an interpretation of the relevant material that the therapist can meaningfully and truly indicate to the patient that he has acquired some sense of individuation, strength, and autonomy of his own, and is therefore capable of effecting a healthy symbiosis with the patient. This can be signaled only through an interpretive effort, which simultaneously creates an interaction which is inherently a healthy rather than pathological mode of relatedness. Any other response would on some level continue the pathological symbiosis and further reflect the bleakness and pathological symbiotic needs of the therapist. Rectification of deviations in the basic ground rules and boundaries which effect a pathological symbiosis or parasitisim, and correction of errors which express these kinds of pathological needs in the therapist, are basic background interventions upon which a sound interpretation can be offered.

Therapist: She had gone out the night before the day she stayed in bed. She was with Arnold and with somebody who knows Arnold's girlfriend. This was the night after she had gotten the post card. This person knows Arnold's girlfriend and she was concerned about how she looked. Would this guy go back to the girlfriend and say, You're right; she doesn't look good.

Actually, she went on to say that everything went all right. She had a good time. And the next day, she woke up and she kept thinking about Alan. And she just couldn't get out of bed. She was thinking that maybe things could have been much different, in terms of their relationship. Maybe they would still be together if she had been nicer to him. She feels that she's been going backwards. She's looking for an apartment in a building owned by this center, and she feels she's going backwards because both Arnold and Alan were involved with this center. And now Alan is going to have a house.

Langs: Any brief comment?

Discussant: The patient is working over how she might have kept her relationship with her former husband, and not lost him. Then she says something about living in an apartment owned by this center. I could hear these associations as derivatives related to the Kleenex, as a way the therapist has of holding on to his patient and offering her a concrete part of himself so there is no sense of separation. But I feel that the material organizes far better around the pending forced termination. It's as if the patient is saying she feels she has done something wrong or bad which has led the therapist to plan to leave her, and that she will undo the loss by moving in here, so to speak.

Langs: Yes, the derivatives seem to become somewhat more meaningful in respect to the pending forced termination. And yet, even though the patient now alludes to this center, there is still no specific reference to treatment. The resistances have lessened in one respect, generating clearer representations for the derivative complex. They continue in full force with respect to the representation of the major anticipated intervention context, however. On the whole, the resistances remain at a level above the midpoint of five on the scale I suggested earlier in this course, in that they do not as yet facilitate or permit an interpretive intervention.

In these circumstances, we must undertake another measure which should not be overlooked. If we do not eventually hear some clear representation of the intervention context, it would be necessary for us to reexamine the material and to consider possible reformulations. Such is the influence of major resistances: they lead you to doubt your formulations, to wonder if you're missing something, and to reassess. You become uncertain of yourself and you actually lack the power to intervene. Resistances may have paralyzing, at times even devastating, effects on the therapist. Interactionally, they often function as an expression of the patient's aggression and destructiveness, and as disruptive projective identifications.

Again, to specifically synthesize the point at hand: resistances are indeed based in part on intrapsychic defenses, and constitute efforts to resolve intrapsychic conflict and to deal with disturbing unconscious fantasy constellations. Resistances also stem from introjects of the therapist and reflect compromises related to unconscious perception constellations. Thus, resistances have dynamic functions for the patient's inner psychic economy, but in addition, have dynamic functions within the spiraling communicative interaction. These interpersonal effects have been experienced by every therapist and analyst, yet have received little consideration. Bird (1972) addressed them, though I have seen little in the way of investigation by others. Nonetheless, these interactional influences are often a major motive for the patient's resistances. Obstacles to treatment, expressed not only through gross behaviors but through communicative resistances, stand high among the patient's weaponry. They may express both aggressive and seductive needs, serving as a way of thwarting the therapist as well as a means of seducing him into inappropriate interventions and involvements. We must keep a careful eye on these interactional effects.

As with all such phenomena, once we have made a silent formulation in this sphere, to consider ourselves on firm ground we must obtain validation from the patient's associations and cognitive material. Certainly, we would want such support before interpreting these effects to the patient. Otherwise we would risk intervening based on subjective experiences and without available derivatives from the patient. The effects of countertransference are often considerable under such conditions, and all interventions which deal with interactional pressures, processes, and contents should have firm backing in the patient's associative material.

These remarks, of course, touch upon metabolizing and interpreting projective identifications. The model for this type of interpretation is quite similar to the one we developed a moment ago for dealing with the patient's symptoms. In this case, the indicator is some type of interactional projection from the patient, though beyond that, the interpretation is always related to an activated adaptive context and a coalescible derivative complex. The processing by the therapist of pathological interactional projections is more likely to be necessary with borderline and psychotic patients, and is one difference in therapeutic work with more severely ill patients. But notice: the principles are the same. It is mainly in the material and the shape of the intervention that distinctions emerge. Hopefully, we will have an opportunity with our case presentations to apply these principles to an example of projective identification in order to clarify the techniques involved.

Two additional comments. First, in mentioning the destructive and hurtful aspects which underlie the patient's resistances as they influence the therapist, I want to remind you that simultaneously, or sometimes alternately, resistances are also unconsciously designed to protect the therapist. In part, every interactional resistance has a function of this type, in that it is designed to join with the therapist in effecting certain types of defenses against otherwise threatening material. Once we are in touch with the interactional aspects of resistance, their role and functions—as interactional projections, means of effecting role- and image-evocations, and harmful or seductive of the therapist, or helpful and protective—obtain full consideration.

Secondly, returning directly to this material, let's remember that we are continuing to monitor the patient's associations as a commentary on the therapist's silence. There is a sense now of the negative effects of this silence. This should lead us to question the use of this intervention, and to search again for possible ways to actively intervene.

In principle, you will find that there are situations in which the patient offers no bridge to therapy whatsoever, and where there is no major break in the framework. We review the material from the patient and conclude that there is no possibility of intervening. Nonetheless, the patient begins to complain through derivatives, and sometimes even directly, about the therapist's silence. Often, this means that the patient has placed you in a bind: she has not given you the means to interpret, and yet she demands that you speak. Such a problem is quite common with certain types of patients, many of them Type B-C narrators, who go on and on about emotionally-laden material which either fails to coalesce around a pertinent intervention context, or which unfolds in an hour in which there is no meaningful representation of that context. When this occurs over an extended period of time, the patient sometimes becomes directly critical. Powerful efforts are made to engage the therapist in a manifest content form of relatedness—itself a resistance designed for pathological symbiotic gratification and to seal off Type Two derivative communication. Frequently, the patient offers many manifest associations regarding the therapist, and engages in extensive efforts to directly show him how to do his work. This is done without a shift to meaningful derivative communications, and as a rule does not constitute a nonneurotic, valid therapeutic endeavor, which is almost always expressed by the patient through indirect expressions.

Under these circumstances, the therapist often experiences powerful interactional projections and self- and image-evocations which generate a strong wish to respond actively—and sometimes, quite directly—to the patient. Often, the wish is to prove that the therapist is not helpless in the face of the disturbing demands made by the patient. There is usually a split here so that the patient expresses a manifest wish for an intervention, yet generates a communicative network which does not permit interpretation or rectification of the frame. Thus, if the therapist speaks out, he does so defensively to reassure himself, to gratify himself interpersonally, and for a number of other reasons. Often, he is dealing with an unmetabolized projective identification, highly toxic and destructive in nature, which is essentially dumped back into the patient through the erroneous intervention.

As we well know, the patient unconsciously perceives the implications of the therapist's erroneous intervention in these very terms. While she may manifestly express her sense of gratitude or relief, the derivatives almost without exception will revolve around the therapist's weaknesses, his failures in containing, his fearful need to speak in the absence of meaning or to generate meaning when it has been destroyed, and his own need for a manifest content form of relatedness which can seal off the underlying chaos of the therapeutic interaction and provide both participants with pathological symbiotic satisfactions.

This type of situation is among the most difficult to handle in psychotherapy. The first step is extensive silent validation of your hypothesis that the material does not organize meaningfully around sufficiently well represented adaptive context, and that the derivative complex is indeed fragmented and devoid of meaning. It is the uncertainty of the situation which evokes considerable anxiety in therapists. Actually, it is just this type of interactional projection and evocation which the patient unconsciously wishes to create in the therapist.

With this particular patient, it is my hypothesis that we are dealing with someone who is resistant within a Type A communicative mode rather than using the more obliterating, nonderivative Type C style and defenses. I say this because there are many meaningful derivatives, and I suspect that eventually, left to her own resources, she will provide a useful bridge of link to therapy. It is also clear that the therapist himself is contributing to these resistances.

Nonetheless, at this point in the session, as the patient expresses her symptoms and describes regressive feelings and the possibility of acting out, at a moment when the indicators have become strong and the derivative network remains entirely resistant, it may be possible for you to experience the sense of frustration that patients of this kind can generate in their therapists. When this occurs with the typical Type C patient, it is necessary to bide your time until a sound interpretation is feasible. But with some of these patients, the hostility and direct assault is so great, the pressure to speak and the fear of losing the patient are so intense, that a countertransference-based intervention is difficult to resist. Nonetheless, if you adhere to basic technical precepts under those conditions, the patient will often eventually generate interpretable material.

I have no ready answer for this dilemma. Our consideration of the maturational mode of relatedness between the patient and therapist does, however, provide additional perspective. The patient may well be representing the pathological symbiosis between herself and the therapist through her allusion to obtaining an apartment in this medical center complex. There appears to be an overall sense of compromise: on the other hand, the patient wishes to maintain the pathological symbiosis as a major means of alleviating the separation anxieties and other aspects of her neurosis which are currently being mobilized, while on the other hand, she seems to be moving toward meaningful communication related to these issues and a possible effort to modify the pathological relatedness between herself and the therapist.

Therapist: She was saying that she is going backwards. If she would still be with Alan, she would have a house. Instead, she is looking at housing in this center. Her present boyfriend is a student here. Maybe she should be alone. Maybe she shouldn't be with anybody. Maybe that's the answer for her.

Alan is bothering her now. But Alan didn't want her for herself; he wanted her for her family. Alan's parents were divorced right after he was born, and he really just wanted to be a part of her family. She's not convinced that he liked her for herself. And she was always afraid when she went out with him that she wasn't going to live up to the way he described her.

Discussant: It seems to me that the present boyfriend, since he's involved with this center, may also constitute a pathological symbiotic object for the patient, and a means of representing that particular aspect of the relationship with the therapist. I found support for this formulation in the patient's comment that Alan wants her for her family rather than for herself: this could well imply an unconscious perception of pathological symbiotic needs within the therapist which interfere with the patient's individuation.

Langs: That's excellent. It seems that you are now integrating a number of levels of listening and conceptualizing in a very meaningful way. There is no need for me to add to your comment.

Therapist: At this point I intervened. I said to her that it seems that no matter how many people give her positive reports on how she is, she still has to change her image of herself—she's still not satisfied with it.

Langs: There is still a little time. Who will analyze this intervention?

Discussant: I would call it an attempt at a general interpretation. It reflects listening on a manifest content and Type One derivative level. There may be a vague indicator in respect to some disturbance in the patient's self-image, but there is no use of an adaptive context and virtually none of the derivative complex.

Discussant: Once again, it is critical of the patient, and divorced from the therapeutic relationship. Because of its repetitive qualities, I wonder if the patient doesn't experience it as some form of pathological projective identification. On that basis, I would postulate that it is a Type B or Type B–C form of communication from the therapist.

Langs: That's excellent.

Therapist: I can see now how empty my intervention was. I was trying to help her with her problems in achieving any secure sense of self-esteem. It seems so empty now.

Discussant: It also locates all of the problems in the patient. It is my impression that this type of undisciplined intervening abounds in work with narcissistic patients.

Langs: There was a mixture here of confrontation and superficial interpretation. Hostility is a consistent aspect of confrontations, a point we have seen again and again. The hour is short. How did the patient respond?

Therapist: She continued to talk about how she felt about Arnold. I can see no response that confirms my intervention. In fact, the session ended with her repeating what she had already said.

Langs: Well, there was no cognitive validation. We don't have time to hear the specific associations, but it would seem that the patient offered little in the way of commentary on your intervention. Apparently, she continued her comments about Arnold as a derivative way of conveying her impression that the therapist is using her for his own needs—e.g., for supervision—rather than as a way of taking care of her therapeutic needs. This is another theme pertinent to the forced termination. Patients often say through derivatives that their therapist has used him or her for his training, and once he is finished, he drops them. It is an experience which evokes a considerable sense of depression.

Time is up. Thank you for an excellent presentation. We'll begin with a new case next week.

Chapter Four

THE INFLUENCE OF
DIAGNOSIS ON TECHNIQUES
OF INTERVENING

Therapist: This is a thirty-one year old graduate student at this center. I have been seeing him for about a year and a half, and I probably will be leaving at the end of the academic year. Our sessions are twice weekly.

I will begin with the session prior to the one on which I would like to focus. It was curious how the session started. He was about six minutes late. As the time came for me to see him, I became particularly sensitive to this. I'm also sensitive to the fact that he's been consistently late for quite a while, but not markedly late. In fact, it is generally only a minute or two.

He came into the session and started talking about his being late. He raised the questions, Why do I always manage to come just after the session starts? Why can't I be on time? How come it is difficult for me to be even a little bit early?

Then he recounted this little vignette. He tells me: Today of all days, I got here ten or fifteen minutes early. I registered downstairs (where he has to go in order to come up to my office which is on the ward). I was feeling well and waiting for the elevator to come. But something called me away and made me go check my mailbox, which is at the other end of the building. So I went to check my mailbox, and I ended up getting into this brief conversation with this girl, and by the time I got up here, it was late again.

Then he said, Once again, I just can't seem to get here before you start. There is something about waiting around here that is just difficult for me, and yet I can't express what it is that is difficult. I am puzzled by the whole thing.

At this point I made a comment. I said, There is some reason why you need to keep me waiting, rather than allowing me to keep you waiting.

Langs: Let's proceed cautiously. We know nothing of the previous hour. Nonetheless, it will be possible to develop some comments and silent hypotheses.

Discussant: Had you told the patient you were leaving the center?

Therapist: Yes, I had. In fact, he will be getting his doctorate around the same time. He has already accepted a position at a university in the south.

Discussant: Had you told him where you were going?

Therapist: I'm not sure. I know that I told him that I would probably be leaving the city. I should also add that this particular session took place immediately after a conference I had in my office with the ward staff. This is a regular weekly meeting, and every so often it would run over and he would have to wait. I decided, partly because of what I have learned here, that it was not possible to expect him to come in to see me on time if I couldn't be on time, so I made his session fifteen minutes later. That was done two weeks before the hour I have started to describe. I would expect that to be a background adaptive context for this session. I had rectified a bit of this frame, even though I had to do it by making a change in the framework itself.

Langs: Who will comment?

Discussant: On the surface, without knowing an adaptive context, I found the material flat and empty. Despite the fact that it pertained to the treatment situation, it seemed quite hollow. I realize that a particular adaptive context might lurk behind these associations, and that if I knew it, I might be able to find a great deal of meaning. It just led me to wonder whether surface rumination bears any relationship to communicative resistances.

Langs: The point for the moment is that you are distinguishing the surface qualities of the patient's associations from their possible communicative qualities in light of an adaptive context. Until now, therapists have focused almost entirely on the manifest attributes of the patient's associations. Some would therefore see these associations as too detailed and reality oriented, unimaginative, and therefore as resistant. Others might suggest that, since the associations relate to the patient's lateness, there is considerable meaning and importance.

A few other brief comments. First, rumination of this kind may well be a means used by a patient to maintain a pathological symbiosis with his therapist. I mention this in order to demonstrate another relationship between resistances and maturational mode of relatedness. To the extent that a patient wishes to maintain and preserve this type of relatedness with the therapist, he may resist meaningful derivative communication while simultaneously cooperating and appearing nonresistant on the surface.

Secondly, even though we lack definitive clinical data—though there is some support in this initial material—I would like to propose that a therapist who keeps a patient waiting past the appointed hour, and who is involved with another group of individuals during the time set aside for a patient's session, is in some way creating a parasitic mode of relatedness. There is a sense of exploitation and a disregard for the patient's needs reflected in such behaviors, and it is this which characterizes the parasitic mode of relatedness—an entirely selfish expression of need which is gratified at the expense of the other individuals.

Discussant: If we simply take the adaptive context which we now know—the fact that the therapist had often been late to the sessions himself and that he had recently corrected the situation—it seems to me that this material does have some sense of communicative meaning. It would appear that the patient is still working over the therapist's involvement with the staff and the way in which he would delay seeing the patient. The patient seems to have introjected these attributes and is showing the therapist how it feels. He could have been on time and he ends up with distractions, getting his mail and talking to a girl. It's not a complicated derivative complex, but there does seem to be some evidence of meaning.

Langs: To complete your effort, would you identify the indicator and adaptive context for the hour, in light of the little that we know?

Discussant: I would see the therapist's lateness and rectification of the frame as both the indicator and the adaptive context. They are both represented by the patient's lateness and his comments about his problem in getting to the sessions on time.

Langs: While there might well be other more pertinent and recent intervention contexts, the particular background context we have identified does indeed seem to meaningfully organize this material, though only to a limited extent. It provides us with a model or an exercise in listening and formulating. We will soon find out how pertinent that context is for this session.

As we can see again, in order to develop a silent intervention and decide whether to offer it to the patient, it is necessary to formulate the material at hand. You have proposed—and I would agree—that the indicator and adaptive context for these associations (within the limits of our knowledge) is the therapist's past lateness, specifically due to meetings with a group of people in his office, and his recent decision to rectify part of the situation by seeing the patient fifteen minutes later. This context is represented through the patient's lateness and comments about his tardiness, a form that could readily lend itself to the development of an interpretation. This is so because the key element—lateness—is manifest in the material, and the main defense is simply one of displacement—from the therapist onto the patient himself. This reflects an introjective process which might well lend itself to interpretation.

At this point in the hour, an intervention of this kind could not specifically relate the patient's associations and behavior—his interactional acting out, if you will—to the therapist's lateness since the patient has not provided us with such a bridge. However, it would be feasible to allude to the problem of lateness, to develop some of the derivatives around that issue without specifically confining oneself to the patient's lateness alone, and to thereby help the patient to bypass the communicative resistance through which he avoids a direct reference to the therapist's past latenesses.

The derivative complex is indeed, for the moment, not very well developed. It certainly demonstrates that the patient has effected an introjective identification with the therapist, and it conveys something of the irrationality involved when a therapist makes a commitment to a patient and then fails to keep it because of a group meeting. The sense of frustration, the inability to effect a change in the other person's behavior, the puzzling qualities, and even the sense of absurdity are all conveyed in these manifest associations to which we give derivative meaning in light of the therapist's behaviors.

Now, I must add several points; I want to say a bit about each. First, we must relate this material to the additional adaptive context and indicator which we know about. Second, we should discuss briefly the nature of interactional acting out. Finally, we will want to say something about the listening process as it pertains most immediately to the development of formulations of silent, and sometimes offered, interventions.

I will begin with the third point first, since my last remarks are closer to this particular issue. As we have been working with resistances and interventions, there is an aspect of the listening process that has become much clearer to me. It is a dimension I have already discussed with you, but its importance has only now fully registered. In fact, it occurs to me that it probably was no coincidence that our seminars on the listening process (Langs 1978a) actually began with a discussion of this very factor. I refer to the importance of developing a full appreciation of the unconscious implications of each active intervention context in each session. This includes, of course, a need to understand the meanings and functions, manifest and latent, of each and every one of your interventions.

While we enter each session without desire, memory, or understanding, we soon cast about for meaning, context, implications, and such. We allow the patient's ongoing associations to guide us, and we readily include our own responsive and free associations.

We divide ourselves, remaining open to unanticipated possibilities on the one hand, while on the other, we attempt to give some organization and meaning to what is already available.

A critical aspect of this process is identification of the most cogent adaptive contexts for the session at hand. Once recognized, it is critical to freely allow yourself to formulate the implications of the precipitants. We have done so repeatedly in this course, and I offered an example of this kind just a moment ago, referring to the implications of the therapist's group meeting in his office, and being late for sessions because of it. Let's do this as an exercise. In addition to the implications I already derived from the patient's material, who will suggest other possibilities?

Discussant: It is a hostile act.

Discussant: It implies that the patient is not especially important to the therapist.

Discussant: Since it is a staff meeting, it may expose the patient to people he knows from the center. It therefore implies a disregard for the patient's privacy and his right to total confidentiality.

Discussant: Doesn't it also mean that the therapist can't manage his schedule very well? The patient could infer from that something to the effect that the therapist has difficulties in handling his life, inner and outer.

Langs: This is excellent. As you can see, the implications of a powerful adaptive context, especially when it takes the form of a major break in the framework, are complex and multiple. This brings me to a qualifying point: every effort should be made to identify the implications of an intervention context in their relative order of importance. To do this, you must rely on your own human sensitivities and on a capacity to more or less identify those qualities of a particular context which are likely to be most traumatic to the patient.

I must add once again that in carrying out such an effort, it is essential to remain open to the influence of the patient's material.

The patient himself will bring to the fore implications of a particular context you yourself have missed. And because of his own inner needs and vulnerabilities, he may well give major importance to an aspect of the context that most other persons would find relatively insignificant. The main purpose of developing the implications of an adaptive context is not to generate a rigid constellation of meanings, but instead to loosely identify those which appear to be most important and to remain open to clarification from the patient. At the same time, as we saw when we discussed the decision as to which of two activated adaptive contexts is probably most important to the patient, we may find that a patient is willing to respond through derivatives to certain aspects of an adaptive context and that he is quite defensive in his reactions to other aspects.

In sum, the patient may be right in what he is most strongly responding to—directly, and especially on a derivative level—or he may be defensive. In order to decide, you must evaluate the importance of what the patient is working over through derivatives, and compare this with the other possible implications. Often, you will intervene based on what the patient has to offer. Only when the patient fails to move on and deal with other important implications—assuming for the moment that the situation has not been rectified—would you feel confident that highly critical resistances are in operation. No patient can deal with everything at one time, and defenses do have adaptive value.

It would seem here, for example, that the patient's sense of helplessness, the therapist's hostility and disregard for the needs and person of the patient, and the possible exposure of the patient to third parties, might loom especially large in terms of the implications of this particular adaptive context. The patient himself adds a quality no one has mentioned until now, though I touched upon it indirectly. This type of delay of the beginning of the session is, according to the patient, a crazy and irrational act. It is what I would term a minipsychosis or a mini-psychotic act, out of keeping with reality but occurring in a nonpsychotic person. It is a type of response that is on a par with what I term neurotic delusions and neurotic hallucinations—easily repaired breaks with reality which are readily modified when subjected to specific reality testing.

I trust the therapist will forgive me this particular characterization of his behavior—though of course, it is not I whom he must forgive, but the patient. Within the context of a secure framework, the patient will often attempt to drive the therapist crazy and to lead him into mini-psychotic acts of this kind. Here, the therapist himself has expressed such a behavior. Often, it provides the patient with a critical opportunity to projectively identify into the therapist the patient's mini- as well as more pervasively psychotic parts of his personality. However, when this occurs in a form which the patient is unable to control, it is likely to have the unconscious implication of an attempt to drive the patient crazy. In contrast, the therapist's effort to rectify the frame would constitute a cessation of such efforts, and might provide a framework within which the patient's own craziness would unfold. As such, the act of rectification could pose a considerable threat to this patient, which may account for his own mini-psychotic behavior as reflected in the way in which he was late for this particular hour.

I sometimes think of the formulation of the various implications of an intervention context as the development of receptor sites—a preparedness to receive certain types of derivatives. Such preparedness fosters their recognition and even helps you to identify additional implications for which you were not initially prepared. These sites may also exert a bias so it is equally important to maintain an open mind and to reevaluate your formulations. As always, we must maintain a state with both fluid and partially fixed qualities.

Let's now extend this exercise by identifying the second known adaptive context for this material. Once recognized, we can assess its implications and then relate it to the material from the patient to this point. Who can identify it?

Discussant: It must be the pending forced termination.

Langs: Yes, and what implications occur to you?

Discussant: Well, we've been working over this issue for a while now. Forced termination implies hostility, helplessness in the patient, a disregard for his therapeutic needs, the selfish use of the patient by the therapist, and an exploitation of the patient—to name a few that occur right off the top of my head.

Langs: Yes. We can add that you have just characterized a form of pathological relatedness which could be best characterized as parasitism of the patient by the therapist. Here, inappropriate needs within the therapist are gratified entirely at the expense of the patient whose own therapeutic needs are disregarded.

Discussant: There could also be a sense within the patient that he has been seduced only to be discarded.

Langs: Yes, pathological symbiotic and parasitic relationships are infused with the gratification of inappropriate instinctual drive needs, including a variety of unconscious fantasy constellations derived from the therapist's countertransferences. Individuation requires a mastery of such pathological drives and a resolution of superego pathology. As I have stated before, it is important to interdigitate our thinking regarding the maturational level of object relatedness with the other dimensions of the therapeutic interaction, both intrapsychic and interpersonal.

Returning to this clinical material, how do our expectations tally with the associations from the patient? And which implications does the patient himself add?

Discussant: Through derivatives, the patient seems to be saying that the therapist's behaviors—the pending forced termination and his repetitive lateness—are highly frustrating and senseless; they are crazy or irrational and quite provocative. This seems to support the notion of a parasitic mode of relatedness. I can see now that there is a similarity between the therapist's repetitive lateness for the sessions and the pending forced termination, and that the patient is stressing how they make no sense from his vantage point.

Langs: Yes, you are quite right. For whatever reason this patient seems to be emphasizing for the moment the irrationality of the pending forced termination. He is also saying that the anticipation is driving him crazy. Furthermore, he is indicating that it is necessary for him to actively perpetrate on the therapist the very qualities of these adaptive contexts which are most disturbing to himself. He is also indicating that he has a need to protect himself from total submission to the therapist, from an acceptance of a relatively secured framework, and from a clear-cut commitment to treatment.

This now leads me to the patient's interactional acting out. In terms of indicators, context, and derivatives, how would you categorize his lateness to the session?

Discussant: It is an indicator. It may also be a secondary adaptive context, a disturbance stemming from the patient.

Langs: Yes, it has become clear that virtually every adaptive context—and when I use this term alone, I mean, of course, primary adaptive context—is also an indicator. Similarly, every secondary adaptive context—disturbance of treatment and of the therapeutic relationship introduced by the patient—would also be an indicator. This implies that disruptions of the communicative interaction by either the therapist or patient are always important indicators. This also leaves one final category—symptoms within the patient and disturbances in his relationship with others outside of treatment—as a group of indicators which tend, by and large, to constitute secondary rather than adaptive contexts.

We see, then, that there is indeed an overlap between the concept of the adaptive context and of indicators. This is not surprising since both imply the need for adaptation by the patient. The main distinction, then, is whether this need is generated primarily by the therapist or produced primarily by the patient or someone or some incident in his outside life.

I have termed the patient's lateness to the session a form of *interactional* acting out, because we have clear evidence of the contributions from the therapist through his own lateness to the sessions. We must acknowledge this as source for this gross behavioral resistance, and recognize the importance of rectifying the therapist's contribution. In addition, it will prove necessary to interpret the implications of the behavioral resistance in the light of current adaptive contexts, doing so transversally and interactionally.

Of course, the therapist has at present already rectified his contribution in terms of his own lateness to the hours. What then, could be his contribution? Or am I in error in calling this an interactional form of acting out?

Discussant: It seems to me that the pending forced termination could also have this effect.

Langs: Exactly. This implies that the pending forced termination is a form of acting out by the therapist, however rationalized and necessary. The patient responds in kind, partly because of what the therapist is doing and partly because this is his own way of dealing with such behaviors in others.

In formulating the implications of an intervention context, it is extremely useful to decide whether the context includes a modification of the framework or not. I want to make this point clear, since you will find that when a context does indeed involve an infraction of the ground rules, it will always contain a basic constellation of implications pertinent to the disturbance in the therapeutic environment. Such deviations imply a loss of boundaries, a sense of hostility and seduction, uncertainty as to the realities of the therapeutic relationship and setting, a sense of being poorly held and contained. Whatever the specific implications of a particular deviation, these more general qualities will always be present as well. It is possible to develop a group of receptors and expectations whenever the framework is broken, and to find that they function quite well as a way of helping you to understand the patient's material.

Of course, dynamic considerations and the evocation of specific unconscious fantasies and perceptions will also be a part of the patient's response. It may be possible to develop receptor sites in anticipation of relatively common fantasy and perception constellations. In fact, we have been doing exactly that for the two adaptive contexts we reviewed, by suggesting various unconscious perceptions and introjects which might be generated within the patient on the basis of these deviations. It is somewhat more difficult to anticipate universal fantasy responses. Here, these might include experiences of disappointment in the parents; poor parental care; hostile acts by parents; anal issues in respect to punctuality and control; oral issues in terms of the greed of the therapist; and even phallic issues in terms the therapist's showing power by holding a group meeting in his office. The dynamic possibilities are endless, and as a rule it is best to allow the patient to select through his derivative communication those dynamic and genetic issues which are most important to him.

I have now covered the points I wanted to make. Let's summarize through an evaluation of the level of the patient's resistances in light of the two contexts we have identified. And then let's turn to the therapist's intervention.

Discussant: There is the gross behavioral resistance of the patient's lateness. That seems to have considerable importance. He seems to be acting out a number of unconscious fantasies and perceptions, rather than communicating them through words. Communicatively, it seems to me that the patient is showing moderate resistance. As you said, there is a reasonably good representation of the adaptive context of the therapist's lateness, but there is virtually no representation of the pending forced termination. The derivative complex shows medium level resistance. I would have to conclude that the level of resistance is actually somewhat higher than I first suspected.

Langs: I would agree. Now remember, there may well be an additional adaptive context which would yield an entirely different evaluation regarding the level of the patient's resistances. Nonetheless, we have carried out a very useful exercise.

Now, let's turn to the therapist's intervention. As you will recall, the therapist said, There is some reason why you need to keep me waiting, rather than allowing me to keep you waiting.

Who will analyze it for us?

Discussant: Unconsciously, it seems to me the therapist is addressing the issue of the mode of relatedness, though he fails to do this through interpretation. I hear this intervention as a way of telling the patient that that issue is who will be the more parasitic. By pointing this out without an interpretation, there will be no resolution of the parasitic mode of interaction.

Langs: While I do want to get to other aspects of this intervention, and to begin always with its formal definition, your comments are quite well taken, and especially cogent in light of our discussion of the maturational level of relatedness which exists in this therapeutic interaction. Who for the moment will help us to begin at the beginning, so to speak?

Discussant: I hear this as an attempt at a general interpretation. The level of listening is that of Type One derivatives; this is a rather obvious inference. There is an attempt to deal with the indicator of the patient's lateness, but there is no use of an adaptive context or of the derivatives.

Langs: I hope that you can all see—and I strongly suspect that this is a function of how you have been taught—that there appears to be a repetitive pattern in respect to your efforts at intervening. They seem to be confined to questions, confrontations, and quite general interpretations. They will sometimes deal with obvious indicators, though often neglecting crucial ones, and virtually never deal with an adaptive context or derivative complex. There is a sense of emptiness, of Type C barriers, of generality, of absence of instinctual drive derivatives, and of attention to the surface. There is also the impression that each of these interventions could have been said to virtually any patient—they lack specificity.

I must add that you share with experienced therapists and analysts many of the attributes of current practice when it comes to intervening. The difference is that some analysts tend to make more extensive use of the derivatives by translating them into isolated dynamics and genetics, almost always in terms of unconscious fantasies and memories. They virtually never make use of an adaptive context, and are variable in respect to the use of indicators. Their work is largely on a manifest and Type One derivative level, as is your own; and like you, they virtually never obtain Type Two derivative validation of such efforts.

What about the communicative properties of the intervention?

Discussant: It attempts to deal with some aspect of the therapeutic relationship. But without the use of a specific intervention context, it therefore blames the patient for the problem without acknowledging any contribution from the therapist. It implies transference when we would find nontransference, or a mixture of both.

Discussant: Wouldn't we also categorize this as an attempt to interpret a resistance?

Langs: Yes, an attempt to interpret a behavioral resistance. But we are moving toward the conclusion that it is an erroneous effort at interpretation.

Once you have established some basic principles of intervening, it becomes relatively easy to recognize when you have made a mistake. Upon reflection, we realize that we have asked a question, or made a confrontation, or responded with a nonneutral comment.

On another level, we now have a systematic approach to the communicative qualities of an intervention. We can review whether we have addressed an indicator and an adaptive context, and made full use of the derivative complex. We can ask if we have tried to balance our intervention with both perceptions and fantasies, and have maintained a transversal quality. And we can even search for possible missing or missed indicators and adaptive contexts.

Suppose we have indeed alluded to what we feel to be the best representation of the indicators and adaptive context, and have done the most we could with the derivative complex. How then are we to detect errors in intervening? After all, these are only formal categories. They may be misused. The material may have been misevaluated. Something may have been missed or heard incorrectly. The especially difficult problem of organizing the derivative complex in terms of its adaptive implications may have been handled badly. There are any number of possible mistakes. How are these to be discovered? This is an important task since it implies the presence of countertransference-based communications from the therapist.

My answer is neither especially profound nor easy to apply. There is an enormous resistance with respect to a therapist's narcissistic investment in his own interventions. The principles and techniques we might use in essence require a full application of the validating process and a search for clear-cut Type Two derivative validation. *In its absence,* we must conclude that we have made an error and make every effort to identify its expression, and trace its sources within ourselves.

In addition, we may accept any representation of a negative introject as a signal to investigate our interventions for mistakes. The same applies to any regression or remission, or symptomatic expression. Any sign that things are amiss calls to the search for errors.

Sometimes, the signal occurs subjectively as some sense of dissatisfaction with the intervention or eventual awareness that a mistake has been made. Perhaps the best principle is to assume the presence of some measure of error in every intervention, and to maintain a quiet and consistent effort to monitor subjective responses and the material from the patient for indicators which will help you to locate your mistake. Without being masochistic or self-defeating, permit the assumption of error to guide your evaluation of the patient's responses to your effort. On that basis, much will be revealed.

One final exercise. We now have an adaptive context in the form of a therapist's intervention. Who will provide us with receptor sites—implications to which the patient may well respond?

Discussant: It follows from our formulation of the intervention that the patient will feel blamed for his badness and feel that the therapist is attempting to exonerate himself. There is also avoidance of the pending forced termination, and a suggestion to the patient that his derivatives are meaningless. The patient may feel he hasn't been listened to, and that the therapist has a need to deny his contributions to his—the patient's—problems.

Langs: Yes, you have put things together quite well. Allow me to revise what you have said in order to study this intervention as the offer of a Type C barrier, a lie-system. It reflects the use of a Type C communicative style in the therapist, with perhaps a shading of the Type B mode—projectively identifying into the patient unmetabolized aspects of the patient's own aggression as dumped into the therapist through the patient's repeated lateness and description of how avoidable it was. In addition, there may be interactional projection of the defense mechanism of denial,

also incorporated from the patient's associations and not understood—unmetabolized.

To characterize this intervention in terms of the offer of a lie-
barrier system, I would say that the therapist is proposing that he
and the patient seal off the pending forced termination as well as
his other countertransference inputs. He is suggesting that they
place all of the badness and difficulties within the patient, and see
the patient as vengeful. Based on the patient's own associations,
the effort is made to place all the craziness within the bipersonal
field into the patient and to deny its existence within the therapist.

This particular lie-barrier system is designed to seal off the
underlying chaos stemming from the recent rectification of the
frame and from the therapist's countertransferences. We would
expect a relatively masochistic patient to accept the onus of such a
lie-barrier system, while the more paranoid patient would object. It
will be interesting to see exactly how this patient reacts. We
actually know nothing of his presenting complaints and character
structure. Certainly, if we had such data, we would be able to say a
great deal more; but let's stick to the limits the therapist has
imposed upon us and see what we can do within them.

Discussant: Before we continue, I would like to ask a question.
How would you formulate the curative effects of a valid interpretation?

Langs: I have great hopes that we will be able to observe such an
intervention during this course, and derive the answer empirically.
To respond in theory, a neurosis derives from unconscious fantasy
and perception constellations. It stems from irrational interactional and intrapsychic experiences, which lead to symptomatic
responses and characterological disturbances which are maladaptive and cause suffering.

The structure of the symptom itself or the characterological
difficulty is complex. Some of the elements condensed into a
symptom—a term I will use for all types of psychopathology—
include the effects of unconscious perceptions and introjects, internally and externally prompted fantasy constellations, unconscious conflict, contributions from the three macrostructures—id,

ego, and superego—disturbances in the self-system, and distortions in self- and object representations.

This kind of discussion tends to get wordy and all too metapsychological, far too divorced from clinical referents. But as a model which I hope has some clinical meaning, it implies that by securing a therapeutic environment and offering valid interpretations-reconstructions, it is possible for the therapist or analyst to generate a curative introject and a level of cognitive understanding that permits conflict resolution, modification of pathological defenses and superego inputs, taming of pathological instinctual drives, a more balanced and healthy self-system, and amelioration of the pathological effects of the unconscious fantasy and perception constellations. A valid interpretation is curative in part because it establishes the therapist's relatedness with the patient as a form of healthy symbiosis. This in and of itself can have a salutory effect on the nature of the patient's object relationships. This must, however, be supplemented by specific cognitive insights.

In this context, allow me to add to my previous comments about the type of lie-barrier system offered to the patient by the therapist at this moment. This material supports the thesis that some forms of lie therapy are extremely parasitic of the patient, especially so when a lie-barrier system attacks and blames the patient, places the onus on him for the difficulties within the bipersonal field, and otherwise exploits him. It is my impression that all too often this type of relatedness is effected between therapists and their patients in present-day psychotherapy.

Although I could elaborate further, please accept that as a brief answer.

Discussant: Since we are covering a number of unresolved issues, I would also like to ask where you would place interventions of a type we have not as yet discussed. I refer here to therapists who actually touch their patients and who become involved with them socially.

Langs: Yes, to offer a comprehensive classification of interventions, we would actually have to consider the wide range of behaviors in therapists which might not occur to those of us who maintain a relatively secure and stable therapeutic environment. Therapists who touch their patients, have intercourse with them, or socialize with them probably consider such interventions supportive and helpful. Undoubtedly others know full well that such interventions are entirely or largely self-serving and destructive but engage in them nonetheless. But if we are interested primarily in well-meaning therapists, there are many interventions used in present-day practice which deserve some special categorization.

If we wish to avoid side issues, we might simply propose that there are a series of noninterpretive interventions which would obtain a general consensus as to their obvious and blatant harmful effects. These would include, besides those I have already mentioned, such behaviors as giving or accepting gifts from patients, suddenly discharging a patient, attacking a patient verbally or physically. The effects on the patient can be devastating. Hopefully, we will not have a chance to explore such a response here. Nonetheless, more subtle forms of this type of intervention are not uncommon.

Physical contact and interventions of a comparable nature are undoubtedly a form of parasitic relatedness through which the therapist exploits and damages the patient. In general, patients who accept such a mode of relatedness are intensely needy themselves. Often, they are hopeful of a pathological symbiosis or parasitic interaction and in need of a wide range of masochistic and other self-destructive gratifications. The apparently widespread existence of such treatment relationships testifies to the extent to which lie therapy and noninsightful efforts at symptom alleviation are sought by patients and therapists alike.

Discussant: What about insight?

Langs: Insight is an important subject, and certainly relates to interventions. There are several recent papers on this subject (e.g., Baranger and Baranger 1966, Hatcher 1973), and it is often touched upon in clinical writings. But by insight we mean affective-cognitive understanding, and for me, the literature on this topic is yet to be written. Until now, it has been based on a psychoanalytic approach that does not include Type Two derivative validation. Because of that flaw, discussions of intellectual versus affective insight leave me cold. The assumption is made in almost all of these writings that the therapist has intervened correctly, and surface agreement is applied as the relevant criteria. For me, this is no measure of insight, and resistances to insight cannot be identified or understood on that basis.

From the communicative approach, insight would be a form of conscious understanding and integration, with cognitive and affective elements, which stems from an interpretation-reconstruction or, more rarely, from the experience of a sound management of the framework or a self-interpretation by the patient himself. True insight would have to entail the integration of Type Two derivative communications pertinent to a currently activated adaptive context. In its best form, it would shape up as a selected fact through which the patient himself was able to meaningfully integrate previously disparate experiences and observations, in a manner that enables him to resolve some aspect of his neurosis and symptoms. Insight would therefore be but one factor in the development of adaptive structural change and symptom alleviation.

Discussant: It seems to me that often, when we think that we are imparting insight to the patient, we are actually attempting to destroy meaning and relatedness, to either generate lie barriers or projective identifications. It's rather disorienting to attend this seminar, to realize how much has to be revised.

Discussant: Since we are dealing with unresolved issues, I would like to ask if the right interpretation is always helpful.

Discussant: And is a wrong interpretation always bad?

Langs: Well, I see that we have managed to accumulate a number of unresolved problems. Some of them, as I said, are not especially pertinent to the clinical material at hand. Nonetheless, they all pertain to the subject of intervening.

Is the right interpretation always helpful? The question is ambiguous as to helpful for whom: the patient or therapist, or both. If we assume that you mean by the right intervention one that is, in our appraisal, correctly formulated, and which would, if offered, obtain Type Two derivative validation (and you can see how difficult it is to talk theoretically about a right interpretation if it has not been offered to the patient), then I would say that a correct interpretation is, in some ways, always helpful to both the patient and the therapist.

As for how it helps the patient, it generates a positive introject and a segment of cognitive insight. It provides him with adaptive tools he previously lacked. It therefore gives him both understanding and ego strength, and helps to resolve an aspect of his neurosis.

A correct interpretation is also always helpful to the therapist in that it will almost always contain a small sector of self-understanding, of insight, for him. It will have a positive internal effect, derived from the patient's validation and ultimate benefit. It will confirm the therapist's image of himself as helpful and as doing his job well. It is, in a few words, a rewarding experience.

Why then my hesitation? Well, the problem lies in the disturbing qualities of the truth. In essence, an introject from a truth therapist can be quite disruptive for a patient's mental equilibrium. The positive introject destroys some measure of the patient's defenses against the prevailing negative introjects within his psyche. It evokes envy and disequilibrium. The opportunity to renounce pathological maladaptations may create anxiety, as will any situation in which familiar, though costly, adaptive tools are in jeopardy. The opportunity for symptom alleviation will also evoke responses from the pathological components of the superego, largely based on guilt and on masochistic needs which demand satisfaction.

It seems to me that these subsidiary effects are secondary, and do not detract from the helpfulness of a correct interpretation. Nonetheless, they must be kept in mind because, overall, a patient may respond to a validated interpretation with anxiety or other symptoms based on these secondary consequences, and may then feel that he is not being helped.

On the object relationship level, as I have already indicated, a correct interpretation implies the development of a healthy symbiotic relationship between the patient and therapist. While this creates thrusts toward relative autonomy and individuation, it also generates significant separation anxieties that frustrate the patient's inevitable wishes for pathological merger or fusion. It follows that on this level too, a valid interpretation is growth-promoting even though evoking anxiety; and while it fosters the development and growth of the patient, it does so in the face of noticeable persecutory and separation anxieties.

To turn this around, we can also see that the wrong interpretation—one that does not receive Type Two derivative validation—consistently generates a negative introject within the patient, and in addition, fails to provide him with insight and affect-laden understanding. It has major destructive attributes, but the patient may nonetheless respond in a manner that leads him to feel he is being helped. He may find symptomatic relief through the lie barrier, through the horrendous introjects of the therapist that reassure him that he is less sick than the therapist, and through the opportunity to respond therapeutically to the therapist's expressed countertransferences.

As you can see, much of the difficulty revolves around the notion of what is *helpful.* It reminds us that symptom alleviation may be based on insight derived from sound managements of the framework and valid interpretation-reconstructions, but it may also be derived from poor management of the framework and from erroneous interventions. For many reasons, it is my impression that not only does most symptom alleviation in current psychotherapy and psychoanalysis stem from poor framework management and erroneous interventions, but also that there are relatively few patients who would have it otherwise—who are capable over extended periods of tolerating the truth and utilizing it for insight and symptom relief. Patients and therapists alike are more than prepared to surrender the enormous adaptive values and growth potential embodied in the truth as it pertains to neuroses and therapy, and to accept the expediency of lies, falsifications, and barriers. It appears that the human mind, when it comes to emotion, is designed for lie-barriers far more than the truth.

Our main thesis on an object relationship level is that an erroneous interpretation or intervention is designed to parasitize or effect a pathological symbiosis with the patient. It maintains the patient's pathology in the object relationship sphere, even though it sometimes serves to reassure him and mollify his anxieties regarding separateness and the inevitable dread of relatively independent functioning which appears to exist in all persons.

I think it is quite important to recognize the seemingly therapeutic effects of erroneous interventions, and the pathological mode of relatedness and lie-barrier systems which they effect. Momentary and even more lasting symptom alleviation says little of the basis on which it is achieved. It is my impression, based on my reading of the literature, on supervisory experiences, and on my own self-analytic efforts, that there are powerful needs within all persons for these immediately gratifying forms of pathological symbiosis, perhaps more so than for the frustrating, growth promoting, healthy symbiosis essential to sound and effective therapy.

Discussant: I've been thinking over your comments on lies and truths. It seems to me that in terms of truth or falsity, you make one evaluation on a manifest level and a different one on a latent level, in terms of derivatives.

Langs: Exactly. On a manifest level, truth may involve correspondence with surface reality and self-evident propositions. On a latent level, truth as I have defined it in respect to psychotherapy and psychoanalysis involves the spiraling communicative interaction and the patient's neurosis. Because of this, it is possible for both patients and therapists to utilize manifest truths *functionally* as expressions of dynamic, interactional, and latent lies. Surface truths can function as *nonderivative* lie barriers, which do not reflect in disguised form the underlying truth, or as *derivative* lie barriers which do contain in some distorted way reflections of the underlying truths. This determination depends on an evaluation of the material in terms of the prevailing adaptive contexts.

Again, my use of the terms lie and truth always alludes to the level of unconscious communication, and to derivative implications organized around a pertinent intervention context. The lies I allude to are usually unconscious lies, often unintentional and seldom recognized. They are not deliberate and, of course, there is absolutely no moral implication. Remember, it is the intervention context, an actuality, filled with implications, which is at the center of the truth within psychotherapy. Our definition of truth therefore involves the extent to which the patient is in some meaningful manner working over those truths or instead, attempting to seal them off and obliterate them.

Discussant: Can't you also say that there is truth about external reality and truth about internal reality?

Langs: Yes, and of course, these need not coincide.

Therapist: I must say that I did not want to make this intervention. I consciously did not want to make it. I can't quite put it together, but basically there has been a pattern with this man in which this kind of thing has happened repeatedly—his being late and my making a comment even though I preferred to be silent.

Langs: Your remarks bring up another point. In this course, we often do not have the therapist's subjective feelings and thoughts. In the session, it is important that you pay attention to these experiences.

For example, we hear the patient saying something about his wanting, but being unable, to be on time for the session. His lateness is beyond his control; it takes place despite his best conscious intentions to the contrary. He does something he doesn't want to do.

Next, we hear that the therapist intervened even though he didn't wish to. It seems to me that the therapist would experience an uncanny feeling in hearing these associations from the patient while knowing that he has, in the past, intervened in ways he preferred to avoid. On that basis, he would do well to postulate some type of unconscious perception within the patient, and be careful to manage and to rectify that type of error—speaking when he prefers to be silent.

In this type of situation, it is usually impossible to interpret the unconscious perception because the patient will not allude to it directly or represent it with sufficient clarity in derivative form. Instead, learn from the patient subjectively, benefit from his therapeutic efforts, and show your appreciation by appropriately and silently modifying your approach. Actually, that is all the patient asks of you; an active interpretation is often superfluous. We must learn to value efforts of this kind, and to not overidealize interpretive work. A great deal that is successful in psychotherapy and psychoanalysis stems from the therapist's silence and his private, silent self-curative efforts.

I see our time is getting late, but perhaps we can hear a bit more of the session.

Therapist: I just want to add that I had intervened because he had become silent. And I did so because of a desire to move him and a feeling that he wasn't moving. He seemed to want to sit with this pattern which has existed throughout therapy, and which I probably haven't dealt with well enough. He tends to not pursue his problems and often to not associate.

Discussant: It sounds as if the patient has placed into the therapist a sense of frustration and resistance, and that the therapist had a need to projectively identify these disruptive qualities back into the patient.

Discussant: I wonder too what the effect could be on this patient that the therapist has his office on a ward in which there are many grossly psychotic patients.

Langs: Yes, that too is an often unrecognized background context.

Notice that the therapist was responding to some major behavioral resistances: the patient's lateness and his silences in sessions, as well as some sense of failure at working over some seemingly pressing problems. The latter appraisal was made in terms of manifest contents, and is one that we would have difficulty in accepting. The former constitute important behavioral resistances, and certainly we would all agree that they require interpretation, as well as rectification of the frame, if relevant.

Based on our formulations to this point, the therapist has rectified part of the disturbance but is actually unable to do so with the other break in the frame—the pending forced termination. In addition, he has in all likelihood been intervening on a manifest content and Type One derivative level—technical errors which also could be corrected.

The material was beginning to develop around a possible derivative complex pertinent to the two adaptive contexts we have discussed, and it might have been possible—if the derivatives became less disguised—to show the patient here that his lateness and silences are responses to the therapist's own latenesses and the pending forced termination. You could then add that these two experiences are frustrating and enraging the patient, driving him to distraction and prompting vengeful and self-protective responses. But to offer this interpretation, we would need a clear representation of the adaptive context of the pending forced termination. Lacking that, we could either remain silent and therefore not add to the patient's burdens by making an error, or develop the interpretation around the therapist's earlier latenesses with strong hints that there is another, interrelated context, to which the patient is also responding.

As you can see, I have once again outlined an interpretation of a behavioral resistance. These are often far more easier to interpret than communicative resistances, which usually must be dealt with by means of patient silence and holding. I have taken these resistances as my indicator, used the adaptive contexts of the therapist's latenesses and the pending termination as the precipitants, and organized the derivative complex in light of those contexts. With the two contexts as the fulcrum, the lateness and silence are given meaning. Be sure to include all relevant perceptions and fantasies, and to try to touch upon both spheres. Behaviors of this kind have a multitude of implications, and it is important to restrict yourself to those which the patient has represented.

Allow me to stress that last point. In the intervention we heard, the therapist proposed that the patient's lateness was an effort to keep him waiting as an alternative to his waiting for the therapist. As I heard the material, the patient did not represent this particular meaning vis-à-vis his lateness. Instead, through these manifest associations organized as derivatives, he assigned both his own and the therapist's lateness qualities of absent-mindedness, inability to manage, interest in a girl, and absurdity. Using these derivatives, we would interpret the indicators of the patient's own lateness and silence as constituting an introject of the therapist and an expression of the patient's own inner fantasies in the terms I have just described, organizing these derivatives around the two prevailing intervention contexts. One might silently postulate the presence of an effort at projective identification, but first I would want some clearer representation of interactional pressures in the patient's material.

Notice too that, by isolating the major themes and organizing them around the prevailing adaptive contexts in order to clarify the meanings of the indicators, we can detect a possible dynamic factor in the patient's lateness. His interest in the girl which could represent, along the me/not-me interface, an unconscious introjection of the therapist's use of the group meeting as a defense against homosexual fantasies and anxieties he may have in his relationship with the patient; and in addition, of course, it could also represent the patient's own anxieties in this sphere. In preparing an intervention and attempting to shape the derivative complex as an adaptive response to the intervention context, it is important for us to formulate the presence of defenses, superego pressures, instinctual drive needs, and such. But remember, these are still at the stage of silent formulations.

I have tried to stress the concept of not introducing your own ideas into the patient's material. This is not meant to preclude your own free-floating associations, hunches, and flights of fantasy. Rather, all such impressions must be checked against the patient's own associations. Those which have validity will find some derivative echo in the patient's material. The ultimate offer of an interpretation of a gross behavioral resistance must be founded only on the available derivatives in the session. It is often tempting to refer to a prior session, but we have already established the principle that each hour should be his own creation. If you are correct, it will be sufficient, and your comment will obtain Type Two derivative validation.

Therapist: I can add a bit more. I have experienced this kind of thing before with this patient. What he does is that he shrugs his shoulders, takes on a puzzled look, and clams up. He becomes silent and I have the feeling that if I don't do something, either I am going to go crazy or he is going to go crazy. I have a sense of needing to contain a certain chaos, perhaps even a psychotic chaos.

Langs: Yes, you are now identifying many subjective influences on the timing of interventions. Your candid comments also help to illuminate some very practical issues in response to the timing of interventions. Until now, I have confined myself to formal indicators in the material from patients. In the real world of clinical sessions, these cognitive factors interact with a variety of subjective feelings, thoughts, and needs within the therapist.

Ideally, we intervene at the behest of the patient's therapeutic needs, not because of our own. If we have a feeling of chaos and disorganization, we must first determine where it is located. We must, for example, be certain that this is a sound appraisal of the state of the patient, and not our projection of something within ourselves into him. Even when we experience the chaos and disorganization within ourselves, we must identify its sources within the bipersonal field. We must embark upon an effort at self-analysis. And we must tolerate and contain the frustration and disturbance until we can understand and interpret it. This is what we mean by the metabolism of a projective identification. But it is crucial not to assume that these feelings of psychosis and chaos have been placed interactionally into you, as the therapist, by the patient. It is entirely possible to feel quite crazy primarily because of factors within yourself, a countertransference-based intolerance of silence and nonconfirmation, for example. Everything experienced within the bipersonal field is an interactional product, and you must trace the sources from both yourself and the patient.

Since all too often, therapists intervene because of their own therapeutic needs rather than those of the patient, I have offered extensive guidelines in order to safeguard against the use of such interventions. In actual practice, you will often feel sorely pressed to wait for a well-represented indicator and adaptive context, and a meaningful derivative complex. You effect a kind of compromise: instead of screaming at the patient, you attempt to offer something that resembles an interpretation. But the effect is nonetheless that the patient experiences it like he is being screamed at and blamed, and will sense your inability to contain and metabolize disruptive projective identifications and moments in treatment.

I can't repeat this principle often enough: Do not automatically atribute your own internal chaos to projective identifications from the patient. Sometimes the Kleinian literature gives that impression. More recently, there have been distinct exceptions to this trend. For us, there can be no substitute for analyzing the sources of such an inner state in both ourselves and in our patient.

Discussant: Since it's getting late, and we probably can't do much more with this clinical material, I wonder if you can add to your remarks about the differences in how we intervene with patients suffering from different kinds of psychopathology. I think we all have many questions in that area.

Langs: Taking the ambulatory schizophrenic patient at one extreme and the neurotically functioning character disorder at the other, I will characterize the areas of communality and of distinction in the communicative approach.

I have had so little to say on this subject as yet, and have been able to discover several reasons why. First, I realize that regardless of where a patient stands on the diagnostic continuum, he will respond to certain consistent ways to sound therapy as well as to alterations in the framework and errors by the therapist. Because the communicative clinical approach is significantly different from current practices, the presentations offered by our therapists consistently involve issues in these two areas. And because patients are consistently and overridingly sensitive to these problems, which become the adaptive contexts for virtually all of their derivative communications, our clinical work has studied the implications of these factors for the psychotherapy of all patients. While it has been possible to explore all the other dimensions of psychotherapy despite this biasing factor, it has led to a relatively greater consideration of the expressions of the therapist's psychopathology than is usually the case.

It is a validated clinical observation that current practices reflect countertransferences, and that the psychotherapies we have been observing often involve an unconscious working over of the pathological inputs from the therapist. Fortunately, our therapists do not appear to be psychotic and most of them seem to be functioning quite well, whatever the nature of their neurosis. As a result, the pathological inputs they have placed into the bipersonal fields in which they work, and into their patients, have been within a relatively narrow range with respect to the nature of the psychopathology involved. Most of their inputs have not been psychotic or even borderline, but neurotic in the narrow sense of the term. Consequently, there has been a tendency toward a relatively narrow range of responses in your patients to these disturbances.

Some of these considerations also apply to the patients. We have not heard the presentation of an overtly psychotic patient, or one who is noisily borderline. Most of these patients have been suffering from severe characterological disorders or relatively well managed borderline syndromes. It might be that in a well secured bipersonal field, and with valid interpretations, these patients would appear much sicker. In general, you will find that when a therapist's countertransferences predominate, many patients respond by mobilizing their adaptive resources and actually appear more healthy than they otherwise seem to be. In addition, under conditions where the framework is modified and the therapist's countertransferences predominate, the patient often has a major opportunity to projectively identify his own craziness into the therapist and will do so quite effectively, often appearing far more stable than he does under other conditions. Also, we know, it is dangerous for the patient to reveal the depths of his sickness under these circumstances.

Of course, these conditions can also have the opposite effect. With a rupture of the holding environment, the input of major countertransferences by the therapist, and major breaks in the framework, the patient may respond with uncontrolled regression, and appear quite ill. I am sure you have all had such experiences, and we did hear of one or two situations where this seemed to be a factor. However, such patients often abruptly leave treatment. Just as often, the therapist prefers to not present such situations.

Turning now to other reasons why I have not focused on the interplay between diagnosis and technique, as you know, much of what I have had to say has taken the form of exploring previously unrecognized issues, dimensions of therapeutic interaction, qualities of the framework, and matters of technique which have been relatively neglected or erroneously conceptualized by earlier writers. In addition, my approach has largely been empirical, and has therefore depended upon the material which you have presented to me. Despite that limitation, I have been surprised by the broad applicability of the carefully defined precepts we have developed, and by my own sense that only rarely has the issue of the patient's diagnosis—or that of the therapist, which is quite another, though related, matter—come to the fore with sufficient force to require an extended discussion.

To me, the clinical data speaks for itself. I believe that if an issue had arisen in respect to a patient's response to an intervention or his behaviors within therapy that called for a modification in our techniques based on the diagnostic considerations reflected in his behavior, we would have taken up such problems in detail. The fact that such a discussion has not materialized suggests that among the factors which influence our techniques, the diagnosis of the patient ranks quite low. It may well be that instead, the diagnosis of the therapist has a very powerful influence, a subject I have discussed by indirection.

To come directly to the issue, it seems to me that the most cogent discussion I could offer would focus on the influence of the patient's basic character structure rather than on specific symptoms. As we all know, phobic, obsessive, hysterical, anxious, and other symptoms may appear in both schizophrenic and nonschizophrenic patients. While some therapists advocate alterations in basic technical procedures in the presence of specific symptoms, I can see virtually no basis for such recommendations, and feel certain that the techniques advocated would not find Type Two derivative validation in the patient's responsive material.

The most common deviation in this respect is to offer advice to phobic patients, even pressure them to confront their phobic situation. As Brenner (1969) pointed out, the rationale for this type of noninterpretive intervention, a directive, is not well founded, nor is its value clinically documented. There is every reason to believe that sound therapeutic work with such patients remains the optimal approach, and specific deviations are unnecessary and even detrimental.

Another common example of proposed modifications in technique involve the report by patients, or direct evidence of, delusions and hallucinations. As we know, these experiences may occur in borderline and even neurotic patients, but are characteristic of the psychotic disorders such as schizophrenia. Such noninterpretive interventions as hospitalization, reality testing, advice giving, and other types of manipulations have been advocated. It is not my purpose here to review the pertinent literature, nor to discuss each of these recommendations specifically. I simply want to address this particular problem by offering a summation of my clinical experience, whatever its value.

First, I should make clear that I am not proposing that technical measures that cause a major break in the framework, such as hospitalizing an acutely psychotic patient, should be entirely discarded. Such a conclusion is obviously absurd. However, the communicative approach indicates that many hospitalizations can be avoided, that they stem from interludes in treatment to which the therapist has contributed significantly because of his countertransferences, and that regressions of that particular type often take place because the therapist has failed in a major way to offer the patient a secure therapeutic setting and basically interpretive approach.

In general, it appears that there is a sense among therapists that the more ill and regressed is a patient, the greater the necessity for deviations from the standard framework. A variation on this unfortunate and erroneous precept is to the effect that the more the therapist approaches the treatment situation with a psychotherapeutic rather than psychoanalytic approach, the greater the flexibility with which the ground rules should be created and explicated. Actual clinical practice shows that, to the contrary, it is the psychotic patient who most needs the remarkable, inherently supportive qualities of a stable holding and containing therapeutic environment and therapist. But these patients themselves are most likely to attempt to modify the very qualities of the therapeutic setting and of the stance of the therapist which they most need. In fact, this is one way in which some differences appear in work with psychotic patients.

I hope that these statements come as no surprise to you, and that you can anticipate the reasons for this last observation. In essence, psychotic patients have difficulties in maintaining their capacity to delay, to deal with their intensely pathological instinctual drives and pathological introjects, and on the whole to manage their rather disturbed inner mental worlds. As a result, they make many kinds of efforts to seek direct gratification, whether through an hallucinatory experience or through an interaction with their therapist. They are frightened of a rather steady therapeutic environment and of a therapist who does not gratify their immediate needs, since they often entertain conscious fantasies that any buildup of their instinctual drive tensions and any free play of their primitive and pathological introjects will result in their annihilation. Their anxieties and fears are extreme, and their coping measures are powerful, primitive, and founded upon immediate gratification. They therefore attempt to impose these qualities onto the therapist and therapeutic setting, and do so with considerable force. Much of what they communicate contains strong, primitive, and toxic projective identifications which are difficult for any therapist to metabolize, manage, and interpret.

In effect, these patients live their lives by attempting to effect framework deviation cures in their relationships, and they do exactly that with their therapists. They have their own therapeutic environment in mind, despite its pathological and destructive components, since they greatly dread any other set of conditions. Among the reasons they fear a secure therapeutic setting is that it creates the very conditions under which they are likely to regress and experience the most primitive aspects of their inner mental lives. The therapeutic hold, as you know, is not only supportive, but is also designed to create the conditions under which the patient may reveal, analyze, and work through the basis for and expressions of his psychopathology. Since the inner disturbance is greatest among psychotic patients, it follows that it is they who will most intensely dread a secured therapeutic environment.

There is, of course, a striking paradox. The patients who most need the secure hold have the greatest reason to fear it. Some therapists have suggested compromises in basic technique designed to spare the patient a fearful regression. However, application of the listening process under these conditions shows that the patient unconsciously often views such modifications in the frame as reflecting highly murderous impulses in the therapist and his countertransference dread of a regression within the therapeutic interaction. It may be possible to offer such patients a lie-barrier system on this basis; though the risks are considerable, it would appear that in actual practice, this is what is done in virtually every instance. It remains to be seen just how much patients of this kind can tolerate and work within a sound therapeutic environment.

I have only preliminary impressions to report, and they suggest wide variations in this regard. Some psychotic patients will make massive efforts to destroy the basic therapeutic environment from the first moment of their treatment, and when these fail, take flight.

They are usually Type B–C communicators. Other psychotic patients, while they also attempt to disrupt the therapeutic setting, experience something highly favorable and insightful when the therapist maintains the frame, and noisily and disruptively continue in therapy to their considerable gain. These patients are, as a rule, Type B–A communicators.

Psychotic patients are more likely than neurotic patients to enter treatment with a compromised therapeutic environment in mind. They usually attempt in striking ways to establish their own conditions of therapy, and to blatantly modify those that are proposed directly and indirectly by the therapist. These patients attempt to break the frame in countless ways—the fixed frame as well as the therapist's anonymity, neutrality, utilization of interpretive interventions, and basic mode of relating. They are quite frightened of Type Two derivative relatedness and make repeated efforts to establish a manifest content interaction, sensing the safety of the lie-barriers inherent to this level of relating.

But make no mistake, through their derivatives, these patients universally express their need for and appreciation of a stable therapeutic environment and an essentially interpretive approach from their therapist. There is usually a major split here: a manifest clamor for deviations, and a contrasting latent appreciation for the therapist's capacity to contain the highly disruptive and pathological projective identifications, which often have virtually assaultive qualities, and to maintain both the basic environment and interpretive approach.

It remains to integrate object relationship considerations into this discussion. Patients at the more pathological end of the continuum show an inordinate need for either a parasitic or pathological symbiotic mode of relatedness with the therapist. It is this type of object relationship they have experienced, virtually without exception, with parental figures, especially their mothers. They have come to rely on this mode of relatedness for the pathological instinctual drive satisfactions and the pathological superego sanctions afforded them in this way. Both their neurosis (in its broadest sense) and their ability to maintain some sense of equilibrium depends in large measure on establishing this type of relatedness with the therapist—as well as with outside figures. And while these patients are unconsciously aware of the many detrimental aspects of this type of relationship, the level of their anxieties and of their fantasy and perception formations are such that they virtually dread annihilation without this type of pathological bond to the therapist.

While relatively neurotic patients have lesser versions of these needs and anxieties, the differences in this sphere emerge in the finding that the more severely ill patients will make more pervasive efforts to effect a pathological mode of relatedness with the therapist. They respond with intense anxiety, and even with gross behavioral—and, less often—communicative resistances when the therapist offers them a healthy symbiosis. On the surface, they protest loudly and make extensive efforts to compromise the therapist, much of it, as I have said, through effecting alterations in the ground rules and boundaries of the therapeutic relationship— the basic core of the maturational form of relatedness between the patient and therapist. The therapist is often hard pressed to interpret these efforts. The outcome often depends upon whether the patient is a Type B–A or Type B–C communicator. The former provides the therapist with interpretable derivatives which represent his unconscious wish for a more healthy form of symbiosis, while the latter will not do so. This last group of patients are determined, sometimes consciously and always unconsciously, to parasitize, exploit, and destroy the therapist; they have little interest in self-understanding, growth, and individuation. There is a major unanswered question whether these patients have the capacity to work analytically toward a healthy mode of relatedness, or, regardless of the therapist's behaviors and interventions, will remain insistent upon their need for a pathological relationship with the therapist and refuse any other alternative.

Empirically, the highly disturbed patient will more often attack the ground rules and boundaries of the therapeutic relationship, and the therapist himself. If the therapist is parasitic, the patient will often respond with a parasitism of his own. On the other hand, if the therapist seeks a pathological symbiosis and lie-barrier mode of relatedness, the patient will often join him in satisfying these pathological needs. There is a great terror of the secure framework despite the almost desperate need on another level for such a secure hold and containing environment. In addition, these patients often express themselves through highly disruptive projective identifications designed to rid themselves of primitive inner disturbances rather than for understanding, and for parasitism and pathological symbiosis rather than a healthy symbiosis which can lead to growth and insight.

In response to these attacks, the therapist should, of course, maintain his basic faith in the patient, in the ideal therapeutic environment, in the more healthy modes of relatedness, and in his own capacities to hold and contain and interpret. Knowing that these resources offer the best opportunity for the patient to meaningfully resolve aspects of his psychopathology—and to develop new resources and no longer be a helpless victim of his impulses and needs—the therapist attempts to adhere to the usual basic principles of technique to the greatest extent possible. He does so with sensitivity, tact, and a full appreciation for the morbid anxieties and primitive conflicts and introjects within his patient. He manages the frame at the behest of the patient, with full use of his derivatives, so that he does not offer arbitrary and countertransference-based directives, or engage in aggressive confrontations and self-defensive behaviors.

The therapist should be capable of accepting the patient's deviations, and of rectifying the framework as the material permits; it should be quite unnecessary for him to propose any basic alterations in the frame. In actual practice, at times of utmost emergency, the therapist may be forced to deviate, though a retrospective investigation of such interludes generally reveals the presence of major countertransference inputs.

While on the whole, the same basic principles of technique apply to both the psychotic and neurotic patient, in actual practice, since the patient in so many ways determines the specific nature of the therapist's intervention, you will find that a therapist working with a psychotic patient will intervene quite differently. With the psychotic patient, there will be much more in the way of metabolizing projective identifications, of managing acute ruptures in the frame, and of dealing with the basic issues and ramifications pertinent to the fundamental therapeutic environment. In fact, work in this sphere—rectification and interpretation—will not only be much more frequent with the psychotic patient, but will also provide such patients with their most meaningful insightful interludes.

There will also, of course, be considerable differences in the type of contents which are worked over in these two groups. For example, you will find in psychotic patients much more in the way of pregenital conflicts, pathological introjects, basic disturbances in identity and in self-systems, major problems in ego functioning, highly primitive superego and drive expressions, and such. Expressions of such pathology shape the nature of your interventions, in regard to both content and form.

In managing the framework impingements from these patients, and interpreting the Type Two derivative implications, it is well to maintain the principle of interpreting resistances, defenses, and ego dysfunctions before other types of material. I wish to emphasize only two points in this respect. First, interpretations rather than confrontations offer the best means of dealing with disturbances in ego functions; it is critical to help patients understand the unconscious basis for their failures in reality testing, object relating, and coping abilities. Secondly, whenever you interpret these Type Two derivative implications, it is well to include models of more appropriate functioning when they are available in the patient's material.

Often, especially in the face of a delusion which pertains directly to oneself, therapists have considerable difficulty in maintaining an interpretive stance and secure framework. They often succumb to defensive reality testing which sets aside the interpretive process, and, instead of strengthening the patient's ego, weakens it. This effect derives first, from the negative introject communicated unconsciously to the patient, and secondly, because the very failure of the therapist's containing capacities reflects an ego weakness which is also introjected by the patient.

While my remarks are incomplete, I hope they offer you a sense of the communicative view in respect to the similarities and differences in the techniques we apply in our work with psychotic as compared to neurotic patients. Our guide throughout is the patient's *derivative* communications, whatever his diagnosis. All patients are capable of such expressions. And on that basis, having tested a series of precepts in terms of Type Two derivative validation, we may conclude that in general, it is essential to maintain the same basic therapeutic stance with all patients; and the differences in actual therapeutic work arise almost entirely from differences in the form and content of expressions in these patients.

One final comment, if I may, about this material. If we think for a moment of the patient's lateness as a response in part to the adaptive context of the therapist's having secured an aspect of the frame, we could then organize the patient's derivatives as unconscious transference fantasy–memory constellations which express the patient's concerns and pathological reactions to this measure. It would appear that fears of intimacy and homosexual fantasies and anxieties are unstable in this regard. In a secure therapeutic setting—which, of course, does not exist here—much of the therapeutic work is motivated by the patient's largely unconscious anxieties, conflicts, fantasies, memories, and *distorted* perceptions as evoked by the valid image of the therapist's sound holding-containing and interpretive capacities. There is disturbance and trust, while in a deviant setting there is disturbance and mistrust. Both, however, can lead to sound therapeutic work, though the latter requires rectification as well as interpretation.

We will continue with this patient next week. Thank you for your presentation.

Chapter Five

THE TIMING OF INTERVENTIONS

Langs: Could the therapist begin with a brief resume?

Therapist: The patient is a graduate student at this center who will be leaving the area to begin a job at the end of the year. I too will be leaving at that time. More immediately, I had shifted the hour of his session fifteen minutes later because I had been late as a result of a ward staff meeting I held in my office. Actually, there were people coming out of that meeting whom he knew.

He was about six minutes late, and began this session by saying, God, I don't know exactly what this is all about, but I had even gotten here early today. I was ready to hit the button for the elevator to come up, and something just took me away.

He said, I'm late again and I really don't understand quite why. I registered at the front desk, was ready to come up here, and somehow I just ended up going off and checking my mail which is at the other end of the building. I bumped into somebody I knew—a girl—and we got into a little conversation, and now I'm late again. It's difficult for me to be on time here. And certainly even more difficult for me to be early.

There was a long silence which I broke by saying, Then there's a reason right now why you need to keep me waiting, rather than allowing me to keep you waiting.

Discussant: I found the intervention ambiguous. Was the therapist alluding here to the silence as something that was keeping him waiting, or to the patient's lateness?

Therapist: I felt that I didn't have enough information to know what his lateness meant, or even what his silence meant. For me, this was a preliminary interpretation.

Langs: As some of you know, we discussed this intervention at some length at our last meeting. We will therefore not attempt to formally identify its manifest and communicative properties. However, this brief discussion brings up several points worth commenting upon.

One of our listeners, in a sense identified with the patient, found this intervention ambiguous. It is important that in expressing himself, a therapist should be as clear and precise as possible. Therapists have always honored the principle that the shorter the intervention, the more succinct and clearly defined, the better. As you have undoubtedly realized by now, I accept such a tenet as self-evident, though in actual practice I believe it is often necessary to make a relatively complex intervention—though, of course, it should be offered as sparsely as possible.

After all, we have found that preliminary interventions, such as questions, clarifications, and confrontations, tend not to have the anticipated effect of producing more meaningful material from the patient, and tend to be introjected in negative ways. The only intervention to have received Type Two derivative validation which could be characterized as at all preliminary in nature is the playback of selected derivatives around an unmentioned adaptive context, and one that usually pertains to a break in the fixed frame. Beyond that, we have found that the most facilitating response with which we are able to help the patient to modify communicative resistances is the judicious use of silence. As a result, you will find that there are many sessions in which silence is the only intervention which will receive Type Two derivative validation from your patients or which, upon repeated evaluation, is appropriate to the material at hand despite resistance.

In sessions where you do have a basis for intervening, your response will almost always take the form of an interpretation-reconstruction to which may be added, as needed, an effort to manage the framework. The intervention will include the best representations of the indicators and adaptive contexts which are most pressing, and an explication of the derivative complex in terms of its unconscious meanings and functions—its adaptive and maladaptive qualities in response to the context.

As such, it is likely that you will have quite a bit to say to the patient. It is therefore important to develop a capability to automatically organize your comments in a way that takes the patient from the prevailing indicator to the evocative context, through a clarification of his responses, their dynamic meanings, and their genetic counterparts—all depending, of course, on the available derivatives from the patient in that particular hour. Although you will virtually always begin your intervention with a reference to either the indicators or the adaptive context, the context is ultimately the organizing force. There is a good deal to cover, but if you use a broad cause and effect model, and string together your comments with logic and precision, the patient will be able to follow you not only on a conscious level, but unconsciously as well.

Discussant: We have always been taught to promote the development of the patient's material by asking questions, or through confrontations and clarifications. You have made clear your preference for silence as a means of facilitating the emergence of meaning in the patient's associations. How do you account for this difference in approach?

Langs: Through careful attention to the patient's *derivative* responses to these various interventions. The patient is our guide, and his indirect, disguised responses are critical. Questions, clarifications, and confrontation, consistently fail to evoke Type Two derivative validation, and, in addition, they virtually never foster the development of the patient's derivative expressions. These techniques are based on manifest content and Type One derivative listening and the intervening which follows on that basis. The techniques I have been proposing are based on Type Two derivative listening and intervening.

The active group of interventions—if I may use that term for questions, clarifications, and confrontations—do not promote the further unfolding of the patient's *derivative* responses to the adaptive context he is working over at the time. Instead, they tend to introduce a traumatic or countertransference-based context which often enough becomes a new focus for the patient's derivative reactions. Certainly, there may be a melding of his reactions to both contexts, but the active group of interventions nonetheless tend to complicate the picture rather than promote its more naturalistic unfolding on the patient's terms.

In addition, the active interventions often promote and intensify the patient's use of communicative defenses, all too frequently rendering material which was beginning to unfold meaningfully no longer potentially interpretable. While the patient's superficial response may seem meaningful, the implications are virtually always linear and simplistic. The more convoluted and derivative meanings are usually obliterated as a result of evoked interactional defenses within the patient. The patient often focuses on the manifest question or confrontation, and his surface associations lose much of their richness and disguised implications. Direct communication is promoted, while indirect expression is sacrificed. The outcome is usually a mixture of confusion and defensiveness. Quite often, the result of active interventions, which themselves reflect use of the Type B or Type C communicative mode in the therapist, is to prompt the use of Type C barriers in the patient, or more rarely a responsive, uninsightful, unmetabolized projective identification.

Try to maintain the perspective that the communicative approach is essentially a Type Two derivative approach, while most present-day therapeutic practice is based on manifest content and Type One derivative listening and intervening. This will help you to anticipate that the communicative approach will derive distinctly different technical precepts. In a sense, the guide for classical analysts is the patient's conscious reactions, while the guide for the communicative analyst or therapist is the patient's latent or derivative responses. As we have seen throughout this course, vast implications stem from this basic difference.

Discussant: This also touches upon the timing of interventions. With the usual approach, we tend to intervene as soon as we see something to question or confront. With your approach, interventions seem to be called for much later in the session.

Langs: These are all important questions, though something seems to be making it difficult for us to get beyond this particular point in the presentation. I suspect that the therapist has made the kind of intervention which is typical for this group, and perhaps for therapists at large.

In attempting earlier to discuss the timing of interventions, I realized that, while we can develop some precepts, the variables are so great that, ultimately, it comes down to the art of psychotherapy and the gifts of the therapist. There are many situations which will fit into distinctive precepts, and they can serve as a guide for most sessions. But there are also sessions in which the patient's communicative expressions and resistances are such that fine decisions must be made and some small measure of disagreement is inevitable. Most situations can be measured against these tenets, and a consensus can be reached; more rarely, there will be situations where more than one possibility exists. At the very least, however, we should be able to reach a consensus that a particular session offers several alternatives.

The specifics of timing can be identified in terms of several possibilities. First, you might intervene where the patient offers a bridge back to therapy. Second, if the three elements of the communicative network are clear and full, you might intervene at a point when there is an especially meaningful derivative. Third, you might intervene at a point where you feel the network has a sense of fullness. And fourth, you might intervene when, after communicating at a low level of resistance, the patient begins to show major communicative resistances and the material is becoming stale. In this last instance, you would require an earlier link or bridge to therapy through which you could connect your comments to the prevailing adaptive context.

These are ideal models of intervening. There are many additional possibilities. With a powerful indicator, in the presence of major communicative resistances, you will intervene with the best available representation of the intervention context and the most meaningful elements of the derivative complex. In the face of powerful indicators which include major gross behavioral resistances and threats to terminate or disturb the treatment situation in some critical way—significant threats to the alliance sector—it may prove necessary to intervene as soon as some meaningful material is available. Under these types of pressure conditions, in the presence of highly disturbing projective identifications from the patient, there is a powerful tendency within therapists to respond noninterpretively and with major alterations of the ground rules. These are consistently revealed to be major technical errors, and tend only to further aggravate this type of crisis situation. They are experienced by the patient as failures within the therapist in his metabolizing and interpretive capacities; they generate negative introjects; and they only further reinforce the patient's Type B–C communicative mode. At such junctures, the therapist and patient become identical in important pathological ways, and the latter's psychopathology and maladaptive coping mechanisms are only reinforced.

When the indicator corresponds to a break in the fixed frame, you will want to intervene either with the representation of the adaptive context and the implications of the derivative complex, or with a playback of selected derivatives organized around the missing adaptive context when it has not been clearly represented. Under these conditions, it is important to remember that a break in the frame created by the patient is *not* a primary adaptive context but a secondary context; and the deviation itself is a response to a particular context of a prior intervention. All too often, therapists intervene by organizing the patient's material around his break in the frame, actual or proposed, rather than locating the precipitant in a previous intervention. By excluding this critical context, the intervention becomes either a pathological projective identification or a Type C barrier. It does not obtain Type Two derivative validation from the patient.

There are special difficulties to intervening in two extreme kinds of situations: (1) where the patient is in a state of crisis and attempting to assault, stir up, or in some other way seduce or threaten the therapist; and (2) those in which there is a high level of communicative resistance. Under the latter conditions, many therapists feel hard pressed to remain silent, abhorring the void reflected in the patient's Type C communicative mode—a void which not only endeavors to destroy intrapsychic and interpersonal links, but also constitutes an unconscious effort to treat the therapist as if he did not exist. Inherent is a wish to confound the therapist, to attack him by having him doubt his abilities to understand and integrate the material, and even to think, and to isolate him and deprive him from the minimal hold, nourishment, and support inherent to a patient's *meaningful* free associating. These insidious qualities often constitute a rather disturbing projective identification, sometimes what I have termed a negative projective identification or the interactional creation of a void (Langs 1976b). They tend to produce a state within the therapist that is difficult to metabolize and tolerate. This is especially true because therapists develop strong needs to express themselves after long periods of silence and passive listening. We wish to reaffirm our identities and coping capacities. Deprived of such moments, we may become restless and agitated; all too often, we intervene erroneously, primarily as a way of dealing with our own inner tension and anxiety. Such interventions constitute failures in containing and in understanding, and will be experienced as such by the patient.

In the more agitated situation, you have disturbing projective identifications which can be metabolized into interpretations. However, in the presence of major communicative resistances—the Type C communicative mode—you have far more subtle and indirect forms of destructiveness to metabolize, and you do not have the opportunity to produce a sense of discharge or closure, of resolution through the formulation and offer of an interpretation. Instead, you must remain silent, relying on an internal value system which supports the use of silence for however long it is appropriate. You must be capable of that particular kind of inner nurturance in order to survive what can be long periods of intense communicative resistances from one or more patients in your practice.

In this context, I would like to share with you some impressions I have developed with respect to the characteristics of patients who remain in long-term psychoanalysis or psychotherapy, and outline what I believe to be a rather typical course of such treatment situations. Now that I am gaining some extended experience with the communicative approach, I have a preliminary sense that this type of therapy could shorten the duration of most therapeutic experiences. There is some evidence that extended treatment situations often go on for many unnecessary years because of unrecognized countertransference inputs from the therapist or analyst.

We can begin with the Type A patient, who usually presents with acute symptoms and is therefore motivated to search for and express the highly threatening derivatives through which he can gain insightful understanding. In the opening phase of therapy, he may attempt to modify the framework, but benefits greatly from the therapist's capacity to maintain a secure hold. Primarily around these frame issues, and in response to additional intervention contexts which may arise, he produces an interpretable derivative networks and begins to resolve his symptoms through the insights offered by the therapist. He tolerates well the interpersonal barriers and frustration of symbiotic needs imposed by the therapist's management of the frame and by his valid interpretations.

Eventually, this type of patient shifts to a Type C communicative mode or leaves treatment. If he stays on, he often becomes quite comfortable within the therapeutic situation, finding considerable security and gratification in the holding environment and the healthy symbiosis offered by the therapist, and presents now as a Type C narrator. He engages in a great deal of Type One derivative self-interpretations, through which he appears to modify his more pathological lie-barrier systems, becoming more flexible and adaptive. Eventually, through embedded derivatives, he will allude to his readiness for termination, and when this is picked up by the therapist, there is a final period during which the separation issues are analyzed in light of his intermittent return to the Type A communicative mode. I suspect that all of this can be accomplished with most patients—neurotic, psychotic, or borderline—in one to three years.

The same sequence applies to the Type B–A patient, whose opening phase is far more violent than with the Type A communicator, and whose impingements upon the framework are more frequent and intense. Nonetheless, patient containing and holding and sound interpretive interventions based on the meaningful communicative networks which they also make available to the therapist enable them to soon settle down into the therapeutic situation and continue quite comfortably. More of these patients than those who use Type A communication will terminate therapy after the initial working-through phase. They have resolved their symptoms, remain concerned about the eruption of a rather violent psychotic core which remains only moderately well defended, and prefer to terminate rather than risk a fresh regression. This choice, which often takes place mostly on an unconscious level and which can be interpreted to the patient, deserves extensive consideration in future studies of the therapeutic process. While it is my belief that the therapist must adopt a position which favors assisting the patient to gain as much insight as possible, he can certainly also respect—though not pathologically reinforce—his patient's sense of having achieved a new level of adaptation without wishing to take further risks, which are indeed considerable. As therapists, we tend to overvalue the pursuit of truth, and to deny many of the terrifying and tumultuous aspects of this endeavor within the therapeutic situation. While we should not adopt a position which supports a patient's pathological defenses, we should have a clear perspective on the choices which a patient must make in entering and remaining in psychotherapy. In some situations the risks outweigh the possible gains.

The Type B–C patient will either destroy the framework of therapy in the opening weeks of treatment, or terminate prematurely in response to the sense of persecution he experiences when the therapist maintains the frame in the face of his assaults. Some of these patients shade into the Type C patient, and effect a compromise in which they continue to more quietly attack the basic therapeutic hold, while maintaining their own lie-barrier systems and engaging in nonderivative communication. Some of these patients may stay in therapy for months, creating one crisis after another, though only rarely do they produce an interpretable communicative network and gain any sense of understanding. These patients dread the activated psychotic part of their personalities which threatens to erupt in ways they experience as tantamount to self-annihilation. They therefore attempt to maintain their fragile Type C barriers and to attack the therapist's handling of the therapeutic environment, knowing quite well unconsciously that to do otherwise would be to experience the secure hold which would encourage a therapeutic regression. They seek out many pathological forms of merger and symbiosis, and tolerate poorly both the therapist's functioning as separate and any pressures toward their own individuation. They wish to merge or flee.

The psychotic core in these patients is quite primitive, and often these patients have considerable difficulty with impulse control. Awareness implies action; and action implies destruction, seduction, and loss of control. Their dilemma is acute and intense, and many of these patients terminate prematurely rather than risk the derivative expressions of the psychotic part of their personalities.

A small group of Type B–C patients provide the therapist with sufficient islands of Type A communication to permit interpretation of the sources and dynamics of their intense anxiety and dread, enabling them to eventually develop more secure derivative and nonderivative defenses, and to continue in therapy.

Finally, there are those patients who begin treatment as Type C communicators. As a rule, they are not suffering from acute symptoms, and often, they have been pressured by someone in their family or environment to enter therapy. Much of their psychopathology is characterological and the suffering is usually located in those who relate to them, rather than within themselves. They drift about in therapy for a while, sometimes obtaining pathological symbiotic gratification, and only occasionally shifting to a Type A communicative mode. Often, they will simply accept the secure therapeutic environment and hold, showing little in the way of meaningful derivative expression and seldom raising frame or other issues. Though little direct insight is offered to them, they seem to benefit from the secure hold and to engage in some degree of self-interpretation which enables them to soften and make more flexible their lie-barrier systems. Some of these patients, as they experience a symbiosis with the therapist which is both pathological and non-pathological, will sense the onset of a therapeutic regression and either prematurely terminate therapy or shift for short but important periods of time to Type A communication.

Each of these types of patient pose particular problems for the therapist. The Type A patient requires an ability to interpret, while the Type B patient needs a therapist who can metabolize and interpret intensely destructive pathological projective identifications and role- and image-evocations. The Type C patient, as I said, must have a therapist who is capable of dealing with voids and the destruction of meaning and relatedness, and of maintaining judicious silence for long periods of time.

Discussant: I have begun to realize that very often I say things to a patient for my sake rather than his. Sometimes I realize my own needs only after I have made an intervention. Then I recognize it has something to do with what is going on within myself, and that I have something to figure out.

Langs: I suspect that some of this understanding has developed because you have been able to use the criterion of Type Two derivative validation in response to your interventions, and because you are becoming more sensitive to your own inappropriate needs and interventions as a therapist.

Discussant: I have also learned that it is important to listen long enough to develop silent hypotheses and to see whether the patient's material adds to them in any way, validates them. By doing that, I have slowed down considerably in my rate of intervening, and I have also discovered many mistaken formulations.

Langs: Yes, an important principle in respect to intervening is to develop a silent intervention first, and to then allow the patient's continuing associations to help you to further shape and reshape the proposed comment. You must remain open to the need for revisions and even for the possibility of major errors to the point where you must discard all that you have been developing. Under those last conditions, it is necessary to generate a new silent intervention. Ultimately, you impart to the patient only those interventions which meet the criteria of potential validity and which have already received preliminary validation through continued, silent listening.

Therapist: Coming back to this material, the patient had referred to his lateness directly. I took that as an indicator, though I realized, as we discussed it last week, that I was not working with an adaptive context—for example, my own earlier lateness and the pending forced termination—and that I made virtually no use of the derivatives in the patient's association.

Discussant: Some derivatives were available. The patient said that he somehow felt he wasn't responsible for his lateness—implying that the therapist was responsible. There is considerable truth there, since the therapist has created conditions which have encouraged the patient to be late. I guess we would have to put it this way: a gross behavioral counterresistance has contributed to a gross behavioral resistance.

Discussant: The patient was late because he lingered to talk with a girl he knew. I heard that as a representation of the adaptive context of the therapist's lingering with the people in his staff conference to the point where he kept the patient waiting.

Langs: Yes, in principle, we search for all available indicators, and evaluate their representations. Then we search for all possible intervention contexts, concentrating on those which are more immediate and compelling, such as recent breaks in the frame. As for adaptive contexts, we must be prepared for layering: a clearly represented context may cover a more threatening context which is represented with greater disguise. You listen to the derivative complex in light of the known contexts. Which do the derivatives most illuminate, and to which do they seem least pertinent? How critical is what the patient has revealed, and how important is the material against which he is defending himself? These are all delicate evaluations, to be made primarily by using the patient's associations and their derivative implications as your guide, supplemented by your own assessments.

For the moment, to review some of our discussion from last week, there is a clear indicator here in the patient's lateness. There is a disguised representation of the therapist's lateness in the patient's allusions to his own lateness, and perhaps a highly disguised representation of the adaptive context of the pending forced termination in the reference to the mail room. There is a direct representation of the absence of total confidentiality in the patient's mention of having stopped to sign in downstairs before going up for his session. Each of these contexts is represented with varying levels of disguise, though the total impression would be a level of representability around three or four, and therefore a rather strong level of communicative resistance—around six or seven—in respect to representing the activated intervention contexts.

The derivative complex also appears to be relatively weak in meaning, though some is present. It too could be rated at a level of about three, which would suggest the presence of strong communicative resistances in this area as well.

As I recall the material, there was also some reference to something taking the patient away from the therapy—another highly disguised representation of the pending forced termination. Other possible manifest associations which contain meaningful derivatives include the patient's comment that he doesn't understand why he is late, his bumping into a girl he knew, and that it is difficult for him to be on time or early. Overall, I would say that the derivative complex deserves a rating of two or three, and not higher; there is a high degree of communicative resistance.

We know that the therapist intervened at this point. Based on the communicative approach, would we have intervened?

Discussant: While there is a relatively strong indicator, there is a high level of communicative resistance. I would have to conclude that we would not intervene; that instead, we would remain silent and permit the patient an opportunity to resolve his resistances.

Langs: I would agree. There is a strong interactional component to these resistances, and the therapist has tried to rectify some of his contribution. He has not, and cannot, rectify the contribution which derives from the pending forced termination. Because of this, these communicative resistances may be insurmountable for long periods of time. They are further reinforced by the lack of confidentiality to which the patient alluded in derivative form.

In principle, it would be best to sit back and see how the patient deals with the anxieties, conflicts, and introjects involved. Remember, we know nothing of the immediate adaptive contexts derived from the previous hour. They too might be contributing to these communicative resistances. We are attempting to use this material to develop principles and models, and we will not be in a position to study its implications in depth because we lack the prior session or two.

Discussant: You seem to be implying that there is nothing that the therapist can do through an active intervention to alter these communicative resistances and thereby obtain material for interpretation. I can see where that follows from the principles and observations you have developed in this course. Yet I can't help wonder if there isn't some intervention other than silence which would modify this patient's defenses. I almost said "break down" his defenses, but I quickly realized that if I had used that phrase, I would have been answering my own question in the negative.

Langs: Exactly, and despite the decision to change your wording you have done just that. Your language tells us that an active intervention would be an assault on the patient's defenses, and while something might give—though often the patient only reinforces and intensifies his defensiveness—the patient's main response would be to react to your assault. The problem of modifying his communicative resistances so he could work over the prevailing adaptive contexts would either be set aside or complicated. A confrontation of that kind would actually be another version of the therapist's lateness and of the pending forced termination, and because of that, the type of intervention you propose would be experienced unconsciously by the patient as a new traumatic intervention context which would only unconsciously reinforce his current impressions and reactions—including his resistances—rather than modify them.

Notice the principle involved. If you evaluate an intervention in terms of its manifest implications, you might have reason to believe that a confrontation with a defense will lead the patient to give it up. On the other hand, when you evaluate an intervention in terms of its unconscious implications, you discover that quite the opposite is true—the intervention itself is a new version of the very danger situations which prompt the patient's defensiveness in the first place. This is why active interventions of that type do not resolve resistances or generate Type Two derivative validation. Something changes on the surface, and this has mistakenly led therapists to believe that confrontations do indeed alter a patient's resistances. However, a communicative analysis reveals that these changes actually reflect the development of new resistances or a derivative working over of the new, traumatic intervention contexts. That segment of the patient's resistances which has been directed against a prior danger situation or conflict remains in force, and is actually further reinforced by the confrontational intervention.

Perhaps as therapists we still entertain secret and unconscious fantasies of omnipotence, a belief that we can always change our patients with our words regardless of their hidden implications and our behaviors. Because such fantasies imply active measures, we also tend to overvalue active interventions. In reality, such active efforts are, indeed, sometimes quite constructive and capable of effecting adaptive change within our patients. But we must come to realize that there are many situations in which change can be effected only through our silence and holding. Anything more active only aggravates the situation.

It is necessary for therapists to tolerate their helplessness and even impotence at times. Possibly further extensions of the communicative approach may lead to active techniques which obtain Type Two derivative validation, but all I can say is that many of my supervisees, and I myself on rare occasions, have attempted to apply a wide variety of such techniques without success. Without exception, they have failed to resolve the communicative resistances; they have, instead, generated negative introjects and consequences of the type I have already identified.

This type of problem is especially noticeable in the Type C patient who accepts the ideal therapeutic environment as constructed by the therapist, makes no effort at modification on his own, and accepts for long periods of time the therapist's necessary silence. While these patients may on occasion manifestly complain of the therapist's silence, they often accept the holding qualities without protest when the silence is, indeed, well founded. The only available adaptive context is the therapist's appropriate silence and holding-containing function. And because these patients find nurturance or safety in those elements, they do not respond to them with especially meaningful derivatives. I have seen some patients of this kind who have obtained considerable benefit from therapy despite the fact that the therapist seldom intervened at all. These are puzzling therapeutic experiences which deserve further study.

Therapist: In this situation, I would agree that my intervention was premature. I can see that I spoke for my own safety and sense of well being, rather than for the patient's; that it came out of a need within me and basically, from an inability to tolerate his lateness, and much of his silence.

Langs: Your comments serve as a reminder that every intervention must be understood on one level as a response to the adaptive context of the patient's associations. The material which precedes an intervention can be taken as the immediate stimulus, though it is necessary to weigh that element against the rest of the patient's associations and behaviors. As such, it is a major clue and organizer of the derivative implications of the therapist's intervention.

In principle, a valid intervention deals with the adaptive context implications of the patient's material through a sound interpretation which illuminates the unconscious meanings of the patient's associations and behaviors to the greatest possible extent, and which deviates from that goal to the least degree feasible. Sometimes, your own personal needs and anxieties, as stirred up by the patient's material, may best be resolved by the interpretation which most effectively serves the patient's therapeutic needs. On other occasions, this is not the case: a valid interpretation would do far more for the patient than for the therapist. As a rule, every valid intervention should offer some type of implicit and inherent therapy to the therapist, even though it is in the main a coincidental effect.

We are dealing with matters of degree. The less validity an intervention has, the greater the countertransference input. These are interventions offered primarily to satisfy the therapist's pathological (inappropriate) needs rather than those of the patient, and they have highly personal and idiosyncratic implications in light of the adaptive context from the patient. Every follow-up analysis of an intervention should investigate the immediate precipitant, and evaluate the extent to which that adaptive context has evoked a countertransference-based response and the extent to which it is valid.

Discussant: Is the patient's silence always a resistance? It seems to me that silence has meaning at times.

Langs: We already have acknowledged that all resistances have meaning. Gross behavioral resistances are measured by the patient's adherence to the fundamental rule of free association and to the other ground rules of therapy. In fact, we may identify gross behavioral resistances as any departure by the patient from the basic framework as defined by the therapist. While disruptive on the surface, such behaviors do indeed always have function and meaning, the nature of which is determined through an evaluation of the prevailing adaptive context and derivative complex.

Discussant: I made this comment because talking can be a resistance too. There are some analysts who say that being able to sit in silence and to be safe and comfortable with the analyst is almost a goal of treatment for the patient.

Langs: Your comment reveals the extent to which the definition of gross behavioral resistances, and communicative resistances as well, is dependent upon your formulation of the nature and goals of therapy. Within a communicative framework, I am proposing definitions and implications based on the criterion of Type Two derivative validation of the therapist's interventions.

Discussant: I was thinking about the obsessive patient who adheres to the fundamental rule, but in a sense violates it by sticking too close to it. Perhaps we need to revise our concept of the fundamental rule and state that what is essential is whether the patient communicates derivatives of unconscious material.

Langs: Rumination is often viewed as a gross behavioral resistance, and usually it has that particular function. Still, obsessiveness has function and meaning, whatever its resistance qualities. In that part of your comment, you were addressing behavioral resistances.

In the final part of your remark, you are alluding to communicative resistances, an aspect that I hope I have defined sufficiently clearly by now. I would agree that, on the surface, the fundamental rule deals with gross behavioral resistance—whether or not the patient is free associating, saying whatever comes to mind. Communicatively, or beneath the surface, the fundamental rule proposes that the patient express himself in terms of prevailing intervention contexts and meaningful derivative responses, to the point where they can be interpreted.

I made a comparable point when we were talking about the therapeutic alliance (Langs 1980), when I spoke of the manifest and latent alliance sector—surface cooperation and communicative cooperation. The ground rules define the patient's cooperative and nonresistant behaviors, and therefore pertain to gross behavioral resistances. The ground rules, however, also have meaning for the communicative and unconscious alliance, and we could take the trouble to define that sphere for each basic tenet. We have already done so for the fundamental rule of free association. We could do the same for the requirement that the patient pay his bill and come to his sessions on time. In these situations, the gross behavior is self-evident, though the unconscious implications remain to be specified.

To stay with our central topic, then, our discussion has led us to restate the distinction between gross behavioral and communicative resistances. And we would apply these concepts to the therapist as well with respect to his counterresistances.

Discussant: In these terms, the basic resistance is absence from a session and premature termination, rather than silence. But then suppose someone has to go to a family function which is very important?

Langs: Absence from the session is a gross behavioral resistance. However, we never simply take such behaviors at face value; we explore their basis within the patient and his life, and in terms of contributions from the therapist. It becomes easy to make these principles seem a bit absurd, but judiciously applied, they make an enormous amount of sense and will serve you well. Whatever its cause, absence is a resistance or obstacle to therapy; but simply do not prejudge its implications. Allow the patient's material to guide you. Incidentally, you will find that many highly rationalized absences reveal, in light of the patient's responsive associations, that underneath they are reactions to critical adaptive contexts, often in the form of modifications by the therapist of the basic framework.

Discussant: It seems helpful, then, to look at resistances the way Freud looked at instincts, in terms of their sources, aims, and the object involved.

Langs: Yes, that is a way of characterizing what I have tried to do: to identify the sources within patient and therapist, the aims or functions, and the person toward whom the resistance is directed— empirically, almost always the therapist.

Discussant: It is evident that we have a problem in working through the communicative definition of resistance. We have always thought of resistances as intrapsychic and as expressions of the patient's defenses in his relationship with the therapist. Now we learn that there are interactional and interpersonal factors, and the situation becomes more difficult and complicated.

Discussant: If I may return to the clinical material, I think it's fair to state that the therapist's discomfort with the patient's lateness and silence prompted a confronting, general interpretation designed unconsciously to reproject the disturbance felt by the therapist, unmetabolized, into the patient.

Langs: That's quite a mouthful. It is quite accurate, however. We don't want these words to lose their clinical meaning and become functionally meaningless. In essence, your point is that the patient had done something to upset the therapist and the therapist, instead of understanding and interpreting the source of the disturbance and the implications of the patient's behavior in that light, intervened in a somewhat accusatory manner as a way of placing the disturbance back into the patient. This is certainly an example of a Type B communicative style in the therapist. The intervention is designed as a lie barrier against contributions from the therapist to the patient's lateness and silence.

Discussant: Would you have intervened at this point?

Langs: Not at all. I would have been evaluating the indicators, and would recognize the importance of dealing with the patient's lateness and silence. I would be searching for the relevant adaptive context, and attempting to derive meaning from the derivative complex. I would take in the pressures of his silence and of his sense of absurdity, and attempt to metabolize it toward meaning. Even if the silence were extended, I would probably not intervene because of the high level of communicative resistances.

If the silence went on for a long time, I would consider this a level nine or ten indicator, and would make the best intervention possible in light of the material. Only at that point might I say that the patient has fallen silent and mentioned his lateness; that these reactions seem to stem from something he is experiencing in treatment which is absurd and beyond his control, something which touches upon the theme of being taken away and of being involved in talking to someone else rather than getting to the session.

In that way, I would be offering the best representations of the intervention context and the best available playback of derivatives around the adaptive context of the therapist's recent lateness and the pending forced termination.

This is how we work with well-disguised representations of contexts and a relatively poor derivative complex. Two indicators are clearly represented, while two others—the therapist's lateness and the pending forced termination—coincide with the adaptive contexts. Under these conditions, you do your best with the derivatives available, and intervene only when the indicators are extremely intense. This hypothetical example constitutes one of the most difficult types of therapeutic situations a therapist will have to face. Sometimes, the indicators are far more disturbing, such as a patient's threat to terminate. Unconsciously, the high level of communicative resistances is designed to keep the therapist at bay, and prevent him from effectively interpreting. This is often a threatening and frustrating situation, but its best management involves adhering to the interpretive principles we have been developing.

Discussant: I must confess that I might have been inclined to say something to the patient like, You're still keeping me waiting. I realize now that an intervention of that kind is entirely divorced from the principles you have offered. Communicatively, it is critical and hostile. It's a destructive confrontation. On reflection, I certainly did not like the way it sounded, and I'm sure that the patient would feel the same way. It places the entire onus of the problem on the patient, and serves to deny my contributions. Sometimes we reassure ourselves that we have used a kind tone, as if to deny the underlying hostility.

Therapist: In reviewing my notes, I found that I often have confronted this patient. Consciously, I was attempting to prove to him that he has an unconscious—if I may put it that way—to show him he's doing things he's unaware of. But I'm no longer certain of the utility of that approach, and I immediately recognize that the confrontation not only denies what I am contributing to the patient's resistances, but also could be applied to myself. There is much that I am doing with this patient of which I am unaware.

Langs: If I may, I would like to suggest that we get back to the material.

Therapist: Okay. He responded to my intervention with a long silence.

Langs: The gross behavioral resistance is unmodified. This is an initial level of nonvalidation.

Therapist: But then he sort of winds himself up and begins by saying, You know, it makes me think of something that happened last week, with Betty. (Betty is his current girlfriend.)

Langs: Does she have anything to do with this center?

Therapist: She certainly does. She's a social worker here.

Langs: The question comes from listening to this material and attempting to formulate derivative implications.

Therapist: The patient went on to describe what had happened. It had taken place the morning of the session. He had spent the night at her apartment, which Betty shares with another woman who also works at this center, as a secretary. Betty, who works in the emergency room, has to get up pretty early in the morning. Meanwhile, my patient has a nice, easy job in a laboratory and can sleep very late.

Anyhow, what happened is rather peculiar. He described it in the same tone of voice as when he mentioned the craziness he experienced when he suddenly found he couldn't go up the elevator to wait outside of my office; but that he had to do something else first. In any case, he found that after Betty got out of bed, he couldn't get himself out of bed. And there was a problem with that. The problem was that there was this other woman around, and she was okay. But once she left the apartment, he didn't have a key to lock the apartment when he left. The regular lock was broken; there was a deadbolt but he didn't have the key.

In his own semiconscious way, he was aware that if he stayed in bed, he would not be able to lock the apartment. Yet he persisted, and he's not sure why. He was aware that there would be stirrings toward this other woman in the apartment, but he said that she was a friend of his, and that he felt comfortable with her. It wasn't a particular issue about his being seen in the apartment. They had all had a good time the night before. He didn't feel uneasy about seeing her per se, but he just couldn't quite get himself out of bed.

Very shortly after this woman left he bounded out of bed, somewhat anxious about the whole thing because he did it so suddenly. He put it on himself that he was going to have to leave Betty's apartment without a key, and he didn't know what to do. Luckily, he was near the center. So he ran to Betty, to her office. And that's interesting because he had met her there the first time they had seen each other, and he felt comfortable there. He ran up to Betty and said, Gosh, what am I going to do? I don't have a key. Just give me a key and I'll run over and lock the apartment and then bring the key back to you. And her response was, Forget it, I can do it myself later. Then she went on to tell him that he gets too upset about these things and shouldn't worry about them at all. He should just go home or go to his laboratory, and she would take care of it. She even told him that there was a superintendent who was always in the lobby, and he could have locked the apartment.

Here, he said to me, Gee, why didn't I think of that?

This took up a lot of the session.

Langs: Since you paused, let's all pause, and comment on this material.

Discussant: I found it ruminative, detailed, and boring.

Discussant: I felt there was much too much detail, and that there was a gross behavioral resistance despite the fact he was free associating. I also felt I could generate a little bit of meaning in light of the two intervention contexts of which we are aware: the therapist's former lateness and the pending forced termination. It's well disguised, but I think that I could discern that the patient is working over some kind of issue about being left, about wanting to linger on, about getting in touch with someone who has left him, and about being unable to cope with separation.

Langs: As an initial formulation, that is quite good. In developing a general impression with respect to the degree of communicative resistance, remember that as therapists we are prone to want to see and develop meaning, and less open to experiencing a sense of nonmeaning. I say that because even though you can develop some degree of implication here, and find some meaning to these derivatives, it is important that you experience how well disguised they are, and, therefore, how high the patient's level of communicative resistance is. Based on your general comments, we would suspect that the level of clarity and coalescibility of these derivatives is somewhere around two or three, and that therefore, the resistances are quite strong.

Can anyone be more specific now?

Discussant: I find that I have to take each adaptive context separately. I'll begin with the therapist's lateness, which I think is best represented by the patient's tardiness in getting out of bed.

Langs: Yes, and please notice that this is a disguised derivative which involves a relationship outside of therapy and which lacks a link to the therapist. Nonetheless, we do have a general bridge to therapy in the patient's initial associations, during which he discussed his problem in coming on time to the session. That was, however, the last we heard of therapy or the therapist.

Discussant: I'll try the intervention context of the pending forced termination. It seems to me the best representation is the pressure the patient felt in having to get out of bed on time.

Discussant: What about the social worker? Isn't it possible that she is serving as a substitute for the therapist, especially in anticipation of the forced termination?

Langs: Yes, but that would be part of the derivative complex, and perhaps even an indicator since it contains postulated qualities of acting out. Try to maintain a clear distinction between matters of representability—how something is portrayed in disguise—and derivative reactions, which are disguised responses to the adaptive context. It is wise to begin your formulation by identifying the *clearest representation* of the indicators and adaptive contexts, with direct allusion being the clearest form. With each of these elements of the communicative network, passing *manifest* allusion is ideal.

Next, you identify the conscious and unconscious implications of the intervention context. It is important to determine not only which adaptive context the patient is most clearly representing, but also which of the many unconscious implications and communications contained within the context are being represented. We cannot treat intervention contexts as single elements, but must instead recognize their complexity and the need to identify the most compelling implications conveyed to the patient. Once these have been identified, we organize the responsive derivative complex as adaptive and maladaptive reactions to one or more particular aspects of the activated contexts. It is here, of course, we devote our overriding interest to indirect, derivative expression. In interpreting, we can then be as definitive as possible.

Both of our known adaptive contexts are here represented through relationships outside of therapy, and with a moderate to strong degree of disguise. Few of their specific implications are conveyed. We may conclude, then, that there is a rather strong level of resistance when it comes to the representation of the main adaptive contexts.

What of the derivative complex?

Discussant: I already mentioned an implication of the girlfriend. There is also the business of staying in her apartment, which could express the wish to be closer to, or live with, the therapist. Then there is not wanting to leave, not wanting to be able to lock the door—the fight against finality—and the urgent need for the girl-friend, who here, I believe, represents the therapist.

For me, this material does not organize especially clearly around the adaptive context of the therapist's recent latenesses. Instead, I hear these derivatives as reactions—I would have to say both perceptions and fantasies—to the therapist's leaving.

Langs: Yes, you have done an excellent job. It is difficult to organize this material along the me/not-me interface without knowing the therapist's prior interventions. In principle, this material may also reflect unconsciously communicated anxieties within the therapist who is fearful of separating from the patient, afraid to finalize the pending termination, and who has an anxious need to hold on to him. We could decide who this material applies to more cogently only if we had heard the presentation of the recent sessions, especially the theapist's latest interventions. My main point for the moment is to encourage you to not simply assume that this is entirely the patient's fantasy constellation, and to leave room for possible unconscious perceptions.

There may well be major elements of transference in the narrow sense; the patient may be fearful, in need of a replacement figure, and anxious about the separation. If this were to prove to be the case, then the patient's use of detail and of communicative resistances would attack mainly the representation of the adaptive context, less so the communicative complex, and could be accurately

said to constitute *transference resistances*—behavioral and communicative obstacles to therapy based on pathological unconscious
fantasy constellations which pertain to the therapist. In such a
situation, we would, of course, offer an interpretation of a transference resistance. I have presented one such intervention, and will
offer another one at this point. Remember, I am not saying that
this is the intervention I would offer to the patient; I would most
likely respond far more transversally. I would want to take into
account both my own contributions as validly perceived (nontransference resistances) and the patient's responsive distortions and
extensions into pathological fantasies (transference resistances).

In any case, as a model, we could say to the patient that he began
the session by describing a powerful need to be late and that there
was also a long period of silence. He then went on to talk about his
situation with Betty and to touch upon his feelings about being left
by her early in the morning, his reluctance to leave her apartment,
his inability to lock up, and his urgent need for her help. Earlier,
he had spoken of how something just took him away from the
session, how ridiculous everything seemed, and how he was delayed talking to someone. In the main, leaving and being left seems
to be central, in some way to be connected to treatment, and seems
to have something to do with both his lateness and his silence.

I might have developed this particular intervention as a silent
intervention; I would probably have included something that would
have implied that he might have been responding to my having
been late as well. This is, in a sense, a transversal interpretation in
that it leaves room for contributions from both the patient and
therapist, and from transference and nontransference. It leans toward the transference contribution to the gross behavioral resistances, while saying virtually nothing about the communicative
resistances. In that respect, it would be difficult to say to the patient
at this point that these same factors prompt him to avoid clearer
expressions of the issues within treatment that are setting him off.
The closest I come to that in this intervention is pointing out that
leaving and being left is a major influence at the present time.
There is, as far as I can tell, for the moment no clear representation
of the communicative resistances, and the interpretation has had to
concentrate on the behavioral resistances. Nonetheless, this work

should lead toward either a modification in the communicative resistances, or material which would permit their interpretation.

I hope that you all felt that the intervention was quite sketchy, very tentative, and weak. Remember, the patient's communicative resistances are the key factor and they are based in part on an unmodifiable pending break in the frame—the forced termination. In that light, if the material did not become clearer, I might have offered this intervention as a way of letting the patient know that I can appreciate the issues which are leading to his acting out and his resistances. It is this type of effort that I would characterize as a preliminary interpretation, offered with a full recognition of its tentative qualities, but presented to the patient as a way of helping him to understand his battle against treatment and the therapist, and to realize that the therapist himself is in touch with the issues. This sense of being understood, of incorporating a positive introject, often motivates a patient to modify communicative resistances and to express himself more clearly. This is one way of strengthening the communicative alliance and of fostering a sound sense of trust.

Clinical sensitivities and judgment would be a major factor in the final decision to intervene. The issue is whether we intervene in the face of major communicative resistances, with a well-disguised representation of a critical adaptive context and indicator, and a moderately clear and coalescible derivative network. As I think about it, I would opt for intervening primarily because the indicator involves a major break in the fixed frame which is undoubtedly impairing the communicative qualities of the bipersonal field. Were it not for this factor, I would allow the patient to work out some of his communicative resistances on his own before I would intervene. Since the unmodifiable deviation creates conditions under which this is unlikely, a preliminary interpretation of this kind is called for. It is a type of interpretation which is best reserved for special circumstances of this kind.

As you can see, the decision in respect to intervening in the presence of major communicative resistances is often complicated. You must weigh the state of the framework, and be prepared to intervene more frequently when there is a break in the frame. In addition, whenever there is a major resistance, communicative or

behavioral, if the derivative network permits any measure of interpretation, it is well to do so rather than wait.

As for the timing, I would have been waiting for a fresh bridge to
therapy. Lacking that, a particularly cogent derivative would have
served quite well. In its absence, at the point at which the story
trailed off, I might have waited for the next derivative in the hope
of something fresh, and failing that, might have then intervened
anyhow. I want to allow sufficient time for the patient to respond
in order to enable him to work through the interpretation in the
session and for me to observe the extent to which Type Two
derivative validation appears. I would also be able to further evaluate the intensity of the patient's resistance in light of my intervention.

Finally, since we have not integrated a full consideration of the
maturational object relationship dimension of this material into
our discussion, allow me to introduce several comments. A pending
forced termination implies a parasitism of the patient by the therapist, largely because of its distinctly exploitative and self-serving
attributes. In a clinic setting with many framework deviations, it
quite likely shifts the primary level of object relatedness from that
of pathological symbiosis to parasitism.

While the material is not conclusive in this regard, the hour may
well have a parasitic quality in that the patient has disturbed, and
did not in general gratify, the therapist. A relationship with a
social worker at this center speaks for some type of pathological
symbiotic tie to the therapist in two ways: first, as a derivative
means of representing some of the qualities of the pathological
relatedness between the two members of this therapeutic dyad, and
second, as an actual, probably pathological, substitute for the
therapist who is leaving. For the moment, we must take these as
silent hypotheses in need of Type Two derivative validation.

Perhaps the clearest quality to this material on a developmental
object relationship level is the patient's derivative representation of
his failure to achieve relative autonomy and individuation, and of
a pathological symbiosis as conveyed by the need to stay in bed and
then panic about locking the apartment, needing the social worker
to assist him. There are clear infantile qualities to these representations and behaviors, and these derivatives could be mentioned
when the therapist eventually intervened, though for the moment

their specific connections to the treatment situation have not been fully defined.

Therapist: In the session, he went on to say that all of this must have somethig to do with his neurosis. (I don't know where he picked up this term.) He said, I have the feeling that this is important. But I can't, for the life of me, figure out what the heck is going on. At this point, he shifted and went back to ruminate again about his coming late to his session.

Langs: As you can see, the shift is uninformative and does not help. I would have intervened at that particular point, for the reasons I have already stated.

Therapist: At this point, he himself made the connection between somehow being late and getting out of bed and now being late in coming to see me. He said, I don't mind being on time, but there's something about having to get up early and having to get here early, something which I don't like at all.

Langs: I just want to call to your attention the patient's effort at Type One derivative formulation or self-interpretation. This is quite common and many therapists will join their patients in this type of relatedness, effecting what is often a mutually satisfying form of pathological symbiosis. Incidentally, virtually all self-analytic work undertaken by patients within their sessions is on a manifest content or Type One derivative level. As I mentioned, it is my impression that these efforts, undertaken within a secure frame, enable these patients to soften their lie-barrier systems to a point where they are far more flexible and adaptive. Clearly, they cannot arrive at the truth as we have defined it, since they do not attempt to deal with prevailing intervention contexts.
Our time is almost up. Is there much more to this session?

Therapist: Yes, a good deal more.

Langs: Then we can stop now, and ask you to complete the presentation next week. Any final comments?

Discussant: I notice that you did not get into any psychodynamic issues in your intervention.

Langs: That's an astute observation. In our discussion, I certainly should have alluded to certain possibilities, though in all likelihood I would not have done so in commenting to the patient. Do you have something in mind?

Discussant: In being late, he's indicating he'd rather stay with the girls. There must be some homosexual issue here. He was also afraid to talk to the janitor. He's afraid to talk to his male therapist. Something in that area.

Discussant: I also felt that he was late because he didn't want to be seen by people he knew that attend the conference with the therapist. I saw the anxiety related to confidentiality. He didn't want to get out of bed because he didn't want to be seen by the woman in Betty's apartment.

Discussant: But there too he was protecting himself against possible sexual fantasies.

Langs: I have been examining the general topic of communication from a psychoanalytic viewpoint. I have come to realize that it is far easier, cognitively and emotionally, to understand and formulate direct meanings and obvious inferences—Type One derivatives—than Type Two derivatives related to adaptive contexts. The literature abounds in such efforts, books for the lay public are filled with them, and patients and therapists work with each other in that way day in and day out. In line with this, it seems relatively easy, once you learn this type of decoding, to detect indications of the patient's homosexual fantasies and anxieties—inferences which I think are quite pertinent in this material.

But there is something else. When it comes to emotional communication, expressions pertinent to neurosis, we have to search for indirect and convoluted expressions. Direct inferences are simply not enough. And all too often, they can serve as lie barriers to the more threatening convoluted implications of a particular set of associations.

I say this because our discussant has offered a Type One derivative formulation stated entirely in terms of the intrapsychic dynamics of the patient, without any allusion to an activated adaptive context. This formulation is interesting and well stated, and no doubt has some degree of validity as another transference factor in the patient's lateness and silence.

However, we must recognize the presence of two adaptive contexts: the therapist's lateness and the pending forced termination. And we must take into account the me/not-me interface in listening to this material. We must be prepared to suggest that the therapist's participation in the forced termination is viewed by the patient, rightly or wrongly, on an unconscious level as a flight from homosexual anxieties in his relationship with the patient. More particularly, we must recognize that the patient unconsciously perceived the therapist's lateness and his own need to stay with the group in his office as a defense against homosexual fantasies and anxieties. Whatever the contribution from the patient to that particular perception and unconscious belief, there is strong reason to suspect that it has valid elements. Here too we are operating within a limited field of knowledge, and it may well be that the nature of the therapist's other interventions have given the patient considerable support for that particular hypothesis.

Thus, the theme of lingering with a woman postulated as a defense against homosexual fantasies and anxieties must be applied to both therapist and patient, and to the therapist before the patient. The homosexual constellation is both perceptive and fantasied, and contributes as a source of the patient's resistances derived from both himself and the therapist.

Because there is only a single derivative in this area, I would have not included that particular dynamic implication in my initial intervention. To do so might increase the patient's resistances rather than decrease them. On the other hand, avoidance could also increase the patient's resistances since it communicates from the therapist a wish to be protected in this area—another illustration of how interactional resistances are unconsciously designed to protect the therapist. Perhaps the best compromise would have been to include a passing reference to the fact that the patient had delayed coming to the session because he had been talking with a young woman. This might suffice as a compromised way of alluding to that particular derivative without overly threatening the patient. Much would depend on the point reached in treatment, the type of work done previously, and my impression of the importance of that particular derivative. As for the latter, I must stress that, upon reflection, I would have to view it as extremely important since it is a major expression of instinctual drive related conflicts and perceptions. If I had omitted this association and its implications in my silent formulation, and had detected its absence, I would have taken that observation as an indication of some type of counter-transference difficulty and engaged in a period of self-analysis. Therefore, not including it in my proposed silent intervention has to be seen in similar terms, and I fully accept your having pointed out this particular omission to me.

It is important to move beyond general framework issues to recognize how they involve specific unconscious fantasies, perceptions, conflicts, and such, which do indeed relate to instinctual drive expressions. In the past I often have identified this area when omitted in interventions of therapists and analysts, and in some small way I have illustrated this type of error in my own proposed intervention. It is critical to be sensitive to the existence of such derivatives, however well disguised, and to at least consciously formulate them as a basis for deciding whether to include them in intervening. In principle, if the patient's additional derivatives permit, a specific interpretation of underlying homosexual fantasies and perceptions as a contributing factor to the patient's lateness and silences should be made.

As long as you maintain your intervention at the level at which the patient has expressed himself, using a derivative of this kind is a way of showing the patient that you can metabolize and interpret such material, and that he should feel free to more clearly express himself in this regard so as to work through both the perceptive and distorted aspects. As I indicated, I might allude to the patient's having lingered with a girl rather than coming to my office, much as he had lingered in bed in the presence of a young woman. The derivatives are rather weak, yet crucial. They offer the most compelling dynamic expressions in respect to the patient's resistances. Certainly, in order to interpret fully, it would be necessary to refer to these instinctual drive derivatives.

A complete interpretation would include a direct reference to the indicators; an allusion to the best expression, however disguised, of the prevailing intervention contexts; and a playback of derivatives which would include the instinctual drive expression we are now discussing. This would address one important unconscious fantasy-perception constellation filled with dynamic import which is serving as a source of the patient's resistances. The intervention would imply that because of unconscious perceptions of unresolved homosexual anxieties and fantasies within the therapist, and because of comparable anxieties and fantasies within the patient, it has been necessary for the patient to be late to his session, to linger with a woman, and to establish a series of communicative resistances designed to protect both himself and the therapist from expressions in this area. As you can see, this instinctual drive conflict involves both perceptions and fantasies, and is an unconscious motivating factor in both the gross behavioral and communicative resistances. No interpretation could be viewed as complete without at least touching upon these derivatives. They are also the only available instinctual drive expressions related to the pathological symbiosis and parasitism we have postulated to exist between this patient and therapist, and would therefore deserve mention when interpreting in this area too.

Your point also raises the issue as to how to deal with such material early in therapy. The principle of not intervening or omitting allusions to particular derivatives might be invoked by some therapists. As I mentioned quite early in this section of the course, my own clinical experience is so limited in this area, and the criteria of validation so difficult to evaluate, that my impressions remain tentative, and my opinion keeps changing a bit. At present, I am inclined to believe that it is preferable to touch lightly upon such derivatives in an intervention, rather than to omit them. While even the most indirect allusion can frighten the patient, avoiding such derivatives is also threatening. I think it is best to carefully show the patient that you have heard his derivative communications and are prepared to deal with them, rather than implying a need for avoidance. With sufficient tact and discretion, I think now that the best approach is to include such derivatives, no matter how threatening or primitive, and to do so on the level at which the patient has presented the material. It is my impression that the communication of such derivatives is a sign that the patient is prepared to deal with the relevant intrapsychic and interpersonal issues, as long as his defenses are respected. The use of a light touch appears best at all times, especially early in treatment. I particularly object to therapists who are fearful of touching upon such derivatives early in therapy when they are quite clearly expressed in the patient's material. I believe this to be a countertransference-based anxiety rather than a valid approach. As Gill (1979) in particular has pointed out, a common failing among analysts involves not interpreting early transference (i.e., relationship) resistances in light of available material. The communicative approach actually fosters such interventions and renders such interpretations especially cogent and useful to the patient as a way of resolving initial gross behavioral and communicative resistances. They should be used to the fullest extent possible.

One final exercise: What is the patient's commentary on the therapist's intervention?

Discussant: The patient is not going to take responsibility. Perhaps he felt like a little boy because of the intervention.

Discussant: Perhaps he saw something seductive in the therapist's comment, or perhaps he experienced it as a defense against underlying homosexuality.

Langs: Yes, along the me/not-me interface, the intervention reflects the therapist's wish to deny his partial responsibility for the patient's silence and lateness. It also treats the patient as a child, reprimanding him and holding him accountable entirely for what he has done. There could also be something potentially seductive in the intervention; or it could serve as an expression of, and defense against, underlying homosexual countertransferences and transferences. The sense of penetration may, on the other hand, have stirred up homosexual fantasies within the patient.

Discussant: I think the patient also detected the sense of discomfort in the therapist. He describes a situation where he felt uncomfortable, was afraid of having sexual fantasies, and therefore hid and withdrew. The intervention may have had such qualities for the patient.

Langs: Yes, these are all seemingly valid unconscious perceptions. There is almost an unconscious interpretation from the patient to the therapist, to the effect that he is uncomfortable alone with the patient in his silence because of unconscious homosexual stirrings. Undoubtedly, the patient shares these with the therapist, but for the moment the derivative interpretation is offered mainly to the therapist and less so by the patient to himself.

Discussant: There is also the fear that someone will get into the apartment. This could reflect the fear of penetration or a sense of having been penetrated by the therapist's confrontation.

Langs: Yes, and notice too that the patient, through the comments of his girlfriend when he went to see her, holds up to the therapist a model of a good intervention. Through derivatives, he advises the therapist to take it easy, to slow things down, and to realize that they can manage, that nothing so terrible will happen. There is someone available who can lock the door, a possible derivative reference to the supervisor. With a bit of control and patience, the situation can be managed.

In respect to intervening, it would not be possible for the therapist to comment on these derivative bits of advice, since the patient has not clearly represented the adaptive context of his intervention. He did come back to the subject of his lateness, but this constituted only a weak bridge to therapy. In the area of the adaptive context of the therapist's last intervention, there are strong resistances regarding the representation of the context itself, though the derivatives have some measure of meaning. Under these circumstances, the best intervention by the therapist would be to silently understand the derivative implications of the patient's material and accept his advice, conveying implicitly appreciation of the patient's therapeutic efforts by correcting the disturbing qualities of the work.

Discussant: I sense also that the patient is reacting to interventions in the previous hour. As you said, without knowing much about the session, we are missing some important adaptive contexts.

Langs: Yes, that is why I hope to get through this session in order to establish a context for the therapist's presentation of the following hour. Since it has come up so often, do you recall anything about the hour prior to the one you are now presenting to us?

Therapist: Yes, I had been quite active in the hour. It was really a verbal onslaught on my part. I had been trying to show him ways in which he was acting out certain kinds of needs and certain indirect ways he had of expressing anger. I think there was validity to my view of his behaviors, but the way it came out in the session, I found it rather stilted and forced. I was far too attacking.

Langs: Well, on your own, you could organize the material up to this point in the hour in the adaptive context of your confronting and hostile interventions. In essence, we could see that the patient experienced them as senseless, that his lateness was an attempt to protect himself from your onslaught, and that staying in bed was an expression of his need for safety in the light of your hostility, and perhaps, on some level, seductiveness. The homosexual implications take on strong aggressive overtones, and we can better understand the patient's dread of penetration—he had already experienced some rather destructive and penetrating interventions in the previous hour. His silence too was an effort to protect himself from further attacks.

In this light, the patient's behavioral resistances take on strong interactional implications as defensive and communicative responses to your hostile confrontations. And you can see that the patient does not represent very clearly the adaptive context of your excessive interventions in the prior hour. In fact, the greatest level of communicative resistance in his material is in this area. At best, it is portrayed in his overanxious flight to his girlfriend and in his fear that someone would break into the apartment. In this light, we could use the general bridge to therapy to point out to the patient that whatever has stimulated his lateness and silence, it also has to do with the sense of someone being out of control and of someone in danger. However, you can, I hope, experience the weakness of that representation and the intervention we derive from it, and recognize the major resistances which the therapist's countertransference-based interventions have evoked.

In general, a significant proportion of high-level communicative resistances derive in major ways from countertransference-based interventions by the therapist. A smaller proportion of such resistances arise in the presence of the offer by the therapist of a secure therapeutic environment which evokes intense dread and anxiety in the patient.

Discussant: To clarify a point I would like to resolve, would you say that we are observing a Type A field?

Langs: Yes. The gross behavioral and communicative resistances we have been discussing today are being worked over by the patient within a Type A communicative mode. The therapist's only intervention to this point had qualities of both the Type B and Type C mode, but the patient did not accept the Type C barriers offered by the therapist and continued to express himself with moderately strong resistances of the derivative type. That is, it is possible not only to formulate the unconscious basis for these resistances, but also to find expressions of their sources, meanings, and functions. These are derivative rather than non-derivative (Type C) defenses and resistances. There is decipherable, disguised meaning. It formed the basis for our silent interventions and created the potential for interpretive work. If the patient had been using the Type C mode, it would have been far more difficult, even impossible, to formulate a tentative interpretation.

We will look forward to hearing the balance of this session next week. Thank you.

Chapter Six

THE PARTIALLY
CORRECT INTERPRETATION

Discussant: We usually start with some clinical material, but I wonder if I could begin today with a question. As I have been listening, it seems to me that you are making two major points about how we should study an intervention after we have made it. Both are done through our subjective reactions and an evaluation of the patient's subsequent material. One area has to do with dynamic issues, the unconscious meaning and functions of our intervention, its communicative style and such. The other has to do with whether the intervention is valid. And it is there that I have a question.

I will admit that it's a strange way of looking at the problem, and that I may sound a bit radical, but I wonder if it is really necessary to look for validity in the patient's responses. In other words, shouldn't we be so sure of any intervention that we make that there's no need to look for validity? In that case, all we would have to do is examine the patient's response and the dynamics of that response, and do our work from there.

I've always assumed, as you have taught us, that we should look for validity. But then I thought about the way I work. I have found that I go over an intervention that I will make, and decide that there is a good fit, and then make the intervention. My entire approach to the patient's reactions to those interventions is a study of the dynamics of his response. In actual practice, I never really look over that reaction in order to determine the validity of what I have said.

If I ever feel I really made a mistake in terms of my understanding, as you say, of the adaptive context and how the patient is responding to it in terms of the derivatives he is presenting, have made a mistake in judgment, I usually recognize that on my own and not based on the patient's material. I discover it because I look at the timing of the intervention, the reasons I intervened, and I take a close look at myself as to why I responded as I did to the patient's material. That's usually where I go, rather than looking at the patient's associations for the validity of what I have said.

Discussant: I have had some questions in the same area. Basically, I now monitor my own interventions and the patient's responses on two levels. On one level, I do listen more now for derivative comments on the intervention, and carry that over into the following session. But there is also a sense of belief and passive acceptance that occurs, that makes you believe this is right, and that you have put things together quite well. And then it becomes a question of how well the belief is maintained in the patient's communications. But I see that aspect on a different level, one that has nothing to do with the particular contents, or even with the derivatives that are being expressed by the patient. Somehow, it's the feeling tone of the session that tells you whether you are on the right course.

Discussant: As I understand it, Dr. Langs, it would be your assumption that the interpretation always becomes the primary adaptive context for the patient and he is necessarily going to respond to it. You also postulate that the patient is able unconsciously to validate or invalidate what's been said. You assume that the patient's unconscious—if I may put it that way—is not going to lie. And I'm not so sure about that. I see it as an empirical question. What appears to be validation could be nonvalidation and vice versa.

Langs: I agree right off that these are all empirical questions. I have tried throughout this course to document the basis for my formulations of a patient's material, and to always do so through Type Two derivative validation. I may not have provided you with data which is convincing beyond reasonable question, or your questions may reflect uncertainties about your own clinical work and observations. Whatever their source, I think they are representative of questions which many therapists would raise.

To respond briefly, it seems to me that your last point, that validation may actually constitute nonvalidation, reflects the chaos that would follow if we lack specific criteria of validation—a chaos I believe exists in most therapeutic situations. You may be referring here to conscious agreement, the type of response upon which most of the sparse literature on this subject is based. I therefore must remind you that I have defined validation quite carefully in the listening part of this course (Langs 1978), and have done so in terms of derivative responses—Type Two derivative validation— which reveal entirely unexpected fantasies or facts which give new meaning and order to previously disorganized and uncertain material.

Your statement that a sense of certainty in the therapist should constitute a kind of proof that an intervention is correct reflects the conscious and unconscious attitude I have found among many therapists and analysts. I referred to this earlier as the narcissistic investment in our interventions, and would consider your statement representative of an inappropriate or pathological form of that narcissism—a sort of grandiosity not uncommon in the field.

I would be less concerned if you indicated that you had made careful efforts at silent, Type Two derivative validation before offering an intervention, but still not accept that as sound. It seems self-evident that empirical validation must ultimately be based on the actual offer of an intervention to the patient, and on an in-depth assessment of his reactions. Your comments suggest that the correctness of an intervention need not matter, that what really counts is the dynamics of the patient's responsive communication. You seem to be touching upon the so-called therapeutic work with Type One derivatives in which purported dynamics inherent to the patient's associations are inferred from the material without any consideration of an adaptive context. Recently, a senior analyst reviewed a paper of mine, and could not in the very least understand the distinction between Type One and Type Two derivatives. I mention this because it is very easy to slip into Type One derivative formulations, and to develop implications which are divorced entirely from the patient's associations. This is quite common today, and it lacks the interactional qualities and understanding I have been teaching you.

Your subjective evaluation of an intervention has meaning and can be helpful. Analysts who question their own work have tended to restrict themselves to this sphere. This level of reassessment is clearly chancy, especially so when you are comfortable with an intervention and when the countertransference constellation has influenced your basic attitudes toward the patient and manner of formulating and intervening—your basic style of working. There are many expressions of unconscious countertransference constellations which go unnoticed by therapists and analysts because they are inherently a part of their character structure and approach to therapy. Without careful monitoring of the patient's material, there is almost no conceivable way that such therapists could identify these problems.

In addition, if you assume that your intervention is correct, you will view regressions, direct objections and contradictions, a lack of elaboration in the material, and other disruptions as signs of resistance, sometimes constituting negative therapeutic reactions. The literature on the latter topic entirely lacks psychoanalytic criteria of validation on which to base the formulation of a subsequent paradoxical regressive response to a correct intervention. And since the validity of the intervention is so crucial to that type of formulation, the total lack of comment on the issue of validity reflects a broader disregard of this problem among therapists and analysts.

It was entirely through empirical observation that I began to realize that the patient's derivative communications are a resource of commentary on the therapist's interventions, including their precision and usefulness. In all innocence, I thought that this resource would be immediately welcomed and established as important to the validating process. But resistances and questions inevitably arise, and, as we see today, clinical proof must be repeated again and again.

Freud, in his paper on constructions in psychoanalysis (1937), adopted a rather loose attitude to the question of validation: a denial by the patient could be appropriate or defensive, and erroneous interventions tend to affect the patient like water off a duck's back. I think that I have clearly established in this course that this is simply not the case: erroneous interventions constitute dynamic inputs which patients consciously and unconsciously work over in many ways.

If I were to characterize my own clinical observations, I would state my conclusions this way. On an unconscious level, through derivatives, a patient will virtually always find some way of confirming and elaborating correct interventions, and of contradicting and indicating the failings in an incorrect intervention. There will also virtually always be an expression of a positive introject with a correct intervention, and of a negative introject with an incorrect one. My formulations in this area were developed when I found that I was able to evaluate the correctness of an intervention, and its unconscious implications, in a way that led to a conscious statement which was consistently supported in remarkable and usually self-evident ways in the patient's derivative communications. On that basis, it proved possible to learn to rely on the patient's derivative commentary.

By and large, we must realize that the patient's derivative communications virtually always speak to the truth rather than lies. Why should this be? Certainly, I have seen unconscious misperceptions; it is possible for a patient to create derivative misrepresentations. However, these are extremely rare reactions, often to a therapist's efforts to secure the framework, endeavors which threaten the patient and prompt this type of defensive reaction.

Some of the confusion in this area comes from the observation that, under emotional stress and in the presence of disturbances in the holding environment, virtually all patients shift to Type Two derivative communication, and make use of the Type A communicative mode—however temporarily. This seems to express their wish to understand and master the truth. And yet, once the truth is interpreted to them, patients differ in their responses. Some offer extended Type Two derivative validation of the rectifications of the frame and interpretations involved, and extend the therapeutic work considerably in the direction of truth-seeking. Others offer a brief and immediate form of Type Two derivative validation, but quickly shift to the Type C mode and to the use of lie-barrier formations. Both consciously and through derivatives, they protest against their own and their therapist's quest for the truth, and their material will obstruct further pursuits in this direction.

As I have said before, there is an overwhelming amount of clinical evidence to indicate that on an unconscious level a patient knows and appreciates the ideal therapeutic environment, just as he knows and appreciates a valid intervention. The former seems to have something to do with basic human and nurturing needs, perhaps some need for a healthy form of symbiosis which may well provide the only soil which can support growth. As for the latter, the patient may unconsciously sense qualities of fit, explanatory power, insightfulness, momentary relief, conflict resolution, modifications of pathological introjects, and a variety of processes which which account for his sensitivity to issues of validity. It seems to me that it will require careful scrutiny of many responses to interventions in order to determine the specific unconscious sensitivities and capabilities which account for these clinical observations.

Discussant: I want to make clear that there are times when I realize that I have made a mistake. But I do that during, or more usually after a session, when I begin to ask myself why I made the intervention and whether it was really based on what the patient was saying. And I ask myself if I have intervened because of some need of my own, or some problems I have been working through. But the examination comes through self-scrutiny rather than from the patient.

Langs: Yes, I understand. But I see no inherent reason why you should limit yourself to self-scrutiny. Why not make use of the patient's direct and especially derivative communications? Throughout this course, I have tried to show you the rich resource involved, and I will not repeat my arguments here. In principle, it seems to make considerable sense to make use of all possible resources.

Discussant: You have given me a sobering perspective on much that I read and on a good deal of my supervision. The assumption always seems to be that an intervention, especially if it comes from a senior analyst, is inherently correct. And now, I have begun to wonder about that assumption. It smacks of autocracy. The patient can never be right, only the therapist. And I realize too that many patients submit to therapists of that kind, gratifying their masochistic needs and whatever else. It really raises serious questions about the field of psychotherapy for me.

Discussant: How often do you feel your interventions with your own patients are not validated? I'll tell you why I ask. It sounds like you feel that using the adaptive context and the communicative approach will lead to a clinical situation in which most of your interventions are validated.

Langs: Exactly. This has been borne out in my own personal work and in the efforts of supervisees who have successfully applied these principles. We all obtain a very high incidence of indirect, Type Two derivative validation, in both the cognitive and interactional spheres.

In this connection, I should state explicitly that communicative therapy, if I may call it that, is highly effective. It requires securing the therapeutic environment which, for all patients, is *implicitly* supportive and ego-enhancing, and depriving of pathological symbiotic satisfaction. The subsequent interpretive work carried out in the course of such therapy provides the patient with specific insights and adaptive resources with which to resolve specific unconscious conflicts and introjective disturbances as a basis for the adequate resolution of their neurosis. It creates implicit pressures toward individuation and mature relatedness.

In this context, I would like to share with you some recent initial observations on the course of communicative therapy. It is my belief that they raise some new and important questions about the nature of psychotherapy, its duration, and the sticky issue of the differences, if any, in what is accomplished through psychotherapy as compared to psychoanalysis.

As far as I can tell, there are two major reasons patients make use of the Type A communicative mode and risk anxiety and disturbance, the loss of symbiotic ties, and the exposure of the psychotic parts of the personality—of course, all in the service of true growth and adaptive symptom resolution. The first is the presence of acute emotional symptoms and conflicts, and the second is any modification in the basic therapeutic and holding aspects of the therapeutic relationship and environment created by either patient or therapist. Many patients enter therapy with an acute emotional disturbance and express themselves initially in the Type A communicative mode. In good hands, they do so largely around the therapist's efforts to secure the framework and mature relatedness. In this way they express their own unconscious needs through actual attempts to generate modifications in the frame and to establish a particular level of pathological relatedness. This expresses critical therapeutic needs within the patient, and provides opportunity for specific relationship responses (e.g., maintaining the ground rules) and interpretations organized around the intervention contexts related to the therapist's handling of the framework issue and the patient's derivative responses.

To follow the course of therapy with this group, what appears to happen next is that there is eventually an experience of some measure of symptomatic relief. The acute symptoms quiet down and more chronic or subacute difficulties, if they exist, continue to find expression. With the crisis over and the frame and relationship now secured, these patients settle into therapy and shift to the Type C communicative mode. In this way, they ask of the therapist only that he be present and maintain the therapeutic environment. They then engage in free association and in direct self-interpretive efforts. Virtually all of these endeavors take the form of Type One derivative interpretations. Much of this occurs in this form because there is no acute break in the frame, no sudden satisfaction of pathological symbiotic needs, and the therapist is not, for the moment, making errors in intervening. He is holding the patient, as he must be held, and containing whatever is being communicated, though not responding with active interventions since none are called for. He is, on an object relations level, offering a healthy, growth-promoting form of symbiosis. If we term the opening phase of such a therapy the crisis phase and recognize its characteristic Type A communicative mode, we could term the second phase the quiet or lying fallow period and accept the Type C communicative mode as characteristic.

The self-interpretations which the patient offers himself during the quiet phase, since they are not based on a conscious realization of an intervention context or on Type Two derivative understanding, actually constitute the generation of lie-barrier systems. This had led me to reexamine lie-barrier formations, and to discover, not surprisingly, that some of these obliterating defenses are quite rigid and pathological—hard and maladaptive—while others are quite soft, serviceable, and touch upon the underlying truths or are less rigidly and pathologically maintained.

It seems clear now that all human beings need at times to make use of flexible lie-barrier systems, and that they cannot tolerate too great or too extended exposure to the emotional truth as activated by meaningful adaptive contexts. Lie-barrier systems, as is true of derivative defenses, can be pathological or relatively healthy. In the light of these considerations, I would not even assume that derivative defenses are healthier than lie-barrier defenses. Instead, it now seems to me that both are necessary, and that each can be relatively pathological and maladaptive or healthy and adaptive. The nature of the trauma and of circumstances, the patient's mode of relating and his basic communicative propensities—among many other factors—appear to determine which type of defense is used at a particular moment.

In any case, during the middle or quiet phase of therapy, the therapist's responsibility is to not intervene, to provide a holding-containing mode of relatedness for the patient, and to afford him an opportunity to modify his pathological lie-barrier systems. Most patients appear to make very good use of this situation, and show considerable additional symptomatic improvement—including characterological and behavioral changes—during this phase.

At times, there is an intrapsychic or interpersonal disturbance which creates an acute therapeutic need within the patient. You will find that at such junctures, he will make an effort to modify the framework or evoke a noninterpretive intervention. This conveys both his mobilized wish for pathological symbiotic gratification and his need for deeper understanding. Depending on his response—whether he holds the frame and frustrates the symbiotic wish or deviates and gratifies it—the therapist's reaction is taken as the intervention context for the patient's responsive derivative communications. It is then necessary to offer an interpretation of this constellation in terms of the prevailing indicators and intervention context, and of the patient's derivative material. If the therapist has deviated, rectification is also necessary. Based on the insight and positive introjects generated in this way, the patient soon returns to the holding therapeutic work of this phase.

Of course, the quiet period can also be disturbed by counter-transference needs within the therapist. Most often, this leads to an erroneous intervention, a context which the patient then works over until the situation is rectified and interpreted. Sometimes the patient shows little derivative response to the therapist's vacations during this period; however, in patients sensitive to separation issues, this experience will serve as an important intervention context and lead to interpretable derivative networks.

In all, after a period of some months—in total, perhaps a year or two—most of these patients will begin to consider termination through passing thoughts and derivative communications. When, in light of some intervention context, the therapist interprets the patient's wish to terminate and some of the derivative implications, there will usually be a shift for a while to the Type A communicative mode. We can term this the acute phase of termination, and it usually lasts several months, during which the patient from time to time responds meaningfully to the anticipated intervention context of the end of treatment. The rest is spent in Type C communication with continued Type One derivative self-interpretations.

This is, I believe, a relatively typical course of therapy with a communicative psychotherapist. Some of these patients, after mastering the acute opening phase of therapy, will leave treatment. It is their preference not to work over the residual and now quiet psychotic part of the personality and other unconscious fantasy-memory constellations and conflicts, nor do they wish to deal with further issues in object relating. They prefer to accept the immediate gains and carry the therapeutic work no further. Other patients settle so strongly into the secure environment and therapeutic symbiosis with the therapist that they show little inclination to give it up. They have established an equilibrium which depends upon the therapist and his capacity to maintain the holding-containing (healthy symbiotic) mode of relatedness, and are reluctant to risk the acute turmoil of the termination phase. However, in light of relevant intervention contexts, these anxieties can be interpreted in terms of derivative responses. This enables these patients to enter the acute termination phase and work through their reactions to the end of therapy.

With respect to entering treatment, the Type C and Type B communicators approach therapy somewhat differently from the Type A communicator. The Type C group includes those patients who do not show an acute initial disturbance and enter therapy primarily because of some external circumstance or because of a deep but readily concealed concern about maintaining their equilibrium and lie-barrier systems. These patients have effective and rigid defenses against the psychotic part of their personality, and against other acute intrapsychic and interpersonal disturbances. They begin treatment as Type C communicators, readily accept the holding environment and relationship, and settle into the quiet phase of therapy—often for extended periods. Only from time to time will they generate a framework issue on their own. Even with termination, only a small number of these patients become acutely disturbed and shift to Type A communication, and the rest do so only sparingly. As a result, their therapeutic gains—remarkably, these are often quite extensive—are derived from efforts at self-analysis through Type One derivative self-interpretations, which enable them to soften their lie-barrier systems. When these efforts involve derivative lies, it is my impression that some of the unconscious fantasy, memory, and introject systems are also modified. Nonetheless, this is not done directly, and the truth of the ongoing communicative interaction and of the patient's neurosis is seldom consciously realized. On the object relationship level, they seem content with the therapeutic symbiosis and eventually appear to mature.

The third group of patients include all Type B communicators. There are two subgroups here. Both are difficult and highly disturbing for the therapist. The first is the Type B–A patient, who enters therapy in a somewhat agitated state. He makes powerful efforts to modify the framework and otherwise projectively identify into the therapist much of his own inner turmoil and of the agitated, poorly defended psychotic core with which he is struggling. Surprisingly, many of these patients actually function rather well in business, but characteristically they do so only at the expense of others since they are engaged in extensive projective identifications—dumping, riddance, and such. They relate in intensely symbiotic and parasitic ways as well. Some of them are psychopathic and prone to living out. Some show little agitation and, instead, reveal passing hints of underlying vulnerability through neurotic delusions, highly rigid defenses, and an overriding need to effect an intensely pathological symbiotic or parasitic mode of relatedness with the therapist. Most of these patients fall into the borderline and ambulatory schizophrenic diagnostic groups, though only some show impulsivity, poor judgment, a propensity toward immediate gratification, and striking intolerance for relationship boundaries.

These are characteristics of all Type B patients. I started to describe the Type B-A patient since we must distinguish him from the Type B-C patient. All of these patients make use of dumping lie-barrier systems. All of them protect themselves from highly threatening psychotic parts of the personality. All have significant problems in object relating. As a result, they all welcome the therapist who offers a secure holding environment and healthy mode of relatedness as someone who can be trusted, and who can contain their pathological projective identifications and help them to manage internal stress. At the same time, however, such a therapist is a great threat, not only because of the mobilized envy they experience, but also because the secure therapeutic environment will create conditions of frustration and a potential for a therapeutic regression, and thwart their pathological symbiotic needs. Thus, the therapist is seen as both ally and enemy.   •

Under these conditions, the Type B-A communicator will engage in active efforts to disrupt treatment, dump into the therapist, and modify the ground rules and mode of relatedness. Simultaneously, he will represent in a meaningful manner the activated intervention contexts and provide the therapist with a relatively meaningful derivative complex. Because of the propensity of these patients toward action-discharge, the communicative network is often fragmented and incomplete. Nonetheless, these patients communicate in a manner that permits specific interpretation and which directs the therapist toward the necessary rectifications of the frame. After weeks or sometimes months of this type of interplay, the Type B–C patient eventually begins to settle down, and sometimes even shifts to the Type C communicative mode and into the quiet phase of therapy. However, as a rule, this phase will be interrupted from time to time by active efforts of pathological projective identification, often as attempts to modify the frame and disrupt treatment. In addition, it is generally more difficult for therapists to hold and contain these patients and their disturbing communications and interactional efforts; and technical errors are more frequent. Consequently, there are frequent periods of Type B–A communication, and important interpretive and management work is carried out, much of it in the context of these errors in intervening.

Eventually, these patients will enter longer quiet phases in which the agitated and intense qualities of the pathological projective identifications have lessened. However, termination will probably renew their psychopathology since they are almost universally highly sensitive to separation issues. The final phase of treatment is therefore often quite tumultuous, but nonetheless it is possible to effect a secure finish to their therapy. There are strong signs that most of these patients do quite well once they have survived the termination experience and understood how it impinges upon and stirs up the psychotic part of their personalities, their merger forms of relatedness, and their primitive dread of annihilation.

Unquestionably, the most difficult patient to enter psychotherapy is the Type B–C communicator. Characteristically, these are patients with acutely disturbing psychotic cores or with massive defenses designed to keep that core totally encased. They are often more parasitic than symbiotic. While they show derivative communications which indicate some wish to explore and resolve their basic pathology, their overwhelming need is to entirely avoid such possibilities. Even on a derivative level, these patients show an enormous terror of a secure therapeutic environment and of the truth as it exists within themselves and the therapeutic interaction. Throughout their lives, they have resorted to highly obliterating lie-barrier systems, and they wish only for the therapist to reinforce these barriers and to justify the patient's own pathological mechanisms and mode of relatedness. As a result, these patients engage in massive interactional projections, efforts to break the frame, pressures on the therapist to engage in noninterpretive measures, and attempts to compromise the treatment situation in every conceivable manner. They carry out these behaviors in sessions in which they do not clearly represent the prevailing intervention context or present a highly fragmented, virtually meaningless derivative complex. Their purpose is to destroy truth and meaning, and any significant sense of mature, communicative relatedness to the therapist. In a sense, they enter therapy only to destroy its truthful attributes and to have instead, some form of symbiotic misalliance and lie-barrier therapy.

In the absence of interpretable material, the therapist is virtually helpless in face of the onslaughts of these patients. Unconsciously, it is their intention to destroy the therapist and his interpretive and relationship capacities. They are remarkably accomplished in these efforts, and often make the therapist feel helpless and incompetent. Efforts on his part toward establishing boundaries and in generating interpretive interventions are experienced as destructive persecutions. Errant deviants and noninterpretive interventions afford the patient a malicious sense of triumph, while endeavors to silently hold and contain the patient tend to increase the conscious rage and destructive efforts. The more competent the therapist seems to be and the more capable he is in attempting to maintain a secure therapeutic situation and relationship, the more intense the patient's envy and dread, in his consequent destructive efforts.

Quite rarely these patients offer, at best, highly fragmented derivative complexes and passing representations of an intervention context. Interpretation of this material will usually lead to Type Two derivative validation. However, this is almost immediately followed by manifest denial, and intense efforts to destroy the hard-won insight and to negate its positive effects and implications.

Many of these patients will terminate therapy within the first few weeks, in part because they have been unable to destroy the therapist in any other way. They also feel that they will not survive, must take flight from, any possibility of truth therapy and of nonpathological relatedness. Nonetheless, efforts at compromise in treatment have so far failed to ameliorate this type of situation.

They simply lead the patient to experience the therapist as someone who is as sick as himself.

It is my impression that the dilemma posed by these patients is most clearly stated from the communicative approach. It remains for future clinical studies to discover whether there is some constructive way of working with more of these patients. Even though the communicative approach enables us to understand what happens with these patients, we cannot expect to keep every patient in therapy and to cure everyone who comes into our offices. Every therapeutic procedure has its limitations, and it may well be that many patients of this kind cannot be effectively helped with the communicative approach. Let's leave the matter open for future study.

Discussant: Is there any effect on these patients due to previous therapeutic experiences?

Langs: By and large, all such prior therapeutic experiences have unfolded as some form of lie therapy with considerable pathological symbiotic gratification. This tends to reinforce the patient's wish for lie-barrier systems, symbiosis, and the avoidance of the truth. As a result, it is extremely difficult to engage these patients in truth therapy. And yet, if the therapist is sensitive to the underlying issues, it may well be possible to work them through and enable the patient to accept this new approach. Lie therapy tends to reflect a fear within the therapist of the patient's inner mental world, and to reinforce the patient's comparable dread. It is symbiotically gratifying—in its pathological sense—as well. It is an attractive form of uninsightful work and leaves residua which require extensive interpreting in order to enable the patient to work with the truth.

Discussant: I have seen patients shift into some type of uncontrolled regression in response to my efforts to compromise or deviate in the face of pressures of the kind that you describe from the Type B-C communicator. I am now aware that these efforts characteristically generated negative introjects. Before now, it was easy to work on a manifest level and to rationalize such measures as

supposedly supportive and sympathetic. It was only when I began
to analyze their implications in terms of the patient's derivative
communications that I realized just how destructive I had been.

Langs: Yes. Work of that kind is based on a split within the
therapist who operates almost entirely on a manifest level, and
splits off his own and the patient's derivative communications. It
supports a comparable split in the patient. The lie-barrier systems
may either enable the patient to momentarily seal off the underlying chaos within himself and the therapist, or can evoke an
uncontrolled regression based on the negative unconscious perceptions and introjects of the therapist. Unconsciously, the patient
senses the therapist's failure to contain and hold, to effect a healthy
symbiosis, and to understand the truth. It is my impression that
many unnecessary psychiatric hospitalizations have taken place on
this basis.

Discussant: Oddly enough, I keep coming back to a point you
made in the listening part of this course. It had never dawned on
me that patients could enter therapy not wanting to understand
themselves and not wanting to achieve insight. Certainly, I knew
that some patients engaged in denial or tried to locate their own
pathology in someone else, like a spouse. But I never realized the
extent to which they wished to destroy meaningful and healthy
relatedness between themselves and me, and to not communicate in
a meaningful fashion. I was taught that associations have meaning, and it is our job to discover them.

Langs: Yes, even in situations where patients become Type A
communicators in the face of an acute disturbance or a break in the
frame, they may respond with defenses and lie barriers on the
receptive side. Truth sending is characteristic under these conditions; truth receiving is not. The patient makes a decision, unconsciously determined, whether to face and work through the truths
within himself and the therapeutic interaction, or to take flight
with obliterating lie-barrier systems. Here, too, we need a great deal
of clinical research to establish the determinants of such a decision.
Clearly, the therapist's commitment to the truth is an important
factor, but there are undoubtedly many factors within the patient,

as they exist dynamically within himself for the moment and as they have evolved from his past. One aspect involves the extent to which he can accept or tolerate nonmerger modes of relatedness.

Still, this is a choice to which every patient is entitled. The more primitive and potentially uncontrolled the psychotic part of his personality, the more he dreads separation and individuation, the more likely he is to opt for lie therapy. Some of these patients pursue the truth even in the face of intense dread and anxiety. The communicative approach offers us a means of sympathetically understanding the dilemma each patient faces. With truth comes unique adaptive resources and growth, and with lie-barrier systems come risky and usually fragile obliterating defenses and pathologically symbiotic forms of relating. Some of these can be effective and can enable a patient to function reasonably well. We must learn to respect the decision of each patient in this regard, while always helping them to understand both its unconscious basis and its full implications. Once you know something of the terror and dread associated with the truth, and its concomitant, related sense of separateness, you can work quite humbly with these patients in an effort to enable them to make the best possible decision for themselves, and can accept their solution with the best available perspective. There are fine lines to be drawn here. It is important not to support even on an unconscious level the patient's dread of the truth and separateness, and yet accept the flight taken by patients who are absolutely convinced that they will be psychologically annihilated if they attempt to deal with these problems.

Discussant: At times, I hear you saying that most patients are truth patients. At other times, I hear you saying that most patients are lie patients.

Langs: I do not as yet have sufficient clinical data to say. What I have been trying to convey is that in the face of an acute intervention context, virtually all patients are truth communicators. Once these truths have been expressed through meaningful derivatives, some patients are truth receivers and will work over and through the full implications. Other patients are lie receivers and will erect lie-barrier systems against validated truths, rather than work further with them. While at one time I felt that the vast majority of patients were lie receivers, I now have the impression that there may be something more like a fifty-fifty division.

In this connection, I want to make clear that in situations in which there are subacute and chronic symptoms, and long-standing breaks in the frame, patients will tend to fluctuate in regard to communicating meaningfully in response to these intervention contexts. As a result, there will be periods of low communicative resistance which alternate with periods of high communicative resistance. In the former situations, interpretations and rectifications are feasible; but with high communicative resistances it is important for the therapist to remain silent and to not add intervention errors to the patient's burdens.

Discussant: In these comments, I now hear you saying that there are more patients who wish to seek the truth than I believe you had indicated earlier.

Langs: Yes, my impressions continue to change as these issues are clarified. If I had to make a brief statement, it would be to the effect that in acute emotional crises, both patients and therapists—all human beings—tend to become truth senders and to some degree both truth and lie receivers. They work over the truth with meaningful derivatives, but do not permit themselves a full conscious realization of these truths—direct awareness of the adaptive context and the meanings of their derivative responses.

Discussant: Would you clarify the implications of these distinctions for our study of resistances?

Langs: I will try to respond briefly.

In developing the concept of communicative resistances, it becomes clear that we are utilizing Type Two derivative or Type A communication as the model of nonresistant expression. I believe this is a sound model, as long as we recognize certain qualifying factors. Thus, in the face of an acute intervention context, we would expect the patient to respond with a meaningful representation of the intervention context and an equally meaningful and coalescible derivative complex. Failure in either sphere would be viewed as resistance, and we would then determine whether the defenses involved were derivative defenses (resistances within the Type A communicative mode) or nonderivative, lie-barrier defenses (defenses within the Type C communicative mode).

The same criteria of resistance can be applied in respect to the patient's responses to intervention contexts which extend over several sessions or longer. There will indeed be periods of low resistance during which rectifications and interpretations are feasible, as well as periods of high resistance during which such efforts cannot be effected. A key to evaluating resistances is the ease with which material permits interventions.

The problem, as I see it, arises in the middle or quiet phase of therapy. There, by the standards of the Type A communicative mode or of Type Two derivative communication, the patient is indeed resistant. But by a variety of criteria related to therapeutic progress, the patient is making important gains. There appears to be a contradiction. Nonetheless, I believe that it can be readily resolved by recognizing that some resistances are highly adaptive, while others are essentially pathological. Or it may well be we have to redefine resistances according to the phase of therapy and the patient's therapeutic needs for the moment.

To state this in a more elaborate way, during the quiet phase, the patient seldom responds meaningfully to the intervention context of the therapist's silence or to the occasional separations which come about because of the therapist's vacations. It therefore seems reasonable to suggest the presence of resistances. However, we must evaluate what the patient is accomplishing while he is being resistant. If we recognize that this is indeed part of a quiet phase of self-interpretation, we would think of these resistances as relatively benign or nonpathological. Indeed, there are defenses in operation and the therapist experiences some type of opposition. But it appears to be a necessary opposition and period of defensiveness, rather than a primarily pathological one.

Technically, we have no choice but to accept these resistances since the patient's material does not permit their interpretation. It is my impression that pathological resistances occur in the context of acute intervention contexts and involve sessions in which the patient will soon communicate in a manner which reveals the unconscious basis and structure of the resistance. On the other hand, with nonpathological resistances there is no acute intervention context and the basis for the resistance is not revealed in the patient's associations. The therapist has no choice but to continue to hold and wait until interpretable material emerges.

Discussant: When you say that most patients and therapists appear to be lie receivers, I gather that you mean unconsciously and are not referring to conscious and deliberate lies.

Langs: Yes, I hope that is quite clear. The categorization of lie communicators and lie receivers is based on a specific definition of the lie, and entails unconscious rather than conscious lies. It refers to all efforts to depart from the truth as it is unfolding at the moment in terms of the ongoing communicative interaction. Remember, conscious lies may function as derivative truths, while statements which correspond to reality and on the surface appear truthful, may be part of lie-barrier systems.

Discussant: What happens, then, when you make a seemingly valid intervention to a lie patient? Since they are prone to unconscious lies, doesn't it follow that they will fail to validate even a correct intervention?

Langs: Your question is an excellent one. I would very much prefer to use a clinical situation of that kind in order to derive the answer. Since such a situation may not arise, I will respond briefly at the risk we are getting too far from clinical referents.

When a lie patient is utilizing the Type C communicative mode, he has virtually destroyed all meaning—i.e., all derivative meaning—in his associations. If the therapist takes up any of the contents and attempts to interpret them, he has joined the patient in his lie-barrier system and is attempting to afford meaning when none is present. The therapy becomes a sham and there is often a lie-barrier misalliance.

The only resource available to the therapist under such conditions is to interpret the patient's destruction of meaning and relatedness. This implies an interpretation of the patient's lie barriers, including indications of their presence and functions. In principle, this can only be done when the patient represents an adaptive context—even if it is the therapist's silence and his maintenance of a secure frame—and provides coalescible derivatives pertinent to the presence of the lie barriers. But, at the moment the patient does that, he has become a truth patient, and therefore permits interpretation of his previous state.

Sometimes, in the presence of highly defended representations of the adaptive context and derivative complex, there is sufficient truth to be able to interpret major lie-barrier systems. However, there are other interludes during which there are no meaningful representations of the prevailing context or of the lie-barrier system itself, and your only available intervention is silence.

My comments regarding the quiet phase of therapy should provide you with an added perspective in this regard. In a way, lie patients unconsciously communicate in a manner that requires only holding and containing, and not interpretations. They may do so for many reasons, such as their fear of the truth, their need to reinforce lie-barrier systems, or their need for a holding environment and a quiet form of symbiotic relatedness during which they can carry out self-therapeutic work. It is important to realize that lie-barrier patients are expressing some particular therapeutic need of their own. We can respect this need and interpret its meanings and functions entirely at the behest of the patient—i.e., when he is ready to explore and modify it. It is important not to be so over-committed to the truth and individuation that we lose all perspective on the patient's need for lie-barrier systems and pathological merger. There is every reason to believe that truth therapy offers more than lie therapy to all patients; but it is important to recognize the inevitability of compromises in some cases, and further, that truth therapy can be effected only when the patient himself is prepared to engage in it. Our efforts at securing the frame and in making initial interpretations are designed in part to provide the patient with the insight and capacity to relate which will enable him to engage in such therapeutic work.

Discussant: When a patient is using lie-barrier systems, why not simply confront him with his noncommunicativeness?

Langs: Because empirically, an intervention of that kind is experienced as intrusive, as a reflection of countertransferences, and as a failure by the therapist to hold and contain. As a result, it does not help the patient to resolve his lie-barrier systems; instead, it offers a lie-barrier system from the therapist which often reinforces the one used by the patient. On another level, an intervention of that kind can evoke a sadomasochistic misalliance which pathologically gratifies the patient rather than helping him to resolve his defenses.

Allow me to make another point. I have been able to demonstrate many of these tenets from the clinical material presented here. It seems to me that ideally your response should be mixed: those points which are convincing should be integrated into your thinking and should be applied in your own therapeutic work. But points about which you have some question should lead you to test out your own hypotheses. As long as you sincerely believe that you are doing the best you can for the patient, even an erroneous intervention is reasonably well tolerated; the patient unconsciously recognizes your basic sincerity and concern, even as he responds to your mistake. Sincere and dedicated efforts of that kind might lead to a personal realization that your proposed modification of the basic tenets taught here is not useful or valid, and should be discarded; on the other hand, as you try out various modifications in these basic principles, you may be able to discover techniques which have been missed up until this point and help us to solve some of the difficult problems I have identified. Many of my students have tried to adopt one modification or another with patients who present themselves with an enormous fear of a secure framework and of truth therapy. Up to this point, all of these efforts at compromise have failed. But this does not imply that we should not keep trying, or that there is no possible solution. We need such explorations, though they must not be exploitative; they must be carried out with sincerity and honest intention.

Our classification of truth patients and lie patients addresses overriding tendencies and the patient's basic attitude toward the truths of the communicative interaction. The criteria involve primarily the patient's expressive and receptive modes, far more than conscious attitudes toward treatment and the therapist. In fact, there are lie patients who consciously express their wish to understand the truth, while unconsciously destroying all semblance of truth which emerges in the communicative interchange. And there are truth patients who consciously protest against therapy, while expressing themselves meaningfully through derivatives.

In general, lie patients will from time to time express themselves truthfully, thereby permitting an interpretation which they validate through Type Two derivatives, though they quickly resume their Type C mode of communication. You must learn to expect this type of therapeutic work, and to tolerate long periods of high resistance measured by the Type A communicative mode standard. As I said before, these patients are asking only for your holding and containing capacities, and for your silent patience. They need the benefit of the therapeutic symbiosis. They do not wish for erroneous interventions and need the time to work something through within themselves, even if it is done in terms of more flexible lie-barrier systems.

Allow me to stress again that some lie-barrier systems are flexible and adaptive, while others are pathological and destructive. Certainly, there may well be a residual symptom or two, some minor characterological disturbance, and some sense of difficulty in patients who function through the use of major lie-barrier systems. But this type of nonderivative defense can be quite serviceable, and I suspect that it has always served mankind. We must be reminded again and again that truth is a superb resource but painful and difficult to utilize. Lies may be a liability, but they can also help us to get by and function effectively. In fact, it seems likely that it is only when lie-barrier systems fail or become intensely pathological that people become motivated to do something about them.

One final point. I have only recently realized that Type A patients—truth patients, if you will—virtually always express unconscious truths through derivatives of whose implications they themselves are unaware. This realization was long in coming because, as a therapist, I saw it as my role to indicate to patients those pertinent truths which they had expressed in derivative form and had not realized themselves. This of course, is the definition of an interpretation, since it always involves the implications of an activated intervention context.

I have found it extremely rare for patients to represent an adaptive context, to then communicate a meaningful derivative complex, and to then take the final step of integrating the two into a conscious realization. This almost never happens. To me, this

implies that the truth is tolerable only if expressed without awareness, and almost unbearable if expressed along with direct awareness. I mean by this the near-simultaneous derivative expression of
underlying truths, and the conscious recognition of their nature.
As a rule, the latter type of realization, if it is to occur at all, takes
place after the adaptive context is no longer active and the patient
has a sense of safety in respect to facing the true meaning of his
responsive derivative communications.

Discussant: While you are covering these subjects, I wonder if
you could get back to some further comments about the differences
and similarities between psychotherapy and psychoanalysis. When
you speak, you almost never make a distinction between the two
therapeutic modalities. And even though you have made some
comments in this respect, I keep wondering what that means.

Langs: Well, I can see that we have built up a good deal of
tension and many questions. This is something like the good and
welfare part of a business meeting. I will respect your needs, and try
to comment as briefly as possible.
Both psychotherapy and psychoanalysis are a special form of
relatedness which takes place under highly distinctive conditions
and which has an unusual and specific goal: the insightful resolution of a patient's neurotic symptoms—once again, I use neurosis in
its broadest sense. As such, the communicative interaction within the
two therapeutic modalities is highly comparable, different only to
the extent of the influence of the face-to-face mode where it is used
in psychotherapy and the lesser frequency of sessions in that particular treatment modality.
Psychoanalysis as it is practiced today is a form of lie-barrier
therapy. Our ideas about the greater effectiveness of analysis, its
ability to probe deeper, and its capacity to generate more stable
structural change than psychotherapy, will need a complete reassessment once analytic practice has shifted toward becoming a
form of truth therapy. The comparisons between psychotherapy
and psychoanalysis have, until this point, been based on lie therapy forms of both modalities.
Having now practiced truth analysis and truth therapy—to use
those terms in their narrow sense—and supervised some of each

(though primarily truth therapy), I have some new impressions. They are mainly questions that have not been asked before and tentative hypotheses that deserve investigation. I wonder, for example, whether any patient can tolerate an extended period of truth analysis. Now that I can appreciate the unbearable qualities of the truth, it is my belief that actually no one can experience its impact over too long a period of time. Connected with the ultimate realization of our own death and of highly primitive fantasies and perceptions, the anxiety would become unbearable and the psychological effects more disintegrating than integrating. Truth can be growth-promoting only in small doses and within a secure framework.

It is therefore not surprising to realize that by and large, the patients who stay in truth analysis for long periods of time are those who soon become Type C communicators, and then permit only periodic interludes of truth therapy. They benefit in the various ways from the holding-containing efforts of the therapist during this quiet phase of their analysis. They engage, as I said, in derivative and nonderivative self-interpretations which are Type One derivative in nature and therefore involve lies rather than truths. However, they often become almost addicted to the security of the therapeutic situation and to the therapeutic symbiosis involved, and they show considerable disturbance at the prospect of termination. They may then shift to an intense period of truth therapy upon which a sound ending of their analysis can be based.

Much the same applies to truth psychotherapy, though generally it is offered in smaller doses and there is the relief afforded by the one to six days between sessions. The question arises whether truth analysis does indeed probe deeper to provide the patient with more lasting adaptive resources, or whether, because the periods during which the truth is actually worked over becomes so widely spaced, much the same can be accomplished by truth psychotherapy. This is an important question for which I do not have an answer. My own impressions lead me to place far more value on truth psychotherapy than might others, and to raise serious questions as to how much more effective truth analysis actually is.

Perhaps the latter modality is best used with patients who are extremely disturbed, even suicidal, and who are willing to accept a secure therapeutic environment and to communicate in the Type A mode. These patients also have an intense underlying symbiotic need which requires *implicit* gratification as a way of helping them to stabilize, and the more frequent sessions may more readily supply them with these important holding, containing, and inherently nurturing qualities.

In any case, I now have a great respect for what can be accomplished with truth therapy. In light of the extensive cost of truth analysis, I feel that we need fresh extended empirical investigations designed to determine what additional benefits, if any, accrue under those conditions as compared to truth therapy. What I have in mind is best represented by four-times-a-week analysis and two-times-a-week therapy, though it would also be applied to analysis five times a week and therapy once a week. The latter modality is greatly underestimated in terms of its potential and what it can actually deliver when carried out as a form of truth therapy. Perhaps three times a week therapy-analysis is the best compromise.

All I ask is that we attempt to take a fresh look at these issues. As therapists and analysts, we cannot be self-serving when it comes to an evaluation of each treatment modality, its conditions and its results. As I said, I really do not as yet know the answers. There are far too many variables to develop definitive impressions in even five to six years. I think instead that if we are free enough to ask these compelling questions, we will eventually develop fresh insights, and on that basis, offer the best possible treatment modality—all things considered—to each patient.

Discussant: I am trying to sort something out. On the one hand, you are saying that most patients, given their natural tendencies, are lie patients unless they are under great stress. On the other hand, you have indicated that in response to errors by the therapist, most patients speak the truth. Is there a contradiction there?

Langs: I don't think so. As I said before, the natural lie-barrier tendency appears when the therapist is not making errors and has secured the framework. There seems to be a natural tendency to respond with the truth when there are disturbances in that environment and when the therapist is in error. Your question helps to make this point much clearer: emotionally, we lie when we feel secure, and we speak the truth when we feel disturbed. Remember, as with all of these discussions, we are talking about adaptive context and derivative responses, or their absence.

Discussant: It sounds as if there remains some question as to the percentage of patients who can actually tolerate very much in the way of truth therapy.

Langs: Yes, I have tried to outline the factors and issues involved. No patient can tolerate too much truth therapy, but many will engage in important periods during which such work is carried out both expressively and receptively. In addition, it is my belief that if the public were educated, and if therapists were educated as well, that percentage would increase considerably. As matters now stand, virtually every patient knows on some level that they can find a lie therapist, and this simply encourages them to take flight from the truth. Often, this is a quite unfortunate development, since the patient could gain a great deal by staying with the truth therapist. But I must tell you, they virtually never look back. Those who take flight are so relieved to seal off the truths within themselves and the most primitive parts of their personalities, that they almost always reinforce this defensiveness with an extensive use of denial and splitting. They simply do not permit themselves to realize what they have done and why they have done it.

As therapists, I believe that not only must we unrelentingly, though tactfully, pursue the truth, but we also have the responsibility for enabling as many patients as possible to accept and work within the truth therapy modality. I say this because there is no doubt that once the truth is worked through, the gain is enormous and the results have the least possible degree of liability. Still, we must avoid value judgments and as I said before, recognize fully the values and liabilities of both truth systems and lie systems.

Discussant: I don't want to put you on the spot, but how many truth therapists do you think exist in this country or even in the world?

Langs: There is no doubt that the natural tendency is to become a lie therapist rather than a truth therapist. It is for that reason that

I have said that there is no such person as a natural or born therapist as defined from the communicative approach. My review of the literature suggests that truth therapists are extremely rare, if they exist at all beyond those who have begun to study and integrate the communicative approach.

Discussant: This discussion reminds me of a patient who, after talking initially about a crisis he was in, was unable to say anything while in session with me. It had to do with his background and his fear that, by verbalizing, he would actually lose his feelings. He wasn't psychotic and came from a very religious background. Relationships would panic him, especially when he was helping others. Yet he was helped by simply sitting in the room with me. He did leave therapy, but he called me about other things. On the one hand, this leads me to believe that the holding environment can be extremely helpful, but it also makes me wonder if you're not being too strict about who is helped and through what means.

Langs: Misunderstandings are inevitable in this type of discussion, especially in the absence of immediate clinical material. Your summary of what happened with this patient is so incomplete we can make no judgments whatsoever. All I would say in response is that you have misunderstood me if you believe I am trying to imply that lie therapy can be of no help to patients. There appears to be considerable evidence that this is not the case, and as I said earlier, I have a great deal of respect for what can be accomplished by lie therapy—despite the risks involved. I am cognizant of the limitations of that therapeutic modality, the liabilities it incurs, the vulnerability of its results, and the unpredictability of its course. I think there are many dangers to lie-barrier systems, but at times they can indeed serve both patient and therapist quite well. Some such systems appear to be rather flexible and adaptive, while others are rigid and infused with pathology.

Discussant: I wonder how large a practice I could develop if I did only truth therapy.

Langs: That's a question raised by my students all the time. It is an open question, though it is sobering to raise it. I have no answer for the moment, except to say that there are many patients who will accept and work quite effectively within the framework of truth therapy.

Discussant: Do you have to lie to a lie patient to help him? Must you meet him on his own terms, or does that simply reinforce his lie tendencies?

Langs: I am pleased to hear these questions. Until recently we never dreamed they existed. Many I cannot answer in any definitive way. They need empirical determination.

As I said before, some of my students have attempted to provide lie patients with lie therapy, hoping to modify the conditions as the treatment proceeds and to shift eventually to a truth therapy modality. I have found that almost all patients tolerate such a shift when the initial lie therapy was inadvertent and based on ignorance in the therapist. All of my students go through a transition period of that kind, and while some patients consciously protest, all patients show a deep understanding and appreciation, expressed derivatively, of the implications of the rectifications of the framework. Such work is extremely salutary for both patient and therapist. Type Two derivative validation is abundant and it is usually a very moving and constructive experience on both sides.

Now, what of a therapist who is a truth therapist, and who deliberately attempts to modify the conditions of treatment and to utilize lie barriers? Will the patient in some way sense the deliberate contradictions between the therapist's understanding and his actual practice, and experience the split involved? Will the therapist himself be able to tolerate the patient's derivative reactions to his deviations, responses which are filled with their negative and destructive implications?

Remember, the lie therapist is partially or totally deaf to the patient's derivative communications, and does not consciously realize, at least most of the time, the destructive implications of his interventions and mismanagements of the frame. Contrasting awareness of these issues poses great difficulties for the truth therapist, and it would probably alter the effects of his efforts to deliberately use a lie therapy modality. Nonetheless, I await reports on this type of therapeutic effort before reaching any final conclusions. I am skeptical, to say the least. I myself am incapable of knowingly offering any type of lie therapy; instead, I attempt to dole out the truth with utmost sensitivity and caution. Finally, I must add that, as you begin to realize and experience the need in all human beings for lies and barriers, and the related and not unrealistic dread of the truth, your attitude toward lie therapists and lie therapy softens considerably and becomes quite sympathetic, even as you remain opposed to its use.

Discussant: There is a need, then, to properly conceptualize lie therapy, and to see whether there is some reasonable way it can be used with certain patients.

Langs: Yes, it seems inescapable that we must know the truth about the therapeutic process, whatever that may be. And then we must be open to a consideration of all types of therapeutic modalities.

By the way, our discussion of the developmental object relationship between the patient and therapist, and the type of relatedness necessary for sound and insightful therapy, provides another type of tentative support for the thesis that psychotherapy and psychoanalysis are on a single continuum. To state this thesis in its essence: the pathological forms of symbiosis and parasitism are inherently inimical to cognitive insight, constructive positive introjective identifications, and the growth, individuation, and relative autonomy which are derived in this way. It follows that all forms of therapy must be founded on a healthy symbiotic mode of relatedness or they will fail the patient in important ways. As we have already seen, there is a significant correlation between a sound and effective interpretation and a healthy symbiosis between therapist and patient. In particular, in the absence of such symbiosis, even the best interpretive efforts will be undermined because of the pathological gratifications afforded to the patient and therapist.

Well, in its own way, this has been a most stimulating discussion. Perhaps we can now turn to some clinical data and give these ideas a sense of substance.

Therapist: Well, as you may recall, I was in the middle of a session. I will pick up where I left off, applying the principle of continuing without memory, desire, or understanding.

The patient had described how he had delayed getting out of bed while at his girlfriend's apartment, and was then unable to lock the door. He came running to this center where his girlfriend, a social worker, has an office in the emergency room. She responded to his problem by saying to him, Why do you have to be so nervous and anxious about this sort of thing; why do you even have to worry about it? I'll go back and lock up. And why didn't you just tell the janitor to lock the door. You know he's there.

In the session, he said to me, Why do I behave like this? It was getting fairly close to the end of the session by this time, so I whipped into action. I began by reminding him about the difficulties we've had in the past about the starting time of the sessions. And how, at times, I have been late and not reliable. And also, very frequently, he had been late and had missed sessions entirely. And I said that he had certain feelings about being delayed and also about being exposed to the people who had been in this room, in the meeting, people whom he knew.

And I told him that I thought that he was doing a number of things here. He was responding to a feeling of being imposed upon—that he had to see these people come out of the room and put up with my lateness. I said that this is somehow related to his relationship with Betty; he was responding to a sense of demandingness on her part that he get out of bed and to a sense that she might pull back from him; and he felt angry about her demands to get out of bed. And I said that he also feels angry about now having to come to sessions on time with me.

I then added that basically the solution he had found to this problem is to leave the door open; by delaying getting out of bed, he could come and go, and leave Betty's apartment as he pleases. But also, he would like to be able to come and go as he pleases with my sessions and doesn't like the demand that I put on him to come at a certain time. And part of this has to do with certain feelings of anger he has about the way things were handled before.

And finally, to round it all up, I made a comment about how he felt something about being left, that Betty had left him in the morning and that he had certain angry feelings about that, and I'm also leaving him and he has feelings about that (the pending forced termination). And he deals with that, on the one hand, by exposing her by leaving the door open, and on the other hand, by lateness with me.

That was the end of my intervention.

Langs: You present some very practical work for us to do in this seminar. So, who will begin our evaluation of this intervention?

Discussant: It sounds like a confrontation to me.

Discussant: It also has interpretive qualities, an effort to make the patient conscious of feelings and problems of which he is, at the moment, unaware.

Langs: Yes, it is a mixture of a confrontation and a rather general interpretation, though there is an effort to be specific as well—perhaps more than any previous interpretation we have heard.

What type of interpretation is this?

Discussant: It would seem that the therapist is attempting to show the patient that there is some link between his reactions to his girlfriend and his responses to the therapist himself. I would have to consider this a transference interpretation.

Langs: I believe that you are using the term transference here to refer to an intervention which touches upon the therapeutic relationship, a type of intervention I would call a *relationship interpretation*. I believe that we will find upon further analysis that this is indeed an effort at such a relationship interpretation, in that it contains elements of both transference and nontransference. Such interventions are designed to make the patient conscious of previously unconscious fantasy (transference) and perception (nontransference) constellations, and their influence on his relationship with the therapist, his relationship with others, his symptoms, and such.

We can clarify this point by further categorizing the nature of this intervention. Who will continue?

Discussant: The level of listening here seems mixed: there is use of manifest content and Type One derivatives, but also some effort to develop Type Two derivatives.

Langs: Yes, you are quite right.

Discussant: The indicators in this session, as I recall them, include the patient's lateness and a period of silence. I am not sure, but we might have reason to believe that the patient was acting out something when he was unable to lock his girlfriend's apartment. In the main, I think that the gross behavioral resistances are the main indicators.

Discussant: What about the therapist's previous interventions? Didn't we learn that the therapist had been quite confronting in the previous hour, that he had pressured the patient in a rather hostile way? In addition, I seem to recall a brief intervention in this hour, to the effect that the patient was trying to keep the therapist waiting rather than having to wait himself. That intervention, since it was essentially erroneous, is both an adaptive context and an indicator.

Discussant: There is also the pending forced termination.

Langs: Yes, we have a series of indicators ranging from gross behavioral resistances to technical errors by the therapist, to the pending forced termination. We also heard something last week that brought up a lack of confidentiality to this treatment, a concern which was represented early in the hour when the patient alluded to signing in with the secretary and which comes up again in a more disguised form through the reference to the social worker. This issue appeared also in the therapist's intervention when he mentioned the people in the group which met in his office, some of whom the patient knew.

In ranking the intensity of indicators, we first take their accumulated force. Then we also try to rank them separately so that we will be certain to deal with those which are most pressing. But in addition to our own subjective ratings, we must also pay attention to the extent to which the patient himself represents and responds, directly or indirectly, to the different indicators. This will help to determine both those indicators with which we will be able to deal through interpretation and how we will actually allude to them— manifestly or by indirection.

As you can see, in the average session there usually are several indicators, though often one will be far more outstanding than the others. We have already discovered that there are often several adaptive contexts as well. It is important to be able to develop the therapeutic skill of running through these indicators and contexts, ranking them in order of importance, and ascertaining the best representation of each. On that basis, you are able to identify points of major communicative resistance, and decide whether it is possible for you to deal with those defenses, and to determine whether and how you will intervene.

Who will run through this exercise here?

Discussant: I would rate the accumulated indicators at about seven on your scale.

Langs: Yes, I thought of seven or eight.

Discussant: Among them, I would think that the pending forced termination is the most important, and the therapist's recent lateness—I don't believe you included that in your last summary—as next important. I would give lesser ratings to the recent interventions, though hostile confrontations in the previous hour deserve to be included in the therapist's ultimate, responsive intervention if they are represented by the patient. The issue of confidentiality is also important, but I would imagine that the therapist could deal with that only if it was clearly represented in the material.

Langs: That's an excellent survey. What about the representations of the indicators?

Discussant: The patient mentioned his lateness, but not the lateness of the therapist. He did not mention the pending forced termination, at least as I heard the material. He didn't refer to the issue of confidentiality directly, but represented it through the reference to the secretary and his girlfriend. The patient also did not mention the therapist's recent interventions.

Langs: Yes, the therapist introduced in his intervention a number of indicators which had not been mentioned by the patient and which were either not represented at all or with considerable disguise. He therefore did not adhere to the principle of allowing the patient to create the session and to put into the therapist all of the elements needed for an intervention, responding primarily by integrating the separate fragments.

Discussant: I'll take on the intervention contexts. These seem to correspond with many of the indicators: the therapist's lateness, his hostile interventions, his role in the lack of confidentiality, and the pending forced termination. Except for the possibility that the patient was acting something out, most of the indicators correspond to the prevailing adaptive contexts. Because of that, it seems unnecessary to repeat the way in which each is represented.

Langs: You are quite right, though it would be well for us to scale the level of communicative resistance in respect to each adaptive context.

Discussant: Well, the therapist's lateness is represented by the patient's lateness, and I might give that a four or five because it includes the theme of lateness but does not refer to the therapist. The pending forced termination is probably best represented when the patient mentioned his girlfriend leaving the apartment, and I would give that a score of four or three—alluding to clarity of representability, the converse of the level of resistance—because it is a well-disguised reference to being kicked out of treatment and it has no link to the therapist. As to the therapist's interventions in the previous hour, I am at a loss to see how it is represented at all.

Discussant: Perhaps it is conveyed in the patient's sense of pressure and in an earlier reference to how he himself does things quite irrationally, without being able to control them. Based on the difficulty we are having in seeing these associations as representations of that particular context, I would guess that it ranks at a level of two or three in respect to representability. I suspect on that basis that it has been subjected to rather intense communicative resistances.

Langs: These exercises, as I call them, seem to be moving along much more quickly now. The accumulated effect might be summarized as a situation in which there is a relatively high level of resistance in respect to the patient's representations of the activated intervention contexts, corresponding to a low level of representability. There is a general bridge to therapy, but no specific links— the latter term reserved for connections to therapy and the therapist which are contained in specific representations of a prevailing adaptive context.

What now of the communicative network?

Discussant: I thought that the therapist forced things a bit. As I heard this material, it seemed rather well disguised. We discussed this last week, though I don't remember all the details. It was my impression that the material organizes best around the pending forced termination, and that it reflects the patient's reluctance to leave treatment, his wish that the door would remain open so that he could come back, and his feelings of separation anxiety. However, I don't think these things can be pointed out to the patient at this time in any meaningful way. I would have to say that the level of resistance is fairly strong in respect to the derivative complex.

Langs: This is somewhat confirmed in the fact that I share with you the impression that the therapist did indeed force matters too much, based largely on the fact that he found it necessary to introduce the adaptive context himself without using representations from the patient. He did this largely because of the absence of either direct allusions to these contexts or well-represented derivatives in the patient's associations.

Let's turn now to the intervention itself. Does it meet the criteria of an interpretation? And what about its communicative properties?

Discussant: It is an attempt to deal with indicators, to identify some important adaptive contexts, and to work with selected derivatives. I would say it meets the criteria we have established for an interpretation.

Langs: Yes, and this reminds me that, for us, virtually every interpretation is a relationship interpretation—primarily transference, primarily nontransference, or transversal, a mixture of both.

Discussant: While it meets the criteria, I found the intervention awkward and pressing. This touches upon a point you made last week, that an interpretation may have the correct attributes, but its contents may be in error or it may be shaped incorrectly. My criticism of the interpretation would be that the therapist introduced elements which the patient had not mentioned, and that it centers around a sense of anger which I did not detect in this material.

Langs: Yes, the patient appeared more confused than angry, though the therapist has a right to postulate the influence of an unconscious affect. However, such an inference should be based on the patient's derivative communications and represented in the material, rather than arrived at as a Type One derivative in the form of an inference based on the therapist's subjective evaluation or feelings.

Discussant: The intervention did not include any reference to the patient's separation anxiety and his wish to be able to come back to therapy once it has ended. In addition, I found the therapist's efforts to link this material to his own lateness, and to his exposure of the patient to people he knew, quite forced and only minimally derived from the material in the hour.

Langs: Yes, one of the most difficult appraisals of our interventions pertains to the extent to which we have remained faithful to the material from the patient and not introduced our own notions. In principle, we must undertake such an evaluation and attempt to remain as close to the material as possible. We should take departures as countertransference-based errors, and anticipate the patient's unconscious working over of their implications.

Before we attempt further criticisms, I think we should at least pause and appreciate the positive qualities of this intervention. I do not remember another presentation in this course in which a therapist attempted to identify an activated adaptive context, deal with the related indicators, and shape the derivative complex as a response to the context. However rough around the edges, the fact that the therapist intervened in keeping with these principles is to be applauded. It is no small accomplishment. I would predict that the patient will appreciate his efforts despite the qualities of prematurity and the intrusion of the therapist's own associations. There is something genuinely truthful in the technical sense about this intervention. Even though it is a bit ahead of the patient, I must predict that he will show some type of Type Two derivative validation even though he may, in addition, work over and respond to the countertransference elements. Still, the therapist is to be congratulated for his effort.

Discussant: Forgive me for not lingering with praise, but I must say that I found the intervention far too long for what the therapist had to say, and confusing at times. The pressure also had some quality of projective identification.

Discussant: Nonetheless, this was an effort by a therapist to use the Type A communicative mode.

Langs: So it was. And certainly there are mixed features here, many of which you now have defined.

Notice too that the therapist made an effort to deal with the patient's resistances. We would therefore call this a *relationship resistance intervention*, an effort to deal with interactional defenses. It included an attempt by the therapist to identify his contributions to the patient's behaviors, as well as those factors which stem from the patient himself. As such, it had transversal qualities—another achievement for which I think the therapist deserves our congratulations.

In all, then, our evaluation is that this is an effort to generate an interpretation which is likely to obtain Type Two derivative validation, though it reflects a variety of countertransferences as well. We therefore anticipate a mixed response.

Discussant: For me, the main affect in this session was anxiety or panic, rather than a feeling of anger.

Therapist: I sensed the anger from the sleepy quality of the session and from some of the rumination.

Discussant: But he ran over to the Center in something of a panic, and left the door open.

Therapist: But I heard it as a kind of groggy-eyed disorientation which had an unconscious meaning. He kept asking, Why do I keep forgetting?

Langs: These subjective impressions should be validated through derivative expressions in the contents of the patient's material. The sense of anxiety seems more evident than the anger, though the hostility could be latent to this material. In principle, I would suggest that you not intervene unless the patient clearly represents such qualities in his own affects and verbal associations. This is one way of validating subjective impressions and it will safeguard against inferences which are countertransference-based. I think we could all sense a provocative quality to his behavior, but in order to interpret it to the patient we would want to have some derivative representation of that aspect.

Discussant: My emphasis on the sense of anxiety had to do with the way in which his girlfriend told him there was an obvious solution to the door problem. He seemed confused, and he's all over the place; he doesn't seem to know if he's coming or going. I felt that his girlfriend did something therapeutic for him, and that I would have addressed this aspect of his material.

Langs: Try to not drift away from organizing around adaptive contexts when making such formulations. Certainly, you may get impressions divorced from context, but eventually you not only want to find a representation of a particular impression in the patient's associations, but also a meaningful relationship to an activated intervention context. Remember, there is no true meaning in a session without a link to a context.

Discussant: Incidentally, isn't his sense of anxiety an indicator?

Langs: Yes, any type of symptomatic response is indeed a therapeutic context. Indicators are any sign within the patient that something has created a therapeutic need, a need for an intervention from the therapist. Remember too that we have classified foreground and background indicators: those which are immediately pertinent and activated, and those which are long-standing and perhaps not immediately intensified in a particular session.

Therapist: Oddly enough, I thought that his lateness was an adaptive context. I now realize that I was confused, that it was an indicator and a secondary context, not a primary adaptive context.

Langs: I may have contributed to that confusion quite early in our work, but it is a distinction which I now hope is quite clear to you: primary adaptive contexts derive from your interventions as a therapist, and are the central organizers of the patient's material. Disturbing or disruptive behaviors on the part of the patient are *secondary* contexts, and must be understood as reactions to primary contexts which derive from the therapist.

Therapist: I also now realize that I expressed an unconscious truth in my intervention, without recognizing what I was talking about at the time. I had begun my intervention by talking about demandingness, and in a sense I now realize that, unconsciously, I was alluding to the adaptive context of my interventions in the previous hour.

Langs: Yes, that is an important realization. We spoke about demandingness in general, without linking it to your interventions—and actually, the material would not have permitted such a link. As you now well know, within the therapeutic interaction it is quite viable for the patient to express derivative truths, but the therapist must state them manifestly and explicitly. Your intervention did, however, contain both direct and derivative statements of the truth of the therapeutic interaction.

Discussant: Last week, we also spoke of the adaptive context of the therapist's effort to rectify the frame. I simply mention it because it did not come up in this discussion.

Langs: That is a point well taken. Among the multiplicity of contexts, that particular precipitant seems to rank rather low for the moment. If the rest of the field were secure, and there was no pending forced termination, the patient's sense of anxiety might have been more readily linked to his fear of regression within a relatively stable and sound therapeutic environment. It may well be a factor, but it would be difficult to interpret this aspect to the patient since there are other, more pressing issues.

The complexities of this intervention are staggering. Remember that this is what the patient heard, and it might well have had a similar effect on him. It is well to state again the principle that interventions should be as clear and concise as possible, though they should also be as complete and thorough as the material permits.

How did he respond?

Therapist: His response was a sort of embarrassed laugh. And he said, I'm not angry with you. Then he seemed to blush.

Langs: We are now in the area of validation. We hear first a conscious denial, and it may be accurate or it may not. Some of the discussants felt that anxiety rather than hostility was the prevailing affect. The patient may be directly correcting the therapist. He also responds by invoking a negation. We may begin to wonder if he is attempting to refute the entire intervention, but we must be prepared to listen to his derivative response before drawing any conclusions.

Therapist: And he said, Things are going very well now; I'm much happier with my girlfriend.

Langs: I always get a bit anxious when I make a prediction in a seminar, all the more because for once, I predicted some type of

Type Two derivative validation. So I am relieved to hear this next association: a derivative representation of a positive introject.

I cannot recall such a representation in any other hour we have heard—sessions in which, as you know, I consistently evaluated the therapist's efforts as largely erroneous and countertransference-based. I am, of course, absolutely delighted that my evaluation of the positive qualities of this intervention is borne out in the patient's first derivative communication. I have been waiting all year for a moment of this kind, and I am quite gratified that I was able to predict when it would appear and that a member of this group was able to make it happen. This is a very satisfying moment indeed.

Therapist: He went on: Things are going well with her. I seem to have finally developed a fairly decent relationship with a woman.

Langs: Just listen: at long last, something decent has happened. I suspect that this is one of the first efforts by this therapist to apply the principles developed in this course in his work with this patient. And the patient is delighted.

There is another important point. It is barely perceptible, but I believe it to be present nonetheless. The patient chooses his girlfriend to derivatively represent his relationship with the therapist, doing so in a manner which would justify the formulation that he views himself as the woman in the relationship with the therapist at times, while at other times he may view the therapist as feminine and himself as masculine. In any case, there is a possible further latent homosexual implication here.

Now, this could be based on both unconscious perception and unconscious fantasy. However, since it arises in the context of interactional validation—as a reaction to a partially correct intervention—we would have to hypothesize that the transference component is primary for the moment. This implies that the therapist's intervention was largely valid and did not express a latent homosexual countertransference; it is the patient who is introducing this element because of some unconscious fantasy constellation and pathological inner need. This formulation is in keeping with the principle developed earlier from other clinical data to the effect that valid interventions evoke transference responses in patients, while countertransference-based interventions evoke nontransference reactions (Langs 1980a).

You might say that, in addition, the therapist's need to introduce his own associations had a penetrating and latently homosexual quality. I would agree, but would also point out that in comparison to his interventions in the previous hour, which were blatantly confronting and apparently intensely, though latently, homosexual, this particular intervention shows considerable mastery of the unconscious homosexual countertransference and now leaves room for the patient to stress his own homosexual fantasies and problems.

Finally, on an implicit level and to some degree directly, this intervention may be viewed as an attempt to interpret aspects of the pathological symbiosis, though much of the burden for this mode of relatedness is placed onto the patient for the moment. Nonetheless, as an effort to clarify and resolve these symbiotic qualities, the interpretation itself actually communicates to the patient the therapist's wish to move with him toward a more healthy form of symbiosis. There is some evidence that the patient has unconsciously perceived these efforts in his allusion to a more mature way of relating to his girlfriend, a communication which stands in contrast to the patient's earlier indirect stress on the infantile qualities of that twosome. The former material appeared, of course, prior to the therapist's intervention.

In principle, all valid interpretations unconsciously or implicitly express the therapist's wish to maintain or establish a healthy symbiosis with the patient. This is true whether or not specific pathological symbiotic needs are subjected to immediate interpretation, since sound interventions inherently create a sense of healthy separateness between the patient and therapist.

Therapist: He went on to say: I'm just not angry with you. I feel fine with you. And that's how the hour ended.

Discussant: It seems to me that we discussed the homosexual problem here last week. He had a need to stay with a woman and that made him late for his hour. I therefore felt that in his reference to the girlfriend at this point in the session he was trying to tell the therapist that he's not homosexual, that he has heterosexual relationships.

Langs: Yes, but that is a Type One derivative inference. It does not take into account the adaptive context of the intervention.

Time is very short now, and it would be nice to hear the beginning of the next hour. We have for the moment a situation in which we obtained interactional Type Two derivative validation, but not cognitive Type Two derivative validation. This may represent the mixed response I had anticipated: the positive aspects of your intervention are incorporated and represented interactionally through a positive unconscious perception, while the confusing and negative aspects evoke the absence of cognitive confirmation.

Therapist: Since I am completing this presentation, I would like to mention that I have actually gone against my supervisor innumerable times with this case. He has paid no attention to the framework and has even preferred that it remain loose and ill-defined. Instead, I have tried to tighten the frame and the patient has become quite angry. In fact, he seems to be in a homosexual panic right now.

Langs: Unfortunately, we are not in a position to evaluate such a summary comment. We know nothing of the prevailing contexts, though I do realize that you are suggesting that they involve a further securing of the therapeutic environment. That may be, but without specific material, we cannot determine the source of those anxieties.

Can you give us a bit of the next hour?

Therapist: The next hour he came in with a very interesting dream. He said that he had suddenly decided to visit his two daughters who are in Atlanta. He had split up with his wife for several reasons. She had had several affairs and had become involved as well with a woman.

In the dream, he finds himself on a trip with a strange person whose face he can't see. And this person has a machine gun and is shooting up all these people. Then he goes to visit his daughters and they come out with their hands up. He awoke at the moment in the dream when this person began to shoot his daughters.

Langs: Since time is short, allow me to comment. In the adaptive context of the interpretation of the previous hour, this dream is certainly one of nonvalidation. The introjects are negative and destructive, and the patient seems to be responding to the hostile and penetrating qualities of the intervention, the confronting aspect as it echoed the more violent confrontations of the previous hour.

The information you provide us in respect to the dream shows again the underlying theme of homosexuality. There is an unconscious perception here of the therapist's violence, though it is carried to such an extreme that we would have to say that there is a transversal quality to this material, and that it seems to extend well beyond the destructiveness of the therapist. We would therefore wonder if the dream does not also refer to violent unconscious fantasy constellations within the patient which pertain to the therapist. But you see, a forced termination is a violent and even psychologically murderous act, a form of destructive parasitism, as I said before. I must therefore add that much of these derivative communications must be seen to constitute valid unconscious perceptions of the implications of that activated intervention context.

Incidentally, the dream now makes clear the underlying affect of rage and destructiveness. Some of it undoubtedly related to the pathological mode of relatedness dominant here. It is an example of what I meant when I said that hostility should be represented in the associational material before we allude to it in an intervention. Of course, there is no way of knowing whether the patient is now reacting to the destructive aspects of the therapist's interpretation, or whether the underlying rage had been present all along.

There are many other qualities to this dream worthy of discussion. Unfortunately, we will not be able to hear the balance of this session or extend our discussion of the material beyond what has already been said. It is certainly a dramatic moment, filled with a sense of violent projective identification, with which to end this particular presentation. I feel quite indebted to the therapist for the clarity and frankness with which he has presented his material. Again I want to congratulate him on his efforts to offer this patient a sound interpretation, however flawed. I think most of you know now that it takes a great deal of inner and outer management capacities and ego resources to intervene in this way.

Chapter Seven

THE LOCUS OF
INTERPRETIVE WORK

Langs: We'll begin with a new presentation today.

Therapist: This patient is a young woman, a physiotherapist by profession, who has had problems in her relationship with her boyfriend, who happens to be an accountant who works at this Center. When she first came to therapy, things were not going well in their relationship and a lot of it has had to do with the way she was treating her boyfriend. She seemed to be driving him away, though she had a feeling that he was a guy who really cared for her and who might really be willing to have, and was appropriate for, a long-term relationship. She wanted to understand what was going on.

  The sessions I am going to present occurred after a year and a half of therapy. At the time, I was seeing her twice weekly, and we had changed our office twice. Manifestly, most of the issues she brought up focused on two major areas: the relationship with her boyfriend, and secondarily, her relationship with the people at work, particularly a woman who was in charge of the program with which she was affiliated. She described conflicts with this woman which were similar to those with her boyfriend, and concerns about her ability to perform well on her job, about her skills, and about her future. She was also trying to decide whether to move in with her boyfriend, which she did after a few months of treatment.

During the first phase of therapy, she was primarily a trainee. She received financial support from her mother in small amounts. Her father had divorced her mother when she was four years of age and later remarried and had children. She and her mother have a mixed emotional relationship: they are very close, but they are always fighting. She has an older brother and a younger sister, though lately she seldom sees them.

In terms of the therapeutic relationship, her style, especially at the beginning, was to present a problem and expect me to take over and make decisions for her, to tell her what to do and to give her some secret answer as to why she acts the way she does—to tell this to her and then everything will be better. The model of therapy she had in mind is based on an earlier treatment experience, because of enuresis, when she was eight years old. Her mother was openly concerned about the patient's sexual identity because she tended to be quite tomboyish. She remembers the therapy as a pleasant kind of experience, and how her therapist told her at one point that her symptoms would disappear, and that's exactly what happened. Her therapy was terminated and was a wonderful success, and this is what she is now waiting for.

At the time of these sessions, the patient had been dealing for many months with the question of whether she should get engaged to her boyfriend. He had on many occasions intimated that he would be interested in marriage, but she had been undecided. Her major concern has been the fact that the previous year she met a rather attractive, domineering kind of guy, who treated her rather shabbily. Nonetheless, she was powerfully attached to him, and after that relationship broke apart, she was not able to get him out of her system. She talks about him and still feels a tremendous sense of passion and attachment, which she tries to suppress though it tends to crop up periodically. He lives in a nearby city and has not done too well, and they still share a number of mutual friends so she has some indirect contact with him. That whole situation is, in her point of view, one of the reasons she can't commit herself to her present boyfriend, largely because of all these powerful feelings she has for her previous boyfriend.

Turning now to the session before the one I want to concentrate on, I must say that my notes are sketchy. She began that session by talking about a job interview in which she had to demonstrate her capabilities as a physiotherapist to a rather large group of people. She had been very anxious about it, but felt she had done fairly well. And they had told her directly that she would be given serious consideration.

She talked about a particular man who was part of the panel; he seemed to be gay, but apparently was the husband of a woman, also present, who appeared to be very powerful, middle-aged, and important. The patient wondered about how the two of them might be as a couple. It seemed as though they were a very awkward kind of couple, yet when he spoke and made several suggestions, he was quite firm and effective—not at all awkward.

She went on to talk about how she feels when she is doing her job in front of others. She really loosens up and feels that there is no holding back, and she can really get into her work with abandon. She came home from the job interview and had thoughts of having sex with her boyfriend, and seemed to be turned on by the whole experience. When her boyfriend did come in and they did have sex, it was okay, but nothing fantastic, which is what she would expect. She talked about her sense of abandonment and associated it to the problems that she has in never being able to have an orgasm in intercourse. She said that she felt that if she could have that kind of abandonment, it might occur. (Here she was using the word abandonment to mean losing herself.)

On the day of the session, she had had some thoughts about having an affair, of picking someone up at an upcoming party that her boyfriend could not attend because he had to work late. She had actually never done anything of that sort, but has had continual fantasies about one-night stands. She also talked about getting stoned with a friend of hers and began to have some questions about whether she might have homosexual feelings for this woman; she was somewhat anxious about that.

Then she referred to the fact that her present boss, a woman, had once made some comment about being attracted to the patient, that the patient seemed to be attractive to her. The patient talked about how she felt revulsion in response to that idea. She could never trust that woman, whose name was Patricia, nearly enough to have a sexual relationship with her. She asked me if she had ever told me how this woman with whom she had gotten stoned the previous night had almost had sex with her boyfriend. It was a very awkward situation. The patient had actually initiated the idea, but her boyfriend refused and said maybe some other time. She wondered if I had perhaps asked her about what had attracted her or excited her about the idea of the three of them having sex.

Langs: On the surface, this is a rather interesting presentation, and it offers us considerable material. I will comment upon the question of determining the level of resistance in a moment, but first I must ask you if these process notes faithfully reflect the transactions between yourself and the patient, since they indicate that you were entirely silent—at least up until this point in the hour.

Therapist: Actually, I had said a lot, but I don't have my interventions recorded. As I remember, they were mostly in the form of questions, asking her to elaborate here and there.

Langs: So, it will not be possible for us to have a sense of this material in terms of what actually transpired during the hour. Do you think, then, that it is possible to discuss the issue of resistances?

Therapist: No.

Discussant: You have often talked about how difficult it is to organize the material from the patient when we do not know anything about the previous hour, and especially about the therapist's interventions. It is also difficult to comprehend the material when we do not know the therapist's interventions in the session at hand, and I believe that this is true both in respect to unconscious implications as well as resistances. In fact, as I listened to this material, I had the feeling that there was a lot here, but that I couldn't be sure, so much of it was manifest. I had trouble generating derivatives. And certainly, you hear a lot about homosexuality, having affairs, and sexual threesomes, so we have a sense that the material is loaded. But I kept feeling that I couldn't organize it, and then I realized that I was experiencing a lack of one or more adaptive contexts. It led me to recognize that I am actually becoming accustomed to the communicative way of listening. I tend to get lost without it. In the past, I would have readily formulated this material around the patient's continuing problems with her sexual identity, and suggest the presence of major homosexual conflicts. I might have even then gone on to link those conflicts to her hesitation in marrying her boyfriend. At this point, I get a kind of empty feeling with such formulations; somehow, I know that something very important is lacking.

Langs: Your comments are well taken. Without the activated adaptive contexts, there is a tendency to formulate this material manifestly or in terms of Type One derivatives, almost exclusively in terms of the patient's isolated intrapsychic fantasies and conflicts.

Discussant: But you also told us that we could monitor this material in a general way around the conditions of treatment. This may involve background contexts, but I did hear some very tentative Type Two derivative meanings.

For example, the patient was talking about being on exhibit in a job interview where she had to perform. This could refer to the lack of confidentiality in the clinic, especially since her boyfriend works here. It may be that she stays in treatment because she finds the conditions stimulating and is even prepared to have a *ménage à trois*, possibly with the therapist and his supervisor. The homosexuality may involve the seductive qualities to the treatment setting and therapist, and be a way of representing it, or may be a defense against heterosexual fantasies and perhaps even perceptions related to him.

Discussant: With the turn of the year, the problem of another pending forced termination arises. This could be prompting sexualized fantasies in this patient who may wish to be able to get closer to the therapist and even seduce him.

Langs: All of this is extremely tentative. Some of the patient's material may also be a reponse to the therapist's repeated questions, his efforts to establish a manifest content and pathologically symbiotic form of relatedness with this patient, and the patient's unconscious perception that this involves some kind of defense against an erotic countertransference. Even there, we would have to know the specific questions, their unconscious implications, their timing and such, before we could really establish any sense of meaning and function to this material which would be likely to obtain Type Two derivative validation.

Let's not dwell on these problems, but instead I will ask the therapist to continue so we can soon have material which we can discuss more cogently.

Therapist: The patient started to talk about watching two people having sex. She asked me if she ever had told me about a time she worked as a physiotherapist on a locked psychiatric ward, and how she felt a very high sense of sexual tension, and how she and her supervisor were turned on by what was going on there. She had volunteered to work on the ward, but then felt maybe that she was doing it for a turn-on, and she felt bad about that.

Here I made a reference to an earlier session and told her that what she was talking about reminded me of a fantasy that she had described on several occasions. It was a sexual fantasy that she had about masturbating in front of a large group of men. Describing her work on the ward, she had emphasized how many of the staff and patients were taken by what she was doing, and they had been watching. I therefore told her that this particular experience seemed to be similar to her fantasy. (Unfortunately, this was right at the end of the session, and she made only a very brief response which I did not record.)

Langs: Well, we now have an intervention. Let's analyze it as a way of preparing for the following hour.

Discussant: This seems to be a confrontation, a direct comparison between a conscious fantasy and an actual experience. The level of listening is manifest.

Discussant: I have little sense of the indicators in this session. There may be something symptomatic in the patient's smoking pot with this woman, though not necessarily. There may be some sense of homosexual anxiety or even panic, but without knowing the therapist's questions, I'm not sure where to locate the sexual anxieties or what their nature might be. There is the thoughts the patient is having about an affair, which could be a form of acting out. And there is also the general indicator of her indecision about getting married. For me, it's all rather vague and difficult to assess.

Discussant: We are also postulating as an indicator a pending forced termination.

Langs: Perhaps we are fortunate in having this experience. I hope that it has led you to realize that you are severely handicapped in evaluating the material from any patient without knowing the therapist's interventions, the adaptive contexts for the patient's associations and behaviors. The formulations we are now making must therefore be quite tentative, since we are lacking a critical dimension of the therapeutic interaction.

Discussant: In some way, we might say that the therapist was trying to deal with indications of sexual conflicts within the patient, though I would agree that without knowing the contexts, we might be doing the patient an injustice—these conflicts may be more intense in the therapist than in the patient. If I may say so, a presentation of this kind is extremely protective for the therapist. It almost forces you to locate all of the problems and pathology in the patient since the therapist himself is virtually absent.

Langs: Yes, and now extrapolate your impressions to the therapeutic and analytic literature, and recognize how often this is done. This is another way of bringing to the fore the enormous prejudice within therapists toward locating the pathology of the bipersonal field within their patients, and in denying their contribution to that pathology.

Discussant: Clearly, the intervention does not deal with an adaptive context, nor is there any effort to generate a derivative complex. Two manifest elements are simply brought together.

Langs: Yes, and there is an important point about derivatives to be made here. The manifest content at hand is sexual, involving a masturbatory fantasy of a highly exhibitionistic nature, in which the patient in a sense performed in front of others and was sexually stimulated. Many therapists would take such manifest contents and believe they were dealing with derivatives because of the instinctual drive quality of this material. In error, they would call these conscious fantasies and surface reactions derivatives of the patient's sexual conflicts, or of the patient's sexual anxieties and her problems with her sexual identity. They might even call this material a derivative of the patient's poor controls over her sexual impulses and fantasies. In this way, both the therapist and the therapeutic interaction would be excluded.

For me, this is an idiosyncratic way of using the concept of derivatives, despite its prevalence. It uses this material to establish what I have termed *translation derivatives*, the rendering of direct inferences, some of them quite broad and general, based on the patient's manifest associations. It might even be better to simply term these *direct inferences* from the manifest content, rather than to invoke the concept of derivative expression at all. As you know, we have abundant clinical evidence that these linear inferences, while containing a measure of accuracy, do not define truth within the therapeutic interaction. All too often, they are used primarily as lie-barrier systems designed to seal off such truths, especially those which pertain to the therapist. Interpretations made on the basis of such direct inferences do not obtain Type Two derivative validation.

The term derivatives should be reserved for what I have called *indirect interactional derivatives*: specific implications, disguised or encoded within the patient's manifest associations, which constitute a response to an activated intervention context. While manifest contents contain only partially revealed fantasies, perceptions, and introjects, the definitive implications of such contents can be identified only in light of an adaptive context. It is these derivatives which constitute the communicative medium of neurotic expression and form the underlying basis of neurotic symptoms. Symptoms themselves are based on derivatives and the patient unconsciously works over his neurosis in such terms. Remember, many inferences from manifest contents do not even involve derivatives. In essence, a specific manifest sequence of associations constitutes a derivative representation of an underlying sequence which has its own definitive contents, meanings, and functions.

Discussant: It is apparent that the intervention does not in any way refer manifestly to the treatment situation or therapeutic relationship. It also introduces an association from the therapist, and it therefore extends beyond the patient's material in this particular hour.

Langs: Which communicative mode would you postulate here?

Discussant: It could be the Type C mode, an offer of some kind of barrier to something that is going on within the therapeutic interaction.

Langs: I would agree. Any other comments?

Discussant: Well, it was suggested in an earlier seminar that we should look at material which prompts a seemingly erroneous intervention. Maybe the therapist was trying here to move toward an interpretation because the hour was nearing its end. But it might also be that he experienced some similarity between the psychiatric ward and his office, and sensed unconsciously that the patient was saying something about her relationship with him and how she finds it sexually stimulating. While that certainly is a tentative hypothesis, it is in keeping with the way in which the therapist intervened so that he could place all of the sexual anxiety and tension in the patient, not himself.

Langs: Though tentative, that is an excellent formulation. Yes, it is always critical to review the adaptive contexts within the patient's material which prompt an intervention—valid or not.

Lacking the specific intervention contexts for the patient's material, we may find little validation in the session we are about to hear. On the other hand, it may well be that you have become so sensitive to listening and formulating in terms of the therapeutic interaction that much of what you have said will find some type of Type Two derivative validation in the next hour, despite the limitations in the presentation.

Therapist: As I hear it, the group is proposing that this material must have something to do with the therapeutic interaction and with myself. Yet we also know that this patient is in great conflict about whether or not to marry. I am wondering why you prefer to go to her relationship with me rather than her relationship with her boyfriend. It seemed to me that there were strong reasons to believe that this material reflected the patient's reactions to this possible, single, heterosexual commitment.

Langs: Once again, we come back to contrasting hypotheses: (1) for interventions to be validated through Type Two derivatives, they must pertain to adaptive contexts within the therapeutic interaction; or instead, (2) cogent adaptive contexts and responses by the patient as they pertain to outside relationships can be confronted or interpreted to a patient and find significant confirmation. We are nearing the end of this course and I welcome the challenge. I trust that we will agree that we will allow the patient in the following hour, primarily through her derivative communications, to indicate her choice as to the realm of primary meaning. We will also allow her to respond to your intervention, and we will attempt to ascertain whether there is some type of meaningful confirmatory reaction, or instead, an unconscious effort to get you onto the right track and to deal with the communicative interaction. As you can see, we are back to the question of whether a therapist can intervene meaningfully and effectively with respect to outside relationships, or if such interventions consistently constitute the offer of Type C barriers to critical and chaotic transactions.

Discussant: I am curious about some problems related to this discussion that involve the purpose and nature of therapy. After all, the patient is coming for a particular purpose which she states as wanting to get at her problem with her boyfriend. To what extent does that become a somewhat constant adaptive context, something she has to get into again and again? For instance, the last intervention the therapist made is an attempt to get into this area, and there is something that he wants to uncover and make manifest to the patient. She herself must have a certain expectation, probably throughout the whole therapy, that this is what therapy is about and that he's going to pull something out of her or get into something of this kind. Her expectations can also be thought of as a context for the entire therapy, even on a session-to-session basis.

Langs: Well, here you are using the term context in a different way than we use it in the communicative approach. You are talking about the patient's conscious (though not unconscious) fantasies and expectations of what therapy will be like. Of course, this helps to shape the treatment situation, including the patient's associations and, at times, the manner in which the therapist intervenes. These are part of the patient's intrapsychic set and will reflect positive ego attributes as well as psychopathology.

A good deal of analytic work can be carried out with the patient as she responds to intervention contexts based on her expectations, and in addition, on the communicated expectations of the therapist. As used by me, expectations are conscious *and* unconscious for both participants, and for the therapist. They involve the basic contract, the ground rules and setting, as well as the nature of the intervention efforts. Often, the patient's expectations help to shape gross behavioral and communicative resistances to the unfolding of treatment.

To cite an extreme example, let's say the patient expects the therapist to direct or advise her, as in this case. Her efforts to obtain such responses will constitute gross behavioral resistances, which may be accompanied by communicative resistances. Nonetheless, in the adaptive context of an interpretive intervention or attitude in the therapist, or in his efforts to secure the frame, these endeavors by the patient form part of a derivative complex which can be meaningfully interpreted to her, and which will have a significant bearing on her psychopathology. At the same time, some aspects of the patient's expectations will contribute to the alliance sector, manifest and communicative, and help to foster the therapeutic unfolding and interpretive work.

However, the patient's conscious, manifest expectations must be understood in the light of activated intervention contexts. It is no exception to the rule that true meaning involves such contexts, and that all manifest expectations and associations must ultimately be understood in terms of their derivative implications. In this way, you will not simply and naively go along with the patient's expectations or attempt to correct them directly and consciously. Instead, you will observe when they are expressed in a particular session, and determine their unconscious meanings and functions, and be in a position to interpretively resolve their pathological, underlying implications and their role in the patient's resistances.

I must address another implication in your question and comment. You seem to be uncertain whether I agree that the patient's manifest wish to resolve her conflicts in her relationship with the boyfriend is a therapeutic goal on which both she and the therapist can agree. This is a major aspect of the patient's stated complaint, and you seem to be asking whether the therapeutic work should be designed to help her resolve it. This implies that you believe that the communicative approach I have been developing here would move in some other direction.

I can recognize the source of confusion here. The communicative approach acknowledges the patient's manifest complaints, and is designed to help the patient resolve them, whether they are symptoms, characterological problems, or whatever—as long as they are emotionally founded. However, the essential point in this approach is that insightful and adaptive resolution of such difficulties is best effected through an analysis of the unconscious structure or basis for the patient's neurosis, rather than through some direct and manifest discussion of the patient's problem or offer of Type One derivative speculations as to its supposed basis.

The communicative therapist has come to realize, based on empirical findings, that the patient's neurosis will be mobilized within the ongoing communicative interaction. As a result, effective interpretations will take that interaction as the point of departure. This means that interpretations of the patient's derivative responses to intervention contexts will directly expose aspects of the patient's unconscious fantasy and perception constellations which pertain not only to neurotic reactions in the relationship with the therapist, but also to her neurosis in general—including, in this case, its influence on her relationship with her boyfriend. When the patient becomes aware of the underlying factors in her indecision and sexual conflicts, and whatever else, she can resolve the pertinent conflicts and modify the relevant pathological introjects through which new adaptive resources will enable her to handle the situation far more realistically and effectively.

Often, it is possible to begin with an adaptive context within therapy, trace the patient's derivative responses and then link them to related problems in her relationship with her boyfriend—all carried out in keeping with the patient's derivative communications. At times the insights will derive entirely from material related to the therapeutic interaction; but at other times, direct connections to the problem with her boyfriend will emerge in the session and will permit specific interpretation in light of prevailing adaptive contexts and derivative response within the treatment relationship. Thus, there are two ways in which these problems are approached: indirectly, through an analysis of the neurotic aspects of the patient's reactions to the therapeutic interaction; and more directly as this type of analysis is simultaneously linked to expressed problems. In no case, however, has it been found in the communicative approach that it is possible to effectively analyze and interpret the unconscious basis of the patient's difficulties through interventions which exclude any connection to the ongoing therapeutic interaction.

In sum, the communicative approach is indeed designed to help the patient resolve her problems with her boyfriend, but proposes to do so through an analysis of its unconscious sources pivotal to which is a consideration of the patient's reactions to prevailing adaptive contexts within the therapeutic interaction.

Discussant: There is another point to consider: she had these problems before she came into therapy.

Langs: Well, I can sense an upsurge of doubts about the communicative viewpoint, which may be based on some failure on my part to offer convincing validation. It may also be a function of something about this material, which is so intensely instinctual, or even a response to the pending termination of this course. Whatever its sources—and I'll leave each of you to self-analysis—I would suggest that we now hear some clinical material, so we may answer these and other questions based on specific clinical data. Patients do, of course, have their neurosis before they come into treatment, though it is sometimes considerably expanded because of the unconscious countertransference contributions of the therapist. However, the patient's meaningful neurotic responses almost immediately became organized around the relationship with the therapist and his interventions.

Therapist: I wanted to mention that I had not as yet informed the patient that I would be leaving the clinic. The session I reported was on Tuesday, and the following Monday was our next session. In it, the patient said that she hadn't been able to sleep for five days. Last night, she had been able to sleep. She didn't know why she couldn't sleep for five days.

She said that on Tuesday she was feeling real good, she got a massage and got dressed up, and really felt like a woman. She then went to this party that she had mentioned in the previous session, expecting to go home with someone else. Her boyfriend was at his office. At the party, she met this friend or acquaintance of hers, named Ted. He was someone that she was never particularly close to or attracted to, but she spent some time with him at the party. Afterwards, she went back with him to his apartment but she couldn't go through with it—having sex with him. He wasn't very sensitive about it, either, and she left after spending some time there, after having a drink with him. She said that later (and it wasn't clear as to when), she had also made love with her boyfriend, after which she had started to cry because she wasn't deriving much pleasure from it. She hadn't had an orgasm. The next day she told her boyfriend about going over to Ted's apartment. Here I said, You told him?

Langs: We have several tasks at this point. First, we must review the material up to this point in the hour in order to both evaluate the level of resistance and to see if it helps us to decide the degree of validity of an intervention pertinent to the patient herself and her relationships outside of therapy. We also have to discuss this particular intervention in some detail.

Discussant: It was my impression that the therapist's intervention had absolutely no effect on the patient's plans. Also, I heard nothing in this material which extended or clarified his confrontation, and saw no sign of validation.

Discussant: But maybe the patient would have gone to bed with this fellow Ted if the therapist hadn't intervened.

Langs: There is a sense of uncertainty in that there's no telling what might have happened in the absence of an intervention or how the intervention influenced the patient's behavior. You are dealing with inferences which cannot form a basis upon which to establish the validity of the intervention.

Discussant: For me, the material is flat and I would be inclined to agree that the intervention in the previous hour was not validated. The flatness could reflect a gross behavioral resistance, though I can't be sure. On the surface level, she might be moving toward something meaningful in respect to her relationship with the boyfriend. For once, I can experience the uncertainty in determining resistances in terms of the manifest flow of the material.

Discussant: I am struck with the fact that this patient has apparently not referred to therapy or the therapist through all of last session, and in this hour as well. I see two possibilities. One is that the treatment situation is not especially relevant, a point that I know Dr. Langs would dispute. Another possibility is that the patient is being highly defensive. In terms of the definition of communicative resistances which you have provided us, I sense the presence of a high level of defensiveness even though I have not tried to define it more specifically.

Discussant: I have tried to organize this material around the adaptive context of the therapist's previous intervention regarding her masturbation fantasy. In light of this context, there would be an indicator based on its erroneous qualities, at least as we have evaluated that particular confrontation, and an unconsciously communicated wish by the therapist to steer clear of his relationship with the patient. The patient acted out in a sense against her boyfriend, and that's a possible indicator which is represented manifestly. I have to say that any possible indicator related to the therapeutic relationship is not manifest; if it exists, it is represented with considerable disguise. My conclusion would be that there is a high level of communicative resistance in respect to the representation of the adaptive contexts pertinent to treatment.

Langs: I would agree. At best, you might tentatively formulate that the patient represents the seductive and self-revealing qualities of the therapist's intervention by her involvement with Ted and her revelation of that fact to her boyfriend. The level of representability of the context is quite low, a two or three, and therefore the level of resistance is quite high.

Discussant: It seems to me that there is also a high level of resistance in respect to the derivative complex. As someone said, there is no bridge whatsoever to therapy. The derivatives are general, indicating that someone in the therapeutic field is struggling with inappropriate sexual needs and has a need to reveal it to another person, perhaps a third party. This could be an unconscious perception of the therapist, it could say something about the patient herself, but whatever it's about, I find it extremely unclear. I would therefore suggest that the resistances are quite high here as well.

Langs: Yes, we have a situation which justifies the evaluation of a high level of communicative resistances in respect to the representation of the indicators and adaptive contexts, and in regard to the meaningful implications of the derivative complex.

I can only speculate that formulating a high level of resistance would run contrary to the evaluation of many classical therapists, who would believe that, because the patient is talking about her sexual conflicts and behaviors and revealing herself to her boyfriend, the material is quite meaningful and eventually would prove interpretable in terms of these outside relationships.

What about the intervention?

Discussant: It seems to be a question with confronting qualities. It brings her behavior into question. It certainly is a response to manifest content listening, and it treats as the indicator for the session the fact that the patient made a confession to her boyfriend. There is of course no reference to an intervention context or a derivative complex.

Discussant: But isn't the therapist attempting to imply to the patient that her self-revelation is worthy of further exploration?

Langs: That's one of its communicative implications. What else?

Discussant: It implies a criticism of the patient, and of course, it directs her away from the therapeutic interaction.

Langs: Yes. In that connection allow me to backpedal a bit. We formulated a high level of communicative resistances, and an uncertain level of gross behavioral resistance—perhaps relatively low, since the patient is free associating and being cooperative. We did not, however, attempt to define the motives for the patient's resistance. What might they be?

Discussant: We know that the therapist in the previous hour asked repeated questions about the manifest contents of the patient's material, each time steering clear of his relationship with the patient. I would therefore have to believe that the patient's own avoidance of her relationship with the therapist is an interactional defense, as you termed it, and that in part it is prompted by an introjection of the therapist's defensiveness.

Langs: Yes, repeated questions of that kind would constitute not only a cognitive barrier, but also the projective identification of an active defensive barrier designed to seal off any direct and even meaningful derivatives pertinent to the therapeutic relationship. The therapist's defensiveness, his failure to sit back and contain the material until the patient's derivatives show the way, has created a need system within the patient for a complementary type of defensiveness reflected in her communicative resistances.
What else?

Discussant: I wonder if the patient isn't struggling with some type of sexual fantasies and conflicts which have something to do with the therapist, and which lead to this type of compromised communication: derivatives regarding her sexual fantasies and anxieties, her sense of overstimulation and concern about controls, without any link to the therapist.

Langs: Yes, but we would also have to postulate the presence of counterresistances in the therapist which are contributing as well to the patient's resistances. These counterresistances may well be motivated by some type of erotic countertransference; at the very least, that is the patient's perception. These run complementary to the patient's own erotic tranferences and nontransferences, that is, her own erotic fantasy constellation and her unconscious perceptions of the therapist in this sphere.

In all, there is considerable evidence that the patient and therapist have created a bastion through which they have sealed off allusions to the therapeutic relationship and interaction, motivated by their mutual conscious and unconscious sexual fantasies and perceptions, and related anxieties and conflicts. Once again you can see how the patient's communicative resistances are designed to protect the therapist from manifest and derivative associations which might threaten him, and evoke within him both conflict and anxiety. Most interactional resistances, since they are generated at the unconscious behest of the therapist, serve in part a protective function of this kind.

Discussant: I tried to understand the timing of the intervention. I am aware that the surface approach can offer little in the way of guidelines. But trying to understand what prompted the therapist to intervene, his adaptive context, I can only sense that he experienced some anxiety in regard to the patient's self-revelation. I sensed that he is revealing an interest in triangles on his own part as well.

Discussant: I was puzzled why, for example, the therapist didn't question the patient about her decision to go back to Ted's apartment, and why instead, he suddenly picks up on this particular issue. There seems to be no principle behind this type of intervening.

Langs: I am glad that you can sense the arbitrary qualities in the usual approach to resistances and the timing of interventions. The lack of sound precepts creates the potential for a great deal of self-revelation on the part of such therapists.

Discussant: Isn't it possible that unconsciously the therapist was conveying his concern about the lack of confidentiality in this treatment?

Langs: Yes, his concern about his patient's revealing secrets could well imply a concern about the conditions of treatment, and especially the lack of confidentiality in his own presentation of this material to his supervisor. As such, this intervention would constitute a derivative lie barrier, since it touches upon an important intervention context for this therapy. While such communications from the therapist fall short of the necessary conscious and direct delineation required for a sound interpretation, a therapist's capacity to touch upon issues of this kind through derivative lie-barrier systems may have some small constructive influence on the patient. We should at least be open to this possibility—namely, that this is one of the ways in which the therapist offers lie-barrier systems which may be more flexible and adaptive than those which the patient is presently using. However, often this is not the case, and the therapist's lie-barrier systems are infused with pathology and distinctly maladaptive. In general, their offer to the patient, however unconsciously, will tend to reinforce the patient's own pathological defenses and use of maladaptive lie-barrier systems.

Discussant: There are a couple more qualities to this intervention. It is an attempt to have the patient elaborate on a manifest content rather than any effort to interpret a resistance. Our formulation would lead to the conclusion that it is the offer of a Type C barrier against any connection to the therapeutic relationship, and as such, we would have to say that the therapist has been quite effective in establishing these barriers in both himself and the patient.

Langs: Yes, we can state all of these as silent hypotheses, but sooner or later we need Type Two derivative validation. I have seen a number of presentations of this kind in which therapists have intervened so actively in respect to outside relationships, repeatedly at points where the patient's derivatives are moving toward less disguised allusions to the therapist and treatment situation, that it becomes virtually impossible for the patient to produce a link to therapy of any kind. None of these efforts receive any form of Type Two derivative validation, and often lack even surface confirmation. There is usually a sense of repetitiveness and staleness when listening to such material, and it is my belief that this is one type of therapeutic work which produces treatment situations which go on for years accomplishing little that is meaningful.

On rare occasions, in anticipation of presenting to me, one or two therapists of this kind have sat back and allowed the patient an opportunity to communicate more freely. Much to their surprise, links to therapy soon began to emerge. In this session, the therapist sat back for a while, though eventually he did intervene on a manifest content level. We will soon see if this leads to clarification or to further resistances. In time, we'll also see whether a bridge to therapy appears.

Discussant: But what if the therapist is addressing himself here to possible masochistic behavior on his patient's part. Why would we then feel that this is an erroneous intervention?

Langs: We keep coming back to basic issues of listening and of technique which seem not to have been resolved by this course. I sense a kind of split: in your discussions, you are able to apply the communicative approach quite well, while your questions show continued uncertainties and the need to justify manifest content and Type One derivative therapies.

If this does represent a masochistic behavior on the part of this patient, the analysis of this behavior should rely on an understanding of the patient's derivative communications in light of an adaptive context within treatment. Your suggestion excludes the possibility that a most critical determinant of this behavior is based on an introject of a set of communicated masochistic needs within the therapist. The communicative approach would leave open both possibilities, while your approach would immediately locate the psychopathology in the patient and deny its presence in the therapist, as well as any influence on his part. In addition, the therapist's particular question has a confronting quality, with its critical tone. On an unconscious communicative level, it actually places the patient in a masochistic position as the victim of the therapist's criticism. Paradoxically, then, while manifestly hoping to pursue and resolve the patient's masochism, the intervention unconsciously reinforces those very elements in her personality. It is these unconscious communicative qualities that are consistently overlooked in the type of approach some of you are advocating.

Discussant: I see room for disagreement. I think that you could help the patient a great deal by using this kind of confrontation of masochistic behaviors based on a harsh superego. While it is confronting, it is a different kind of person doing the confrontation than, say, the critical and overbearing parents of the patient's past.

Langs: Here too we must allow the patient's responsive derivatives to decide. You are assuming that the patient will experience the therapist inherently as different from the parents, while I would think it likely that instead, an intervention of this kind will unconsciously be experienced by the patient as an actual repetition of the harshness of the parents—a confirmatory pathological interaction which supports the patient's pathological introjects and psychopathology. As I have said before, my own extended clinical observations have validated that particular thesis repeatedly.

Discussant: But the therapeutic relationship takes place in a different environment than that which the patient has come from.

Langs: You are making an assumption rather than examining the actual qualities of the therapeutic environment and the nature of the therapist's interventions to see if this is really the case. I appreciate your openness since I think it is important for us to hear about your reservations and doubts. They also reveal what I believe to be prevailing attitudes in the field today. Both Loewald (1960) and Dewald (1976), in writing of the differences between the therapist and patient, and between the therapist and earlier pathogenic parental figures, assumed without question the presence of such differences. As an empiricist, I make no such assumption. My clinical observations support the conclusion that in a high percentage of instances, there are many areas of similarity between the therapeutic environment and the early home environment, and between the implications of the therapist's interventions and the pathogenic qualities of the earlier relationships. There are also differences; as a rule the therapist does indeed express himself in different ways from these earlier figures. But the totality is such that the patient experiences divided communications from the therapist, sensing a split to which he himself responds in split fashion. The patient introjects and works over the therapist's psychopathology and the similarities between the therapist and the parents, while simultaneously experiencing, working over, and expressing some appreciation for the therapist's efforts to be different—actually different and nontraumatizing and hopefully, even helpful, or at least genuinely concerned and dedicated. These mixed perceptions are often reflected in a communication to the effect that somebody has been very hurtful even though he tried not to be so. You hear that kind of commentary again and again in clinic patients, and in patients with therapists who are trying to do their best, but who are nonetheless providing some form of lie therapy.

Discussant: It seems to me that something disturbing has happened in the therapy. After all, the patient could not sleep for five days after the session, or at least until the night before she was to see the therapist.

Langs: Yes, there is a sense that something is amiss. Remember, we don't know the therapist's interventions in the previous hour, except for one comment at the end of the session. Incidentally, the sleeplessness is a symptomatic indicator and we would hope to be able to eventually intervene in a manner which would help the patient to understand its unconscious basis.

Discussant: We have not said much about value judgments on the part of therapists. This occurs to me because we really don't know whether the patient is being honest in clearing the air, perhaps concerned that the boyfriend might find out about her little involvement with Ted. On the other hand, she might have been behaving masochistically or self-destructively. I had the feeling that a value judgment was involved, rather than an approach through which we would let the patient's material tell us whether this particular behavior is destructive.

Langs: Many comments are made about the potential dangers of imposing your own values as a person and therapist upon the patient. The communicative approach is designed to safeguard against such impositions to the greatest extent feasible by allowing the patient's derivative communications to be the means through which such evaluations are made. Our concern is for the patient's suffering, and our interest is focused on the unconscious basis for her neurosis. We attempt to provide her with the therapeutic environment within which such expressions can be safely conveyed to the therapist and subjected to interpretation. We leave it to the patient to work through the relevant insights and introjects, and to decide how she will respond.

Discussant: I thought that letting her boyfriend know about Ted was her way of dealing with some kind of conflict about going to his apartment. And the therapist's question can be looked upon as a way of bringing this particular conflict into the therapy in order to analyze it, rather than have her act out one side of the conflict. It's an effort to analyze in the place of the patient's acting out.

Langs: I sense a great need for the patient's responses to this intervention at this point. Several of you seem strongly invested in the rationale for questions and confrontations of this kind, justified in the belief that it constitutes an effort to analyze and to understand. Manifestly, those goals are clearly what the therapist had in mind. Issues arise in respect to the question of whether these goals can be achieved in that manner or if it requires a different type of approach: silence, waiting for the patient's derivative material, an effort if possible to interpret the prevailing communicative resistances, a need to rectify the therapist's contribution to these resistances, and an ultimate understanding of the unconscious basis for the patient's behavior based on an analysis of her responses to the prevailing adaptive contexts within therapy.

This intervention was made before we learned more about the implications of the patient's confession. It fixes the problem within the patient, something some of you feel is quite necessary at this point. I have already stated my objections to this approach, focused as it is on the manifest contents of the patient's associations and on the belief that in some way the patient will be able to consciously express herself in a way that will illuminate this issue. This reflects the assumption that conscious realizations lead to the resolution of a neurosis, rather than understanding based on unconsciously determined derivative communication.

Let's realize once again how, though we are focused now on intervening, the key questions involve the basics of the listening and validating processes. In a way, this particular therapeutic interaction, focused as it is by both patient and therapist on the patient's relationship with others outside of treatment, has encouraged you to raise serious questions regarding the communicative approach. It may well be, as I said, that this material will not permit a convincing resolution to the problems you raise; only time will tell.

Discussant: Why can't we postulate that both levels are true: there is a problem with the boyfriend and a problem with the therapist.

Langs: The issue is, Which is central? And also, can you interpret these conflicts entirely in the context of the relationship with the boyfriend, and obtain Type Two derivative validation? I thought that I had established beyond question that interventions of that kind fail, and consistently serve the defensive and other countertransference needs of the therapist. For some of you, this proves not to be the case. We must therefore turn again to the patient as the ultimate unconscious supervisor and ask her to resolve our dilemma.

Discussant: I guess that I have not resolved in my mind your position that there is a single basic technique which should be applied to all patients. It seems to me that if you sit back with certain types of patients, you get nowhere.

Langs: We are moving too far from clinical data. We know nothing of the basis of your impressions, while you know a great deal about how I have established the position and technical principles which I advocate.

Discussant: I was simply trying to say that, with patients with harsh and overbearing superegos, there is a necessity to confront that harshness so the patient can begin to grow in therapy, and then be able to do the kind of exploratory work that you advocate.

Langs: Let's now hear from the patient—and therapist.

Therapist: Well, she responded by saying, Yes, I did. The fact that I went back to the apartment with Ted didn't really bother him, but he got angry about the fact that I had chosen to go with Ted of all people, since he doesn't particularly like him and he isn't a particularly attractive kind of guy. And the fact that I even almost considered staying with him, and sleeping with Ted, that was something that bothered him, that I had chosen Ted. When I told him that we had held hands, he got very angry, and shouted at me, which was typical for him. And he said, Why are you telling me this? He got very upset about that.

Langs: As I listen to this material, I continue to attempt to establish a perspective on the many questions that are being raised today. I think it is important to remember that most of your own clinical observations are based on manifest content and Type One derivative listening, formulating, and evaluating. As such, your questions are inevitable. I thought we had sufficiently developed and validated the communicative viewpoint, that its validity was well established. Of late, I have begun to realize that I am so embedded in that particular approach, and have so clearly tested out its formulations and found the consequences so constructive and convincing, that I sometimes fail to go back to basics to explain the intermediary steps. Still, a concept such as Type Two derivative validation is transversal in this special sense: it offers a form of confirmation that should be quite acceptable to present-day therapists, while simultaneously establishing a critical criterion which leads without question to the communicative approach and almost immediately validates many of its tenets.

Here, we must take these first associations as the patient's *commentary* on the intervention, and sort out her valid and distorted unconscious perceptions and fantasies. In doing so, we are adopting a principle that should make sense to the classical therapist, even though in actual practice he does not, as a rule, listen to the material which follows his intervention in this particular manner. He often feels that once he has made an intervention, it has validity since his intentions are clear to him and are, in his opinion, constructive. It then becomes a matter of listening to whether the patient responds to the intervention with elaboration, most of it on the surface, or does not—in which case, he often invokes the concept of resistance and tries to understand why the patient is battling against his wisdom. Even on those occasions where he more avidly attempts to determine whether the patient's response validates his intervention, he will usually extend and interpret the patient's material in ways which reflect a bias directed toward finding confirmation, and will tend to consider any segment of nonconfirmatory material as based on transference distortions.

I would venture to say that with a question of the type just offered, the average therapist would consider his intervention to be relatively innocuous and simply observe where it leads. Such communicative qualities as the way in which it focuses the patient on her relationship with the boyfriend and away from the therapeutic interaction, the way in which it selects a particular aspect of the patient's material and behavior as the locus of the question, and the consequence that the therapeutic work will take place in terms of manifest contents and perhaps their direct implications—all of that would, as far as I can tell from the literature, be entirely overlooked. In addition, the concept of the patient's responses as a commentary with both valid unconscious perceptions, as well as possible distorted fantasies, would not be entertained.

I am reiterating points that I have made in previous parts of this course primarily to refresh your memories and to restate some of the distinctions between the classical and communicative approaches. The average therapist would simply hear this material as constituting a direct response to the therapist's question, and as reflecting a continued elaboration of the details of what transpired between the patient and her boyfriend. How might we hear this same material?

Discussant: That the therapist was behaving in the same way as the patient's boyfriend. It seems to me that the therapist's unconscious, but easily detected, communication to the patient was that she was into this sexual acting out with Ted and she never went through with it, and that he's surprised she told her boyfriend, and that they will have to struggle with this material in the session. In a sense, the patient felt criticized, and that response is reflected in the fact that her boyfriend is reacting in a critical way.

Langs: I would not be able to agree with all that you said, though the last part of your comments moved in the direction that I think reflects an important aspect of this commentary. Taking the therapist's intervention as our adaptive context, and recognizing its harsh and questioning qualities as we formulated them before we heard the patient's associations, the material about the boyfriend can be seen as reflecting an unconscious perception of the therapist's criticism of the patient's behavior. This constitutes the valid core of this material, and it appears to shade into some degree of transference distortion in portraying the therapist as totally enraged. Nonetheless, the *how could you do that?* quality of the question is beautifully portrayed in these associations.

I hope that this formulation is quite clear. Remember, in advance of these associations we formulated the communicative implications of the therapist's intervention and now we find that through her derivative communications—the latent implications of her manifest associations—the patient is expressing a set of qualities that are strikingly comparable to those we identified directly. This constitutes a secondary form of Type Two derivative validation—indirect and disguised confirmation—of our formulation. We do not assume that our communicative evaluation is inherently correct, but leave it to the patient's associations to decide. For the moment, for example, the material confirms the hostile and confronting qualities of the intervention, but not the interest in threesomes which some of you proposed. Later associations may support that impression or they may not. If they fail to do so, we must accept nonvalidation for the moment, attempt to evaluate its basis beginning with the likelihood that we have been in error, and await further material to clarify the situation.

Discussant: On another level, in terms of what the therapist was wondering about when he made the intervention, it seems to me that the intervention works. He wanted to show the patient that she was being provocative, and we learn that her boyfriend took her comment in that way.

Langs: Yes, there is indeed that kind of surface elaboration here. As I said before, this particular material is striking for the way in which it continues to appear to support formulations made on a manifest content basis, with some small measure of Type One derivative implication. We still await a sequence of associations which would support one level of listening while contradicting the other. For the moment, it appears to be a matter of choice: listening to this material along the me/not-me interface, you can locate the problem entirely within the patient, entirely within the therapist, or within both. You could say that the patient was being provocative, that the therapist had been provocative, or that they both had been provocative. The communicative approach has validated the principle of dealing first with the valid elements in the patient's material as they pertain to the therapist before considering distorted elements. Nonetheless, this position requires new validation through this material.

Therapist: She went on to say that later her boyfriend had said to her, You are always acting like a masochist.

Langs: Here too the same problem exists: Who is the masochist? The patient, the therapist, or both? Who is inviting attack? I am impressed with the extent to which this material does not permit a definitive resolution of this problem. I think that there is a consistent element here that demonstrates how easily a therapist could justify a continued formulation of this material around the patient's sadomasochistic problems, without feeling a need of any kind to link this material to himself or to the therapeutic relationship.

Discussant: It occurred to me that her style is one of teasing and provoking. Because of that, I would want to avoid any type of confrontation, because it would simply play into her style of relating.

Discussant: Also, an interpretation of the patient's masochistic needs, her provocativeness, would involve something that she already has heard before.

Discussant: The commentary here is that the therapist is a masochist, that he seems to provoke the patient again and again through his interventions.

Langs: Yes, but let's hear more.

Therapist: At this point, she went back to what is for her a traditional theme, doing so in a kind of standardized way. And she began to ask, Why can't I decide about marrying my boyfriend, why is it so hard for me? And she went through the familiar pros and cons, saying again that he's such a nice guy and yet she can't decide about it. She went on: I could live with him. I could live with him forever, but I just can't decide to marry him.

At that point I said, It seems as if you can only go so far, both in the relationship with him in general and more specifically, in your sexual relationship. You can live with him, but you can't take the further step of marrying him. And you can have a sexual relationship, but you can't go on to have an orgasm in intercourse. Something seems to be stopping you.

Langs: Who will comment?

Discussant: On the surface, in respect to gross behavioral resistances, the material became flat and empty. Now this could mean that the patient became defensive at the point at which she began to appreciate her own masochism, and that her fear of her masochistic needs prompted the sense of resistance. On the other hand, it could imply a nonvalidation of the therapist's intervention—his question —and a commentary that it was now being seen as the same old stuff and keeping her in limbo. I was struck by the patient's dilemma: she can live with her boyfriend but not marry him. In a way, I could connect that to the therapeutic relationship: she can have therapy with the therapist in the clinic, but will soon be facing a forced termination. In addition, therapy in a clinic has a certain quality of not having the therapist as your own. He belongs to the clinic; he has a supervisor; and there is no direct commitment to the patient, except as made through the clinic.

Langs: Yes, we can monitor this material as Type Two derivative commentaries, much of it valid, on the basic conditions of the therapeutic relationship. On that level, the patient's inability to make a final decision could well be a Type Two derivative perception of the therapist's difficulty in understanding and interpreting this material in a definitive manner. As you know, it is my thesis that this would require the use of silence to the point where the patient's derivatives would more clearly show—as I would expect— that these unconscious communications pertain to the therapeutic relationship.

Discussant: One thing is for sure: on a communicative level, there continues to be a high level of resistance in respect to the representation of the adaptive context. There is still no bridge to therapy. In our discussion, we were able to organize a set of coalescing derivatives, so I think that we would have to say that the resistances are moderate to low in that respect. But I am amazed by the absence of any reference to the therapist or therapy here. In my own work, this seldom happens. And in the presentations we have heard in this course, if my memory serves me, the therapy or therapist has come up again and again.

Langs: Yes, your comments are well taken. This is quite unusual. However, I have seen this type of misalliance develop in case presentations where the therapist has had a powerful need to intervene repeatedly in terms of outside relationships and to keep the patient away from all possible unconscious perceptions of the nature of his therapeutic work. In any case, who will now help us to evaluate this intervention?

Discussant: It is mainly a confrontation, but there is some kind of shading into an interpretation by suggesting to the patient there are things that she doesn't understand about her own behavior.

Langs: Yes, it has the qualities of a preliminary interpretation, based on confronting the patient with certain facts of her behavior. It suggests that there are unconscious factors involved, but they are not specified.

Discussant: The level of listening is manifest, but the hint is that there is some type of Type One derivative which would account for the manifest material. As for its communicative qualities, it deals with the indicator of the patient's problems in deciding whether to marry or not. There is no consideration of an adaptive context within therapy, and the implied adaptive context is the problem the patient is having in her relationship with her boyfriend. It doesn't really meaningfully organize the derivatives, except to link up some rather similar aspects of the patient's behavior.

Discussant: I was struck by the superficiality of the point being made here: the patient can't commit herself to her boyfriend and she is unable to achieve orgasm in intercourse. Perhaps it is true that when someone is not committed to another person, they are less likely to have an orgasm during intercourse. Somehow, for me, it doesn't address unconscious determinants. I say that even though the therapist is hinting that there is some underlying basis for this problem. There is nothing in his intervention which illuminates those particular factors.

Discussant: Once again, the therapist has intervened in terms of the patient's outside relationships, here between herself and her boyfriend. There is no effort to deal with the sense of resistance we heard in this material, either on the gross behavioral or communicative level.

Langs: Yes, and in principle, the critical decision is whether to remain silent or to interpret the unconscious basis for the gross behavioral and communicative resistances. This decision depends, of course, on whether there is material available for interpretation. As we know, it is more common to have a represented adaptive context and meaningful derivative complex available as a way of interpreting gross behavioral resistances, such as the patient's empty ruminations, than it is to have such material available in the presence of communicative resistances. In the latter situation, we need a momentary lessening of resistances in order for an interpretable network to emerge.

Let me state here a rather simple principle to serve as a guideline. The therapist should intervene whenever he has a sufficiently strong indicator, and a directly represented or thinly disguised expression of an activated adaptive context accompanied by a coalescing and meaningful derivative complex. In essence, then, the therapist should interpret whenever it is called for and he has the means to do so.

This tenet can prove quite helpful in a session where, for example, you have a strong indicator and a directly represented adaptive context and know that you must wait for the derivative complex to develop. Or in another hour, you might have a strong indicator and a meaningful set of derivatives, and will need to wait for a good representation of the intervention context. Knowing the ingredients you need for a good interpretation helps in effecting good timing to your efforts.

Sometimes, you will have a situation where there have been strong gross behavioral and communicative resistances, and then the patient shifts temporarily to produce a meaningful derivative network. Under these circumstances, you will have to choose between interpreting the resistances—which you should do if at all possible—and momentarily bypassing them in order to interpret the available derivative implications of the patient's associations in light of a different, but pressing, indicator and intervention context. In principle, as I said, it remains important to interpret defenses and resistances first, other types of material second.

Returning to this situation, it would appear that the therapist felt that it was necessary for him to bypass the patient's resistances and to make a confrontation which had some of the qualities of a general interpretation. However, this effort does not meet our criteria of a sound or complete interpretation: it did not deal with many pressing indicators, failed to establish the best representation of an adaptive context within the therapeutic interaction, and did not offer a meaningful shaping of the implications of the derivative complex. Within the communicative approach, the principle would be to attempt to combine both efforts when the material permits: to always begin with an interpretation of the unconscious basis for resistances and then shade into the meaningful aspects of the patient's neurosis, her unconscious perception and fantasy constellations, as revealed by the material. In principle, attempt wherever possible to interpret rather than bypass resistances. As a rule, when there is a meaningful derivative network, the unconscious basis and implications of resistances are in evidence.

Discussant: Based on our formulations, we are postulating again that the therapist has intervened through the Type C mode, reinforcing the bastion erected by himself and the patient against communications more directly related to the therapeutic interaction.

Langs: Yes, we continue to find considerable evidence of such efforts.

Discussant: The intervention also contained an unconscious communication of the therapist's perception of the patient's progression in the session. First, she offered up some spicy material about the party and the boyfriend, but then she closed herself off and gave the therapist stereotyped material. It was as if she was unable to continue with the session; she couldn't follow through there as well.

Langs: Yes, but you left out the therapist's intervention. The therapist pressured the patient to remain on the surface. While she did continue with more affect-laden and instinctual drive-laden material for a while—you are quite right—she soon trailed off. But remember, you are offering us a manifest observation. The question remains, in terms of dynamics: Does it characterize the patient alone, or the patient and the therapist? How much of this is coming from the therapist's interventions? This is an interactional product. We must first formulate the therapist's contribution, and rectify it within the sessions, before we will be able to determine the extent to which this reflects the patient's own propensities.

Notice too that this intervention once again places all of the psychopathology within the bipersonal field in the patient, and emphasizes the extent to which *she* has a block and cannot permit a fully satisfying relationship or sexual experience.

Well, we have characterized the communicative implications of this intervention. I would only add, in keeping with a remark already made, that it is also unusual for us to hear a presentation which the therapist intervenes repeatedly without any reference to himself or therapy. The avoidance is intense on both sides, patient and therapist. It remains to be convincingly shown, however, that this indeed, constitutes a pathological bastion rather than an appropriate way of working with a patient whose problems supposedly have nothing to do with the therapeutic interaction.

Therapist: She said, But the sexual aspects of things are just not so important. Not in making a decision about getting married. I was talking with my friend Susie and I spoke to my sister, and none of them understand.

Discussant: Here the patient says that no one understands her. Would you consider that a Type Two derivative validation of your formulation that the therapist has not understood this material?

Langs: Yes, I certainly would. However, to be entirely fair, we must recognize that the patient may be saying that the problem is not so much the *area* of the intervention—i.e., in terms of the patient and her relationship with her boyfriend—as it is a sense that the therapist had not correctly put together the implications of the patient's associations. We must remember again that an interpretation, even when it meets the criteria we have established from the communicative view, may be incorrect in content though correct in form. Still, in this situation, there seemed to be accuracy in what the therapist had said, so it does seem unlikely that this forms a basis for the patient's feeling of not being understood. We would then have to look elsewhere, and suspect, now perhaps a bit more strongly, that it has to do with the very basic qualities of the therapist's approach, especially his failure to allow the material to unfold to the point where its relevance to the therapeutic interaction could emerge and be interpreted.

Therapist: Just to add to what you are saying, I do hear her saying that what I am emphasizing is not as important as I think. That's still rather vague, but it is there.

She went on: I was talking to Susie and she even said that I should marry my previous boyfriend. She had said it back then when I was going with him. She just can't understand. It is very hard for me to decide about getting married. It is not just the fear of divorce. I think I would have married my old boyfriend, but at this point, with my present boyfriend, I just can't decide.

Here I asked, How are Jack and Richard different? (Jack is the name of her old boyfriend; Richard is her present boyfriend.)

Discussant: I heard what you would call an embedded derivative, which brings up the problem of forced termination: the reference to divorce.

Discussant: If Susie is a representation of the therapist, you might say that the patient experiences his interventions as superficial and as confusing.

Discussant: The intervention is a question, and it has all of the qualities of the previous question: it is arbitrary, it falls outside of the therapeutic relationship, it is on a manifest level, and it probably serves as a Type C lie barrier.

Langs: I must say that it is my belief that we are now hearing a type of therapy which is quite common among practitioners. It must be an approach which this therapist has been taught through his work at this Center. You will notice that he makes an initial intervention—a confrontation hinting at unconscious factors— and when the patient's material proves unilluminating, he goes on to a different question. In all fairness, I suspect that he now wants to bring out a point, a ready inference about Jack and Richard, and their effect on the patient. He pursues his own line of thought without support or validation from the patient, even on a manifest level. If probing one area leads nowhere, then try another. But this can be done only if you continue to obliterate the unconscious communicative implications of this style of working and of each specific intervention. And this is exactly what is done in most therapeutic situations.

It is interesting to now hear a couple of derivatives which hint at the validity of the position I have established. They are, at best, faint whispers. But I begin to sense that the patient has had enough of this bastion, which she has helped to sustain for at least two sessions, and may now slowly and tentatively shift toward an unconscious working-over of the pathological contributions from the therapist and from herself, and perhaps she may soon become engaged in unconscious curative and rectifying endeavors. It may well be that I am allowing myself to be encouraged by communications that are all too weak, since it is quite clear that this patient could easily resume her almost total support of the bastion. Still, the possibilities become more interesting.

Therapist: She went on to give me a rather monotonous version of how Jack and Richard were different, things she had already said before. She was always passionately attached to Jack, and really, whenever she would see him, she would do whatever he wanted. In contrast, Richard is not that way; she would not go along with him if he simply asked her. She said that she realizes she has been trying to get Richard angry with her, and she just doesn't know why she is doing it.

Langs: We are drawing toward the end of our time today, so I will make a brief comment. Notice that there are now additional Type Two derivatives pertinent to the unconscious communicative interaction. In particular, there is the comment that she would do whatever Jack wanted, because of her sense of passion. This is in keeping with my formulation that she has joined the therapist in the bastion, and she now adds that it relates to unconscious sexual fantasies and needs—certainly in herself, and in all likelihood, within the therapist as well.

Her comment that she is trying to get Richard angry with her may also constitute a reflection of an unconscious perception of the therapist and the implications of his interventions. These are all highly tentative silent hypotheses, but it does seem clear now that the patient's derivative communications are offering more support than previously for our communicative evaluation.

Therapist: Here I said to the patient, It seems that you want to be forced to do things. You think that if you have no choice, if a man were to force you, you could get married and perhaps also you could have an orgasm.

Langs: Is there much more to this session?

Therapist: Yes.

Langs: Well, perhaps it will be well to keep us in suspense. Let's evaluate this intervention and stop for today. We can continue with this material next week.

Discussant: This sounds to me like an interpretation.

Langs: Yes, and it is to the therapist's credit that, right or wrong, he used simple, nontechnical language in developing his intervention.

Discussant: The level of listening is Type One derivative. The indicator remains the patient's problems with her boyfriend. The adaptive context the therapist used lies within that particular relationship and in no way pertains to therapy, and there is an attempt here to shape the derivatives around some type of need within the patient to be forced, perhaps to be needlessly attached, or even raped. It seems to me as I heard the intervention, the therapist was moving toward establishing certain kinds of rape fantasies within the patient which exist for her as conditions for sexual gratification.

Discussant: I am a bit concerned about the accuracy of the intervention. It wasn't clear to me that Jack forced the patient to do anything at all. It seemed to me she was saying that she herself was ready to surrender to him, and that he really didn't have to push her into anything. Her attachment seems more to someone who had little concern for her and who was heading toward failure.

Langs: Yes, your comments bring up the important point of recognizing the extent to which our interpretations constitute important decisions regarding the implications of the patient's material. As you can see, it is easy to read things into the patient's associations, and it becomes critical to test out such silent hypotheses before intervening. As I have been listening to the presentation, I have had the impression that the therapist has tended to make interventions before validating them silently. Whenever possible, it is really essential to obtain such Type Two derivative validation before intervening. In fact, you would do well to avoid interventions which have not found unexpected support in the patient's continued associations.

We can establish another principle from this material. To the extent that the necessity of being forced is not the patient's condition for attachment and orgasm, but a misreading by the therapist of the patient's material, the intervention offered here would derive more from the therapist's needs and fantasies than from the patient's material. I myself had not heard the theme of being forced as central to these associations, but I do think we would need to hear more before we could be certain. Misreading the patient's material can be self-revealing and reflect important countertransferences. Here, the intervention might reflect the therapist's own hostile and even rape fantasies, or his own unconscious need to be forced into something in order to achieve gratification. It could also reflect the therapist's unconscious realization that his own style of intervening is forcing, a self-revelation which the patient might unconsciously detect and now work over.

It seems to me that as the patient has begun to produce more meaningful derivatives, the therapist has responded with a greater exposure of his own countertransferences. This may well be coincidence, but it may not. The material has not become richer on the surface, but it has become richer in its derivative implications as they pertain to the therapeutic interaction. And it may well be that the therapist was unconsciously sensitive to this development, and that he had both a strong need to intervene—once again in connection with the patient's relationship with others. In addition, his own countertransferences may have been activated to the point where they received clearer derivative expression in his intervention to the patient. This is therefore quite a fascinating moment in this session.

Therapist: I was also using here some previous material from earlier sessions which I did not present.

Langs: Yes, I understand. This is very often the case with such an intervention. Nonetheless, in addition to the principle that each session should be its own creation, it is material of that kind, taken from earlier sessions, which facilitate the expression of the kind of countertransference constellation which I am postulating to have been reflected in your comment.

Discussant: The sense of coercion could also allude here to the pending forced termination.

Discussant: I felt that this was a premature intervention, and I too was not certain that this is really what the patient was doing. I would say that she was looking for a response from Richard, and perhaps from the therapist, but I didn't hear the theme of being forced into orgasm or into marriage.

Langs: Well, let's end on that note of uncertainty. We will have to wait until next week to see what follows, and to see whether the patient, through her own unconscious creativity, will help us to resolve the many pressing questions which this therapeutic interaction, and our discussion of it, has raised. I have always found it to be a sound principle that critical questions which arise in the course of a presentation will be answered by the patient's derivative communications. In the context of this therapeutic interaction, this patient may well be an exception, though there is some reason now to anticipate that she too will once again demonstrate the remarkable unconscious perceptiveness and therapeutic capacities within all patients who enter into psychotherapy or psychoanalysis.

Chapter Eight

MODIFYING
COMMUNICATIVE RESISTANCES

Langs: As I recall, we were in the middle of a session. Why not take up from the point where you left off?

Therapist: This was the session in which the patient had complained of insomnia, had gone to a party and went home with an acquaintance, and had then told her boyfriend who had blown up. She also had had relations with her present boyfriend, Richard, but kept thinking of her old boyfriend, Jack.

That's the point where I had left off in the presentation, I had just made an intervention to the effect that she wanted to be forced to do things and that she thought that if she had no choice and were forced to marry Richard, she might be able to have a lasting relationship with him—just as she seemed to feel that she had to be forced in order to have an orgasm.

Her response was that it wasn't by force that she had decided to stay with Jack (her previous boyfriend, a very charismatic fellow with whom she had lived briefly).

Langs: Much of the session and our discussion quickly returns to mind. Some of us felt that you had made a mistaken intervention in suggesting that the patient felt forced to comply in her relationship with Jack. Quite directly, the patient herself has now confirmed our impression that you had developed an erroneous, Type One derivative implication. As I said last week, to safeguard as much as possible against such errors, it is advisable to develop a silent hypothesis, and subsequently to find clearcut support and even Type Two derivative validation, before offering an intervention to the patient.

Therapist: She went on to say, Well, maybe I really didn't decide. I was so swept off my feet by him that maybe I really didn't have a choice. The thing is, he really derived a lot of pleasure from our relationship, but I didn't get too much pleasure out of it. And I don't want to just get pleasure from someone else's pleasure. Maybe it really wasn't love for him; maybe it was all sick.

Langs: What can now be said, from the patient's initial response to this intervention?

Discussant: I too had felt last week that the therapist was off a bit in the inferences he drew for the intervention. I probably don't have the same reasons for thinking that way as you do, Dr. Langs, but in any case, I now think that what she may be saying in a fairly honest way is that she is not going to go along with his intervention just to make him happy. For me, there was something truthful in what she said. It was honest, instead of a submissive and bullshitting response—for example, just agreeing with the therapist, and going on about how her whole life has been one situation after another where someone has forced her to do something. I would have seen that as rather insincere and as just going along with the intervention. Instead, it sounded like the patient was beginning to work with the intervention rather than blindly going along with it.

Discussant: Shouldn't we remember that her manifest response was one of disagreement. We can think of the rest of her associations as an effort to say more about her relationship with this fellow Jack, or as an unconscious commentary on the intervention.

As far as I'm concerned, I'm beginning to hear more and more derivatives which make sense as commentaries on the intervention, especially in terms of the patient's unconscious perceptions and introjects. In the adaptive context of the last intervention, I hear the patient saying that the therapist is trying to sweep her off her feet in order to gratify himself, and that she doesn't want to continue to go along with him in that way. She gets no pleasure from it; she's gotten something through identifying with the therapist which is now becoming unsatisfactory. She concludes that maybe she hasn't loved the therapist all along, maybe it was all sick. That seems to fit with our discussion last week.

Discussant: It certainly fits with the idea presented by Dr. Langs that this is a misalliance based on unconscious erotic transference and countertransference fantasy constellations.

Discussant: There is another odd point, which is helping me to become convinced that the communicative evaluation makes more sense than any effort to understand this material in terms of manifest content and Type One derivatives. As I remember, Dr. Langs had suggested that the patient was now shifting from going along with the bastion and misalliance to undertaking efforts to rectify and interpret its presence and implications to the therapist. It's kind of amazing to hear the patient now say something about how she got no pleasure from going along with this fellow Jack and that maybe her motives are suspect, and to then comment that maybe it's all sick. It's as if she is now saying she doesn't want to continue to go along with the therapist in their misalliance; she realizes how sick it is, and wants the therapist to realize it as well. In a general way, I wonder if that could not be an example of a general unconscious interpretation.

Langs: That's an excellent appraisal. I have little to add to it. I simply want to connect the evaluation of the communicative qualities of these associations in light of the intervention context with our consideration of resistances. The point here is to realize that it is impossible to determine the level of communicative resistances without knowing the implications of the adaptive context of the

therapist's most recent intervention. Here too the difference between the communicative and classical approaches may be further
defined.

First of all, I would not agree with the discussant who said that,
if the patient had agreed with the therapist's comment about her
need to be forced in order to be gratified, she necessarily would be
responding on a false note merely out of submissiveness. After all,
if the therapist had been correct in his reading of the Type One
derivative inference of this material, and if the patient wished to
respond honestly, she would have to agree with the surface of his
comment. As it stands, the intervention was actually designed to
serve as a lie barrier against truths which lay within an entirely
different sphere. It was a derivative untruth, an incorrect appraisal
which revealed in disguised form realizations I have already identified in respect to the therapeutic interaction.

The evaluation of surface agreement or disagreement by the
patient in respect to the therapist's intervention is a difficult process. As Freud said (1937), negation of that kind may often be
highly defensive, and yet, at times, it may be quite valid. It is an
unreliable criterion of the validity of the therapist's efforts. Only
the patient's subsequent associations can tell you whether the
negation will stand up, and this involves two levels: first, whether
the patient's material manifestly supports her denial; and second,
whether it contains Type Two derivative validation of the intervention despite the conscious denial. As you know, in response to
an erroneous intervention, the patient will not provide Type Two
derivative validation, but he will reveal derivatives of a negative
introject, quite often attempt to correct the therapist, and interpret
the basis within the therapist for the error.

So, there is little evidence of gross behavioral resistances here.
The patient continues to associate; she initially disputes the therapist's intervention, though she becomes tentative at least in respect
to the issue of choice. An unwary therapist might feel that he is
helping the patient to realize a previously unnoticed need and
fantasy, and that she had been defensive at first and then confirmatory. He would feel that the patient had been resisting a bit, only to
offer some type of confirmation through a realization that she felt
she did not have a choice in her relationship with Jack. This would
be judgmental and uncertain, and of little relevance to the real

problems within this treatment situation—at least, as I have formulated them. And I believe now that I am obtaining some level of validation for my hypotheses.

Here, material which seems ambiguous and uncertain on a manifest level can be evaluated communicatively to reflect a familiar pattern in this patient: failure to clearly represent the adaptive context and link it to the therapist, while providing a relatively meaningful derivative complex which contains some degree of resistance.

The communicative approach offers a far more reliable means of measuring resistances on both manifest and latent levels, and to recognize those which can ultimately be subjected to meaningful interpretation. For example, what unconscious factors are revealed here which could help to account for the patient's communicative resistances?

Discussant: As I hear it, the patient seems to be saying that she avoids clear expression of the adaptive context of the implications of the therapist's interventions out of some kind of love for him, possibly because she wants to feel swept away by his efforts. The implication also is that she is doing so to give the therapist pleasure, and to gratify his erotic countertransferences.

Langs: Exactly. And if the patient provided you with a meaningful bridge to therapy, you might well be able to interpret this particular communicative resistance. In essence, you would be able to tell the patient that she seems to have been avoiding connecting all of this material to her relationship with you, the therapist, because she sensed that somehow you wished for her to maintain such an avoidance; and you and she were secretly being gratified by her submitting to you as she had submitted to Jack—though she was now saying that she believes that there is something sick about this type of gratification, defensiveness, and avoidance.

In its bare essentials, that would constitute an interpretation of a relationship resistance. It deals with the *indicator* of the resistance and the bastion that the patient and therapist have formed; it identifies the pertinent *intervention context*, in respect to which I might have added more about the specific interventions involved once the patient had more clearly represented them, and it defines the implications of the relevant *derivative complex*. Notice too that the intervention is made transversally primarily in terms of implied valid unconscious perceptions, leaving room for the possibility of later identifying the presence of additional distortions. The key point is to understand that the implications of the derivative complex in light of the activated adaptive context are integrated as a means of identifying the unconscious meanings, function, and basis for the indicator—here, the resistance. To turn this around, the resistance itself is interpreted in light of an activated intervention context and the patient's responsive derivative reactions.

This material also can be used to illustrate the interplay between resistances and developmental modes of relatedness. While the clinical data is somewhat thin, it can be proposed as a silent hypothesis that the patient is indicating through derivatives her unconscious perception of the therapist's wish—and undoubtedly her own as well—to effect a pathological symbiosis in the treatment situation. She indicates that confronting, questioning, and somewhat self-revealing interventions of this kind are designed on one level to effect such a symbiosis and perhaps even a parasitic mode of relatedness. Such efforts can, as we have seen, prompt strong resistances in a patient who wishes to maintain such pathological symbiotic gratifications and to avoid the more painful pursuit of cognitive insight and individuation.

At other times, a patient may respond quite meaningfully to a therapist's efforts to secure a pathological symbiosis and therefore be in a state of relatively low resistance on both the gross behavioral and communicative levels. However, the meaning of the material at such moments will be evident only if organized around those intervention contexts through which the therapist is endeavoring to create or maintain a pathological mode of relatedness. At such junctures, a sound interpretation of these resistances would simultaneously provide the patient with cognitive insight and with the interactional experience of the therapist's wish for a healthy symbiosis. Both would contribute to positive introjective identifications with the therapist and movement toward insight and individuation. In essence, then, the resolution of resistances often is founded upon the renunciation by both participants of a pathological mode of relatedness.

Discussant: To continue the discussion we had last week, it seems to me that I could make a case for some kind of validation of this intervention. The therapist told her that she wanted to be forced into a relationship and into sex in order to have a lasting involvement and an orgasm. The patient now says that being forced means having to accept love and enjoyment, and to have pleasure. She was also able to realize that she felt that she had no choice in her relationship with Jack. To me this implies that we have helped the patient to increase her knowledge of herself.

Langs: Well, I can see that you are still not convinced by the Type Two derivatives which this patient is beginning to generate and which fit so nicely with our communicative formulations of this material. You would therefore locate the so-called insight into being sick entirely within the patient, and experience it as a genuine realization instead of a derivative lie. Actually, it is quite helpful to have your comments, since they once again represent the way in which many therapists would hear this material. The comment about sickness would not be examined along the me/not-me interface, but on the manifest level as alluding to the patient. To provide you with a convincing argument to the contrary, we would have to repeat virtually everything that has been stated in this course. Instead, I will again remind you that your own thinking is linear and direct, and that my thinking is convoluted, indirect, and based on an appraisal of the spiraling communicative interaction. At the very moment when you formulate insight, I would formulate the presence of a meaningful derivative lie: the realization by this patient of sickness within herself is serving here, I would hypothesize, as a derivative lie barrier to the realization of the sickness within the therapist and within the patient's interaction with him.

Please remember that every moment of insight must be evaluated in light of the prevailing adaptive context for its derivative implications, and not simply accepted at face value. This too is one of the differences between the classical and communicative approaches. Many moments of apparently expanded self-knowledge actually function as reflections of a *decrease* in the spheres of self-awareness and understanding others. The communicative approach indicates that unconscious insights in the patient as to the nature of the therapist and therapeutic interaction, if not made conscious to the patient, will not lead to an effective, adaptive widening of her understanding. Please recognize that point, since the implications of a derivative lie from the patient are usually not clear to her. The underlying truth contained in such a communication must be made conscious in order to have adaptive value for the patient or therapist.

Discussant: Even though it might serve as a barrier, it seems to me that this type of insight gives the patient a structure, something to understand, which she can then work through more thoroughly.

Langs: I cannot agree. The so-called insight involves ideas that are dynamically untrue for the moment; even as they pertain to the patient, they may actually serve as a lie barrier to some other truth.

On a manifest level, she realizes something about her relationship with Jack, which perhaps she had never seen before and related to its pathological qualities. I realize that you are pointing to that as being potentially positive. I think that a great deal of therapeutic work is based on a belief of that kind, and is supported by your type of thinking. But I do not believe that any type of resolution of a neurosis can take place on that basis; and the unconscious fantasy and perception constellations which account for the patient's sickness will not be modified by apparent surface realization. Functionally, it is sterile, and will not serve the patient in a meaningful way. It is the kind of manifest or Type One derivative pseudo-insight that is often reported in the literature.

At this point in the material critical truths about the therapist are being avoided on a manifest level, but are gaining clearer representation in the patient's derivative communications. This implies that her communicative resistances are lessening at this point in the session. The realization about sickness within herself, then, has validity only in light of its derivative meanings with respect to the therapist. It occurs at a moment when the patient functionally is in many ways less sick than the therapist, and not essentially sick at all in a communicative sense.

We also have here an example of an effort at self-interpretation developed primarily in terms of manifest content and Type One derivatives. It is by no means a good instance of the type of spontaneous self-interpretations which patients make on their own throughout therapy. Here, there is considerable influence from the therapist. However, I want to point out the level at which the patient explained things to herself. You will find that, especially in the middle phase of communicative therapy, patients engage in extensive self-interpretations on a manifest content and Type One derivative level. I believe these interpretations help them to develop flexible derivative and nonderivative lie-barrier systems which serve them adaptably, and which require the holding environment of the therapist to have such a positive influence. More rarely, a patient will develop a Type Two derivative self-interpretation, though my own observations indicate that these tend to be relatively simplistic and almost never elaborated in a manner comparable to a sound interpretation offered by the therapist.

Let's notice now the basis on which the communicative resistances have been modified. How would you account for the change in the derivative implications of the patient's material, the lessening of disguise and the heightening of meaning?

Discussant: This certainly did not take place because the therapist had become silent. It seems to have something to do with his interventions. I am trying to understand what the relationship could be. After all, our formulations indicated that he was trying to not only promote but even to intensify the patient's communicative resistances. Maybe she is now reacting against those efforts.

Langs: Yes, but again we must entertain divergent hypotheses: (1) that the therapist's interventions, in ways unclear to us, helped the patient to modify her defensiveness and communicative resistances; or (2) that his interventions have produced a paradoxical effect, in that they were designed to shore up these communicative resistances and the patient has reacted against these pressures by making initial efforts to modify their influence. This shows you once again how complicated the therapeutic interaction can be. We recognize a lessening of communicative resistances, and we have to account for it, through possibilities that are virtually self-contradictory: it came about because of effective therapeutic work, or it developed because the therapeutic work was deteriorating.

This is why we must continuously attempt to formulate the specific implications of the communicative interaction at each major juncture. We develop silent hypotheses and await their validation, and we attempt to formulate the material which follows in light of our constructions. Once we have taken this next step, we must subject our tentative conclusions to further validation from the patient's derivative communications, and consider alternative hypotheses if need be.

The therapist, of course, made no effort to interpret the factors in the patient's communicative resistances or to rectify his contributions to them—largely because he did not recognize their presence and, beyond that, he was not concerned with manifestations of gross behavioral resistances. He heard what seemed to him to be meaningful material, and he raised questions, made confrontations, and eventually proposed a general interpretation focused on the patient's inner difficulties.

Now, it is within the realm of possibility that this probing and interpretive work has led to a loosening of the patient's defenses. It is our goal to understand the basis for this change. There is the suggestion before us that it could arise from an initial level of expanded self-awareness and insight within the patient, an experience that would encourage her to communicate and analyze previously repressed material. This formulation is quite out of keeping with the hypotheses we developed from the communicative viewpoint, but it deserves to be tested in the material which follows.

From the communicative approach, the implications of the intervention contexts suggest a continuing and intense effort on the part of the therapist to seal off all of the ramifications of the therapeutic interaction which may be reflected in this material, and which might emerge were the therapist to hold back and to not offer repeated questions and other interventions in respect to the patient's own, isolated mental life and her relationships with others. Our postulate is that the patient's communicative resistances are interactional resistances which are receiving strong reinforcement from the therapist's interventions.

But notice something else. At the point where we began to suspect that the therapist's interventions had become more powerfully determined by his unconscious countertransference fantasy constellations, more revealing of his own unconscious needs and perceptions of his techniques with this patient, the patient herself began to express clearer derivatives pertinent to the therapeutic interaction. In essence, when the therapist made use of derivative lie barriers which contained significant implications for the therapeutic interaction, the patient herself made use of a comparable type of communication. When the therapist states these matters indirectly we call them lie barriers, and here we term them derivative lie barriers. When the patient does so, we term them derivative communications. We could just as easily consider these to be the patient's own lie barriers, her lie-barrier systems.

In this particular therapeutic interaction, there is a strong similarity between the lie-barrier systems used by both patient and therapist. In the early part of this session, there was more a sense of nonderivative lie barriers in both the patient's associations and the therapist's interventions, based largely on a concentration on the manifest content of the patient's narrative of the week's events and her related associations. At this point in the session, both appear to be using derivative lie barriers with important implications for the ongoing communicative interaction.

Now that I have made this particular formulation, I realize that it is another way of understanding why both patient and therapist have been able to so intensely exclude their own relationship from their manifest transactions. The shared lie-barrier system is the bastion we had identified earlier. In some way, it satisfies both of their pathological needs—defensive and instinctual.

I would therefore hypothesize that there is a circular interaction here, in which the patient began to modify her communicative resistances and expressed more revealing derivatives, after which the therapist changed in a similar direction. While he did not reach the level of a meaningful manifest interpretation, his own counter-resistances softened and changed from being largely nonderivative to becoming more derivative. In response, the patient's own derivative expressions became more meaningful—i.e., her communicative resistances lessened.

This sequence provides us a unique kind of understanding of the factors which modify resistances within patients. Here, it is based not so much upon a rectification by the therapist of his contribution to the resistances, and subsequent interpretation, but instead arises out of a counterreaction within the patient to an intensification of the therapist's input into her resistances.

To pause and summarize, communicative resistances may be modified by the therapist's silence, by the silent rectification of his contribution to those resistances, by a sound interpretation of the nature and function of these resistances in terms of unconscious fantasies and perception organized around a particular activated adaptive context, and as a paradoxical or counterreaction to and intensification—and perhaps to the continued expression—of the therapist's contribution to the patient's interactional resistances. It is important, then, to ascertain as clearly as possible the actual underlying basis to this type of decrease in communicative resistance. Similar principles would apply to fluctuations in gross behavioral resistances, and I suspect that the four possibilities we just applied to communicative resistances would also apply to the determinants of a lessening of behavioral resistances.

If I may finish this line of thought, what would account for an *increase* in communicative and gross behavioral resistances? Since the question is hypothetical, I will simply attempt to answer using the model already proposed for the decrease in resistances. This means that an increase in resistances could arise because of the therapist's inappropriate use of silence, an erroneous intervention, the failure of the therapist to rectify his contributions to the patient's resistance, new pathological inputs from the therapist which create or reinforce the resistances within the patient, and paradoxically, as a response to a correct interpretation from the therapist. This last would be a form of negative therapeutic reaction, but would, as I said earlier, by definition, have to be preceded by an initial sign of Type Two derivative validation, after which the communicative resistances set in. This type of phenomenon sometimes takes place because of the anxiety evoked by conscious insight in the patient, a kind of shock wave in which the repercussions and implications of newly found understanding evokes a temporary period of defensiveness.

Conscious insight, while the foundation of flexible adaptive resources, also entails the realization of previously repressed fantasies and perceptions which have been defended against because of their tendency to evoke anxiety and other disturbing affects and conflicts within the patient. Their conscious realization is bound to create a temporary disturbance which will require interpretive working through. During such an interlude, there may be a period of increased defensiveness and resistance invoked by the patient as an effort to defend against the newly activated realizations, conflicts, and affects.

Discussant: I've been thinking about your point about how the patient's realization that she acted in some kind of a sick way with her former boyfriend, Jack, cannot be viewed by us as genuine insight. In one sense, I think that the particular proposed piece of understanding was actually at odds with the reality of the situation between the patient and the therapist. It served to deny those realities, so I fail to see how it could be helpful to the patient.

Discussant: But suppose she is right, that her relationship with Jack had been sick?

Langs: Then it is a realization that will take on definitive meaning and function as true insight when it is linked up to an adaptive context within treatment. Eventually it might prove possible to interpret this particular realization as having been based on an unconscious perception of the therapist. Then, in some way you could show the patient that she too had behaved in a comparable and sick way—whatever that means in specific terms—in her relationship with Jack. It is my impression that only then could the insight about the patient vis-à-vis Jack serve her in constructive fashion.

Let's not fail to recognize that the term *sick* is being used in a highly ambiguous way which does not lend itself for the moment to specific meanings and functions. It may imply that the patient inappropriately submitted to Jack, surrendered herself unrealistically, or overidealized him. There may well be some type of narcissistic pathology here, but we must reach it in a meaningful manner by means of an intervention context which takes into account the disturbance within the therapist as well as the patient. Without that, true or false, it remains a pseudo-insight.

Through these discussions, I am gradually developing a perspective on the therapeutic effects of lie therapy, including psychoanalysis and psychoanalytic psychotherapy. While in need of specific empirical investigation, it seems likely that these treatment modalities, when successful, provide lie-barrier systems which are either pathologically gratifying or more flexible and adaptive than those with which the patient entered treatment. They are developed through pseudo-insights and the kind of paradoxical effects we described when identifying the factors in an increase or lessening of a patient's resistances. The same principles apply to fluctuations in symptoms. In essence, a symptom may be exacerbated or undergo remission in response to essentially valid or invalid interventions by the therapist. It is only through an analysis of the material organized around prevailing intervention contexts that we can identify the actual sequence and the underlying basis for the change.

Discussant: I have been thinking about the concept of interactional validation—that a positive introject is confirmation and a negative introject is nonconfirmation. It seems to me that you run into a problem here. You seem to be saying that the scientific truth is when the patient likes you and the scientific lie is when the patient doesn't like you.

Langs: No, I don't think that a positive introject reflects being liked by the patient. It is simply a valid introjective identification with the functional attributes of the therapist, reflecting adaptive and constructive activity. In fact, some patients will develop an intense dislike for the therapist who has intervened correctly because they are deeply disturbed by the truths involved and because the positive introject, as I discussed previously, can create terrible intrapsychic disequilibrium and envy.

Discussant: But waiting for the patient to come up with some kind of good figure immediately attaches the value "good" to a scientific observation. You can end up tailoring your therapy so the patient will have all these good feelings about everybody and about you.

Langs: But please understand, you are now confusing indirect and derivative communication with manifest content—direct feelings and attitudes. You will find, as Strachey so clearly observed (1934), that any conscious effort to be good to the patient, to be liked by her, and to have her think well of you, will be experienced unconsciously as destructive and actually generate a negative, not a positive, introject. The term positive introject is used here in a descriptive sense without a value judgment as to goodness or badness. The good quality is simply descriptive of positive functioning and a criterion. It is not a value judgment, but an empirical finding.

Discussant: But I think you are getting mixed up and confusing the accuracy or correctness of an intervention, with the question of whether it is helpful. For instance, there are a lot of correct statements that can be made, but I think that what you are saying is that they may be correct and not helpful, or correct and yet serve as a way of covering up some other truth. I believe the validation you are looking for is to the effect that it was helpful to the patient.

Langs: There are several problems here. We already know that incorrect interventions can seem helpful in that they produce some type of symptom alleviation, largely through lie-barrier systems. We also know that a validated intervention, correct and accurate by our criteria, can be temporarily disturbing for the patient and only ultimately prove to be symptom alleviating. That is why I have settled upon Type Two derivative validation, cognitive and introjective, as the essential criterion for the correctness of an intervention. It is the one measure which seems to correlate most clearly with the predictions made from the communicative viewpoint, and which leads to truly unique elaborations and, ultimately, insights within the therapeutic interaction. It is a means by which a neurosis may be resolved in a lasting fashion; but there are many additional vicissitudes which the patient may have to go through before achieving that result. But virtually all other criteria of the correctness of an intervention have serious flaws and prove unreliable. Type Two derivative validation is the most reliable means we have of gauging the correctness of our therapeutic work.

Discussant: In this sense, validity appears to be a way of saying that an intervention is accurate in the sense that it is stating a truth about the patient, his fantasies or perceptions.

Langs: Yes, and the most pertinent truth within the bipersonal field at the moment, stated sensitively, meaningfully, with tact, well timed and well put.

Discussant: Will a patient inclined to lie therapy nonetheless communicate in some derivative way a positive introject after a correct interpretation?

Langs: Yes, and he will do so because for the moment he has expressed the truth and is prepared to validate it. Usually, such a patient will quickly reconstitute his lie-barrier system, and destroy the meaningful qualities of the therapeutic experience. But nonetheless, his immediate reaction will contain a derivative of a positive introject if the intervention has been correct.

Discussant: I keep thinking about the question of how to deal with lie patients, especially when they are nonderivative liars. It seems to me that the entire technique developed from the communicative approach requires derivative communication.

Langs: Yes, that is indeed an important theoretical and technical question. However, the communicative approach makes it possible to identify the nonderivative liar, and to await those moments in which his resistances are modified so that meaning is revealed and can be interpreted. The question seems to be whether you can work meaningfully with a patient who is in actuality destroying meaning and relatedness. Any effort to deal with the content of such material is to pretend that there is truth to the patient's lies when none exists functionally. Clearly, that type of approach is bound to fail.

But aside from trying to tell the patient that he has destroyed meaning and relatedness, at a time when he has a need to obliterate

any meaningful implications of your presence and your interventions, what can you possibly do? The patient's defenses and
resistances are such that he would also destroy the truth of that confrontation. All I can say at the moment is that I have a strong impression that these patients are unconsciously seeking to be held
and contained, to be patiently tolerated, and that they wish for a
steady kind of therapeutic symbiosis as a way of building sufficient
strength to tolerate the communication of derivative truths. As I
said at an earlier meeting, beyond that formulation, I am quite
open to further suggestions.

Discussant: It seems to me that you preclude the patient from
having a paranoid kind of response to you when you make a
correct intervention.

Langs: I do not believe that I preclude the patient from having
any type of response whatsoever to a correct or incorrect intervention. I am trying to summarize a series of empirical observations,
and to draw some conclusions, principles, and hypotheses on that
basis. Somehow you seem to have misunderstood and to believe
that I am trying to impose these ideas upon the patient. Not at all.
Technically, I impose virtually nothing upon the patient, though I
do offer a specific type of holding environment. Still, I don't insist
upon his acceptance of that environment or the ground rules
which create it; he is free to accept or reject what I have to offer. I
never confront a patient by directive and in all instances—and I
really do mean without qualification except for the extremely rare
emergency—I work from the patient's material and its derivative
implications. If something is to be rectified, the effort comes from
the patient's associations and is not introduced unilaterally by
myself.

As a matter of fact, I have already postulated the basis for a
paranoid response to a correct intervention. It would be an interpretation which receives Type Two derivative validation, and
which generates a type of insight and positive introject which is
experienced by the patient as persecutory. I have already shown
you that the truth may be persecutory, and I have also indicated
how positive introjects may have the same qualities. They threaten
to destroy the patient's defenses against negative introjects and his

use of defensive denial and repression. They threaten the patient's psychic equilibrium, and some tinge of paranoid response is not at all uncommon after initial Type Two derivative validation.

Discussant: There is another difficulty in testing your hypotheses. We have been working almost exclusively with incorrect interventions, and have had little chance to observe a correct intervention.

Langs: A couple of weeks ago, one of our presenters offered an essentially valid intervention which did obtain Type Two derivative validation through the emergence of a positive introject. Of course, it would be helpful to have further interventions which we evaluate as correct in order to more carefully observe the patient's direct and derivative responses. There are several such instances in my papers (see Langs 1978) and you might wish to review that material. Remember, my main purpose here is to develop principles which can be applied to your own therapeutic work. While helpful, it is not essential to illustrate all possibilities. Nothing would please me more, but I myself do not find it especially disturbing. I know that it has been for some of my students and readers, but many others have been able to find sufficient reason to believe in the validity of the principles of the communicative approach and apply them in their own work, discovering its utility in both understanding and curing the patient.

Discussant: Until now, if I see a negative response, even a paranoid response, in the patient's material after I have made an intervention, I have not necessarily thought that I made an incorrect intervention. It could be, but there could be other reasons for that type of response.

Langs: Well, I have offered at least two rather different possibilities just a moment ago. We need specific clinical material to give this discussion real meaning. I think we have taken it as far as we can on a hypothetical basis. I would therefore like to return to our presentation.

Therapist: To continue: She had just said that maybe it really wasn't love with Jack, maybe it was sick. She went on: I did everything for him that he wanted. Here I said (referring to material from an earlier session), It was as if you were his slave (meaning Jack's slave). She said, But I did it voluntarily. Then there was a pause, and she said, You know, I really feel better. It's as if a weight has been lifted off my shoulders.

Langs: Well, we must certainly pause here in an effort to determine the basis for the patient's sense of relief. Who would like to comment?

Discussant: The intervention is either a confrontation or interpretation, depending on the nature of the material from the earlier session. In terms of the present hour, it has the qualities of a Type One derivative interpretation. Once again, it places the entire sense of pathology within the patient, avoids the therapeutic interaction, stands unrelated to any issue of resistance, and offers a Type C barrier in respect to the therapeutic relationship. On that basis, we might suggest that the patient feels better because she is prepared now to accept the barriers, the lie barriers, offered by the therapist.

Discussant: The therapist seems to be attempting to extend his effort to help the patient see that she wishes to be forced into intercourse and into relationships in order to experience gratification. Now he is trying to point out to the patient that she also wishes to be enslaved. Isn't it possible that her sense of relief comes from understanding herself a bit better?

Langs: We certainly must entertain that hypothesis. However, I do want to point out that the earlier intervention regarding the patient's wish to be forced and coerced received little in the way of confirmation. Some of you did feel that the patient elaborated a bit on that theme and realized that there was something sick in her relationship with Jack. In principle, it would be well to ask of the patient a more unique and definitive form of validation, such as the revelation of a previously unknown incident, behavior, or fantasy which extends your intervention in totally unanticipated ways—in effect, a selected fact (Bion 1977, Langs 1978a).

In the absence of this kind of Type Two derivative validation, it is extremely important that you question your formulation and intervention, make efforts at reformulation, and attempt to avoid further repetition or variations on a nonvalidated intervention. It may well be that in this instance, the therapist had felt encouraged by this material and therefore continued to pursue this particular theme. Nonetheless, it might have been wiser to have sat back and experienced the lack of definitive validation, and attempt to scrutinize this material and your subjective reactions for clues as to what it is that may have been missed or misstated. Remember, the therapist had to invoke a derivative from a previous hour, and this is often a sign that the material in the present session has not validated his intervention and that he is now reaching back into the past for support. A more appropriate attitude would be to accept the absence of confirmatory material in this session and to attempt to reformulate.

Discussant: Does her sense of feeling better constitute a derivative of a positive introject? If it does, I would suggest that this particular criterion is not foolproof and that relief can come in the absence of a validated intervention.

Langs: There is no criteria of validity which is entirely foolproof and works with a hundred percent consistency. Some therapists would take any sense of relief as a suggestion of a positive introject, though others might question that particular expression. The response actually falls more clearly into the realm of immediate symptom relief, a lessening of the patient's sense of anxiety and tension. We already know that such reactions may come not only from the experience of a valid intervention, but also from the offer by the therapist of a strong lie-barrier system. The differentiation must be made on the basis of your formulation of the patient's material and the unconscious implications of your interventions prior to the sense of relief, and then validated or revised based on the patient's subsequent associations.

In this situation, the therapist may well be pursuing a line of thought which has meaning and validity for the patient and which will help her to better understand herself and deal with her emotional problems. The alternative hypothesis is that by introducing material from a previous hour and by alluding to the theme of enslavement, and by focusing on the patient's relationship with Jack, the therapist has offered the patient a lie-barrier system which will now more effectively seal off the implications of the ongoing therapeutic interaction.

We have already formulated that the patient was producing less disguised derivatives relevant to the therapeutic interaction and the therapist, and this particular intervention could have one of several effects in light of that trend. For one, it could steer her away from the interaction and prompt an intensification of communicative resistances. Second, it could be viewed unconsciously as a message to her to lessen her enslavement to the therapist, and to communicate still more freely. On this level, this would be a derivative lie intervention which reflects the therapist's unconscious awareness of the patient's enslavement to himself, and to some degree his enslavement to the patient. It may thereby constitute an unconscious realization which provides the patient some sense of relief. A third possibility is that the patient now believes that the therapist strongly insists on not recognizing the implications of this material for her relationship with him, and that the mounting anxiety which accompanied the lessening of defense-resistances here has been brought under control through the unconscious awareness within the patient that the bastion will prevail.

Therapist: I want to point out that this is an extremely atypical statement for her. In any case, she said, Right now I am thinking, maybe it would be a good idea to get married. It doesn't seem like such a bad idea.

I intervened again, and said to her that something seems to have happened here to make her feel differently about things.

Langs: Who will comment?

Discussant: It seems to me that the patient was getting a message from the therapist that she had inappropriately enslaved herself to Jack, and that she should be free of such tendencies. For me, that is a clear representation of the disadvantages of a pathological symbiosis.

Discussant: On another level, there is a kind of avoidance of the therapeutic interaction which offers the patient a sense of denial. This could encourage her to think of getting married, an act which also would protect her against any erotic perceptions of the therapist and inappropriate feelings toward him. The patient began this hour with a sense of intense sexual need, and we have hypothesized that it reflects both introjections of the therapist and her own fantasies and wishes toward him. None of this has been interpreted to her. Instead, the message has been: Don't ask to be forced, don't be a slave. This seems to lead her to think of getting married.

Langs: Yes. You are attempting to summarize aspects of the spiraling and primarily unconscious communicative interaction. I would also agree with the previous discussant: the patient seems to be suggesting through derivatives that both she and the therapist recognize the need to resolve the pathological symbiosis. It is important to realize that on an unconscious level, the patient seems to be suggesting that the therapist is pressuring her to become the functional therapist and, as such, the *symbiotic provider* or *giver*. We can reserve the terms *symbiotic receiver* or *recipient* for the person in the dyad who obtains the major share of gratification, pathological or nonpathological.

As we can see from this material, it is possible on an unconscious level for the patient to become the symbiotic provider and the therapist the symbiotic recipient. This shift parallels our earlier conception of the *designated patient* becoming the *functional therapist* at a time when the *designated therapist* becomes the *functional patient*. It is most important that we not assume the manner in which the patient or therapist actually functions when a therapeutic (healthy) or pathological symbiosis is effected within the treatment situation. Instead, we must make such evaluations through an in-depth analysis of the patient's associations and the therapist's interventions. Not surprisingly, most analysts who have written on this subject and applied it to the therapeutic and analytic processes and experiences have simply assumed that the patient's pathological symbiotic needs are greater than those of the therapist, while in contrast the communicative therapist would make this determination on an empirical basis.

Discussant: Many therapists would take the patient's sense of relief and decision to get married as a confirmation of their interventions in this hour.

Langs: Yes. They would do so despite the absence of any other type of validation, including Type Two derivative confirmation. Their surface goal would be to enable the patient to resolve her conflicts about getting married, and if this occurs, they would be satisfied and really uninterested in the unconscious basis for the patient's decision.

It is my impression that many marriages of patients in treatment take place at the behest of the therapist's unconscious, countertransference needs, rather than through genuine insight—a point made in an early and relatively unrecognized paper by Barchilon (1958) on countertransference cures. Patients frequently act out on the basis of the therapist's unconscious needs, in order to defend themselves against valid unconscious perceptions of the therapist. They do so on the basis of unconsciously offered defensive formations which stem largely from the therapist and usually go entirely unrecognized. This is another way of indicating why symptom alleviation is not a criterion of valid therapeutic work. It simply indicates that something has happened within the therapeutic interaction to lead to a particular result. The basis for that outcome can only be determined by an analysis of the unconscious communicative interaction.

Discussant: The intervention is another confrontation, and is based on Type One derivative listening.

Discussant: These interventions seem rapid and frequent. From your comments, Dr. Langs, I sensed that you feel that it is better to sit back and to allow the patient's derivatives to generate meaning or reflect the underlying implications of what has taken place. An intervention of this kind focuses the patient consciously on what is taking place, and I suppose it would interfere with her derivative communications.

Langs: Yes, it would. Learn to intervene only after a silent formulation and planned intervention has received Type Two derivative validation from the patient's continuing associations. And once you have spoken, sit back and allow the patient's material to convey the validity of your intervention, its implications to the patient, where it has been correct and where it has gone off into error. As we have seen, there is so much to monitor and evaluate there should be little time for repeated questions, confrontations, and repetition of unvalidated interventions.

The intervention which the therapist just made is one that I would have entertained as a silent question. I would then have allowed the patient's associations to have answered it. However, there is one important quality to this intervention which no one has commented upon.

Discussant: It is the first reference that the therapist has made to therapy. He said, Something seems to have happened here.

Langs: Exactly. I sense that the most critical level of communication in this session is quite beyond the awareness of both the patient and therapist. The patient seems to have detected certain defensive needs in the therapist, certain implicit and more deeply unconscious messages in his interventions, and has responded with the thought of marriage. It occurs to me that it would be a possible solution to the pending forced termination, and that the unconscious dialogue does have a bearing on that issue.

Unconsciously, the patient wishes to be enslaved to the therapist, and to remain in treatment. And unconsciously, the therapist suggests that such enslavement is inappropriate, preparing the way for his departure. The patient detects this clue, and opts now for a piece of acting out: marriage to someone at the Center in preparation for the loss of the therapist. Now, the therapist has a sense of disquietude, senses that something is the matter, and tries to have the patient locate it consciously and directly in the therapeutic interaction. He asks her to identify what is happening between them. But this task should fall to the therapist himself and to an analysis of the derivative implications of the patient's material and of his own interventions.

Discussant: In keeping with that, I heard this intervention as a command or a directive, which in some small way could enslave her at the very point at which he is attempting to show her that such needs are pathological.

Therapist: She said something which was nondescript, and then was silent for a minute or two. I guess her initial comment was something to the effect that getting married is something she's been thinking about a long time. She then went on: I don't like to be pressured though.

Discussant: Her comment about not liking to be pressured seems to be a Type Two derivative validation of the formulation that these interventions are creating pressure for the patient.

Therapist: She continued and said, This physiotherapist that I met is Denise's husband. (Denise is someone who works with her at her present job.) This guy came on to me at the party the other night.

Discussant: Is the patient saying that she feels a sense of relief because the therapist is pressuring her, and coming on seductively toward her?

Discussant: In a way, the inappropriate qualities of the therapist's interventions seem to make the patient feel attractive and wanted sexually.

Langs: Yes, I think that the pressure was building within the patient in respect to her efforts to move toward less disguised derivatives pertaining to her relationship with the therapist. She unconsciously viewed the therapist's intervention as reflecting his own difficulties in containing his own inner pressures and un-conscious—perhaps conscious—sexual feelings toward the patient, his erotic countertransferences. With that, the patient feels a sense of relief, which might well constitute her response to her own successful projective identification into the therapist. She also moves toward a decision which could protect both herself and the therapist from the mounting pressures within their relationship. That would be my tentative formulation.

It is also interesting that at the point where the therapist finally alludes to treatment, the derivatives in the patient's material, as they reflect a commentary on his intervention, now seem far more readily understood than earlier in the session. This may be the continuation of a trend we had identified at the midpoint in this hour, or it may be a lessening of communicative resistances in response to the first hint from the therapist that he is prepared to examine the therapeutic interaction with this patient.

I had suggested a number of means through which the patient's communicative resistances could be lessened. This is a variation on one type of sequence I had identified earlier: namely, that the moment at which the therapist, even unconsciously, introduces a preparedness to deal with the deeper truths within the patient— here, her unconscious perceptions and fantasies about the thera- pist—the patient responds with clearer derivative communication, and eventually provides a bridge to therapy which would facilitate an interpretation. Here again, the interpretation could involve the communicative resistances themselves, as well as other aspects of the patient's unconscious fantasy and perception constellations.

At this point, it would be possible to propose, as a silent inter- pretation, that the patient's thoughts about marriage (an indicator which takes the form of what we believe to be a type of acting out) and her feelings of being pressured and of someone coming on strong, are related to her perceptions of the therapist and his interventions. These are comments which she feels are both forcing and seductive, and which lead her at one moment to become protective and to think suddenly of getting married, while at an- other moment to more clearly indicate the actual ways in which she is experiencing her relationship with the therapist.

As you can see, this tentative intervention is rather weak. For one thing, the material lacks for the moment a clear representation of the patient's communicative resistances, without which it would be difficult to offer an interpretation in that sphere. If the patient were to represent these resistances, it would then be possible to show that they are a reaction to the therapist's pressure and seductiveness.

My proposed intervention is intended, for the moment, to deal with the patient's sudden decision to consider marriage and to help her to recognize and work through her disturbing unconscious perceptions of the therapist, which are based on Grade Two deviations and perhaps on some additional deviations in respect to the fixed frame. Much of the material centers around the patient's unconscious perceptions of the therapist's erroneous efforts at interpretation and the communicative qualities reflected in these efforts. The adaptive context corresponds to these indicators which refer, of course, to the therapist's interventions. As we know, the patient has still not represented these contexts in sufficiently clear form to permit interpretation, so she continues to show a high level of resistance in that regard. But the derivative complex continues to show increasing clarity, especially in regard to the patient's unconscious perceptions of the therapist. The resistance level there is lessening and it might permit, at the very least, a playback of derivatives if there was a clear enough representation, however disguised, of the prevailing intervention context. Otherwise, I would not play back these derivatives, since it has not been established that they pertain to a fixed framework issue.

My preference would be to take the derivative clues and interpretations from the patient, to learn from them, and to stop intervening in this erroneous manner. It is my belief that such a step would enable the patient to further resolve her communicative resistances, since their input from the therapist will have lessened, and on that basis, the material would become less disguised or readily open for interpretation.

Discussant: If we are trying to trace out introjects, I would see this material as reflecting a negative and seductive introject.

Langs: Yes, there may still be something in the background that is positive for this patient, perhaps simply based on the therapist's concern and his efforts to understand—however insufficient. The other side of the situation is much clearer, in that the patient fails to validate the therapist's interventions and does indeed introduce a negative introject based on her unconscious perception of the therapist's efforts.

Note that the therapist's question, about what could be happening in the therapeutic relationship to have changed things for the patient, is a manifest stimulus for this material. The patient does not offer any direct speculation, but instead quickly shifts to derivative communication. And as I said, her derivative comments are now more clearly related to our own evaluation of the communicative properties of the therapist's interventions. And they still speak to the notion that the patient's impression that the therapist finds her attractive is gratifying for her in some way.

Discussant: Why do you call this a negative introject? What is negative about the sexual overture?

Langs: Inevitably, clinical judgment is a factor in our evaluation of material. My own comment is meant to imply a tentative and silent hypothesis, but I base it on the image of physical contact, and on the image of a husband's friend coming on in a seductive manner to the patient.

Discussant: But for her, this is pleasurable.

Langs: Yes, and it is our responsibility to determine the underlying basis for this sense of gratification. The question is whether I am making so-called value judgments, or clinical judgments which pertain to the implications meant by the patient. In principle, we make every effort to limit ourselves to the inferences which the patient intends, both consciously and unconsciously.

It may well be that I have added something from within myself, and from my countertransferences. I do not think so; I believe that we could reach a consensus in respect to the implications of this material. In any case, I would not have intervened on the basis of these inferences, which are, by the way, supported by my evaluation of the unconscious implications of the adaptive context of the therapist's recent interventions. To safeguard the accuracy of the inferences I have made, I would not feel secure in these judgments unless the patient's further material offered some Type Two derivative validation.

Discussant: This might be an oedipal triumph, and she may feel happy about it.

Langs: That may well be one level of dynamic implications for this material, but it would have to be related to the therapeutic interaction for it to have cogency at this moment. There seems to be some resistance against monitoring this material in terms of unconscious perceptions and introjects of the therapist. There is still a tendency in some of you toward maintaining a focus on intrapsychic dynamics within the patient divorced from the ongoing therapeutic interaction. With the communicative approach, we first establish the patient's unconscious perceptions of the therapist and the resultant introjects, after which we go about understanding what they portray of the dynamics of the therapeutic interaction and the therapist's functioning. Only then do we examine the implications of this material in respect to the patient's fantasies and conflicts, in terms of the adaptive context from the therapist which have evoked them, attempting to understand their genetic implications for the patient.

Discussant: I only wanted to suggest that this man who was seductive could be a positive figure for the patient, since she finds him stimulating and interested in her. I simply wouldn't assume that he is a negative introject because he has been seductive.

Langs: Your question takes us into the realm of the nature of neuroses, and of valid and distorted conscious and unconscious perceptions. Your line of thought would imply that anything which gratifies the patient would generate a positive introject, by which I mean a helpful, constructive, nontraumatizing figure who helps to give the patient general ego strength and adaptive resources which derive from the process of internalization. It is difficult for me to see how this kind of seductiveness could have that type of effect.

Perhaps my earlier definitions of positive and negative introjects have not been stated clearly enough or have been insufficiently understood. A negative introject, then, is one which is disruptive intrapsychically. It is traumatic and threatening to the patient, disruptive to her ego functioning, and likely to promote maladaptive responses. This particular image of this man, which of course we have not as yet established as having been internalized within the patient—I have only been speaking hypothetically—would suggest that the patient would continue to seek satisfaction by making herself attractive to married men, including the husbands of her friends. I somehow thought that we would readily agree that such behavior has rather strong maladaptive qualities and can create considerable suffering for the patient and others. However, your comments indicate that this particular aspect of interpreting— understanding the implications of the patient's material—is open to considerable subjective judgment, to countertransference bias, and undoubtedly must be influenced to some extent by the therapist's own value systems. In that case, it seems insufficient to suggest that we should restrict ourselves to clinical judgments and clinical values, to the question of whether or not the particular adaptation might cause the patient suffering. We must recognize those points where the slightest aspect of our own values, social and otherwise, could be influencing an interpretation, see to it that we are aware of this factor, and take the trouble to carefully scrutinize its influence. In addition, we can safeguard against too great an influence from this particular human factor by insisting on derivative validation of a formulation or judgment in the patient's subsequent associations before presenting it to the patient.

Discussant: What if this patient has in her history a series of figures who actually overstimulated her, who led her to sexualized relationships and superego figures? Here she would be saying, You are acting like someone who is trying to help me and I appreciate it. And like all the figures in my past, I will now sexualize my image of you.

Langs: But here you have not made the critical distinction as to whether the patient's experience of the sexual qualities of the therapist's interventions is valid. You have excluded the therapist's unconscious communications, and the possibility that they are in actuality seductive and a reflection of erotic countertransferences. Therapists seem to have difficulty with actualities which pertain to themselves and which are not directly and consciously stated or reflected in their overt behaviors. They have this problem especially when it comes to their evaluation and perception of their own interventions, though they seldom seem to have this difficulty when it comes to the implications they derive from the patient's material.

As I have said before, the therapist's behaviors may on some level constitute an actual repetition of a past pathogenic interaction, here in the form of overstimulating the patient or behaving seductively. It is only when this is not the case, both manifestly and latently, that we can propose that the patient herself has introduced the sexual element into the relationship and into her perceptions of the therapist. The former situation is essentially nontransference, while the latter is essentially transference. In this particular session, I think we have a mixture and that the interplay falls somewhere toward the middle of the continuum.

I think the therapist is in some ways pressuring the patient, being seductive, but in the main, attempting to protect himself against the sexual implications of the therapeutic interaction. It is because the defensiveness is so central here that it has been difficult, I think, for some of you to appreciate that factor underlying his interventions. On the other hand, the therapist has not been overtly seductive, and has tried to show a reasonable interest in the patient's sexual conflicts and behaviors. It is here that the patient seems to begin to distort and to show the influence of her own unconscious transference fantasy constellations, viewing him as blatantly seductive—as touching her and coming on strong in a sexual sense.

In intervening, it would be important to express yourself in a manner that shows an appreciation of these transversal qualities, and which accepts whatever the therapist should be responsible for, while also placing appropriate responsibility within the patient. All of this must be done implicitly rather than as some type of confessional.

I would like to illustrate specifically here, even though the material does not entirely facilitate such an intervention. Nonetheless, to propose a model, once the adaptive context has been represented, we might say something like this to the patient: You have now connected these images of someone coming on strong, pressuring you, and being seductive with the way in which I have been intervening. It seems apparent that you have sensed something

pressured and sexual about my comments. You convey this perhaps most clearly in your comments about the physiotherapist.
You yourself seem to be quite stimulated by all of this, and this
seems to be reflected in your wish to go to bed with someone other
than your boyfriend.

Something as direct as that. This is an intervention in which
you do not immediately imply that the patient is totally distorting
her impressions of your intervention and misperceiving based on
her own pathological inner needs. You are directly descriptive in a
way that implies a certain degree of validity to her perceptions, and
similarly hints at some measure of distortion. I expect that the
patient's subsequent associations would enable you to more clearly
indicate whatever was valid about her unconscious perceptions of
your interventions. This is what I mean by a *transversal interpretation,* it traverses two spheres primarily because there is truth on both
sides.

Discussant: I don't see how you can say to the patient, Yes, there
is a kernel of truth in your perceptions, that I am trying to rape and
enslave you, and to inappropriately seduce you.

Langs: Your comment helps me to see the kind of anxiety that
can be evoked within a therapist when it comes to accepting as
valid an unconscious perception by the patient of some type of
countertransference, erotic or otherwise. It is a frightening prospect; in fact, it is so threatening that most therapists never acknowledge such a possibility and totally deny the unconscious
implications of their interventions. For you, implicit acknowledgment conjures up the image of blatant confession and even a
new level of sexual assault of the patient. To the contrary, I am
proposing here an acceptance of the truth, efforts to self-analyze
and resolve the basis for your own difficulties as a therapist, and
implicit acceptance of the patient's perceptions when they are
valid. I am not proposing explicit acknowledgment or confes-
sionals. In fact, your characterization shows how explicit acknowledgment can often be experienced by the patient as a further
seduction and pressure. Only rarely, under unusual circumstances,
such as forgetting a session, is it necessary to directly acknowledge
an error. And even then, it is important to not reveal to the patient

the basis for the mistake, whatever that may be. That should be your own province and subjected to private therapeutic work, and not conveyed to the patient in a way that would inappropriately ask her to become not only the functional but the designated therapist.

Therapist: Well, here, I came on strong and interrupted her. She was describing what had happened with this man, and I repeated her comment that he was her friend's husband, being uncertain that that had been the case. She responded by saying, Yes, he is Canadian and he is a physiotherapist. I had needed some help preparing for job interviews and had asked him to demonstrate a particular technique. My mother always thought that it was a little strange that I allowed a male physiotherapist to demonstrate on me, but I told her that this is the way things are. I explained to her that it was typical in the field, and that it is not at all sexual.

Langs: We have here the introduction of the genetic figure who is undoubtedly most pertinent at this moment to the communicative interaction. Once again, it is difficult to be clear of the implications of the mother in this context. She appears as the person who is questioning a possible sexualization of a teaching situation, and prompting the patient to explain that physical contact within a therapeutic context needn't be sexual.

How are we to understand this communication? For one thing, it must be seen as part of a commentary on the therapist's last interventions, especially his question about the physiotherapist. On another level, I would see this as a model of rectification, an effort by the patient to propose that clear-cut boundaries be established between herself and the therapist, that the unconscious sexualization of the relationship, possibly on both sides, be eliminated as much as possible, and that treatment be afforded a neutralized, nonsexual quality. Remember, there is a striking contradiction here: The patient claims that the physiotherapist is not involved in something sexual, but then goes on to describe how he was seductive at the party.

There is no evidence that the model of rectification derives from a shift in the therapist's interventions. It may well be a response to his allusion to the treatment situation, and a continued expression of meaningful derivative communication in that area. In any case, the ambiguity of this material can be taken as a reflection of continued communicative resistances. There is still no clear representation of the intervention context, though the patient does move a bit closer to it with an allusion to a therapeutic relationship. On the other hand, the derivative complex, while it now includes a model of rectification and an unconscious interpretation to the therapist, has a sense of ambiguity which suggests moderately strong communicative resistances.

Therapist: This was near the end of the session. She said a bit more about the physiotherapist coming on to her at the party, and how she just couldn't wait to get away. She went on: He started to talk about the emotional experience of doing physiotherapy. And he said how wonderful I was in making contact with people, and it was clear that he was just coming on to me. I just withdrew from him totally and I'm never going to consult him again.

Langs: There is little more to add for the moment on the subjects of resistances and interventions. I would like, however, to show you that this material offers Type Two derivative validation for an earlier formulation that I made in respect to this therapeutic interaction. I had suggested that the therapist was being perceived validly as someone who was coming on strong and seductively, and that the patient appeared to respond with strong communicative resistances. This appraisal is reflected in this last piece of material, which now includes the patient's own unconscious awareness of the extent to which she has entered into a protective withdrawal with the therapist. True, she begins to develop some meaningful derivative communications, but the session is nearing its end and she has not sufficiently modified her communicative resistances to the point where this material can be integrated and an interpretation offered. I continue to sense a strong sense of defensiveness in this patient, despite the fact that I could discover derivative meaning in her associations. And here too the communicative resistances are designed to protect both patient and therapist.

Her comment that she would never consult this physiotherapist again could also be a derivative of the pending forced termination. It suggests to me that an important unconscious motive for these communicative resistances is related to the conditions of treatment in this particular clinic, and to patient's anticipation of an interruption of her therapy and the departure of the therapist. This remains a tentative, silent hypothesis—though now we have found some repetitive derivative support.

By the way, shutting the physiotherapist out and not going back to him at all is an extreme model of rectification. The patient is implying here that if the therapist is unable to control his seductiveness and pressures, it would be best for the patient to terminate the treatment. This may be connected to her thoughts about getting married. On the surface, this would be a means of justifying the termination of therapy and of dealing with many of the underlying transference and countertransference issues.

All of these comments are quite tentative. We are observing a bipersonal field in which communicative resistances remain at a rather high level. This often implies the presence of a basic disturbance in the communicative properties of the field, and I have tried to identify its basis as much as possible in the course of these discussions. It is one of the problems of an impaired communicative field that it creates difficulties in being able to conceptualize the basis for that very disturbance, especially when there is no recent, blatant break in the fixed frame.

Discussant: I find something interesting here. She was probably naked for the physiotherapy demonstration and found nothing sexual about the situation. Then she is at a party and she finds that sexual, and wants to run away. I think that is quite fascinating.

Langs: Well, it is a surface observation. You are hinting at possible Type One derivative implications. While working with a patient in psychotherapy, I would strongly recommend that you not infer meaning without linking the material to an adaptive context within the therapeutic interaction.

Therapist: At this point she was silent again for a minute or two. I said, You seem to have withdrawn here as well.

Langs: Our time is nearly up, so I will comment briefly. Notice here the continued use of confrontation. For a second time, the therapist has now commented upon what seems to be taking place between himself and the patient. This might have a strong effect on her, though it could, as she now seems to hint, paradoxically prompt an intensification of her defensiveness and resistances.

The intervention is on a manifest content level, and has none of the properties of an interpretation that we have developed. But notice that on the most superficial level, the therapist is drawing a parallel between the patient's behavior with the physiotherapist and her behavior with himself. The unconscious implication could go along either side of the me/not-me interface, and be perceived by the patient as a confession by the therapist that in some way he recognizes the similarity between himself and the physiotherapist, or as an implication that for some distorted reason the patient is viewing him as such. These are the kind of implications that should be stated directly and interpretively to the patient, and organized around the adaptive context of the therapist's many interventions in this hour. I continue to sense that the most important transactions between this patient and therapist are occurring on an unconscious level and through unconscious communications on both sides. This statement by the therapist is a true observation which is serving as a derivative lie barrier.

Therapist: She said, I am feeling better about marriage and about the possibility of getting married. It is just so frustrating to keep going into this material. I open up so many wounds, and I just want to put them aside already, so I can decide whether I can get married. I want to file them away. It seems that I am just picking at them here over and over again.

Here I asked her, You don't seem to think that I can actually help you with these things? She said, That is kind of what I mean. But what more can I say? I've shown you all my innermost secrets here and there is nothing more I can tell you about. I said, You don't think I'm able or actually want to help you with the things that are bothering you. You experience me as being like all men who just want an emotional experience for themselves, to get their own kicks, and in the process to use and eventually to discard you, like Jack did in the past and as now you are describing this physiotherapist.

Langs: It seems clear from this intervention that quite consciously you were experiencing a strong need to connect this material to the patient's relationship to yourself. You took the patient's comment about how frustrating it is to go over this material again and again as a bridge to therapy. It is important to realize that it was you who had brought up the therapeutic relationship twice and that the patient had responded in a minimal way with her own rather glancing allusion to the treatment situation.

Who wishes to comment briefly?

Discussant: Well, this is certainly an attempt at interpretation, of the kind that we have called in the past a transference interpretation. It reflects listening on a Type One derivative level, because it does not allude to a specific intervention context. Maybe it bridges Type One and Type Two derivative listening. There is a strong attempt here to use a derivative complex, though I sense that the therapist has forced a great deal into his comments with little basis in the patient's material.

Langs: Yes, I think that the therapist is now intervening in the right area, but somewhat prematurely and without sufficiently shaping the intervention in keeping with the specific material from the patient. There is still a sense of pressure here, some difficulty in containing capacity, which the patient will undoubtedly experience on an unconscious level.

On the other hand, you are now trying to help her to understand that there are important issues in her relationship with you. Your intervention has a transversal quality in that you don't directly challenge the perceptions of yourself which you identify to her, but simply play them back as derivatives organized around the way in which she is experiencing her relationship with you.

In principle, if you had included a specific representation of one or more intervention contexts, it would have given your intervention considerably more cogency. The point is that you did not attempt to deal with the communicative resistances which attacked the patient's representation of the adaptive context. Instead you bypassed them and essentially alluded to her derivative communications and suggested that they pertain to yourself.

In all, it is an interesting intervention. It shows that you are attempting to apply the principles we have been developing in this course, and suggests a problem that I have seen before—a tendency when first doing this kind of work to intervene prematurely at a point where you realize that a particular set of derivatives must have something to do with yourself. It takes considerable time, patience, and understanding to sit back and really let the patient put all of the elements you need for an intervention into you before speaking out.

Therapist: She responded by asking, Why is it I need men so much, but I can't trust them? Then she was silent for the last minute or so.

Langs: Let's hear how the next session began.

Therapist: She said, I didn't want to come today. I left the last session feeling depressed. I am just frustrated. I don't see the point of going on. It has been a long time that I have been in therapy, and it can go on forever, and I still can't decide whether to get married or not. I just don't know what is going on.

Discussant: This sounds like an attempt on her part to prepare for the pending termination. I wondered too whether the therapist's intervention, since it finally addresses the therapeutic relationship, didn't place the tension back into the patient and lead to her feeling of depression.

Langs: We will have to hear more of this session next week in order to see whether any aspect of the therapist's intervention received Type Two derivative validation. These initial associations suggest that the patient saw the therapist's comment as a confession of helplessness, and as a reflection of his own belief that he is unable to help the patient. And I think that there was something important to that perception, that the therapist himself experienced that particular quality, and that it was a factor in his attempt to interpret the patient's unconscious perception of himself as someone who is using her and plans to discard her. It seems important to realize that the intervention implicitly dealt with the pending forced termination, without referring directly to that issue. And it may well be that that particular aspect of his comment has had the greatest meaning for the patient, and that it is in that particular area that she will respond most meaningfully.

Therapist: I will say this much about today's discussion. I had a sense that I had been too forceful in this session, and that somehow she took that to mean that I was pressuring her to get married.

Langs: Well, there could be rather extensive unconscious countertransference fantasies and perceptions underlying that particular realization. Thank you for your presentation and we look forward to hearing a bit more next week.

Chapter Nine

COUNTERTRANSFERENCE
AND INTERVENING

Langs: Let's get right into the clinical material and begin without desire, memory, or understanding. This is our final meeting, and if questions occur to you in the course of our discussion, please bring them up. Also, by all means raise any last minute issues or concerns which have occurred to you.

Therapist: Well, I had begun to describe a new session. She came in and said that she didn't want to come today. She had left the previous session feeling depressed and she just continues to feel that frustration. She really doesn't see the point, it's been a long time that she's been in therapy. This could go on forever. She still can't decide about her marriage. That's what she came into treatment for.

She then went on to talk, in a rather typical way for her, about the difficulties in making that decision. She likes this guy, her present boyfriend, but she is still tied to this previous boyfriend. She doesn't know, she really can't make up her mind, she just can't decide. Then she said, I really don't know why I am so angry and I don't even know who I am angry with. I said, It sounds like you are angry with me.

Langs: I have been thinking about this last presentation. I have a kind of *déjà vu* experience here in that I seem to recall that the listening process part of the course (Langs 1978a) ended on a similar note of uncertainty after a series of highly convincing presentations and discussions. It remains to be seen what our patient and therapist will offer to us on this last day.

Actually, I don't feel badly about ending on a note of uncertainty. There are many therapists who feel that the communicative approach is so well defined that it claims to have solved all of the dilemmas of psychotherapy and to propose principles for every conceivable situation. While the communicative approach has offered some previously unrecognizable solutions and also a means through which many previously confusing situations could now be understood, it has also identified new dilemmas and problems which are in need of clarification and resolution.

So—to paraphrase Freud's comment to Dora (1905)—while I may be deprived of the satisfaction of a final opportunity to prove once again that interpretations must pertain to the therapeutic interaction, I nonetheless expect that we will have an opportunity to clarify other issues as we proceed. This is already in evidence.

Who would like to comment on the material and on the intervention?

Discussant: The adaptive context was easy for me to recall. The therapist had made a rather strong intervention, saying that her seductive allusions to men who use her and drop her referred in some way to himself. We had suggested that the intervention was premature and that the patient had not provided a clear link to therapy or given the therapist sufficient reason to shape the derivatives in terms of her relationship with him. We felt that there was truth to the intervention, but that it might have been too shocking for the patient. In addition, I believe we said something about a derivative reference to the pending forced termination, an issue we believe to be an active one, though unconsciously for both the patient and the therapist.

Well, if my formulation is accurate, the patient now shows a new level of communicative resistance. She seems depressed or disturbed by whatever it is that the therapist had stirred up. She conveyed some derivatives that separation is on her mind, and even connected it to her thoughts about getting married. But then she begins to ruminate. She's angry about something, and I would agree that it is with the therapist, though it seems to me that his last intervention was a bit premature.

Langs: Well, let's stay for a moment with the patient's material. Surface rumination is usually a sign of both a gross behavioral and communicative resistance. Whenever we identify the presence of a resistance, we must try to formulate its underlying basis. Greenson (1967) stressed the importance of determining the motives for a resistance in order to arrive at its unconscious basis. This is also true in Freud's (1914) writings on the subject, and the same principle applies in the communicative approach.

Discussant: It seems to me that we are postulating that some of the resistance stems from the premature qualities of the therapist's intervention, and his indirect allusion to the forced termination.

Discussant: With the patient's comment about being angry, it might also be that she is angry with the therapist because of his intervention and perhaps because of the anticipated termination, and the anger is creating some kind of anxiety and conflict which the patient wishes to defend herself against. The anger itself might lead her to be resistant in order to frustrate the therapist.

Langs: I am glad you made that last point. You are proposing that this is an interactional resistance, with inputs from both patient and therapist. The motivational systems, which form the unconscious basis for the resistance, also derive from both participants. Resistances are motivated interactionally and reflect interactional motivations within the patient. By this I mean not only that they are stimulated by the therapist's interventions and receive additional impetus from within the patient, but they are also a response to the therapist and are designed to have interactional effects upon him. As you may recall, this is a point which Bird (1972) made: resistance may be designed consciously and unconsciously to thwart, frustrate, and hurt the therapist. Because of this, this last association may well be a derivative of the patient's unconscious perception of the function of these particular resistances.

Discussant: It seems to me that the patient is now providing a bridge to therapy by discussing a disillusionment with treatment. She still does not represent a specific adaptive context, but it seems to me that now the derivative complex is considerably less meaningful and has been subjected to a greater degree of resistance.

It seems clear that patients can apply defenses either to the representation of the adaptive context or to the level of meaning in the derivative complex. Sometimes they are defensive in both areas, sometimes in one but not the other, and sometimes in neither. I begin to wonder: Is there a communicative, or rather resistance, style involved? Do patients tend to show a consistent pattern of communicative resistances? Do these patterns change, and if so, what influences these changes?

Langs: You actually touch upon a problem that I have been pondering over the last couple of weeks. As a matter of fact, I had planned to bring up that issue today myself. I had not introduced it earlier because I had been unable to garner sufficient clinical observations to provide a definitive answer. I'm not even sure I have a tentative answer, but you have raised an extremely important and interesting question.

When I think of how readily I have been able to identify trends using the communicative approach, my inability to come up with a definitive answer despite efforts at observation for some weeks now strongly suggests to me that patients do not show a characteristic pattern in this respect. If this is the case, I would think that much depends on the nature of the intervention context and on the dynamic and genetic implications it has for the patient. That is, I would expect patients to more frequently represent an adaptive context related to a disturbance in the fixed frame than to do so with even continuous interpretive errors. That particular expectation is borne out in this presentation, and is in keeping with our observations over the last two weeks.

In addition, I would expect the derivative complex to be especially meaningful when a disturbing intervention context touches upon areas of great sensitivity to the patient, and upon conflicts and fantasy and perception constellations which are especially pertinent to his neurosis. When a context relates to the fixed frame, it is also likely to produce a relatively meaningful derivative complex.

It is my current impression that Type C patients tend to apply defenses in both spheres: in respect to the representation of the adaptive context and in regard to the derivative complex. They will often suddenly refer to the therapist's silence or to an error in technique rather directly, instead of gradually and through derivatives. Further, at such moments the derivative complex may be quite fragmented, except for rare occasions when it is coalescing, and the patient has unconsciously chosen to express himself through the Type A communicative mode. I am not certain of the determinants of these fluctuations and variations, and very much hope that they will be subjected to further clinical observation.

The discovery of communicative styles indicates that patients tend to segregate into those who tend in general to show relatively minimal communicative resistances, or those who do so in a derivative manner that lends itself to interpretation—the Type A patient—as compared to those who show a high level of communicative resistance in all spheres, often using nonderivative defenses—Type C patients. Your question seems to touch upon variations within the Type C group, and I have not found any consistent pattern.

With this patient, who appears to be a Type A patient expressing derivative resistances, we have seen that she consistently attacked the representations of the intervention context in the previous hour. As our discussant indicated, she now seems to be more directly representing that context, though not the therapist's specific interventions, and showing more resistance in respect to the meaningful nature of the derivative complex. This implies that she has shifted the locus of her primary resistances. In this respect I think we can identify one factor: at the point where the therapist moved directly into interventions related to the therapeutic interaction, the patient responded by obliterating meaning in the derivative complex and alluding in a general way to the therapeutic situation. Overall, it seems to me that her resistances have spread from the area of the adaptive context to the derivative complex, lessening slightly if at all in the former area.

Remember, in principle the intervention context is the traumatic, rarely gratifying stimulus for the patient's responses. Resistances in this area constitute a wish to not identify the source of the patient's adaptive reactions. On the other hand, the derivative complex contains these adaptive and coping responses, and representations of the meanings of the context. When they are relatively meaningless and therefore resistant, they reflect an effort on the part of the patient to seal off rather than represent the disturbance, in a sense to deny the impact of the context on herself and her inner mental world.

This reminds me of a point that has become clear to me in respect to the listening process. I have found that it helps to conceptualize the derivative complex by identifying the nature of the traumas contained in an intervention context. It is useful to ask yourself the question, What is it that has traumatized the patient? What is the nature of the disturbance and what conflicts are likely to have been stirred up? What are the issues with which the patient is coping? In that light it is sometimes easier to organize the derivative complex as both reflecting the patient's unconscious perceptions of the unconscious nature of the precipitant, and the patient's efforts at coping and adapting.

What about this intervention?

Discussant: It sounds like a cross between a confrontation and an interpretation. I guess it is mainly an interpretation, an effort to make the patient aware that her anger is directed at the therapist even though she has not directly said so. She has been saying that she is frustrated about therapy, but not that she is angry with the therapist.

Discussant: This also sounds like a cross between Type One and Type Two derivative level listening. No adaptive context is identified so it really is not a true Type Two derivative intervention. There is also no use of a derivative complex, simply a comment on the patient's sense of anger.

Discussant: It sounds premature to me, like the therapist didn't wait for a new bridge to therapy.

Langs: Yes, but he did have a prior bridge. Still, I believe you are right. In a way, this intervention is an attempt to identify an unconscious basis for a resistance within the patient, an effort at a relationship resistance interpretation. It neither states that the anger is appropriate or inappropriate. In the former case it would be a nontransference resistance interpretation, while in the latter instance, a transference resistance interpretation.

In any case, the main indicator seems to be the patient's dissatisfaction with treatment and her ruminative resistance. The adaptive context is omitted, which would serve as a warning that it is absolutely critical in interpreting relationship resistances to organize the intervention around represented contexts within the treatment situation. The intervention also does not make use of the derivative complex, and in principle, it should.

A correct interpretation should integrate all of the patient's meaningful material, not deal with an isolated segment. This is an important principle, since there is a tendency among therapists to pick and choose in isolated fashion, rather than finding an interpretation which serves as a selected fact by integrating all of the scattered associations from the patient.

This type of intervention, in which the therapist suggests that a diffuse feeling of anger, or even anger expressed at someone else, actually reflects anger at himself, is quite common in the field. Many therapists would consider this to be a transference interpretation since it deals with an affect directed toward the therapist. Some would feel that the interpretation does attempt to deal with an apparent resistance.

The problem with this kind of intervention is that it is sudden, not built up gradually from the patient's derivative communications, and it is speculative in circumstances where the patient would probably eventually provide sufficient material to permit the therapist to make his point with more certainty. As a sudden effort to link an affect with the therapeutic relationship, it is usually experienced by the patient as intrusive, speculative, and self-revealing by the therapist. It is often subjected to direct denial and frequently reinforces communicative defenses, rather than lessening them. It is too disconnected from the rest of the patient's material; even if true, it does not clarify the basis for the anger and its relevance to the patient's resistances. Such matters should not be left unstated, or for the patient to wonder about.

A full interpretation would have identified the specific indicators (here, the communicative and gross behavioral resistances), linked them to represented intervention contexts, and attempted a meaningful integration of the entire derivative complex designed to show how these resistances constituted an effort to cope with the adaptive context—here, for example, the intrusive qualities of the therapist's previous interventions and his passing reference to the end of treatment.

Discussant: While I may not be able to validate this impression, it seems to me that the therapist first avoids his relationship with the patient entirely. Then he suddenly confronts her rather blatantly with it, in a premature manner, and it seems to depress her and frighten her off. Either way, the unconscious need seems to be to avoid any meaningful working over of the therapeutic interaction. It leads me to suspect that the same countertransference constellation can lead to avoidance or to premature confrontation or interpretation.

Langs: Exactly. While tentative, your point is well taken.

Discussant: I want to be clear about something. As I see it, the clearest representation here of an adaptive context would be the patient's comment that treatment could go on forever, a derivative of the pending forced termination. I wonder too whether the reference to anger could not allude to the therapist's intrusive intervention at the end of the previous session. She may be sensing something hostile in his approach and introjecting that quality into herself.

Langs: Yes, it is always important to apply the me/not-me interface to the patient's associations.

Discussant: There was also something nebulous about the intervention, which was reflected in the patient's confusion and uncertainty. We could also postulate that the intervention could have been a defense against depression within the therapist, which the patient experienced as an introjective identification.

Langs: These are all tentative hypotheses. They make a good deal of sense, but require Type Two derivative validation. But let's not forget that their tentative qualities reflect the relatively high level of resistance within the patient at this particular juncture.

Discussant: It seems to me that an intervention of this kind, while possibly a true statement, serves as a Type C barrier against the more specific aspects of this particular therapeutic interaction. It also has a nonderivative quality, and I wonder if that would not encourage the patient herself to communicate in a nonderivative manner and to establish her own lie-barrier systems.

Langs: In principle, when dealing with gross behavioral and communicative resistances, it is important to utilize the patient's communications whenever they facilitate an interpretive intervention. Sometimes, these resistances appear in nonderivative form, and as I have said before, they then require the silent holding and containing of the therapist. It is important to not propose meaning when meaning has been destroyed. It is preferable, instead, to seek a means of interpreting the destruction of meaning, since that is the only truly meaningful interpretation possible under those conditions.

Discussant: It seems to me that the message from the patient that therapy is not progressing is an important communication and reflects the patient's unconscious perceptions of the therapist's intervention in the previous hour.

Discussant: Isn't is also true that when you tell a patient that he is angry with you, you imply that the me/not-me interface does not apply, and that you are not angry with the patient and she has not introjected any sense of anger from you?

Langs: Yes, that is another important, detrimental consequence of this type of isolated intervening. It disregards the derivative complex, which includes the me/not-me interface as applied to all of the patient's associations.

Therapist: As I heard it, I was trying to help her understand why she was experiencing difficulty in coming to the session. I was trying to point out that it was based on her sense of depression, and that there was a sense of anger underlying the depression.

Langs: Yes, but once again you develop your thoughts without organizing them around a specific adaptive context. Her reluctance to come to treatment and her thoughts of terminating are, indeed, gross behavioral resistances. I hope that the model of interpretation which I have offered will enable you to respond somewhat differently in the future under these conditions.

We all agree that there are important resistance indicators in this session, and differences arise as to how best handle them. In the actual session, I would have remained silent rather than intervening at this point. I would have been aware of the gross behavioral and communicative resistances and waiting for the patient to more clearly represent the most pertinent intervention contexts and to fill in the derivative complex. If I felt that the threat of termination was high, I would then feel a responsibility to offer the patient the best possible intervention in light of her material. But it would certainly be structured around the representations of the indicators, which are fairly direct in this hour, the best representations of the contexts, and the most meaningful qualities of the derivative complex.

Here, for example, I might be formulating a specific tentative interpretation to the effect that her depression, reluctance to come to treatment, and feelings of frustration seem in some way connected to her perceptions of my interventions in the previous hour (a point in need of representation in this material), and to the theme of therapy ending or going on forever (the best available representation of the adaptive context of the pending forced termination). These particular concerns seem related to her sense of anger (which, I would hope to show her, derives from an unconscious perception of the interventions in the previous hour as well as from her reaction to the anticipation of the end of treatment).

In this way, I would have met the requirements of an interpretation. And in the actual hour, by preparing a silent interpretation of this kind, I would be able to experience whatever it is I am lacking in order to offer it to the patient, and would be more likely to hear the derivatives which I need as the patient continues to associate. I also would remain open to other possibilities, trying carefully not to become too invested in a particular formulation, especially when there are so many gaps in the patient's material in respect to Type Two derivative support.

Discussant: As I understand it, functionally, this last intervention is incomplete. It touches upon a possible truth without fully stating its context and total implications.

Langs: Yes, it is an unusual kind of lie-barrier, in that it has a certain ring of truth, but is so significantly incomplete as to interfere with a clear definition of the actual unconscious issues which exist between this patient and therapist.

Therapist: Well, the patient responded angrily, You always bring things back to here. And I know that you really don't know anything. You really don't know the answer to whether I should get married or not. And you never said you did, so how could I be angry with you, since I really couldn't have expected that of you? It's just like with Patricia (who is the head of her physiotherapy department), where I would get angry with her because of things she would do, and she wasn't really doing them in order to hurt me, though it seemed as if she did. And why should I have gotten angry with her because she never changed on the basis of my anger.

Discussant: It seems to me that the patient wants little to do with the therapist's lie-barrier system.

Discussant: I often get that response from patients when I try to link up their material to myself. I've learned in this course that, often, this is based on the fact that I have intervened prematurely, and have not waited for sufficient derivatives and for a meaningful bridge to therapy. I hear less of this complaint in recent weeks, since I have changed my technique.

Discussant: I can hear this patient's response to the intervention in two ways. On the one hand, she does elaborate on her feelings of anger, now directing them at the therapist and using the excuse that he tries to bring himself into the picture. On another level, she seems to be saying that she really is angry, but that she feels there is no sense in expressing it directly because it has no effect on the therapist.

Langs: Yes, that last point is an important commentary on the therapist's interventions, and more broadly, I believe, on the nature of this therapeutic interaction. It helps me to finally understand why we have had so much difficulty in obtaining Type Two derivative validation for our hypotheses, and in establishing in a convincing manner that the therapeutic interaction itself is central to this patient's conflicts and concerns—and to her neurosis as it is activated at the moment. This derivative may prove very helpful in enabling you to recognize the validity of the communicative hypotheses. It is certainly the patient's way of unconsciously explaining to me, and to her therapist, why she has not responded to his countertransference-based interventions with more active corrective and curative efforts.

In essence, the patient seems to indicate that she has no basis upon which to expect anything constructive from this therapist. For some reason not specified for the moment, she nonetheless continues in therapy, maintaining a tie which must be something like her relationship with her boss. I must emphasize that her manifest complaint, that the therapist does not provide her with an answer about marriage, implies that the therapist has not been able to offer this patient sound interpretations. These are her direct and derivative observations, and they may have considerable validity. They do not, for the moment, leave room for the kernels of valid effort reflected in several of the therapist's recent interventions, but it sounds as if this type of work has never been sustained and that the patient has good reason to believe that nothing will change.

Our lack of knowledge of the course of this therapy seems to have limited our understanding of the patient's material. All of this changes now that the patient tells us that it is pointless to get angry and expect help; her friend, a representation of the therapist, never listens and never changes. The patient reveals a critical motive for her communicative and gross behavioral resistances, one that we might have detected sooner had we known more.

The patient is telling us that she has engaged in unconscious curative efforts toward the therapist for a long time. She informs us that these efforts have failed to modify his countertransferences, and she has lately become angry and depressed because of it; and she is now entertaining thoughts of giving up on the therapist and therapy and turning to an acting-out solution to her conflicts through marriage. She claims it is pointless to communicate derivatives of valid unconscious perceptions of the therapist's errors, since these go entirely unheeded. She engaged during the last session in a bit of unconscious therapeutic work, but then withdrew when the therapist intervened in a way that reflected his failure to understand the implications of her material.

We must postulate that this patient feels deeply hurt and disappointed, since she is not acknowledging the kernel of sound effort in the therapist's recent interventions. She appears to be reacting to his intrusive, sudden style and his failure to crystallize interpretations around meaningful adaptive contexts. She may also be reacting to his alternation between reinforcing the bastion against the therapeutic interaction through questions and comments in respect to her outside relationships, and sudden shifts to confrontations and superficial interpretations pertinent to the therapeutic experience, though divorced from specific adaptive contexts. In any case, it is her claim that resistances are justified as a way of protecting herself from further disappointment and because it is pointless to attempt to communicate through derivatives to this therapist.

These are, indeed, harsh implications, but we would have to know a great deal more before establishing any sense of distortion in them. Based on what we do know, I believe that there is much that is valid here, though I also suspect that defensive needs within the patient deny any constructive effort by the therapist—a defensiveness that I suspect stems from the additional trauma of the pending forced termination.

In principle, then, interpretive and framework management failures by the therapist may prompt strong gross behavioral and communicative resistances, justified in the patient's mind because of the difficulties within the therapist. When such failures are repetitive, the resistances may become fixed. Any effort to interpret their basis without rectifying the therapist's contributions would have virtually no effect on the patient's communicative style. This helps to explain why there was little change in this respect in this sequence, despite a valiant effort by the therapist to interpret the disturbance within the therapeutic relationship. The patient feels that she is being asked to serve as a functional therapist, but that it is pointless to do so if the designated therapist fails to benefit from being in the position of the functional patient.

I have discussed elsewhere the patient's interventions to the therapist, and only wish to remind you that such interventions are responses to the adaptive contexts of the therapist's interventions, and they contain significant elements of valid curative intentions. Because relatively little material is available to the patient, they tend to be offered on a general level, to be influenced to some extent by the patient's own dynamics and personality, and almost always to be communicated on a derivative level. They tend to be quite perceptive and valid, and only rarely mistaken, in contrast to the patient's conscious efforts at intervening which are characteristically in error, highly defensive, and distorted. Finally, as Searles (1975) so cogently pointed out, it is extremely painful and damaging to patients when their unconscious therapeutic efforts go unheeded by their therapists. This sense of hurt, disappointment, and anger, as well as hopelessness, is certainly reflected in the last communication from this patient.

Discussant: I am beginning to see your point. I would agree that here, despite the elaboration of material in respect to the patient's sense of anger, there is no sense that the intervention was experienced as valid. It is striking to hear the patient tell the therapist that he doesn't know any of the answers, and that she has given up on expecting him to have any. I am aware that some therapists would take this to mean something in the restricted sense of alluding to his advice about whether to get married, but I am no longer that naive. I would formulate this as a commentary on the intervention and on the therapist's work in general. I feel quite depressed when I hear this kind of thing from patients and I must admit that I do hear it more often than I would like.

There is something else that I have been mulling over. I've been thinking about your emphasis on derivative communications, and your statement that this is the medium of neurotic expression. In terms of Freud's distinction between primary and secondary processes, I was wondering whether what you term neurotic communication is based on primary process mechanisms.

Langs: That's an excellent observation. I have considered that possibility for some time now, though I have maintained a distinctive characterization of the processes involved in neurotic communication largely because I find the concept of primary process mechanisms somewhat incomplete as an explanatory concept. Nonetheless, Freud's (1900) distinction between conscious, logical mentation as governed by such laws as causality (secondary process mechanisms), and mental processes which take place outside of awareness as governed by a different set of laws or principles, is undoubtedly fundamental. For Freud, primary process mechanisms included symbolism, condensation, displacement, and considerations of representability—the mechanisms of dream work. There is an absense of logical relationships and a disregard for reality testing. Freud was able to show that both dreams and neurotic symptoms are based on ʾunconscious fantasies which operate according to primary process mechanisms.

Efforts to clarify the distinction between primary and secondary processes, and to specify the nature of the former mode of functioning, are well beyond the purview of this course. Suffice it to say that all neurotic symptoms are based on unconscious processes—fantasies, perceptions, and introjects—which exert their influence in keeping with primary process mechanisms. In addition, the means through which the patient expresses himself to the therapist as it pertains to his neurosis is similarly governed. As a result, we must pay attention to the patient's derivative rather than manifest communications. The surface of his associations are governed by and large by secondary processes, and even when there are breaks in logic, their underlying basis is not revealed on the manifest level. On the other hand, the latent meanings of manifest associations—the disguised derivative expressions—are developed based on primary process mechanisms, and analysis or decoding will consistently reveal the nature of the patient's unconscious functioning—including both fantasies and perceptions.

Clearly, an interpretation designed to reveal the unconscious factors in a disturbance in the patient's communications to the therapist, must be based on derivative listening and an understanding which takes into account the special laws of unconscious or derivative communication. Efforts to work on the surface and in terms of secondary processes can only be designed to avoid or cover

over these more threatening, irrational, and often primitive derivative expressions.

This is a difficult area to conceptualize and clarify. Despite the predominance of irrational mechanisms, derivative communications involve functions which are often highly sensitive and perceptive, and quite in touch with reality. We have seen many examples of this in the patient's valid unconscious perceptions of the implications of the therapist's interventions. These perceptions are not permitted to enter awareness and to be worked over consciously, but are experienced outside of awareness and thereby subjected to disguised expression.

Try to be clear about this point: A patient may incorporate accurately perceived communications from the therapist, including many of their unconscious implications, yet not allow these impressions to register consciously. Repressive and perhaps denial defenses are operating, usually supported by other mechanisms. Because this information enters the mind without conscious awareness—and sometimes, after direct awareness which is repressed—it is then subjected to unconscious processing, identified as primary process in nature. As a result, when a patient, for example, correctly unconsciously perceives hostility in a therapist's intervention, he speaks of how his father seemed inappropriately angry last night. The unrealistic element is not in the perception of the therapist, but in the way in which the patient experiences his perception—e.g., as not belonging to the therapist but to his father. It is in the expression of the perception that the distortion takes place. In this way, you can recognize that primary process mechanisms may be applied to what are initially either valid or in themselves distorted perceptions or fantasies.

Discussant: I am reminded of another question. It seems to me that all deviations from the ideal frame or therapeutic environment constitute resistances when the patient participates, and counter-resistances when the therapist does so. Am I correct in that impression?

Langs: Yes, you are quite correct. Many resistances are expressed through gross behaviors which entail deviation in the ideal or optimal set of ground rules.

On a dynamic level, many resistances function as avenues of pathological defense and inappropriate gratifications for the patient, and often for the therapist as well. Such gratifications reinforce the patient's neurotic maladaptation and symptoms, and therefore interfere with efforts to work over these symptoms in a communicative fashion toward insight, understanding, and overall, a different, constructive type of adaptation. These qualities are inherent to the concepts of acting out and acting in, gross behaviors which similarly gratify and reinforce the patient's neurosis. In addition, all deviations offer the patient gratification of his pathological symbiotic needs. When this occurs, work toward insight and individuation is usually slowed down or set aside.

Discussant: I wonder if you would say a word or two about the distinction between derivative and nonderivative defenses, and between adaptive and maladaptive lie-barrier systems.

Langs: The communicative approach reveals two basic types of defensive formations in patients, derivative and nonderivative. The former type of defense is based on unconscious fantasies and perceptions, and communicates in some disguised way this underlying structure. It is a type of partially failed repression, for example, which leads to a compromise formation in which the presence and unconscious implications of the defense itself is revealed in disguised form.

On the other hand, there are defensive formations which serve as barriers and which obliterate both the underlying unconscious fantasies and perceptions, as well as any representation of the unconscious basis for the defense itself. With derivative defenses, compromise prevails and meaningful disguised expressions of the entire underlying unconscious fantasy-perception constellation can be detected. With nonderivative defenses, this entire underlying constellation is virtually obliterated and covered over. Clearly, there is another continuum here with relatively pure forms at either extreme, and gradations in between. It is an area in need of extensive clinical investigation.

As for adaptive and maladaptive lie-barrier systems, it seems clear now that both derivative and nonderivative defenses and resistances can be relatively adaptive or relatively maladaptive.

There is, I believe, some tendency for nonderivative defenses to be more primitive, to rely more on splitting and denial than derivative defenses which utilize more sophisticated protective mechanisms such as repression and the group of obsessive defenses. In addition, there is a group of defensive formations which may be described as lie-barrier systems in that their main characteristic is an effort to cover over or falsify the underlying conflict and fantasy-memory constellation, rather than represent it.

Defenses and resistances as conceived in present-day psychoanalysis are thought of almost entirely in terms of compromise formations which permit derivative communication. In contrast, lie-barrier systems are uncompromising, and are impervious barriers designed to cover over and misrepresent. The first group of defenses convey representations of underlying (unconscious) truths, while the second group does not do so and attempts to substitute in their place misrepresentations and falsifications. I have tried to show the clinical referrants which enable us to distinguish these two types of defensiveness and resistance, and recognize that here too we need more clinical investigation and discussion.

Finally, those lie-barrier systems which prove flexible, easily modified, and which are likely to give way to derivative defenses are those which I have termed adaptive or soft lie-barrier systems. Those lie-barrier formations which are rigid, intensely maintained, quite often a defense against an activated psychotic constellation, and unlikely to give way to derivative defenses and communication, are those which I have termed hard or maladaptive lie-barrier systems. There seems to be a period in every extended psychotherapy during which the patient on his own works over his lie-barrier formations and softens them based on Type One derivative pseudo or false insight. During this time, the therapist usually has no choice but to be silent and to maintain a holding and containing attitude. These new lie systems tend to be more flexible and adaptive and to enable the patient to manage better his own inner mental disturbance and his relationship with others. The specific mechanisms involved also require further investigation.

Please continue.

Therapist: Unfortunately, I have rather sketchy notes for the next part of the session. But I think this was because she began to ruminate, as she has done so often before, about how she can't really hope to change very much from the therapy, and that she is really not sure whether she will ever be able to make up her mind about getting married. And she went on and on about how it's still the same old problems and how she's back to where she started. There was a lot of rumination and many periods of silence, two of which were quite long.

Discussant: I could make a somewhat different formulation of the patient's ruminations. It seems that she is trying to protect the therapist against her anger. She says that she can't get angry at him because she has no expectations. She wants to spare him her anger.

Langs: Yes, on some level, this material could be seen in that way. But again, try to be specific when you develop a formulation of that kind, and link it to a particular intervention context. And always apply the me/not-me interface. In that way you could also suggest that the therapist's interventions are designed to protect the patient, just as her denial and rumination, while it frustrates and thwarts the therapist, serves to protect him against a deeper sense of rage and disappointment.

Your comment helps to highlight the transversal qualities of resistances when it comes to wishes to help and harm the therapist. Therapists have been so preoccupied with the hurtful effects of these resistances that they fail to identify the well-meaning side. Ruminative resistances of this kind take the power and sting out of the patient's associations and interactional projections. They form an effective nonderivative lie-barrier system which has a protective function for both the patient and therapist.

I must say that the only protective function I see in the therapist's interventions is reflected in his failure to identify the specific adaptive contexts for the patient's derivative associations. In that way, he spares both himself and the patient definitive realizations of many types—sexual, aggressive, and much more.

Therapist: There were also some expressions of anger again, though they were rather vague and indirect. She then became silent for about five minutes. And I said, Is your silence an expression of anger?

Discussant: While this is a question, it also implies an interpretation. It is an attempt again to deal with a gross behavioral resistance, but lacks both an adaptive context and a derivative complex. It has that barren and speculative quality that we saw in the previous intervention when the therapist suggested that the patient must be angry with him.

Discussant: It is mainly on a Type One derivative level. It also has a fragmented quality, in that it helps the patient to keep everything separate and to integrate nothing.

Langs: And like all questions, it is also an attempt to move the patient away from derivative communication despite the use of inference. I fear that once again it will justify the feeling within the patient that her unconscious interpretive efforts go to naught with this therapist. Remember, her derivative comment about how her boss never changes was an unconscious interpretation to the therapist. His present intervention will reveal again that he has not understood the patient's derivative meaning. Her depression might well intensify, as might her own Type C lie-barrier formations.

Discussant: In some way I connected this interaction with the desertion of her father in her childhood. It could well have been the model for her experience with the therapist. She might have wanted to hold onto her father, and have been totally disappointed when he did not listen and abandoned her.

Langs: That's certainly an interesting association, and a tentative hypothesis worthy of maintaining as open for validation. It undoubtedly has a great deal to do with her reaction to the pending forced termination. It would also help us to understand her sensitivity to this issue: needing to express derivative responses in anticipation of its occurrence, she also needs to defend herself against too open an expression of the relevant issues.

Therapist: She reacted angrily again, and said, All you say is that I really have nothing to say. I've said it all. And then she motioned as if she wanted to leave. I then said, In the previous session, there was something that was really bothering you, and I didn't make it go away. I didn't help you. What you had expected from me was that either I act like other men, or that I would take over and take the problem away, like Jack used to do. If not, that I would just reject you outright, as he also did.

Discussant: The therapist has repeated his confrontation of the patient with her sense of anger. The patient invokes an introject through which she says that she herself has nothing to say. She's said it all, the therapist has said it all—the same thing over and over again. And then she wants to leave, as if she feels there is no point in staying.

Her threat to leave the session must be a level ten indicator. As I heard him, the therapist now attempted a Type Two derivative interpretation, using the intervention context of having disappointed the patient in the previous hour. He suggested that either he would be helpful or would be seen as rejecting. Much of that comes from the previous session. But there was little to work with in this hour. In fact, I wonder how Dr. Langs would have intervened at that point.

Langs: We have our greatest technical problems when gross behavioral resistances coincide with communicative resistances. To some extent, this appears to be the situation here. I have found this combination to occur most often in the presence of either major countertransference difficulties and counterresistances within the therapist, or in situations where a therapist is endeavoring to secure the frame with a patient who is attempting to deviate, and the patient enormously dreads the secure therapeutic environment and the exposure of an activated psychotic core.

In this situation, the patient prepares to leave the hour. This provides us with further validation of our silent hypothesis regarding her anxiety about the pending forced termination. This is a derivative behavior which does not, however, permit interpretation linked to that particular anticipated intervention context. By and large, the prevailing adaptive contexts—the therapist's recent interventions and their implications, and the pending forced termination—are poorly represented here, a communicative resistance which makes interpretation difficult. The derivative complex is somewhat meaningful and coalescing, though highly disguised.

If the patient were to begin to stand up to leave the hour, I would offer the best possible interpretation available for the moment. I might say something like this to her: You seem to be working over some sense of anger and frustration in response to the ways in which I have been intervening here, and to something that has to do with therapy going on forever or being interrupted abruptly. (These appear to be the best representations of the activated adaptive contexts and as a rule, they should be the point of departure for an interpretation or playback of derivatives.) You were talking of your boss, Patricia, whom you felt was provocative and hurtful, and unresponsive to your anger and other reactions. You were also talking about how it is pointless to say anything here. It seemed that you were implying that what I have had to say has had little effect upon you, must be entirely negated, and that what you have been communicating to me has been similarly disregarded. Your reaction is to move to interrupt the hour as a way of expressing your sense of depression and hopelessness, and of expressing in action something related to your concerns about the continuation or ending of the therapy.

As you can see, this is a rather tentative, not very specific, interpretation which makes use of as many information elements as are currently available in the derivative complex. It identifies the immediate therapeutic context—the indicator of the patient's wish to leave the session prematurely—and moves from there to the identification, at the level expressed by the patient, of the motivating intervention contexts, and the patient's perceptions of, and reactions to, these contexts as they illuminate the unconscious implications of the indicator.

Leaving the hour prematurely is, of course, a type of resistance, and once again it takes the form of an enactment and an attempt to modify the fixed frame. This is therefore an interpretation of a relationship resistance that has elements of both transference and nontransference, though apparently the latter predominates. While offering this interpretation, I would be preparing to engage in self-analysis in order to rectify my own contributions to this resistance. One aspect, the pending forced termination, I cannot rectify, and that will continue to motivate the patient in the direction of acting out resistances—since it is in itself an acting out form of counter-resistance.

Discussant: As I heard your interpretation, you used these derivatives to show the patient her unconscious perceptions of the therapist, hinted at some fantasies, and possibly stated something of the patient's reaction to the prevailing contexts. In general, does the derivative complex contain anything more?

Langs: The derivative complex contains all of the patient's unconscious perceptions and fantasies, as mobilized by an activated adaptive context. It also contains activated memories—the genetic element—as well as indications of the patient's efforts at adaptation—defensive and otherwise. In essence, then, the derivative complex is the patient's adaptive responses to an intervention context, and within these responses are perceptions, fantasies, memories, introjects, dynamic stirrings, superego representations, and defensive efforts—in sum, all of the dynamic, genetic, intrapsychic, and interpersonal implications mobilized by a particular context.

Discussant: It seems to me that the therapist's intervention is too vague, and that it is a derivative lie system. It contains another indirect reference to separation but does not get around to the specific issue of the forced termination. It also identifies the source of the patient's disappointment as the therapist's failure to take over and remove her problems. That is a derivative of his interpretive failures, but at the same time it has a defensive and accusatory quality. It's as if the therapist is saying that the patient's expectations are unrealistic and infantile, when our own formulation was to the effect that it is not especially childish for a patient who is operating as a functional therapist to expect or hope that the designated therapist will benefit from her unconscious efforts.

Langs: Exactly. This is where you can experience the hurtful qualities of treating a problem in terms of transference and distortion, at the very moment when there are important valid and nondistorted reasons for the patient's reactions. This comes from having to desperately select derivatives from the previous hour, and also from being quite unclear as to the nature of the ongoing communicative interaction. As long as you fail to attempt to define the specific unconscious implications of each of your interventions, you will not correctly understand the patient's material. You will constantly shift to Type One derivative formulations as a defense against Type Two derivative implications.

Discussant: Oddly enough, the patient could feel relief in having to leave the therapist because, in reality, he has not been especially helpful.

Discussant: I can also see the disadvantage of lie-barrier systems. The therapist focuses on the patient's disappointment that he did not take over in the previous hour. There is a derivative of the separation problem, but it is not directly confronted or interpreted. This patient, whom I suspect has little in the way of resources with which to deal with separation issues, is left with no option but to marry her present boyfriend in order to deny the loss of the therapist. If, instead, this material were permitted to unfold, the therapist could eventually interpret the nature of the patient's fantasies and anxieties. In addition, he would be able to show the patient that he himself has a capacity to deal with such issues. However, when they both avoid the problem and interrupt the development of clearer derivatives in this area, the patient is bound to feel that this is a frightening subject, for the therapist as well as for herself, and to feel hopeless and without resources.

Langs: Yes, there are many disadvantages to lie-barrier systems, and you touch upon some that are quite important. It remains to be seen whether the patient will accept the particular lie-barrier system offered by the therapist, invoke her own lie-barrier system, or make a desperate effort to express the truth. At this juncture, the last possibility seems least likely. The middle possibility, developing her own lie-barrier system, seems most likely. In a way, I think she expressed that very effort in her threat to leave the hour. That would constitute a derivative lie barrier through which she would hope to projectively identify into the therapist the unbearable separation anxieties she seems to be experiencing without any assistance from him.

Therapist: With a lot of feeling, she said, You certainly didn't help. She was then silent for several minutes.

Langs: Even her silence now is an expression of the separation issue and a defense against it.

Therapist: Then she went back to ruminating about whether to get married. She said: I just can't make up my mind; what am I going to do? I really haven't learned anything. I just keep going over and over this stuff; this could go on forever.

Langs: For the moment, she has little use for the therapist's lie-barrier system, and does not turn to the issues she introduced from the previous hour. Her own lie-barrier system seems to be more empty, ruminative, and formless than the one offered by the therapist. Notice too that there is no sense of validation of these interventions, an observation which would dictate caution and the need to reformulate.

Therapist: Well, I simple reintroduced my lie-barrier system when she said, This can go on forever. I said, Like a bad marriage.

Discussant: This seems to be an effort at interpretation, though I'm not sure what the therapist is trying to imply. I can see where he took this from the patient's associations, but it seems to me that once before, he made an association of this kind which the patient could readily experience as reflecting his fantasy as well as hers.

Discussant: He also continued to introduce derivatives of the issue of separation, now selecting the theme of marriage to do so.

Therapist: Yes, one of her main fears about marriage is that it might end, that she would not succeed and that she would end up getting divorced.

Langs: You can each see how easy it is to move away from intervention contexts, and into Type One derivative interventions. In a way, you have now shifted from your own lie-barrier system to hers, picking up the rumination about marriage as if it were meaningful, when for the moment, it appears to be a derivative lie barrier which relates to the forced termination issue.

It has been difficult for you, as therapists, to bring some of your derivative insights up to the level of direct consciousness, and to thereby effect a sound interpretation. Remember, it is one of the unique qualities of therapy that the patient can function constructively through derivatives, while the therapist must show his adaptive resources through manifest understanding.

Therapist: She had an extreme and emotional reaction to that particular intervention. She said, Why did you say that? Does that mean that you think my getting married to Richard is a bad idea? I know you'll never say this outright, but maybe that's what you mean. And now this makes it worse because I am more confused than ever before. She went on in that vein a little bit and then said: I came in angry and I am still angry. And then there was a silence. The time was up for the session, and I told her so. And she left angrily, without saying goodbye, which in the past always meant that she was furious.

Langs: Notice the unpredictability of a patient's response to interventions made on the manifest content or Type One derivative level. In her own way, she is actually attempting to get you to recognize that there are unconscious implications to your interventions. She picks a rather obvious representation, so it is important to realize that it has more extensive implications, and undoubtedly reflects another therapeutic effort on her part designed to help you to recognize that you are expressing far more than you realize.

I see that time has been moving along. Are there any questions about the reading or about the basic concepts we have developed in respect to resistances and interventions?

Discussant: I found things a lot easier, if somewhat unsatisfactory, with a more superficial definition of resistances. It has become clear to me that the analytic writings on the subject involve what you call gross behavioral resistances—surface evidence of defensiveness—and lack any sense of what you have described as

communicative resistances. It led me to wonder how much attention you yourself pay to gross behavioral resistances.

Langs: I have tried to show that both gross behavioral and
communicative resistances have importance. The communicative
therapist would sometimes find considerable meaning in material
evaluated by the classical therapist as reflecting gross behavioral or
surface resistances. This often occurs when the classicist believes
that the patient is avoiding a particular subject or suspects acting
out. It would be especially the case when the patient is talking
about events of daily life to a therapist who believes that his work
must be based on the communication of conscious fantasies and
material which directly pertains to himself. The classical analyst
lacks definitive criteria of resistance, and bases much of his thinking on manifest content and Type One derivative considerations,
and on a definition of transference that centers primarily on direct
allusions to the therapist or analyst.

On the other hand, the communicative therapist has derived
empirically a set of criteria for meaningful communication, in
which derivative expressions related to the patient's neurosis are
central. He is therefore open to all types of associations and behaviors from patients, and primarily interested in investigating the
extent to which the indicators and adaptive context are meaningfully represented, and the degree to which the derivative complex
contains definitive implications of various kinds.

Gross behavioral resistances often involve threats to the alliance
sector and to the treatment itself. They are manifest signs that
something is amiss. Here, the communicative approach adds one
main point: it is critical at such times to search for possible and
likely contributions from the therapist to the patient's behaviors.
This implies a need to treat all resistances as interactional, accepting the idea that some resistances have an absolutely minimal
contribution from the therapist, while others turn out to be his
major responsibility.

Discussant: We know that resistances reflect the patient's psychopathology and character structure. Is there any correlation between specific types of communicative resistances and clinical diagnosis?

Langs: I have given that question some thought, though perhaps not as much as I should. From the communicative approach, diagnostic considerations are relatively unreliable guides. We find that there is little correlation between communicative style and diagnosis, except perhaps for the finding that certain types of obsessive patients tend to be Type C ruminators. But we know too that this kind of obsessiveness can appear in patients with a relatively neurotic character structure, as well as in patients with borderline and even schizophrenic disturbances. As I said earlier in this course, the main diagnostic consideration from the communicative viewpoint involves the extent to which a patient shows ego dysfunctions and related primitive superego and self psychopathology. This implies diagnostic considerations which modify the specific contents of the therapist's interventions, though not the basic principles of intervening.

There are other possible correlations which I can comment upon in a rather tentative way. There are some borderline and schizophrenic patients who are strongly inclined toward projective identification, and these fall into the B–A and B–C communicative classifications, depending on whether there is on some important level an interest in understanding or simply a need to get rid of contents and tensions. Some hysterics communicate in the Type B mode as well, though not all.

I have seen no correlation between diagnosis and the communicative area in which the patient's defenses operate most intensely— the representation of the indicators or adaptive context, or in respect to the derivative complex. I have been quite impressed with a different kind of finding, namely, that highly naive and sometimes quite ill patients prove capable of using the Type A communicative mode, especially in response to breaks in the fixed frame. It is quite surprising and impressive to find extremely meaningful communications in such patients, but this is often the case.

Discussant: I would like to be sure that I understood a particular point which has impressed me. The communicative approach shows, as I understand it, that resistances within the patient, behavioral or communicative, can arise from two usually intermixed sources: unconscious perceptions and unconscious fantasies. As I understand that particular point, you are therefore modifying the classical view that resistances correspond to intrapsychic defenses.

Langs: I like to think of it the other way around, that these clinical observations modify the classical view of defenses, which should now be considered as essentially interactional with a crystallization intrapsychically in a particular person—patient or therapist. I would also stress that resistances based on unconscious perceptions are found to be far more difficult to modify than those based on unconscious fantasies. This is true because the resolution of such defenses requires rectification within the therapist so that he is no longer contributing to and reinforcing the patient's defenses. Also, the therapist who unconsciously fosters a resistance within the patient is usually seen as dangerous and not to be trusted, and his need for the patient's defenses is usually unconsciously perceived by the latter. This further motivates the patient to maintain the resistance rather than modify it. In addition, it is likely that a therapist will have something of a blind spot to those resistances in his patients to which he has contributed and for which he has some unconscious need. Analysts have commented that resistances in patients sometimes arise in response to the therapist's or analysts's errors, but they have by no means appreciated how often this occurs, the specific technical problems such resistances pose, and the essential interactional nature of all defenses and resistances.

Discussant: Since time is short, I wonder if we could not hear the beginning of the next session. This course has been especially meaningful to me because it is so entirely clinical. I think it would be more profitable for us to continue that way to the very end.

Langs: I agree. I like the image of going off into the sunset while still in the process of examining some last fragments of clinical data. If there are no other pressing questions, let's hear as much of the next hour as we can squeeze in.

Therapist: Okay. She came in and she was very quiet and subdued; remember, this is six days later. And there was a deviation in the frame in that we started five minutes early. She was there early and I walked through the waiting room about that time, and I saw her there, and I said, Okay, we can start now.

Langs: Who will comment briefly?

Discussant: I have several reactions. For one, I wonder if this kind of thing has occurred before, and whether the patient's complaints about treatment also involve intervention contexts related to the therapist's failure to maintain a stable framework. I also see this particular intervention—the deviation—as some kind of response to the adaptive context of the patient's threat to leave the previous session before her time was up.

Discussant: It could also have meaning in terms of the pending forced termination. In a way it acts out some type of fantasy that separation can be overcome or denied, while at the same time, it communicates something about the uncertainty of the framework itself.

Therapist: I ended the session five minutes earlier as well. In any case, she was quiet and then talked in a very low voice. She said, Well, the first thing is that Richard and I got engaged. It didn't directly happen, but it just sort of happened. Also I decided to apply to dental school in the fall. (This had been an interest of hers for some time.)

Langs: As we had noted, it would be critical to understand the unconscious basis for these two decisions. We have already developed that theme, so I will say very little about it, except to point out how seemingly constructive decisions and changes in a patient's life can develop through lie-barrier therapy as well as from truth therapy. After all, we know that the particular decisions have been made in the context of considerable turmoil within therapy, and we have seen little in the way of validated interpretations.

The immediate adaptive context for these first associations is a break in the fixed frame. It's as if the patient is saying that the therapist has his way of dealing with the disturbances in treatment and the pending forced termination, and the patient has hers. Each has his own lie-barrier system, and each appears determined to maintain it until the end.

In a way, this is a very interesting moment. Of course, we would want to hear the patient's subsequent associations in order to determine her own unconscious perceptions and communications of the implications of these two decisions. This material could reveal basic flaws or suggest some degree of soundness to both decisions. In addition, it would take a number of additional sessions to fully clarify the underlying factors, and several years to see just how they work out. Even if the two decisions are an effort to establish a lie-barrier system designed to seal off chaotic truths within the therapeutic interaction, the adaptive aspects involved might well be sustained and the general outcome for the patient quite favorable.

We would have to know a good deal more about this therapy in order to determine whether the positive aspects of these two decisions arise from some type of constructive therapeutic work which we did not have an opportunity to observe. We did see that the therapist had made efforts at interpretation which approached the truth, though it did so with limitations and all too often through derivative truths—unconscious rather than conscious realizations. And there are undoubtedly other positive inputs based on his basic attitude and concern for the patient.

However, there is no doubt that in addition there have been segments of misalliance and bastion, the offer of lie-barrier systems, inappropriate alterations in the basic framework, erroneous interventions, an effected pathological symbiosis, and all too soon the forced termination will be the crowning blow. We must recognize that some of the inputs into these decisions are undoubtedly based on those particular qualities of this therapeutic interaction.

All of this may provide us with some insight into how patients can derive some small measure of positive introject from the kernels of valid therapeutic work offered by a therapist. But in addition, this material seems to indicate that patients can also react to the psychopathology and countertransferences of the therapist, and to his therapeutic failings, with a powerful mobilization of their own resources—at least on a behavioral level. These efforts may be founded on the use of lie-barrier systems, and may lack true qualities of growth and flexible adaptation, yet they could prove gratifying and constructive to the patient despite their underlying flaws. Here again the material from the patient would reveal the strengths and weaknesses involved. Nonetheless, on a behavioral level, we are now reminded that apparent progress can take place in the face of a considerably flawed psychotherapeutic experience.

Discussant: In that context, I wondered if the therapist's intervention of the previous hour—about how the patient seemed to see her relationship with him as some kind of bad marriage—influenced this patient. Her conscious thought was that the therapist was trying to discourage the marriage or to indicate that it was sick in some ways. She then reacts by becoming engaged. On the surface, this could reflect her wish to dispute the therapist, while under the surface, she may have detected a countertransference need of his own and responded by now offering a defense for both of them—her engagement to Richard. I would agree with Dr. Langs that this did not follow a period of insight and working through.

Langs: Yes, you may well have touched upon some of the unconscious dynamics in the patient's decision to get engaged. She indicates that she experienced it as all quite beyond her control, which may well be how she is experiencing the therapist's interventions and the pending forced termination. Whatever the immediate stimulus, I think it is quite likely that it also touches upon qualities within this therapy which have existed for some time—a point which the patient made in the previous hour.

Discussant: I wonder too if this was the patient's reaction to what she experienced from the therapist. After all, he had begun to directly confront and interpret the problems in her perception of himself and in their interaction. It is as if the patient found that unbearable, and had to immediately turn to her boyfriend for protection. Perhaps the decision to get engaged was an effort to deal with projective identifications from the therapist which the patient was unable to contain and metabolize.

Langs: Yes, and this response is supported by the therapist's own tendency to deal with disturbing introjective identifications through action as well, which is reflected in seeing the patient five minutes early. In this way, he is unwittingly supporting the patient's own tendencies toward action and pathological symbiosis at a critical moment. This is a strong reminder of the implications of the fixed frame and of how deviations serve to reinforce the patient's own pathological tendencies. It is also important to recognize that the patient's action takes place in a setting in which mastery through interpretation has by and large not been offered to her.

Therapist: To continue, she said, I was at the movies with my friend Susie. And when I came home from being at the movies with her, I thought that Richard was still at work at the hospital and I felt very sexy. But I came in and Richard was there, and I was kissing him, and I was really being very passionate, and it seemed to frighten him.

Discussant: Along the me/not-me interface, wouldn't you say that this refers to both the patient and the therapist? The patient herself seems to have been frightened by the therapist's passionate interventions, while she may well feel that the therapist in turn is frightened by her sexual material and passion.

Langs: Yes, you are implying that this material is quite meaningful when organized around the prevailing intervention contexts. But remember that her style is to not represent the adaptive context with sufficient clarity to lend itself to interpretation; she concentrates her defensive efforts in that sphere. The same applies to the indicators for the moment. In contrast, she seems to be developing a rich and coalescible derivative complex filled with both unconscious perceptions and unconscious fantasies. This material is transversal—it does indeed apply to both herself and the therapist. Remember too that there is an immediate context here: the break in the fixed frame.

To clarify a bit, the indicators which are not represented are those which pertain to therapy. The indicator which *is* represented involves the patient's engagement and her decision to apply to dental school. The critical intervention contexts derive from the therapeutic work over a long period of time and its characteristics as revealed in the last session and in this hour. The specific immediate contexts would have to be identified and their implications stated. These would serve as the immediate organizers of this material.

I feel quite fortunate in our decision to hear a bit more material. There is an important model here. The central contexts are the therapist's interpretive failures, his impassioned efforts to interpret material related to the therapeutic interaction, his shift from repetitive questioning about her sexual conflicts and experiences outside of therapy to confronting interventions in respect to the therapeutic relationship itself, and the pending forced termination. Time does not permit the identification of the unconscious implications of each of these contexts, but we can summarize them in the patient's words: they have stimulated the patient sexually and are seen as reflecting some kind of sexual arousal within the therapist; and they have frightened her and are seen as expressing fears within the therapist. On the basis of these and other implications of the therapist's interventions, the patient is now attempting to resolve the realistic and intrapsychic problems and conflicts posed by these contexts. It is in this respect that I can stress again the importance of identifying the most critical intervention contexts to which the patient is attempting to adapt.

To simplify matters a bit, the patient here is attempting to cope with the anticipation of the sudden loss of the therapist and with his passionate, pressured, interventions. She does this by becoming passionate with her boyfriend, and by becoming engaged to him. She finds a safe substitute for the therapist and a way of protecting herself from the sense of loss, as well as providing herself with a person toward whom she can feel openly passionate without guilt or anxiety. She finds in Richard, as well, someone who seems frightened and put off, which enables her to locate the anxiety in the other person and to deny her own sense of fright. These are all implications of the derivative complex, and reflect the patient's coping mechanisms in response to the disturbances evoked by the intervention contexts.

Now comes the final step in preparing to intervene: using the communicative network—the context and derivative response—to illuminate the unconscious implications of the indicators. And we have been doing just that. It is these unconscious perceptions and coping efforts which account for the patient's decision to become engaged. The decision to go to dental school may have additional implications, such as her wish that the therapist would himself seek more education, and a wish on the part of the patient to heal herself. These too are derivative responses to the prevailing adaptive contexts which illuminate that particular indicator. These last hypotheses are far more tentative, but I offer them as a further model of how we use our understanding of the communicative network as a conceptualization of the unconscious basis for indicators and therapeutic contexts.

Therapist: She went on: And then I started to cry. I was really sorry that I had done this to him, he seemed so cowardly and broken down. And then Richard started to cry and we were both crying, and then he said to me, I have something for you. And I said, No, I'm too scared. Okay, go ahead. And then he gave me the ring. And they were both tearful and didn't say very much. She said, I really felt I was in a twilight zone during that entire scene. It was all very strange. And I said to him, But you know, you never actually asked me. So he did. And I said that I would. And after that, we just kind of hung around and we didn't rush out to tell anybody about what we had done. I didn't call my sister, though I usually would call her to tell her about anything that happened. She would be the first one if something of much less significance occurred. I didn't call her and we waited two more days and then we finally did call up some people and tell them. And even then, I was just so scared about it, just scared in general. We called my mother and sister and then Richard's mother—his father is dead— and they weren't so excited about it. It seemed that they had expected it all along. And what was funny was that I found myself thinking about how this would hurt Jack. And how my father would be hurt too.

Here I asked her a question: What were you thinking? She said, It was just that I couldn't get them out of my system, both Jack and my father. It seemed that nothing had changed. I still felt the same way.

Langs: Well, we now have a Type Two derivative validation of our main hypothesis: that this decision was not based on insight and adaptive structural change, but on the patient's need to protect the therapist, whom she saw as cowardly and broken down, and to protect herself because of her own weakness in dealing with the issues within the therapeutic interaction.

I am well aware that the boyfriend presented the ring to her. Nonetheless, I am attempting to formulate implications of the patient's decision to agree to the marriage, and her feeling that nothing had been resolved. Despite the fact that these associations contain many details, they are nonetheless meaningful on the derivative level.

The technical problem remains her failure to provide a specific bridge to therapy and a definitive representation of the intervention contexts. The closest she comes is her image of being very passionate—an unconscious perception and representation of the therapist's rather intense interventions toward the end of the last hour. There is little sign for the moment of a representation of a break in the frame. Perhaps the best the patient does in this regard is to allude to her sense of not being in control of what was going on—a nonspecific representation at best. As you can see, in both instances, the level of representation is quite low and the level of resistance is quite high.

Today's discussion of acting-out forms of resistance lead me to attempt to crystallize a number of ideas I have had in respect to the concepts of, and distinctions between, defenses and resistances. I have already defined some of the differences. I am reminded of Stone's (1973) comments that defenses may be seen as specific intrapsychic mechanisms, while resistances are more complex, behavioral units. I have tried to indicate that both defenses and resistances are interactional products, with both intrapsychic and interpersonal elements. Now, I want to add to these thoughts.

It occurs to me that the notion of an entirely intrapsychic defense-resistance is an extreme conception which, while it has served us well, has also interfered with developing some important perspectives. There is no doubt that such defenses exist, such as repression, isolation, projection, and the like. However, at no time do these defenses operate entirely at the behest of the ego and as simple protective devices. Instead, they are called into play unconsciously by the patient—I will focus for the moment entirely on the patient—at the behest of forces which include contributions from the id and superego, that is, the instinctual drives and the individual's self- and value systems. They function in interplay with introjects as well. As a result, when we describe the operation of intrapsychic and interpersonal defenses—and perhaps the two always work together—we are identifying situations in which the defensive aspects of a particular behavior or intrapsychic-interactional effort appears to be primarily defensive. Nonetheless, we should also identify the ways in which the particular defensive mechanism— even at the level of repression, projection, and the like—simultaneously gratifies instinctual drive needs and superego requisites.

With this approach, we immediately recognize the unconscious gratification available to a patient through primarily defensive operations, and through his resistances. When defenses and resistances operate maladaptively, these gratifications are also pathological. When they operate effectively and out of adaptive necessity, the satisfactions are nonpathological. The key evaluation involves identification of contributions from each of the three macrostructures and from introjects, and distinguishing the intrapsychic and interpersonal aspects.

Discussant: Please allow me to clear up a bit of confusion I have been experiencing. Perhaps I will state my understanding of the problem I want to clarify, and you can tell me if I have it right. I have been thinking about the representations of the intervention context and the implications of the derivative complex. For one thing, I fully understand that some manifest associations may be loaded with derivative meaning, while others are quite barren—as measured by the implications which can be derived from an activated adaptive context. I therefore can understand that some associations are highly defensive and resistant, while others are far less so. Am I correct to this point?

Langs: Yes, please continue.

Discussant: I began to get a bit confused when I realized that the most important communications from a patient are expressed indirectly through derivatives. What confused me was the realization that I was learning to look for an undisguised representation of the intervention context. I resolved the problem by telling myself that we need a manifest representation of the adaptive context in order to interpret, but this does not preclude our understanding that context in terms of its unconscious implications. On the other hand, we also need a meaningful derivative complex in order to interpret, and it is there that manifest elements have little meaning. I hope you can see the dilemma I was experiencing.

Langs: Yes, I find it a common bit of confusion in many therapists who are just beginning to work from the communicative viewpoint. But you have stated the resolution quite well: we rely upon the representation of the adaptive context to be direct or minimally disguised, and to therefore provide us with a manifest link to the therapeutic interaction. The derivative complex is almost entirely encoded and includes all representations of the implications of the intervention context, as well as the fantasies, memories, introjects, and other adaptive responses evoked in the patient. Actually, we divide our attention to the patient's associations and establish two requisites for interpreting: a manifest link to treatment as it pertains to the adaptation-evoking intervention from the therapist, and a coalescing derivative response.

As you can see, it is possible to have many derivative representations of an adaptive context, and yet not be in a position to interpret the patient's perceptions and reactions because he has failed to provide you with a link or bridge to therapy. When the connection to therapy appears in the derivative complex, we generally have a nonspecific *bridge*. When it appears in the representation of the intervention context, we have a specific *link* in that the patient has identified the major source of his responsive communications. In practice, then, the ideal communicative network includes a direct allusion in passing to the adaptive context and a shift to a rich variety of indirect communications which provides us with a meaningful derivative complex. Thus, we need both a direct reference to therapy and indirect allusions.

Discussant: Allow me to mention another point which I think could benefit from further comment on your part. When we discussed the listening process, we did eventually include empathy, intuition, and other relatively automatic and sometimes unconscious modes of taking in impressions from the patient. Now, in discussing interventions, it is clear to me that you assume that they must be done with all due empathy, and perhaps sympathy as well. Some therapists advocate direct interventions based on their empathic responses to the patient. My impression in this course is that such interventions are highly speculative, and that they can often be an expression of some type of countertransference. What role, then, does empathy play in intervening?

Langs: I have not said much about empathy largely because I have little to say that is new, and, as you said, I have already made it clear that it is one among many tools with which we experience the patient and through which we develop our formulations. Interventions should be offered with a tone of concern and based in part on empathy. However, your question does lead me to caution you regarding possible misuses of empathic experiences within the therapist.

Remember, whatever you experience based on a temporary and trial identification with the patient, and on immediate affective sampling and knowing, should eventually be examined cognitively, and validated in the material from the patient. It is unwise to intervene on the basis of an empathic experience without cognitive representations in the patient's material, since such efforts are indeed open to major countertransference influences. All too often, empathy is invoked as an explanation for an erroneous nonvalidated intervention, and we must therefore be quite cautious in our use of this important and somewhat automatic capacity.

In addition, a full sense of empathy with the patient and his communications can take place only when the therapist has some sense of the intervention context to which the patient is reacting. As a result, interventions which rely in part upon empathic responses will nonetheless be organized around activated adaptive contexts. This approach is usually overlooked by therapists who advocate direct interventions based on empathic experiences in the therapist, and who, as a rule, operate on a manifest level and make no effort to validate these impressions. Such purported empathic sensitivities are often mislabeled, and allude actually to experiences which arise more from the therapist's own inner difficulties than from a sensitive in-depth reading of the patient. An isolated sense of subjective empathy in a therapist is a Type-One derivative or manifest experience. It can only be given full meaning in light of a relevant adaptive context. In its absence, the empathy can be highly defensive and an expression of counterresistance rather than therapeutic sensitivity.

Let's now hear a bit more of this material.

Therapist: Here I asked her, Did you think about the effect of what you had done on other men as well? She was silent briefly and then said, I was curious about how you would react. And then she was silent and I asked, What did you expect? She said, I don't know. And I said, You told me what you did as if you were breaking very terrible news. And I wonder whether you expect that once you had chosen Richard, all other men would reject you. She said, Well, I have next to face Ted because he has been teaching me the guitar, and I'm scared about that. (Ted was the fellow she had held hands with at his apartment after a party.)

She went on: I also began to wonder about my mother's former husband, and her not being remarried. It's really funny that I thought about it. And also I was thinking about the fact that all my woman friends are without men now, and what did I do to deserve to get married, to have a man? I'm just so frightened about the whole business. Then I started to think about what I would call Richard's mother. He has a stepfather. Should I call him Dad? I was really scared about that. Here, she became tearful, adding, But I was also happy about it as well.

Discussant: It seems to me that there is a mixture of communicative resistances and isolated islands of revelation. Somehow, this all has to do with her parents' divorce and with feelings she has about both her mother and father. This must be the genetic connections to whatever she is experiencing in therapy, though as I heard the material, I could not entirely piece it together. Most of it seems related to the pending forced termination, but there's now a kind of vagueness which gives me a sense of diffuseness and resistance.

Langs: There is much in this material which each of you will have to work over on your own. I hope that you made note of the therapist's interventions, through which he led the patient to himself, rather than waiting to see whether she would provide a bridge or maintain resistances in this respect. Once the patient expressed her curiosity about how the therapist would react, he pursued the matter directly. She did not provide meaningful surface associations—did not especially join him in manifest content relatedness—though he seems to have revealed how he felt by telling her that he experienced her as breaking very terrible news. There may well have been such a quality to this material, but it is far from the only quality which the therapist could have identified. It seems to reveal some of his own conscious and unconscious responses and to have a rather nonneutral sense. Certainly, the therapist's comment that other men would reject the patient for chosing Richard can be seen as an unconscious countertransference-based fantasy: the patient has abandoned him, the news is terrible, and he will reject the patient in turn.

Beyond that particular unconscious communication, which I am organizing around the adaptive context for the therapist of the patient's announcement of her engagement, lies once again a derivative allusion to the pending forced termination. The therapist seems to repeatedly sense that separation is an issue, but is unable to offer a direct, consciously stated interpretation in that respect, partly because the patient's material remains resistant. As you can see, the therapist's premature interventions help to promote that resistance, and the defensiveness is once more an interactional product.

Let's hear more.

Therapist: She said, Richard is just so good. But I'm still afraid of what's going to happen. He thinks in terms of a fifty-year marriage. And I just don't know about that. Here I said to her, You expect that if you commit yourself to him, you will lose all your relationships with other men. Not only that, you will lose some of your relationships with other women as well, out of envy. So the man you would have to commit yourself to would have to be some kind of superman, just as you had hoped Jack would be. He would have to be someone who would be able to provide enough to make up for all the other losses that you would have to put up with.

Langs: Because time is short, I will take the liberty of making selected comments. I will emphasize points that I have not been able to adequately develop until now. It should not surprise us that at a point at which a patient brings in an announcement of this kind, so filled with powerful implications, that we should have a special opportunity to study the therapist's interventions.

We have here an attempt at interpretation, based on Type One derivative listening. The indicator is the announcement of the engagement; the adaptive contexts within treatment are totally obliterated and ignored by the therapist; and the derivative complex is shaped in a manner which speaks more for countertransference than for the quiet and comfortable reshaping and integration of elements scattered throughout the patient's associations.

I appreciate the therapist presenting this material to us in such detail. He must know that there is ample evidence he was quite disturbed by the patient's announcement of her engagement. We find that in his dismissal of adaptive context listening, and in the seemingly arbitrary timing of his interventions. But he does give us an opportunity to hear a rather extended intervention which bears only a minimal relationship to the patient's material, and considerable relationship to some of the unconscious countertransference constellations we had already formulated based on his earlier interventions. In fact, that particular effort at interpretation tends to offer a type of Type Two derivative validation of my formulations about the therapist in a rather convincing manner.

With all due respect, but out of our necessity to know ourselves as therapists, allow me to point out that the therapist seems preoccupied with how the patient will lose her relationships with other people, men and women, because she has chosen Richard. You can see how easy it is for a therapist to select one or two manifest or derivative associations, and to build his own story on that kind of a foundation. Sometimes, of course, many therapists endeavor to respond entirely in terms of the patient's own associations. But because of countertransference needs, the problem arises in the ease with which it is possible for a therapist to pick up a particular element, and elaborate it on the basis of his own fantasies, rather than those of the patient.

The therapist's reference to envy, which was perhaps implied in the patient's comments about why does she deserve a man when her women friends do not have one, is a kind of Type One derivative inference which can be quite self-revealing. It very much sounds as if he envies the patient for having a man, and that he himself is lacking in such gratification and stability. There is a sense too that the therapist is expressing through derivatives contained in his interventions some sense of losing an important symbiotic partner.

In this context, I would like to stress the importance of self-knowledge, of sticking with the material from the patient, and of formulating silent hypotheses which must obtain Type Two derivative validation before you speak. These are important safeguards against inevitable expressions of unconscious countertransference fantasies, and especially against extension into preponderant countertransferences in a manner which I believe we are observing here.

For example, if the anxiety had to do with the loss of other attachments, or the fear of envious women, we would have heard additional derivatives which indirectly support these hypotheses. We should not force meaning from the patient's associations—an effort which again implies the influence of countertransference fantasies. Instead, sit back and allow the continuing associations to represent contexts and generate derivatives in a manner that virtually insists on meaning and function. This offers both ourselves and the patient as much protection against countertransferences as humanly possible.

The more you offer interventions based on single associations, immediate hunches, or on formulations that have not received Type Two derivative validation, the more likely is the countertransference influence. At a time when a patient presents a major piece of news, whether it's traumatic, acting out, or threatening to therapy, it is especially important to maintain basic principles of listening and intervening, and to engage in self-analytic work in response to a silently formulated intervention long before it is offered to the patient.

The interpretation that the patient wished for some kind of superman to compensate for all of her losses introduces an image which is clearly not in the patient's associations and which once again arises from the therapist. No matter how accurate, the fact that the therapist introduces this theme before the patient does so suggests countertransference pressures. It is important to not be ahead of the patient, and to allow the patient to lead the way. Contained here in this aspect of this particular lie-barrier intervention is another derivative allusion to the patient's need to cope with the pending forced termination. Once again, however, this is expressed unconsciously rather than manifestly by the therapist.

In all, then, we would have to postulate that the patient placed into the therapist a projective identification and cognitive material which created considerable inner tension and conflict within himself. There is evidence of anxiety and depression, perhaps guilt, and a sense of conflict and loss which apparently mobilized his countertransferences to a point where he had considerable difficulty in managing their influences. This resulted in a need to intervene in a manner which offered the patient a type of lie-barrier system, but which at the same time seems to be an extensive expression of derivative truths about the therapist. In fact, my sense here is not so much of a nonderivative lie-barrier system as it is of derivative lies and derivative truths. The problem lies in the fact that this should be the communicative province of the patient rather than the therapist, and that it constitutes an appeal to the patient to permit the designated therapist to become the functional patient, and for the designated patient to become the functional therapist.

Therapist: Well, she responded by saying, I don't expect to lose all my friends. That shouldn't happen. I really don't think you're going to dump me either.

Langs: I want to point out how the kernel of truth in your erroneous intervention, which derivatively touched upon the pending forced termination, has produced the clearest derivative representation of that issue we have heard. Derived largely from countertransferences, your effort constitutes a pathological projective identification into the patient. However, while it does indeed have some destructive effects, it can also have its constructive side. It reflects a failure in the containing capacity of the therapist, and asks that the patient contain and metabolize toxic material which the therapist is unable to master. To the extent that it touches upon and mobilizes aspects of the patient's anxieties and conflicts, it can also lead—though it is a hurtful and risky route—to constructive therapeutic work.

It is important to have that perspective, especially when, through self-monitoring and monitoring the material from the patient, you decide that you have made a mistake. You can accept the negative consequences and work them over with the patient as her derivatives permit, but you can also expect to discover some bit of useful consequences for the patient. This appears in the form of a lessening of certain aspects of her resistances, in providing you with material which could now be interpreted even though it was previously refractory to intervention, and through the ego enhancing qualities of her unconscious awareness that you have recovered from your errors and that she is working well as a functional therapist. That last positive feature should be quite coincidental, but would also require some *implicit* indication on your part that you have benefited from her derivative therapeutic efforts.

As you can see, the patient contradicts the therapist on the manifest level. Her comment that she doesn't think he is going to dump her is filled with derivative implications: that he should control his sense of rejection, that there is a pending forced termination, that she is defending herself against being abandoned by the therapist, and that she herself has, on some level, abandoned him first.

Therapist: She continued to talk about her fears about what was going on, and said that she doesn't want a fanfare about this engagement. She went on: I think I'll go crazy facing everything I have to face in the next few months.

Langs: Yes, especially within therapy, and the engagement is an attempt to protect herself from going crazy. The same association reveals an unconscious perception of the therapist's anxiety and loss of control; his countertransferences give the patient a sense that he is going crazy with all that he has to face in this session.

Therapist: She was then silent for five minutes. I finally said, You're very quiet. She said, I'm scared. I don't know what to say. And I said, Were you scared to tell me? She replied, I almost didn't come. I was afraid to tell you. And maybe I won't go to see Ted today so I don't have to see him as well.

Here I said, It sounds as if you were experiencing what's going on as if you're running a gauntlet. You have to face each person's anger and envy, and you're afraid you're going to be dumped by all these men in particular. Is that what you expected from me? She said, No, but I thought of dumping you and now I've made my decision. I thought of dumping you because I finally made the decision, which is the reason I came here in the first place. And perhaps in the process to learn something about myself.

She was silent and then continued: I guess things don't have to be different. I can still have other relationships as well. When I told Patricia, my boss, she was critical of my taking a ring from him because there was just something corny. Later she called me up and wished me the best of luck. This is something I have always wanted, every girl's dream. I guess I'm old-fashioned. But I'm still very frightened about what's going on.

And that's how the session ended.

Langs: You are seeing an example of how erroneous interventions, through the pressures of projective identifications which they create, can lead to a lessening of communicative resistances in some areas. This is part of our learning that resistances are modified not only through sound interpretations of their unconscious basis, but in all sorts of other ways, including some that involve the therapist's countertransferences. All too often, the therapist will take a diminition of surface resistance, such as the patient's revealing her thoughts about wanting to terminate treatment, as a sign of sound therapeutic work. Clearly, fluctuations in resistance, since they are open to pathological and nonpathological influences within both the patient and therapist, cannot be used as a criterion for valid therapeutic effort. This is a similar tenet to the one we proposed regarding the vicissitudes of the patient's symptoms. The same principles apply in both respects.

In principle, too, it is well to not repeat an intervention under any circumstances, and to not add to it unless you have obtained clear indications of Type Two derivative validation to your first comment.

There is far too much here for us to discuss in any comprehensive way. The patient shows a sensitive unconscious perception of the therapist's interventions when she talks about Patricia as being critical and as jealous or envious. The envy is implied, but I am not suggesting that I would have interpreted it to the patient. It is the patient's way of offering Type Two derivative validation of some of my earlier formulations.

We have a moment or two; if there are no questions, tell us how the next session began.

Therapist: She started by saying that she was thinking about what we had discussed yesterday. She had not been aware of some of it. She went on to talk about how nobody seemed to be excited about her engagement. Everyone is kind of blah about it. Richard called his brother who said to him, I hope you know what you're getting into.

Langs: Well, unfortunately time does not permit us to hear further material. Some of this is certainly an unconscious perception of the therapist's reaction to the patient's announcement of her engagement.

Therapist: Let me say this much. The issue of her terminating treatment prematurely came up twice after this, and I'm sure it was on my mind during that last session, and that I was concerned about how to prevent it. I think that subsequent material bears out the formulation that the forced termination is a trauma that she was working on, and against which she had to protect herself. I can see now that I did have difficulty interpreting in this area, and that I was stirred up quite a bit when she announced her engagement.

Langs: Thank you for your comments and especially for such a clear and detailed presentation. It has provided us with some fine material with which to end this seminar. I am delighted that we have ended our work on a strictly clinical note—and with quite a flourish at that. I must express my gratitude to each of you for your contributions to the work that we have done; it has been an especially innovative experience.

Part II

Chapter Ten

THE CLASSICAL POSITION
ON RESISTANCES

THE THEORETICAL DEFINITION OF RESISTANCE

There is a remarkable degree of consistency to the basic conceptual definition of resistance in the classical psychoanalytic literature. No sooner had Freud developed a conception of the nature of neuroses and the type of analytic work which could lead to their resolution (Breuer and Freud 1893–1895), than he developed some sense of the importance of the extent to which a patient cooperated with or opposed his therapeutic ministrations. His theory of the structure of resistances was intimately related to his ideas about the basis for emotional problems, and his viewpoint as to the nature of the analytic process also soon became intertwined with his thinking on the analysis of resistances.

To clarify Freud's conception of resistance, we must first understand his thinking on the nature of neuroses. From the start, Freud offered a unique definition of the factors underlying neurotic symptoms. The following elements were emphasized: early childhood traumas and seductions (later, early childhood *fantasies* of trauma and seduction); the continued influence of the memories derived from these experiences, which operated primarily on an unconscious level; and the presence of intrapsychic conflict—opposing forces, one side directed toward action, discharge, or expression, and the other toward inaction, protection, and defense. At the heart of the neurotic problem are ideas incompatible with the main body of the patient's thoughts and feelings, and these are fended off by protective defenses which find expression in the form of opposition to the analyst. This arises largely because the latter's efforts are designed to enable the patient to become directly aware of the incompatible ideas which are at the root of his symptoms. Often involved in this opposition are the moral standards of the patient and his efforts to avoid painful conflicts and affects.

It was in the context of presenting and discussing the case material which formed the basis for his contribution to the *Studies on Hysteria* that Freud first used the term resistance. He wrote: "In the course of this difficult work I began to attach a deeper significance to the resistance offered by the patient in the reproduction of her memories and to make a careful collection of the occasions on which it was particularly marked" (Breuer and Freud 1893–1895, p. 154).

The material which precedes this prophetic realization was drawn from Freud's work with Fraulein Elisabeth von R., during which Freud encouraged the development of pictures and ideas by pressing on his patient's forehead. He found that, at times, her behavior fulfilled his highest expectations and led to a virtually chronological unfolding of a particular theme. At other times there were impediments: she would maintain that nothing occurred to her and sometimes this led Freud to break off their work together in the hour. However, Freud soon realized that something was taking place in his patient, that some idea or picture had occurred to her that she was not prepared to communicate to him and which she tried to suppress. She was either applying criticism to the idea—which, as Freud put it, she had no right to do—or she found it too disagreeable. Freud therefore pressured her to realize that something must have occurred to her, and without fail, something would then be revealed. As Freud put it, she would never be free of her pains as long as she concealed anything.

We have here both a monumental insight, and the seeds of basic concepts of resistances and the techniques used to resolve them. Focusing for the moment on the theoretical definition of resistance, it is well to realize that his delineation was based primarily on Freud's observations of his patients' rather direct opposition to him and to the stated procedures of analysis. While analysts later recognized the presence of subtle and even silent resistances (Glover 1955, Greenson 1967, Stone 1973), virtually every definition of resistance offered through the years is phenomenological and behavioral—a statement of direct, usually surface, opposition.

In the course of his psychoanalytic writings, Freud identified, defined, and clarified the basis for resistances. As early as 1900, he stated: "One of its rules [of psychoanalysis] is that *whatever interrupts the progress of analytic work is a resistance.*" Freud, in a footnote, pointed out that reality might create exceptions to this rule; but his basic definition has been echoed by those who followed him. Glover (1955), for example, saw resistances as existing throughout the whole of the analysis and as a reflection of the defensive function of the mind. Citing Freud as quoted above, Greenson (1967) stated: "Resistance means opposition. All those forces within the patient which oppose the procedures and processes of analysis, i.e., which hinder the patient's free association, which interfere with the patient's attempts to remember and to gain and assimilate insight, which operate against the patient's reasonable ego and his wish to change; all of these forces are to be considered resistance" (pp. 59–60).

Similarly, Sandler and his coauthors offered this definition: "The concept of *resistance* is concerned with elements and forces in the patient which oppose the treatment process" (p. 71). Stone also paraphrases Freud's 1900 definition and defines resistance "as anything of essentially intrapsychic nature in the patient which impedes or interrupts the progress of psychoanalytic work or interferes with its basic purposes and goals." (1973, p. 46).

Despite the simplicity and relative uniformity of these definitions, a thoughtful response rather quickly raises important issues. The definition implies agreement in at least two fundamental areas: first, the nature of neuroses, their structure and functions; and second, the procedures through which a neurosis is best resolved. A third qualification is somewhat different: the decision that a patient is being resistant is made by the analyst or therapist, and therefore depends not only on his definition of neuroses and of analytic and therapeutic procedures, but also on factors immediate to the therapeutic interaction itself, including much that is subjective and that lies within the therapist.

Once identified, it is self-evident that each of these qualifying factors is enormously complex and would require separate, extended study in order to develop a clear consensus and a basis upon which clinical judgment, that a patient is indeed in the state of resistance, could be made. Another problem arises with the realization that it is quite possible to develop a theoretical framework for, and definition of, resistance, and yet to have difficulty in identifying its clinical referents. Granted the uncertainties involved, it is small wonder that much confusion and controversy exists in the relevant analytic literature once writers move beyond the relatively simple and broad definition of resistances described above. In the face of such potential and actual difficulties, many therapists have simply adhered to the simple gross behavioral definition of resistance and have probed no further.

In recent years, there has been a growing awareness among analysts that resistances may exist in forms other than those that are directly observable, such as silences and absences from sessions, and which may escape the immediate notice of the analyst. Glover (1955) indicated that from the descriptive point of view, resistances may be divided into those which are obvious and crass, and those which are unobtrusive. He went so far as to state that the most successful resistances are silent and that the main sign of their existence is our unawareness of them—a confusing point with which Stone (1973) later took issue. Similarly, Greenson identified a wide range of phenomena which constitute the clinical appearance of resistances and also mentioned silent resistances, which he felt were subtle, difficult to pin down, often recognized when the analyst is thinking about the patient away from the analytic situation, and sometimes discovered only after many hours with the patient and in the context of a certain distance from the analysis. He suggested that these particular resistances are essentially characterological in nature. Stone (1973) saw the more obvious resistances as falling into the "tactical sphere" in that they deal with the manifest process phenomena of ego resistances. He suggested that other resistances, which are relatively silent, fall into the "strategic sphere" in that they relate to the depths of the patient's psychopathology and personality structure, and to his total reactions to the analytic situation and the person of the analyst. He believed that this second type of resistance is most clearly represented in a failure to achieve symptomatic change, the omission of decisive material from the patient's free associations or from his transference neurosis, and in an inability by the patient to accept the termination of treatment.

Speaking hypothetically, then, classical psychoanalysts have suggested that resistances may be overt or silent. The latter occurs with patients who apparently are cooperative and free associating, and with whom the analyst or therapist senses some type of hidden opposition. While gross resistances could readily lend themselves to clinical definition, silent resistances pose major problems, both in respect to the clinical evidence for their existence and the techniques with which they should be handled.

TRANSFERENCE RESISTANCES

A special class of resistances are purported to be among the most common seen in patients in analysis, though their status in psychoanalytically oriented psychotherapy has barely been considered and, as a result, opinions are far from uniform. These resistances have been termed *transference resistances*, and they are most broadly defined as opposition to the work of analysis within the patient which derives from his relationship with the analyst.

It is impressive to realize that Freud actually crowned his first discussion of resistances with the realization that they may stem from a disturbance of the patient's relationship to the physician (Breuer and Freud 1893–1895, pp. 301–302). In this respect, he initially saw three possibilities: a sense of personal estrangement in the patient's relationship with the analyst, such as when the patient feels neglected, unappreciated, or insulted, or has heard unfavorable comments about the analyst. The second involves a dread of becoming too accustomed to the physician personally and thereby losing his independence or perhaps even becoming sexually dependent upon him. And the third is based on the patient's fear that she is *transferring* onto the analyst distressing ideas, arising from the content of the analysis, through a false connection between the analyst and persons important to the patient in her life, present and past.

Freud was here characterizing distinctive sources of resistance within the patient's relationship with the analyst, only some of which are based on transference in the sense of a displacement onto the analyst from an important genetic figure. The other two sources of resistance seem, on the surface, to involve more realistic anxieties and conflicts. The distinction suggests that Freud did not view all resistances which arise in the context of the analytic relationship to be based on transferences, a point which remains to this day unclear for many therapists.

In his postscript to the prematurely terminated analysis of Dora, Freud not only crystallized his theoretical definition of transference, but also immediately recognized that transferences form the basis for the most serious threats to the work of analysis. Freud stated, "Transference, which seems ordained to be the greatest obstacle to psycho-analysis, becomes its most powerful ally, if its presence can be detected each time and explained to the patient" (1905, p. 117). It was at this juncture that Freud most clearly realized that the analysis of transference resistances—whatever that implies—is at the heart of analytic work and that the means through which patients oppose the analytic procedure are extremely important in themselves.

In respect to psychoanalysis proper, there is virtually unanimous agreement among later writers that transference resistances are indeed a major and necessary locus of analytic work. Discussions of resistances concentrate on those which derive from "the transference." For example, Greenson (1967), after devoting ninety pages to the general subject of resistances, within which transference resistances are repeatedly considered, nonetheless included an additional section on this subject in his discussion of transference. Greenson explicitly stated that this group of resistances are the most important, frequently obstruct analytic work, and that more time is spent with their analysis than with any other aspect of analysis. Greenson's theoretical definition of this class of obstacles is founded on his definition of transference. The latter was seen as the experience of feelings, drives, attitudes, fantasies, and defenses toward the analyst which do not fit him but repeat reactions to significant persons of the patient's early childhood, unconsciously displaced. Any obstacle to analytic work drawn from this source would be defined as a transference resistance.

Sandler and his associates (1973) similarly identified transference resistances as obstacles to analysis which are based on thoughts and feelings toward the therapist which arise because of the patient's tendency to reexperience repressed earlier important attitudes, feelings, and experiences instead of recalling them. Stone's discussion of transference resistances (1973), however, raises a number of theoretical issues and suggests a more complex interplay between transference and resistance.

To summarize the basic theoretical position of classical psychoanalysts, resistances are constituted by all obstacles within the patient to the process of cure. Those impediments which arise in connection with the patient's relationship with the analyst or therapist are termed transference resistances, and are a major locus of analytic work. The role of resistances in general, and transference resistances in particular, in psychoanalytic psychotherapy is ill-defined. The consensus appears to be that resistances are continually present in psychotherapy, and that transference resistances may emerge but are more difficult to analyze and less often the basis for interpretive or other types of therapeutic endeavors. Nonetheless, in both analysis and psychotherapy, since resistances constitute obstacles to cure, their identification and analysis is a first-order therapeutic task.

SOME CRITICAL ISSUES

On a theoretical level, the basic definition of resistance is open to many qualifications. There is, as I have suggested, an intimate interplay between the psychoanalytic conception of neuroses and that of the analytic process which leads toward symptom resolution and constructive characterological change. I have already identified one of Freud's earliest models of neurotic disturbances, in which he emphasized the role of conflict, defense, and the strangulation of affects. Freud later elaborated the conflict theory, detailed the role of unconscious fantasies and memories in such conflicts, and generated the structural theory in which a central concept was that of the ego's function in mediating between the demands of the id, superego, and reality. More recently, analysts have developed a complex conception of ego psychology, an elaborate theory of object relations, and an extended concept of self and narcissistic pathology. To their structural and oedipally centered theory, clinical psychoanalysts have added a prestructural and preoedipal dimension. This has been in response to expanded clinical observations, especially in respect to patients with severe psychopathology.

At the cornerstone of the psychoanalytic theory of neuroses is the critical role of unconscious mental contents and processes in symptom formation (using this term in its broadest sense). The minimal outline of the nature of neuroses developed here is offered, not as a format for a discussion of that important subject, but merely as a way of sketching the nature of the illness with which the analyst or therapist must deal. While in actual practice each patient and each session should enable a therapist to empirically rediscover one or another elements of this theory, all too often the theory itself, ossified and reified, has dictated clinical thinking. In any case, the practitioner enters a session with some concept of the disturbance he is attempting to help the patient to resolve, and this has a distinct influence on his appraisal of the extent to which the patient is resisting the therapeutic work.

For example, therapists without conviction in regard to the role of unconscious memory and fantasy constellations in the creation and maintenance of neuroses have a different concept of the indications of resistance from those analysts who feel that analytic work must concentrate on the derivatives of these unconscious contents and processes in order to produce an insightful resolution of the patient's emotional disorder. To illustrate briefly, and to demonstrate the extent to which theoretical concepts influence the appraisal of resistance, we may turn to a recent chapter on this subject by Blanck and Blanck (1979).

In the context of a discussion of patients with relatively severe psychopathology based on pregenital disturbances derived largely from the symbiotic phase, these authors suggest that borderline patients be permitted to telephone the therapist during vacations, and that they be given slips of paper with telephone numbers which can serve as transitional objects. Another device of this kind involves sending the patient a postcard during a vacation.

In a case example, the Blancks suggest that a postcard helped a particular patient deal with her sense of despair and depression during a specific separation experience. They saw the postcard as reestablishing a much needed object image which enabled the therapist to enter the formerly "closed shop" of the narcissistic unit—i.e., the patient's mental world—in a way that is consistent and dependable, and which served as a catalyst for development. When this patient began arriving late for her sessions, the authors suggested that to regard this behavior as a resistance, traditionally defined, would have been damaging. Instead, the therapist regarded the lateness as a stepping away and when this was suggested as such, the patient grinned. This was seen as her first unopposed expression of independence (pp. 156-157).

While this vignette touches upon the issue of adaptive aspects of resistance—a topic which will be discussed toward the end of this chapter—there is little question that many, perhaps most classical analysts would adopt a position that this patient was showing a major behavioral resistance. There is some confusion as to definition, since a behavior such as lateness, which clearly limits or disturbs the therapeutic process, may have additional implications. Nonetheless, the issue does not appear to be resolved by stating that this lateness could be identified as a gross behavioral resistance whose nature was primarily adaptive. The problem would remain that many analysts would suspect that this behavior reflected a *maladaptive* resolution of underlying conflicts and fantasies, rather than a sign of truth growth and independence. Necessary here is material from the relevant sessions to provide a means of investigating the unconscious basis and implications of the lateness.

On its face, being late for sessions does not seem to be an act of genuine and constructive independence, but instead speaks for some disturbance within the bipersonal field. It is to be stressed also that the clinical vignette illustrates a prevalent approach to resistances in terms of overt behavior with virtually no sense of the presence of underlying unconscious fantasy and perception constellations, either in the structure of neuroses or the nature of resistances.

A radically different conception obtains from the vantage point of the communicative approach. The clinical example cited, while skeletal, is revealing in that the adaptive context for the patient's lateness can be identified as the postcard sent to her by the therapist. One unconscious communication, among many contained in the postcard, is a lack of faith in the patient's ability to cope and a need to infantilize and force dependency upon her. The lateness, then, would be viewed as a maladaptive response through which the patient expressed her protest against the therapist's efforts to merge with—or seduce—her through an action which interferes with the therapeutic work, but which nonetheless lends itself to meaningful interpretation.

As can be seen from this example, resistances have an oppositional or disruptive quality which other material or behaviors do not possess on a phenomenonological level. As noted above, classical analysts are now aware that patients who appear to be cooperative, and with whom there is no evident opposition, may nonetheless be more subtlely working against the therapeutic goals. Here too theoretical bias often influences the appraisal of resistances. Analysts who maintain the importance of unconscious processes and contents would see silent or subtle resistances in patients who fail to include important genetic material or critical dynamic dimensions, such as oedipally-tinged associations, in the course of free associating over an extended period of time. Those analysts and therapists who view transference and transference resistances as the main or exclusive arena for the expressions of the patient's neurosis, and therefore as fundamental to successful therapeutic work, would propose the presence of resistances in the absence of such material. In the other direction, analysts with a particular theoretical bias, such as a special interest in the narcissistic transferences and self pathology (e.g., Kohut 1971, 1977), would experience a relative absence of resistance when they are able to formulate the patient's material in such terms; while an analyst not so inclined might find the same associations devoid of derivatives of relevant unconscious fantasies and memories, and therefore conclude that the patient was in a state of severe resistance.

In practice, then, expectations in the therapist or analyst based on his theory of neuroses are to some degree inevitable. It is self-evident that technically such anticipations should be kept to a minimum and should be subjected to interpretation and to subsequent Type Two derivative validation in actual sessions with patients. In the absence of this type of confirmation of efforts to interpret resistances, the therapist's formulation of the basis for obstacles to therapy should either be discarded or revised. Unfortunately, methodology of this kind is lacking in the classical psychoanalytic literature on resistances in particular, and in clinical writings in general.

Requiring Type Two derivative validation would lead to a number of reformulations of the present psychoanalytic theory of neuroses, though this important topic cannot be pursued here. For the purposes of this chapter, we will accept as psychoanalytic any theory of neuroses which includes a formulation of unconscious processes and contents, and use that criterion as the broad standard of classical psychoanalytic thinking.

Based on both direct clinical observations and on the theory of neuroses derived, and eventually stated somewhat separately, from such observations, classical analysts have developed a theory of the psychoanalytic process which includes indications that it is proceeding reasonably well. Every therapist and analyst enters his sessions with his patients with such a theory in mind, and with some degree of awareness of the hallmarks of a good hour as compared to one which goes poorly and is filled with resistances. While it should be accepted practice that the definition of resistances should be validated in each session through the interpretations made by the therapist, all too often there is no evidence whatsoever of such efforts. Instead, the concept is invoked arbitrarily, as seen in the work of those analysts who suggest its presence whenever their anticipations of the development of a so-called transference neurosis, of pertinent types of genetic material, and of certain kinds of projections by the patient fail to materialize. In this way, psychoanalytic theory has dictated clinical postulates which are self-fulfilling and lack much needed verification. As a consequence, analysts often fail to agree clinically in respect to the manifestations of resistances because of differences in their conception of the processes of analysis and cure.

As Klauber cogently pointed out (1968), underlying this entire discussion is the fact that the decision that the patient is resisting the analytic process is a subjective one within the analyst. It is broadly influenced by all aspects of his personality, including value systems, residual psychopathology, and creative sensitivities. This is evident in the brief vignette presented above, which also touches upon the issue of the definition of acting out, a common form of resistance first identified by Freud (1905, 1914) and seen by classical analysts as an especially common form of resistance—the use of action and behaviors in place of both remembering and cognitive-affective, verbally founded analytic work. With the recognition of the adaptive aspects of certain actions and behaviors by the patient, the decision as to whether a particular behavior constitutes a resistance is often based on subjective factors. The communicative approach proposes to resolve much of this uncertainty by basing this decision on an understanding of the derivative complex pertinent to a particular behavior. In a more limited way, within the classical approach, an effort is sometimes made to understand the patient's associations in connection with a particular behavior, as a means of evaluating its implication. Too often, however, this work is limited to manifest meanings and Type One derivative formulations.

RESISTANCE AND DEFENSE

A final theoretical issue concerns the relationship between resistances and defenses. Are resistances in essence the expression of the patient's intrapsychic defenses in his relationship with the therapist or analyst, or do they involve something more than the patient's defensive armamentarium? Freud's emphasis was on the overlap between resistances and intrapsychic defenses. His main thesis was to the effect that the same intrapsychic defenses which contribute to the compromise formations leading to the patient's symptoms find expression in the patient's resistances (e.g., Breuer and Freud 1893–1895, Freud 1914). However, while analysts have subsequently accepted the presence of an intimate connection between resistance and defense (e.g., Glover's [1955] use of the term defense-resistance), most have suggested that the two terms are not synonymous (Loewenstein 1954, Greenson 1967, Sandler, Dare, and Holder 1973, Stone 1973). In the main, these writers point out that defenses are essentially intrapsychic and genetically founded, while resistances defend the status quo of the patient's neurosis, and oppose the analyst, and the analytic work, and even the patient's reasonable ego. It follows that resistances may derive from and be expressed through behaviors heavily laden with instinctual drives and masochism pertinent to unconscious guilt. In general, then, resistances are seen as having a wider scope and using a more complicated and broader variety of mechanisms than those involved in the usual classical conception of defenses. While the ultimate purpose in resistance is indeed defensive, other qualities, such as the wish for direct instinctual drive gratification, may contribute or even predominate.

It would seem that classical analysts have failed to benefit from the evident incompatibilities between their theories of defense and of resistances. The former has remained an essentially intrapsychic conception, with an overriding emphasis on the patient's use of a variety of inner protective mechanisms—e.g., repression, projection, isolation—which are mobilized to defend against anxiety-provoking instinctual drive wishes. Much of this is carried out at the behest of the superego and external reality. This line of thought, which concentrates on issues of intrapsychic conflict and unconscious fantasy-memory formations, has been challenged by Kleinian analysts and others who have written from an object relations viewpoint. These analysts have presented cogent arguments for a more balanced conception of defenses, which would take into account both intrapsychic and interpersonal or interactional factors and processes. This would lead to a revision of our understanding of the basic intrapsychic defense mechanisms, much of it based on a recognition of the role played in their development and sustenance by important object relationships and interactions with others, and mediated through complicated introjective processes. This approach also would expand the classical conception of defenses, which is so exclusively intrapsychic, into interactional defenses, such as projective and introjective identification.

It would also become necessary to resolve a considerable degree of conceptual and terminological confusion. A distinction must be made between *defenses* in the narrow sense (defined psychoanalytically in terms of intrapsychic and interactional mechanisms, and their behavioral and psychic consequences) and *defensiveness*, a more descriptive term which would embrace any self-protective behavior. Defensiveness takes a variety of forms and includes behaviors that can accent the use of defenses in the narrow sense, thereby stressing defensive needs and their gratification, or involve major superego and instinctual drive satisfactions. These actions and intrapsychic maneuvers usually are a consequence of vectors from all three macrostructures.

By and large, in the classical writings, resistances draw their parallels with defensiveness both in being relatively descriptive and by alluding to behaviors which are obstructive and in some way oppose or disrupt the analytic process. It follows, then, that resistances are multiply determined, and that defenses in the narrow sense may play a major, but not exclusive, role in their formation. Further clarification would follow from a study of the interrelationship between the operation of intrapsychic and interactional defenses and defensive behaviors.

In summary, classical psychoanalysts are in basic agreement in respect to the behavioral definition of resistances as all manifestations of a patient's opposition to the therapeutic work and process. There is also a consensus about the presence of relatively silent resistances whose definition has been quite elusive. The assessment of resistances in the patient is based on subjective judgments within the analyst, and appears to be strongly influenced by his conception of both neuroses and the therapeutic process. Clarity can be brought to some of these problems by turning to the practical question of the clinical referents for resistance.

THE CLINICAL REFERENTS OF RESISTANCE

The clinical signs of resistance have received considerable attention, though studies have been restricted to gross behavioral resistances and a number of underlying issues have largely escaped notice. Freud postulated that any type of defense could operate as a resistance in psychoanalysis, though his basic concept of resistance pertained to certain types of behaviors in the patient, such as silence (i.e., any interruption in the flow of the patient's free associations) and gross acting out, primarily through interfering behaviors within or outside of the analysis. Freud postulated the presence of resistance and acting out in regard to Dora's premature termination of her analysis (1905) and wrote more extensively on the subject in his basic papers on technique (1914).

In essence, Freud saw acting out as constituting a form of resistance by repeating a past pathogenic interaction in some form in the relationship with the analyst or with some outside figure, designed for instinctual drive gratification and defensive purposes. At first, Freud conceptualized defense mainly in terms of efforts to avoid the painful recollection of traumatic unconscious memories which form the basis for the patient's neurosis, in consonance with the early model of the analytic process as focused on the recall of unconscious fantasy-memory constellations. In subsequent years, as the nature of analytic work was reconceptualized and extended, such goals as enabling the patient to understand the dynamic factors in his neurosis, to analyze the implications of his immediate interaction with the analyst, and to develop adaptive mastery and inner structural change through other forms of insight were introduced. With this widening of the concept of curative factors in psychoanalysis, the purposes of resistance were also seen in a broader light. Resistances were understood to be directed not only against the recall of pathogenic childhood memories, but also against the anxieties and dangers inherent to an understanding of the dynamic conflicts and unconscious fantasy-memory systems pertinent to the patient's symptoms.

It was soon recognized that conscious awareness of previously repressed fantasies is almost always accompanied by some degree of anxiety and conflict, disturbances related to the factors which prompted the use of repression and other defenses in the first place. Awareness of intrapsychic conflicts—and of unconscious perceptions—while highly adaptive, once integrated and understood, is anxiety-provoking at the point where previously maintained defenses are modified (Stone 1973). Thus, resistances are understood to be directed against conscious awareness related to the sources of conflict and the recognition of unconscious fantasy and perception constellations. These direct realizations may pertain to the past or present, to dynamic configurations or genetic sources, and may involve the analyst as well as others. Together, they constitute a series of motives for resistance which lead to obstacles such as silence and acting out.

Finally, a number of Kleinian analysts and several classical psychoanalytic writers such as Dewald (1976), Gill (1979), and Langs (1976b) have indicated that in addition to the curative aspects of cognitive-affective insight, the patient is able to achieve some degree of adaptive symptom resolution through a series of processes which involve introjective identification with the well-functioning, correctly interpreting analyst. While this has many implications for the understanding and analysis of transference and transference resistances, of special and generally unrecognized importance is the sense that the well-functioning analyst himself, through the ways in which he establishes and maintains the framework and intervenes to the patient, offers himself as a relatively resistant-free model. His capacity to interpret entails a renunciation and resolution of counterresistances, an implication which the patient unconsciously experiences and introjects. The analyst comes to stand for the renunciation and resolution of resistances within the patient, and serves as a model of a person functioning with healthy rather than pathological defenses. These particular introjects form a foundation upon which the interpretive and cognitively insightful work with resistances can be especially effective. In all situations in which the analyst is unable to properly interpret and maintain the framework, and in which he unconsciously expresses both his counterresistances and his unconscious need for resistances within the patient, verbal interpretive work will have virtually no influence upon the patient's resistances.

It must be noted, however, in keeping with the critical point made by Strachey (1934), that all this must transpire implicitly and unconsciously and derive from sound interpretive work. Any effort by the analyst to deliberately hold himself up as some kind of a model or to try to directly suggest that the patient stop using a particular resistance will generate a defensive, resistance-prone introject which will actually unconsciously reinforce the resistances.

With this as our background, we may now turn to the clinical description of resistances. Glover (1955) detailed most of the well known forms of gross behavioral resistance and Greenson (1967) catalogued them in some detail. Glover included silences and absences, direct avoidance of topics, and use of trivia, and other evident forms of opposition. By and large, there is general agreement that all behaviors of the patient which directly disturb the flow of his associations and the progress of the analytic work should be classified as resistances. In addition, however, virtually everyone who has written on the subject has pointed out that the patient may utilize any type of behavior, action, or aspect of free association as an obstacle to the therapeutic procedure. The decision that a resistance is present must be based on some other clinical consideration beyond obvious disruptions. However, such statements of criteria as the patient does not get well or the analysis seems stalemated lack the definitive sense needed for such decisions. It is in this area, of course, that we are dealing with the clinical manifestations of silent or strategic resistances. Disturbances in the production of derivative expressions pertinent to the patient's neurosis—a major criterion of resistance in the communicative approach—is almost never considered, except for obvious states of rumination and the avoidance manifestly of seemingly important topics, present and past.

In addition to behaviors which are obviously disruptive to the therapeutic work, the main clinical criteria of resistance are founded upon the psychoanalytic theory of neuroses and of the therapeutic process. Several problems surface with a careful sifting of the many complex aspects of this particular dimension. I will focus on two such issues: first, the influence of the definition of transference on the assessment of resistances; and second, the evident discrepancy between the psychoanalytic theory of neuroses and the theory related to the nature of analytic work which emerges through a consideration of this area.

In a previous work (Langs 1980a) I pursued the clinical definition of transference. I concluded that in the classical psychoanalytic literature the term mainly refers to direct allusions to the analyst and analytic setting, and to relatively transparent displacement figures—though the latter are quite infrequent in the vignettes presented by analytic writers. On the whole, *manifest* fantasies about, attitudes and feelings toward, and references to the analyst are taken as expressions of transference. By and large, the defensive component in such so-called transferences is restricted to the mechanism of displacement from an earlier figure onto the person of the analyst. These manifest communications about the analyst are not viewed as *derivatives* of *unconscious* transference fantasies, in the sense that they themselves are disguised representations of an underlying constellation. Instead, such material is taken at face value and is seen as essentially undisguised, though subjected to displacement.

This approach is considerably different from that proposed first by Melanie Klein (1952), in which every communication from the patient is viewed as a derivative expression related to the therapeutic relationship—to "transference" in its broadest sense. On this basis, *all* of the associations from the patient are treated without exception as disguised derivatives, and the patient's material is understood not only in terms of distorting fantasies and memories, but also in terms of unconscious perceptions of the therapist or analyst.

In the classical approach, the material from the patient is overridingly understood as pertaining to transference and therefore to pathological and distorted communication. While efforts have been made to segregate a so-called real relationship which is undistorted, the role of the actual direct and indirect, conscious and unconscious, communications from the therapist in generating adaptive stimuli for the patient has been neglected. In particular, there has been a notable failure to appreciate the unconscious communications contained in the therapist's interventions, and the patient's ongoing introjection of these expressions—including the nondistorted reactions which follow on this basis.

In sum, then, the clinical definition of resistances relies heavily upon the clinical definition of transference. In the classical literature, the clinical referents for transference are direct references to the analyst or obvious displacements, and the material involved is understood primarily in terms of displacements rather than inherent disguise. In addition, most of the patient's associations are formulated as expressions of transference—pathological unconscious fantasy-memory constellations which pertain to the analyst—and often, transference is used as a term for the total relationship which the patient has with the therapist. Little room is afforded the nontransference component of this relationship, and most of what the patient expresses is not examined for valid, nonpathological unconscious perceptiveness or other forms of indirect but adaptive functioning.

The writings of analysts such as Calef (1971) in regard to patients whose resistances take the form of the apparent absence of a transference neurosis can be better understood in this light. Implied is the absence of direct allusions to the analyst in a form taken to represent displacements from past figures. Often this entails a failure to significantly refer to the analyst on a conscious level. It does not, however, take into account disguised, derivative communications regarding the analyst, which can be identified primarily through the communicative viewpoint.

Similarly, analysts who maintain that sound analytic work requires the development of a transference neurosis appear to be using the active presence of conscious fantasies about the analyst as a criteria for such a neurosis. While much has been said, though little written, about the relative absence of patients who manifest a full blown transference neurosis, this leads to a conception through which borderline patients who are consciously preoccupied with their analyst, both sexually and aggressively, would be taken as model patients in terms of the development of a transference neurosis. Much confusion has arisen from defining transference neurosis in terms of direct allusions to the analyst. While there is evidence that some patients are highly defensive in respect to their *unconscious* transference constellation, it would require a study of this subject from the communicative viewpoint to clarify the relevant issues. (For an initial effort, see chapter 11.)

It is expected, then, that the patient will express his neurosis in his relationship with the analyst "in the transference," as the classical analyst puts it; and the level of resistance is often gauged by assessing the extent to which the patient openly, rather than through disguise, expresses his feelings and fantasies toward the analyst. Extreme resistance is understood as reflecting massive defensiveness to a point where there is a complete failure to refer directly to the analyst (Gill 1979). On this basis, what might be termed in the loosest sense "associational resistances" are defined mainly in terms of the extent to which the patient *manifestly* refers to the analyst. On this basis, concepts such as "resistances to transference" (i.e., the avoidance of direct allusions to the analyst) have been proposed. Other overt transference resistances are seen as arising from threatening feelings or fantasies toward the analyst which are themselves either manifest in the patient's associations or available through elicitation or confrontation.

Randomly selecting Greenson's first clinical illustration of transference resistances we are presented with an example of the defensive search for direct "transference gratification" from the analyst and the way in which libidinal factors produce resistances. The patient, a depressed woman who overate, was often sadly silent because she wanted the analyst to talk to her. The speaking meant that the analyst was willing to feed her, and if this and related wishes were gratified, she would be able to work; if not, she felt empty and unable to communicate. Later in her analysis, she felt strong sexual impulses of an incestuous nature toward the analyst.

> She came to her hour in a flirtatious, frivolous mood, determined to provoke me into some kind of sexual play, even if it were only verbal. For a period of time she refused to work with this material; she demanded that I first had to indicate some reciprocity in my feelings. Still later in her analysis, she refused to produce analytic material unless I prodded her. . . . All these different urges became a source of resistance, until she was able to relinquish her desire for satisfaction. Only then was she willing to establish a working alliance and attempt to work analytically on her different instinctual impulses toward me [the analyst] (1967, p. 249).

As can be seen, the interference with the analytic work described here is based on *conscious* feelings and impulses directed toward the analyst. While Greenson acknowledges the presence of an unconscious element, such as an underlying incestuous factor, the resistances he describes are understood in terms of the patient's manifest associations which are not themselves seen as disguised derivatives of possible unconscious perception and fantasy constellations, but mainly as displacements from past relationships.

Many present-day classical psychoanalysts believe in the validity of interpreting derivatives of unconscious fantasies and memories in material which pertains entirely to outside relationships. They therefore posit the presence of resistances when patients obstruct the flow of such communications or appear otherwise defensive in that area.

Again, the first example used by Greenson (1967, pp. 62–63) in his general discussion of resistances is representative. In the context of a discussion of gross behavioral resistances, specifically of the manner in which affects may indicate resistance, Greenson describes a patient who began his hour by stating that the night before he had experienced "a great sexual thrill—in fact, the greatest sexual pleasure" of his life with his new bride. Greenson was struck and puzzled by the patient's hesitant description, however; the words and feelings did not fit. Taking this as an indicator that some resistance was at work, Greenson eventually commented that, "It was a great thrill, but yet it was also sad." Initial denial was followed by associations that the wonderful sexual experience signaled the end of something: "a good sex life with his wife meant good-bye to his wild infantile sexual fantasies which had lived on unchanged and unfulfilled in his unconscious mind."

In another vignette, a physician in analysis began speaking in medical jargon. He referred to his wife's painful protruding hemorroids which developed prior to a planned trip. The news caused the patient unmixed displeasure and he wondered whether the hemorrhoid could be surgically excised and whether they would have to postpone their vacation. Greenson could sense the latent anger and, as he puts it, he "could not refrain from saying: 'I think you really mean that your wife's hemorrhoids are giving you a pain in the ass.'" The patient responded angrily that the analyst was right, and a son of a bitch. He said he wished they would cut them out of her, and added that he can't stand these women and their swellings that interfere with his pleasures. This was connected to the patient's mother, whose pregnancy had precipitated his infantile neurosis at age five (p. 66).

It appears that within the classical literature there are two classes of resistances: those which involve allusions to the analyst and which are termed transference resistances, and others which interfere with the development of material believed to be unrelated to the analytic relationship, for which no specific term has been coined. Perusal of the clinical vignettes in these writings reveal an impressive amount of subjectivity to these evaluations. Seldom does an analyst require that a patient *represent* his resistance through some type of derivative expression before the offer of a confrontation or interpretation of the resistance, and confrontations are far more common than interpretations. Much of this work is developed on the basis of direct impressions. Little use is made of the patient's derivative communications, nor are these interventions and the patient's reactions subjected to examination for Type Two derivative validation. It seems that at any point that the analyst or therapist senses some disturbance in the smooth flow of what he believes to be meaningful material, he will invoke the concept of resistance and search for its intrapsychic basis within the patient. While lip service is afforded to the possibility that some behaviors or interventions of the analyst may contribute on occasion and momentarily to a resistance in the patient (Greenson 1967, Sandler, Dare, and Holder 1973, Stone 1973), the reported clinical vignettes virtually never address this issue. When they do so, they minimize the importance of the analyst's role (see, for example, Lipton 1977).

Most classical writings on psychotherapy propose that it should be centered on the patient's life experiences and outside relationships; the vague clinical criteria that any disturbance in the flow of the therapeutic work is a signal of resistance appears to characterize the writings on this subject. In this treatment modality, gross behavioral indications of such obstructions are the main signs of resistance. Not only are many of the more subtle forms of resistance missed in the psychotherapeutic situation, but also many gross behaviors, which in analysis would be viewed as reflecting resistances, are taken far less seriously. In part, this trend is an expression of the thinking of many therapists in regard to their work with borderline and schizophrenic syndromes. These attitudes have been illustrated above in the vignette presented from the work of Blanck and Blanck (1979). It is far more likely, for example, that a patient's telephone call requesting to change an hour—say, because of a conflicting appointment with another doctor—would be viewed as an expression of resistance in a patient in psychoanalysis than it would be in a patient in psychotherapy. Nonetheless, many analysts would see such a request as realistic rather than resistant, though some would examine the clinical material in the subsequent session for the evidence of a need in the patient to disturb the therapy. However, the impression generated by the writings is that many analysts would change the hour and thereby join in with the acting out of the apparent resistance, failing to realize that this change would influence the patient and his subsequent material.

Clearly, we need an extensive reevaluation of the basis on which analysts and therapists determine (and validate) the presence of resistance in the patient's free associations, and especially in his behaviors—many of which impinge upon the basic ground rules and framework of treatment. There are indications that analysts, both knowingly and inadvertently, have evoked and supported a wide variety of resistances within their patients, and that they have as yet failed to develop specific clinical criteria for their detection. This is particularly true for transactions which pertain to the ground rules of analysis, especially of psychotherapy, and for the resistances within patients who appear cooperative on the surface and engaged in meaningful free associations.

THE DIMENSIONS OF RESISTANCE

In a tribute to the complexities of the nature of and basis for resistances, the classical psychoanalytic literature reveals a wide variety of classifications of pertinent factors. I will review those which have stood the test of time and appear to be most meaningful.

As indicated above, resistances have been divided into those which are gross, crass, and overt on the one hand, and those which are silent and more subtle on the other. In the present volume, I have termed the first group *gross behavioral resistances* and the second, *communicative* (see chapter 11).

Greenson has offered the most thorough listing of gross behavioral resistances. He includes silences, the patient's not feeling like talking; qualities of affects such as their absence or inappropriateness; aspects of the patient's posture; fixations in time so that the patient speaks only of the present or past; extensive associations related to trivia or external events; avoidance of topics; rigidities in respect to the style of free associating and behaviors related to the analytic situation; the use of the "language of avoidance" such as clichés, technical terms, or sterile language; lateness; missing hours; forgetting to pay the fee; the absence of change; boredom in the patient; a consciously kept secret; acting out; and frequent cheerful hours. To these could be added some other gross indicators: verbalized opposition to the therapist or analyst; repudiation of interpretations; attempts to manipulate other aspects of the ground rules; and other behaviors of this kind. These constitute the ways in which disturbances and opposition to the analytic work appear in the patient's behaviors and associations.

Classification by Source

Where do resistances stem from? Once resistances have been identified, it becomes necessary to understand their basic sources. Such efforts have led to a variety of classifications, some of them quite confusing and actually on different levels of conceptualization. Freud set the tone in this respect by identifying five major types or sources of resistance (1926):

1. Repression resistance, whose clinical manifestations reflect the ego's usual defenses against anxiety and the related intrapsychic and external danger situations and conflicts which evoke such responses.

2. Transference resistance, which Freud saw as comparable to repression resistance but involving the analytic situation and the analyst himself, and which expresses the reanimation of a repression which should have been recollected.

3. Gain from illness (so-called secondary gain), another form of ego resistance.

4. Id resistance, which necessitates working through and reflects the tendency of instinctual drives to maintain their forms of expression.

5. Superego resistance, which originates from the sense of guilt or the need for punishment, and opposes every move toward success, including the patient's recovery through analysis.

In essence, Freud was suggesting that resistances could be classified in terms of primary and secondary gain, that is, in terms of basic defensive mechanisms and those which are utilized to maintain equilibrium. Next, he was indicating that resistances could be divided into those which pertain directly to the analytic relationship, and those which involve other kinds of dangers. And finally, he was propsoing that resistances could be classified in terms of the three psychic macrostructures in respect to their source: the ego, id, and superego.

It is well to pause here with a brief comment from the communicative vantage point. It seems likely that gross behavioral and communicative resistances are compromise formations—adaptive responses with inputs from each of the psychic agencies and external reality, including object relationships. The analysis of the sources of a resistance would therefore attempt to take into account each of these factors, and to identify which is predominant. Inherent to such considerations would be the primary and secondary gains derived by the patient from his neurosis.

Problems arise, however, in respect to Freud's distinction between repression resistance and transference resistance, which, in general, is maintained to this day. The assumption is that resistances may arise within the patient in the course of analysis or therapy that are not related to unconscious fantasy (and perception) constellations which pertain to the analyst. This has also been taken to imply that interpretations can be made in respect to such resistances without allusion to the therapeutic interaction. It follows, in theory at least, that important therapeutic work can be undertaken in either sphere—as it pertains to the therapist or to outside relationships.

On a manifest level, it is evident that patients may become resistant as they begin to approach fantasy material related to persons other than the therapist or analyst. In chapter 11, I will stress the importance of unconscious perceptions, and certainly some degree of disruption in the therapeutic process may also derive from unconscious perceptions related to outside figures, in addition to the influence of unconscious fantasy-memory formations. In both cases, it therefore often appears clinically that a disturbance in a relationship with an outside figure is proving disruptive to therapeutic progress.

From the communicative viewpoint, these considerations have validity, but only up to a point. Observations from the communicative vantage point indicate that there is almost always some contribution from the therapeutic interaction—transference and nontransference—to apparent repression resistances (a term, then, that should be reserved for resistances which seem to emerge primarily in response to material pertinent to relationships other than with the therapist or analyst). This contribution is often critical to the unconscious basis of the primary repression resistance, and unless it is rectified where necessary (in those situations where unconscious perceptions and introjects play a significant role) and the relationship component (transference and nontransference) analyzed, the repression resistance will not be modified. In practice, this means that virtually always some link should be made to the therapeutic interaction in interpreting repression resistances.

Glover (1955) maintained Freud's classification in respect to the forms and sources of resistance. Greenson (1967) also accepted this classification, although he offered several additional means of identifying distinctive aspects of resistance. He suggested that resistances can be identified in terms of fixation points—oral, anal, phallic, and oedipal—or more broadly: preoedipal, oedipal, and postoedipal. This would depend not only on the content of the material being defended against, but also the form in which the resistance is expressed and the nature of the fantasy constellations involved.

Resistances also can be organized by the major defense used by the patient in creating his obstruction, that is, in terms of repression, isolation, reaction formation, projection, projective identification, and others—a point elaborated in some detail by Anna Freud (1936). As a rule, character resistances—a term used to emphasize the patient's characteristic modes of defense and disruption—are usually included in this category since they reflect the patient's habitual mode of dealing with the internal and external world (W. Reich 1928, 1929, 1933; Greenson 1967).

Yet another classification of resistances can be developed in terms of diagnostic catgories. Here, typical forms of resistance, as seen in schizophrenic and narcissistic patients, and in the neuroses and neurotic character disorders such as hysteria, obsessional neurosis, and depression, could all be identified and used as a basis for understanding the ways in which patients attempt to disrupt the therapeutic process. Diagnostic considerations would influence not only the form of resistance, but also the sources. They would also play a role in anticipating the intensity of resistances and the likelihood of dealing with them analytically. They need not, however, suggest any essential deviation in the basic technical approach to resistances beyond their interpretation as defined in the classical approach. Such efforts should, however, regularly include the rectification of all contributions from the therapist or analyst, and a full consideration of the role of interactional and introjective (unconscious perceptive) processes, in addition to that played by unconscious fantasy constellations.

Greenson (1967) also identified ego-alien and ego-syntonic resistances, and made note of the special difficulties that arise in attempting to analyze and modify the latter.

Sandler and his associates (1973) offered ten sources of resistance: (1) those due to the threat posed by the analytic procedure and its aims, which threaten the patient's usual adaptations and which are best termed repression-resistance or defense-resistance; (2) transference resistances; (3) resistances deriving from secondary gains; (4) superego resistance; (5) resistances arising from faulty procedures and inappropriate technical measures adopted by the therapist (which could lead to a breakdown in treatment if left unnoticed); (6) resistances which derive from threatening consequences and real difficulties in the patient's relationship with important persons in his environment that are based on the changes brought about by the analysis; (7) resistances prompted by the danger of cure and the resultant loss of the analyst; (8) resistances due to threats to the patient's self-esteem because of the analytic work: (9) resistances due to reluctance to give up past adaptive solutions (which include so-called id resistance); and (10) character resistances.

As can be seen, this classification touches upon aspects of resistance which derive from different facets of psychoanalytic theory and various levels of conceptualization. It might be possible to suggest a synthetic reorganization: resistances may arise in the relationship with the analyst or because of outside relationships; they may arise from immediate defensive or secondary gains which stem from the patient's symptoms; and they may arise from various aspects of the patient's structural makeup and character. Resistances within the therapeutic relationship may stem not only from within the patient, but also from within the analyst—a point recognized by these authors, though given insufficient attention. Finally, resistances may also arise from any factors which lead the patient to maintain present adaptations, including his relationship with the analyst and specific kinds of interaction with others.

In identifying so many different ways of organizing the sources of resistance, it becomes easy to lose sight of the importance of unconscious dynamic factors in the form of fantasy and perception constellations. A classification could therefore be proposed which states a continuum of sources of resistance with unconscious introjective-perceptive factors at one extreme and unconscious fantasy-memory constellations at the other. It would take into account resistances which arise within the therapeutic interaction (primary resistances; the major sources of obstacles), as well as those which arise in outside relationships (secondary resistances). It would also take into account contributions from the id, ego, superego, and reality (object relationships), including the implications of the conscious and unconscious factors within the patient and in his relationships with others, including the therapist. Disturbances due to the fear of losing the therapist, to blows at self-esteem, and to wishing to maintain present relatedness and adaptations, could be easily classified. But the overriding importance of unconscious factors in the development and maintenance of resistance, as they exist within both the patient and therapist, would also receive full consideration.

Classification by Motive and Form

Resistances, since they reflect many dimensions of the patient's adaptive responses and their relevant genetics and dynamics, can be classified in many additional ways. I will add just two: the motives for resistances and their basic forms.

In general, analysts have suggested that the motivational factors tend to correspond to those need systems within the patient which prompt defensive behaviors. Since I have discussed this aspect in an earlier part of this chapter, I will confine myself here to indicating that it ultimately must be recognized that resistances derive from need systems arising not only from within the patient, but also as a result of his object relationship with the analyst or therapist—and secondarily with others.

Freud (1926; see also Arlow 1963) identified a hierarchy of intrapsychic motivations which prompt defensive and other mental mechanisms and behaviors designed to protect the individual and to promote adaptation. He noted such danger situations as the actual loss of the object (in particular, the mother) and related separation anxieties, the fear of losing the love of the object, castration anxieties, and the fear of punishment. He saw anxiety as a signal generated (or experienced) by the ego in the face of a danger situation, to which the ego responds with protective mechanisms. Later writers identified additional, relatively primitive anxieties such as the fear of annihilation or mental disintegration, as well as those which pertain to an individual's needs for narcissistic supplies, and more elaborate aspects of superego anxieties. In addition, other signal affects, such as depression and shame, were postulated as additional motivations for defensive and other adaptive responses, intrapsychic and behavioral, all of which could play role in stimulating resistances in patients.

To these intrapsychic sources we must now add interactional sources of danger and the related affects—those which arise as a result of the patient's object relationships (Sandler and Joffe 1969, and Sandler and Sandler 1978). Here the role of conscious and unconscious perceptions and of introjective mechanisms must be recognized and understood. Need systems which derive from object relationship have considerable importance in the patient's use of defenses, and in the development of resistances as well. These will, of course, interact actively with internally derived need systems within the patient.

It should be stressed that the model of the closed intrapsychic mental system must now be discarded for one that takes into account both intrapsychic and interpersonal-interactional processes. There is no such entity as an isolated intrapsychic need system or motivation, nor do interpersonal and interactionally derived motivations exert their influence per se; instead, they interact with factors within the patient in never-ending, spiraling sequences. These apply to the therapeutic interaction as they apply to all other relationships. Full recognition of this type of interplay would accord a central role to the ways in which therapists can and actually do play a critical role in many resistances observed in patients (see chapter 11).

As for the *forms* of resistance, we have already identified the most common distinction, that between gross behavioral and so-called silent resistances. The communicative view suggests three such categories: (1) *gross behavioral resistances,* which are self-evident disruptions in treatment; (2) *communicative resistances* which are revealed through an analysis of indicators, adaptive context, and derivative complex; and (3) *subtle resistances,* which involve behaviors in the patient which are not obviously disruptive and yet express in some form major obstacles to the therapeutic process. This last group of resistances characteristically involve modifications in the basic framework, the ground rules of therapy or analysis, whose resistant nature often eludes the therapist or analyst. They also entail resistances which are unconsciously suggested to the patient by the therapist, or fostered in some manner because they serve countertransference-needs. They often involve major blind spots in the therapist, and require a careful utilization of the listening process for their detection. In chapter 11, I will further clarify this particular grouping of resistances.

A final variation on the classifications already offered—and clearly, these tend to overlap considerably—would involve the extent to which the major motives for a resistance derive from the therapist or from the patient. This is another way of restating the communicative finding that all resistances are both interactional and intrapsychic, and that the major need-system involved may arise primarily from the patient or from the therapist, and always entails some degree of intermixture.

It can be seen from the various ways of classifying resistances that they constitute highly complex behaviors, gross and subtle, action-oriented and communicative, which constitute prime therapeutic tasks. All resistances involve the therapeutic relationship to some degree, and most derive their primary motives from the therapeutic interaction, whether mainly from the patient or from the therapist. We should therefore now turn to a more careful consideration of this particular aspect of resistances.

RESISTANCES AND THE THERAPEUTIC RELATIONSHIP

As discussed briefly earlier in this chapter, classical psychoanalysts have accorded considerable importance to the relationship between resistances and "transference." It behooves us now to more carefully examine the interplay between the patient's relationship to the therapist, with its transference and nontransference components, and the development of resistances. Transference was defined by Freud (1905, 1912a) in an ambiguous manner, referring to both conscious and unconscious fantasies and reactions on the part of the patient toward the analyst. While it should be self-evident that transference involves pathological, distorted, and distorting *unconscious* fantasy and memory constellations, most of the subsequent writings on the subject have utilized *conscious* fantasies about the analyst and obvious displacement representations. As a rule, the only psychic mechanism applied to such transference material is displacement. Conscious fantasies are taken as whole cloth, and as direct expressions of feeling, fantasies, and other kinds of reactions derived from earlier relationships with important genetic figures. Conscious fantasies about the analyst are not understood as inherently derived and disguised material which represents some underlying unconscious fantasy system, and in most instances are not viewed as derivative communications. In addition there is no room in such thinking for the patient's undistorted and realistic perceptions and reactions to the analyst. These are somehow relegated to the so-called real relationship, rather than being understood as one component of every communication to the analyst, whether directly about the analyst himself or about others. The concept of transference, then, highly prejudices the analyst's picture of the patient, the implications he derives from his material, and his conception of resistances. Quite broadly, it favors a view of the patient's associations as essentially pathological.

This approach can be readily demonstrated by turning to the many illustrations offered by Greenson (1967) in his discussion of transference resistances. Typically, the clinical material involves conscious feelings and fantasies toward the analyst which prompts the patient to oppose the procedures of the analysis. The reader may recall the vignette alluded to earlier to this chapter as part of the initial discussion of the interplay between transference and resistance, in which a patient was silent in her analysis because of sexual impulses toward him. There were direct demands for satisfactions from him. All of this was discussed on a manifest level, and in addition in terms of apparent genetic implications.

In another illustration (pp. 267–268), Greenson describes a male patient who found fault with whatever the analyst did in the analysis; his silence was regarded as oppressive and his interventions as irritating and hostile. In a dream, someone was listening to the radio commentator, Gabriel Heater, who had the voice of doom. In associating, the broadcaster was linked to the patient's father and how his homecoming changed the atmosphere at home—he was a wet blanket and spoiled the fun for the patient. As he approached, the patient would always become irritable and hostile.

Struck by the parallel between the patient's behavior toward himself and his reactions to his father's homecoming, Greenson suggested to the patient that as long as he kept silent in the hour and let him talk, and as long as it was early in the session, the patient enjoyed the analytic situation just as he enjoyed being at home with his doting mother and sisters. At the end of the hour, the patient began to anticipate his analyst's interruptions of his secret fun at home. He could anticipate the analyst's intervention as he anticipated his father's return. Greenson's interpretations were therefore like the voice of doom connected to his father's return home, and announced the end of the patient's pleasure with his mother and sisters.

Greenson found confirmation for his intervention when the patient added that, in all honesty, he had to admit that his father's homecoming was painful only to him, that his mother and sisters looked forward to it. The material was seen as an illustration of a reenactment of a past family interaction by the patient with the analyst, and discussed as a form of transference resistance.

In this vignette, representative of classical psychoanalytic writings, transference resistances are formulated in terms of opposition to the analyst, without any sound consideration of the nature or validity of the interpretations. There is an implicit assumption of the correctness of the analyst's work, and, further, that the patient's opposition must be based on an unconscious fantasy or memory derived from the past and displaced into the present. It is the patient's conscious feelings and attitudes toward the analyst which are seen as a sign of resistance, and in this way, the analytic work is concentrated on gross behavioral oppositions to the analysis. The unconscious element is formulated entirely in terms of a genetic incident and a displacement from the past, and the patient's manifest associations are not in themselves treated as derivative representations. In addition, as we have repeatedly seen, the interlude is formulated in terms of resistances based on transference, distortion, and displacement, without any consideration of adaptive contexts, valid unconscious perceptions, and derivative communication. Possible interactional qualities are thereby excluded.

In general, this type of resistance is formulated as a defensive effort within the patient designed to obliterate his awareness of the pertinent feelings and fantasies about the analyst, impressions of which he would be relatively directly aware if the resistance were to be resolved. Occasionally, when the defense involves displacement, the resistance is seen as an effort, by means of conscious feelings or actions, to shift to another person reactions which actually involve the analyst. In these situations, displacement maintains the patient's lack of awareness of his fantasies toward the analyst, though they are expressed directly with little or no disguise. Once the displacement has been recognized, a second displacement from an earlier genetic figure is postulated to account for the reaction to the analyst, which is now located more directly within the therapeutic relationship.

Once clinical referrents for transference and transference resistance are understood, the writings on this subject in the classical literature become considerably clarified. Thus, Gill (1979) has emphasized the distinction between (1) resistances to the awareness of transference and (2) resistance to the resolution of transference. Both Greenson (1967) and Stone (1973) adopted a similar position. Daniels (1969) also attempted to specifically define this particular point.

The first type of resistance is called *defense transference,* while the second type is termed *transference resistance* (Gill 1979). In the first situation, it is the transference that is resisted, while in the second, the transference does the resisting. The former involves implicit or indirect references to the tranference which must be made explicit or direct through interpretation. The latter involves interpretations which enable the patient to realize that the now explicit transference includes a determinant from the past.

By and large, the determinants of transference as defined in these writings are assumed to be almost entirely within the patient. Recently, Gill (1979) has stressed the importance of identifying aspects in the here-and-now situation with the analyst, and in the latter's attitudes and behaviors, which form a basis for the patient's transference manifestations. Gill follows Freud (1914) in also emphasizing that resistances are not only designed to prevent remembering, but also involve repetitions through actions in the relationship with the analyst. These can involve not only motoric behaviors, but cyclical repetitions expressed in attitudes, feelings and intentions. Gill stresses the importance of encouraging the expansion of transference within the analytic situation, largely through the analysis of resistances, to the awareness of transferences which exist in both the patient and analyst. Here, then, counterresistances are noted, though the subject receives no elaborate consideration.

The basic concepts of resistances which apply to the awareness of conscious and unconscious fantasies and other reactions toward the analyst, and those which apply to the analytic resolution of such transference constellations, find considerable support in the communicative approach. However, this viewpoint adheres to the basic definition of transference in terms of *unconscious* and pathological fantasy-memory constellations, and recognizes an additional source of resistances based on nonpathological unconscious perception-introject constellations (which may subsequently be subjected to distortion). As a result, its total conceptualization of the subject is somewhat different from the classical approach.

I will devote part of chapter 11 to a discussion of the areas of overlap and distinction. Suffice it to say here that throughout his excellent and unique discussion of the immediate precipitants of the transference, Gill (1979) maintained an exclusive emphasis on the transference component to the patient's responses. The role of unconscious perceptions is neglected, and his stress ultimately is on the patient's direct awareness of a fantasy which derives from a displacement from a past figure. However, Gill's effort to demonstrate to analysts that transference (as he defines it) is ever-present, that it is an aspect of all of the patient's associations, and that it derives from stimuli in the here-and-now (i.e., from adaptive contexts from the analyst), could provide a basis through which classical analysts could begin to utilize the communicative viewpoint in their basic thinking. For the moment, Gill's paper is exceptional. But neither he nor any other classical psychoanalyst besides myself has yet attempted the integration of the communicative approach.

In summary, by analyzing the relationship between transference and resistance, classical analysts have identified three major possibilities: (1) resistances may reflect defenses erected against awareness of conscious and unconscious pathological fantasy-memory constellations; (2) they may entail defenses erected against the analysis and understanding of transference manifestations and their

genetic basis; and (3) they may arise when transferences (defined
here as clinically conscious fantasies and reactions to the analyst)
may be used as defenses against other transference and nontransference reactions to the analyst (e.g., Daniels 1969).

Resistances and Countertransference

As noted, classical analysts have given only lip service to the
possibility of resistances within the patient which arise primarily
from the analyst's inappropriate attitudes and interventions. These
are regarded as quite rare, though difficult to recognize since they
involve the analyst and his errors (Sandler, Dare, and Holder 1973).
There is little indication that classical analysts would accept the
thesis that every resistance within the patient receives some input,
however small, from the analyst, and that such inputs are part of
the continuing, spiraling, conscious and unconscious communicative interaction. Further, there are many types of resistance-evoking
errors, especially those which involve mismanagements of the
ground rules and framework, which are totally unrecognized in
present-day classical writings. Little effort has been made to develop
a listening process through which this particular source or resistances could be identified, and thereby rectified and interpreted.

One quality of the interplay between countertransferences and
resistances within the patient is perhaps best illustrated in the
recent paper by Lipton (1977). Writing of "resistance to the transference," Lipton notes that there are two forms: one in which the
self-representation remains intact and the transference is alluded to
by displacement (the usual, classically conceived form); and another in which the self-representation is changed by means of a
transitory identification with the analyst. To illustrate the latter,
Lipton uses a vignette in which he offered a patient who appeared
ill the use of his personal thermometer. In the following hour,
when the patient described herself as hopelessly incompetent and
as having betrayed her client (the patient was an attorney), Lipton
interpreted this material as an identification with himself. Through
negation, the patient connected this to the offer of the thermometer
and described a series of conscious fantasies about how rash, intimate, irregular, and incompetent the analyst would feel for "going
physical" on her. Lipton then writes: "Now, with the identification

out of the way, the transference configuration which we already knew something about became clear" (p. 469). The intimacy which the patient wished for with the analyst, and regarding which she had anxiety lest he feel guilty that he had done her irreparable harm, was seen as an aspect of the transference connected with her child-hood relationship with her father.

On a practical level, many analysts deny unconscious, and some-times conscious, implications of countertransference-based inter-ventions. In this instance, Lipton proposed that the offer of the thermometer is not part of analytic technique, but rather a part of the personal relationship between analyst and patient which can-not be codified. Despite the abundant indications of conscious and unconscious perceptions and introjects stemming from such inter-ventions, the classical approach to this type of interlude would either ignore the contribution from the analyst, or, as presented here, view these contributions as coincidental and creating ob-stacles within the patient which must be disposed of in order to arrive at true transference implications. The effort is made to reduce this incident to a replay *by the patient* of an earlier patho-genic, genetic experience with her father, a position which denies the extensive ramifications of the analyst's interventions.

In this and similar ways, expressions of counterresistances in the analyst are treated as if they were transference resistances, and problems within the therapist are handled as if they existed within the patient. A more accurate approach would acknowledge, rectify, and interpret the analyst's contributions to the patient's resistances, and allow subsequent material to reveal other distortions. In this way, the analyst's actual repetition of the father's past pathogenic behavior would be corrected and interpreted as such. Only when additional material of a clearly distorted nature was introduced, would the interpretation propose that the patient, in some patho-logical way, is misperceiving or reacting inappropriately to the analyst based on a displacement from her father.

Despite the importance of Lipton's recognition, as a classical psychoanalyst, of introjective mechanisms within patients as part of their relationship with the analyst—a point I have expounded for some years, and which has been stated by many Kleinian analysts (see Langs 1976c)—his contribution has serious limitations. An effort that might have served as a bridge between the intrapsychic-projective view of transference, which still dominates the classical analysis, to the communicative viewpoint in which introjective and projective processes are both given their full due, becomes instead an attempt to ultimately deny the implications of these introjective processes and their influence on the patient's resistances.

THE ADAPTIVE ASPECTS OF RESISTANCE

Implicit to the classical psychoanalytic writings on resistance is some appreciation of their adaptive aspects. Viewed basically as efforts to cope with danger situations and with all factors which threaten the patient's psychic equilibrium, their value to the patient is self-evident. Stone (1973), in particular, stressed the affirmative aspects of resistance and their self-protective role. He also noted their importance in maintaining a sense of personality cohesion and narcissistic balance.

Recognition of the adaptive importance of resistances softens the classical therapist's approach to their analysis; it leads to an appreciation that the full adaptive value of resistances be counterbalanced against their maladaptive aspects. It also asks for a sense of patience and understanding in the analyst, who through his interpretations, usually implies that the patient modify or give up his resistances and expose himself to the underlying dangers in the hope of effecting new and more constructive modes of adaptation. Modifications of resistances lead to psychic disequilibrium, and require the patient to develop new modes of coping.

Some analysts, however, have drawn unjustifiable conclusions from the recognition of the adaptive value of resistances (e.g., Blanck and Blanck 1979; see above). Resistances are adaptive in the sense that they include healthy and flexible adjustments—i.e., all efforts at coping. Some of the confusion stems from the failure to distinguish nontransference from transference resistances, since the former often reflect sound adaptation while the latter are basically inappropriate and maladaptive. Thus, defensive responses to an analyst's countertransference-based interventions are often reasonably protective for the patient, while resistant reactions to valid interventions tend to reflect the latter's psychopathology. Still, any defensive-resistant effort may have pathological aspects even while serving as a means of coping. It is a technical error for a therapist to accept or sanction resistances in a patient, and forgo their necessary analytic exploration and resolution—even in selected instances.

As obstacles to sound analytic process, all resistances are inherently detrimental to optimal therapeutic outcome. With full respect for their protective value to the patient (and, at times, to the therapist), they require careful analytic work designed to promote their insightful resolution. Transference resistances always express pathological defenses and other types of disruptive behaviors which have their counterpart in the patient's daily life. As such, their analytic resolution consistently leads to not only important extensions of the therapeutic process, but also to symptomatic improvement within the patient and in his relationships with others.

TECHNIQUES FOR ANALYZING RESISTANCES

Classical analysts appear to agree that resistances must ultimately be interpreted to the patient in terms of their source and meanings, including their dynamic and genetic implications. Greenson (1967) has presented the most careful delineation of the techniques involved. He suggested four steps to this process: (1) demonstrating to the patient that he is resisting, showing its presence and form; (2) identifying how the patient is resisting, including its main manifestations; (3) arriving at what the patient is warding off, usually in terms of conscious and unconscious fantasies and memories; and (4) determining why he is doing so—identifying the motive for the resistance. Much of this work is carried out through a sequence entailing a confrontation of the patient through which the resistance is demonstrated, a clarification of its more apparent implications, and then the interpretation of its nature. This last includes an interpretation of the motive for, as well as the mode of, resisting. In essence, the analyst demonstrates to the patient that he is resisting and why, what it is that he is resisting and how. Ultimately, this process, according to Greenson, should always include an analysis of the prevailing transference resistance.

To illustrate, Greenson (p. 105) describes a patient who reported a successful "marital experience" with his wife the previous night. His speech was then rather restrained, concerned making love to his wife, and shifted to rather innocuous events. Here, Greenson asked what the patient meant by "marital experience," to which the latter responded with hesitation, realizing that he wanted the analyst to be more specific. Greenson was able to point out that the patient seems bashful when it comes to talking about sexual matters. The patient went on to describe his difficulties in talking about sex. In this way, he had begun work on his resistances.

In a later reference to the same patient (pp. 112–113), Greenson describes how the analytic work sought to uncover the impulses, fantasies, and historical events which were associated to his talking about sexual matters. The patient described that sex was considered dirty and a forbidden subject at home, and then thought of the analyst as a stranger and authority. Greenson interpreted to the patient that, as soon as he had mentioned sex, he—the analyst— had become a father figure and the patient, a little boy. In this way, a general resistance was interpreted as a transference resistance.

In interpreting the nature and sources of resistances, every dimension of the therapeutic interaction, and of dynamic and genetic factors, may be brought into play. However, classical analysts have not especially paused to develop clear or strict criteria of validation for their efforts to analyze resistances nor have they examined the unconscious implications of their interventions. Much of this work is carried out directly and on the surface, and it is taken for granted that the analyst's interventions are valid and without major countertransference elements. The pursuit is directed toward the intrapsychic basis of the patient's resistances in almost all cases. Not surprisingly, the techniques used in analyzing resistances reflect the theory of their nature and structure, and that developed for understanding the therapeutic process itself.

A SPECIFIC CLINICAL COMPARISON

As we have seen, a study of virtually any clinical vignette would reveal some degree of difference, often of major proportions, between the classical and communicative understanding of resistances. I have selected, as basis for a specific illustrative comparison, a presentation by Greenson (1978, chapter 20), first, because it deals with the detection of errors of technique and therefore provides a unique basis for understanding the analyst's contribution to the patient's resistances; and second, because Greenson provides the reader with detailed clinical material of a kind usually lacking even in clinical presentations. The more usual discussion of resistances (not the main focus of this particular chapter by Greenson) would concentrate almost entirely on intrapsychic factors within the patient and offer little in the way of clinical material through which the reader could make an independent evaluation.

Greenson's presentation, "The Use of Dream Sequences for Deecting Errors of Technique," is quite rich, and I shall focus only upon the material pertinent to the present chapter. The interlude involves a male patient, Mr. Z, who was in his second analysis with Greenson because of a lack of close relationships with both women and men, feelings of sadness and inadequacy, and a sleep problem. The patient took barbiturates to sleep, and Greenson had repeatedly interpreted the taking of the sleeping pills as a resistance to the analysis: a form of magic designed to replace the analysis and blot out the analyst's interpretations, and an attempt to avoid thoughts and feelings which the patient had when he lay awake, especially hateful and loving feelings concerning his mother and the analyst, whom he felt brought about or disturbed his sleep.

The patient began an hour by reporting that he had not taken any sleeping pills and had been more aware of his fantasies. He had been angry at Greenson and wondered why he listened to him. His workday had been wasted.

The patient reported a dream of being in an apartment. His mother was around. In a closet, he found a hatbox with a hat that was odd and too large for him. Even with fiddling, it did not fit. Then there was another hat with a capelike fabric like they wear in the Foreign Legion; it then became an overseas cap. There was also a reference to the biggest manufacturer of artificial food sent to Europe or Africa.

The hat reminded the patient of something sexual and of penises. The first hat was like one his grandfather had owned. The second was like those worn in World War II, and the patient had been thinking of his years in the navy. He went on to say that he was annoyed with Greenson and felt that he was responsible for his not sleeping. Greenson made him give up the sleeping pills and that made him worse. Mr. Z was prepared to not sleep and also to not free associate. There were more feelings of hostility: the patient felt that something had been taken away and he had gotten nothing back. He felt the analyst didn't know what he was doing.

Here, Greenson intervened and suggested that the patient was enraged with him for suggesting that his analysis would go better if he gave up the sleeping pills. The patient was questioning this and wondering if Greenson knew what he was doing. Greenson inquired about the hat not fitting and not belonging to the patient.

The patient associated to European hats and to his stepfather, whose closet was full of them. He was a man who looked crazy and who kept getting worse all the time, and the patient hated him. The stepfather constantly invaded the patient's privacy with his nudity, entering the living room completely naked at times. He had a hat the patient liked to play with when he was a kid. Associations led to a French army captain whom the patient had befriended during World War II and who had been shot and killed by a Senegalese guard.

At this point, Greenson felt there was too much material and inquired about the manufacturer of the artificial food. This led to associations related to a company of this kind in Santa Monica. (Greenson now mentions in parentheses that he lives in Santa Monica and that the patient came to see him at his home where he works in the late afternoon.)

Before proceeding further, we would agree with Greenson—though some might not—that taking sleeping pills constitutes a gross behavioral resistance. As yet, Greenson is unable to formulate the sources and meanings of this resistance beyond those indicated early in his summary—impressions which cannot be validated from the present material. It is interesting, however, that the point at which Greenson felt overwhelmed by the patient's material, he asked a question which led to associations from the patient which have the clearest relevance to the analysis—the Santa Monica manufacturing firm. In this way, a fundamental deviation in the ideal therapeutic setting is identified, though at the implicit behest of the patient, and parenthetically. At this point, the communicative therapist would recognize a critical deviation in the fixed frame and a major background intervention context. In contrast, many classical analysts would see this as a relatively unimportant detail (as did Greenson), and merely a vehicle through which the patient was able to reveal the "transference" implications of his dream and associations. Nonetheless, from the communicative viewpoint, we would credit Greenson with considerable *unconscious* sensitivity in inquiring into the manufacturer of the artificial food, and raise the possibility that on some level he may have sensed that there was something unreal about the therapeutic setting or situation.

At this point, the communicative therapist would review this material in light of the revealed intervention context. He could offer an immediate tentative though silent hypothesis as to a number of unconscious sources and meanings of the patient's use of sleeping pills as well as his decision to stop taking them. He would also discover some rather compelling elements in this derivative complex which seem to be strongly related to this particular framework issue.

In essence, the sleeping pills are a break in the fixed frame—in the use of free associations within each session as the fundamental basis for cure. As such, it is a version of the therapist's modification in the ideal therapeutic environment through which he makes use of an office within his home rather than one in a private and professional setting. The therapist's deviation inherently invites and supports the patient's break in the frame. In this light, the patient's decision to stop taking the sleeping pills is an important *model of rectification* and suggests that on some level, and for reasons apparently unavailable in this material, events which probably took place within the therapeutic interaction have prompted efforts on the part of the patient to unconsciously work over this particular framework issue.

In support of these formulations, we have the patient's anger toward the analyst and his questioning of his techniques. The dream takes place in an apartment and alludes to his mother who may be an important *nontransference* figure in respect to the violations in boundaries implied in the home-office arrangement. The hat which does not fit conveys the patient's unconscious perception that something is not right. The analyst is represented in derivative form as a big manufacturer, but of *artificial* food. The communicative studies of the therapeutic environment have shown that this type of deviation in the fixed frame destroys the illusory play space essential for analysis and creates a setting which is unreal, artificial, and often dead. It is also highly seductive and presents a situation in which the boundaries of the analytic relationship are blurred. This is in keeping with the patient's associations to something sexual and his continued feelings of annoyance toward the analyst. It is striking that the patient then expresses his wish to not free associate, a comment which may well reflect his sense of danger under the conditions described. His sense that he is getting nothing back may well refer to the analyst's blind spot in respect to the framework issue.

Greenson's intervention focused on the patient's *manifest* associations and is based on translation derivatives. It constitutes a Type One derivative effort at interpretation and inquiry. The patient's comments about the craziness in his stepfather appears to be another nontransference expression of his view of the analyst in respect to the setting and the nature of his interventions which, evaluated from the communicative viewpoint, have not dealt with the critical prevailing adaptive contexts. There is striking support for this in the patient's association to how the stepfather invaded his privacy with his nudity—a striking derivative allusion to the self-revelations which take place in a home-office setting and to a lack of clear-cut boundaries under these conditions. The association clearly implies the patient's unconscious sensitivity to the homosexual implications of these conditions. This particular sequence ends with the allusion to the captain who had been shot, an element that probably condenses the patient's sense of danger under these conditions, his rage at the analyst for creating the setting and for failing to intervene in that particular area, and the deadness of the analytic situation within a deviant environment. There was some confirmation of the initial silent hypotheses described in the patient's subsequent allusion to Santa Monica.

In working with material of this kind and in this way, there is always the danger of misinterpretation, overinterpretation, and of appearing to overformulate. The efforts made here are offered primarily as models and as a means of providing a number of definitive contrasts in the classical and communicative analytic positions. While an attempt will be made to indicate sources of Type Two derivative validation for the communicative theses suggested by this material, freedom will be taken to offer some speculations which will not especially find significant substantiation. The purpose is to promote thoughtful reconsideration rather than total conviction.

In any case, to summarize, the communicative analyst would propose that the patient's use of sleeping pills and his thoughts of not wanting to free associate find an important source in the home-office arrangement, and in the patient's unconscious perception of the analyst as dangerous, homosexual, exhibitionistic, and failing to provide the necessary privacy for a sound therapeutic environment.

Returning to the vignette, Greenson intervened at this point and pointed out the patient's fury at the analyst for taking away his sleeping pills. The anger was seen as keeping the patient awake, and Greenson stressed the shift in the patient's fantasies without the pills, from self-destruction to hostility toward the analyst. This led the patient to question if the analyst knows what he is doing since he has taken something valuable away from the patient. Greenson stressed the newness of the hatred for the analyst and suggested that the patient felt that he, the analyst, had become a dangerous person. This was connected to his stopping the patient from taking the sleeping pills and to the patient's fear that the analyst would get to know too much about him. The patient seemed afraid that the analyst will hurt him like the guard who killed the French captain he was supposed to take care of.

It is interesting that this particular intervention is organized around the adaptive context of Greenson's apparent, noninterpretive efforts to have the patient stop taking sleeping pills. Although this is a cogent intervention context, it will take us too far afield to reorganize this material in light of this precipitant which contains deviant, noninterpretive efforts. Suffice it to say that, to the extent that Greenson had offered directives to this patient, many of the implications of his intervention would overlap with the meanings of the home-office arrangement. With this context, there would, however, be considerable stress in the patient's unconscious perceptions of Greenson in terms of hostility and danger, a point which Greenson touches upon to some extent in his own interpretation. Nonetheless, the communicative approach has shown that modifications of the fixed frame take precedence over partially erroneous interventions. Because of this, Greenson's interpretation would be seen as either incomplete or incorrect in not dealing with the most important adaptive context within the bipersonal field at the moment. This formulation finds a degree of validation in the patient's initial response to this intervention: he tells Greenson that he is not listening to him. This appears to be an introjective identification with the analyst who has not heard the most important *derivative* meanings in this material and who has not recognized the most critical intervention context.

The patient went on to say he wanted to leave and didn't want to be there. Greenson suggested that the patient didn't really want to work in the analysis, to free associate and expose his real fears and desires which he had hidden from himself and from the analyst for so many years with the sleeping pills. The patient had the feeling that Greenson was going to betray and destroy him. In asking the patient to give up the sleeping pills, Mr. Z reacted to the analyst as if he had taken something valuable away from him.

Greenson attributes the patient's resistances in this session to his directives regarding the sleeping pills. There is some truth to this formulation, though we must note that the suggestion that the patient is hiding something fails to recognize the patient's view that Greenson is missing and hiding something from himself. Further, the comment that the patient feels that the analyst is going to betray and destroy him alludes to tentative feelings rather than the patient's conscious and unconscious perceptions that the directive, and the break in the frame, are forms of betrayal and destruction, and that these have actually taken place in reality. In typical fashion, transference rather than nontransference is stressed.

Overlooked once again in this intervention is, first, the patient's failure to offer the analyst Type Two derivative validation of his initial and subsequent interventions; the critical adaptive context of the home-office arrangement; and the likelihood that the patient's newly expressed resistances are primarily nontransference in form, in that they appear to be a response to an essentially erroneous intervention as well as to the continued impairments in the framework. In the communicative view, this material illustrates the extent to which countertransference-based interventions can lead to heightened resistances within the patient. This last intervention also demonstrates the extent to which classical analysts treat material exclusively in terms of fantasies and intrapsychic difficulties within the analysand, an approach that fosters the use of considerable projection and projective identification by the analyst into the patient.

Mr. Z reacted sarcastically to this last intervention, criticized Greenson for his explanations, and told him that he did not understand what Greenson was saying. Greenson could repeat it over and over but he still wouldn't listen or comprehend. Maybe the analyst was right, but it just didn't touch him. This was followed by a silence and the hour ended. It is a response which suggests an introjective identification with an analyst who has failed to properly listen and comprehend.

Greenson reported that he was dissatisfied with this hour and was annoyed at both the patient and himself for not getting more out of it. He felt that he had failed to recognize that the patient wanted to provoke his anger, and Greenson was discontented and angry with himself.

The next day Mr. Z came a few minutes early. (Does this imply that the hour was started before the appointed time?) The patient again hadn't slept well and felt that Greenson had been telling him that he was a fraud. He felt Greenson had seemed to be irritable and he felt that he was being hostilely jabbed. He also felt that Greenson was arguing with him and trying to degrade and humiliate him. He qualified these feelings, but then added that he he didn't need Greenson and wanted to say, "The hell with you. Goodbye!"

Mr. Z then reported that he had dreamt he was walking outside a building. It was an odd combination of a residence and a barn. It was shabby and, through a window, Mr. Z could hear someone talking inside. He was outside and thought that the man should be aware he was being overheard.

The voice was connected with a manager of a company with whom the patient no longer did business. There was a lot of fraudulent behavior in that business. The sleeping pills enabled the patient to hide certain wishes and fears—he was fraudulent. Overhearing the man reminded the patient of hearing his mother and stepfather quarreling. He was angry with Greenson and resistant, and felt that this led Greenson to be annoyed with him. The patient said that he couldn't go on being a failure in business.

Greenson intervened and pointed out the patient's awareness of resentment toward him. He acknowledged that he had been angry with the patient the day before, especially when the patient had said he wasn't listening and found him incomprehensible. In the dream, Mr. Z felt the man should have been aware he was being overheard. Greenson connected this to the patient's "overhearing" his anger and suggested that the patient retaliated by changing his office at home into a shabby combination of house and barn.

It can be seen that Greenson made use of the adaptive context of his countertransference-based anger toward the patient. He attempted to interpret the material in this light, though he did so through a self-revelation. The allusion to the home-office was viewed as a form of fantasied retaliation and not adopted as an important intervention context.

From the communicative viewpoint, the patient's early arrival calls attention once again to the framework of therapy. His feeling that he is a fraud may well be based on an introjective identification with an analyst who purports to do genuine therapeutic work under conditions which make this impossible. The reader will find a striking parallel to this communication in a vignette reported by Lipton (1977), described earlier in this chapter.

Here, the patient had consciously perceived Greenson's hostility and degradation in respect to his interventions in the previous hour. However, the *derivative* implications of this material pertain to the degrading and humiliating qualities of the home-office arrangement.

Much of this is confirmed by the dream, which clearly alludes in derivative form to the dual functions of Greenson's house. The patient sees this as shabby, and as a situation in which his privacy and confidentiality are violated. The question of being overheard may refer to the patient's belief that Greenson's office was insufficiently soundproofed, as well as to sounds and voices which he was able to hear either while waiting for his session or during the hour itself. Clearly, the primal scene qualities of the home-office arrangement are represented dramatically for a second time in this material.

The patient responded to Greenson's intervention which, it should be noted, did approach the home-office issue, doing so through a derivative lie-barrier intervention. Mr. Z stated that he had changed and had become more capable of telling Greenson when he got angry. Greenson's interpretations were of no help to him when he got so angry. Their relationship must be straightened out or he will never make improvements, certainly not through interpretations alone. Greenson's interpretations are of no meaning when he—the patient—has such hostility.

Greenson agreed with the patient and indicated that he should have simply pointed out the patient's anger and fears in response to asking him to stop taking the sleeping pills. He acknowledged that he had become annoyed when the patient refused to listen and suggested that the patient started to degrade him by not listening in return. Mr. Z said he was not at all aware of degrading Greenson, but added that he often felt that Greenson did not know what he was doing. Greenson said that the dream about the house-barn must relate to his combination home and office, the allusions to shabbiness and bad repair an attempt to degrade him in retaliation for the fantasy of being humiliated by his analyst. Once again, this was linked to Greenson's taking away the sleeping pills.

Notice here how the allusion to the home-office is linked to an intrapsychic fantasy within the patient. From the communicative approach, it would be treated as an actuality filled with unconscious implications serving as an adaptive context for the patient's perceptive and fantasied responses. Oddly enough, even though Greenson had acknowledged being angry with the patient, he treated the patient's sense of humiliation as a fantasy rather than in any way a valid appraisal. He also did not, of course, connect the sense of humiliation to the ramifications for the patient of the home-office arrangement.

The patient spoke of all the errors he had committed during the day (another postulated *introjective identification* and valid unconscious perception of aspects of Greenson's erroneous intervention). Greenson then interpreted the patient's *projection* of hostility and self-reproaches onto the analyst as making him untrustworthy and unreliable. This led Mr. Z to experience fears that the analyst would hurt, kill, and humiliate him, which interfered with his ability to relate openly to Greenson and to free associate.

This is, of course, an attempt to interpret the unconscious sources and basis, as well as functions, of the patient's resistances. The intervention is couched in terms of the patient's projections and intrapsychic fantasies; in no way does it deal with the realities of the analyst's interventions and their unconscious implications, or of the home-office setting.

Mr. Z went on to associate about fears of abandonment and depression. After a while, he mentioned that he had come early one day to his session, and had overheard Greenson's wife on the phone. He hated coming early and overhearing things in this house, and would feel terribly embarrassed. Greenson now adds in brackets that he has no waiting room in his house, and that if the patient comes early, the housekeeper opens the door and the patient is invited to sit in the living room, adjacent to the treatment room. This particular revelation serves as an additional selected fact which meaningfully organizes aspects of the patient's material which previously seemed rather disconnected. In a striking way, it offers Type Two derivative validation that the theme of the father's nudity in the living room is indeed a representation of qualities of the home-office arrangement, and that the material related to over-hearing others also pertains to this situation. The housekeeper is, in addition, a third party to treatment who exposes the patient and helps to account for his sense of humiliation.

Greenson suggested that Mr. Z both hates and likes overhearing the analyst's wife. Greenson recognized himself as the manufacturer of the artificial food, and added that while Mr. Z may resent hearing his wife's voice, Greenson thinks he likes to look into the living room and see what's going on in there.

The patient spoke about Greenson's wife's voice and of the living room. The man's voice which the patient overheard was like Greenson's. Greenson responded with another interpretation of the patient's mixed feelings toward him, as both good and fraudulent, and suggested that he and the patient alternate as to who is good and to who is bad, competent or incompetent. This was traced again to Greenson's annoyance the previous day and the patient's need to retaliate.

There are further interchanges which I will not detail here. Greenson believed that a good deal has been accomplished in this second session and felt that he and the patient were working effectively now. He went on to describe in a more condensed fashion several hours which followed. The patient referred again to the living room and to his fear of doing real associating. There is an allusion to Kafka, regarding whom Greenson had expressed some personal opinions. In a later session, the patient reported dreaming of carrying a dictating machine, and of someone trying to taunt and tease him by manhandling the machine which the patient took away from him and got to work. The patient associated to a dictating machine he sees on Greenson's desk—another break in the frame which strongly suggests the absence of total confidentiality and firm boundaries to the analytic setting.

In the final session reported, the patient described a dream of being in a small room the size of Greenson's consultation room. In order to go to the bathroom he goes to another part of the room and locks the door. A husky Negro working man enters in order to use the phone and the patient lets him do this. The intrusion occurs two or three times.

It seems clear that this patient continued to the end of this excerpt to work over his unconscious perceptions and fantasies as they pertain to the home-office arrangement. He attempted in various ways to indicate the unrecognized but actual implications of this analytic setting, and the manner in which it contributed to significant resistances within himself. The patient's efforts to lock the door constitute another representation of the much needed rectification of this framework, a point which goes unheeded by Greenson. Instead, the patient is seen as wishing to resist and keep private much that has to be exposed in analysis. The actual source of this interactional resistance in the breaks in the frame are set to the side, and intrapsychic sources are proposed instead. While both play a role, rectification of the former is the only basis upon which work with the latter could prove effective.

I have tried through this vignette to illustrate some of the differences in the ways in which to formulate the nature, sources, and functions of resistances when approaching material from the classical and communicative viewpoints. The latter centers on prevailing intervention contexts, treating them as realities fraught with unconscious implications on both the realistic and fantasied levels. In contrast, the former stresses almost exclusively the patient's intrapsychic fantasies and defenses, and his projections and distortions, with little attention to the introjective and nondistorted (perceptive) side of his experience. In addition, the clinical decision as to whether the patient is resisting strongly or minimally is quite different in these two approaches. At several junctures in this material, Greenson suggested the presence of powerful resistances, while the communicative evaluation revealed a clear-cut representation of the home-office adaptive context, and a highly meaningful derivative complex—i.e., a low level of resistance.

CONCLUDING COMMENTS

The classical psychoanalytic investigations and views of resistances would benefit considerably from fresh empirical observations. These endeavors should be founded on an approach which sets to the side theoretical prejudices and premature conclusions, and relies upon an unencumbered listening and validating process as a way of rediscovering the sources and natures of resistances. The present classical position is too fixed in its intrapsychic focus, relative denial of contributions from the analyst, and study of transference resistances primarily in terms of conscious rather than unconscious fantasies about the analyst.

While there are signs of discontent and of a broadening understanding, these appear to be isolated islands which have not been picked up by most classical analysts and which do not appear to have influenced, as yet, the main lines of thinking in this area. For example, Bird's (1972) realization that resistances are often used to attack the analyst, or to retaliate for countertransference-based hurts, could open the way to an understanding of the realistic object-related sources of resistances and the realities of their consequences. It could also lead classical analysts to a more careful consideration of the interactional aspects of resistance. Similar trends could derive from Gill's (1979) stress on the immediate precipitants for resistance, and from Lipton's (1977) recognition of introjective-identificatory factors in these obstacles.

There is extensive evidence that resistances are critical expressions of the patient's psychopathology, and that their analysis is a first-order therapeutic task. Such work not only generates insightful inner change, but also deals with the major threats to treatment and to the therapeutic alliance. Since classical analysts tend to stress an ultimately interpretive approach, a full appreciation of the analysis of resistances could lead to a clearer recognition that it is this type of therapeutic work which is best designed to establish and maintain the sound therapeutic alliance. The alliance concept is in some ways the obverse of resistance; all too often manipulative measures have been advocated as means of establishing a sound alliance. The psychoanalytic investigation of resistances should serve as a clear reminder that a strong therapeutic alliance must derive from two sources: the appropriate concern and interventions of the analyst, and the analytic resolution of resistances within the patient (and analyst, if necessary). There are signs that analysts will sometimes respond to resistances with manipulations and noninterpretive interventions, though the bulk of the literature advocates a relatively interpretive approach. This is in contrast to the work with the therapeutic alliance, where all too often interpretive efforts are set to the side. A fuller appreciation of the implications of the resistance literature could well form a basis for a more cogent and sound approach to problems which may arise in respect to the alliance sector.

Chapter Eleven

THE COMMUNICATIVE
APPROACH TO RESISTANCES

This chapter* presents an integrated summary of the communicative approach to resistances. The emphasis is on those aspects of resistance which are conceptualized differently from the prevailing classical viewpoint (see chapter 10), and the techniques which follow from an understanding based on both interactional and intrapsychic considerations. While there are many areas of overlap between the classical and communicative approaches, only passing mention will be made of them; the stress is on areas of reformulation and especially on differences in technique, which will be clinically illustrated.

Resistances are essentially constituted by all behaviors and associations from the patient which in some way oppose or interfere with the procedures and processes of therapy or analysis.** These obstacles pose some threat to the treatment situation itself and to

*This chapter is an extensively revised and expanded version of the paper, "Interactional and Communicative Aspects of Resistance," which appeared in *Contemporary Psychoanalysis*, vol. 16, no. 1, January 1980, pp. 16–52.
**The term therapy here alludes to both psychoanalytic psychotherapy and psychoanalysis unless otherwise specified. The concepts presented here by and large apply equally to both treatment modalities.

therapeutic outcome; as such, they constitute first-order indicators for intervening. As products of the bipersonal field and therapeutic interaction, they must be understood in terms of contributions from both patient and therapist even though they are expressed by the former. Their unconscious and conscious determinants may be viewed along the type of continuum typical for factors within the therapeutic interaction: at one end, resistances which derive primarily from within the patient; and at the other, those that stem primarily from the therapist. Since neither exists in pure form, all resistances have both intrapsychic and interactional components. It seems best to think of all resistances as *interactional resistances*, and then to sort out contributions from the patient and the therapist. However, before such work on resistances can be carried out, we must develop a clear means of recognizing their presence.

ESTABLISHING THE PRESENCE OF RESISTANCE WITHIN THE PATIENT

The formulation that a patient is in a state or expressing some form of resistance is a subjective assessment; it is usually based on the therapist's feelings and his inner state, as well as evaluations of the patient's material. Such an assessment is under the influence of inputs from both the patient and the therapist, and while it constitutes a decision of the latter, it is nonetheless a product of the bipersonal field.

The clinical and theoretical criteria through which resistances may be defined are insufficiently developed in the analytic literature. Several factors can be identified: (1) the subjective feelings of the therapist and his sense that in some way the patient is opposing or sabotaging his therapeutic efforts, proving refractory, or undermining the therapeutic work and goals; (2) blatantly disruptive behaviors; (3) specific associations from the patient which speak for his own awareness that he is opposing the therapeutic process (communications which must, however, be examined for their *latent* implications, especially for Type Two derivative meanings in light of prevailing adaptive contexts); and (4) the therapist's theory of the therapeutic process by which he measures the extent to which the patient is cooperative or oppositional.

Given such complex criteria, and the tendency of therapists to consider resistance almost entirely in terms of obvious manifestations and manifest content communications, confusion seems inevitable. The present discussion will attempt to offer relatively definitive criteria of resistance. However, we must begin with a brief delineation of the communicative theory of the therapeutic process in order to have a sufficient background for further discussion. It should be kept in mind that this is an *empirically derived* theory, which itself must be validated in every session with each and every patient to the greatest extent feasible. It is a distillate of meaningfully related clusters of clinical observations, and not a set of abstractions which should then be imposed upon clinical observations. We must remain open to discordant observations which would call for a revision of the theory. Nonetheless, therapists have some set of expectations and an effort to define them in a broad sense will help to orient us.

The therapeutic process, the nature of a positive therapeutic interaction, and the means of symptom alleviation or resolution, allow many levels of definition. It is necessary to be highly selective and to identify elements which lend themselves to determining the relative presence or absence of resistance. Oddly enough, we will quickly discover that each effort to identify particular dimensions of this process meets with immediate indications of exceptions to the rule. Although some general categorizations are feasible, it seems likely that there is no single process of cure, and that each patient-therapist interaction develops its own means when it is successful.

The simplest approach is to state the ground rules of therapy, and to suggest that adherence to these rules would indicate a lack of resistances. In a sense, this is what Freud actually did (see chapter 10), and on this basis, the patient's silence became the hallmark of resistance. This approach can be expanded in several important ways.

The ground rules of psychotherapy, as I have defined and empirically tested them elsewhere (Langs 1975b, 1979), include the establishment of definite and set hours, length of sessions, and frequency of visits; there are also fixed fees, and set positions for patient and therapist, with the patient either on the couch or sitting face-to-face opposite the therapist; the patient's adherence to the fundamental rule of free association—a commitment to say everything that comes to mind; the therapist's neutrality, anonymity, and use of neutral interventions geared toward interpretation; total privacy and confidentiality; and the rule of abstinence as it applies to both participants.

On this basis, it is possible to state that the patient is resistant when he does not adhere to these basic tenets—when in effect, he modifies the ground rules of treatment. Similarly, counterresistances could be defined in terms of the therapist's deviations from these tenets. A number of gross behavioral resistances may be identified, such as silences, absences, a shift from the chair to the couch or vice versa, and acting in and out—the latter which are forms of inappropriate gratification which violate the rule of abstinence (in itself a tenet which is difficult to define empirically).

Basically, classical analysts have used these criteria of resistance in most of their writings. Nonetheless, some therapists believe that failure to adhere to these basic ground rules need not constitute resistances, and because of this, disagreements arise readily in respect to the issue of their definition.

The communicative approach indicates that virtually all such deviations by patients do indeed constitute oppositions to the therapeutic procedures and disruptions of the therapeutic process. This is true not only by manifest definition; in addition, there is consistent correlation between behaviors of this kind and Type Two derivative material from the patient which reveals conscious and unconscious efforts to disrupt the treatment process. Deviations are often responses to intervention contexts which involve technical errors by the therapist, such as erroneous efforts at interpretations, the use of noninterpretive interventions, and quite frequently the failure to maintain a secure frame—i.e., the patient responds to the therapist's deviation (a counterresistance) with a deviation (resistance) of his own. The resistance aspects of these behaviors stand as such, in spite of recognizing the adaptive or maladaptive value they may have for the patient, and despite the realization that quite often these behaviors are interactional products to which the therapist has contributed the greater part.

Clinically, this particular standard of resistance, as with all such standards, is not to be applied rigidly to a particular therapeutic interlude. Instead, the patient's communicative network as it is organized around the indicator of a break in the fundamental ground rules of treatment should be examined for unconscious meanings and implications. It will be found quite consistently, as stated above, that such material, understood in light of a prevailing adaptive context, reveals not only conscious opposition to the therapeutic procedures but unconscious opposition as well. This material is often filled with meaning pertinent to the unconscious motives for the resistance, and with other dynamic and genetic implications.

It follows from this discussion that psychotherapy is defined in terms of its ground rules, and that the fundamental framework of treatment is an offer to the patient of a setting, hold, container, and relationship with inherently therapeutic qualities, a set of conditions under which the curative process can unfold. This is not to propose that the setting itself is the exclusive vehicle for cure, though as I will discuss below, this may sometimes be the case. But the basic conditions for treatment are an essential context for sound interpretive work, which, of course, is primarily the responsibility of the therapist. Failures in this realm constitute counterresistances, and they can promote significant resistances within the patient.

Using the ground rules of therapy to define resistance is not sufficiently comprehensive to take into account all manifestations of opposition to treatment. While it might be feasible to extend the implications of such ground rules to the point where they could be all-inclusive, it is well to realize that it is possible for a patient who manifestly cooperates can still be in a state of resistance. Clearly, not every patient who is free associating, paying his bill on time, and appearing punctually for all sessions, is in a state of nonresistance. We therefore will need criteria for *communicative resistances.* While it is possible to suggest that subtle or hidden opposition to the therapeutic procedure is inherently an alteration of the rule of abstinence, it seems best to use the ground rules of therapy as gross indicators of resistance and to study them on a manifest and behavioral level, and to establish separate criteria for communicative resistances.

A second broad set of criteria for resistances could evolve from a conception of the curative process itself. The most basic psychoanalytic conception in this regard can be stated as follows. Adaptive structural change evolves from effectively meaningful insights into unconscious processes and contents which form the basis of neuroses. It is therefore the working-through and integration of the therapist's interpretations which produce cure. Such a definition implies, in turn, that the patient provides the therapist with the necessary material for interpretation. In a sense, this could be expressed either through behaviors or verbal-affective associations, with the provision that the behavior itself is such that the patient is willing to and able to understand its implications when interpreted. It may well be that certain behaviors are carried out without such qualities and that they directly gratify the patient or provide avenues of discharge which preclude insight. Despite this caveat, this particular definition of the curative process would center on the determination by the therapist as to whether the patient's communications, whatever their form, ultimately permit interpretation.

Clearly, there are many uncertainties when this delineation of the curative process is used as the basis for evaluating the presence or absence of resistances. There is not only the therapist's subjective evaluation, but also his cognitive ability to comprehend the material and to determine the possibilities of interpretation. While the classical approach has done little to define the criteria for intervening, the communicative approach has been able to develop rather specific guidelines. It is far more feasible to ascertain the extent to which the patient is providing analyzable derivatives in this light as compared to the classical approach, and it is here that the delineation of communicative resistances plays an important role. Nonetheless, the definition of communicative resistances is based mainly on the criterion of the therapeutic process which states that its advancement relies on the patient's unconscious cooperation in producing interpretable material.

This position leaves room for the evaluation of such issues as whether the patient's associations reflect meaningful unconscious dynamics, and whether there is an alternation between current issues and important genetic material. Interpretable material implies an ability to illuminate, to the extent necessary for symptom alleviation, the dynamics and genetics of the patient's neurosis as they specifically unfold in the context of the communicative interaction. This latter proviso is included because of the empirical finding that validated interventions arise only when organized around critical intervention contexts within the therapy.

This description of the therapeutic process recognizes the importance of insights into the dynamics and genetics of the patient's neurosis, and would include both intrapsychic and interactional mechanisms and factors. The question remains, however, whether this is the only vehicle for sound, adaptive cure based on lasting structural change; and this latter concept must be clinically defined for a discussion such as this to have clear meaning. While it is well beyond the scope of the present presentation, we might simply state that such criteria would be founded upon behavioral changes which are founded upon the Type Two derivative validation of the therapist's interventions, and on derivative communications which reveal positive, flexible, and adaptive changes within the patient. Both conscious and unconscious insight would be involved.

The communicative approach has shown that there are several other curative factors within the therapeutic experience. The first relates to the ground rules, setting, containing, and holding capacities of the therapist—abilities which can be distinguished from, and overlap with, his efforts at interpretation. There is clear evidence that a sound holding environment (in essence, adherence to the ground rules of therapy) in itself has curative value for the patient, that, at times, patients can accomplish dramatic and sound symptom resolution entirely without interpretations from the therapist. In earlier works (Langs 1976b, c), I suggested that these effects derive from the ego-enhancing qualities of the secure hold and from introjective identifications of the positive capacities of a therapist capable of sound holding and containing measures— often, in the form of silence in situations where the patient's associations do not call for interpretation. I would supplement this clinical observation with another tentative hypothesis: namely, that under these conditions, patients may themselves work over aspects of their neurosis, doing so largely through the use of Type One derivative interpretations and manifest content realizations. I have the impression, which must be subjected to careful clinical investigation, that the derivative and nonderivative lie-barrier systems derived in this way tend to be relatively nonpathological. They may be termed *soft* or *flexible* (adaptive) lie-barrier systems; but they are not Type Two derivative selfinterpretations, and do not constitute a sensitive understanding of intervention contexts and derivative responses. They are able to promote symptom alleviation, even while based on a type of false insight which touches upon elements of intrapsychic truth while simultaneously denying interactional truths.

Although it is difficult to validate, I have recently developed the thesis that the vast majority of clinical insights into the nature of neuroses and into the therapeutic process itself involve otherwise valid realizations which were arrived at in clinical situations in which they served *functionally* as lie-barrier systems, derivative and nonderivative lie formations designed to seal off more chaotic truths pertinent to the ongoing therapeutic interaction. Most of our understanding of neuroses has been derived in this manner, a proposition that can readily be made by studying the clinical vignettes in the psychoanalytic literature. Therapists who adopt and use this understanding may themselves apply these insights as lie-barrier systems in their own clinical work, failing to realize the counter-resistances involved.

Returning to our main theme, the postulate of the therapeutic effects of a secure hold and of the therapist's containing capacities leads to a conception of resistance which is unlike that defined in terms of the ground rules of therapy. All situations in which the patient accepts the therapist's holding and containing efforts—his management of the framework and ability to contain uninterpretable material (leaving aside for the moment material which can be interpreted)—would constitute a state of relative nonresistance. Efforts to disrupt the therapist's holding and containing capacities, and to modify the framework, constitute expressions of resistance. We would include not only the patient's own alterations of the basic ground rules, but also situations in which the patient attempts to overload the therapist with material beyond his containing capacities. This would happen only when the associations proved uninterpretable, and would constitute a special form of communicative resistance: an inundation of primitive or instinctual-drive derivatives which cannot be interpreted in light of an intervention context. This type of resistance, once identified, also shows how delineation of the curative process can lead to the recognition of previously unnoticed forms of resistance.

At this point, another complicated but important issue must be joined. It must be recognized that patients vary in their needs for specific interpretations. Some patients require relatively few, while others need many. As a rule, such needs are expressed through efforts by the patient to modify the framework in order to create an intervention context in the form of the therapist's maintenance of the boundaries and ground rules of treatment. They then react to this particular context with derivative material which permits interpretation. Sometimes, patients will attempt to evoke erroneous interventions in a therapist largely through the Type B communicative style which contains great interactional pressures. If the therapist makes a mistake—to which, of course, he contributes significantly himself—there then exists another adaptive context which will require interpretive response and rectification.

It can be seen, then, that some patients benefit considerably from the therapist's holding and containing capacities. Others do so for lesser periods of time, primarily in the middle phase of therapy, and create issues which require interpretive responses at other times. By and large, these patients do not show gross behavioral resistances during these interludes, though at times their material does become somewhat hollow and repetitive on the surface.

It follows, however, that it would be somewhat misleading to postulate the presence of important communicative resistances in patients during these holding interludes. While they are certainly resistant in the sense of not conveying material for interpretation, they are not resistant in accepting the holding environment and benefiting from it. During these interludes, these patients tend to develop their own direct and Type One derivative interpretations, often to the point where noticeable adaptive symptom alleviation is achieved. As long as such efforts take place within a sound framework, the lie-barrier systems which the patient develop tend to be flexible, less pathological than previous barrier defenses, and functionally useful.

Before deciding on the question of the presence of communicative resistances, we need a full appreciation of a patient's communicative style, the stage of psychotherapy, and the nature of whatever the patient may be accomplishing. There is strong evidence that all patients require a period of lying fallow, a phase in which they communicate using the Type C mode. Thus, the criteria of resistance established on the basis of the pursuit of insight and the availability of interpretable material (or of guides with which to rectify the frame when necessary) cannot be accepted as relevant to all clinical interludes. We therefore need specific indications of adaptive structural change and of effective self-interpretations—the development of flexible lie-barrier systems—by the patient. It is insufficient simply to identify the presence of communicative resistances; it must also be discovered whether there is an activated adaptive context within the bipersonal field. In the presence of such a context, a failure by the patient to represent the context in his material and to provide meaningful derivative communications would constitute communicative resistance. In a holding environment where such an active and disturbing intervention context is absent, the realization that a patient is not representing a meaningful intervention context or expressing coalescing and interpretable derivatives, would not lead to the conclusion that there is evidence of communicative resistances.

Furthermore, each patient has his own style of working with his therapist toward adaptive symptom resolution. Patients unconsciously create therapeutic and interpretive opportunities, largely by creating framework issues. Those patients who need interpretations do just that, while those who need holding and containing will accept the healthy and secure therapeutic symbiosis as such. It is important, however, to be certain that a patient is not obliterating and avoiding an active intervention context, since this will be crucial to knowing the extent to which the Type C mode is essentially adaptive, as compared to pathologically defensive and maladaptive. The communicative approach indicates that while gross resistances are easily identifiable and consistent in their manifestations, communicative resistances can only be determined in light of a full consideration of the presence or absence of an activated intervention context.

These comments imply another dimension of resistance which deserves to be specified. We have been studying to this point the expressive side of the patient's cooperation: the extent to which he conveys analyzable derivatives or simply does not do so because he is benefiting from the holding environment. We must also turn to the receptive side of the patient's cooperation, and recognize that a critical aspect involves the extent to which the patient meaningfully accepts, introjects, and changes on the basis of the therapist's interpretations, holding and containing efforts, and rectifications of the framework.

In practical terms, the receptive side of the patient's cooperation with the therapist includes his ability to understand interventions, both interpretations and management of the therapeutic environment. Operating on a conscious and unconscious level, this includes acceptance and integration of valid interventions, and engagement in the process of working through as it is geared toward developing new and healthier adaptations. The hallmark of cooperation in this sphere is the patient's creation of a new adaptive context to which he responds with meaningful and interpretable derivatives which then furthers insightful therapeutic work.

Many resistances occur on this receptive side. Some of them are, of course, due to factors within the patient, such as symbiotic and masochistic pathology which give rise to genuine negative therapeutic reactions in which the patient validates an intervention with Type Two derivatives and then regresses, attempts directly to disrupt the treatment process, or indirectly fails to extend the insights just gained. At times, blatant denial follows the direct and indirect acceptance of the therapist's intervention. However, it must be kept in mind that manifest disruptions of the patient's acceptance of the therapist's interventions can also be based on the latter's erroneous efforts. While the first group of resistances are essentially transference-based, the second group are nontransference resistances which are derived primarily from the therapist's countertransferences rather than from the patient's psychopathology. It requires a careful evaluation of the therapist's interpretive and framework management efforts to distinguish these two groups.

A third essential factor in the curative process stems from the therapist's valid interpretations and his maintenance of the holding environment. These efforts lead to positive and ego-enhancing introjective identifications with the well-functioning therapist. As Strachey (1934) made clear in his first extended discussion of this important topic, these adaptive introjects arise only in the presence of the therapist's sound functioning in terms of his responsibility to maintain the therapeutic environment and interpret to the patient. Deliberate and naive efforts to be a so-called good object, and to behave in seemingly supportive ways, actually constitute failures in the therapist's basic responsibilities, and consequently are universally experienced unconsciously in terms of negative, destructive, failing introjects.

Based on this aspect of the therapeutic process, we would have two criteria of resistance: (1) the wish to disrupt the therapist's hold or capacity for interpretation as a way of interfering with inevitable positive introjective identifications; and (2) the need to destroy such positive introjects after initially showing their presence. The latter form of resistance is especially noticeable, for example, with depressed patients who will validate an interpretation both cognitively and interactionally—the latter in terms of speaking of some type of positive figure—only to subsequently destroy the positive introject and its influence. Because these resistances attack the therapeutic process in one of its most essential areas, their understanding and interpretive modification is exceedingly important though quite difficult. Involved are the threatening qualities of positive introjects, including their capacity to disrupt denial defenses within the patient which are maintained and directed against existing negative introjects.

There is a fourth means of cure which has been identified through the communicative approach, though present findings are highly tentative and need clarification. This process involves the patient's unilateral development of soft or flexible lie-barrier systems. Such efforts take place in patients who are capable of accepting the holding environment, but who do not produce interpretable communicative networks. They are usually Type C narrators, and consciously engage, from time to time, in efforts at self-interpretation, much of it in terms of manifest content and Type One derivatives. There is preliminary evidence that such lie-barrier systems can prove adaptive when they involve sound understanding, despite the fact that functionally they are serving as lie-barrier formations against chaotic truths within the therapeutic interaction. It is essential for the therapist to not participate in the development of such lie-barrier systems. If he does, the systems will almost always tend to become hard and inflexible, and quite pathological. The therapist's stance must be that of holding and not interpreting, providing the patient with a serviceable space or environment within which he can shore up his more adaptive defenses. The key problem here is determining whether the patient is developing adaptive or maladaptive lie-barrier systems, and whether it is feasible for such a patient to become accessible to the truth. As noted above, this determination is based on a search for activated intervention contexts. This type of therapeutic gain will occur only in the absence of major and unresolved adaptive contexts.

One final consideration is pertinent. If the therapeutic process is defined as an effort to arrive at the truth of the patient's neurosis as it is activated within the therapeutic interaction, a different though overlapping set of standards with which to measure resistance would be required. This particular definition would integrate other criteria developed in terms of the patient's acceptance of the holding environment and his production of analyzable derivatives which he subsequently comprehends and works through. It would also involve indications of constructive introjective identifications, but it would not accept efforts by the patient to develop lie-barrier systems of any kind.

The pursuit of truth as defined here (Langs 1980a, chapter 12) is probably a standard of the ideal therapeutic process. As a result, it would lead to an ideal or optimal set of criteria for determining the presence of resistances. Patients who attempt to resolve their neurosis through the acceptance of a holding environment *without* the production of analyzable derivatives, and those who hope to develop adaptive lie-barrier systems *without* access to the underlying truths which are thereby sealed off, would be patients who are expressing important forms of resistance. It follows that the therapist would make every appropriate effort to analyze such resistances and enable the patient to arrive at the rich adaptive resources which can be developed only through the integration of various types of truths pertinent to his neurosis and to the ongoing therapeutic interaction.

This implies continued maintenance of the holding environment and the use of interpretations only when feasible. When the patient does not produce analyzable derivatives, active intervention is impossible. Such an effort would not lead to genuine insight and to the adaptive modification of the defense-resistances involved. Instead, it would reflect failures in the therapist's functioning which would generate countertransference-based negative introjects and prove to be an additional unconscious source of further resistances within the patient. Consequently, it may be that resistances in certain patients cannot be interpretively modified, and must be accepted by the therapist. Such patients will not make optimal use of the therapeutic environment and of the potential for insight and adaptive structural change, but will instead generate some type of compromise in which lie-barrier systems, hopefully adaptive, play a role. As a rule, such patients will engage in some measure of analytic work when significant framework issues arise, including termination. In general, they tend to become involved in extremely isolated and constricted periods during which they pursue the truth, spending the rest of their time in therapy developing and elaborating upon—sometimes softening—their lie-barrier systems.

We may conclude, then, that the definition of the therapeutic process may take as its standard either the ideal therapeutic procedure—the pursuit of truth—or the practical finding that some patients engage in this pursuit to a significant degree, while others do not. The therapist's conclusions regarding the patient's resistances will vary in keeping with differences in these two standards. However, the technique of listening and intervening would remain the same; both standards involve evaluations of activated intervention contexts and derivative complexes, viewed in light of indicators.

Theoretically, it seems preferable to adopt the ideal standard, and to view all departures from it as some form of resistance. This encourages the therapist to pursue interpretive efforts wherever possible, and to not accept, and especially to not join, the patient's search for lie-barrier systems. Within that context, realizing that some patients will not risk the pursuit of truth will provide an important perspective in regard to his resistances, and promote the understanding that some resistances cannot be modified through interpretive work.

Still, there is a fine but crucial line between accepting the limitations of the analytic process and actively supporting, consciously or unconsciously, the patient's resistances. This is especially pertinent in light of the finding that every patient requires a period of Type C communication during which he accepts the holding environment and does not actively engage in analytic work directed toward insight. Even those patients naturally prone to use the

Type A communicative mode will develop periods of Type C communication, during which they make use of their residual lie-barrier systems. There is considerable evidence that truth as it pertains to the patient's neurosis and the therapeutic interaction is extremely burdensome and threatening, and that it will be sought after only as much as is absolutely necessary, and no more. By and large, it is at times when the framework has been broken, by either patient or therapist, and other periods of acute symptom remission and life crisis, that patients tend to express themselves in the Type A mode.

SUBJECTIVE FACTORS IN DETERMINING THE PRESENCE OF RESISTANCES

We have reviewed a number of criteria which may serve as standards for determining the presence or absence of resistances. This problem can also be approached in terms of the specific determination by the therapist of whether a patient's associations and behaviors provide meaningful material for interpretation. This standard depends heavily on the therapist's conception of the implications of the patient's communications. Clearly, therapists who believe that the patient's manifest associations have meaning for his neurosis, and that addressing the surface of the patient's material can lead to symptom alleviation, will focus on the manifest implications of the patient's associations and arrive at determinations regarding resistance on that basis. Despite the fact that such work does not involve unconscious processes and mechanisms, and runs contrary to the most basic psychoanalytic conception of neuroses, there is ample evidence that many analysts and therapists work with their patients on this level, far more often than generally realized. Many therapists have adopted this type of approach as part of their fundamental therapeutic efforts.

Similarly, therapists who work primarily with Type One derivatives, with intrapsychically focused inferences derived from the patient's material, will have another set of criteria of resistance. These would involve impressions of the availability of derivatives which can be translated into underlying themes without any allusion to an adaptive context. Finally, therapists who have found that only analysis of Type Two derivatives organized around specific intervention contexts produces meaningful, insightful cure will have their own criteria of resistance.

The therapist's subjective evaluation of the patient's material also depends upon the manner in which he listens to and organizes the patient's behaviors and associations, and on the type of validating process, if any, that he applies to his interventions. The manifest content therapist will take the patient's direct agreement with his interventions as a sign of low resistance, paying little attention to the patient's subsequent material for unconscious implications related to validation or its absence, and to resistance. A Type One derivative therapist will accept virtually any extension of his intervention, no matter how repetitive or unoriginal, as validation, and will consider any new material to be a reflection of the correctness of his intervention. He will not examine the patient's fresh associations for unconscious commentaries on the intervention and for the possibility that such material is designed unconsciously either to correct or cure the therapist, or to interpret to him the nature and basis of an error. New material is accepted as a sign of low resistance and not examined for its *functional capacity*—for its implications in terms of the spiraling communicative interaction.

In contrast, the communicative therapist will require a selected fact or truly unique response to his intervention as a basis for its confirmation. Such material will of necessity shed new light on the patient's neurosis and serve to organize previously disparate material, giving it new meaning in terms of some type of constant conjunction. Following such validation, he is then in a position to observe whether the patient continues to elaborate upon the newly discovered realizations, or begins to obstruct the communicative interchange. Throughout this sequence, the communicative therapist has specific criteria of resistances as they apply to the patient's associations and their *derivative* implications. These will be discussed in greater detail below.

For the manifest content and Type One derivative therapist, the patient's manifest disagreement or failure to extend a Type One derivative-based intervention is virtually always taken as a sign of resistance. There is little indication in the psychoanalytic literature that such therapists are prepared to take this type of nonconfirmation as a genuine indication that their intervention is in error. As a result, they are virtually unable to distinguish between resistances evoked by their mistakes and those which derive primarily from valid work and the patient's intrapsychic anxieties and pathological unconscious fantasy constellations. They tend to be highly prejudiced toward formulating resistances in the presence of nonconfirmation, and relatively refractory to other possibilities.

In contrast, the communicative therapist will accept the absence of Type Two derivative validation of an intervention as an indication that he has been in error. The disturbance in the positive flow of the therapeutic process is not conceptualized immediately as a transference resistance. At times, when the patient reacts to the error with meaningful derivative communication and with a clear representation of the erroneous intervention context, such a therapist would see the patient in a state of relative low communicative resistance, while another type of therapist might think otherwise. Other times, when the patient's subsequent associations are nonrevealing, the communicative therapist would formulate the presence of nontransference resistances and recognize his own contribution to their presence. It is to be stressed that when instead, the patient unconsciously works over a pathological introject based on a countertransference-based intervention, and becomes involved in unconscious interpretations and correctives directed toward the therapist (thereby engaging in efforts to place the therapeutic process and the therapist back on the right track), these efforts, understood in light of the prevailing adaptive context, reflect a relative absence of resistance. On the whole, in this area there is considerable divergence between the prevailing classical and communicative viewpoints, as I discussed toward the end of chapter 10.

There are many other subjective factors, far more difficult to define, in the therapist's evaluation that the patient is in a state of resistance or that a particular communicative interlude or behavior reflects resistances. Many of these can be minimized by developing clear-cut criteria of resistance on gross behavioral and communicative levels. Other factors involve influences that touch upon problems related to countertransference. These would include the therapist's general value systems, his understanding of acting out, the nature of his personality and character structure, and his particular feelings toward a given patient. Ideally, the therapist should be aware of these factors and minimize their effects on his understanding of the patient. Nonetheless, such elements may play a role in these evaluations, and should be searched for whenever the therapist makes a determination that an important resistance exists within the patient.

Another, overlapping factor involves shared countertransference-based attitudes, theories, and clinical practices through which certain types of associations and behaviors of the patient are identified as resistances primarily because of a prevailing attitude or value within the field. I have already alluded to instances of this kind in my discussion of therapists and analysts who work on the manifest content and Type-One derivative levels. In a different vein, many resistances expressed through deviations by the patient in the ground rules and framework tend to be missed on this basis.

It would take us too far afield to attempt a listing of errors of this kind. They involve critical blindspots and sources of inappropriate defensiveness and gratification for the therapist which are detrimental to the patient and which unconsciously contribute to and reinforce his own resistances. Errors in evaluation of this kind can be recognized only if a therapist applies the stringent criteria of Type Two derivative validation to interventions which involve purported resistances, and through application of the basic listening process during periods assessed as low in resistance. Efforts of this type could rather quickly lead to important revisions in the classical psychoanalytic view of resistances, and redress many wrongs done to patients in the guise of confronting resistances (see Klauber 1968).

These considerations touch upon the classification of resistances into those which are overt and those which are silent. The insights generated by the communicative approach suggest that all resistances find actual expression within or outside the therapeutic interaction, though either as gross behaviors or on a communicative level. In this light, the silent resistances described by classical psychoanalysts, and for which Glover (1955) proposed the questionable criterion of the analyst's lack of any awareness of obstacles to the therapeutic process, in fact appear to be resistances which have been expressed by the patient on a communicative level, but of which the therapist is unaware. Silent resistances, then, are a product of the therapist's counterresistances, his blind spots and prejudices which lead him to fail to realize the resistance implications of a particular behavior or sequence of associations. As a rule, such resistances exist for a long period of time and lead to either a seemingly successful termination which takes place based on the development of lie-barrier systems rather than through genuine insight and structural change; or to any one of a number of negative outcomes such as a stalemated therapy, failure by the patient to resolve his symptoms, exacerbation of symptoms or development of new disturbances, crises in treatment, and precipitous and premature terminations.

The identification of resistances which classical analysts tend to miss depends on basic revisions in their understanding of the therapeutic process and of neuroses. The communicative approach has been designed as such a corrective, and there is considerable evidence that it provides a sound basis for the identification of resistances which greatly diminishes the incidence of failures to identify their presence. Almost entirely, resistances which are missed by a communicative therapist go unrecognized because of specific countertransferences.

MANIFESTATIONS OF RESISTANCE

Previous studies of resistance have used as their criteria selected failures by the patient to comply with the ground rules of therapy, certain types of voids in the patient's manifest associations, a number of qualities of these associations such as repetitiveness and the absence of dreams, and a broad, ill-defined group of behaviors termed acting out and acting in. The emphasis has been on the patient's behaviors, crass and subtle, with little attempt to judge the presence and meanings of a resistance through an analysis of the patient's associations. Some of these signs of resistance are behavioral while others are communicative, though the latter is confined to the manifest level.

Through the communicative approach, we arrive at two basic categories of resistance: *gross behavioral expressions* and *communicative*. The former involve all types of failures to comply with any of the basic ground rules of therapy and manifest disturbances in the patient's associational flow—e.g., repetitiveness, direct opposition to treatment, and silences. The second group can be identified only with an analysis of the communicative network. While both groups of resistance indicate some type of opposition to analytic

procedures, each has a distinctive constellation of properties. With
each, the expression of resistance may be carried out knowingly or
unwittingly, consciously or unconsciously.

Gross behavioral resistances entail any subtle or crass behavior
which suggests opposition to, or bypassing of, the basic therapeutic process. With the standard of adherence to the ground rules,
it becomes relatively easy to identify one group of gross behavioral
resistances: they involve a break in the basic framework of treatment. While each such resistance has specific implications depending on the particular ground rule which is violated, it shares a
number of attributes seen in all modifications in the frame. Gross
behavioral resistances involve a variety of efforts to achieve direct
gratification of pathological instinctual drive needs as well as
pathological superego sanctions and the reinforcement of pathological defenses. Ruptures in the therapeutic environment also
function as resistances in producing symptom alleviation through
framework deviation cures (Langs 1979) which stand in direct
opposition to efforts directed at insightful symptom relief. All such
endeavors prove to be means of reinforcing the patient's neurosis or
modifying his symptoms without insight, and of attempting to
obtain direct gratification in the relationship with the therapist in
a way that precludes the search for sound insight, which is founded
on the frustration of such needs—the rule of abstinence.

Other behaviors, such as monotonous free associations and certain types of involvements with persons outside of treatment, are
more difficult to identify as expressions of resistance with any
degree of certainty. This type of behavior may, however, function
as a resistance at one juncture in therapy and not at another. In
these situations, the therapist must turn to the communicative
network in order to determine, first, whether the derivatives reveal
unconscious resistances latent in the behavior, and second, whether
the behavior is associated with a resistant communicative network.
In each instance, some form of resistance is undoubtedly involved.
In contrast, when the unconscious implications of a particular
behavior appear to be adaptive or to communicate meaningful
derivatives which can be submitted to interpretive analysis, or
where the accompanying derivative network itself yields meaning,
the conclusion must be drawn that the behavior is relatively adaptive and essentially nonresistant.

Gross behavioral resistances may be enacted with or without a conscious wish to disrupt treatment. In either case, however, it is always based on some unconscious fantasy or perception constellation, and analytic resolution depends on the specific identification of these underlying factors. Conscious resistances are ego-syntonic, while unconscious resistances are often ego-alien. In either form, the resistance qualities must be identified through an analysis of the accompanying derivative network.

Gross behavioral resistances are *indicators for intervening, therapeutic contexts.* Since they entail disruptions of the therapeutic procedures, they require analytic resolution before meaningful interpretations are feasible in any other sphere. As a rule, the presence of such resistances constitutes a means of maintaining a maladaptive resolution to the conflicts which underlie the patient's neurosis. As such, they markedly diminish the patient's motivation to deal with his intrapsychic and interactional problems in any other way, especially through the pursuit of insight and understanding.

Communicative resistances are also first-order indicators and therapeutic contexts. As such, they convey the efforts of the patient, usually unconscious, to destroy meaningful communication and potential for interpretation. As is true for gross behavioral resistances, they are unconsciously designed to protect the patient—and therapist—from danger situations, and from threatening unconscious fantasy and perception constellations. They provide, however, an especially difficult therapeutic challenge in that their presence interferes with understanding and interpretation. The difficulty is one of degree: in the presence of major communicative resistances, often no intervention is possible—especially when the framework is already secure; in the presence of a relatively low degree of resistance, however, it may be possible to develop an interpretation based on the meaningful material which escapes the patient's defensive operations.

Both gross behavioral and communicative resistances indicate efforts by the patient to interfere with the therapeutic process. As such, they reveal little of their unconscious meanings and sources. On occasion, the particular form that a resistance takes reflects an aspect of the underlying unconscious fantasy or perception constellation, and therefore is inherently meaningful. In such cases, the resistance itself is a meaningful part of the communicative network. This situation often obtains in the presence of nontransference resistances based on the therapist's countertransferences; the patient often unconsciously chooses a form of resistance which is a facsimile or disguised version of the therapist's counterresistances. For example, when a therapist incorrectly extends a session, the patient is often late for the next hour. In the absence of this type of input from the therapist, lateness or periods of silence in a session may reflect the patient's tendency to utilize denial and obliterating defenses against unconscious fantasies and perceptions which are threatening his awareness. However, it is well to recognize that such meanings are quite thin and unsubstantial, and that the meaningful interpretation of resistance requires a coalescing derivative complex and will not find substantial validation through simple, direct derivative translations.

COMMUNICATIVE RESISTANCES

The total *communicative network* includes *indicators* for intervening derived from the therapeutic interaction and from the life of the patient, the prevailing *intervention context* (adaptive context), and the *derivative complex*. If we identify the ideal communicative network, we can use it as a standard against which to measure the presence of resistances and their strength.

We begin with indicators. It is essential that the patient express in some form his external life concerns, problems within the therapist and therapeutic interaction, and the disturbances in his own inner mental state which require interventions from the therapist. Each session has the potential for being a mini-analysis in which one or more indicators are interpreted to the patient, or handled through necessary rectifications of the framework. It is through such work that insightful symptom resolution is built.

In the ideal session, the patient finds some means rather early in the hour of indicating the most important disturbances with which he is currently dealing. He might mention a quarrel with his wife in which he behaved irrationally, a symptom of anxiety, or he might have missed the previous hour. Indicators may be categorized as (1) those which arise from the therapist's errors, and more rarely, his correct interventions, in terms of both managements of the framework and interpretations; (2) those which stem from the patient's efforts to modify the framework; (3) those reflected in other gross behavioral and communicative resistances; and (4) those which arise from disturbances in the patient's inner mental life and his relationship with others outside of therapy. Passing mention of a problem of this kind, and early evidence of one or another form of resistance, presents the ideal opportunity for interpretive work pertinent to the patient's illness.

Resistances are in evidence primarily when the patient fails to mention or clearly represent an activated indicator. Most commonly this resistance arises when the therapist has modified the framework. Because of the dangerous unconscious perceptions and introjects generated under these circumstances and because of the patient's own investment in framework deviation cures, it is common for the patient to repress all allusion to that particular type of indicator. Repression may also be applied to symptoms within the patient and to other disturbances within the therapeutic interaction. Conscious feelings of resistance may also be suppressed, and sometimes patients knowingly conceal indicators for a variety of pathological reasons.

In general, this is the sphere of communication within which resistances tend to be the least powerful. Nonetheless, some patients produce meaningful derivative communications in the absence of an indentified indicator; more frequently, indicators are repressed when there are powerful resistances directed against the remainder of the communicative network. Failures to represent indicators suggest that the therapist and patient are in unconscious collusion and have produced a misalliance or framework deviation cure, affording the patient powerful lie-barrier systems through which his neurosis and other expressions of pathology have been sealed off. This type of massive repression may also take place when a patient is enormously threatened by the therapeutic hold and proc· ess, and by the primitive qualities of his own inner mental world. He responds by erecting intense lie-barrier systems which obliterate the communication of indicators, and sometimes even the experience of them.

The second element in the communicative network is the adaptive context—the intervention context, and more specifically those aspects of the therapist's interventions which are evocative of, or most pertinent to, the patient's neurosis. So rarely will a neurosis-related adaptive context pertain to some outside event or relationship, that we will concentrate here on intervention contexts and their representation in the material from the patient. It is this aspect of the derivative network which proves to be most crucial to the possibilities of interpretation. Because of this, when the patient applies defense-resistances to the representation of the activated adaptive contexts, interventions are often difficult to make and sometimes it proves impossible to do so without violating important technical principles—which would constitute a countertransference-based intervention which would become a new intervention context overshadowing the precipitant under repression.

In the ideal communicative network—i.e., one with little or no resistance—the intervention context will be mentioned by the patient quite directly, either in its entirety or through some reference to a fragment of the precipitant. Usually this is done in passing, as though the patient hardly noticed the context or had hardly responded to it. Characteristically, the patient's defenses are such that the largest part of his reaction to a neurosis-related adaptive context takes place on an unconscious level, and is therefore reflected in derivative communications rather than in conscious thoughts and fantasies. On occasion, however, such a context may be mentioned specifically and the patient may include some direct associations, though always, if the material is to be related to the patient's neurosis—i.e., to unconscious fantasy and perception constellations—he must soon shift to indirect communication.

When the intervention context is alluded to manifestly we have a situation of undisguised representation and a relatively low level of resistance. All other representations of the intervention context contain some degree of disguise. It has proved helpful for the therapist to evaluate the degree of distortion in terms of a ten-point scale, with ten involving the clearest representations of the context and the lowest levels of resistance. A direct reference to the context, then, would receive a rating of ten, while a context which appears virtually unrepresented in the patient's associations would receive a rating of zero. This type of scaling provides the therapist with a sense of the relative weight of resistances with which he is dealing, and fosters interventions and rectifications of the framework in the resistance sphere before all other types of therapeutic effort.

In addition to direct representations of the adaptive-intervention context, there are the following additional possibilities, listed in order of increasing defensiveness and disguise: (1) representation by displacement to some other aspect of the therapeutic interaction aside from the main intervention context; (2) representations of the context through experiences and relationships outside of the therapy; and (3) the absence of any apparently meaningful representation of the intervention context.

The evaluation of the presence and implications of an adaptive context in the actual clinical situation often proves to be a complex determination, one that is distinctly an interactional product. The therapist enters the session without desire, memory, or understanding. The patient's behaviors and associations begin to prompt the recall of the previous session, which the therapist experiences both at the behest of the patient's material and in terms of his own tendencies toward remembering. The patient provides two types of clues in respect to a particular adaptive context: direct or indirect representations of the context itself, and communication of a cluster of derivatives which point to a given context. This latter is best conceived of as the communication of a *preconception* (Bion 1962), an unfulfilled, tension-producing cluster of associations that can be organized, understood, and given a sense of closure only through the identification of a particular adaptive context which unites the material into a meaningful whole and thereby yields a *saturated conception*. To these are added the therapist's own recollections of the prevailing context which may be highly accurate or quite defensive. Clearly, a sorting process is required in which both the material from the patient and the therapist's subjective reactions are repeatedly assessed.

In the usual clinical situation, there is more than one major adaptive context. While at times, a single context overshadows all others, there are more often, two or more contexts, whose implications need to be identified and which require ranking in order of importance—an effort made on the basis of the patient's material and the therapist's own subjective evaluation. It is characteristic for the patient to represent one context while repressing the other, thereby subjecting the latter to resistances. Often, the derivatives will organize relatively well around the clearly represented context, providing it with considerable meaning in terms of both fantasy and perception constellations. The clinical decision, then, revolves around the importance of the represented adaptive context-derivative complex, as compared to the constellation which has been subjected to repression-resistance. Here, the therapist must use his own human sensibilities and his sense of order of importance in respect to context, modifying his thinking based on a careful evaluation of the patient's derivative communications. In intervening, it is well to deal with the material which lends itself readily to interpretation, and to offer some hint as to what is being left out. It is here that important nuances of clinical judgment come into play.

One of the most vital aspects of this type of evaluation is the need to fully comprehend the unconscious communicative messages contained in the adaptive-intervention context. The therapist's attitudes, silences, managements of the framework, and verbal-affective interventions are actualities filled with unconscious meaning, and an essential part of the spiraling communicative interaction between patient and therapist. The patient's conscious, and especially his unconscious, reactions cannot be formulated without a full appreciation of these implications. The therapist is guided here through efforts at self-analysis and intuitive self-knowledge, and by the patient's responsive associations—especially his derivative communications. The latter are *not* treated as inherently transference-based, and therefore distorted and pathological, but instead are viewed as *commentaries* on the intervention at hand—a mixture heavily laden with valid unconscious perceptions and introjects, to which are added distorting and pathological components. These are *transversal* communications which bridge a number of polarities: transference and nontransference, truth and falsification, introjection and projection, defensiveness and revelation. Ultimately, it is the therapist's capacity to understand the patient's material, to know himself and the implications of his interventions, which prove crucial. Full appreciation of the therapist's unconscious communications to the patient, expressions to which the latter is exquisitely sensitive, is a much neglected aspect of the listening process. Without it, any attempt to evaluate the nature and extent of the patient's resistances must prove either limited or essentially erroneous.

Since both the indicators and the derivative complex constitute, as a rule, adaptive responses to the manifest and latent implications of the intervention context, it can readily be seen how the latter is vital to the possibility of interpretation or rectification of the frame. While it is possible to intervene in the absence of a clearly represented adaptive context (especially when it involves a modification in the fixed frame, through the playback of selected, pertinent derivatives; see chapter 12), resistances of this kind are often quite successful in precluding sound interventions from the therapist.

The derivative complex, which contains the disguised expressions of the patient's unconscious perception and fantasy constellations as they pertain to an activated intervention context, is the final major component of the communicative network. Its dimensions are complex and varied. As we know, associations and behaviors which are afforded specific meaning in light of an intervention context are termed *Type Two derivatives*. The ideal derivative complex contains what I have termed *coalescing derivatives*, group of associations which illuminate through indirect communication various dimensions of the patient's valid and distorted perceptions of, and responses to, the activated context.

Coalescing derivatives bring to light such diverse reactions to a precipitant as the patient's unconscious perception of the therapist's unconscious communications and his underlying motives; unconscious interpretations to an errant therapist; Type Two derivative validation to a therapist who has intervened correctly; representations of the genetic meanings of the context for the patient; distorted and distorting responsive fantasies and behaviors (transference); and allusions to the unspoken implications of the therapist's interventions for the ongoing therapeutic interaction. In all, these are meaningful clusters of derivatives that illuminate the implications of the adaptive context from many vantage points, and which reflect in essence the patient's adaptive and maladaptive responses. It is especially important that the unconscious aspects, and those elements which allude to important instinctual drive derivatives and dynamics and to critical genetic factors, be allowed to unfold. Finally, it is essential that the meanings derived be organized around the prevailing intervention context and not treated as isolated derivatives—translation derivatives or Type One derivatives, as I have termed them. In all, the comprehension of the derivative complex draws upon the therapist's knowledge of his patient, unconscious processes and contents, and himself, in terms of the totality of his understanding of the psychology of human behavior and communication.

There is a final element to the derivative complex which is related to the presence or absence of resistance. In order to intervene, the therapist requires a *link* or *bridge* to the therapeutic relationship or situation. The *link* is conveyed when a patient represents an adaptive context either directly or through some derivative related to the treatment situation. The *bridge* is a relatively nonspecific allusion to the treatment situation. It enables the therapist. to connect all of the material to the therapeutic interaction, and when a bridge appears toward the latter part of a session, it especially facilitates an interpretation or effort to manage the framework. The absence of a bridge is an expression of resistance.

To summarize, on the communicative level, the relatively nonresistant patient expresses the indicators for the hour quite directly, represents the adaptive context manifestly or with little disguise, offers a set of diversely meaningful, coalescing derivatives, and provides a clear-cut bridge between the associational network and the therapeutic interaction. Such material is ideal for interpretive or framework management efforts. Various degrees and types of communicative resistances can be identified by recognizing the presence of obscuring factors in each of the three major components of the communicative network, factors which make intervening problematic.

Evaluation of the level of resistance in the derivative complex poses a number of problems. The patient's defenses may so disturb this complex that it is flat and empty. The associations may prove to be nonilluminating vis-à-vis the prevailing adaptive context. The material may be relatively unrelated to the context, or fixed and repetitive, involving the replay of one or more manifest themes in a flat and empty way that deprives the associational complex of any sense of depth, variation, or nuance. At other times, the derivatives may be fragmented and scattered, providing little in the way of organizable latent content and involving dispersed communicative elements that cannot be coalesced meaningfully around the prevailing precipitants. At other times, there may be a rich and varied level of manifest associations which nonetheless do not give unified latent meaning to the implications of the prevailing adaptive context. We need a classification of communicative resistances as they apply to the derivative complex; but the blunting, fragmenting, and dispersed types of derivative complexes characterize some of their major forms.

Resistances may also attack the meaningful links between the indicators and the adaptive context, and between the adaptive context and the derivative complex. The connections between these separate but related pairings may be obscured, fragmented, or nonexistent, making it difficult to establish a clear-cut connection between the adaptation-evoking stimulus and the patient's derivative responses—symptomatic and communicative. Another common gap occurs when the patient fails to provide a bridge to the therapeutic relationship in the latter part of the hour, especially in the presence of heavily disguised allusions to the prevailing neurotic adaptive context.

In sum, the patient's resistances may attack one or more components of the communicative network, or the relationship between these components. It is essential to evaluate the level of expression and clarity of the patient's latent or derivative material; and its inverse is the level of resistance. This type of evaluation brings to the fore the therapist's thinking about the patient's resistances and defenses, and promotes an interpretive and rectifying approach. It also must be stressed, as will be discussed presently, that it is important to maintain an interpretive approach to these resistances, endeavoring to identify their unconscious sources, functions, and meanings by taking the prevailing adaptive context as the point of departure. It is somewhat easier for therapists to interpret gross behavioral resistances in the presence of an essentially nonresistant communicative network, and far more difficult to interpret the basis for communicative resistances themselves. It is also quite frustrating for a therapist to be confronted with critical gross behavioral resistances in the presence of a highly resistant communicative network, a situation which is often ominous for the future of the treatment. Nonetheless, it is essential that the therapist have faith in the patient's own ability to resolve his resistances. It is also well to recognize the disturbing, counterresistant aspects of confrontations and other inappropriate interventions in response to these overt and communicative obstacles to the therapeutic process.

WHAT IS BEING WARDED OFF

From the communicative approach, we may develop three inter-related categories which pertain to the protective and adaptive aspects of resistance and to the specifics of what they ward off. A resistance may, by design, protect the patient—and often, the therapist—from: (1) threatening perceptions of the therapist; (2) threatening fantasies about the therapist; or (3) threatening perceptions and fantasies related to persons outside of the therapeutic relationship, but which usually have a significant bearing on the therapeutic interaction. In each category, the fantasies or perceptions may be conscious or unconscious. Inherent to this classification is the distinction between intrapsychic and interactional sources of resistance, though the interplay of the two is fully acknowledged. This classification would also permit an understanding of all resistances designed to obstruct the analytic resolution of both transference and nontransference fantasies and responses, and allow for understanding the ways in which manifest allusions to the therapist are used in the service of resistance.

Perhaps the most broadly overlooked source of resistances within the patient lie within the interventions of the therapist—adaptive-intervention contexts. These may arise in response to a valid or incorrect interpretation, as well as to the therapist's efforts to either secure the frame or his deviation from the ideal therapeutic environment. Responses to correct interpretations and securing of the framework are characterized by Type Two derivative validation, while the other two categories of interventions do not receive this type of confirmation.

A correct interpretation exposes the patient to the therapist as a sound figure, to a new level of understanding in respect to the therapeutic interaction and to the patient's own inner mental world, and to an unconscious positive introject. This type of experience is growth-promoting, ego-enhancing, and productive of new and more constructive levels of adaptation and conflict resolution.

However, in addition to these positive effects, this type of interlude poses a series of threats for the patient which usually evoke resistances. Most common among the sources of this type of resistance is the patient's envy of a well-functioning therapist, his dread of the loss of his previous level of adaptation (however maladaptive), his fear of functioning with new resources, and his dread of further regression and analytic work. Conscious insight often produces a sense of disequilibrium and disturbance, especially as it fosters the patient's realization of previously unrecognized or repressed problems within himself and in his relationships with the therapist and others. There is also considerable danger of disequilibrium evoked by the introjective identification of a good object (the therapist), where equilibrium has been based on the use of defensive denial and other forms of defensiveness that tolerate and seal off the influences of negative introjects. Realization of a positive introject can therefore have devastating consequences, an experience which promotes further therapeutic work, though as a rule it initially stimulates the mobilization of strong defenses and resistances.

An incorrect interpretation is countertransference-based and constitutes a projection, projective identification, and expression to the patient of the therapist's own psychopathology and pathological unconscious fantasies and perceptions. It contains elements from each of the psychic macrostructures, and may also function as the offer of a Type C lie-barrier system designed to wall off disturbances within the ongoing therapeutic interaction. In response, the patient will become engaged in unconsciously therapeutic and curative efforts, though he will also attempt to exploit the therapist's countertransferences for purposes of both resistance and pathological gratification.

It is in this sphere that the therapist's counterresistances and his broader countertransferences contribute significantly to the patient's own resistances. There is a maxim that the best resistance a patient can utilize is one which is offered or sanctioned by the therapist (Langs 1976b). Patients are exquisitely, though unconsciously, sensitive to such offers, and will characteristically exploit their presence.

Resistances which arise as the result of erroneous interventions may entail, therefore, the unconscious sharing of defensive formations with the therapist, in terms of either derivative defenses such as repression, or obliterating and nonderivative defenses such as Type C barriers and some forms of denial. These resistances may also be a response to the threat experienced when the therapist makes a mistake, when he interactionally projects aspects of his own pathology into the patient, and when he otherwise expresses himself in terms of his own pathological needs rather than the therapeutic needs of the patient. Extreme forms of this type of reaction are seen when the therapist responds noninterpretively with such interventions as questions, clarifications, confrontations, and especially noninterpretive interventions such as advice, manipulation, and the like (see chapter 12). These resistances are based on valid perceptions and introjections of the therapist and his pathology, and often constitute the most *adaptive* response possible under the circumstances. This last point deserves emphasis since therapists seldom appreciate the constructive qualities of resistances which stem from their own countertransference-based interventions. Any attempt to attack such resistances through confrontation, or by interpreting their purported meaning without addressing the sources from the therapist, is bound to fail. Often, such efforts, which constitute further countertransference-based interventions, lead to an intensification of the patient's resistances, sometimes to the point of premature termination.

Resistances commonly arise in the adaptive context of the therapist's efforts to create and manage an ideal therapeutic environment. Efforts to create a secure setting and to rectify the therapist's own breaches in the frame, as well as those which arise from the patient, constitute framework management interventions (e.g., maintaining responsibility for a missed session, keeping hours as agreed upon rather than changing the time of a particular session, or correcting a mistaken bill). They are a class of interventions which have strikingly contradictory implications for each patient. These measures offer the patient an optimal therapeutic environment and hold, and a safe space for the unfolding of the therapeutic work and the expression of his neurosis-related derivatives—both perceptions and fantasies. In addition, however, such a setting constitutes conditions under which the patient will adaptively regress and experience the most disturbing and primitive aspects of his inner mental world, as well as highly disturbing unconscious perceptions of the therapist. It follows that this optimal setting also poses a series of specific dangers to the patient, and he will defend himself against these threats with resistances.

These particular obstacles to the treatment situation are often constituted through efforts by the patient to unilaterally modify one or more of the ground rules, and to thereby alter the therapeutic setting in the direction of a framework deviation cure, (Langs 1979). The communicative approach has shown that such efforts to alter the frame express in all cases some degree of resistance, and that the therapist's appropriate response is to both interpret the implications of the patient's proposal or behavior and to maintain the security of the setting—all at the behest of the patient's derivative communications, which consistently point in these directions. Thus, while we may clearly establish the importance of clear-cut boundaries and a secure setting for the treatment process, it is critical to not overlook the dangers they create for the patient and the ways in which they become the source of usually quite analyzable resistances.

While framework management responses by the therapist in the direction of securing the frame characteristically obtain Type Two derivative validation, those interventions in which the therapist accepts a patient's deviation or invokes a modification of the frame himself will typically generate nonvalidating responses and negative introjects. This type of intervention is countertransference-based and generates resistances whose sources are comparable to those seen with erroneous interpretations. (The secure frame is comparable to a correct interpretation.) However, because the issues pertain to the basic therapeutic hold and environment, and to the core matrix of the treatment relationship, the patient's resistances are likely to be more intense in this area than with an erroneous interpretation, and more fixed as well—at least until the framework has been rectified and the necessary interpretations made. It seems likely that the largest overlooked source of resistances within patients arise from the therapist's acceptance or invocation of a deviation in the framework, and from the dangers so derived. Typically, the situation alternates between highly resistant communicative networks and the presence of gross behavioral resistances, and interludes in which the patient communicates through intensely expressive derivative networks whose meanings and functions can only be properly understood in terms of the adaptive context of the prevailing contribution by the therapist to the break in the frame.

After resistances within the therapeutic interaction are recognized, rectified, and interpreted, access to and therapeutic work with primarily intrapsychically founded resistances is feasible. In this sphere, the therapist will be dealing with a hierarchy of danger situations ranging from separation to castration, with disturbing affects such as anxiety and depression, and with fantasy-memory constellations which form the genetic and contemporary basis for intrapsychic conflict and ego dysfunctions. Together, they promote the expressions of pathological instinctual drives, all of which may prompt resistance responses.

Every conceivable type of unconscious fantasy, memory, and introject, and every type of disturbing perception and content may evoke resistances within the patient. These can be recognized and understood through an analysis of the communicative network, and must always be organized around an activated adaptive context. The communicative approach has demonstrated that conceptualizing resistances in terms of isolated and dangerous intrapsychic fantasies, conflicts, and anxieties are erroneous; such Type One derivative formulations are designed primarily to seal off more chaotic disturbances within the therapeutic interaction—often threatening unconscious perceptions of the therapist. In contrast, formulations which are developed in light of a prevailing intervention context and which touch upon the evoked intrapsychic pathology of the patient (transferences) lead to validated interpretations.

A study of the unconscious communicative interaction demonstrates the presence of some element of countertransference in every intervention by the therapist (Langs 1980a). He is therefore always contributing in some meaningful way to the presence of resistances in the patient, and it is encumbent upon the therapist to ascertain his own contribution to each resistance before dealing with those sources which arise primarily from within the patient. This work is also founded on an evaluation of the therapist's interventions, and a search for his own gross behavioral and communicative counterresistances as they are expressed in his attitudes and interventions. That which is warded off by resistances entails not only threatening contents and conflicts within the patient, but also threatening contents and conflicts within the therapist as perceived, validly and with some degree of distortion, consciously and unconsciously, by the patient.

In this light, we can better understand what is meant by resistances against the expressions of transference. Here we are defining transference in its narrow and classical sense as alluding to *unconscious* fantasy constellations which pertain to the therapist. Such fantasy constellations, which include critical dynamic conflicts and genetically founded disturbances, prompt resistances designed to ward off all of the attendant inner dangers. They are also designed to ward off the recollection of early childhood traumas and the patient's responses to them, behaviorally and in fantasy. All such material, since it pertains to the sources of anxiety, depression, and disturbance within the patient, poses some degree of threat and will evoke resistance responses. However, it cannot be emphasized often enough that the analysis of these resistances must nonetheless always take as its point of departure an activated adaptive context.

There is a special class of resistances to which some classical analysts seem to be alluding when they refer to resistances against the transference or against the expressions of transference (see, for example, Gill 1979). Here, as Stone (1973) pointed out, we are dealing with unique sources of anxiety which arise at the moment of the conscious realization of a previously repressed or unconscious fantasy. While such an experience is potentially highly adaptive, making available levels of understanding previously inaccessible when the fantasy was under repression, this type of conscious realization is also the source of considerable anxiety, shame, and other disturbances. It is here that the patient's responsibility to say whatever comes to mind, and to express all the conscious feelings and fantasies he has toward the therapist, prove to evoke resistance. Characteristically, however, these are superficial sources of defense; attention to the patient's *derivative* communications will reveal additional unconscious sources—some in terms of deeper unconscious fantasies, and others in terms of threatening unconscious perceptions of the therapist.

Similar but more intense resistances arise at the moment of a conscious realization of a previously *repressed perception* of the therapist, especially when it involves error or disturbance on his part. There is a special, enormous threat when the patient, who has accepted the responsibility, must report all associations of a valid realization regarding the therapist, one which would disturb both the patient and the therapist himself. The danger is compounded by the fact that the therapist has erred, often through some type of deviation in the frame. It renders uncertain the boundaries of the therapeutic relationship and creates a strong and realistically founded sense of mistrust. When the therapist is in error, he is hurtful of the patient, sometimes dramatically so. He is a truly dangerous figure, and the threat of even more extreme transgressions is ever-present. In light of these factors, we can readily understand why patients would tend to repress disturbing unconscious perceptions of their therapists, and some patients will often consciously suppress such realizations.

Among the sources of resistances, and the motives which prompt their utilization, two relatively neglected elements should be stressed. First, there is the patient's dread of the most primitive aspects of his own inner mental world, as well as of terrifying unconscious perceptions of failings, communicated difficulties, and pathological unconscious fantasies within the therapist. Second, there is the universal need for merger and fusion, the wish to maintain highly pathological symbiotic ties to the therapist.

Acceptance by the patient of proper therapeutic procedures, including an interpretive approach and the maintenance of a sound therapeutic environment, deprive the patient of pathological symbiotic gratifications. These then evoke resistances which are characteristically designed unconsciously to restore the pathological symbiotic interaction. Because many therapists have comparable counterresistances and pathological needs, the resistant nature of such efforts is often overlooked. This leads therapists to make many unnecessary deviations in the ground rules and to offer a wide range of noninterpretive and nonneutral interventions which are unconsciously designed to serve the therapist's counterresistances and to foster the patient's own use of certain forms of resistance. Paradoxically, many of the techniques proposed in the analytic work with psychotic, borderline, and narcissistic patients preclude the analytic resolution of the primitive and persecutory anxieties and fantasies experienced when symbiotic relatedness is threatened, and instead tend to unconsciously gratify the pathological symbiotic needs of both patient and therapist alike. Such satisfactions will also interfere with the therapist's recognition of the patient's resistances—and, of course, his own counterresistances as well.

Resistances which can be categorized in terms of defenses directed against the analysis of the transference as defined in the classical literature, would be seen communicatively in terms of defenses against the analysis of both transference and nontransference, distorted and nondistorted, reactions to the therapist. It is important to distinguish these two modes of therapeutic work as it pertains to the patient's relationship with the therapist, and to recognize the continuum on which they exist. Resistances which arise against the resolution of unconscious transference constellations would derive from a multitude of intrapsychic sources, including the patient's reluctance to forgo the pathological gratification derived from unconscious transference fantasies. Such therapeutic work also implies the ultimate termination of treatment, a prospect against which many patients erect substantial resistances. Obstacles directed against the therapeutic process which arise from the analysis of unconscious nontransference perceptions and their elaboration are of considerable importance, and their presence has already been discussed above.

In all, then, resistances are designed to ward off threatening unconscious perceptions of the therapist and threatening intrapsychic conflicts, fantasies, memories, introjects, and the like. The specific nature of what is being warded off can be formulated correctly only in light of an activated adaptive context, and the interpretation of this aspect of resistance depends upon a conceptualization of the derivative network in which the adaptation-evoking stimulus is central.

WHY THE PATIENT IS RESISTANT

The motives for resistance can be readily understood, as just described, in light of what is being warded off. Resistances are motivated by the patient's need to deal with danger situations and by efforts to achieve pathological instinctual drive gratification and pathological superego sanctions. Intrapsychically founded resistances arise in the presence of a secure framework and in response to interpretations from the therapist which are relatively countertransference-free. All of the need systems and motivational factors which stimulate the patient's use of defenses in dealing with intrapsychic and interpersonal conflicts and problems will, under such conditions, prove pertinent to the reasons for which a patient becomes resistant.

A second motivational source for resistances lies within the therapist. This type of motivational system has been described by Sandler and Joffe (1969) and Sandler and Sandler (1978), among others. It entails the development of need systems and motivations within the patient which are primarily derived from disturbing (and gratifying) stimuli emanating from their object relationships, and especially the object relationship with the therapist. It is important now to extend our conceptualization of object relational, interactional, and introjective motivational systems deriving primarily from the patient's relationship with the therapist, in terms of a broad theory. In this respect, the therapist may, through countertransference-based interventions, convey to the patient a wide range of need-motivational systems of his own, ranging from wishes directed toward the patient to those which pertain to his own intrapsychic disturbances. The therapist may therefore intervene in a manner which expresses his own need for pathological instinctual drive gratification, superego sanctions, or pathological defenses, which arouse comparable or related needs within the patient, and which may prompt the development of resistances.

One form of interactional resistance has been described by Baranger and Baranger (1966) as *bastions* of the bipersonal field. These are repressed, denied, or split-off sectors of the communicative field and relationship which are set aside through unconscious collusion. Through this means, certain aspects of the therapeutic interaction, often relevant to the therapist's countertransferences or to some aspect of the patient's material in respect to which the therapist has developed counterresistances, is sealed off from the communicative interchange. This particular type of interactional resistance is one form of therapeutic misalliance designed to undermine insightful therapeutic work and to achieve symptom alleviation through some other means.

Interactional resistances are quite difficult to identify, since they are based on unconscious contributions from the therapist, who experiences strong counterresistances to their recognition, and must develop a sensitivity to his own contributions to the patient's resistances and to his countertransferences in general. Any sense of disturbance or stalemate, and any suspicion of resistance within the patient, calls first for an investigation of possible contributions from the therapist, carried out simultaneously with an evaluation of factors within the patient. These efforts can be developed not only through the therapist's own self-scrutiny and self-analysis, but also with the assistance of the patient's associations—communications which can be organized as derivatives and commentaries pertinent to the activated adaptive-intervention contexts from the therapist. These commentaries prove to be an extremely useful guide for the sensitive therapist in search of his own contributions to the patient's resistances.

There is another constellation of motivations which, in general, has eluded classical analysts. It is comprised of the distinctly primitive anxieties, including the dread of annihilation and the fear of the psychotic part of the personality. This constellation is a derivative of the universal infantile psychosis which may be relatively well or poorly mastered by a particular patient or therapist—and which has been recently discussed by Grotstein (1977a, b). These primitive anxieties render dangerous the pursuit of the truth of the patient's neurosis as activated within the therapeutic interaction. It seems likely that classical psychoanalytic theory and technique has been designed to some extent as a defense against such primitive anxieties and the primitive fantasy-perception constellations which they involve, and that the formulations and interventions of classical analysts have served on one level as Type C barriers against these universal disturbances.

Similar considerations apply to issues of fusion and symbiosis, in that much of classical analytic and therapeutic technique is unconsciously designed to permit pathological fusion and symbiosis, and to interfere with healthy individualization. It is common to find shared resistances-counterresistances in these areas, and to discover pathological needs of this kind, for example, in therapists who fail to recognize the resistance functions of breaks in the framework. On this level, all such deviations gratify the pathological needs under consideration, and thereby lead in part to failures to recognize the resistance implications in such techniques and in the patient's efforts to modify the frame.

The communicative approach permits the identification of what may be termed mini-psychotic behaviors (irrational behaviors and communications from an otherwise neurotically functioning patient or therapist), neurotic delusions (gross distortions of reality which are constricted and temporary, and which occur in an otherwise well functioning individual), and neurotic hallucinations (momentary sensory misperceptions in an otherwise well functioning individual). Such behaviors and communications reveal their primitive implications in the light of an activated intervention context, especially when they are understood and not merely dismissed as inconsequential. However, it requires a consistent sensitivity to, and monitoring of, the unconscious communicative interaction to identify these behaviors in the patient or therapist, and to fully appreciate their ramifications.

Resistances derived from these primitive sources are often a factor in disorganized and chaotic therapeutic situations. There is some evidence that the primitive unconscious fantasies and anxieties involved in this sector of the personality of the therapist provides a basis for important counterresistances and erroneous interventions, especially laxity in regard to the management of the therapeutic framework and hold. It seems that many deviations in the framework constitute minipsychotic acts, which are designed as well to defend against the psychotic part of the personality. In addition there seems to be a deep *unconscious* appreciation in both patients and therapists in respect to the extent to which a secured framework creates the conditions under which the manifestations of the psychotic part of the personality will find expression. It is anxieties of this kind which lead to resistances in the patient expressed through breaks in the framework, and the counterresistances in the therapist which often take a similar form. The well-managed framework interferes with pathological symbiotic gratification; in its absence, the patient's and therapist's primitive separation anxieties become quite prominent.

As might be expected, patients with the most primitive forms of psychotic fantasy formations and symbiotic needs, who have the least degree of control over such wishes, fantasies, and perceptions, prove to be the most resistant to accepting a secure therapeutic setting and opening themselves to the experience of these primitive elements of their personality. In general, the borderline and psychotic patients are most fearful of this type of therapeutic environment, and show resistances in response to a therapist's offer of such a setting. While these patients find considerable strength in the therapeutic hold and containing capacities of the therapist, they experience a simultaneous dread of separation and of the unleashing of the psychotic aspects of their inner mental worlds. The separation experience itself is perceived in primitive, persecutory, and terrifying terms.

Some of these patients are able to benefit from and appreciate the positive aspects of a secure therapeutic environment to the point where they are able to tolerate both separation and primitive expressions, and benefit from their analytic understanding and resolution. Others have little faith in their own ability to cope with this aspect of their personalities, which has contributed in a major way to their symptoms and functional impairments. They will not risk the potential separateness and regression which takes place under these conditions, preferring to prematurely terminate and flee the treatment situation, especially when their own efforts to modify the frame—through requests for medication, for extra sessions, for direct advice, and the like—are responded to with interpretive efforts which do not afford the direct gratification and protection the patient is seeking.

There is a particular group of patients who enter therapy appearing to function relatively normally or neurotically, and who show such an enormously disturbed response to the offer of a secure hold, that the therapist quickly becomes aware of their fragile defenses, often in the form of Type C barriers, which have been serving to seal off an underlying, active psychotic core. These patients become acutely disturbed and resistant when a sound therapeutic setting is offered. Some prove capable of tolerating the separation and regression which follows, and prove to be strong Type A communicators capable of extensive insightful therapeutic work. Others become panic stricken and either attempt to permanently modify the framework or take flight. Much depends on whether these patients, who typically become resistant on a gross behavioral level and thereby threaten the continuation of the therapeutic work and the therapy itself, continue to provide the therapist with a meaningful communicative network which permits pertinent interpretation.

In general, four groups of patients can be recognized in terms of the type and extent of resistances they develop when offered a secure therapeutic environment: (1) those who panic over the prospect of separateness and regression, and the exposure to the psychotic part of their personalities, and who either permanently modify the framework or take flight from treatment; (2) those who become frightened by the regression and separation, but nonetheless make relatively benign efforts to modify the frame and prove receptive to its maintenance and to the therapist's interpretive efforts; (3) patients who more quietly accept the holding environment after initial efforts to alter the frame, and who either become Type A communicators because of some pressing need to actively resolve their neurosis, or Type C communicators; and (4) patients who settle into the therapeutic situation quite readily, with little sense of disturbance or efforts to modify the basic therapeutic environment.

It may be stated broadly that patients in the more agitated—Type B—group tend to generate resistances through modifications in the fixed frame, while patients who are less actively stirred up will express resistances on a communicative basis while accepting the basic environment. With each type, an interpretive approach must be maintained. While the first group tends to provide interpretable derivative networks, they are greatly influenced by realistic fears. They make use of resistances as a way of maintaining their equilibrium and sanity, and must decide between exposure to nonfusion and dreaded fantasies, memories, and perceptions on the one hand, and on the other, the possibility of flight, fusion elsewhere, and their independent use of Type C barriers, however unstable. For these patients, meaning and understanding are dangerous, and many prefer the destruction of meaning and relatedness to the dreaded implications of meaningful interaction.

Another group of patients develop a different type of resistance which is also difficult to resolve interpretively. These patients accept the therapeutic holding environment, and settle in as Type C communicators, often as Type C narrators. They show little in the way of gross behavioral resistances, though their communicative resistances are powerful. The safety of the therapeutic environment reinforces their previous failing Type C barrier-defenses, and they show little wish to modify these nonderivative forms of protection to the point where their underlying psychoticlike disturbance will be experienced and become accessible for analysis. Their acceptance of the therapeutic hold and the therapist's containing capacities has strong symbiotic qualities, which the therapist is often hard-pressed to determine as essentially pathological or nonpathological. Much depends on continued listening and observations of the patient's symptoms or characterological disturbance, and deciding whether the patient's lie-barrier systems are becoming more rigid and pathological, or more flexible or adaptive.

Technically, since there is seldom material available for interpretation, these resistances are difficult to resolve. These patients seem to benefit greatly from the therapist's holding and containing capacities, and shift only occasionally to Type A communication—in face of an acute life stress, an unexpected disturbance within the treatment situation, and sometimes a vacation by the therapist. With this type of patient, the most pressing issues in respect to their resistances is enabling them to sufficiently work through their neurosis to the point of a suitable termination of treatment.

RESISTANCES IN EACH TYPE OF BIPERSONAL FIELD

Each of the three communicative styles and bipersonal fields—A, B, C—involves distinctive forms of gross and communicative resistances, provides special qualities to the relationship between the two forms, and calls for specific technical approaches.

In brief, the Type A field is characterized by the relative absence of gross behavioral resistances or their well modulated, readily controlled, and analyzable expression. The Type A patient tends to express his unconscious fantasies and conflicts verbally and with due affect, and his resistances tend to appear on the communicative level. From time to time, there will be a major behavioral resistance, but as a rule, the communicative network reveals its unconscious meanings and functions. Sources of resistance within both the patient and the therapist are communicated in derivative form, and prove interpretable. Based on a reasonable degree of self-analysis and on an understanding of the patient's material, it is usually possible for the therapist to rectify his contribution to these resistances, which are typically based on misinterpretations and occasional, relatively minor, mismanagements of the framework. (It is to be remembered that a broad use of Type A communication requires a secure framework and a capacity for holding and interpreting in the therapist; it may however take place in the face of an acute break in the frame, though then, only in regard to the deviation itself and for a restricted period of time.) On the whole, these patients provide the therapist with the clearest opportunity for the analysis of behavioral resistances in terms of their unconscious determinants in both patient and therapist.

In the presence of a behavioral resistance, the Type A patient will, within a session or two, usually devise an hour in which, however scattered, there will appear a definitive reference to or representation of the prevailing adaptive context, a group of coalescing derivatives, a statement of the major indicators, and a bridge to the therapeutic relationship. Such a communicative network permits interpretation: an allusion to the main therapeutic context, the identification of the neurotic adaptive context and its communicative implications as experienced in the patient's responsive and adaptive unconscious fantasies and perceptions, and a full delineation of their dynamic and genetic implications. Such an interpretation indicates the unconscious motives, sources, and functions of a behavioral resistance, and the unconscious fantasies and perceptions on which it is based. This type of work approximates the classical model of the analysis of resistances. The relevant defenses are *derivative defenses* in that they are expressed through disguised communication, and structured in terms of compromise formations with contributions from the id, superego, and ego. They are resistances which have structure and meaning, the nature of which is defined by the associated communicative network in the manner just described.

On a communicative level, the Type A patient tends to show the fewest resistances. When faced with an especially threatening intervention context, defenses may temporarily be directed at one or more of the three basic communicative components, though most commonly the resistances are concentrated on one particular element. These communicative blocks do not last long and the patient often spontaneously resolves and modifies their use on his own, returning to meaningful communication. In these situations the most important intervention by the therapist involves silent rectification of any detectable contribution that he has made to the patient's defensiveness. This type of withdrawal of support is often sufficient to enable the patient to resolve the resistance and shift to meaningful communication. In addition, this approach is technically best because of the lack of material for interpretation; often enough, it suffices. In the face of a persistent resistance—usually directed at representations of the intervention context—the playing back of the derivative complex organized around the unmentioned and poorly represented precipitant (usually a framework issue) generally leads to a resolution of the resistance.

It is with the Type A patient, then, that behavioral resistances are usually accompanied by a meaningful communicative network. With these patients, resistances have a sense of depth and complexity, and of implication, that tends to be lacking in the other two communicative fields. These resistances are layered, structured, and filled with understandable and interpretable unconscious meaning, both in regard to the nature of the resistance itself and to whatever is being defended against or warded off. It is, as I said, this type of resistance with which classical psychoanalysts are most familiar.

There are two kinds of Type B patients. With one group, projective identification and action-discharge is used in the service of both riddance and understanding. In the second group, the excretory and barrier functions of their use of interactional projection predominates, and there is virtually no quest for understanding. In keeping with this distinction, the behavioral and communicative resistances contained in the projective identifications of the first group prove ultimately to be analyzable. While these patients often communicate in a distinctly pressured, fragmented fashion, and create resistances which tend to be highly disturbing to their therapists, they manage eventually to meaningfully represent enough of the communicative network to permit an interpretive response. Often, this development requires several sessions during which the therapist's main intervention takes the form of patient, tolerant, and silent waiting, expressions of his holding and containing capacities, until the point where he is able to metabolize and understand meaningfully the relevant communicative network.

Many of the resistances expressed by these patients involve strong interactional pressures and efforts at disturbing role- and image-evocations, directed toward the therapist. The roles and images involved are typically discordant with the therapist's usual self-image and behaviors, and tend to be difficult to contain and to respond to with understanding and, ultimately, interpretation. These patients engage in what may be termed violent forms of acting out and acting in, and much of the destructiveness—and occasionally, open efforts at seduction—is expressed directly toward the therapist. The latter must maintain an openness to the introjection of these disruptive projective identifications, and maintain his capacity to metabolize their implications toward interpretive responses. With patients in this first group of Type B communicators, identified as Type B-A, the therapist's expectation of an eventual admixture of Type A communication—the representation of an interpretable communicative network—is helpful in enabling him to maintain a sense of hope that ultimately each particular disturbing interlude will prove resolvable through insight. This enhances his tolerance for these highly disturbing projective identifications, a feeling which tends to be lacking and unjustified with the second group of Type B patients.

However, even with the Type B-A patient, the therapist will often experience their resistances as personal attacks and threats. The actual conscious and unconscious qualities of resistances, directed toward not only the disruption of treatment but also the harm or disturbance of the therapist, is most keenly experienced. While true of all forms of resistance, those which involve interactional projection tend especially to evoke defensiveness and counterresistances in the therapist, as well as unmetabolized, responsive pathological projective identifications directed toward the threatening patient. As a result, the analysis of resistances in the Type B patient requires not only a cognitive ability to formulate, understand, and interpret, but also depends on the therapist's capacity for *reverie* (Bion 1962)—his ability to contain, tolerate, and metabolize or detoxify the disturbing interactional and object relational—parasitic—pressures experienced with these patients.

The second kind of Type B patient, Type B-C, shows, even on an unconscious level, no viable interest in self-understanding and sound therapeutic work. These patients are often suffering from major symbiosis-related pathology, and an agitated psychotic core whose derivatives continuously threaten to reach consciousness, terrify the patient, and disrupt his functioning. Their defenses are fragmented and they repeatedly resort to violent projective identifications as an evacuatory effort designed to rid themselves of acutely psychotic disturbances, often paranoid in nature. Their need for merger and fusion experiences is inordinate, and much of their agitation is designed unconsciously as a means of satisfying such wishes. As a result, with this type of patient, a relatively secure frame and an interpretive approach by the therapist is experienced as a persecutory threat and abandonment designed to terrify the patient and to unleash his primitive introjects as well as their highly pathological and destructive unconscious fantasy-memory constellations. A parasitic mode of relatedness is typical.

As a group, these patients manifest highly intense and disruptive gross behavioral resistances. Typically, they attempt to modify the basic framework of therapy either unilaterally or by engaging the therapist in a deviation. They become enraged and directly attacking when a therapist maintains the frame and attempts to interpret. Often, they disrupt these interpretive efforts and disclaim any interest in understanding, seeking only some form of immediate gratification or merger. Sometimes they will be silent for prolonged periods, will directly oppose cooperative therapeutic work, and frequently threaten to terminate treatment. Typically, these agitated behavioral resistances are not accompanied by a coalescible communicative network, but instead appear in the presence of fragmented and somewhat disorganized associations. On the rare occasions when interpretive material is available, the patient usually will initially validate the therapist's intervention if it is correct, only to subsequently destroy the perspective gained in this way. Little or no understanding persists, nor is it used to modify through insight the prevailing behavioral resistances.

These patients are terrified of sound therapeutic work, and deeply mistrustful of both themselves and their therapists. They often generate resistance crises of ominous proportions, seeking to projectively identify into and to harm or disturb the therapist, failing even on an unconscious level to engage in meaningful communication and efforts toward comprehension. The prognosis in these situations is quite poor, and sudden termination is often the outcome. At best, the therapist can offer the soundest interpretations available from the material while maintaining a secure hold for the patient. The therapeutic work must, of massive necessity, center on the major resistances and their unconscious implications. It is well for the therapist to understand the sense of terror within these patients, who find any degree of separation or distance between themselves and their objects a source of inordinate danger, and who feel almost totally helpless in the face of the threat posed by their intensely pathological introjects and unconscious fantasy constellations. Their unconscious perceptions of the therapist, whatever their valid core, are highly mistrustful and paranoid-like.

A gradual resolution and modification of these resistances is feasible only when these patients are able to maintain an initially good image of the therapist with a sufficient positive component to enable them to endure the anxiety and terror involved in the necessary exploratory work. The positive introjects and insights which do accrue based on the therapist's capacity for reverie and interpretation are sometimes silently integrated to the point where these patients are better able to tolerate the violent disturbances within themselves. These patients tend to prefer a poor or even destructive therapist who unconsciously justifies their paranoid attitudes and defenses, and who gratifies their sick needs for fusion. These therapists also facilitate the projective identification and psychopathology of these patients, and encourage the belief that the more disturbed member of the dyad is the therapist. Such a therapist is incapable of creating the conditions under which the patient experiences as his own his intensely pathological inner mental world. For the communicative therapist, these patients are a grim reminder of the realistic consequences of resistance and the dreadful anxieties which they are sometimes designed to help the patient defend against.

There are several forms of resistances in the Type C communicative style, each designed to rupture the interpersonal links between the patient and therapist, to provide healthy or pathological symbiotic gratification, and as barriers to underlying-chaotic and disturbing truths within the patient, and often enough, within the therapist as well. It is characteristic of Type C resistances to be *nonderivative* in form, and to not reveal either their own underlying structure or the material being warded off. They are opaque lie-barrier formations designed to destroy meaning and understanding, and to seal off rather than reveal the underlying threat.

Because of their nature, Type C resistances are very difficult to deal with, and they only rarely lend themselves to interpretation, doing so at those moments where the patient provides some derivative representation of their nature. By and large, their presence requires silent and patient holding by the therapist, during which the patient becomes engaged to some degree in a form of unilateral self-interpretation which functions toward lie-barrier formations and more rarely, true insight.

One group of Type C patients will consistently associate in a flat, noncoalescing, empty manner, showing communicative resistances which tend to attack each of the three major elements of the communicative network. At times, they will represent indicators, an activated intervention context, or offer a few meaningful derivatives, though they will not provide both of these latter elements of the communicative network in the same session. Many of these patients show virtually no gross behavioral resistances. Others will, on rare occasions, especially at moments with potential for acute disturbance, manifest an isolated gross behavioral resistance such as acting out or acting in, prolonged silence, or somatic symptoms. Seldom do these gross resistances unfold in the presence of a meaningful communicative network. This tends to occur in the presence of a sudden break in the framework, initiated by either the therapist or patient, to which the Type C communicator will respond briefly to Type A communicative mode. In general, it is more characteristic for these patients to maintain quiet noncommunication and to destroy rather than generate meaning. They convey unconscious fictions, lies, falsifications, and deceptions, all serving as nonderivative lie-barrier formations. The absence of a full and meaningful, clearly linked communicative network is the hallmark of the Type C style. When the adaptive context is clearly represented, the derivatives are, as a rule, scattered, flat, or empty. When the derivative complex seems coalescible, the pertinent context fails to be meaningfully represented.

From time to time, these patients will make available a metaphorical representation of their resistances and barrier formations, such as allusions to vaults, tombs, tanks, and dead ends, but in order to interpret this material, the therapist must also have available a represented, activated adaptive context. In its absence, an interpretive playback of these metaphors and derivatives may help to begin to modify these very difficult resistances and defenses, but in general they can be offered only in the presence of a break in the fixed frame.

Much of the therapeutic technique available in response to these types of resistances involves silence and holding, and the important contribution of not making an error and of not contributing to the patient's defensive style. There is a tendency for therapists to experience with these patients a sense of personal fragmentation, helplessness, stupidity, and impotence. These role- and image-evocations are based on the negative and voidlike projective identifications involved, as well as on the patient's highly successful efforts at destroying any significant sense of relatedness or meaning. They are potential sources for countertransference-based interventions designed not to help the patient understand his resistances, but instead to provide the therapist with a false sense of reassurance and competence. These interventions fail to receive Type Two derivative validation, and are experienced by the patient as failures within the therapist in terms of his holding and containing capacities, and as an indication that the patient's quiet efforts at destructiveness have found a vulnerable response in the therapist. It is quite common for these patients to respond to such interventions with a sense of conscious or unconscious triumph, often consciously identifying the indications of the therapist's countertransference responses and exploiting their presence as a way of berating the therapist in a manner that is seldom interpretable. These are difficult patients and difficult resistances, and require that the therapist maintain his basic holding and interpretive stance, and not deviate out of desperation or guilt. With the overriding and unfortunate stress within therapy and analysis on active and interpretive interventions, therapists are prone to feel inadequate and guilty under such conditions. Instead, they should realize that these patients pose a great challenge to their therapeutic techniques and to their own inner mental balances.

THE DISTINCTION BETWEEN DEFENSES
AND RESISTANCE

The communicative approach provides findings and formulations which offer a meaningful basis for the distinction between defense and resistance. In essence, the term defense alludes to the patient's efforts to protect himself from danger situations, sources of anxiety and discomfort, both intrapsychic and interactional. These protective mechanisms themselves are developed from intrapsychic and interactional factors and operate on the mental, somatic, and interactional levels. Their nature and function should be viewed in terms of the expression of complex unconscious fantasies, memories, and introjects, all of which funnel, as a rule, into a series of characteristic protective devices.

Defensive operations include the classically conceived mechanisms such as displacement, reaction formation, denial, isolation, and projection, as well as specifically interactional defenses, such as projective and introjective identification. They also include complex defensive behaviors, and even the use of instinctual drives and efforts at punishment, when they serve in some way to protect the individual. This type of multileveled and multidetermined conception of defense permits a classification of its intrapsychic and behavioral expressions, as well as an understanding of its multiple sources and functions. It also enables us to realize that defenses can be recognized in terms of specific unconscious fantasies; for example, projection represented in terms of evacuation. This provides a clue to some of the somatic sources on which fantasies are built.

Resistances, derived from similar mechanisms, sources, and functions, may also take a wide range of forms and expressions. The distinction between defenses and resistances docs not lie in the nature of their functions and contents, but rather in the extent to which these mechanisms are mobilized in the service of obstructing the therapeutic work. Clearly, not all defensive operations interfere with the therapeutic process, and because of this, it proves essential to distinguish these defenses from those which are indeed disruptive.

Matters are quite different, however, on a communicative level. There are many interludes during which a patient makes use of intrapsychic and interactional defenses while not essentially attempting to disturb the therapeutic process. These defensive formations produce the disguised representations which produce the much needed derivative complex. When they involve meaningful representations of the adaptive context and the development of coalescing derivatives, the patient is actively defensive but essentially nonresistant. In fact, it is these defenses which permit neurosis-related communication and through which the patient expresses the unconscious basis for his symptoms. At such times, defensive mechanisms and fantasies permit meaningful communicative expression and further interpretive work.

Defenses are more pervasive than resistances, and continue to operate at all times, even when the patient is neither consciously nor unconsciously obstructing the therapeutic work. Resistances, however, may be intermittent and sometimes unnecessary. These distinctions help the therapist to approach the patient's defenses in a more tolerant manner, and to concentrate the interpretive therapeutic work on those defenses which are in the service of resistance and which also prove to be analyzable.

RESISTANCE IMPLICATIONS OF DIRECT ALLUSIONS
TO THE THERAPIST

In terms of prevailing psychoanalytic thinking, direct references to the therapist are usually identified as transferences, and understood in terms of both surface and implied meanings. They are seen as inherently distorted or distorting, and as derived primarily from earlier, genetically important relationships. By and large, the meanings involved are taken at face value, and the postulated unconscious mechanism is simply that of displacement. The emergence of such material is seen as signaling the relative absence of resistances. A formulation is made to the effect that the transference has broken into consciousness, that it has now been stated directly, or that a previously repressed transference fantasy has now reached direct awareness. In all, the patient's conscious fantasies and reactions toward the therapist are accepted as meaningful, as essentially undisguised except for displacement, and they are usually interpreted in light of repressed early childhood experiences—the latter viewed as the unconscious element. Such moments, then, are considered as breakthroughs, and much of the therapeutic work is geared toward confrontations and other kinds of efforts designed to enable the patient to express directly his repressed or suppressed fantasies, feelings, and reactions to the therapist. These expressions are therefore seen as a sign that existing resistances have been resolved, and that the patient is, for the moment, relatively resistant-free. The search is direct, linear, and geared to what has been omitted from available associations—what lies directly beneath, though is not represented.

In contrast, the communicative approach views all manifest associations as derivative, and as representing latent contents and functions. There is no such entity as a simple undisguised break-through of an underlying unconscious fantasy or perception, since some derivative function is always present. Full and consistent consideration is given to the sphere of disguised communication. As a result, the communicative therapist does not use questions, clarifications, or confrontations. He is concerned, of course, with what remains unconscious, but discovers considerable disguised or encoded meaning in what is already available, as long as it is organized for derivative implications in light of an activated intervention content. His technique stresses silence and permitting the patient to shift from one association to another in order to provide distinct but coalescing elements for the derivative complex. He therefore never engages in direct pursuit, but instead interprets the patient's resistances when feasible, and his meaningful material when there is an interpretable communicative network.

While in theory, both classical analysts and communicative therapists believe that the patient represents unconscious contents and processes on a manifest level through disguised representations, the communicative therapist includes perceptions which develop outside of awareness along with fantasy-memory formations. He also will never address a manifest association and treat it simply as a breakthrough of a previously repressed or suppressed fantasy, finding instead that all manifest associations serve, as their most critical function, to represent those processes and contents which remain unconscious. Clearly, no exception is made in respect to manifest allusions to the therapist or analyst.

This type of manifest content is very often a poor carrier of derivative meaning and the vehicle of communicative resistances that are difficult to resolve. There are actually two main possibilities: one in which the reference to the therapist is made in passing and involves the representation of the intervention context which is most critical at the moment; while the other entails extended references to the therapist which are part of a reaction either to the adaptive context to which the patient is reacting manifestly or to some other intervention context which has either not been clearly represented or has been represented through other associations. To clarify, the most meaningful type of direct allusion to the therapist occurs as a reference to a recent intervention, which constitutes an important activated adaptive context. This allusion may be direct or displaced, though it usually occurs in a form that fosters interpretation. With the allusion to the therapist as a nodal point, the remainder of the patient's associations constitute the responsive derivative complex. It has been discovered empirically that extended allusions to the therapist on a manifest level tend to yield relatively little in the way of derivative meaning. Some confusion arises in this regard because a low resistance communicative network requires a direct representation of an intervention context, and therefore some manifest reference to the therapist. It is important to distinguish this from a meaningful and coalescing derivative network; in this respect, direct associations to the therapist have a high valence of resistance.

Many manifest allusions to the therapist are actually a part of the derivative complex, rather than a way of representing an important intervention context. Of course, this determination can be made only when the therapist has a clear picture of the intervention context itself. Once it is established, he evaluates the qualities of the derivative complex by determining the extent of meaning and coalescence. Extended comments about the therapist seldom prove to be part of a Type A communicative mode, and only rarely exist as an aspect of a meaningful derivative complex. By and large, they are part of the Type C communicative style and prove fragmented, scattered, and difficult to organize. This is especially true when a patient refers to some manifest issue within the treatment, and even sometimes to an important adaptive context, and goes on to provide extensive conscious and direct comments, reactions, and fantasies without changing the focus of his associations. Such material tends to be repetitive and flat, yielding little in the way of derivative meaning.

More rarely, associations which pertain manifestly to the therapist do function in light of a particular intervention context, as disguised and derivative communications which reveal important *unconscious* fantasy and perception constellations. Under these conditions, important dynamic and genetic connections are often conveyed. Nonetheless, the use of manifest associations pertinent to the therapist for derivative expressions is quite rare.

Two related findings should be noted in this connection. The communicative approach reveals that many efforts by a patient to consciously interpret to his therapist, to point out his mistakes and to speculate as to their basis, and to suggest alternate interventions, are reflections of major resistances, and tend to lack validity. While it is difficult to make broad generalizations in this respect, therapists who are prone to gross errors and significant mismanagements of the framework are likely to hear direct criticisms from their patients which have an important measure of validity. Even then, such communications tend to serve additional resistance purposes. They are always on one important level derivative communications so that the manifest content expresses some disguised, unconscious fantasy or perception constellation. On the other hand, in a well managed treatment situation, these conscious criticisms of the therapist are almost always expressions of resistance, and, where decipherible, containers of latent unconscious fantasy and perception constellations. Their manifest implications are essentially related to lie-barrier systems and to the destruction of meaning. In keeping with this finding, where the therapist does indeed make a major technical error, the patient seldom recognizes its presence consciously and works it over on a manifest level. Instead, the typical reaction takes place through derivative expression and reflects an *unconscious* perception of the mistake, encoded comments on the patient's beliefs as to the source of the error, and efforts at unconscious, derivative interpretation to the therapist—in addition to tendencies to exploit the mistake.

Despite these findings, conscious criticisms of the therapist are to be taken seriously. While in the service of resistance, they often represent an unmentioned mistake or touch upon a threat posed by the therapist's application of sound technique. They require a careful evaluation of the prevailing adaptive contexts for important countertransference inputs. While therapeutic work with such manifest complaints will seldom lead to Type Two derivative validation, careful listening for the derivative implications of such communications often enables the therapist to recognize unnoticed aspects of his countertransferences.

Similarly, the patient's efforts to understand himself, to formulate and to interpret aspects of his own reactions and associations,

have been discovered through the communicative approach to
function primarily as resistances or as derivative communications
with rather different latent implications when organized around
prevailing intervention contexts. Patients seldom make Type Two
derivative self-interpretations, doing so primarily at time of crisis.
Instead, these efforts are characteristically formulated in terms of
Type One derivatives, and serve primarily as derivative and nonderivative lie-barrier systems. Sometimes, the truths contained in
these insights, even though they function as lie-barrier systems in
respect to the ongoing communicative interaction, have a relatively
soft or adaptive quality and foster some degree of symptom relief.
Nonetheless, such changes are not based on an understanding of
the patient's neurosis as mobilized by the communicative interaction, but tend to involve isolated genetic reconstructions and
dynamic interpretations. It is most interesting to discover the extent
to which patients are capable of such therapeutic work, especially
since it is this kind of therapeutic effort which characterizes most
therapists in present-day practice. These are matters which will be
discussed further in chapter 12.

RESISTANCES AND REALITY

For some time, resistances have been treated primarily as deriving from intrapsychic sources and as part of an inner struggle
within the patient, with little in the way of implications for the
therapist or for reality. While some resistances were understood to
lead to, or be based upon, acting out, these behavioral consequences
were set largely to the periphery. An effort to correct this trend can
be seen in Bird's (1972) study of transference, where he stated that
some resistances are either efforts to harm and disturb the therapist
or counterresponses to his destructive interventions.

It is important to realize that the actualities of the conditions of
therapy influence the mobilization and resolution of the patient's
resistances. As we know, many resistances are expressed through
actual alterations in the ground rules and framework of therapy,
and can be maintained indefinitely as long as such deviations are
not rectified. Many counterresistances of the therapist find comparable expression in modifications of the ideal therapeutic environment. It is here that the reality of the implication of the therapist's
errors and breaks in the frame provide continued unconscious

stimulation and support for the patient's resistances, and create a climate within which these resistances remain relatively unmodifiable.

These trends are in keeping with the findings of Halpert (1972) who reported that the presence of a third-party payer who became responsible for the entire fee of two patients in analysis provided a realistic anchor for resistances which proved entirely unmodifiable until the third-party payer was no longer present. This single and relatively isolated observation found extended support in my own investigations of the therapeutic environment (Langs 1975a, 1979), through which this broader principle was derived: all erroneous interventions and breaks in the framework by the patient or therapist provide a realistic justification for the patient's use of resistances which renders them relatively unmodifiable through verbal-interpretive work until rectification has taken place.

A similar principle applies to acting out—enactments—by the patient, relationship-related behaviors which gratify his neurosis and preclude its resolution through interpretive work. It is important to recognize, however, that most enactments are actually forms of interactional enactment or interactional acting out; and that as long as they derive unconscious sources from the therapist, they will remain fixed and unresolvable. Pertinent here is the realization that patients by and large attempt to resolve their unconscious conflicts and self-disturbances through a single type of adaptive effort. If this moves in such directions as acting out on alterations in the framework, the patient will have essentially no investment in symptom resolution through insightful means. This is another actual consequence of resistances, especially when they are supported by the direct and indirect implications of realities within the therapeutic interaction, and more rarely, in the life of the patient.

RESISTANCES AND THE THERAPEUTIC OBJECT RELATIONSHIP

We may summarize the interplay between resistances and the nature of the object relationship between the patient and therapist—another reality within therapy—with a series of propositions.

1. *The object relationship needs of, and the actual type of relationship effected by, the therapist will influence both his appraisal*

of resistances within the patient and his actual conscious and unconscious contributions to these resistances. This proposition implies that a therapist must be capable of effecting a healthy symbiosis with a patient in order to make consistently accurate appraisals of the level and nature of a patient's resistances. Pathological symbiotic and parasitic needs in the therapist will have a distorting influence on these evaluations. This will occur because many of the patient's resistances, on this level, reflect a mode of relating which satisfies pathological object relationship needs in both participants to treatment. For similar reasons, pathological relationship needs within the therapist encourage certain types of resistances within the patient, geared toward the achievement of inappropriate forms of fusion and merger which serve as a means of obtaining symptom alleviation. Thrusts of this kind prompt the patient to set to the side communicative efforts directed toward insightful symptom alleviation.

Paradoxically, at selected moments, the therapist's pathological relationship needs may lead to a diminution of resistances and to meaningful material from the patient which is, however, almost entirely concentrated around working over the pathological symbiotic tie in question.

2. *There is a strong correlation between the level of the patient's resistances and a pathological mode of relatedness between the patient and therapist.* Patients who have strong pathological symbiotic and parasitic needs will seek the direct gratification of the constellation of fantasies and actual mode of relatedness involved in these two types of relationship; they will show a relative lack of motivation to resolve their neurosis through insightful therapeutic work. In general, acceptance on the part of the patient of a healthy symbiosis is a requisite for insight or truth therapy.

3. *With patients who accept and contribute to a healthy symbiosis, resistances prove to be relatively analyzable; in contrast, with those who insist upon a pathological symbiosis or parasitism, resistances tend to be difficult to analyze and insightfully resolve.* In general, the healthy symbiosis implies a Type A communicative mode and truth therapy, and therefore the presence of derivative defenses and resistances which eventually prove resolvable through sound managements of the framework and interpretations. On the other hand, patients who insist upon a pathological mode of

relatedness tend to generate nonderivative defenses and resistances—obliterating barriers using a Type C or B–C communicative style—which prove refractory to framework management and interpretive intervention. Meaningful communicative relatedness is disrupted or destroyed, and the patient makes every effort to establish a pathological mode of relatedness characterized by the destruction of meaning, and the development of nonderivative, opaque lie-barrier systems.

4. *Efforts to modify the ground rules and boundaries of the therapeutic relationship are among the most common means through which patients simultaneously express their resistance needs and their wish for a pathological mode of relatedness.* Acquiescence to such deviations or deviations initiated by the therapist support the patient's pathology in both of these spheres. In contrast, efforts by the therapist to maintain the therapeutic environment and to interpret the patient's efforts at deviation inherently contain an offer by the therapist of a healthy rather than pathological form of symbiosis.

5. *There is a complex interplay between mode of relatedness and the vicissitudes of gross behavioral and communicative resistances.* A satisfied pathological symbiosis may lead to the relative absence of gross behavioral resistances, though at times, when the patient wishes to extend the satisfactions of the pathological mode of relatedness, gross behavioral resistances may be utilized. In addition, should the therapist begin to set limits on the pathological mode of relatedness, the patient will often respond with gross behavioral resistances such as extended silences, lateness, and missed sessions.

The presence of a pathological symbiotic or parasitic mode of relatedness often leads to intermittent periods of gross behavioral resistance. On the other hand, the therapist's offer of a healthy symbiosis may be accepted by the patient who then shows little in the way of gross behavioral resistances; or, in patients insistent upon a pathological relationship it may evoke a response with intense gross behavioral resistances.

The satisfactions of a pathological symbiotic or parasitic mode of relatedness are such that they tend to produce strong communicative resistances, except for interludes when the patient unconsciously attempts to deal with and resolve the mode of relatedness itself. It appears that the pathological symbiotic tie, the sense of merger, the alleviation of separation anxieties, the gratification of a wide range of pathological instinctual drive and superego related fantasies, and the inherent efforts at symptom relief derived from the mode of relatedness itself, are such that a patient who has successfully effected this form of relatedness with his therapist will tend to show communicative resistances based on his ability to avoid the anxieties and separateness inherent to insightful therapeutic work.

TECHNICAL ISSUES

Throughout this chapter, I have alluded to issues of technique in respect to the handling of resistances. The present section will briefly summarize and integrate these earlier discussions, extending them where necessary.

The therapeutic approach to resistances begins with a tolerance for their expression and an understanding of their adaptive value for the patient. It entails a recognition that all resistances have interactional components, and that the resolution of these disruptive behaviors within the patient requires a full analysis of all factors within the bipersonal field.

In principle, the first approach to resistances involves the therapist's silent listening. In this way, both gross behavioral and communicative resistances are identified. On the whole, resistances are a high-order indicator and reflect a need within the patient for an intervention from the therapist. However, it must be recognized that not every gross behavioral or communicative resistance can be interpreted; often, the therapist has no choice but to remain silent, to hold the patient, to rectify any contribution of his own to the resistance, and to rely on the patient's own curative endeavors.

In terms of specific technique, the first step in analyzing the sources and implications of a resistance involves identifying the intervention contexts which are active for the moment within the bipersonal field. On this basis, the therapist is able to identify the existence of countertransferences and his own contributions to the patient's defensiveness. It therefore follows that the first technical measure in dealing with a resistance involves rectifications of the therapist's contributions, including a brief period of self-analysis in order to insure that the contribution does not surface in some new form. Such rectification is often done silently. When the contribution has taken the form of participation by the therapist in an alteration in the framework, this first technical step will also involve the rectification of the frame, though always at the behest of the material from the patient.

Extensive clinical and supervisory experience indicates that the silent correction by the therapist of his contributions to the patient's resistances, and the quiet assurance that such errors will not find repetition, is the single most important therapeutic tool available in dealing with these obstacles to treatment. It has been found empirically that patients respond to the therapist's resolution of his own contribution to resistance sectors of misalliance on an unconscious level with efforts of their own to resolve the ways in which they have been disrupting the therapeutic process—behaviorally or communicatively. A remarkably high number of resistances disappear in this way, entirely without active intervention.

The rectification of the therapist's contribution is also absolutely essential for the effective interpretation of resistances. Ideally, the goal is to be able to interpret the unconscious sources, meanings, and functions of resistances as revealed in the patient's material. This step provides the patient with definitive cognitive insight and with a positive introject of the well-functioning therapist as well. On the whole, those interludes in which interpretation prove unfeasible, though rectification has silently taken place, tend to lead to positive introjective identifications with the self-correcting therapist, though they may or may not also produce cognitive insight—depending on whether interpretations follow rectification.

The communicative approach has revealed that confrontations of resistances, questioning patients about their presence, efforts at clarification, and especially noninterpretive interventions such as suggestions as to how to remove resistances, virtually never find validation in the patient's material. Consistently, they are unconsciously perceived as expressions of the therapist's countertransferences; and while a specific resistance may be set aside in this manner, new resistances will always emerge based on the newly expressed countertransferences. One type of unconscious collusion is replaced with another. Such techniques do not eventually lead to insight, but instead basically add to the already present interactional resistances within the patient and in the bipersonal field.

The proper intervention in the presence of resistances is an interpretation. Both gross behavioral and communicative resistances must be understood as responses to an activated adaptive context, and interpreted in terms of the responsive derivative complex. Such interpretive work is greatly facilitated when the patient represents, through some derivative, the resistance at hand; this requires then a well represented adaptive context and a meaningful, coalescing derivative complex. Such interpretive work finds consistent Type Two derivative validation, leads to insightful resolution of the resistance, and often of related symptoms.

In actual practice, however, it appears that some resistances do not lend themselves to interpretation. With a Type A or Type B–A communicator, interpretation is usually eventually possible. With a Type B–C patient, not only is interpretation difficult, but the necessary holding process also proves hard to manage because the therapist is under intense interactional pressures. With the Type C patient, interpretation is possible only rarely, and holding and containing is necessary for long periods of time. There is a sense, however, that the resistances seen in all of these patients are necessary and adaptive, however destructive and maladaptive, and that the therapist's ability to tolerate their presence and to allow the patient himself to work them through, has important and critical therapeutic effects.

The classical psychoanalytic model encourages confrontations and attacks upon the patient's resistances as if they were nothing but dangers to therapy and the therapist, and obstructions to be blasted away. The communicative model stresses the necessary and adaptive aspects of resistance. It recognizes a great capacity within patients to resolve their own resistances, either insightfully or without definitive conscious insight. This enables therapists to treat resistances as necessary obstacles to therapy, and to feel far less threatened when they are unable to interpret their sources and implications.

Some resistances used by patients are based on such an extreme dread of their own inner mental world, or on such justified fears of an errant therapist, that they will remain essentially unmodifiable.

Such limitations are reflected in the absence of interpretable material in the presence of a resistance, a situation which always calls for a careful analysis of possible contributions by the therapist.

Acting out and enactments, especially if unconsciously fostered by the therapist, may also so gratify the patient and reinforce his defenses that they preclude, sometimes permanently, analytic and insightful resolution of resistances. It is therefore important to interpret such behaviors in advance of their enactment if the material permits.

TWO CLINICAL EXAMPLES

Many of the ideas and hypotheses presented in this chapter were derived from, and are illustrated in, the clinical presentations which constitute Part I of this volume. Here, I will offer two additional vignettes as a way of illustrating selected aspects of the present discussion.

Miss A

Miss A was being seen in "analysis" three times weekly for episodes of depression and problems in relating to men. She had been in a relatively stalemated treatment situation for a long time, in part based on her analyst's use of many noninterpretive, so-called supportive interventions, including extensive alterations in the basic ground rules and framework. During a period in which the analyst—a woman—had been gradually securing the frame and had become far less active (striving to respond interpretively wherever possible), the patient began a session by reporting a dream in which a mentally defective child, who was in a class she taught, was brought to that class by his mother, who asked Miss A to take care of him. There was a sense of maternal rejection.

The patient went on to speak of how uncontrolled this youngster was in class, and of her misfortune of having him as a student, especially since his siblings in other classes were so well behaved. She had been able to get him to sit for twenty minutes at a time by establishing firm limits, but once he was released from his seat, he went wild. In the dream, the mother had questioned his work in class. The patient, in her session, went on to cast doubts on the mother's capabilities, and then spoke of how critical her own mother was and how she chided the patient for not having married. As the hour grew to a close, the patient complained about the analyst's silence, saying that the session was wasted when the analyst said nothing. Miss A implored her to speak, though the session ended without comment on the part of the analyst.

The patient cancelled the following hour, and began her next session by reporting on how furious she was with the analyst. She told the analyst that her silence had been a deprivation and a waste, that it might be all right for others, but not for herself, and that she wouldn't tolerate it. She had deliberately missed the previous session because she didn't want to be subjected to further silence, and wanted to show the analyst how it felt. She spoke in great detail about feeling rejected and hurt under these conditions.

The analyst intervened. She pointed out that the patient appeared to be experiencing her silence as a reflection of hostility and rejection. The patient then reiterated her feelings of waste, hurt, and the like, again in some detail. Under these conditions she could talk to anyone or to a tape recorder, though she realized that there was something different about seeing her analyst—a chance to get into the depths of things. She remembered a dream: she was teaching at a new school and there were decorations on the ceiling. She asked the janitor to help her get them down, but he refused. In associating, she suggested that the janitor was her analyst, who, through her silence, was refusing to help her. For the balance of the hour, with considerable repetition, she described her anger at her analyst, and her feelings that she wasn't being helpful by being silent.

To focus entirely on aspects of this vignette pertinent to resistances, we may begin our discussion by noting that in the hour prior to the two reported here, Miss A had spoken in great detail about her problems with her mother and with the young man with whom she was living. The analyst had been relatively silent, though she had intervened without using an adaptive context related to the analytic relationship, and had done so on a manifest content level by alluding to some of the patient's conscious conflicts with these people. In this light, we may postulate that in the first session presented here, the patient did not allude to the activated intervention context from the previous hour on a manifest level at any point in the hour.

It is important to identify the best representation of the main contexts in the patient's material. In the first session, this may be the allusion to the uncontrolled youngster—i.e., a representation of the therapist who is unable to manage her own inner state and to confine herself to Type Two derivative interpretations. This is also evidence of a representation of the therapist in light of her efforts to establish firmer boundaries (a positive context in the form of securing the framework) who nonetheless went "wild" from time to time with interventions which lead the patient to question the nature of her work (the mother who questioned her son's work in class). These particular representations are highly disguised and reflect a significant level of resistance—perhaps seven or eight on a scale of one to ten. The representation is not only in the form of a distant derivative, but pertains to an outside relationship.

Since the therapist remained silent in this particular session, her silence became an additional intervention context. We may note that the patient referred to this particular context manifestly. However, the same manifest content serves as a derivative representation of the therapist's erroneous interventions in the previous hour. This too is a well-disguised expression, showing a high level of resistance, in that it represents a mistaken comment by referring to the therapist's silence. This is especially pertinent in that an evaluation of the therapist's silence in this session would support the use of that particular intervention, since, as I will soon demonstrate, the material does not appear to have permitted an interpretive intervention. We can already sense this in view of our finding that the prevailing intervention context has not been sufficiently clearly represented to permit an interpretive response.

Before turning to the derivative complex, we must consider the indicators for this hour. First, there is the presence of a countertransference error placed by the therapist into the patient. With the little we know, it can be postulated that, in terms of unconscious communication, the intervention was designed to seal off allusions to the current therapeutic interaction and place the source of the patient's disturbance in her relationships with outside figures. While some degree of projective identification was probably involved (we lack the details of the hour and of the intervention), there is evidence as well of the offer of Type C barriers to the patient. In this light, the finding that the patient became highly defensive in respect to representing intervention contexts of the kind avoided by the therapist herself, indicates the type of interactional resistances which can be generated by erroneous interventions—of course, with the full unconscious support of the patient.

The second indicator, which emerged in the course of the hour, took the form of a gross behavioral resistance: complaints about the analyst's silence and direct pressures on the analyst to have her speak. In evaluating this type of behavioral resistance, it is critical to determine whether the therapist has missed an important interpretation or rectification of the frame, or instead is intervening appropriately through her silence, holding the patient well and awaiting interpretable material. In the first instance, the gross behavioral resistance is a response to an error by the therapist designed, however obstructively, to alert the therapist to it, and to mobilize some type of response. The fact that the patient does so by challenging the therapist and wishing to not free associate—to have the therapist talk, no matter what she might say—would lead us to stress the resistance aspect of this particular corrective effort. Nonetheless, it is important to maintain a balanced view of such resistances, and to carefully ascertain their sources before completing an evaluation of their nature and functions, and certainly before intervening.

In this instance, the gross behavioral resistance seems to have two sources which stem from the therapist: first, her efforts to rectify the frame, which may be posing some threat to the patient; and second, her erroneous interventions in the previous hour, which lead to a complaint about the analyst's techniques. In each situation, the gross behavioral resistance is essentially a derivative expression of unconscious perceptions of the therapist's efforts and an indirect reaction to her endeavors.

In principle, the more a particular complaint from the patient is unjustified and based on intrapsychic fantasy constellations and transferences, the more the therapeutic work will be focused on efforts to interpret the resistance. Under these conditions, the analyst's contribution is far more subtle, and while it needs rectification, it may be of relatively minor significance as compared to the patient's contribution. It takes a careful evaluation of each intervention context to determine the implications of gross behavioral resistances of this kind.

In light of the main intervention context stemming from the previous hour, we would evaluate the derivative complex as showing a moderate degree of resistance; I have already identified some of the pertinent derivatives. The complaint about the silence is also a derivative response to the error in the previous session. The material suggests an unconscious perception of the therapist as relatively uncontrolled and as failing in her maternal-like therapeutic capacities. It would be difficult, however, to offer this specific interpretation to the patient in light of the poorly represented intervention context. It seems unlikely that a playback of these selected derivatives would lead the patient to the therapist's error in the previous hour, since clinical experience shows that in the absence of an alteration in the fixed frame, such playbacks seldom further the therapeutic work. Despite the presence of both unconscious perceptions and introjections of the analyst's failings and a sense of the patient's own inner experience of defectiveness, and a rather strong indicator as reflected in the patient's protest toward the end of the hour, it would seem that the analyst was not in a position to offer an interpretive response. The therapist could, however, have attempted silently to identify her contributing mistake, and benefit from the patient's appeal for limits and controls by rectifying any other existing breaks in the basic framework. Through such efforts, it might then be possible for the patient to feel more securely held, and on that basis, to modify her main resistances.

There is a resistance quality to the way in which the patient, toward the end of the session, provides a bridge to the analytic relationship. This appears in a form that does not lend itself to understanding and interpretation, but which instead invites a manifest content form of relatedness which would serve the resistances of the patient and counterresistances of the analyst. At best, the intensity of this last indicator might have led to an intervention in which the therapist suggested that there were many allusions to poor class work and poor maternal care, and to a sense of failure, which seem to have been prompted by something taking place in the treatment situation. This would, of course, constitute a playback of selected derivatives around the unmentioned adaptive context of the previous, erroneous intervention. While it might not obtain Type Two derivative validation, it would create such a possibility and provide the patient with an opportunity for eventual cognitive insight. At the same time, it would generate a positive introjective identification with the analyst who is showing her appreciation for some of her own difficulties and the patient's unconscious perception and introjection of these problems.

In light of the subsequent missed session, it seems likely that this particular type of incomplete interpretation should have been made. The analyst's continued silence and failure to intervene can be seen as having not obtained validation since the patient's response constituted acting out through a modification in the fixed frame—a missed session. The absence is, of course, a behavioral resistance. We can identify sources within the therapist in terms of her earlier erroneous effort at interpretation (done without an adaptive context) and her subsequent silence in the following hour, to a point where it appears now that an intervention should have been made. The resistance also receives some contribution from the therapist's unconscious collusion with the patient in the form of a bastion and sector of misalliance designed to seal off much of the communicative interaction. In addition, some degree of resistance may have been unfolding in response to the analyst's efforts to secure a proper therapeutic environment, thereby creating a setting in which a potential therapeutic regression and sense of separateness might well occur in this patient, who in some ways seemed rather terrified of such an experience. Since a secure setting is essential for valid therapeutic work, such measures do not call for correction, but must be dealt with interpretively and with considerable sensitivity, especially with patients fearful of their unconscious perceptions of the therapist and their own primitive fantasy constellations.

The communicative qualities of the patient's associations in the first hour appear mixed. There are indications of Type A communication in light of the potentially meaningful derivative complex, and there is sufficient representation of the intervention context to suggest the use of repression within a Type A communicative mode. Toward the end of the session, there is a shift to Type C communication with repetitive complaints about the therapist, and eventually, a Type B–C mode through which the patient seemed to be projectively identifying some type of disturbance into the therapist, and to be trying to evoke image-role qualities which would generate in the therapist a sense of guilt, inadequacy, failure, and destructiveness. It may well be that the therapist's intervention in the previous hour was experienced as a destructive projective identification, and that in this session, the patient was attempting to reproject this unmetabolized introject into the therapist.

In general, a shift from a Type A mode to a Type B–C suggests a shift in resistances from the use of derivative defenses to nonderivative, Type C barriers. This type of change in the patient's communicative mode is in itself an indicator, and often calls for the best possible available interpretation from the therapist. This is particularly necessary in the presence of relatively violent projective identifications and a mounting sense of lie-barrier formations, with a consequent loss of derivative meaning and a positive sense of relatedness. This shift might have alerted the analyst to a need for an interpretation, a response which might have enabled the patient to insightfully modify her growing tendency toward action-discharge. When the therapist failed to intervene, the patient extended and intensified her use of projective identification, action-discharge, and Type C barriers in the form of a deliberate absence.

Turning to the second session, we can begin more systematically with the indicators. These involve the patient's absence, a gross behavioral and serious therapeutic context, and associated feelings of resentment toward, and disillusionment in, the therapist. The deliberate quality of the absence is somewhat ominous both in respect to the patient's psychopathology and the dangers for the treatment situation. Clearly, the alliance sector has been shattered for the moment by problems stemming from both participants. Finally, there is the therapist's failure to intervene in the prior hour, and based on our revised evaluation of her silence, it would appear that there was a missed opportunity for intervening toward the end of the first session. Taken together, I would propose a rating of nine for these indicators, and would suggest that the patient has an intense need for an interpretive response from the therapist.

Prior to the analyst's actual comment, we have a series of associations which manifestly relate to the analyst herself. While the patient directly alludes to the analyst's silence and latently to the missed intervention (and remember, this is by no means a glaring error), the material also alludes to the earlier erroneous effort at interpretation. As representations of the intervention contexts, there is still a sense of resistance; the manifest qualities of this material suggests the possibility of unrecognized errors by the therapist.

As for the derivative complex, the repetitive complaints about the analyst are relatively linear, flat, and thin. They do not develop a series of divergent meanings and implications, and do not constitute a coalescing derivative network. Such material would be mistakenly understood by many analysts as expressions of "transference," and interpretations would be offered to the patient to the effect that her anger and hostility, and feelings of deprivation, are inappropriate to the current situation and derive instead from the criticisms and deprivations experienced with her mother (using here the allusion to the patient's mother in the previous hour). The postulated unconscious mechanism would be displacement, and the material would be seen as a breakthrough of conscious hostility and criticism toward the analyst which more correctly pertains to the mother. There would be no sense of derivative communication. The possibility of realistic, nontransference factors in the patient's anger, and the likelihood that these manifest associations are serving derivative functions related to some unconscious transference and nontransference constellation, would receive little or no consideration. Therapists of this persuasion would propose to the patient, as this analyst did to some small degree, that her absence was an expression of her rage at the analyst for the deprivations contained in her silence—if they would refer at all to the here and now. They would be likely to attribute the acting out to the patient's conflicts with her mother.

In this situation, then, some classical analysts would deal with the gross behavioral resistance in terms of the patient's manifest anger at the analyst, while others would stress the displaced contribution from the patient's conflicts with the maternal figure. Either way, there would be a failure to develop an interpretation based on an in-depth evaluation of the intervention contexts and the patient's *derivative* communications.

By contrast, we would evaluate these manifest allusions to the analyst as highly resistant, and especially nonrevealing in terms of the derivative complex. There is more of a Type C than Type A communicative quality, and a sense of lie-barrier system designed to break the relationship link between the patient and analyst, and as a barrier to underlying, catastrophic truths within the patient and the therapeutic interaction. Unconscious contents and functions are relatively imperceptible even though the links and bridges to the analyst are offered. The communicative qualities of a cluster of associations cannot be evaluated from the manifest content alone, without studying their variability and their implications vis-à-vis a specific adaptive context.

Turning next to the analyst's intervention, our evaluation would indicate that it was based on the patient's manifest associations— i.e., the patient had successfully engaged the therapist in a manifest content form of relatedness. This level of interaction and intervention is inherently resistant and counterresistant, and a form of misalliance usually designed to seal off the unconscious implications of the patient's material and of the therapist's interventions. As measured by the criteria developed in this book, it must be viewed as essentially erroneous and therefore countertransference-based. It alludes to the adaptive context of the analyst's silence, though not to the prior error. It lacks the use of derivative implications and confines itself to the surface of the patient's associations. It therefore serves to join with and reinforce the analysand's Type C barrier-resistances, and would be expected to have two effects: on the one hand, to reinforce the patient's own resistances, while on the other, to possibly stimulate the patient toward corrective efforts on behalf of both herself and her analyst.

This formulation is confirmed initially when the patient goes on to ruminate further about her anger and her other direct responses to the analyst's silence. The allusion to the tape recorder may well constitute an unconscious perception of the clichéd, mechanical qualities of interventions of this type. Certainly, the responsive material in no way meets the criterion of Type Two derivative validation central for psychoanalytic confirmation—it reveals no new and unexpected truths or selected facts. The tape recorder may also be seen as a metaphor for the Type C communicative mode which has mechanical and unreal qualities, a mode now in use by both participants to the treatment.

Having accepted the offered interactional defenses, the patient next conveys a single and striking derivative, seemingly designed as a meaningful communicative expression: the allusion to getting to the depths of things with her analyst. Here the patient appears to offer a clue to her response to the analyst's efforts to secure the framework, doing so through a heavily disguised communication which hints at her underlying fears and a dread of her inner mental world. This passing comment takes on considerable meaning in light of that particular intervention context.

The dream of the new school follows, a theme which suggests a further reaction to the therapist's efforts to rectify the frame. We see here a situation in which the patient's associations, formulated as derivatives, provide clues to the activated adaptive context to which she is presently responding on a neurotic level. The theme of the new school suggests that the therapist's effort to rectify the frame offers an opportunity for a new beginning and a new form of learning for the patient. It may also be an unconscious directive to the therapist to seek further training in light of her recent error. The decorations on the ceilings may represent a maniclike defense and a flight from the depths. The janitor's refusal to help the patient get these decorations down may imply an unconscious perception that the analyst was now less inclined to help the patient with such barriers and defenses. With this expressed, Miss A returns to rumination and Type C barriers, again in the form of manifest allusions to the analyst.

The formulations based on these associations have a highly tentative quality. These derivatives appear to be fragmented clues which, while showing some tendency toward coalescence, do not build up into a convincing derivative complex. Certainly, the initial silent hypothesis of the patient's fears of her innermost feelings and fantasies found some validation in the subsequent dream. Nonetheless, both the representation of the adaptive context and the derivative complex show a moderately high level of resistance, which undoubtedly made it difficult for the analyst to intervene in this session.

However, there were some Type A and derivative communications, however weak. In the presence of a therapeutic context of intense resistance and acting out, with major threats to the therapeutic alliance and the treatment itself, the therapist was faced with a group of indicators which approached the situation in which it would be best to intervene, if at all possible, rather than to remain silent. There was a thin but complete communicative network: a powerful and represented indicator, an intervention context which was alluded to directly, a clear-cut bridge to the analyst, and several weak but coalescing derivatives—the allusion to the fear of the depths, the recognition of an opportunity for a new beginning, the wish for maniclike defenses and a flight from unconscious processes and contents, and signs of some level of awareness of the analyst's nonparticipation in the patient's defensiveness. While the adaptive context of the therapist's efforts to rectify the frame was represented in a highly disguised manner—primarily through the reference to the new school and to the janitor who would not help the patient take down the decorations—a playback of the relevant derivatives might well have evoked a direct reference to the therapist's efforts along these lines in subsequent associations.

The therapist might have suggested to the patient that on the surface she seemed quite angry about the silence, but was also showing some disturbance in regard to the basic conditions of treatment—reflected in her deliberate decision to miss an hour. She had gone on to speak of having an opportunity to get into the depths of things and had alluded to a new school and to decorations on a ceiling. It seemed that she wanted to reach out for these happy decorations, but experienced the janitor, someone whom she associated with the analyst, as not helping her to get them down. While this might, as the patient was suggesting, refer to the analyst's silence, it also might mean that the patient was perceiving something new about the therapeutic situation and the change in the therapist, who no longer seemed to be cooperating with efforts to decorate things and perhaps cover them over, and possibly to avoid the depths. It would seem that whatever new was happening, it was providing the patient with the chance to move toward the depths of things, that she preferred to move away from such depths and resented the failure of the therapist to help her in such an effort. Perhaps this was why she took flight on her own and missed the hour, and was also threatening the very continuation of treatment.

This particular interpretation is primarily a playback of derivatives organized around the poorly represented and unmentioned adaptive context of the therapist's efforts to rectify the frame. This particular context is the focus of the interpretation primarily because derivative associations point to its importance, while the material organizes quite poorly around the adaptive context of the therapist's silences. The interpretation is designed to understand the unconscious basis for the prevailing indicators, which include both gross behavioral and communicative resistances. The therapist might even have alluded to the patient's repetitiveness and communicative defensiveness, though such comments would have to be based largely upon the complaints about the therapist, an area that might best be left untouched for the moment, since such an intervention would be too confronting. The lack of cooperation between the janitor and the patient might be seen as representing the disturbance in communication within the analysis, and used as a communicative expression through which particular problems could be identified and commented upon.

In essence, then, the gross behavioral resistance of the patient's absence from the session, and the communicative resistances through which the patient had shifted to a Type C communicative style, would have been interpreted here in light of the intervention context of the therapist's efforts to secure the frame, and understood in terms of derivative communications related to the patient's fears of the depths and of the loss of her maniclike defenses. The intervention could also have included a reference to the impression that the patient's anger about the therapist's silence represented a response to the changes in therapeutic technique, which threatened her considerably.

In offering this particular interpretation, we have met the criteria of dealing with indicator-resistances by identifying the pertinent intervention context and the patient's derivative—adaptive and maladaptive—responses. It would remain as a therapeutic task for the analyst to find allusions in subsequent associations to other pertinent adaptive contexts, such as the recent erroneous interventions, and to interpret the present resistances in light of those additional intervention contexts when the material permitted. As a rule, an interpretation of this kind finds Type Two derivative validation and is rewarded with material which covers the unfinished interpretive business at hand. Still, this sequence has provided an opportunity to understand once again the nature of interpretive work in dealing with resistances. These efforts would, of course, be accompanied by further endeavors by the therapist to avoid incorrect interventions. Here, since one of the main stimuli involves the rectification of the frame, there would be no need for a corrective in this regard. Instead, it would be important for the therapist to understand the anxieties evoked within this patient because the framework is being secured, and to interpret the manifestations of resistances accordingly.

Miss B

Let us turn to a second vignette. Miss B was in psychotherapy twice weekly because of episodes of anxiety and problems in forming lasting relationships with men. There had been many alterations in the framework and a multiplicity of erroneous interventions throughout her treatment. She had responded with frequent latenesses and long periods of silence in her sessions. She also made scathing attacks on her boss who seemed to be ineffectual and incompetent, though almost never with clear links to the therapist. These resistances, then, had distinctly interactional qualities, and lacked, as a rule, a connection to a meaningful communicative network. In general, based on contributions from both the patient and therapist, the communicative field shifted about from Type B to Type C, and there were many indications that the frequent deviations by the therapist had created a therapeutic space within which the patient feared to express herself in a meaningful manner.

At the time of the sessions to be discussed here, the therapist had become relatively silent, in contrast to his many active previous interventions which were made as a rule without allusion to an activated adaptive context. He was involved in efforts to generate valid interpretations and to secure the framework. The patient began an hour to which she was five minutes late by reviewing a discussion in the previous session between herself and the therapist about her lateness that day. In the hour, and based on an uncertain cluster of associations, the therapist had pointed out, with some hesitation, that this behavior appeared to reflect a wish to provoke him and a lack of interest in the treatment. The patient now agreed that this was the case, but described difficulties in finding things to say in the sessions and feelings that the therapist spoke mysteriously. She had been at a party with a group of analysts who talked about their patients in considerable detail, and who seemed far more interactive with them than this therapist. They offered judgments and the like, and the patient wished that the therapist would do something similar.

Miss B next reported a dream in which she was at work attending a going-away party for someone. It takes days for the food to come in and the patient can't wait to attack it. It turns out to be dried stuff and unappetizing, like some Japanese fish that she had recently seen in a store. The dream, she went on, had been prompted by a shopping trip and by a strawberry shortcake she had waited to eat at a dinner party. She thought of two men at her previous job with whom she had had affairs: Al, who is a genius but arrogant, and Fred, who is stupid and just can't think or work analytically. She wondered if she is perceptive or impatient.

The therapist intervened, pointing out that Miss B had suggested that there was something mysterious about his comments, which she had experienced in part as critical of her lateness. She had also spoken of other therapists giving more to their patients, and of her appetite, though what was offered to her was inedible. Next, she referred to someone who was unable to follow an analytic approach or framework. All of this, he suggested, must be connected in some way to his recent interventions. The patient replied that she did not mind structuralization and that she felt that the therapist had simply repeated what she had said, adding nothing new.

We may recognize that this particular session begins with a behavioral resistance: the patient's lateness. While we have little information regarding the prior hour, it was the evaluation of the therapist that he had confronted the patient and had made use of Type One derivatives and manifest contents in his comments about the patient's wish to provoke him and her lack of interest in therapy. He realized that he had not based his interpretation of the resistance on an evaluation of derivative responses to an activated adaptive context. Instead, he had placed the responsibility for the lateness entirely within the patient, and his intervention could be seen as an expression of hostility.

In this light, we can recognize that Miss B referred rather quickly in the present session to the specific intervention context of the therapist's comment in the prior hour, doing so manifestly and with, of course, a clear-cut link to the therapist. This is a relatively ideal representation of an activated adaptive context. It should be mentioned, however, that when a patient so clearly represents one context, it is likely that there is an additional active intervention context which is being repressed. While we cannot establish this possibility in the present material because we lack the details of the prior sessions, in the previous vignette we saw that Miss A represented the intervention context of her analyst's silence while repressing, and resorting to highly disguised representations of, the intervention context of efforts to secure the framework and interpretive errors. It is common to find that a patient is reacting to at least two or three major intervention contexts, representing one rather clearly while repressing and disguising the allusions to the others. The therapist must evaluate which intervention context best fits the subsequent derivative material and which appears to be most crucial. He must be prepared to find that a patient's readiness to work over a particular intervention context, while meaningful in itself, can serve as a resistance to working over another and more threatening precipitant.

In this situation, the representation of the intervention context is followed by a group of meaningful, coalescing derivatives related to unconscious perceptions—and possibly fantasies—pertaining to the therapist. There are references to inappropriate comments by therapists who violate the confidentiality of their treatment situations, thoughts of leaving treatment, feeling ill-fed, being gratified and fed, having affairs, a man who is bright and arrogant, and another who is stupid and incapable of working analytically.

We have, then, a Type A field with a sound communicative network, much of it illuminating unconscious factors in the patient's behavioral resistance. We see that the patient is making use of defenses with which to disguise, mainly through displacement, her unconscious perceptions of the therapist as intervening inappropriately, as being bright but arrogant, and as showing a basic difficulty in working analytically. The patient is therefore making use of important defenses which may also include projection (e.g., of the patient's own sexual needs and wishes—though these expressions may also be based on unconscious perceptions of the therapist), while the level of resistance is quite low. We have a situation with a gross behavioral resistance and a relative absence of communicative resistance.

The therapist's intervention is fairly sound, and in fact, appeared in supervision to be the most valid and meaningful interpretation that he had offered this patient in the course of her treatment. It is an attempt to interpret the patient's gross behavioral resistance in terms of its unconscious basis in the therapeutic interaction and as a response to a mobilized intervention context. However, based on the available material, the intervention is somewhat limited since it fails to identify a number of important derivatives.

Ideally, in light of the indicator of the patient's continued lateness and complaints about treatment, the interpretation might have been made that the patient seemed to be responding to the therapist's comment in the previous hour. In some way, she saw the intervention as interactive and self-revealing, as judgmental, and as unappetizing. In a way, it led her to view the therapist on one level as bright but arrogant, and on another as dense and unable to work analytically. She seems to respond to these perceptions by coming late to the sessions as if to avoid their influence and the seductive qualities of the intervention—alluded to in the patient's thoughts about two men with whom she had had affairs.

In this way, the behavioral resistance is interpreted as a response to the adaptive context of the therapist's erroneous intervention, and is based on a series of derivatives which pertain to the patient's unconscious perceptions and fantasies about the therapist. The intervention itself has certain tentative qualities, and we might speculate that some of this arises because the material hints at different, underlying adaptive contexts which would have to be clearly represented and identified in order to complete the interpretation of the basis for the patient's lateness. For example, there are clues that the patient is simultaneously reacting to both the therapist's erroneous interventions and to his efforts to secure the framework. As with Miss A, Miss B seems threatened by the secure frame and by certain perceived dangers in response to the new conditions of her therapy.

To illustrate, if we take these efforts as the intervention context, the patient's lateness can be viewed as an effort to break the frame and seek a framework deviation cure. Her agreement with the previous intervention shows her unconscious appreciation for the therapist's efforts to create a more optimal therapeutic environment. However, the patient is clearly split in this regard, in that she then alludes to a party with analysts who violate their patients' confidentiality and also appear to interact with them in deviant ways. The going-away party may allude to the patient's wish to escape the better secured therapeutic situation. Within such a framework, she may be feeling deprived and hungry. Here, the thoughts of the two men with whom she had affairs would hint at the emergence of unconscious sexual fantasy constellations and the development of a transference constellation far more than one involving nontransference. The inability to work analytically would be a reference to herself, and her fears of this particular type of treatment.

These are, of course, highly tentative formulations and silent hypotheses. The best representation of the indicator-adaptive context of the therapist's efforts to secure the framework is conveyed through an opposite: the reference to the therapists who are judgmental and who have violated the confidentiality of their patients. While it might have been possible to intervene with the derivatives just described with a hint that they allude to securing the therapeutic environment and the patient's wish for a broken frame—an interpretation which would illuminate the function of her lateness—it seems more advisable for the therapist to sit back and await further associations in the hope that the patient's communicative resistances in respect to the intervention context related to securing the framework would lessen. There would then follow a representation of that particular adaptive context which would more readily lend itself to interpretation. In this light, the actual interpretation offered must be seen as only a first step and as a compromise, in that it deals with the more negative qualities of the therapist's efforts without showing the patient her anxieties and other responses to the more positive aspects.

To continue, the patient arrived fifteen minutes late to the next session. Quite uncharacteristically, however, she paid the therapist for the month's sessions at the beginning of the hour. Since the check included payment for the session at hand, the therapist suggested that Miss B hold onto the check and explore her offer. She then apologized for her lateness, blaming an obligation at work. She was starting a new job and wondered if she would be able to manage and to serve well as a supervisor. She had felt that her role was as yet unclear and that she lacked sanctions over her supervisees. She had had more power in her previous job and wondered why she left it, but felt certain that she had not made a mistake. She then spoke of her new boss, who was personable, attractive and competent. She felt sexually stimulated by him and knew she had to keep those feelings separate or they would interfere with the job.

The therapist intervened and pointed out that the patient had been late and had then offered a check at the beginning of the hour, thereby attempting to change their basic agreement. She had gone on to speak of her new job and of the need for cooperation, though the absence of sanctions or ground rules would make matters difficult. She seemed to be having a similar problem with her boss, because there was something sexual there. She was alluding to separating out those feelings, and she related that to the need for ground rules. The patient responded that she felt that she didn't need such ground rules as much as the therapist implied, and she ruminated about the importance of good feelings in her job and the general need for structure. She spoke again of having to control her sexual feelings toward her boss, and felt unable to follow the therapist and quite confused. The therapist then said that the patient was expressing a need for ground rules based on the fear that what she might say in the session would be heard as illogical or nonsensical. The patient said she didn't mind being illogical as long as something comes out of it.

This session begins with a gross behavioral resistance: the patient's lateness. Later we see another type of resistance in the patient's comment that she didn't need ground rules as much as the therapist implied. The latter is a manifest disagreement with the therapist, and may therefore be defined as a resistance since it opposes the therapist's efforts and the therapeutic process as implied in his intervention. We will return to this resistance when we have analyzed this session, although we may note immediately that while many therapists assume that such disagreements are the result of defenses and resistances within the patient, the communicative approach calls for a full evaluation of the validity of the therapist's intervention and leaves ample room for a class of resistances, to which this response may well belong, which may be understood to include all valid and legitimate objections by the patient to the therapist's erroneous interventions and mismanagements of the frame. This is a strong reminder that resistances do not arise exclusively or entirely from the psychopathology of the patient, and that they may indeed reflect sound, adaptive responses.

Faced with the acting out or enactment reflected in the patient's lateness, let us now turn to the communicative network as it unfolded in this particular hour. Early in the session, the patient specifically alludes to her lateness, thereby representing this particular resistance indicator on a manifest level. It is not uncommon with resistance indicators which take the form of acting out by the patient, such as latenesses and absences—and for comparable counterresistance indicators in the therapist, such as his own lateness or absence, or some other break in the frame—to find that the patient represses his allusion to the therapeutic context and fails to represent the indicator on a manifest level. For the communicative therapist, this poses special difficulties since he will respect all of the patient's resistances and attempt to deal with them entirely through rectification of the frame and interpretation. An occasional exception can be made in the presence of a gross behavioral resistance enacted in the immediate hour, though even then, this type of intervention is often met with nonvalidation and strong secondary resistances.

Turning to the intervention context, we find no clear-cut representation in the material prior to the therapist's intervention, and no evidence of a link to the therapist or a more general bridge to the treatment situation. We may sense some meaning to the patient's offer of payment for past sessions as well as the present one, though it would be necessary to await the subsequent communicative network for clarification. In any case, the therapist's refusal to accept the check in advance of the hour, and his suggestion in this regard, constitutes an immediate adaptive context for the session which contains both an effort to maintain a secure framework and a directive which, though it further advocates adherence to the basic ground rules, lessens the patient's autonomy.

Based on the material from the previous hour, we know of two additional adaptive contexts. The first is the background context of the therapist's efforts to maintain and rectify the framework, a group of interventions not described here, though they find renewed expression in the therapist's handling of the check. The second context is, of course, the therapist's intervention in the previous hour, which we have evaluated as mixed in nature: entailing some seemingly valid elements yet incomplete in important ways.

We must recognize, however, that Type Two derivative validation was not forthcoming in the final moments of the session in which the effort at interpretation was made, though attention would have to be paid to the material in the following hour before a final determination of the presence or absence of confirmation could be effected. In this regard, the offer of the check appears, in keeping with expectations, to contain a mixed message: a positive tribute to the therapist on one hand, while also, an effort to modify the frame and restore some sense of misalliance and shared resistance. This derivative appears to confirm, however tentatively, our assessment of the therapist's effort at interpretation. It offers some degree of validation to the hypothesis that the patient is responding in a mixed way to the therapist's efforts to offer a relatively secure therapeutic environment: she is prepared to pay the fee, but attempts to do so by breaking the frame. This particular effort suggests that the patient is quite divided in her response to the newly secured therapeutic climate, paying tribute to it in part, but also attempting to draw the therapist into some type of compromise. In light of this particular derivative, the patient's lateness to the session can be postulated to reflect efforts to modify the security of the framework, unconsciously determined and based on anxiety evoked by the therapist's efforts to secure the treatment situation. In some sense, the behavior with the check is a moderately disguised representation of this context, and a possibility of interpretation exists based on the many complex implications of this initial communication.

There are other disguised but likely representations of this intervention context: the reference to the new job, the importance of sanctions in handling supervisees, the sense of power in the previous job, the absence of a mistake, the attractiveness of the new boss, and the need to keep her sexual feelings toward him separate from the work situation lest they interfere with the job—an especially compelling derivative allusion to an important function of the ground rules which create the basic therapeutic environment. These derivatives not only represent the adaptive context of securing the framework mobilized by the therapist's response to the check, but also constitute a rich and coalescing derivative complex of relatively low resistance, one that lends itself to interpretive efforts.

In the present situation, the therapist might well have prepared the following silent intervention: You were late in coming to the session and then offered to pay me for this month's sessions, though your check included a payment for the present session which had not yet been completed. Your behavior suggests that the ground rules of treatment are on your mind and that you have mixed feelings in respect to maintaining the relatively secure frame. On the one hand, you talk about the importance of sanctions over supervisees, the absence of a mistake, the attractiveness of your boss, and the importance of keeping sexual feelings out of your work relationship so that they do not interfere with your job. This followed my asking you to hold onto the check, and therefore not joining you in a modification of our agreement as to the payment of my fee. As you can see, on the one hand you are attempting to modify the frame both through your lateness and your offer of premature payment, while on the other hand, you are alluding to the importance of clear-cut ground rules and boundaries. You seem quite divided in this respect, wishing to maintain the framework on the one hand, while on the other, attempting to modify it. It appears too that when the frame is secured, you begin to experience sexual feelings and to feel threatened by them.

The last comment in this proposed intervention is tentative and would have been held back awaiting additional confirmatory and coalescing material; but it is nonetheless extremely critical. Much of the prior material describes the patient's unconscious perceptions of the therapist who has secured the frame and reflects the meanings of the new setting—the reference to the new job, an opportunity for growth despite the surrender of a previous power base (a likely allusion to the positive changes in the quality of the therapeutic environment). The patient also states that her role is unclear, and this appears to be a means of reflecting her uncertainty about the new therapeutic situation.

However, these perceptions and adaptive responses do not contain clear representations of the pertinent instinctual drives being expressed by either the therapist or the patient. Sound interpretations ultimately must include both instinctual drive considerations and genetic implications. There is a common form of counterresis-

tance seen in much present-day therapeutic work which is mani-
fested by the omission of specific instinctual drive derivatives in the
interpretations from therapists and analysts. In their place are
comments made about power struggles, wishes to control, dependency needs, and narcissistic hurts. While such comments may well
have their place in intervening, as long as they do not eventually
include allusions to basic instinctual drive derivatives and conflicts, they are lacking a critical component.

The patient's last association in this sequence prior to the therapist's intervention offers the first clear-cut instinctual drive derivative, and thereby reveals an important, specific unconscious motive
for her behavioral and communicative resistances—the latter,
mainly in the form of the relatively poor representations of the
prevailing adaptive contexts. In essence, the patient is indicating
that in the presence of a secure frame and well-functioning therapist, her own unconscious sexual fantasies and anxieties become
aroused, and she experiences a fear of not being able to maintain
the boundaries between herself and the therapist, and of losing
control over her sexual feelings. In the absence of seductive communications from the therapist and in the presence of a direct effort
to maintain the framework, this material appears to reflect *unconscious transference fantasies* whose genetic basis is, for the moment,
not specified. This formulation is in keeping with previous observations (Langs 1980a) that transference manifestations appear in
response to valid interventions from the therapist, while nontransference expressions characterize responses to the therapist's erroneous interventions.

We have here, then, a typical form of transference resistance in its
narrowest sense: behavioral and communicative defenses prompted
by threatening unconscious, pathology-related erotic fantasies
about the therapist expressed through derivatives in the session.
Because the emergence of such fantasies even in derivative form
pose considerable threat for the patient, it would be important for
the therapist to withhold any effort at interpretation until supportive derivatives have emerged. In addition, in intervening, every
attempt would have to be made to be tactful and cautious, lest the
patient respond to the therapist's interpretation with initial Type
Two derivative validation, only to then develop new and stubborn
resistances based on her anxieties about her emerging feelings and

fantasies toward the therapist. It is in this respect that the patient's communicative resistances are protective for the moment. An intervention which would pressure the patient to recognize the implications of her associations for her relationship with the therapist— i.e., to simply set aside the patient's resistances and defenses— might well prove catastrophic. The principle remains that, before intervening, it is best to wait for the patient to modify her own resistances, to provide either a bridge to the treatment situation in general, or a new representation of the activated adaptive contexts with the link to the therapist in evidence. A delicate decision would have to be made if the patient did not modify her resistances in this way, since the silent intervention which I proposed earlier in this discussion would be offered to the patient in this hour. Failure to do so might well be perceived unconsciously by the patient as conveying the therapist's fear of the patient's erotic fantasies. On the other hand, the intervention could well bring into the patient's awareness threatening fantasies which would evoke a new set of resistances. Much would depend on the therapist's knowledge of the patient's capacity to tolerate such fantasies, the state of the therapeutic alliance, and the power of the indicators—the latter implying that the suggestion of major resistances and a significant need within the patient might prompt an intervention in this hour.

Accumulated clinical experience suggests, however, that with continued silence on the part of the therapist, and adherence to the framework, the derivatives would become clearer. This occurs in part because of the ego strength acquired by the patient from the sound efforts of the therapist, a factor which would lead her to modify her resistances. As a result, the necessary context, link, and bridges would eventually emerge, permitting the interpretation already outlined. To state this a bit differently, in the presence of Type A communication from the patient, it is common for him to move independently toward the resolution of resistances especially when he is dealing with an important indicator and adaptive context.

The revelation of the patient's unconscious erotic transference fantasies help to clarify the specific function of her gross behavioral resistances. The lateness can now be seen as an attempt to create distance, and as a specific defense against the unconscious sexual fantasies. The offer of the check is a compromise formation which expresses and gratifies these fantasies through an enactment with the therapist which would create a sector of misalliance precluding analysis of the underlying fantasy constellations. If the therapist had participated in the deviation, the patient would have been justified in developing an unconscious perception and introjection of *his* seductiveness, and would readily conceal her own sexual fantasies and conflicts within that cover.

In respect to the modification of resistances, the therapist's non-participation in the patient's efforts to deviate lead to securing the therapeutic field and permitting the patient to become engaged in Type A derivative communication—of a kind previously quite uncharacteristic, according to the therapist. Unfortunately, he was unable to maintain this stance throughout the hour. Thus, his next intervention regarding the patient's lateness and efforts to modify the frame, her concern about her boss and sexual feelings, and her need for ground rules, is offered without reference to a specific adaptive context and makes use of a very weak link to the therapist. The intervention does not develop the specific issue of the patient's anxieties within the secure framework and in respect to her emerging unconscious, sexual, transference-based feelings, placing these outside of the treatment relationship. The therapist's comment is also confused and confusing, and serves primarily to provide the patient with a displacement and barrier or defense against her specific unconscious sexual fantasies about the therapist. It therefore offers the patient an interactional resistance that seems likely to reinforce her own needs for defense.

In addition to serving as a Type C barrier, this particular intervention has qualities of a projective identification into the patient of the therapist's anxieties and confusion in response to the emerging derivatives of the unconscious erotic transference. It is not uncommon, especially among neophyte therapists, to find that they have difficulty in offering patients valid interpretations, and further, that once they have done so, they tend to become anxious and to regress. They also tend to offer their patients defenses and barriers against the instinctual-drive manifest and latent material which frequently emerges after a correct interpretive effort or the proper management of the framework. Such an outcome is in evidence in this vignette, and the therapist's intervention suggests that he had responded to the sexual material with considerable anxiety and a loss of his capacity to make relatively clear interpretations.

The presence of such anxieties is suggested by the therapist's decision to intervene as soon as the patient had alluded to sexual feelings toward her boss, rather than allowing additional, clarifying associations to follow—including the likely transition to more and more clear expressions related to the therapist. We may postulate that the therapist quickly sensed the danger that the patient's instinctual drives would soon be directed toward himself. Such a build-up is a common consequence of such interpretations when they are offered within a secure frame. This point, as far as I can determine, was first mentioned in Strachey's brilliant paper (1934), in which he discussed the fear in analysts of making mutative interpretations—those which pertain directly to the patient's activated instinctual drive wishes toward the analyst.

The patient's response to the therapist's intervention seems to support some of these hypotheses. There is a direct refutation of an aspect of the intervention, and a shift to rumination. The patient seems to have accepted the therapist's offer of an interactional defense, and to have introjected his own state of confusion. The result is the appearance of new communicative resistances and the lack of a meaningful cluster of derivatives. The allusion to her own need to control her sexual feelings toward the boss may now be based on an unconscious perception of the therapist, who may well have been engaged in inappropriate efforts to control his sexual countertransferences and to shut out the patient's sexual derivatives.

The therapist's final intervention, in which he restated the need for ground rules, may have been directed more toward himself than the patient. He introduced the fear of becoming illogical or non-sensical—of regression and craziness—suggesting again an anxious response to the emergence of the patient's erotic feelings. The patient's final comment—that she didn't mind being illogical as long as something comes out of it—may well have been an effort to reassure the therapist and to remind him that it is essential for the patient to regress in treatment in order to have an opportunity to analyze the relevant unconscious fantasy and perception constellations. The hint is that the therapist too should be able to tolerate such disturbing stimuli in the service of the goals of the treatment.

At this point in the therapy, it would seem that the therapist's counterresistances are far more powerful than the patient's resistances. In this situation, while there is considerable evidence of the therapist's wish for the patient to develop defenses and resistances in respect to the emerging erotic material, the patient responds in a mixed manner: alluding again to the sexual feelings, but developing them no further, and therefore accepting some level of resistance, while suggesting through derivatives to the therapist that this frightening material should be tolerated in order to further the therapeutic work—i.e., that the resistances and counterresistances need to be resolved in order to permit the analysis of the emerging unconscious fantasy and perception constellations. Much of a patient's unconscious therapeutic work directed toward the therapist (see chapter 12) is designed to help the therapist resolve his counterresistances and an expression of the patient's wish to resolve her own resistances as well. Patients tend to fluctuate within sessions and from session to session in respect to their wish to mobilize or resolve resistances. Their wish to resolve them has been greatly underestimated in the psychoanalytic literature; it actually constitutes a major resource for their modification in a well run therapeutic experience.

Briefly, the patient was late again for the next hour. She spoke of her boss's accusation of irresponsibility on her part, because she had taken two days off from work and had failed to prepare certain materials in time for a deadline of which, however, she had been unaware. She then described her relationship with her previous boss which had continued after she had left that job a year ago. He's constantly teasing her about men and making seductive overtures with his body—getting physical, but then pulling away. His behavior is contradictory and weird. He stirs her up, but yet doesn't want to sleep with her. She thought next of another fellow at her former job who was always involved in intellectual masturbation with her. She blew up at him on the telephone today and told him that she was tired of his behavior. As the hour ended, she said that she expected to be away in two weeks for about ten days, and hoped that the therapist could find a replacement for her for those sessions. She then missed the following appointment.

We have here several gross behavioral resistances: the patient's lateness, her plans to cancel several sessions, and her subsequent absence. The ground rule regarding the patient's responsibility for her hours was in the process of being rectified. The patient had, on several occasions, exploited the misapplication of this tenet by missing sessions and expecting, as was stated to her, that the therapist would fill her hours and not charge her for the sessions. This actually had happened several times and the therapist had recently realized how this had contributed directly to the patient's gross behavioral resistances.

These gross resistances constitute major indicators which severely threaten the therapeutic process. On a scale of one to ten, they might be ranked at nine, representing a high need within the patient for an intervention. What then of the communicative network?

The main intervention context of the therapist's anxious, confused, defensive intervention in the previous hour is, of course, not represented manifestly. It is alluded to indirectly, however, through derivatives which do not contain a link to the therapist. Perhaps the best representation of the context is seen in the accusation of irresponsibility and in the patient's missing work. There is also the allusion to the previous boss who makes seductive overtures and then pulls away, and her anger at the fellow involved in intellectual masturbation. Each is a relatively well disguised representation of the context, and none would permit interpretive intervention in full, though a playback of derivatives might have been feasible. Together, they form not only a series of representations of the prevailing adaptive contexts, but also a rich derivative complex. As representations of the intervention context, they reveal a high level of resistances, while as expressions of the derivative complex, they are highly meaningful and suggest a low level of resistance.

In essence, the material suggests that the patient has unconsciously experienced the therapist's countertransference-based response to the emergence of the derivatives of her sexual fantasies as irresponsible, as a flight from work, and as a failure to meet a therapeutic task of which he seemed quite unaware. The material implies that the patient understood that the therapist was creating a therapeutic setting in which her pathology-related sexual fantasies could emerge, only to pull away as soon as this had transpired. Because of this, the patient seems to feel that the therapist is having difficulty managing his own seductive fantasies. He seems to prefer intellectual masturbation to meaningful analytic work.

This material constitutes a group of seemingly valid unconscious perceptions of the therapist, and an extensive endeavor to call the therapist's countertransferences to his attention and to suggest possible reasons for his difficulty. As such, this may be understood to constitute unconscious therapeutic efforts. It is therefore quite interesting to realize, as stated above, that despite the richness of this derivative complex, the patient represses the representation of the intervention context which would permit the therapist, in turn, to interpret the sources of the patient's own resistances. It seems likely that this is due to two factors: (1) her mistrust of the therapist, and her disappointment toward him, including feelings that he is unable to manage the therapeutic situation and her instinctual drive derivative expressions; and (2) the likelihood that the therapist's countertransferences have stirred up within the patient unconscious sexual feelings and fantasies, based on the uncertainty of the boundaries between herself and the therapist, which have led her to become defensive—the transference extensions of the patient's nontransference reaction.

The intensity of these gross behavioral resistances suggests the need for one of two possible interventions. The first is to remain silent, as the therapist did, allowing the patient to experience the security of the therapeutic environment, the absence of further defensiveness in the therapist, and to hope that in the following hour, the patient will communicate a highly meaningful communicative network. The second possible intervention would be to offer an interpretation in the form of the playback of selected derivatives organized around the poorly represented adaptive context of the therapist's erroneous intervention. This could have been done toward the end of the session, since by then the patient had provided a rich derivative complex. It might also have been carried out at the end of the hour, if time permitted, when the patient provided a bridge to therapy by mentioning her plans to be away for two weeks.

To illustrate, the therapist might have begun with the indicators and said to the patient: You are late for today's session and now indicate your plans to be away for two weeks. You seem concerned again about the ground rules of treatment and have a need to alter our basic agreement, as revised in recent weeks. Your thoughts and feelings during this session seem to shed light on your need to be late and absent. You were talking about irresponsibility, missing work, and being unaware. You are alluding to a man who teased you and was seductive, only to pull away after making seductive overtures. You were also talking about a fellow who gets involved in intellectual masturbation and how you became angry with him and tired of his behavior. You certainly seem to have a need to push away these men, just as you are creating distance between yourself and me. Something seems to have taken place which has led you to see me in some way similar to these men and to deal with me in similar fashion.

The interpretive playback of selected derivatives around a critical unmentioned adaptive context, especially when it pertains to the fixed frame (though here, it alludes to a critical error), is important in the therapist's armamentarium for dealing with resistances. While a complete interpretation of the unconscious source and meaning of a resistance is to be preferred, in actual clinical experience we often find that the patient's communicative resistances renders that particular type of intervention unfeasible. When the indicators are not especially intense, the best intervention is silence. However, when they are quite powerful, a playback of this kind is to be preferred. This offers the patient an opportunity to eventually realize the source of her disturbance and resistances, and to recognize as well that the therapist seems to have recovered from his countertransferences and is prepared to deal with the threatening sexual material. It also indicates to the patient that the therapist no longer needs the protection of her resistances, an interactional factor which contributes to their modification. Thus, both cognitive-affective understanding and a modification of the therapist's attitudes and actual needs for the patient's resistances, as conveyed specifically through interpretive work, provide a cognitive and interpersonal basis for the resolution of obstacles within the patient to the therapeutic process.

CONCLUDING COMMENTS

This has been a long and complicated presentation of the communicative understanding of resistances, and the techniques with which they are best resolved. It is hoped that the present synthesis will provide a basis for important revisions in our conception of these defensive formations and in the psychotherapeutic approach to their resolution. It is hoped too that this discussion will provide a stimulus for further clinical research into the many important issues which have been raised, though not entirely resolved.

In summary, the communicative definition regards resistances as all efforts, behavioral and communicative, to oppose or interfere with the process of insightful, adaptive psychotherapeutic cure. It proposes that these responses may be primarily pathological or nonpathological, inappropriate to the prevailing spiraling communicative interaction or, alternatively, quite reasonable, necessary, and adaptive in light of the interplay between the patient and therapist. The definition stresses the source of resistances in factors which arise from within the patient, therapist, and their interaction.

The communicative study of resistances reaffirms their place as a primary focus of interpretive work and as a means through which the understanding of the patient's conflicts, introjects, unconscious fantasies and memories, and unconscious perceptions can be developed as they pertain to his neurosis. Technically, it has been shown that patients are inclined on their own to fluctuate between the intense and modified use of resistances. Spontaneous resolution of resistances depends, however, upon the therapist's ability to provide the patient with a secure therapeutic environment and to rectify his own unconscious contributions to the patient's defensiveness. The patient's capacities in this regard have been relatively unrecognized until now.

Technically, resistances are to be dealt with first, through the rectification of the therapist's contributions, and secondly through interpretations organized around the prevailing intervention context and developed in terms of the responsive derivative complex. Empirically, this approach has been found to provide the sole means of obtaining Type Two derivative validation of the therapist's efforts and a truly adaptive resolution of the resistances themselves. On the whole, resistances have as their most critical source the very intervention contexts which are at the heart of such interpretations.

The identification of communicative resistances has many ramifications. Of particular importance is the insight afforded to silent and previously unrecognized resistances, especially in patients who appear on the surface to be cooperative. The concept also addresses resistances which take place in respect to the patient's derivative communications, the level of expression most pertinent to the meanings of his neurosis. Communicative resistances are also a significant aspect of the unconscious therapeutic alliance which relies upon the patient's derivative expressions, except for moments of lying fallow in order to be held during periods of Type C communication.

Also important is the revelation that periods of nonderivative communication need not speak for resistances in the patient, in that it need not imply opposition to the therapeutic procedures or disruption of sound therapeutic work. There is considerable evidence that patients who require interpretations create interpretive opportunities and express the necessary derivatives and representations of the intervention context so that the therapist may respond accordingly. Patients seem to need quiescent periods, and these must receive specific evaluation in light of activated adaptive contexts in order to determine whether their resistances are pathological or primarily nonpathological and adaptive. This touches upon some of the more interesting aspects of the subject of resistance which have received new illumination from the communicative viewpoint, and which deserve further study.

Finally, the importance of modifications in the basic therapeutic environment as a source of resistances and as a means of their expression has been stressed. In this respect, analytic work related to behavioral and communicative resistances may be understood as standing among the most viable approaches to the patient's defensive style and to his core conflicts, self-pathology, and ego dysfunctions. Loosely stated, as goes our understanding and techniques in respect to resistances, so goes the basic therapeutic process.

Chapter Twelve

THE STRUCTURE AND FUNCTION OF INTERVENTIONS

In contrast to previous studies of interventions, which are based upon classifications derived from their manifest properties and the therapist's or analyst's conscious intentions, the present chapter will reconceptualize the nature and functions of interventions, consequent to a study of their effects as understood from the communicative viewpoint. Unfolding from a multilevel consideration, it will take into account the therapist's *conscious and unconscious* intentions and effects, and will consider interventions as part of the spiraling communicative interaction. In addition, consideration will be accorded to interventions by the patient, both conscious and unconscious.

THE PREVIOUS LITERATURE

The literature related to the analyst's interventions has confined itself almost entirely to the sphere of verbal efforts designed to generate cognitive insight within the patient. This tone was set by Freud, who, with the exception of his paper on reconstructions (1937), did not offer a systematic study of the analyst's interventions. There are virtually no references to interpretations in the

Standard Edition; these are confined to a few brief remarks on the importance of the interpretation of transference resistances (see especially Freud 1913), and scattered efforts at dream interpretation (perhaps best illustrated in his analysis of the two dreams reported by his patient, Dora; Freud 1905). Implicit in Freud's endeavors is the important role of unconscious fantasies, especially transference fantasies, in the patient's symptoms and neurosis, and the use of interpretations of their derivative expression, especially at times of resistance, as a means of making unconscious contents and the related defensive mechanisms conscious to the patient. Throughout these writings, however, there is consistent evidence for Freud's grasp of the need for validation from the patient of both interpretations and reconstructions, essentially through what he termed *indirect material* (Freud 1937).

Perhaps the single paper most often referred to in discussions of intervening is by Bibring (1954), who synthesized the scattered writings on this subject by distinguishing five techniques, verbal and nonverbal, expressed in the behaviors of the therapist and intended to affect the patient in the direction of the goals of analysis. These techniques he designated suggestive, abreactive, manipulative, clarifying, and interpretive.

In brief, *suggestion* refers to the therapist's induction of ideas, impulses, emotions, and actions in the patient, to the relative exclusion of the latter's rational or critical thinking. *Abreaction* alludes to emotional discharge and reliving, through which intense feelings and responses to traumas are ventilated. *Manipulation* includes advice, guidance, directives, efforts to neutralize certain emotional forces, the mobilization of certain conflicts, and a wide range of comparable measures. *Clarification* is any effort by the therapist to enable the patient to see more clearly the nature of his feelings, thoughts, and other communications; it is generally developed on a conscious level and alludes to contents or implications of which the patient is not sufficiently aware. Finally, *interpretations* are an attempt to identify unconscious material, defenses, and warded-off instinctual drive tendencies, related to the hidden meanings of the patient's behaviors and their unconscious interconnections. Interpretations include constructions and reconstructions of unconscious processes assumed to determine manifest behavior. They are the essential vehicle through which the patient is afforded insight, and become effective through the process of assimilation, which is related to working through, and which leads to reorientation and readjustment.

Virtually every work on psychoanalytic technique has regarded interpretation and working through as the ultimate expression of the analyst's interventions, the means through which the patient gains insight and adaptive structural change. While it will not be possible to review the many scattered comments and insights in this area, I wish to single out the contribution by Strachey (1934) since in many ways, it is the paper which most clearly foreshadows selected aspects of the ideas presented in this chapter. In essence, Strachey adopted a modified interactional approach through his understanding of the therapeutic experience, and the nature of the analyst's interpretations. He afforded full consideration to the roles of cognitive insight and positive introjects in consequence of a valid interpretation. It was Strachey who coined the term *mutative interpretation* to allude essentially to an effort at understanding unconscious processes and contents which pertain to communications from the analysand which express an activated instinctual drive wish directed toward the analyst. It was Strachey's contention that this type of interpretation was the most effective type of intervention in the analytic situation, in that it led not only to insights pertinent to the immediate analytic situation, but also to corrective positive introjects which helped to modify the patient's pathological fantasies and images of the analyst—that is, it is the interpretation through which the analyst functions as a good object for introjection in a way that truly modifies the patient's pathological inner mental world. Clearly, many of Strachey's ideas are relevant to the concept of interpretation presented earlier in this volume, and which I will develop in greater detail in this chapter.

More broadly, Greenson (1967) may be taken as representative of the classical psychoanalytic writings on interventions, and on the role of interpretation in psychoanalysis. In his volume on technique, Greenson leaned heavily on the contribution of Bibring (1954). He suggested that the analysis of transference or the transference neurosis is the central therapeutic effort in psychoanalytic treatment. It involves demonstrating the transference through confrontations and the use of evidence; clarification of the transference, which includes at times, a pursuit of the transference trigger; interpretation of the transference in terms of the relevant affects, impulses, and attitudes, which entails tracing the antecedents of the transference figure and a full exploration of the transference fantasy; and the working through of transference interpretations. For Greenson, to interpret means to make an unconscious phenomenon conscious. In addition, he commented on the necessity for validation, and, while not exploring this aspect in any detail, he did note that verification is essential in determining the correctness of an interpretation and that it often takes the form of a patient's adding some new embellishing material.

My own clinical delineation of the therapist's interventions (1973) used and expanded the basic contributions of Bibring and Greenson. However, certain additional trends are evident. First, I included silence among the therapist's basic interventions, to which I added questions, clarifications, confrontations, interpretations, and reconstructions. Second, while maintaining the usual psychoanalytic focus on the formal characteristics and conscious intentions of these interventions, I also alluded to a variety of unconscious meanings and communications inherent in both valid and essentially erroneous interventions. For perhaps the first time in the literature, there was specific consideration of the misuses of the various interventions and of the influence of the therapist's countertransferences in this regard. Third, I offered an extended discussion of confirmation and nonconfirmation of interventions, and attempted to develop specific clinical criteria for the validity of an intervention.

Finally, in a chapter that in many ways is the forerunner of the findings and hypotheses to be described here, I reexamined the therapist's so-called supportive (supposedly positive, though noninterpretive) interventions (1973: chapter 16). Through an investigation of the patient's unconscious (indirect and derivative) responses to such measures, it became evident that they were experienced as destructive manipulations, invasions of privacy, infringements upon the patient's autonomy, and the like, and that despite conscious acceptance on the part of the patient, the unconscious repercussions were uniformly negative.

In the years since publication of the technique books, my studies of the analytic and therapeutic situations have evolved more and more in terms of adaptive and interactional considerations. With the use of the metaphor of the bipersonal field, the unconscious interaction between patient and analyst, and their unconscious communicative exchange, began to take on increasingly greater importance. As this perspective widened, the formal attributes and goals of an intervention, while still critical, were viewed as but one dimension of the therapist's communications to the patient, and their unconscious communicative qualities and functions became the subject of extensive investigation.

The bipersonal field and communicative concepts also led to an elaborate study of the nature and functions of the ground rules or framework of the therapeutic and analytic situations. This led to the specific delineation of a major sphere of interventions that previously had not been separated from the therapist's interpretive endeavors: the establishment, management, and rectification of the frame. Many new hypotheses were generated and validated, leading to fresh perspectives on the therapeutic interaction (Langs 1976b,c, 1978a,b,c). In the course of this work, new insights were developed in regard to many aspects of the therapist's interventions, and these form the substance of this chapter.

BASIC METHODOLOGY: THE LISTENING PROCESS

Attention to the intervening process has led to several addenda to the listening process as developed through a focus on the intaking aspects of the therapist's work. With this in mind, we will touch upon the key points.

The therapist enters each session without desire, memory, or understanding, and allows the material from the patient to foster his recall and the development of initial formulations, in the form of *silent hypotheses*. Until now, the emphasis has been on the extent to which the material from the patient guides the therapist. Recently, however, it has been recognized that the therapist himself must engage in a complicated and creative process in order to generate formulations which can ultimately be interpreted to the patient and find validation.

In essence, the therapist must be of two minds: one entirely open and guided by the patient's associations, especially by their many possible derivative implications; and the other, attempting to abstract formulations based on the therapist's capacities and knowledge which require subsequent derivative validation through the patient's ongoing associations. This implies that the therapist must be capable of metaphorical and abstract thinking, and of developing a formulation which serves as a selected fact, integrating the patient's derivative communications in a manner that generates a new level of meaning and implication. Manifest associations are developed in terms of their first-order themes around activated adaptive contexts. At times, the patient represents the context, thereby facilitating the therapist's efforts at organization. At other times, the therapist is aware of an active intervention context and attempts on his own to organize the derivatives accordingly. In all such instances, the therapist must create a conception at a higher level than the manifest implications of the patient's material. It is this creative act that is the critical interactional product in respect to the formulation of interventions: it is directed partly by the material from the patient, but also stems from the abilities of the therapist. Whenever a therapist is aware of an activated intervention context and begins to formulate the patient's material in terms of derivatives organized around that context, he must remain open to other possibilities and, in addition, obtain ongoing validation from the patient's continuing associations.

Interventions are therefore prepared by the therapist as he listens to the patient, through the development of silent hypotheses which are not imparted to the patient until they have received *silent validation* from the continuing material. There comes a point where the therapist has a clearly represented *intervention context,* a coalescible *derivative network,* and a clear *link* to therapy, all in light of an activated *indicator.* The therapist then will offer either an interpretation or framework management intervention to the patient. This leads to the next attempt at validation, which is primarily a search for indirect confirmation, the revelation of a selected fact which gives the previous material new and integrated meaning which is in keeping with the therapist's intervention. This type of validation, which is essential to psychoanalytic work, takes place in both the cognitive and interactional spheres—the latter in the form of derivatives which represent a positive introjective identification with the effective therapist.

It is to be stressed once again that this type of listening is organized around the conscious and especially unconscious implications of the therapist's interventions, and views the patient's material as adaptive and primarily derivative reactions to these contexts. In keeping with our understanding of the structure of neuroses, the quest in psychotherapy and psychoanalysis is for the patient's derivative communications as they pertain to his neurosis in terms of both unconscious fantasies and perceptions, and as activated in the ongoing communicative interaction. It is this conception of the therapeutic process which leads the communicative therapist to radical changes in his view of valid interventions, and which leads us to discard a number of interventions now in common practice. Since the goal is to create a relationship, setting, and therapeutic approach which facilitates the patient's free and derivative communications, and to manage the therapeutic environment and offer interpretations and reconstructions on the basis of such expressions, the therapeutic techniques involved prove to be different from those used by the classical therapist who tends to pursue manifest contents and Type One derivatives contained in the patient's direct associations.

As a further perspective on intervening, a number of earlier findings deserve explicit statement. First, we must recognize that the communicative approach has consistently revealed that the most significant unconscious communications and adaptive reactions within the patient are derived from his relationship with the therapist and from the latter's attitudes and interventions. It follows that this relationship and interaction must be the essential realm of the therapist's interventions, and that interventions based on outside adaptive contexts and unconscious reactions are in some way related to the therapeutic relationship. In general, material which manifestly pertains to outside relationships serves functionally as derivative communications pertaining to the therapist. Further, most reactions to outside traumas tend to take place on a manifest content and Type One derivative level, and only rarely is it possible to organize meaningfully associations from the patient around an outside adaptive context. When this proves feasible, an interpretation may be called for, though usually an intervention of this kind will also include the additional interpretation of the patient's material organized around an activated context *within* the therapeutic interaction.

In evaluating the patient's responses to interventions, there are two separate but interrelated dimensions of listening. The first involves the determination of validation, as already discussed; the second entails understanding the patient's responsive associations as a *commentary* on the conscious and especially unconscious implications of the intervention at hand. Such commentaries are *transversal* in that they contain first and foremost, *valid* unconscious perceptions and introjects of the implications of the therapist's intervention. In addition, they include distorted and fantasied responses which derive from the patient's own inner mental world and psychopathology. At the same time, this material expresses meanings related to both the patient and the therapist, and must be attended along the me/not-me interface. In all, then, the implications of the patient's associations following an intervention are a mixture of nontransference and transference, and reflect both unconscious perception and unconscious fantasy.

In principle, the formulating process and the actual offer of interventions by the therapist is influenced by the whole gamut of factors which exist within both the patient and therapist, and in their communicative interchanges. Of note is the therapist's capacity to formulate, integrate, and synthesize; his ability to identify activated intervention contexts and to abstract the patient's associations in terms of derivative communications pertinent to those contexts; and his capacity for sensitive, tactful, and well timed interpretations and framework management responses. Much of this is based on the therapist's ego capacities as they pertain to both listening and intervening, and on his knowledge of himself and his fellings, fantasies, and other responses to the patient. All of this is under considerable interactional influence from the patient, both consciously and unconsciously.

To summarize, we have developed a basic methodology for formulating, intervening, and evaluating the patient's responses to interventions. The stress is on derivative communications from the patient, and on understanding the conscious and unconscious implications of the therapist's efforts. Psychoanalytic, Type Two derivative validation in the cognitive and interactional spheres is the hallmark of a correct intervention; conscious insight then follows. Any intervention which does not obtain that type of indirect response from the patient is considered to be incorrect and an indication of a need to reformulate. All of the interventions to be discussed in this chapter have been evaluated on this basis, and in light of the communicative approach and understanding.

Finally, in identifying the basic requisites for an intervention from the therapist, we may keep in mind what the therapist requires in order to intervene. This can be stated succinctly in the following way: for an interpretation and framework management response to the patient, the therapist needs a clear-cut indicator, a directly represented or minimally disguised expression of the intervention context, and a meaningful and coalescible derivative complex. Following these requirements, the therapist is able in each session to develop an understanding of what it is that the patient has made available for intervening, and what is lacking. As we would expect, at times there is a clearly represented context but fragmented derivatives, while in other sessions, the derivatives seem clear in light of a known activated adaptive context, but the patient does not represent the latter element in a form that lends itself to interpretation. Often, the timing of an actual intervention to the patient is decided when the missing component is provided toward the latter part of the session. In principle, it is well to keep this recipe—if we may term it that—as a simple guide in respect to formulating and in regard to the timing of interventions. To further clarify these basic methodological considerations, let us now identify the specific interventions which have obtained general validation from patients, after which we will consider those which do not, as a rule, generate confirmatory responses.

THE BASIC INTERVENTIONS

On the basis of the type of clinical research reflected in the seminars in Part I of this volume, and on many other studies from the communicative vantage point, it has been found that there are only three basic interventions which consistently obtain true psychoanalytic validation, that is, Type Two derivative confirmation. This finding leads, of course, to the exclusion of a number of commonly accepted interventions from the armamentarium of the therapist. It leads to the proposal that therapeutic work should be confined by and large to three essential measures: (1) *silence;* (2) *the establishment, management, and rectification of the framework;* and (3) *interpretations-reconstructions.*

The last type of intervention, which I will call *interpretations* for the sake of brevity, is actually shaped in four different forms depending on the nature of the communicative network available from the patient and his basic communicative style. The subgroups include: (*a*) interpretations proper (the identification of the main indicators, the prevailing adaptive context, and the responsive derivative complex); (*b*) the playback of *selected derivatives,* such as those elements of manifest associations meaningfully related on an encoded level to an intervention context pertaining to the therapeutic relationship, not clearly represented by the patient and generally alluding to a fixed frame issue; (*c*) the metabolism of a projective identification toward cognitive and interactional understanding, carried out in terms of activated indicators, contexts, and derivative responses; and (*d*) the identification of metaphors for the Type C communicative style and its functions, commented upon in light of prevailing indicators, contexts, and derivative complexes.

As might be expected, the first type of interpretation occurs with patients using the Type A communicative mode, while the second is offered to such patients when they are expressing resistances in regard to the representation of an activated intervention context. More rarely, this second type of intervention is offered to a Type C narrator when an important adaptive context has mobilized his responses, though he nonetheless has not clearly represented the precipitant. The third form of interpretation is, of course, a response to the Type B communicative mode and should be based on interactional experiences which are confirmed in the patient's cognitive associations before being imparted to the patient. The last type of interpretation applies to the Type C communicative mode. In general, these interpretive efforts of the therapist occur in two basic forms: definitive and transversal.

I will comment briefly on these fundamental tools.

1. *Silence* is, of course, absolutely basic to the therapist's repertory of interventions. It is filled with nonverbal and unconscious

implications, which may vary from moment to moment and from session to session, within the context of the dynamic interaction between patient and analyst. It implies holding the patient, containing his communications and projective identifications, and permitting him to build the therapist's interventions out of fragments that need only be synthesized and organized. It implies entering each session without desire, memory, or understanding (Bion 1970, Langs 1978b), and permitting the patient to create unconsciously the therapist's understanding and intervention. It implies too a capacity for the adequate management of internal conflicts, tensions, and the like within the therapist, and it certainly conveys a wish to understand and help the patient. It represents the therapist's free-floating attention (Freud 1912), free floating role-responsiveness (Sandler 1976), and openness to the metabolism of projective identifications. It embodies the therapist's wish to listen, contain, understand, and offer constructive help in keeping with the patient's appropriate needs.

It is also self-evident that silence can be misused and inappropriately extended in the service of countertransference needs within the analyst. This occurs in all situations that call for a positive intervention from the therapist, at which point his silence no longer serves therapeutic needs. However, with the exception of preliminary efforts in the technique book (Langs 1973; see also Langs 1976b, for additional references), there has been little effort to empirically delineate the characteristics of appropriate silence and the definitive properties of moments at which its maintenance is no longer tenable. The matter is extremely complex, though it can be definitively stated that the evaluation of the functions of the therapist's silences calls for full use of the validating process. Silence is by far the best way of facilitating the patient's free associations, communication of indirect, derivative contents and mechanisms, and unconscious interactional thrusts; it is the optimal means through which expressions of the patient's neurosis become available for interpretation.

There are, then, two major indications for the use of silence: first, the need to wait and allow the patient to build up a neurotic communicative network, to communicate the role evocations, cognitive derivatives, and interactional pressures that provide the substance through which a positive intervention can be made; and second, the absence of truly analyzable material, of interpretable derivatives, role pressures, and interactional processes. There is a tendency among therapists to intervene more actively under the latter conditions, with the expectation that such interventions ultimately will promote derivative expression by the patient. My own observations indicate that this is a deceptive rationalization and that active interventions under the conditions just described have no such effect. Silence, then, is the preferred intervention in the absence of interpretable material. Inappropriate silences lead to the problem of failures to intervene, a subject that will be discussed when considering countertransference influences.

Clinical supervisory experiences indicate that silence is among the most difficult interventions for therapists to make. There appear to be powerful tendencies toward active intervention to a point where a therapist is prone to deceive himself regarding the presence of the necessary material, only to subsequently discover, in light of the patient's nonvalidating response, that he has intervened erroneously. In addition, it is important to be clear that silence alone facilitates the patient's derivative communications, since the communicative therapist is interested in a coalescible network of disguised elements, rather than the pursuit of direct associations to a single association. Failure to appreciate the importance of this type of scattered or divided representation of a response to an activated adaptive context, and the preference to pursue selected manifest associations for possible underlying meanings, has led to techniques which run contrary to the widest development of the unconscious expressions of the patient's emotional illness.

Once the positive and constructive qualities of silence are fully appreciated, in terms of both its holding and containing attributes—its role in the offer of a sound therapeutic symbiosis—and in affording the patient the most optimal means of expression, this particular intervention should attain its place as the most basic to the therapist armamentarium. On an unconscious level, patients generally appreciate the therapist who is capable of appropriate silence, no matter how long its duration, even lasting weeks or, on rare occasions, one or more months. It is important, however, to continually apply the validating process to the use of silence, and to consistently monitor the material for major indicators, representations of an intervention context, and the presence of a meaningful derivative complex which calls for intervening. In the absence of such a configuration, maintaining the silence is by far the most constructive intervention and experience the therapist can offer to the patient.

2. *Establishing, managing, and rectifying the framework and analyzing infringements* constitute a major group of relatively unrecognized and consistently crucial interventions. Included here is the series of interventions through which the therapist establishes the therapeutic or analytic contract and the conditions of treatment (Langs 1973, 1976b). Interventions in this area also involve responses to efforts by the patient to modify the framework, and in addition, any necessary steps involved in rectifying an alteration in the ground rules. Included here, too, is the announcement of any change in the usual course of the sessions (e.g., a vacation by the analyst), and any other major or minor modification in the basic agreement and tenets of the psychoanalytic situation.

Elsewhere (Langs 1975a,b, 1976b,c, 1978a,b,c), I have rather extensively defined the basic framework of psychoanalysis and psychoanalytic psychotherapy, and have clinically demonstrated and discussed the multiple meanings and functions of its attributes and management for both patient and therapist. In essence, the framework and how it is handled contributes to the basic ego-enhancing therapeutic hold offered by the therapist to the patient, a security that permits therapeutic regression and the unfolding of analyzable expressions of the patient's intrapsychic pathology—primarily within the therapeutic interaction. Similar support is inherently afforded the therapist by these conditions, and both patient and therapist have available a secured container for pathological projective identifications and other pathological communications. In addition, the therapist's handling of the framework is the single most essential factor in determining the nature of the communicative relationship and medium, and the extent to which language will be used for insight and understanding, rather than for pathological projective identifications, or direct symbiotic satisfaction. It also determines the degrees of appropriate and pathological defense and instinctual drive gratification, and the presence or absence of massive defensive barriers.

In essence, then, the manner in which the therapist creates and handles the basic ground rules of the therapeutic relationship is at the heart of the therapeutic symbiosis which provides background—and more rarely foreground—qualities of relatedness which are essential to a well functioning therapeutic dyad. As such, the therapist's interventions in this area are extremely meaningful, both consciously and unconsciously, and the patient is highly sensitive to all such expressions. Similar importance applies to the patient's efforts to accept or modify the basic conditions of treatment.

The ground rules and their management constitute a basic actuality, filled with conscious and unconscious implications, as it pertains to the therapeutic interaction. Deviations consistently function as a means of creating pathological (merger) relatedness and as traumatic adaptive contexts which engender intense unconscious reactions in the patient. As a rule, these responses are split: consciously, the gratification and other pathological implications are accepted by the patient, while unconsciously and on a derivative level, the patient reacts with considerable, even violent objection. Even when applied in emergencies, alterations in the frame are unconsciously experienced ultimately as disruptive and threatening, and are filled with the dangers of merger, seduction, and hostility. The patient sees them as based on countertransference difficulties. They consistently disturb the communicative properties of the bipersonal field and tend to shift the patient's communicative mode toward the Type B or Type C modality, though Type A expressions in response to the deviant intervention context are also common.

Because the ground rules are such basic actualities, alterations in the framework are of the highest order of therapeutic indicators. Their realistic qualities lead a specific type of intervention which has been applied by some therapists, though not accorded the critical recognition which it deserves. I refer to the *rectification* of the disturbed framework—the correction of the deviation in actuality. Clearly, such rectification is essential to any meaningful and accompanying interpretive work; failure to correct an infraction in the ground rules to the greatest extent feasible belies all efforts at interpretation. Situations in which rectification is not feasible—for example, when a patient has been referred to a therapist by another of his patients—may call for termination of therapy, carried out at the behest of the patient's ongoing derivative communications. The problem of which deviations can be fully rectified and which are unmodifiable is in need of clinical investigation. For the moment, it is important to recognize such a possibility, and to realize as well that some of the negative effects of an alteration in the ground rules will remain with the patient without essential change, though much can be done to modify their influence if the frame is rectified and the appropriate interpretations offered to the patient.

In keeping with the material from the patient and using sound principles of interpretation, which will be described below, the therapist should rectify the frame primarily at the behest of the patient's derivative communications. Virtually without exception, he will discover that these contain directives toward, and models of, rectification. To offer a hypothetical example, in a situation where a therapist has agreed to a makeup hour in a particular session, the patient may speak of the ways in which his mother spoiled, overgratified, and overindulged him to the point where he had no sense of his own identity or of responsibility. He might go on to say that his mother was wrong in engaging in such indulgences, and in lacking faith in the patient to handle his difficulties on his own. In a session where the adaptive context of the therapist's agreement to hold an additional session has been clearly represented, the interpretation-rectification intervention can be offered to the patient that he is now indicating indirectly that the decision to hold an extra session is overindulgent and infantalizing, and that it would interfere with the development of a clear identity and with his autonomy. It could then be added that the patient is indicating that this would be a mistake, and on that basis, it seems clear that the additional session should be cancelled.

This model helps to make clear that issues related to the ground rules require a noninterpretive response from the therapist, either in the direction of deviation or toward holding secure the established frame. The therapist's decision in this regard should be based on the patient's derivative associations, which will almost universally indicate that maintaining the framework is the appropriate response and that deviations are pathological. There is a strong tendency among therapists to respond to requests related to the ground rules with direct answers, rather than permitting the patient to go on to free associate so that his derivatives may guide the framework management response of the therapist. There is a related tendency to fail to recognize the extensive implications of such requests, and the critical role played by the therapist's management responses. The basic image of the therapist, his position in regard to the patient's neurosis—i.e., whether he wishes to support or to analyze it—and the definitive nature of the therapeutic relationship are defined in this way. Without exception, deviations gratify pathological symbiotic needs in both participants, while maintaining the boundaries and setting involves healthy symbiosis, and fosters individuation and autonomy.

As a rule, the framework management response should be accompanied by interpretation. Important here is the need to trace a patient's request to modify the framework to an activated intervention context—i.e., to a prior intervention by the therapist. Efforts to modify the frame, and to engage in framework deviation cures, are adaptive responses prompted by adaptation-evoking contexts from the therapist. Not infrequently, an inappropriate deviation by the therapist prompts further efforts to modify the ground rules by the patient.

Because of the importance and neglect of framework management responses, and of interpretations in this sphere, it is well to be reminded again that this dimension of unconscious relatedness and interaction between the patient and therapist is fundamental to all other aspects of their relationship, and to every quality of the therapeutic experience and effort. Adherence to established ground rules is in no sense inappropriate rigidity, but instead offers the patient, and secondarily the therapist, an optimal form of relatedness and setting through which therapeutic needs can be realized. It is of course, in the first session, that the therapist delineates these ground rules, doing so as specifically and as extensively as necessary and feasible. The framework creation is a unique intervention, though it bears a relationship to later framework management responses. While some patients will silently accept the security of the offered frame, others will repeatedly test it and the therapist's capacities to maintain it. At issue is the nature of the symbiotic tie to be developed between patient and therapist, and whether cure will evolve from the analysis of derivatives or from direct, pathological symbiotic satisfaction. In addition, when a patient unconsciously requires a therapeutic response from the therapist, he will often create a framework issue as a way of evoking an actual intervention from the therapist, which can serve as an activated adaptive context which will evoke derivative responses that lend themselves to interpretation.

Any effort on the part of the patient to modify the basic framework (e.g., the wish to change an hour, to have an insurance form filled out, to take a unilateral vacation, etc.) should be met with the basic response of silence (the absence of any direct reaction), permitting the patient to continue to free associate. When under pressure, the therapist must avoid both participation and direct refusal to participate, and must maintain his basic analytic attitude: it is essential that the patient continue to free associate. On that basis, the patient's subsequent material serves as a commentary on his proposal, and will reveal in derivative form both its unconscious meanings and the appropriate response for the therapist, which, remarkably enough, always turns out to be adherence to the established frame. The therapist is then in a position to use the material from the patient as a means of deriving his management response—adhering to the principle of permitting the patient to shape every intervention—and to interpret the unconscious meanings for the patient. The latter intervention takes the form of the interpretation of Type Two derivatives around a prior adaptive context which has evoked the proposed alteration in the frame, and is almost always expressed in the Type A mode. Such work clearly entails additional communications beyond the analyst's interpretive efforts; he has no choice but to establish his position regarding the frame in reality, although it must be stressed again that this can always be done at the prompting of the patient's unconscious communications.

In situations in which there has been a deliberate or inadvertent alteration of the frame, it is essential to both rectify the frame and interpret the entire experience. Rectification is the essential first step, since it is vital to the restoration of the therapeutic alliance and the positive communicative properties of the bipersonal field, as well as to the necessary interpretive work. When the frame has been altered, unconsciously the therapist is seen as dangerous, the boundaries are unclear, the implications of his verbal and behavioral communications are uncertain, and the patient feels endangered and mistrustful. Rectifying measures—e.g., no longer signing insurance forms, shifting hours, or extending sessions, and desisting in nonneutral interventions—should always be accompanied by interpretive efforts. Examples will be provided and discussed in the clinical section of this chapter.

3. *Interpretations-reconstructions* refer to the therapist's basic efforts to make unconscious contents, processes, defenses, interactional mechanisms—fantasies, memories, introjects, self- and object representations, and the like—conscious for the patient within a dynamic and affective framework. It is well beyond the scope of this discussion to pursue the mechanics of interpretation and reconstruction, or to explore many issues involved in the development and offer of an interpretive and reconstructive intervention. Here my focus will be on certain properties of interpretations and reconstructions (I will offer my discussion mainly in terms of the former) which are brought to the fore by the communicative approach. While these two interrelated interventions play a central role in generating cognitive insight and adaptive structural change as the basis for symptom alleviation, interpretations can serve their intended function only if the bipersonal field has a secure frame. In its absence, intended interpretations consistently serve as vehicles for the analyst's pathological projective identifications or as a means of creating Type C barriers.

Based on an understanding of the communicative interaction, it has been possible to develop a specific definition of interpretation, and to propose restricting that intervention to a particular set of qualifications. In essence, all interpretations must allude to an activated indicator or therapeutic context, identify the best representation of the intervention context to which it is related, and identify the patient's Type Two derivative responses to the context as it reveals his reactions to the particular stimulus. There are many other ways in which therapists have endeavored to make conscious for the patient something which was previously unconscious. However, the communicative approach has shown that unless this work is organized around an activated intervention context, even though on some level a truthful proposition, it will serve functionally as a lie barrier to another and more pertinent truth at the moment it is offered to the patient. The truths of the patient's neurosis unfold around the therapeutic interaction, and only those interventions which take into account this particular dimension obtain Type Two derivative validation. Efforts to interpret in terms of Type One derivatives contain a critical element of error and falsification since they do not deal with the spiraling communicative interaction, and with those aspects of the patient's neurosis which are activated within that framework. Of course, it is possible to intervene errone-ously despite the use of the basic tripartite model of interpretation offered here. Such errors can be discovered by analyzing an interven-tion in light of subsequent subjective responses within the therapist and the nonvalidating aspects of the material from the patient—to which he usually adds efforts to correct the therapist.

It must be stressed, then, that many interventions designed to make the patient aware of something regarding which he previously was unaware, while fitting the usual formal definition of interpre-tation, serve functionally within the therapeutic interaction as the offer of Type C barriers, and sometimes as a means of projectively identifying into the patient pathological elements of the therapist's countertransferences. Much of this can be safeguarded against by working interpretively with the intervention context as the ful-crum for intervening. This requires a full analysis of the nature of the therapist's previous interventions, and an understanding of their conscious and unconscious implications and functions. Once the unconscious communications so contained are identified, the therapist is prepared to interpret the patient's subsequent material in terms of both unconscious perception and unconscious fantasy constellations.

It is critical to realize that the communicative approach has established the realm of valid unconscious perceptions as a basic area for interpretation. Because of the threat involved in perceiving traumatic qualities in the therapist, patients quite uniformly—though with notable exceptions—register and express these realiza-tions indirectly and through derivatives, rather than directly and consciously. Such perceptions contribute and reinforce signifi-cantly the patient's neurosis and must be both rectified and inter-preted to the patient. This serves as a basis for the modification of his neurotic responses, and of the common disturbances in the therapeutic alliance and ongoing treatment situation which appear under these conditions. In principle, the therapist interprets unconscious perceptions before unconscious fantasies, and gives full credence to the patient's valid unconcious sensitivities before identifying the pathological implications in his associations and responses.

Interpretation in its four variations is the basic active therapeutic tool of the therapist. These interventions are developed at the behest of the patient's material, and should not be forced. Patients who need holding and an opportunity to lie fallow will not create interactional pressures or other issues which could generate intervention. While it is true that a therapist may intervene erroneously primarily because of countertransference pressures, on an unconscious level patients show a capability of creating an interaction which will produce an interpretation when it is needed, and of permitting matters to remain quiescent when this is what is necessary. As a rule, a patient will create a framework issue or engage in intense interactional pressures when he requires an interpretation from the therapist. Otherwise, ongoing interpretive work is usually organized around the therapist's valid or invalid interventions; either can serve as both an adaptive and therapeutic context in that each evokes simultaneously a therapeutic need within the patient as well as a series of adaptive responses.

The communicative approach indicates that patients need far fewer interpretations than are commonly offered to them in the course of psychotherapy and psychoanalysis. They require instead much more holding and containing and an opportunity to engage in self-analytic work designed to generate more flexible lie-barrier systems, and occasionally insights into the truth. There is some evidence that many interpretations offered by therapists in current practice are in error, and that many major indicators in patients derive from the therapist's countertransferences rather than primarily from their own therapeutic needs. Stalemated and extended therapies appear to be common on this basis. Adherence to the principle of interpreting around activated intervention contexts safeguards as much as possible against this type of countertransference-dominated therapeutic experience.

Every interpretation offered by the therapist is a mixture of valid and distorted comment. A sound interpretation is primarily counter-transference-free, while an erroneous interpretation is dominated by the therapist's pathology. The latter reveals a great deal regarding the therapist's own unconscious conflicts, fantasies, introjects, and such, and generates projective identifications which the patient unconsciously tends to work over and exploit. It also conveys interpersonally some form of pathological symbiotic need. A valid interpretation contains only a modicum of countertransference-based error, though this may at times serve as an important intervention context for the patient's subsequent responses.

An interpretation is a creative act by the therapist. It requires listening on a manifest level for a direct or thinly disguised representation of an activated intervention context. It needs as well an ability to listen to the remainder of the patient's material in a manner which abstracts additional implications and meaning—first-order implications—and then further organizes and specifies these implications in terms of the prevailing adaptive context—second-order meanings. This conceptualization is at a different level from the patient's associations, and requires a capacity for abstraction, metaphorical thinking, and psychoanalytic understanding, and is founded on a resolution of the therapist's countertransferences.

In each session, the therapist, in addition to being entirely open, soon develops some sense of what he would need if he were to interpret to the patient in that particular hour. He listens to the material awaiting a definitive representation of the intervention context, and in its absence knows that he will be limited either to silence or to the selected playback of pertinent derivatives if there is a fixed frame issue. At the same time, he maintains an ear for therapeutic contexts, indications of neurosis and therapeutic need within the patient.

Finally, the therapist knows that he also requires manifest associations from the patient which yield coalescible, derivative, latent, meanings. It is in this area that therapists have the greatest difficulty. The derivative complex contains a number of different components, and some may emerge in one hour, while others may not. On this level of indirect expression, the patient is revealing his adaptive and maladaptive reactions to a dimension of the therapist's intervention. He is conveying his unconscious perceptions of the therapist based on the intervention, as well as the aroused fantasies and memories which it has evoked. He will indicate the important genetic figure connected to the experience, which may have transference or nontransference implications depending on whether the therapist has in actuality repeated a past pathogenic interaction or behaved differently from the earlier figure.

There will also be reflections of evoked introjects, and reflections of the intrapsychic conflicts and other issues aroused by the intervention context. It is here, of course, that the full play of psychoanalytic knowledge comes to the fore, and a therapist's gifts in conceptualizing the most important implications of the patient's response to a context have their greatest test. In general, by maintaining an adaptive viewpoint, and understanding the patient's associations as disguised derivative reactions to an adaptive context, the task is made somewhat easier. A full grasp of unconscious mechanisms, fantasies, and conflicts also enables the therapist to think meaningfully in a way that facilitates an understanding of the derivative complex. Care must be taken not to impose theoretical assumptions onto this complex, but instead to derive anew from the material itself formulations which are in keeping with (or lead to the revision of) accepted psychoanalytic theory. There will always be a mixture of preconceived notions and fresh and open listening and formulating in these efforts, and care must be taken to neither adhere too rigidly to accepted theory, nor to remain so unstructured as to be unable to meaningfully synthesize the available derivatives.

As we have seen, the ideal interpretation takes as its practical point of departure a symptom, resistance, or introjected disturbance derived from the therapist, and identifies the basis for the patient's maladaptive response in terms of an activated intervention context and a relevant derivative complex. In principle, this should be the essential structure of every interpretation.

It is well known that in addition to the cognitive contents of an interpretation, the therapist conveys a great deal in his tone, style, wording, affective investment, timing, tact, and in the other verbal and nonverbal qualities of an intervention. In undertaking to restructure the relatively dispersed or fragmented communications from the patient into a meaningful whole organized around a particular adaptive context, the analyst will inevitably be selective. There is a need for him to be definitive and to be understood without becoming overrepetitive or confusing. If he is to succeed in this, he must not deal with too many facets of the complex communicative networks he faces. This danger of being overinclusive is of course countered by that of being too restrictive. The proper balance falls within a rather ill-defined range, and errors in either direction may be viewed as communicative blind spots.

The possibilities for error here are endless. The therapist may identify a wrong adaptive context or attempt to intervene without having identified the primary adaptive task. There may be interventions based largely on the therapist's associations rather than on the patient's; fragments of the therapist's own fantasies may be introduced, as may material from other sessions which for the moment is dormant within the patient. Other instances of error are the need to exclude particular types of derivatives, and the failure to be sufficiently selective, giving the impression of disorganization and uncertainty. There is a tendency among therapists to avoid instinctual drive-related derivatives, and especially to miss valid and hurtful unconscious perceptions conveyed in disguised form in the patient's associations. It is also common to fail to incorporate and quietly work over threatening and painful role- and image-evocations, especially when these are discordant with the therapist's usual self-image.

In offering an interpretation, the therapist should in principle make use of the most compelling and dramatic derivative associations in the patient's material. Whenever available, he should be certain to identify the genetic figure pertinent to the interaction, doing so in terms of transference or nontransference depending on the nature of the situation. Perceptions must be identified before fantasies, and rectification must accompany the interpretive effort whenever it is required in light of a deviation in the framework or a previous intervention error. Technical terms and generalities are to be avoided, and interventions couched in terms such as problems in dependency, aggression, or sexuality—i.e., nonspecific interventions—are inadvisable. Instead, interventions should be couched in specific *image* terms based on the patient's derivative communications, and should constitute mainly a synthesis of scattered derivative expressions organized around an activated intervention context as it clarifies the unconscious implications of a relevant indicator.

The quiet search for error and countertransference should begin when an interpretation has reached the level of silent formulation and awaits silent validation in the patient's continuing association. If a planned interpretation acquires additional derivative support it can be offered to the patient. Subsequently, the search for countertransference elements receives additional impetus, an effort that is made along with efforts to determine the extent of Type Two derivative validation.

There are four questions which seem particularly helpful in examining a proposed or actually offered interpretation to the patient. While these do not cover all possible errors, they seem to account for most. They are: (1) Have I added anything that was not in the patient's material in this session? (2) Have I omitted anything of significance? (3) Have I organized the interpretation around an activated intervention context and especially around its unconscious implications? (4) Have I made thorough use of the derivative complex, and have I indeed intervened in terms of derivative expression rather than in terms of manifest contents?

The implications and possible errors which can be detected through these four questions are extensive. Any fragment or thread that extends beyond the patient's own conscious and unconscious communications must be seen as derived from the therapist's countertransferences. In time, the therapist must be able to identify relatively quickly his own idiosyncratic contributions. He will be guided by any sense of subjective disturbance or any question he has about what he included or omitted. He will receive additional help from the patient's associations, especially if he attends to them as derivative responses to his interventions—as a powerful commentary which includes valid perceptiveness, as well as possible distortions.

By addressing reality and countertransference before fantasy and noncountertransference, the therapist is guided to a careful search for ways in which he may have disturbed rather than helped the patient. In addition, he should of course, be prepared to identify the valid aspects of his efforts and should know full well when he has made an interpretation which has received Type Two derivative confirmation. The stress should be on derivative listening as always, and the therapist should develop different anticipations depending upon the degree of validity of his intervention, the specific nature of his error, and the specific area of insight which he has imparted to the patient. Subsequent interventions should take into full account the dynamics of the prior intervention situation.

To comment briefly on reconstructions, we can begin by expressing concern for the therapist's tendency to introduce countertransference elements because of the climate of speculation and uncertainty in these interventions and the consequent need to engage in extensive postulation. Second, there is a notable tendency among therapists and analysts to invoke a genetic reconstruction primarily in the service of countertransference-based defenses and needs within the therapist. Clinically, it is not uncommon to discover that a therapist or analyst has introduced a genetic reconstruction entirely divorced from the present interaction, or one that treats current experience almost entirely in terms of the patient's distortions and fantasies. Such reconstructions serve defensive needs in the therapist and are often invoked when he has placed countertransference-based interventions into the bipersonal field, and the patient has introjected and perceived them unconsciously, and is working them over in a rather disturbed climate. The shift to genetics and the past becomes a major invitation to the patient to desist in his conscious and unconscious responses to the therapist's countertransference-based interventions. In this context, when a reconstruction evokes new memories and genetic material, these communications must be understood as having *functional meaning* (Langs 1978b) that pertains not only to the past, but to the current therapeutic experience.

In principle, then, reconstructions should be offered in terms of prevailing adaptive contexts within the therapeutic interaction, and in a manner that accords meaning to both past and present. They should be offered when in a particular session the patient has represented an intervention context, provided a relevant therapeutic context, and offered a derivative complex complete with genetic implications which require only integration and reconstruction by the therapist. This work is carried out in light of an adaptive response to an intervention of his own. The reconstruction should be formulated properly in terms of its transference and nontransference elements, so that full credence is given to ways in which the therapist has himself repeated the reconstructed trauma when this is the case. Alternately, the therapist also identifies ways in which the patient is distorting his view of himself in keeping with the reconstructed experience or fantasy. The reconstructed experience should not be treated in isolation, but should be understood as having been activated by the ongoing communicative interaction. The common practice of including elements from previous sessions should be avoided, since each session should be allowed to be its own creation and a reconstruction should be based on available material in a particular hour. Failure to adhere to this principle will lead the therapist to make countertransference-based selections, to be error-prone, and especially to fail to understand the implications of the genetically reconstructed experience in light of the immediate therapeutic interaction. A review of current psychoanalytic literature reveals that, virtually without exception, reconstructions are divorced from the ongoing therapeutic interaction, and serve functionally as lie-barrier systems rather than expressions of activated truths as they pertain to the patient's neurosis at a given moment in therapy or analysis.

Let us turn now to the three variations on interpreting which take place in each of the three communicative fields.

A. *The playing back of carefully selected derivatives* is an important technical measure that is easily misapplied and helpful only when used in proper circumstances. The main indication for its use occurs when a patient has failed to manifestly or with minimal disguise represent an activated intervention context of which the therapist is aware, and which, as a rule, should pertain to breaks in the fixed frame (largely because it is primarily this kind of repressed or suppressed intervention context which the patient is likely to recover). Often at issue in such interludes are matters such as the therapist's announcement of an unexpected session to be missed or a vacation, some extratherapeutic contact, or some glaring error such as the therapist's lateness to, or forgetting of, a session. Reacting to threatening anxiety, symbiosis, and the like, the patient represses any direct reference to the adaptive context, and his best representation is so highly disguised and resistant that it does not facilitate interpretation. Since the derivative complex organizes meaningfully around the unrepresented intervention context, and because the indicators are quite strong—in the range of eight to ten—the therapist would like to intervene interpretively. The result is an interpretation which omits the intervention context, but which strongly indicates that it is the missing link.

In intervening this way, it should be remembered that the resistance involved is based on significant defenses and efforts at pathological instinctual drive gratification. These should not be bypassed or gratified by the introduction of the missing element by the therapist. The analysis of such defenses is fostered by the therapist's silence until the relevant material has surfaced. At times, however, the missing adaptive context is also a crucial therapeutic context; here there are important reasons to intervene.

In a session of this kind, while maintaining an openness for additional adaptive contexts, the therapist organizes the patient's material around the unmentioned primary adaptive task. Virtually always, the patient's indirect communications will convey a commentary on that context, in terms of both unconscious fantasies and unconscious perceptions. They will be filled with unconscious implications and Type Two derivatives related to the context, and in the later part of the session, sound technique calls for the playback of these selected derivatives in a form that leaves open the possibility of fantasy and perception, as well as allusions to both patient and therapist. This is a quality that is essential to the use of a *transversal intervention,* which alludes equally to seemingly contradictory possibilities.

This type of playback is designed to create a tension state or preconception (Bion 1962) in the patient, which can be alleviated or saturated into a conception only through an identification of the organizing adaptive context. Quite often, the patient responds in a way that fulfills this expectation, permitting subsequent interpretive work around the now identified adaptive context.

The technique of playing back selected derivatives must be confined to those situations where there is a powerful derivative complex and an equally strong, organizing intervention context which has not been sufficiently represented. Failure to adhere to these criteria leads to interventions which, instead of being basically interpretive, have the qualities of either a confrontation or a simple playback of random manifest contents without the clear implica-

tion of a key organizer and coalescible hidden and derivative meaning. These forms of intervening address the surface of the patient's
communications, while playing back derivatives is a transversal
intervention that embodies both manifest and latent contents, and
which is essentially interpretive. Utilized when the patient's
communicative complex does not permit interpretation of the
communicative resistance which has attacked the representation of
the intervention context, it enables the patient to either modify or
maintain the resistance, depending on a number of factors within
both participants. Often, the unconscious communication imparted
by a playback of this kind is that the therapist is prepared to deal
with the patient's unconscious perceptions of his deviation or
erroneous intervention, and to renounce the pathological symbiosis
involved. It is these interpersonal and communicative aspects, added
to the cognitive elements, which enable the patient to modify his
own resistances. Actually, only this way can the therapist indicate to
the patient his preparedness for mature relatedness and open
communication, and his willingness to forgo defensiveness and
resistance in the patient.

Used selectively, this is an extremely useful technique, applied to
patients who are Type A communicators. Occasionally, it proves
useful with Type C communicators who tend to respond to an
acute framework crisis and to other blatant errors in technique in a
partially defensive manner. The playback of derivatives will be
clinically illustrated and discussed later in this chapter.

B. *The interventional processing (metabolism) of a projective
identification* is another important, though potentially treacherous,
form of interpretation which is used when patients are making use
of the Type B communicative mode. It requires a combination of
cognitive and interactional capacities so that the therapist is open
to the incorporation of the patient's interactional pressures, yet
capable of containing and metabolizing them toward an understanding which eventually culminates in the development of a
silent intervention. In virtually all cases, this kind of tentative
formulation should find validation in the patient's cognitive-
associational material before being offered aloud. The therapist's
capacity to insightfully metabolize a pathological projective identification from the patient generates both cognitive insight and a

critical form of constructive introjective identification which is founded upon the therapist's cognitive ability and on his capacity for reverie (Bion 1962) which is reflected in the sound containing capacities necessary for such an intervention.

A similar process takes place in regard to the development of interpretations which find their major source in the object relationship experiences within the therapist as evoked by the patient. Here, the therapist deals with the patient's unconscious efforts to engage him in a pathological symbiosis, and to evoke role-responses, self-images, and other subjective and behavioral reactions in keeping with the patient's unconscious perceptions of the therapist's prior interventions on the one hand, and his unconscious transference fantasies on the other. All these efforts at role- and image-evocation are responses to intervention contexts, and ultimately must be interpreted in that light. Essential is the therapist's ability to maintain a level of signal responses, through which he experiences his tendency to react in a particular way or to have a particular kind of self-image, and yet manages not to act or intervene on the basis of these evocations. Instead, the therapist uses this constricted evoked experience to understand both the patient and himself.

In all instances where the therapist experiences pressures of this kind, he must sort out how much of what he is experiencing derives from the pressures of the patient, and how much stems from his own countertransference and noncountertransference needs. He must also trace the specific stimuli in the patient's material for his inner experience, and, as noted before, organize his understanding of these pressures in terms of previous intervention contexts. The subjective nature of this work requires the silent validation of formulations developed on this basis, carried out in terms of the patient's continuing material.

Interpretations made in this sphere are typically carried out under considerable pressure within the therapist. There is therefore a tendency to react to patients during such interludes with noninterpretive interventions, often in the form of confrontations and self-revealing defensive comments. It should be stressed that there is no substitute for an interpretive response; any other intervention reflects a containing and interpretive failure in the therapist—a form of countertransference. With the Type B–A communicator, interpretations are usually feasible in terms of evident indicators, a represented intervention context, and a meaningful derivative complex. Sometimes it is necessary to use a playback of derivatives, especially when a fixed frame issue is involved. Matters are somewhat different with a Type B-C communicator, since the therapist is usually under enormous interactional pressure—sometimes direct attack—and yet lacks a meaningful communicative network. At certain times, it is critical to maintain a silent containing response, though in the face of major indicators—as a rule, significant resistances and disturbances in the therapeutic alliance are in evidence—the therapist should intervene with as interpretive a response as possible. Often enough, the therapist will discover that he has contributed to the patient's pathological projective identifications with erroneous interventions and mismanagements of the framework which have constituted pathological projective identifications on his part into the patient. Because of this, *rectification* of the technical error and its residual effects is a necessary first step before interpreting; often such measures enable the patient to shift to a more meaningful communicative style.

C. *Interpreting metaphors related to the Type C communicative style* is a special intervention designed to help patients who make use of this particular communicative mode. For long periods of time, the material from these patients is flat and lacking in derivatives, lending itself neither to interpretation nor the playback of selected derivatives. An important determination under these conditions involves whether there is a known, activated intervention context, or whether the therapeutic situation is in a holding-containing phase. In the latter situation, the therapist should continue with his silence, which conveys a series of positive implications to the patient. However, in the former situation, it is important to maintain a search for meaningful representations of the activated intervention context, and for available fragments of the derivative complex. Often, the most meaningful derivatives pertain to the patient's defensive style, and this aspect of his resistance can be interpreted to him in the light of an active adaptive context.

It is to be remembered that all patients will shift to the Type C communicative style for some part of their psychotherapy or psychoanalysis. In the absence of an activated intervention context, the therapist's responsibility is that of silent holding and containing. This phase of "lying fallow" is quite important to the positive outcome of therapy, and should not be disturbed by countertransference-based interventions. On the other hand, when there is an evident intervention context, this particular type of interpretation should always unfold from the adaptive context and should stress the defensive-barrier function hinted at or directly stated. The therapist should remember that he is dealing here with nonderivative defenses, lie-barrier systems which often serve as massive defenses against an active underlying psychotic disturbance and as a means of maintaining a pathological symbiotic mode of relatedness. He should therefore proceed slowly and with tact, though it is important that he interpret when the material permits. Typical metaphors which appear in the derivative complex of these patients are allusions to safes, tanks, walls, dead ends, voids, unrelatedness, lies and deception.

THE TRANSVERSAL QUALITY OF INTERVENTIONS

There is an aspect of intervening that appears to apply to all interpretation-reconstructions, the playback of selected derivatives, and the other forms of interpretations. This refers to the *transversal* quality or form of an intervention, a necessary aspect of technique with which the therapist responds to the patient's *transversal communications* (Langs 1978a). Such communications are characterized by the manner in which they traverse two realms: reality and fantasy, patient and analyst, transference and nontransference, or perception and distortion. Every communication, whether from patient or therapist, has dormant transversal qualites in that it condenses opposite elements of one kind or another (a possible exception occurs in the Type C field, where apparent communications are actually attempts to destroy meaning; but even this is only a tendency, as the attempt is often betrayed by the appearance of Type C metaphors). We will reserve the term *transversal communication*, however, for those associations and behaviors whose heavy investment with ambiguity makes itself felt. When a communication is so experienced, it is almost always found to arise from and to express a specific adaptive context; where this is not found, the epxerience must itself by examined, in the case of the therapist, for countertransference inputs.

Often, when the patient has unconsciously perceived and introjected the countertransference aspect of an intervention from the therapist, the working over and commentary by the patient will be heavily invested in both veridical perceptions and pathological distortions. In intervening, it is essential that the therapist acknowledge the validity of the patient's perceptions, while not neglecting the distorted aspects that derive from the patient's own pathological unconscious fantasies and the like. Similar considerations apply to associations that meaningfully though unconsciously allude to both the patient himself and the therapist—both must be acknowledged through a transversal interpretation.

This position is in contrast to the usual approach to interpretations, especially those related to transference and resistances, which are based on the premise that the patient's communications are essentially distorted and based on pathological fantasies. Such an approach, while it might acknowledge an occasional reality element or adaptive context, views the patient's communications as usually related to himself alone, and to the realm of fantasy. In contrast, other therapists will adhere to the manifest content of the patient's associations, and will deal only with the realistic and nondistorted elements. Occasionally, when there is an acute countertransference input, the focus will be on the therapist's inappropriate communications, often to the neglect of the patient's distorting addenda.

In contrast, the transversal interpretation consistently acknowledges all aspects condensed in the patient's communications—both reality and fantasy. It will be well to label as transversal interpretations all interventions by the therapist which deal with the patient's mixed unconscious responses to an activated intervention context. The contrasting term, *definitive interpretation*, can be applied when the interpretation stresses or refers exclusively to one basic dimension of the patient's response, whether transference or nontransference. In utilizing definitive interpretations, the therapist should be especially careful when the stress is on transference and unconscious fantasy constellations, since there is an ever-present danger of overlooking an important realistic and nontransference element. Nonetheless, when the material meaningfully organizes around an intervention context in terms of primarily transference-based material, such an interpretation will receive Type Two derivative validation.

INTERVENTIONS: INDICATIONS AND TIMING

At present, therapists and analysts have an extremely loose conception of when they should intervene. In general, the principle has been to maintain an interpretive focus on transference resistances, expecting to clear the way for the revelation of core unconscious transference fantasies, memories, and introjects—so-called contents—which are then subjected to both interpretation and reconstruction. This led to the maxim that one interprets defenses and resistances before contents, and is usually supplemented by some vague recognition that interventions are also indicated by ruptures in the therapeutic alliance, acting out, and unexpected symptomatic and regressive episodes.

There is a wide range of *indicators* within the patient, therapist, and therapeutic interaction which suggest that the patient requires an intervention; they may also be termed *therapeutic contexts.* They are the expression of an inner disturbance within the patient derived from some internal or external source—usually a combination of both—which would be best alleviated through an active intervention from the therapist, framework management response, or an interpretation. By and large, the patient expresses a therapeutic need in virtually every session. The goal in the hour, then, is to offer an interpretation of the unconscious basis for, and implications of, the therapeutic context, and to do so in terms of an activated intervention context and derivative complex. In this way, some aspect of the patient's neurosis—his neurotic functioning, and neurosis-related unconscious fantasies and perceptions—can be understood or experientially modified. The actual decision to intervene will depend upon the intensity of the indicators and on the extent to which the communicative complex lends itself to active intervention.

There are five major classes of indicators, which can be organized in a hierarchy based on the extent to which they suggest a therapeutic need within the patient. However, within each of these categories there can arise highly compelling indicators which call for intervention even though the general class tends to be at the lower end of the continuum. The five categories are: (1) interventions by the therapist, more often those that are erroneous and those that involve a break in the frame; (2) efforts by the patient to modify the basic framework; (3) all other forms of resistance, such as acting out; (4) symptoms within the patient; and (5) crises in the outside life of the patient.

Indicators should be scaled from one to ten, with ten representing those situations in which a therapeutic context calls for the best possible intervention available to the therapist despite all limitations to the communicative complex. This would be exemplified by an acute and major break in the ground rules carried out by either patient or therapist, by a suicidal or homicidal threat from the patient, or by a patient's wish to terminate prematurely or suddenly—a form of resistance and rupture in the therapeutic alliance which calls for framework management and interpretive responses from the therapist.

In general, indicators which derive from the patient's object relationship with the therapist, and which are constituted by the therapist's modification of the ground rules and boundaries, and by major interpretive errors, tend to be more powerful therapeutic contexts than, for example, the emergence of symptoms within the patient. This touches upon the extent to which therapeutic need and symptoms arise within the patient based on his interaction with the therapist, and secondarily with those in his outside life. Virtually all symptoms and therapeutic contexts are interactional products, deriving inputs from both participants to treatment. In keeping with basic principles, those elements which derive from the therapist deserve both rectification and interpretation before the therapist deals with indicators which derive primarily from within the patient.

Technically, the patient will tend to report the indicators for a particular session early in the hour. Most indicators are represented manifestly, though occasionally, especially when the therapeutic context involves an error by the therapist in intervening, the patient may repress any direct reference to the context, and instead represent the indicator through disguise. Once conveyed, however, the therapist has a sense of the nature and degree of therapeutic need and can build his interpretive or framework management response around the indicator. In this way, each hour occurs as a kind of mini-analysis, and we have a sense of organization and systematization in regard to the nature of the therapist's interventions and their rationale.

An interpretive response to a therapeutic context involves identification of the specific adaptive contexts and Type Two derivative material from the patient which reveal the unconscious basis for, and meaning of, the activated indicators. This is the essential definition of an interpretation from the communicative approach. It can be seen that the basic purpose of identifying the patient's representation of a prevailing intervention context and Type Two derivative responses is that of revealing the unconscious meanings and functions of a therapeutic context. All sound interpretations and framework management responses will be structured in this tripartite manner: indicator, intervention context, and derivative response.

It can be seen too that all adaptive contexts are indicators, since erroneous interventions create pathogenic introjective identifications in the patient with the therapist which can be truly resolved only by rectification and interpretation. In addition, correct interventions, in addition to their salutary effects, tend to generate paradoxical negative responses in the form of envy, the disturbance of the patient's defenses, and contrasting realizations between the positive introject of the therapist and the negative introjects which presently exist within the patient. Of course, not all indicators are adaptive contexts, since some of these disturbances derive primarily from the patient's own behaviors and the intrapsychic aspects of his symptoms.

The presence of a clearly defined therapeutic context does not place the therapist under a total obligation to intervene. It expresses a need of this kind within the patient, who must then provide communicative material upon which the therapist's response can be based. The therapist must maintain a sense of balance and proportion, evaluating the acuteness of the therapeutic context and the extent to which the material from the patient yields Type Two derivative meaning. As one would expect, in situations of emergency proportions or with major errors in technique, the therapist is more likely to intervene in the presence of relatively strong communicative resistances, as long as there is some degree of representation of the adaptive context and fragments of meaning in the derivative complex. In the absence of an acute therapeutic context, the therapist is likely to intervene only when there is a clearly represented intervention context and a coalescing derivative complex.

Initially even in a crisis, it is best to maintain the basic listening process in order to identify the crucial activated adaptive contexts and to be able to intervene in terms of Type Two derivatives. The therapist should also safeguard his interpretive and management efforts by consistently developing silent formulations and searching for silent validation before intervening. All too often, especially in times of crisis—i.e., in the presence of a major therapeutic context —therapists are prone to premature interventions and to shifts toward manifest content and Type One derivative therapeutic work. Such efforts reflect failures in containing, holding, formulating, and intervening; they will, by and large, fail to resolve the crisis at hand and will add additional countertransference inputs to the original problem. Only sound interpretive work and framework management responses developed at the behest of the patient's derivative communications will prove consistently successful in helping patients to resolve acute symptoms, as well as crises within therapy. Adhering to basic interpretive principles best serves both the patient and therapist at such junctures.

In sum, then, indicators are all elements which signal a need within the patient for an intervention from the therapist—interpretive or framework management. These needs may have either intrapsychic or interactional sources, and can be scaled from one to ten according to intensity. In deciding upon the timing of an intervention, full consideration is given to the nature of the indicator, the clarity and directness of the representation of the adaptive context, the nature of the derivative complex, the presence or absence of a link or bridge to therapy, the patient's prevailing communicative style, and background considerations regarding the status of the therapeutic alliance, the phase of therapy, the overall nature of the patient's psychopathology and resistances, and all other elements pertinent to the immediate therapeutic moment.

Indicators which are constituted by either the countertransference-based and erroneous interventions from the therapist, or a break in the frame created by either participant, call for both rectifying measures and interpretations. When an indicator involves this particular type of problem, it tends to be of high order. At times, rectification may be possible, though not interpretation. However, all efforts to secure the framework should be undertaken at the behest of the patient's manifest and especially derivative communications, and should not be arbitrarily introduced by the therapist. It is there that the therapist must have *faith* in the patient and in his need for a secure therapeutic environment. In the actual clinical situation, the patient virtually always produces derivative directives of this kind. The accompanying interpretive work depends on the nature of the communicative network, as is the case with any effort of interpretation.

Indicators are the most compelling of the several factors which determine the timing of interventions. In the presence of an acute break in the frame, a major rupture in the therapeutic alliance, or an intensely pathological symptom, we have level ten indicators which call for the best possible intervention permitted by the communicative network. Lesser crises range in the seven to nine area of the scale, and call for intervening if at all possible, even in the presence of a somewhat resistant communicative network. Beyond that, with lesser degree of indicators, the nature of the communicative network will be the main determinant.

In our discussion of the techniques related to resistances, we considered issues related to the timing of interventions. The principles we developed are applicable to all types of indicators, and can be stated in essence as follows: communicatively, the key to an interpretation lies in the clarity of the representation of the activated adaptive context which is central to both the indicators and derivative complex. The clearer the representation, the greater the facility of making an interpretation. In addition, there is the need to consider the derivative complex—the material which constitutes the defensively disguised representations of the patient's adaptive responses to the activated intervention context. Here, the greater the extent of meaning and coalescibility, the greater the ease of interpreting.

A nonspecific bridge to the therapy or therapist toward the end of a session facilitates intervening. In general, the therapist can have greater patience with a patient communicating in the Type A mode than with one who uses the Type B mode. The difficult Type B–C mode is often used by patients at times of intense crisis, especially those which evolve in response to countertransference-based intervention contexts with powerful pathological projective identifications from the therapist. Under these conditions, the therapist is often hard-pressed to maintain his basic principles of interpretation. Often, it is feasible to resort to a meaningful and well organized playback of derivatives around a known activated adaptive context. Responses by the therapist which take place on the manifest content level are generally quite ineffective, and tend only to further reinforce the patient's resistances and pathological mode of communication and relatedness.

Finally, with patients who use the Type C communicative mode, the therapist will often maintain his silence for long periods of time until the patient shifts to more meaningful communication. In the presence of an acute crisis, the effort is made consistently to utilize the best available representation of the adaptive context and the most meaningful derivatives contained in the patient's associations.

As noted earlier in this chapter, the therapist has a kind of recipe in mind, and he waits to see whether the patient provides him with the three basic ingredients he will need in order to intervene: a significant indicator, a well represented intervention context, and a meaningful derivative complex. In general, it is best to maintain silence until an initial hypothesis has obtained Type Two derivative validation. It is also advisable to permit the patient who has already represented the adaptive context in a manner which lends itself to interpretation to continue to associate until he has provided the therapist with a rather full derivative complex—i.e., one which contains significant representations of unconscious perceptions and fantasies, as well as genetic allusions and indications of the patient's adaptive or maladaptive reactions. When a patient is communicating meaningfully through the Type A mode the therapist will experience a point at which he has a rather full and coalescing derivative complex. His specific intervention will then be prompted either by a rather striking derivative communication pertinent to the already represented adaptive context, or by a further reference to that particular context or the expression of a general bridge to therapy.

Should any of the ingredients for intervention fail to materialize, the therapist can use a more disguised derivative as a lead-in to the interpretive or framework management response which he has developed and silently validated. It is virtually always feasible to find such a moment if the patient has been allowed to continue past some hypothetical optimal point—i.e., to an extent where the derivatives begin to flatten out. It is best to allow the derivative complex to ripen rather than to intervene prematurely with one or two derivative elements.

Beyond the general principles and more specific guidelines for locating indicators and timing interventions are important considerations of tact, sensitivity, and empathy. However, these must be understood in light of the type of derivative communication which pertains to the patient's neurosis, not naively in terms of surface considerations.

THE VALIDATION OF INTERVENTIONS

Elsewhere (Langs 1976c, 1978a,d), I have offered rather extended comments on the validating process in psychoanalytic psychotherapy and psychoanalysis. It has become increasingly evident that many analysts and therapists make little or no effort to validate either their silent formulations or their actual interventions to the patient. I will stress here only the importance of taking each intervention as the adaptive context for the patient's subsequent associations, and the need to listen to this material, first, as a *commentary* on the intervention—an amalgam of unconscious fantasy and perception, valid and invalid responses offered in derivative form (a variety of *transversal communication*)—and, second, as the means through which the correctness of an intervention is assessed.

In this latter regard, true validation is seen in the cognitive sphere by the report of new, previously repressed associations that lend genuinely new meaning to the prior material. This constitutes the appearance of a *selected fact* (Bion 1962), a realization that reorganizes the previous material so that it yields up a meaning not previously evident. Lesser validation is seen in associations which, in some genuinely new manner, add to the richness of the material under analysis. Direct confirmation of an intervention is linear and nonvalidating, as are its general surface acceptance, comments that extend it in ways already known, and the repetition of earlier material. They call for reformulation and a renewed period of silence on the part of the therapist, so that the patient may assist him in the search for the prevailing adaptive context, the crucial unconscious meanings and functions of his communications, and the working over of the countertransference elements and bias in the therapist's error.

In the interactional sphere, validation is expressed through the report of positive introjects, usually in terms of some outside figure who has functioned constructively or of some reference to a positive attribute of the patient himself. Both cognitive and interactional validation can be achieved only by organizing the subsequent material around the therapist's intervention, thereby throwing into relief the critical Type Two derivatives. Every meaningful and curative intervention should find validation through Type Two derivatives from the patient, and any intervention not so confirmed must be considered in error and explored for countertransference inputs.

DISCARDED INTERVENTIONS

The three interventions I have described should serve all the therapeutic needs of the patient. They are to be maintained even in situations of emergency, although it is evident that in some crises, in part because of the presence of countertransference inputs, the therapist will be at a loss for a valid interpretive intervention and may have to resort to emergency directives. Nonetheless, even though used as a lifesaving measure (and the emergency should be of such proportions), there are uniformly negative repercussions within the patient, many of them expressed in derivative form under the guise of conscious gratitude. Since I have elsewhere established my position on the detrimental consequences of most of the interventions I have discarded (Langs 1973, 1975b, 1976b, 1978a), my discussion here will be brief.

As for methodology, the communicative position is based on repeated empirical tests of the unconscious functions, communications, and meanings conveyed in the actual interaction between patient and therapist or analyst by each of the interventions to be described. Each application is taken as an adaptive context, and the patient's responses studied in terms of Type Two derivatives as commentaries in terms of both meaning and validity.

As we have seen, the communicative therapist finds no need for questions, clarifications, and confrontations. With few exceptions, each of these interventions tends to interfere with the patient's derivative flow and expression. Often, they are designed to direct the patient away from the therapeutic relationship and interaction, and are addressed at a manifest content level. As a result, they constitute denials of the importance of activated intervention contexts, of the implications of the therapeutic interaction and of the therapist's interventions, and of derivative communication which is at the heart of the patient's responses as they pertain to his neurosis. Further, in focusing the patient on a particular association or event, there is a resultant mobilization of defensiveness and a restriction—of the patient's freedom of expression.

In the clinical situation, a remarkable number of questions and clarifications are offered at some point in the session at which the patient is unconsciously working over, through displaced and disguised derivatives, a traumatic aspect of his relationship with the therapist which is usually based, at least in part, on countertransference inputs. The question or clarification is typically directed toward an outside relationship or an aspect of the manifest content. As a result, these interventions constitute the offer of Type C barriers against the more disturbing aspects of the patient's communications as they pertain on a derivative level to the therapeutic interaction. Further, they often constitute defensive and otherwise pathological projective identifications into the patient designed to express or extrude difficulties within the therapist, rather than to illuminate the patient's material. The result is a form of lie-barrier therapy in which manifest content and false so-called insights prevail, and which is characterized by intense defensiveness designed to avoid the implications of the spiraling communicative interaction.

Confrontations have been replaced in the present delineation by the technique of playing back selected derivatives organized around an unspoken adaptive context and by the identification in context of metaphors of Type C barriers and falsifications. The very term *confrontation* conveys a sense of forcefulness and attack that, unfortunately, characterizes all too well a major unconscious function that this intervention serves for many therapists and analysts (see Adler and Myerson 1973, Langs 1973). In addition, despite the conscious intention to use this intervention as a means of developing derivative communication, observations of actual clinical interactions indicate that this seldom proves the case.

Confrontations tend to address the surface of the patient's material, to elicit direct and manifest responses, and to fix the patient on a relatively superficial level of communication. In addition, their use, all too common, without an adaptive context entails the risk of major countertransference inputs, largely designed to gratify the therapist's unconscious pathological fantasies and defensive needs; often harshly seductive, punitive, and attacking qualities prevail. As a result, the patient's material will unconsciously center around the introjection and working over the therapist's countertransferences and the disruptive elements of his confrontation, rather than constructively and unconsciously elaborating in a new and meaningful manner those themes, contents, and defenses relevant to the therapist's manifest intervention.

There are a wide range of noninterpretive and nonneutral interventions that may be classified under such rubrics as supportive, directly responsive, self-revealing, gratuitous, and extraneous. In previous writings (1973, 1975a,b, 1978a,d), I have, based on repeated empirical documentation, demonstrated that such seemingly well meaning interventions evoke responses in the patient that are, as a rule, split: manifestly and consciously, the patient is accepting or grateful, while unconsciously—in his derivative communications— he uniformly experiences the unconscious communications contained in these interventions as seductive, destructive, and nonsupportive, and as a violation of his autonomy, an assault on his ego- and self-boundaries, and a reflection of the therapist's lack of faith in the patient's ego capacities. These interventions are essentially in the service of the therapist's unresolved countertransferences. Rarely, a direct response to the patient is needed (for example, when a patient forgets the date of the therapist's vacation); even then, clarification must be delayed until a full analysis and working through of the unconscious implications of the patient's failure to remember has been completed.

Finally, there is a wide range of inappropriate alterations in the ground rules and framework of the therapeutic interaction, implicit and explicit, that entails interventions that consistently reflect the therapist's countertransferences and which finds nonvalidating responses from the patient. Similarly, repetitions or elaborations by the therapist of an intervention without clear-cut validation are in the service of pathological needs within the therapist, and will evoke further nonvalidating reactions in the patient.

Seemingly innocuous interventions are filled with significant *unconscious* implications and are not to be treated lightly. In attending to the commentary from patients after such interventions, we discover that they are filled with images of ignorant and useless people, and many other negatively toned derivatives of disappointing and disturbing perception-introjects. Virtually all of this is communicated in derivative form unless the therapist becomes involved in repeated and relatively gross errors. Because of the disguised mode of communication, the true meaning of such associations is easily overlooked by the therapist who uses such techniques.

The decision as to which interventions to maintain and which to reject is, as I stated, based entirely on the presence or absence of Type Two derivative validation from patients in response to instances of each type of intervention we have considered. It is not surprising, however, to discover that questions, confrontations, and clarifications are of no use to the communicative therapist in light of the type of listening process he applies as compared to the usual classical approach. His efforts are geared, of course, to the detection of neurotic communications, disguised derivatives pertinent to an adaptive context. It is this type of expression which is, so to speak, the language of the neurosis—more accurately, the mode of expression of neurotic difficulties and their sources. We long ago discovered that this mode of communication requires a relatively secure frame, even though it is often adopted in response to acute breaks in this frame. In addition, there are certain ways in which the therapist can promote the patient's use of this critical mode of expression, just as there are ways in which he can interfere with it.

To understand this point more clearly, we must crystallize the differences in the communicative concept of derivative expression from that which exists in the classical psychoanalytic literature. There are some classical psychoanalysts who believe that they work with derivatives of unconscious fantasies (though almost never with derivatives of unconscious perceptions) in a manner that is comparable to that adopted by the communicative therapist. A careful review of the literature indicates that this is a false impression; there is a basic difference which I have tried to develop elsewhere (Langs 1978a), and which I now wish to make even more explicit.

I will risk a summary statement and general impression in the absence of specific discussions of this issue in the literature. It may be said that for Freud and those analysts who have followed him in the belief that neuroses are based on unconscious fantasy-memory constellations, expressed by the patient through compromise formations and with disguise, the manifest contents of the patient's associations constitute derivatives of latent contents pertinent to these constellations. In their view, the main means of disguise lies within the intrapsychic defenses of the patient. As with dreams, a particular latent thought or fantasy (and perception) is, in this model, initially expressed in some disguised way, perhaps as a projection or quite directly, though displaced. For example, an unconscious wish by a male patient to sleep with his mother derived from his oedipal period may find expression in a relationship with the analyst in the form of a wish to sleep with the analyst's wife. The wish is disguised only in regard to its displacement. Using projection, the patient may believe that the analyst's wife has seen him and wishes to go to bed with him, or may even believe that the analyst himself desires him sexually. With the use of intellectualization, the patient might state that undoubtedly he had oedipal wishes to sleep with his mother, but feeling none of the accompanying affects. As a final illustration, the patient might have sexual relations with a desirable or undesirable woman in a form that lives out the fantasy—again through displacement.

In each of these instances, the unconscious fantasy is available in whole cloth and can be inferred from the manifest content. The patient might state that he wants to be close to a woman, disguising his sexual wish by giving it the form of a wish for intimacy. Or he might mention a fleeting sexual thought about a woman, without describing the details which would show its source in his earlier relationship with the maternal figure. If these wishes were being expressed in the patient's relationship with his analyst, either through homosexual wishes disguised to represent the wish for the mother or through homosexual wishes designed to both express and defend against such wishes, the patient might describe a fleeting thought of being attracted to a man, or a passing wish to be closer to the analyst. Here again it might be possible to suspect the underlying fantasy by developing sensitive inferences from such material.

Based on the theory that defenses can be modified through direct confrontation, efforts at clarification, and by questions, to the point where the previously preconscious or unconscious fantasy can emerge in its entirety into consciousness, classical analysts have applied techniques of this kind in their work with patients. Some analysts tend to become engaged in direct translations of this kind and in inference-making which sets aside specific unconscious fantasy-image constellations in favor of the identification of supposedly unconscious wishes for power, control, and such, thereby carrying out work devoid of specific instinctual drive representations. In all such instances, however, the manifest content of the patient's association are taken as a starting point for direct inferences and translations from the surface to the depths. A dream of a tree implies a phallus; a boat, the maternal body or sometimes, because of its penetrating qualities, the maternal phallus and even the paternal phallus. Anger at his teacher implies anger at the analyst, with its source in anger at either the father or mother.

Elsewhere, I have offered many examples of this type of analytic approach (Langs 1980a,c). In my study of the listening process (Langs 1978a), I termed such derivatives *Type One derivatives*, and gave as their primary characteristics the fact that they are inferences made by the therapist directly from the manifest contents of the patient's associations without the use of imagery or an adaptive context. It is useful as well to term such derivative *inference derivatives* or *translation derivatives,* as a way of highlighting the intellectual and often highly impersonal qualities of this type of effort. While it is not possible to pursue this matter more extensively here, it must be stated that this particular mode of communication is not the means through which neuroses are expressed. It is by and large a highly stultified and clichéd communicative modality to which both patients and analysts turn as a means of constructing lie-barrier formations designed to seal off the more genuinely image-laden neurosis-related mode of communication. In essence, these are defensive constructs which, while couched in terms pertinent to neuroses, organize them in a manner that render them functionally meaningless rather than dynamically explanatory.

The difference between Type One and Type Two derivative formulations has been somewhat obscured by the fact that the elements of language, the individual words and even some of the constructs, are comparable. When arrived at through a Type One derivative effort, these formulations function as critical lie-barrier systems within the therapeutic interaction, a dynamic factor which is absent when these derivations are made in the form of Type Two derivative formulations.

This second type of derivation involves the development of inferences in respect to a number of different and quite separate elements in the patient's associations, and the use of the adaptive context as the essential guide to, and organizer of, the implications developed. To stress the essence of these derivations in terms of the ongoing therapeutic interaction, we may term this type of derivative *indirect image-laden interactional derivatives.*

Type One derivatives become increasingly clear through a concentration of the patient's attention on the details of a single fantasy, thought, or behavior—an effort designed to modify defensiveness in order to reveal more and more of the directly available underlying meaning. In contrast, Type Two derivatives can develop only when a patient is permitted to associate in several different areas or on several different themes, or offers wide variations in his ongoing thoughts and fantasies as they center around a single theme. Rather than encouraging a more intense look at a specific fantasy, Type Two derivative listening is designed to foster spontaneous, unconsciously determined shifts in the flow of the patient's associations and to permit the emergence of a series of rather separate fragments, each containing a meaningful derivative implication decipherable through the identification of the prevailing intervention context. I have termed these coalescing derivatives, and a meaningful derivative complex would contain a large number of fragments which can be integrated into the totality for the moment of the patient's responses to the intervention context. In this work, it is the realization that each information fragment contains a different aspect of the patient's response to the precipitant which proves crucial and which gives depth to the understanding derived in this way. One fragment contains the genetic constellation for the patient, while another alludes to the patient's belief as to the genetic elements relevant to the therapist. Still another fragment involves valid unconscious perceptions of the implications of the therapist's interventions; another reveals the dynamic meanings for the patient in terms of his own unconscious fantasy constellation. Some fragments contain evoked fantasies, while others reveal efforts at active adaptation. Each fragment contains a specific meaning for a particular patient in interaction with a particular therapist in light of a particular activated intervention context. Such meanings are highly personal, entirely interactional, and contain image-laden derivatives of both interpersonal and intrapsychic processes.

Efforts to obtain a concentrated look at an association or fantasy disrupt the more freely flowing associative process needed to obtain meaningful image fragments available for coalescing. Questions, clarifications, and confrontations prove counterproductive and offer lie-barrier systems; they generate interactional defenses which obstruct sound therapeutic work and the production of increasingly clear, less defended expressions from the patient. Other types of non-interpretive interventions, such as direct advice, other forms of so-called support, self-revelations, and such, clearly disturb the flow of the patient's derivative expression, and place disturbing inputs into the bipersonal field and patient which become new intervention contexts. They generate threatening images of, and convey actual disturbing qualities within, the therapist which tend to heighten communicative resistances except for efforts by the patient to work over the therapist's countertransferences.

It must be noted too that there is a form of Type Two derivative formulation which actually involves translation, rather than indirect, derivatives. For example, when a therapist is going on vacation, the patient may recall a period when his mother was ill and in the hospital. If this appears to be the only meaningful association, a formulation which would suggest itself that the therapist's vacation reminds the patient of the loss of his mother. While this is certainly true, it is nonetheless relatively empty and barren, a cliché lacking associative links with other meaningful fragments. As such, it constitutes a translation derivative dressed up in the guise of an interactional derivative, and it will not lead to Type Two derivative validation. A great deal of present therapeutic work is done in this highly general, nonspecific manner, carried out with the use of translation derivatives either totally divorced from an intervention context or based on essentially noncountertransference-based intervention contexts and functionally meaningless responses of the kind just described, dressed up as if to contain meaning when they function to destroy it.

Therapeutic work based on a synthesis of meaningful derivative fragments whose implications derive from a specific intervention context is clearly more difficult cognitively than that based on relatively simplistic translation derivatives. There is considerable evidence, however, that such work is also experienced by all patients and therapists as highly dangerous and anxiety-provoking for a multitude of reasons. Among those already identified are the dangerous qualities involved in conscious realizations of both fantasy and perception constellations which are dynamically active in the immediate moment of the therapeutic interaction at which they are identified; the anxiety evoked by valid unconscious perception of disturbances in the other member of the therapeutic dyad; the dread of the more disturbed and psychotic parts of the personality which are virtually always expressed in their most terrifying forms through Type Two derivatives; and for the therapist, the extensive loss of a lie-barrier system which has served to protect him from highly threatening realizations which relate to his more inappropriate and pathological inputs into the therapeutic interaction. These and other threats involving the loss of pathologically symbiotic relatedness have made it difficult for therapists to appreciate the differences between the two approaches discussed here, and have generated a reluctance to work with Type Two derivative communication. Nonetheless, there is compelling evidence that it is in this realm alone that true insight and sound positive introjective identification can be generated within the patient as a basis for the adaptive resolution of his neurosis.

INTERVENTIONS WITHIN THE THREE BASIC COMMUNICATIVE FIELDS

In the Type A field, both patient and therapist use language and behavior for symbolic communication, illusion, and transition. The patient communicates essentially through Type Two derivatives organized around sequential adaptive contexts. Whether the prevailing attitude is resistance or revelation, in very little time the derivatives necessary to interpret the unconscious fantasies, memories, introjects, and perceptions on which the defensiveness or core fantasy is based become available. In this field, the therapist offers the patient a secure hold and container by defining and maintaining the framework. He then interprets the patient's behaviors and verbal associations, whether they impinge upon the ground rules or serve as a communicative medium. The therapeutic work takes place mainly in the cognitive sphere, though there may be occasional episodes of interactional projection and efforts at role evocation. There is a general sequential alteration between periods of resistance and relevation, with interpretive resolution of the inevitable obstacles and insight into their unconscious sources and meanings, supplemented by similar insight into core fantasies and memories and the like.

The Type A field, then, is one in which silence, interpretations-reconstructions, and occasional management responses to infringements by the patient on the framework prevail. At times of acute anxiety or conflict, these patients may repress allusions to important adaptive contexts within the therapeutic relationship, and the playing back of selected derivatives pertinent to that adaptive context proves a valuable intervention.

In the Type B field, established largely through the patient's use of projective identification and action-discharge, the therapist's main function is to receive, contain, and metabolize toward cognitive understanding the patient's interactional pressures. The silent hypotheses developed in this way should consistently be subjected to validation both through the reception of further interactional pressures from the patient, and through the latter's cognitive material. The major intervention in this field is that of processing a projective identification, and of interpreting in context the implications of role- and image-evocations. At times the playing back of selected derivatives can be important, and quite often management and interpretation of impingements on the framework will also require responses from the therapist.

It is well to remember that projective identification may serve both defensive and revealing functions, and often expresses efforts at resistance. Still, this is a valid mode of communication for the patient, and should be accepted as such so that the therapist can intervene in an interpretive manner. Often the therapist is under considerable pressure to intervene with these patients, and, while he must develop the capacity to silently tolerate interactional pressures until they can be cognitively understood, there will be a need to intervene more frequently with these patients at times of crisis.

In the Type C field, silence is the essential tool for the therapist. While there may be efforts to modify the frame from time to time, characteristically these patients accept the frame as established and make few impingements in any direction. They accept the therapist's hold and the implied symbiosis of the quiescent relationship. There is little or no use in playing back apparent derivatives to these patients in the hope of identifying a hidden adaptive context, since they maintain their opaque defenses and interpersonal distance quite intensely and will seldom provide missing links—in part, because such a relevation would activate the link between patient and therapist.

A limited form of interpretation proves the primary verbal tool for the therapist in this type of field, and can be characterized as identification in context of the patient's metaphors for the barriers, void, destruction of meaning, falsifications, and destruction of relatedness that prevails in the Type C field. Using minor bridges to the therapeutic interaction, these metaphors must be interpreted in light of activated contexts and the nature of the patient's communicative style. Validation is generally found in momentary expression of the tumultuous inner mental world that these defenses serve to seal off.

Work with Type C patients requires great tolerance. Long periods of uninterpretable interludes are experienced by the therapist as resistance and noncommunication. It is critical, however, to distinguish the healthier from the more pathological forms of this communicative style. Thus, in the presence of a known activated intervention context, the use of Type C communication by the patient must be understood as resistant and efforts made to formulate and interpret its basis. On the other hand, in situations lacking an activated intervention context, these periods of apparent noncommunication, and silent symbiotic relatedness without disturbance, may be viewed as necessary interludes in which the patient lies fallow, engages in self-interpretations, and shores up and lessens the pathological elements in his Type C barrier defenses. It is important at such times to refrain from attempting to interpret on a manifest or Type One derivative level, since to do so will be met with nonvalidation and, sometimes, with a sense of triumph by the patient over the therapist who has permitted himself to be fooled by this type of nonmeaningful verbiage. It is in this sphere that the therapist's tolerance and capacity to contain a void—the patient's negative projective identifications (Langs 1978a)—and to accept a relatively nongratifying mode of relatedness, proves crucial. As mentioned, the occasional modification of a Type C barrier will lead to an interlude during which the inner chaos—the psychotic core within patient, therapist, or bipersonal field—will emerge. At such moments, interpretations-reconstructions, playing back selected derivatives around an unmentioned adaptive context, and even the metabolizing and processing of projective identifications will be required. The patient will, however, soon restore the Type C barriers and the therapist must shift back to the use of interpretations in context of the patient's metaphorical representations of the Type C communicative mode.

In all, the therapist's interventions are distinctive for each communicative bipersonal field or particular style of communication by the patient. The timing, pace, and nature of these interventions will vary considerably for each field, and it is essential to identify the patient's communicative mode and work accordingly.

THE ROLE OF NONCOUNTERTRANSFERENCE AND COUNTERTRANSFERENCE

Every therapist has his own style of listening and intervening. Some therapists prefer the Type A cognitive mode and tolerate poorly the Type B and Type C communicative styles in their patients. Others prefer to process interactional projections and are less responsive to symbolic communication. Clearly, the variations are considerable and it is essential for the therapist to recognize his preferences. He must be aware of his capacity or incapacity to tolerate ambiguity or closeness, as well as for synchronized and discordant communication, holding, and containing—to name but a few of the important aspects that deserve fuller discussion.

The therapist must carefully examine, through self-analysis and his understanding of his patient's commentary responses to his interventions, the true unconscious nature and function of his verbal interventions and efforts to manage the framework. He must be prepared to discover in himself the presence of unconscious projective identifications and Type C barriers—psychoanalytic clichés (Langs 1978b,c). These aspects are mentioned specifically because they extend beyond the usual discussions of the influence of the therapist's unconscious countertransference fantasies on his interventions, in which stress is placed on unresolved conflicts, special areas of vulnerability, the misuse of interventions for seductive and hostile purposes, the presence of defensive blind spots, and unconscious wishes for inappropriate gratification.

I wish to emphasize in this discussion a single tenet which, once stated, will seem self-evident. It is a principle, however, that has taken several years to develop, and that requires a departure from the usual view of interventions as essentially correct or incorrect. It is as follows: every intervention made by the therapist—interpretively or in terms of the management of the framework—contains some element of countertransference expression.

To my knowledge, this principle and its many implications, most of which cannot be traced here, has not been explicitly stated in the literature. It implies a continuum of interventions, ranging from those with only a modicum of countertransference to those in which its influence is overridingly significant. It suggests that the timing of an intervention, the material selected for comment, the associations that are not picked up on, the therapist's linguistic style and tone, his use of innuendo or of concrete thinking, and many other dimensions of intervening leave extensive room for the expression of countertransference no matter how essentially valid a particular intervention may be. This implies too that both countertransference and noncountertransference are ever-present in the therapeutic interaction, as are, of course, both transference and nontransference on the patient's part.

There is therefore an element of countertransference in every moment of the communicative interaction, and the patient will respond continuously to this aspect along with his reactions to the noncountertransference elements in the therapist's interventions, including his silences. It becomes essential now to recognize that when we have spoken of a valid intervention we have been characterizing its predominant qualities, just as when we have considered erroneous interventions we have been stressing major countertransference influences—to which, quite often, there has been an added acknowledgement of what I have called a valid core or noncountertransference element (for a more complete discussion, see Langs 1980a).

In evaluating a therapist's intervention, then, it becomes essential to identify both its valid and invalid aspects, and to at least be aware of any measure of error in an essentially correct intervention. It seems likely that it is this continuous stream of countertransference inputs that provides the patient a greater or lesser degree of external and interactional pathology to which he responds in terms of his own both distorted and valid repertory of reactions. This tenet becomes another means through which the crucial importance of therapeutic work within the framework of the therapeutic interaction is established. On the one hand, the countertransference inputs serve on some level as a repetition of past pathogenic experiences and in the actual therapeutic interaction constitute a means, however modified, through which the patient's neurosis is actually restimulated in the present—in a form that is open to analysis only so long as (1) the therapist ultimately becomes aware of the true nature of the unconscious communicative interaction, and (2) these inputs are, by and large, relatively small. On the other hand, the valid, constructive, and essentially noncountertransference components of the therapist's interventions provide the patient previously unavailable adaptive resources, cognitive insights, and inevitable adaptive introjective identifications crucial to therapeutic cure.

Under those conditions in which countertransference factors take on major proportions, a traumatic repetition of the pathological past will prevail, as will an offer of interactional defenses and resistances, of inappropriate and pathological gratification and sanction, and of misalliance and bastion formations. It is the use of the validating process and of self-knowledge that provides safeguards in this respect, and offers a means through which the therapist may detect these elements in his intervening—making use both of the patient's unconscious communications and of self-analysis.

In this context, it can be stated again that every erroneous intervention contains its constructive nucleus, and that the rectification
and analysis of therapeutic interludes related to essentially erroneous interventions may provide both the patient and the therapist
significant opportunity for insight, adaptive inner change, and
growth—as long as the situation is identified and corrected, and is
not part of a repetitive, countertransference-dominated interaction.
Clearly, the optimal therapeutic work takes place in a situation in
which the countertransference elements are a relatively minor component of the therapist's interventions. This provides a setting
within which the therapist's constructive interpretations and
managements of the framework provide a predominantly positive
tone to the therapeutic interaction and to the vital work that
centers around that aspect of therapy which concerns the patient's
introjections of the therapist's pathology and his projection of his
own inner disturbances.

As would be expected, countertransferences may interfere with
each component of the listening, validating, and intervening
processes. If a major indicator is missed—e.g., an unnoticed break
in the frame—the therapist's interpretation may involve the correct
adaptive context and derivative material, but the synthesis of these
aspects of the communicative network will be used to explain the
wrong indicator.

Similarly, the therapist may work with one adaptive context
while the key to the indicators and derivative complex are contained in another context. As we have seen, in the presence of two
important contexts, patients will often represent one context rather
clearly while presenting the other through highly disguised derivatives. It is not uncommon for a therapist to erroneously work with
the more self-evident context, while failing to recognize the one
which has been subjected to greater defensiveness and distortion,
and which is nonetheless more important to the patient for the
moment. Often this occurs because the avoided context involves a
major countertransference input, while the represented context
does not.

In dealing with the derivative complex, among the most common
countertransference-based errors is the formulation of the material
around *fantasy* constellations rather than around an accurate mixture of both perception and fantasy. There is also a common failure

to include critical instinctual drive derivatives, whether they pertain to unconscious perceptions or to unconscious fantasies. Errors in the formulation of genetic connections are also not uncommon, especially when they involve valid unconscious perceptions of the therapist and an actual repetition of a past pathogenic interaction, rather than distortions introduced by the patient.

A useful and practical tool in the search for the countertransference elements in a therapist's intervention is found in the analysis of the material from the patient which preceded the therapist's effort. Often, when an intervention fails to obtain Type Two derivative validation, this kind of analysis reveals unconscious inputs from the patient which have served as a disturbing adaptive context to which the therapist has responded idiosyncratically and inappropriately with an error which yields its considerable implications when understood in light of the precipitants from the patient. Beyond that resource, the therapist can make use of the derivative implications of the patient's subsequent associations and of his own efforts at self-analysis to determine the presence of errors and their unconscious basis.

THE PATIENT'S PROCESSING OF INTERPRETATIONS

It seems surprising to recognize that clinical evidence strongly indicates that patients rarely develop a capacity for meaningful expressive communication which is followed by a careful, similarly meaningful conscious Type Two derivative evaluation. This would be seen, for example, in a session where a patient responds to an activated intervention context with a clear representation of that context and a coalescing derivative network. The capacity in question would be reflected in the patient's ability to subsequently openly receive and register such material and become engaged in accurate self-interpretations of their unconscious implications— based on a process similar to that within the therapist in which the pertinent adaptive context is used to understand the derivative complex, and to illuminate the main indicators. This observation suggests that even with patients who utilize the Type A mode expressively in free associating, there are strong resistances against a Type A receptivity to their own and the therapist's communications. This implies the need for analytic work in this area, and suggests that most patients maintain a state of internal communication in which the receptive mode is closer to the Type C style than the other two modes.

Turning to the patient's responses to valid interpretations, we are faced with a situation in which many determinants influence the final outcome. A valid, well timed, tactful, and sensitive interpretation implies empirically that the patient will respond on one level with Type Two derivative validation, reporting both new, entirely unexpected material and derivatives of a positive introjective identification. All too often a therapist assumes the validity of his interpretive comments without confirmation from the patient, and much of the literature on the patient's resistances to accepting valid interventions and working through their implications—including much that has been written on the negative therapeutic reaction—has not included independent criteria of the validity of the interpretations involved (see Langs, 1976b). In what follows, I will assume a valid interpretation and set aside possible unconscious interactional and intrapsychic factors which could account for the patient's refractoriness to a sound interpretation.

I wish here to stress but a single set of interrelated factors that could adversely influence a patient's response to a valid interpretation. In this context, it is well to recognize that openness to the full implications of interpretive interventions includes a preparedness to experience the relevant anxieties and conflicts, to modify in a meaningful manner the defenses against the disturbances involved, to tolerate the necessary therapeutic regression which often follows, and ultimately to approach the psychotic part of the personality which constitutes the deepest stratum of all psychopathology. It seems evident that such a prospect is both awesome and on some level quite terrifying, in that it requires a secure therapeutic setting and a truly capable therapist, as well as a certain type of trust, ego strength, faith, tolerance of the truth, and capacity for sound maturation within the patient. There are far too many factors involved to explore them in any detail here, though I would stress the choice between tolerating a painful regression in order to effect adaptive intrapsychic change and true growth, as opposed to finding some means of avoiding and closing off the disturbing regressive constellation through avoidance, the development of Type C barriers, the layering over of falsifications, and even actual flight from the analysis (the choice between what I have termed *truth therapy* or *lie therapy*; Langs 1978c).

For many reasons, therapists have in general tended to over-idealize the value of insight, and to minimize or ignore its many burdens. Psychic growth can take place only at great cost to the patient, though it is well to note that it offers a unique form of maturation and singular adaptive resources not attainable in any other way. It is the tolerance for this type of painful openness and working through, which involves the use of analyzable defenses and the affective experience of the most disturbing parts of the patient's inner mental world (unconscious fantasies, memories, introjects, and the like) which characterizes the Type A receptive mode. These patients not only respond with Type Two derivative validation to a correct interpretation, but also carry the therapeutic work forward, albeit in the presence of interpretable resistances and meaningful alternations between revelation and defense. Ultimately, they attain an insightful measure of growth and symptom alleviation, and acquire highly serviceable adaptive resources and flexible defenses previously unavailable to them.

In contrast, there are patients whose receptive mode is characteristic of the Type B communicative style, in that they experience the therapist's interpretations as dangerous projective identifications which threaten to totally disrupt their fragile inner equilibrium. A sound interpretation is experienced as an assault upon the patient's mental balance, and often, as a persecution. Some of these patients express themselves in the Type A mode with highly interpretable derivatives, but then respond to the therapist's intervention with terror, pathological projective identifications, and Type C barriers and flight—all following initial Type Two derivative validation. Others in this group express themselves largely through the Type B mode and experience the therapist's interpretations in a similar vein, once again as violent projective identifications which threaten to destroy their integrity. These patients are prone to respond with extremely violent and directly attacking projective identifications toward the therapist, and they make massive efforts to destroy his equilibrium and the therapeutic situation. A final group who tend to use the Type B mode expressively respond to a validated interpretation with the subsequent erection of intense Type C barriers to the point where their associations and behaviors lose all perceptible meaning, and their sense of relatedness to the therapist is ruptured.

The common thread running through all of these responses is a deep dread within the patient of his own inner mental world, and especially its psychotic core. At times, and far more often than currently realized, there is a comparable dread of unconsciously perceived processes and contents within the therapist. These patient's characteristically contain within themselves extremely persecutory introjects and other violent and disruptive unconscious fantasy constellations, whose realization they believe will lead to psychic annihilation. On some level they are totally convinced that the acceptance of and elaboration upon a valid interpretation would prove unmanageable, produce an openly psychotic regression, lead to violent attacks by pathological introjects who are protected through overidealization, generate an inner assault by fantasied objects which would ultimately lead to their mental destruction, and interrupt a pathological symbiosis without which they are convinced they cannot survive. When the receptive problem is related to highly threatening unconscious perceptions of the therapist, they experience additional fears based on their reading of the implications of his error. Much of this dread is justified by the direct and unconscious implications of the interventions made by a therapist who is having countertransference difficulties.

These patients, then, unconsciously welcome and continue for long periods of time in treatment situations in which truly valid interpretations are either nonexistent or quite rare. In a truth therapy situation, they are ultimately confronted with a choice to either gradually deal with and resolve the psychotic part of their personality (and perhaps of the therapist as well), or to interrupt treatment. With careful interpretive and rectifying work, some of these patients remain in therapy and ultimately, are helped quite significantly; others choose to flee, using a variety of rationalizations. The latter group does so despite a variety of insights into their plight, and nonetheless choose avoidance rather than facing their dreaded inner mental worlds. The factors in this choice, as they exist within both therapist and patient, are multiple and are in need of extensive empirical investigation. For the moment, I would note but one: experiences with previous therapeutic situations in which lie-barrier therapy was the predominant modality tends to strongly favor flight and avoidance reactions when a patient enters a new, truth therapy situation.

Matters are somewhat different in response to an incorrect interpretation. Such interventions may, in light of the ongoing therapeutic interaction, constitute functionally either the offer of a derivative defense or derivative lie-barrier system on the one hand, or a nonderivative defense, or nonderivative lie-barrier system on the other. In response to an erroneous intervention which contains in some derivative form aspects of the missing correct interpretation—e.g., passing allusions to the critical adaptive context or passing mention in some other context of the important elements of the derivative complex—patients often respond in a hopeful manner, and tend to produce derivative material designed unconsciously to foster the development by the therapist of the correct interpretation needed by the patient. As a rule, this type of intervention tends to lessen resistances even though no conscious insight has been developed either into the main issue within the bipersonal field or into the nature of the prevailing resistances. This is especially true if the patient is both a Type A communicator and a Type A receiver. If a frame issue is involved, most patients will respond with this particular communicative pairing. However, with other types of errors, the Type C patient may well become more resistant and not work over the mistake in derivative form, while the Type B–C communicator could well respond with some type of violent projective identification while not producing material that would help the therapist to organize this particular response around his erroneous intervention.

It is in this context that a Type A communicator will engage in unconscious therapeutic efforts toward the therapist, which can be understood only in light of the unconscious implications of the intervention context. Type B–A patients have a similar though more intensely interactional response, while Type B–C and Type C patients are less prone toward such unconscious therapeutic activities unless they involve basic framework deviations.

Responses to nonderivative lie-barrier, erroneous interventions, while they can be classified, tend to be unpredictable. If the lie-barrier intervention reinforces the prevailing lie-barrier system within the patient, or offers an acceptable substitute barrier formation, the patient may well incorporate the obliterating defenses involved and engage in little in the way of corrective or therapeutic efforts toward the therapist. However, if the therapist's lie-barrier system, as offered in the intervention, clashes with that of the patient, the latter may respond with refutation, with corrective efforts, or with some type of compromise formation. In any of these instances, there is a lack of Type Two derivative validation and a prevalence of negative introjects. These remain the hallmarks of a patient's response to incorrect interventions.

THE PATIENT'S INTERVENTIONS

The usual study of the therapeutic situation has considered only the therapist's interventions, while neglecting those of the patient. It is supposed that the patient simply free associates, and that these communications are designed to reveal his inner conflicts, unconscious fantasies, defenses, projections onto the therapist, and the like. A careful investigation of the therapeutic interaction reveals, however, that this characterization is limited, and that the patient will from time to time offer major conscious and unconscious interventions to the therapist and to himself. Since we now realize that countertransference is ever-present, activities of this kind are directed toward the pathology of the therapist and undoubtedly occur at a low level of intensity throughout the therapeutic experience. Major inputs of this type occur when the therapist has placed significant aspects of his own countertransferences into the bipersonal field and patient; they may also occur when the patient wishes unconsciously to offer a model intervention to the therapist, one that neither participant has been able to generate consciously.

As a rule, the patient's valid interventions—i.e., those that the therapist is able ultimately to confirm through Type Two derivatives organized around the adaptive context of the patient's intervention—are offered in derivative form, unconsciously (Little 1951, Searles 1975, Langs 1975a, 1976b). On occasion, the patient will consciously and directly rectify the frame or confront the therapist with an aspect of the latter's implicit psychopathology or explicit errors. A conscious, valid interpretation is extremely rare. However, unconsciously the patient will consistently offer interpretations in derivative form in response to the therapist's pathological inputs;

he will also convey models of valid functioning to the therapist, directives toward the rectification of the frame, and the like. The unconscious resourcefulness of the patient has been insufficiently appreciated. These efforts should be silently accepted by the therapist as offering ameliorating insights and directives. This is feasible, however, only if the therapist tries to be aware of the unconsious communications contained in his own interventions, and if he is prepared to treat his patient's responses to his therapeutic endeavors as commentaries filled with rich and valid understanding—in addition to their pathological qualities.

Finally, we may comment upon the efforts by patients to understand their own material and to question, clarify, confront, interpret, and reconstruct to themselves. As I indicated earlier in this chapter, these endeavors, almost without exception, take place on the level of the manifest contents of the patient's own associations, or in terms of readily available Type One, translation derivatives. Many patients, and they need not be mental health professionals, are quite adept at offering Type One derivative interpretations in respect to their purported dynamic and genetics. Almost without exception, such interventions serve *functionally* as derivative and nonderivative lie-barrier systems, in a manner comparable to their functional capacity when offered by therapists. Strikingly, patients' self-interpretations virtually never center around an activated adaptive context and Type Two derivative responses—perceptions and fantasies. Theoretically, such efforts are feasible in that a patient could well represent an adaptive context, present some related indicators, and then go on to free associate, only to finally, toward the end of the session, make use of reflective awareness to integratively interpret the implications of their free associations in Type Two derivative fashion. The observation that this virtually never takes place attests to the enormous dangers experienced by patients (and therapists) in respect to the full conscious realization of the implications of their derivative responses to activated adaptive contexts—the truth within the therapeutic interaction. This leads not only to failures by patients to understand themselves in Type Two derivative terms, but also to diverse efforts to seek therapeutic situations in which such truths will go unrecognized by both themselves and their therapists. It follows too that where feasible, interpretive efforts should be made that analyze the resistances involved in order to enable a patient to develop a sound model of interpretive work not only as a way of fostering their therapeutic experience, but also as a critical prelude to, and basis for, the inevitable efforts at self-analysis which follow upon any therapeutic experience.

Primarily observations indicate that the most likely time for Type Two derivative self-interpretation is during the termination phase. Often, the patient is quite aware that he is responding to the anticipated completion of treatment—a general intervention context. Some patients, especially those prone to Type A communication or to the use of Type C narration, will offer reasonable Type Two derivative self-interpretations within this context. There is a sense that this is designed unconsciously to exclude the therapist from the interpretive work, and to prevent unexpected and more threatening interpretations. These efforts also appear to have a constructive effect, enabling the patient to enter the post-therapy phase with some ability to engage in further self-interpretive work on a truth therapy level.

In this connection, we may recall the three phases of psychotherapy identified from the communicative approach. The opening phase generally revolves around the therapist's efforts to secure the frame, and will tend to evoke a Type A communicative response from the patient. There is then a middle phase during which patients engage, to a greater or lesser extent, in efforts at self-interpretation which take place usually on the manifest content or Type One derivative levels. While these interventions serve as derivative or nonderivative lie-barrier systems, it seems clear that their development within a secure holding environment enables the patient to modify his more pathological and rigid lie-barrier systems in a manner that permits symptom alleviation and more flexible adaptation—they nonetheless have adaptive value. When there is evidence that this is the case, there is generally no need to attempt to modify the communicative resistances, and the patient's material will not usually permit interpretive interventions. The patient will usually create a framework issue if he requires an intervention from the therapist.

The insights gained by the patient through self-interpretations, when these are made on the manifest and Type One derivative levels, are not statements of the interactional truths which exist within the bipersonal field at the moment. They must be understood as pseudo or false insights, and the therapist should be mindful of their defensive and false qualities, while nonetheless recognizing their adaptive value to the patient.

THE THERAPIST'S DIRECT AND DERIVATIVE INTERPRETATIONS

The material offered in the present seminars (chapters 1-9) has led to the recognition that some interpretations from the therapist are valid in terms of their manifest properties, while others are not. Our standard for this evaluation involves the questions of whether the therapist has identified the clearest representation of the most important activated intervention context, and made use of the most compelling and meaningful derivatives to illuminate the most important indicators. Interventions which are considered to be in error fall into two categories: (1) those which appear to be entirely in error manifestly and latently, and which do not state the critical truths of the ongoing therapeutic interaction even in derivative form—these we may term *nonderivative lie barriers*; and (2) those which are in error manifestly, and yet which contain allusions to important truths within the ongoing therapeutic interaction, though they are expressed in disguised and derivative form in the intervention—the offer to the patient of a *derivative lie-barrier system*. Investigations from the communicative viewpoint have just begun to probe the implications of these two types of interpretations, and here I will present some initial impressions. This will lead us to the more complicated subject of the nature and role of insight in psychoanalysis and psychotherapy, as it pertains to symptom alleviation and structural change.

Whether noninterpretive interventions can ever meaningfully serve as a means of expressing derivative insight is a question in need of further empirical study. It would appear that the traumatic, pathological, and action-oriented qualities of this type of intervention make likely their use as pathological projective identifications by the therapist and entail contributions which would significantly interfere with any useful derivative implications. As a rule, this group of interventions tend to constitute nonderivative rather than derivative lie-barrier systems.

Derivative and nonderivative lie-barrier interventions undoubtedly fall along a continuum. At one end are those erroneous interventions which are filled with derivative truths, while at the other extreme are those which are impervious to the dynamic truths within both participants to the therapeutic experience. Neither type of intervention will appear clinically in pure form, and the middle of the continuum contains increasingly equal intermixtures of these two types of communications from the therapist. It is important both clinically and for heuristic purposes to categorize the main qualities of an erroneous intervention in order to fully comprehend the patient's responses.

Each therapist must familiarize himself with indications of nonvalidation and error on his part, so he is in a position to evaluate his erroneous intervention on the basis of an understanding of the nature of his mistake and the pathological and nonpathological communications so contained. The focus here is on an evaluation of the derivative implications of a manifest error at interpretation. This can be measured against the patient's own expression of derivative truths to the extent that they are available. Often, it is possible for the therapist to recognize that he has indirectly or in passing, or in some specifically disguised manner, touched upon the correct interpretation within the framework of his mistake, in addition to having departed from the most meaningful aspect of the patient's material in ways that are self-revealing. While there is some evidence that patients do benefit in such instances, this clearly does not provide conscious insight, and it is far less satisfactory than a correct interpretation.

The positive and negative influences of a derivative lie-barrier interpretation can be seen, for example, in the excerpt from the work of Greenson (1968) presented in chapter 10. As the reader may recall, after the patient had reported his dream of the residence-barn, Greenson attempted to interpret the patient's rage at him around the adaptive context of the patient's response to his conscious perception that Greenson had been angry with him in the previous hour. Greenson alluded to the patient's feeling that the man in the dream should have been aware he was being overheard, linking it to the patient's "overhearing" Greenson's anger and retaliating by changing his office at home into a shabby combination of house and barn. I suggested that Greenson's use of the adaptive context of his overt anger had only limited validity, and the more crucial intervention context involved the fixed frame: the home-office arrangement, a context which was represented with greater disguise than the patient's perception of Greenson's anger.

Here the patient responded by stating that he had changed and become more open in telling Greenson of his anger toward him. He went on, however, to state that he understood that Greenson did not intend to humiliate him, though that is how it felt. He also added that Greenson's interpretations were of no help to him when he was so angry.

It may be suggested that the salutary effects of this intervention— revealed in the patient's positive allusions to himself—were derived not so much from Greenson's attempt to clarify the patient's reaction to the anger he had perceived, but from the fact that Greenson had touched on the issues of being overheard and the home-office arrangement. Of course, he did not use them as adaptive contexts to which the patient was responding with intense and critical derivatives, but as part of an attempt to formulate the material around the patient's felt need to retaliate against perceived anger. The analyst alludes to an important truth influencing the patient's neurosis, although on a manifest level the reference does not constitute a form of understanding and interpretation. These are defensive derivative formations, and in this instance, probably had an initial positive effect, even though the patient went on to suggest that the analyst's interpretations are of no help to him when the patient himself is angry—a derivative of the patient's unconscious awareness of the failings in this particular interpretation.

Initial observations of this type of effort at interpretation suggest that they do not lead to lasting positive introjects or to useful cognitive insight and the development of sound adaptive resources. They do, however, offer a somewhat positive image of the therapist, and generate a hopeful introject and an expectation that perhaps now that the therapist has touched upon a critical adaptive context in an unwitting or derivative manner, he may soon directly discover its considerable importance. If the therapist fails to move in this direction, the patient often becomes depressed and disillusioned.

The extent to which temporary symptom alleviation may take place based on such hopes is an open question, though this particular form of derivative defensiveness from the therapist may help the patient himself to develop relatively flexible, adaptive lie-barrier systems. This is far more likely than when the therapist intervenes in an entirely erroneous manner, failing to allude directly or indirectly to a critical adaptive context activated within the bipersonal field. Under these conditions, the intervention constitutes a powerfully pathological projective identification and the offer of a nonderivative lie-barrier system which will either promote a regressive response within the patient, or symptom alleviation based on the intense defensiveness reflected in the therapist's intervention.

THE ROLE OF INSIGHT

From the communicative vantage point, much of the literature on insight requires reinvestigation and reformulation. In essence, the hallmark of insight within the patient is a unique realization which serves as the selected fact (Bion 1977) which unites previously disparate experiences and observations, and constitutes a form of affectively-toned understanding of factors relevant to the patient's neurosis. It is essential to state, however, that this type of realization can be considered genuine only when it has been preceded or, more rarely, is followed by a Type Two derivative validation of an interpretation or frame management effort of the therapist, or has been arrived at by the patient through a series of indirect associations which coalesce meaningfully and which lead to unexpected understanding. The validity of such insights lies in their capacity to generate simultaneous positive introjects, to lead ultimately to symptom resolution and characterological change, to growth, and to the development of stable adaptive resources.

By and large, genuine insight does not arise from use of Type One, translation derivatives, nor does it emerge suddenly and inexplicably. While the latter is sometimes possible, in general, functionally useful and meaningful insights arise through an analysis of the patient's derivative communications and from a crystallization of their unrecognized meanings developed in terms of expressed indicators, activated adaptive contexts, and the multiplicity of implications of the available derivative complex. This particular definition would exclude most examples of what is considered to constitute insight in the classical psychoanalytic literature, illustrated recently by the series of papers on this subject in the 1979 supplement of the *Journal of the American Psychoanalytic Association*. Without attempting to develop specific issues and distinctions, it is the contention of the communicative viewpoint that a distinction must be made between true and false insight, and that this is related to truth therapy and lie-barrier therapy as defined in this and previous volumes (see especially Langs 1980a). However, both forms of insight may be functional, though they produce symptom alleviation through rather different means.

Genuine insight arises in the context of truth therapy designed to understand the activated truths pertinent to the patient's—and therapist's—neuroses as they exist in the immediate unconscious and conscious communicative interaction. It requires a formulation which identifies the prevailing indicators and adaptive contexts, and the nature of the derivative complex—the patient's responsive adaptive reactions. By and large, it is feasible only in the Type A field and in the presence of Type A communication within the patient. It requires, of course, a therapist capable of Type A communication and of creating the kind of secure therapeutic environment within which this type of understanding can be achieved.

One of the more surprising findings of the communicative study of insight is that patients almost never arrive at genuine understanding on their own in the course of a psychotherapy or psychoanalysis. That is, patients rarely interpret their own associations as Type Two derivatives organized around an activated adaptive context, and as pertinent to an important indicator. From time to time, patients do indeed attempt to understand themselves, to formulate their material, and to otherwise develop insight. Some of these efforts have already been discussed above when we considered the subject of the patient's interventions. Here, we may note again that studies of these efforts to achieve insight through self-understanding reveal that patients are inclined almost entirely toward the use of Type One derivative explanations and efforts to comprehend the manifest content of their associations. These endeavors, which are strikingly comparable to the work of classical therapists and analysts, can only produce false insight. Often, they touch upon areas of genuine understanding and truth, but these are not dynamically pertinent. *Functionally* they serve to reinforce or develop either derivative defensive formations or nonderivative lie-barrier systems.

There appears to be a natural and inherent tendency among all human beings, patients and therapists alike, which directs them away from interactional derivatives and Type Two derivative understanding, and toward manifest contents and Type One derivative formulations. This suggests the presence of intense anxieties and dangers in regard to the development of Type Two derivative formulations, and a natural tendency toward defensiveness in this regard. This impression is supported by the extent to which both parties to the therapeutic experience consistently prefer to work at a manifest content and Type One derivative level. In this way, both are able to avoid the most threatening aspects of the conscious and unconscious communicative interaction, and of the neurotic and psychotic intrapsychic formations.

Another implication of this finding is that spontaneous, genuine insight, extremely rare in patients, can generally be arrived at only through valid interventions from the therapist. This stresses the role of interpretive interventions in sound psychotherapy, and highlights the necessity of a therapist capable of making Type Two derivative interpretations.

These findings also have their implications for the subject of self-analysis. They stress the extent to which direct readings of dreams, associations, and behaviors on the part of a given therapist in the course of self-analytic efforts have only limited value. Such efforts tend to yield false rather than genuine insights, and to be developed along Type One derivative and manifest content lines. It is possible to generate directly realized insights organized around prevailing adaptive contexts in the professional and private life of a given therapist, but this type of understanding is still quite limited. The most genuine form of self-insight is arrived at through indirect associations which catch the therapist, in the course of his self-analytic work, quite by surprise; it enables him to generate unexpected understanding and integration not available through direct efforts, no matter how intense.

False insight may be generated in many ways. It is defined functionally as a defensive effort designed to cover over or seal off the most immediate implications of the spiraling communicative interaction. It has the formal characteristics of purported understanding which does not organize around an activated adaptive context.

Elsewhere (Langs 1980a), I have tried to identify various types of derivative and nonderivative lie systems which take the form of supposed insight in this kind of way. They include the use of psychoanalytic clichés, genetic reconstructions, and dynamic propositions which are offered in terms of manifest associations from the patient or readily inferred Type One derivatives, without the use of the specific organizing power of an activated adaptive context.

Of course, not all lie-barrier systems are constituted around supposed insight, since many are offered by therapists who do not profess to be seeking understanding, but instead make use of such processes as deconditioning, abreaction, and such. It is, however, especially important to identify those lie-barrier systems which are founded upon hypothetical but not functional truths, and those which make use of the truth functionally to support the development of fictions and the rupture of meaningful interpersonal links—the destruction of true meaning and relatedness. This particular use of the truth in the name of insight is especially nefarious, often difficult to recognize, and in general, unrecognized in the literature. These false insights are often accompanied by intense affects, so it must be stated that direct affective impact cannot be taken as a criterion for genuine insight.

Finally, there are the unresolved questions as to whether a patient may eventually generate a form of genuine, conscious insight on the basis of a reworking of a derivative lie-barrier intervention, arising through self-analytic efforts in response to a derivative or nonderivative lie-barrier intervention, and whether insight may operate unconsciously within a patient or must always be conscious. There are some indications that insight may operate unconsciously within the patient—as well as the therapist—and have some positive influence on his neurosis and adaptive functioning. This particular phenomenon can be identified through derivative communications from the patient which reveal a sense of understanding of which he is unaware consciously, and which is communicated within the context of some type of symptom alleviation. But unconscious insight seems not nearly as effective as conscious insight, and it may well be that the relatively lasting resolution of a neurosis can take place only on the basis of conscious understanding and the relevant working-through process. These are all matters in need of considerable additional clinical study.

INTERVENTIONS AND THE THERAPEUTIC OBJECT RELATIONSHIP

There is a complex interplay between the timing and nature of the therapist's interventions, their conscious and unconscious implications and impact on the patient, and the object relationship effected between the two participants. Some of the more salient features of this interplay may be identified through a series of propositions.

1. *A healthy symbiosis is an essential requisite for a sound and effective interpretation by a therapist.* The ramifications of the pathological symbiotic or parasitic modes of relatedness are such that a therapist who effects such interactions will have major difficulties in correctly applying the listening process to the patient's material, in generating sound formulations and interventions, and therefore in offering interpretations which will obtain Type Two derivative validation. Pathological symbiotic and parasitic needs within the therapist also lead him to generate erroneous interventions designed unconsciously for pathological object-relationship satisfactions. Even if he proves able to offer a technically correct interpretation, the unconscious ramifications of the pathological object relationship with the patient are such that they will contradict and undermine the therapist's manifest intentions. As a result, the patient unconsciously perceives a split within the therapist who moves toward a healthy symbiosis with his valid intervention, while maintaining a pathological symbiosis through other means.

2. *An inherent property of a correct interpretation is the offer to the patient of a healthy symbiotic mode of relatedness.* Thus, the offer of a correct interpretation requires of the therapist a capacity to maintain an appropriate distance from the patient, to renounce wishes for fusion and pathological object relationship satisfactions, and to manage his own pathological object relationship needs and their fulfillment in the actual interaction with the patient.

3. *The establishment and management of the ground rules and boundaries also require of the therapist a capacity to develop and maintain a healthy symbiosis with the patient.* All deviant framework management responses gratify pathological symbiotic and parasitic object relationship needs and must therefore be renounced. All erroneous interpretations, mismanagements of the framework, and noninterpretive interventions constitute on an object-relationship level efforts to gratify and engage the patient in a pathological mode of relatedness. And all manifest efforts to provide the patient with direct support as a purported basis for growth and individuation contain inherently unconscious gratifications and communications which undermine all possibility of true growth, individuation, separateness, and a capacity ultimately for commensal relatedness.

4. *The establishment of a healthy symbiosis or commensal mode of relatedness is inherently curative for the patient, and secondarily for the therapist.* Thus, the actualities of the therapeutic relationship must now be added to the curative factors in psychoanalysis and psychotherapy. A full statement in this respect would identify the following interrelated means through which adaptive resolution of a neurosis is effected: *(a)* the establishment and maintenance of a secure therapeutic environment, including the therapist's management of the ground rules and boundaries of the therapeutic relationship, in a manner which affords the patient ego-enhancing experiences of containment and holding; *(b)* the offer of valid interpretations which produce specific cognitive insights within the patient which then lead to definitive conflict resolution and the development of new and healthy adaptive resources; *(c)* constructive introjective identifications with a therapist capable of managing the therapeutic environment and of sound interpretive work; *(d)* the actual interactional experience of a healthy object relationship with the therapist, symbiotic or commensal, and the growth-promoting, ego-enhancing, individuating qualities of the mode of relationship itself.

Clearly, each of these factors rely upon the other. Thus, a therapist must first and foremost be capable of effecting a healthy symbiosis with his patient before he will have a capacity to properly manage the ground rules and framework and interpret to the patient. Similarly, any response to a patient's behaviors and material, other than relating to maintaining the framework and offering interpretations, constitutes means through which pathological symbiotic and parasitic needs are gratified for patient and therapist alike. It is to be remembered that a commensal or healthy symbiotic relationship between therapist and patient is defined in part through the nature of the therapist's interventions and cannot exist without an essentially interpretive, framework-securing approach. Thus, the experience of a healthy symbiosis and of a therapist capable of renouncing pathological needs for merger and other superego and instinctual drive satisfactions inherent to pathological modes of relatedness, creates one dimension of the curative introjective identifications upon which the sound resolution of a neurosis is founded.

FEAR OF SECURING THE FRAME AND OF MAKING INTERPRETATIONS

The fear in therapists and analysts of making valid interpretations and securing the framework of the bipersonal field is a much neglected topic. It brings us back historically to the landmark contribution of Strachey (1934) and his specific study of mutative interpretations—those involving activated wishes directed toward the analyst. In concluding that particular paper, Strachey wrote:

> Mrs. Klein has suggested to me that there must be some quite special internal difficulty to be overcome by the analyst in giving interpretations. And this, I am sure, applies particularly to the giving of mutative interpretations. This is shown in their avoidance by psychotherapists of non-analytic schools; but many psychoanalysts will be aware of traces of the same tendency in themselves. It may be rationalized into the difficulty of deciding whether or not the particular moment has come for making an interpretation. But behind this there is sometimes a lurking difficulty in the actual *giving* of the interpretation, for there seems to be a constant temptation for the analyst to do something else instead. He may ask questions, or he may give reassurances or advice or discourses upon theory, or he may give interpretations—but interpretations that are not mutative, extra-transference interpretations, inter-

pretations that are non-immediate, or ambiguous, or inexact —or he may give two or more alternative interpretations simultaneously, or he may give interpretations and at the same time show his own scepticism about them. All of this strongly suggests that the giving of a mutative interpretation is a crucial act for the analyst as well as for the patient, and that he is exposing himself to some great danger in doing so. And this in turn will become intelligible when we reflect that at the moment of interpretation the analyst is in fact deliberately evoking a quantity of the patient's id-energy while it is alive and actual and unambiguous and aimed directly at himself. Such a moment must above all others put to the test his relations with his own unconscious impulses. (pp. 158–159)

This is an unforgettable passage whose implications have largely gone untapped. As we know, Strachey's concept of the mutative interpretation involved attempts to understand the unconscious implications of the patient's material as it pertained to activated wishes within the patient toward the analyst, and therefore to the immediate analytic interaction. Strachey was also able to clearly delineate the dual affects of such interpretations: the first in terms of cognitive insight and understanding, and the second in terms of interactional processes through which an ameliorating, unconscious and positive introjective identification of the interpreting analyst served as a corrective influence upon the patient's pathological introjects. To state this a bit differently, Strachey made quite clear that valid interpretations serve to modify the patient's conscious and unconscious fantasies about the analyst, and also to render less pathological the introjects so derived.

To my knowledge, the few analysts who have touched upon this subject have given the matter only passing or insufficient consideration. Bion (1962, 1970) commented upon the analyst's possible use of interpretations to manage his own anxieties, and wrote about the fear of making an interpretation and experiencing the realizations involved. Klauber (1968) in what appears to be the most extensive consideration of this subject in recent years, offered considerable support for Strachey's position. He presented an investigation of the offer of an interpretation which attempted to take into account important factors in the analytic interaction, both transference and countertransference as he termed them. He endeavored to identify those aspects of the patient's transference that might pose difficulties for the analyst to interpret. He stressed implications beyond the content of an analyst's interpretation as they influence the patient, noting such factors as the analyst's unconsciously communicated value system in relation to such matters as the handling of id impulses. Klauber also pointed out that a valid interpretation helps the analyst himself to modulate and handle his own psychic tensions and anxiety in a manner not dissimilar to some of the effects upon the analysand. In general, Klauber tried to identify unrecognized issues which lie beyond the identification of contents for interpretations and which might evoke countertransference difficulties in their offer to the patient.

The empirical studies developed from the communicative approach, and my own experiences as a therapist and analyst, and as a supervisor, have indicated that there is enormous wisdom in Strachey's realization that analysts and therapists experience major difficulties in offering interpretations to their patients, and that this is especially true of what he called mutative interpretations.

Since the essence of a mutative interpretation involves an explanation of unconscious factors in a wish activated toward the therapist or analyst, the definition of interpretations offered in the present volume can readily be viewed as a refinement and elaboration of Strachey's thesis. Unlike the communicative approach, Strachey accepted some secondary function for interpretations regarding outside relationships, and for neutral noninterpretive interventions. However, he strongly objected to so-called supportive interventions on the basis that they generate negative rather than positive introjects, and that they have major detrimental effects. Strachy also neglected aspects of the role of unconscious perceptions and introjections of the therapist, and the need to interpret within this sphere. Still, there is much of substance that is comparable in his position and that of the communicative therapist.

A review of the literature, and direct clinical and supervisory experience indicate that there is a powerful aversion to what I shall term *adaptive context interpretations*. It can be understood in terms similar to those presented by Strachey: this type of interpretation requires a full comprehension of the therapist's contribution to the patient's experience, of the anxieties and conflicts in both participants, and of the dangers and constructive aspects of every dimension of the communicative interaction. It especially requires of the therapist realizations involving the most disturbed aspects of his own personality—the psychotic core—as activated by the interplay with the patient and his material, and requires of him that he deal with mobilized anxieties related to such critical and universal dangers such as separation, death, frustrated needs, areas of inevitable helplessness, and bodily anxieties and damage.

Any intervention other than an adaptive context interpretation provides the therapist with some measure of pathological defensiveness and gratification, and affords immediate relief from tension. Since every therapist has important quotas of unresolved countertransferences, all will experience strong needs in this direction. Beyond that, there appears to be a natural human tendency toward fusion, immediate gratification, and discharge, and toward the development of derivative and especially nonderivative barriers to disturbing evocations; and such tendencies must be understood and mastered for a therapist to be capable of making an adaptive context interpretation.

The therapist's anxieties about offering an adaptive context interpretation center on a fear of the full impact of his communications on the patient, and of the patient's communications—expressed needs and defenses—on himself. Yet it is here that the most dangerous and critical unconscious truths within the communicative interaction reside. Their mastery in the form of an interpretive response offers both patient and therapist a maximal opportunity for growth, independence, and for the adaptive resolution of the mobilized conflicts. It also offers the optimal positive introject for both participants, since even the therapist himself will respond introjectively to his own interpretive efforts and have a salutary response on that basis—just as he will respond to the negative self-introjects when he offers a noninterpretive or erroneous intervention of any kind.

Another danger emerges quite frequently in the course of supervisory work with relatively inexperienced therapists, who often lack sufficient personal therapy to master their patients' material to the point where they can make consistent adaptive context interpretations. Often when such therapists make a correct interpretation, they quickly regress and lose sight of basic techniques, shifting to noninterpretive and confused interventions. There is considerable evidence that this arises because they are unable to tolerate the separation anxieties aroused by the constructive interpersonal barriers contained in a valid interpretation. In addition, they show a dread of the patient's psychopathology, and especially of the psychotic part of the personality of the patient which is, indeed, mobilized in the presence of a secure framework and a valid adaptive context interpretation. It is under these conditions that this type of therapeutic regression takes place. The patient finds considerable insight and strength in a valid interpretation, and mobilizes the strength to express more primitive aspects of his perception and fantasy constellations. This prospect, especially in the borderline or schizophrenic patient, is feared by many therapists, who then use erroneous interpretations and noninterpretive interventions as defenses against this type of sequence. Educated speculation would suggest that much present-day psychoanalytic technique is designed quite unconscioulsy with exactly these purposes in mind.

As a final note, we may include the anxiety in many therapists in respect to utilizing appropriate silence. Here too there is a dread of separation and individuation, and a fear of the regressive potential contained in such silences. Inappropriate interventions provide pathological symbiotic gratification, and a whole range of pathological instinctual drive gratifications and defensive formations which we identified earlier in discussing noninterpretive interventions and mismanagements of the frame.

Rather than maintain a naive and idealized view of the intervention process, we must recognize that it requires considerable self-understanding and inner mastery to respond with the proper therapeutic intervention at various junctures in a treatment experience. Considerable renunciation and perhaps even sacrifice is required of the therapist who wishes to work at this level of effectiveness. The realization of basic anxieties in respect to each of the three critical interventions available to the therapist should help to direct us toward self-analytic work and clinical investigations which will bring us closer to the elusive ideal of consistent and sound therapeutic technique.

CLINICAL MATERIAL

I shall present several condensed clinical vignettes to illustrate the basic techniques of intervening. My formulation will center around these issues, and little effort will be made to discuss other aspects of the material.

Mr. A was in once-weekly psychotherapy with a therapist who had offered family therapy to his brother, sister, and parents. He was now the only member of his family seeing the therapist, and these excerpts took place after year and a half of treatment for periods of depression, problems in dating, and fears of becoming a homosexual. The patient was twenty-seven and single; he taught grade school.

In the first session of this sequence, the patient spoke in great detail of feeling criticized at work, especially by a woman supervisor who had called him irresponsible for allowing one of his classes a free period in the schoolyard. This woman had quarreled with another assistant principal who had attempted to protect the patient, and about whom the patient had had some homosexual thoughts.

After hearing many details, the therapist suggested that the patient was talking about women and men, feelings of irresponsibility, and two people who are fighting over him. The patient felt accused of being irresponsible by the therapist, and stated that he had not behaved in any such manner. The therapist apologized, saying that he had not meant that he believed the patient was irresponsible, but rather that the patient himself was concerned about taking responsibility. The patient agreed that this was a possibility, and he ruminated about his responsibilities at work.

To comment briefly on these interventions: the therapist was unable to identify a specific adaptive context related to the therapeutic interaction, and with some lack of certainty he took as the context the accusation made against the patient at work. In our supervisory discussion, the therapist felt in retrospect that he had probably intervened in the previous hour in a manner that was critical of the patient and irresponsible; this may well have been the primary adaptive task that had evoked this material, which could then be seen as Type Two derivatives related to the patient's unconscious fantasies and perceptions in response to the intervention.

This therapist quite consistently alternated between rather effective and helpful interventions, and sudden lapses during which his responses became noninterpretive, critical, and confused. The material suggests that the two assistant principals represent the patient's unconscious split image of the therapist. Considered along the me/not-me interface, the allusions to homosexuality may be a form of unconscious perception and interpretation to the therapist regarding the underlying basis for his problems in intervening— his unconscious homosexual anxieties and countertransferences. These difficulties serve to mask the patient's own homosexual conflicts and divided self, and would have to be rectified before the patient's pathology could clearly emerge within this bipersonal field.

The unconscious perception of the therapist as having homosexual conflicts which are expressed in the therapeutic interaction appears, based on my knowledge of his work, to be a transversal communication that contains valid perceptiveness and some minor degree of internal distortion—a mixture of reality and perception, nontransference and transference. These comments are of course quite tentative in light of the brief extract offered here, and are offered primarily as models for the type of clinical referents that pertain to the formulations offered in the earlier sections of this chapter.

If we turn now to the therapist's first intervention, which lacked a definitive adaptive context, we can identify it as a type of confrontation with the manifest content of the patient's outside relationships. It was not organized as a playback of selected derivatives around a known unmentioned adaptive context that exists within the therapeutic interaction. The confrontation is designed unconsciously to steer the patient away from that interaction, and to place the burden of prevailing difficulties within the patient—the therapist's contributions are totally set aside. The patient's nonvalidating response seems to allude to the therapist's efforts to blame the patient for the sense of difficulty, and to the irresponsible qualities of this intervention, which failed to take into account derivatives and unconscious communication.

In the face of direct negation, it is well for the therapist to sit back, become silent, listen and reformulate. The therapist's efforts at apology and clarification are noninterpretive interventions which treat the patient's disclaimer in terms of its manifest content, rather than as a derivative communication which serves as a commentary on the therapist's intervention, and which contains both unconscious fantasies and perceptions—especially the latter. It shifts the patient and the therapist to the surface of their respective communications, offers the patient an interactional obsessional defense and misalliance, and creates a bastion which seals off derivatives and more direct communications related to the therapeutic interaction. Rumination follows within the patient, as a representation of these interactional defenses.

In the next session, the patient began by saying that he hated to talk about his sister (whom the therapist had treated); he thought it a waste of time. However, she had threatened suicide because her fiancé had been critical of her and she felt that no one could help her. His mother had said that his sister was fine and the patient had seen her. She told him a dream in which her leg is injured and bleeding; she turns to her mother, who walks away. The dream was depressing, and later his parents fought and the patient felt quite helpless. He remembered times when his father would not allow him to help at work.

The therapist intervened and suggested that the patient had been counseling his sister. He noted that in the dream someone was not being helped, and he pointed out that this sister had been in treatment with him and that the dream must have implications regarding therapy. In fact, he suggested, the image of someone not getting help could tie into treatment, and he pointed out that after the patient had talked to his sister he had become depressed. He also had been unable to help his mother and father, and had recalled his father not allowing the patient to help him. With his sister, he had also been in a helping situation and ended up feeling inadequate and helpless.

The patient agreed that he had been counseling his sister, and thought he deserved a handsome fee. He now felt like crying and remembered a time at supper when he started to wheeze at the dinner table and left for a moment. When he returned, his sister had been given the steak that he wanted and his protests were to no avail—his parents thought he had finished dinner.

In evaluating this session, we must take the prior hour, and in particular the therapist's interventions, as the initial adaptive context for this material. It is striking that the patient began the hour by talking about how he had been wasting his time in therapy—a relatively valid commentary on the prior session and the therapist's interventions. His sister's suicide threat and dream represents, on one level, something of the patient's own depression and bodily anxieties, to which he rather directly adds his own sense of helplessness and the failure of his father to call on him for assistance at work.

However, if we monitor this material along the me/not-me interface in the context of the ineffective interventions made by the therapist in the previous hour, and if we keep in mind the possibility of a latent adaptive context related to the modification in the framework of this therapy that compromised the one-to-one relationship between patient and therapist, it is possible to suggest tentatively that the patient experienced the therapist's need to treat multiple family members as a defense against depressive and suicidal feelings, and as a reflection of his own helplessness. The images certainly convey a disturbance in the working relationship between patient and therapist, and as commentary on the altered frame, the patient seems to be suggesting that under these conditions there is no sense of therapeutic hold and no protection against suicidal fantasies.

As for the therapist's interventions, there was a failure to wait for a bridge to the therapeutic relationship and to identify a specific adaptive context in that area. Had the therapist played back a series of seemingly pertinent Type One derivatives related to the general context of therapy not being helpful, the patient might well have revealed a more specific adaptive context and clearer Type Two derivatives. In general, however, I would recommend continued silence, offering a secure hold, and allowing the patient an opportunity for more meaningful derivative communication.

Rather than adhering to the principle of permitting the patient to build the therapist's intervention in its entirety, the therapist rather dramatically introduced the fact that the patient's sister had been in treatment with him; it was also he who suggested the bridge between the allusions to failures to be helpful and the treatment situation. The intervention also has a transversal quality, in that the therapist alludes both to certain realities regarding conditions of treatment, and to the patient's experience of not being helped—without suggesting that the latter is either well founded or distorted.

Still, the focus is almost entirely on the patient's experience, without any indication of specific contributions from the therapist—a point that I make in assessing the intervention, and not as a suggestion for a proposed intervention. (For the moment, technically, I would have allowed the derivatives to build further in the hope of obtaining a bridge to the treatment situation; failing that, I would have played back selected derivatives taken from the material from the patient with the expectation that he would then communicate with less disguised derivatives, in terms of both unconscious fantasies and perceptions.) Finally, we should note that the therapist intervened in a rather confused manner, scattering his comments and shifting back and forth from one theme to another. This type of disjointed intervention is not uncommon in the absence of a reference to an organizing intervention context, and in itself suggests an underlying sense of helplessness, rather than mastery.

The patient's response to this intervention (which was partially correct, though premature) has another type of transversal quality: it seems both confirmatory and nonconfirmatory. In the main, however, it lacks definitive validation. On the positive side, it may be seen as containing Type Two derivatives related to the prevailing problems in the therapeutic situation; these imply that under conditions in which the one-to-one relationship is altered, the patient is open to illness, and further, that the particular deviation is experienced as favoritism toward the sister and deprivation. As a model, an intervention made on the basis of such a formulation would constitute an effort at interpretation—the identification of a specific adaptive context and the patient's responsive derivative unconscious perceptions and fantasies. In this respect there is a transversal quality in that there is truth to the patient's appreciation of his actual vulnerability under these conditions, and to his sense of favoritism and deprivation, although the oral qualities of his fantasies seem to derive at least in part from within himself. It is an open question whether the therapist could be analytically helpful to the patient after having previously treated his siblings and parents. In all likelihood, this constitutes an unrectifiable alteration of the framework, which, if analyzed at the behest of the patient's derivative communications, could be corrected only by insightful work which progressed toward the termination of treatment—an unrectifiable framework deviation termination therapy.

It is, as I have indicated, a fundamental principle that each intervention should be treated as the adaptive context for the associations that follow, and that the latter be treated as a commentary on the intervention—an unconscious appraisal with mixtures of perceptiveness and distortion. In this context, the patient's acknowledgement of his counseling efforts, and his comment that he deserved a high fee, seem to be a response to the positive elements in the therapist's comment. In supervision, I had previously suggested that the intervention had a valid core; that is, it was an effort to approach the truth of what was really disturbing the patient, though it was undertaken rather prematurely and with some sense of confusion. The patient's response appears to appreciate that mixture: there are the positive elements just noted, an appreciation of the constructive endeavors of the therapist which hint at a new understanding of the consequences of the altered frame. On the other hand, the memory of deprivation implies that there is something lacking in the intervention and that the patient has not been adequately fed—a transversal, oral model of the therapeutic interaction that contains both unconscious truth and unconscious fantasy.

In the next hour, the patient began by saying that he had little on his mind, but was glad to be at the session. He had begun to think about women sexually (a new development), and was masturbating less. He felt he might be responding to the pressures of his mother, who kept insisting that he was doing much better of late—and it was true.

The patient had talked with a young man who was serving as his assistant teacher. He had had homosexual fantasies about being in bed with this man and embracing him, though without having an orgasm. He imagined this student needing help, and helping him sexually. He stopped the fantasy, lest he imagine actual sexual contact.

The patient had been with a friend who had also been a patient of the therapist. For the first time since early in therapy, he described the overt homosexual relationship between the two of them, and how it had developed when they had been classmates and their parents had become friends. Initially, the friend had been the aggressor and the patient had eventually stopped him, only to reinitiate the sexual contact later on. The friend had resisted stimulation to orgasm, but the patient had insisted to the point where they performed mutual fellatio.

The patient was pleased to have told all of this to the therapist, and stated that he now had the wish to go out with a woman. The therapist responded by pointing out that the patient had had a daydream about the assistant teacher which did not reach closure and that he had prevented himself from imagining orgasm. He noted that the patient had gone on to talk about women, fears of exposure, fears of being found inadequate, and a need to cover up. He also pointed out that the patient had emphasized how his friend would not look at his penis and denied having had an orgasm, stressing once again the qualities of hiding and secretiveness.

The patient responded by saying that the image of secrets stirred him up, and he then recalled a series of childhood secrets: finding his father's pictures of nude women and having an erection; not being able to undress in the locker room in high school in front of the guys; having nocturnal emissions that his mother commented on in a humiliating way; being bathed by his mother; and first masturbating with great fears of damaging himself.

We may note that in the adaptive context of the therapist's intervention in the previous session—which entailed an attempt to partially rectify the frame (in actuality, the therapist had stopped all contact with other family members and had also desisted from such practices as note-taking and answering the telephone during sessions) and to interpret the implications of the previously impaired frame to the patient—the patient indicated that he was doing well and described both homosexual fantasies and a previous homosexual relationship with a former patient of the therapist. This material too has a transversal quality, in that it suggests that the patient now feels safe enough to reveal and explore his homosexual relationships and fantasies, largely as an effort to resolve the underlying pathology and to move toward heterosexuality. At the same time, these communications serve as Type Two derivatives in the adaptive context related to the framework, and suggest that the patient had experienced the alterations in the frame as a seduction and as an expression of unresolved homosexual fantasies and needs within the therapist.

In this context, we may briefly note that the patient responded to these efforts with an allusion to the truth. Up until this point, this treatment situation had many of the attributes of lie-barrier therapy, often nonderivative in quality. Quite unconsciously, the therapist had avoided work with the patient's derivative communications and with his responses to the ongoing therapeutic interaction, confining himself largely to manifest content and Type One derivative interventions. On a derivative level, the patient had been quite critical of these efforts, as may be seen, for example in his report of the dream of his sister's injured leg and the mother's walking away from her daughter, rather than helping. It is not uncommon to find allusions to the truth when therapists become engaged in truth therapy, just as references to lies and falsifications, deceptions and such, are not uncommon in lie therapy situations.

In the session, the therapist attempted to play back derivatives around the unmentioned intervention context of the alterations in the framework, but once again in a confusing manner which impaired his efforts to stress the patient's concern about secret sexual contact and needs to cover up. The intervention was stated in a manner that left no room for the patient's unconscious perceptions of the therapist, and did not constitute a definitive interpretation. It is therefore especially interesting to review the many new memories that emerged subsequently. While they undoubtedly reveal aspects of the patient's psychopathology—his overstimulation as a child, the seductiveness of his mother, his intense castration anxiety—it must be recognized also that they function as unconscious communications related to the qualities of the therapeutic situation as experienced under the conditions of this therapy.

Any isolated intervention related to this material that is directed entirely toward the patient's earlier experiences, in order to help him understand the unconscious basis for his homosexuality and fears of women, would include a major defensive element: it would deny the patient's unconscious perceptions of the therapist and the therapeutic interaction which have served as the immediate adaptive context for this material. A more appropriate interpretation would have a transversal quality: it would take the conditions of treatment, past and present, as the adaptive context, attempt to show the patient that he is currently experiencing the earlier deviant conditions as a repetition of the pathogenic past, and detail the relevant unconscious perceptions and their extension into fantasy. The material might permit an interpretation of the patient's awareness of the differences that have been developing with the restructuring of the framework. The therapist could then delineate some of the patient's anxieties within the more clearly defined therapeutic situation—his fears of a therapeutic regression. Technically, however, such an intervention could not be made until the patient provided a clear-cut bridge to the therapeutic interaction. To develop such a communication, the selected playing back of derivatives would serve well, including some allusion to the friend in a way that might hint at the fact that he too had been in treatment with the therapist.

The revelations regarding the homosexual friendship with the patient's friend who was in treatment with the therapist constitutes a form of Type Two derivative validation of the therapist's efforts to interpret and rectify as much as possible the disturbances in the framework of this treatment. This is an entirely new piece of information which serves as a selected fact to help organize aspects of the previous material, and it functions as a further commentary on the implications of the many deviations in which the therapist has been involved. It serves as well as a derivative expression of the patient's unconscious perceptions and fantasies of his relationship with the therapist—including its sexualized pathological symbiotic qualities. As a major transversal communication, the derivative function of this manifest association involves elements of truth and distortion, of transference and nontransference: there is indeed a seductive and pathologically symbiotic aspect to family treatment, and the hypothesis that it satisfies and protects against the therapist's unconscious homosexual fantasies would probably be validated if it could be tested. On the other hand, the therapist had never been directly seductive, was not overtly homosexual, and had made efforts to manage and master expressions of his unresolved homosexual countertransferences. We would therefore have to see this material as containing both kernels of truth and extensive distortions based on the patient's own unconscious homosexual fantasies and conflicts, and their genetic sources. An intervention designed to interpret the implications of this material would have to take into account the diametrically opposed qualities of these associations from the patient—it would have to be stated in transversal form.

In the following hour, the patient described his discomfort in the waiting room (which was in the hospital at which the therapist was associate director), stating that there were too many sick people around. He felt better for what he had discussed in the previous session, and described how well he was doing at work, where he was receiving admiration and was now ready for either a promotion or for a new job at a higher level. His main concern was leaving his job and having a farewell party, during which he might break down emotionally. He had been praised by the principal of the school and had had homosexual thoughts about him. He wondered if he should leave or not.

The therapist pointed out that the patient had said that he felt strange and uptight in the waiting room, and that this was connected to some ambivalence regarding change and his concern about public exposure. He suggested that there were various meanings to the themes the patient was talking about. The patient responded that he had no thoughts of leaving treatment, if that's what the therapist had in mind, and he reviewed again his concern about leaving his job and becoming too upset and crying at a farewell party. His mother had once attended the funeral of a near stranger and had made a fool of herself by carrying on. He thought of his sister's depression and how he still gets somewhat upset when he has to speak in front of his class. There's no place where he can cry—not at home, not with friends, and not in treatment.

The therapist said that the patient had now brought up his mother and sister, and that they were somehow related to facing a problem in changing jobs, speaking in public, and speaking freely. He added that the patient seemed to feel a similar problem here in therapy, where he is unable to cry. The patient responded that actually therapy had changed considerably since the therapist had stopped being a friend. At first the patient hated it and felt betrayed, but now it was working out well. Before, the therapist was a member of the family, but now there seemed to be a change and the patient felt safer. He could talk and he felt more secure when, as just a moment ago, the therapist no longer answered the telephone. Still, there was his fear of revealing himself, and he wondered now if it had been induced by the therapist and if he then took it outside. The therapist said that there might well be a kernel of truth in that, and the patient went on to talk about the recent differences in the therapist, and his own improvement of late. He thought then of his anxieties and of his handshaking, and how he controlled it with strangers. He feels like he keeps up a facade. He is two people living in a shell: one part is a stranger, but confident and liked, and now top dog and interested in women, and doing well; while the other part is the little boy under the covers, masturbating and afraid of exposure.

The therapist said that the patient had mentioned his—the therapist's—involvement with his family and had gone on to talk of exposure, adding that there were two parts to himself: one strong and the other immature. The therapist added that he thought that the patient was referring to therapy, and that he was feeling better about it and safer, and was now revealing more. This was related in part, the therapist said, to his own involvement with the patient's sister and mother, which had been inappropriate and not right.

The patient said that he had been flooded by a number of additional thoughts, but there was time to share only one: he had stopped going to pornographic movies and to the back rooms of pornographic shops where he used to masturbate. He felt he no longer needed them because he now had privacy in treatment.

In brief, the patient appears to be working over his reactions to both the previously modified frame and the currently secured one. The therapist, in his first intervention, played back a series of themes expecting to hear from the patient that he was, indeed, having some thoughts about terminating. It should be noted that the therapist's use of the word *ambivalence* runs the risk of intellectualization and carries with it a certain clichéd quality. It is best to intervene using the patient's language, and to do so without technical terms.

The playback of derivatives was clearly organized around the therapeutic situation and made use of the material from the patient.

It may have been a bit premature, since the intervention context was not as yet clear and there was still a good deal of time available to allow the patient the freedom of direct and indirect expression.

The patient, in response to the therapist's efforts to rectify and interpret the alterations in this framework, rather quickly introduced the theme of termination. The thought has two different qualities. On the one hand, it was conceived as a form of promotion and a sad farewell, while on the other, it involved the image of a funeral and of making a fool of oneself. These associations constitute a form of supervisory Type Two derivative validation of the thesis that rectifying and interpretive work in response to the many unmodifiable breaks in this framework (and the fact that the therapist had seen a friend of the patient is another such deviation) would lead ultimately to the termination of this treatment. Through his own derivative commentaries, the patient is introducing exactly this kind of concept. While there are, of course, other possible implications to this material, it is well to note this particular possible level of meaning.

The patient responded to the therapist's intervention by denying he had any thoughts of leaving treatment. Parenthetically, the therapist felt that there had been considerable improvement in this patient, to the point where such an issue might soon appropriately arise. The expressed fears of humiliation and exposure now appear to relate to the patient's dread of his own inner mental world, which would emerge within the therapeutic situation as secured by the frame. The therapist again played back derivatives, attempting to develop further the patient's insight into his feelings about the previous family therapy and the current therapeutic situation. This led to entirely new material about the patient's experience of the rectification of the frame, associations that reveal considerable conscious appreciation of the differences between the two treatment situations.

The therapist's acknowledgement that he may have contributed to the patient's symptoms, while clearly a constructive and honest effort, nonetheless addresses itself to the manifest content and serves as a kind of confession. This could more adequately have been done within the context of a more definitive interpretation. If we now take this intervention as the adaptive context for the associations that follow, it appears that the patient unconsciously perceived striking variations in the therapist's capacity to intervene:

one moment rather effectively, the next moment based on anxieties. According to the patient's unconscious interpretation, the latter is based on continued unresolved sexual countertransferences.

The intervention—the therapist's acknowledgment of error—is an attempt to address the adaptive context of the alterations in the framework; it alludes to both the patient's unconscious perceptions and his unconscious fantasies. It is somewhat confused once again, and while addressing the contributions of the therapist, it stresses the split within the patient without clearly relating it to the distinct alterations—the split—in the therapist's interpretations and managements of the framework. Still, it seems clear that the patient appreciated the valid efforts contained in this intervention (and they certainly stand in contrast to earlier interventions that failed to appreciate the implications for the patient of the family therapy). The patient's response appears to be a form of Type Two derivative validation in that it reflects an unconscious positive introject of the therapist, who had secured the frame and brought under control a major segment of his unconscious sexual countertransferences. This introject helps modify an earlier pathological introject that had, as the associations reveal, actually contributed to the patient's homosexuality and other perversions. The material suggests that the patient's voyeurism and masturbation had been an *interactional symptom* based in part on the therapist's countertransferences as expressed in the family therapy situation, and in part derived from the family interaction and the patient's intrapsychic conflicts and pathology.

The therapist's final intervention, then, implies the rectification of the framework, and a transversal interpretation of the unconscious fantasies and perceptions involved in the patient's experience of the altered frame. The patient's allusion to his renunciation of pornography validates the intervention through cognitive Type Two derivatives that derive special transversal meaning in the adaptive context of the intervention. It serves as a selected fact (Bion 1962) that provides new meaning to the previous material; it reveals the unconscious sexual implications, both reality and fantasy, for both patient and therapist, of the altered framework.

Let us turn now to another brief vignette.

Mr. B was a young man in psychotherapy for about a year on a once-weekly basis. He was afraid that he might be crazy and had intense homosexual fantasies and anxieties; he had been impotent with women. The therapist was aware that he was having considerable difficulties in treating this patient and found that his interventions consistently seemed to miss the mark and to evoke responses within the patient that reflected a view of the therapist as monstrous and destructive.

The patient began one hour by saying that he felt he was not getting anywhere in therapy. He was ruminating about the daily events of his life without getting into things, as the therapist had pointed out in the previous hour. He bullshits, as the therapist had said, and the therapist was also right when he told the patient that he accuses everyone else of being crazy, when he is really the one who is struggling with these feelings (a gross distortion of the therapist's intervention).

The patient was bothered because he can't really get into what bothers him. He had had a bad scene with his sister and brother-in-law. He had been critical of how his sister had dressed, and she had then told her husband, who became angry with the patient. The patient tried to apologize, but it wasn't accepted. He had been less depressed in the past week, and felt that his sister and brother-in-law had overreacted and had been too attacking in their comments.

The therapist intervened and said that the patient was relating things to the session in the previous week, that he was indicating that the therapist had made him apprehensive and upset, just as his brother-in-law was trying to do.

The patient responded by becoming ruminative again, talking about how immature and selfish he is, how bad he is, and how he did bad things as a child and got his mother angry again and again. When he came to therapy he thought he'd be able to get rid of all the bad things inside himself and become clean and pure, walking the streets free of the bad things inside of him. He thought the therapist would sweep out all of that bad stuff. The therapist responded by saying that he now felt a sense of disorganization as the patient spoke. He suggested that it must relate to the patient's comment about bad things in himself; the bad stuff had somehow gotten out of him, into the room and into the therapist. The therapist went on: he was now coping with a sense of fear, helplessness, and disorganization, which he felt existed in the patient and was now within himself—in the room. The patient responded that he had always been frightened of being crazy and sick, and had always thought of others as nuts. He constantly thinks the other person is crazy so that he himself won't feel crazy.

Briefly, this is a Type B communicative field, which reflects a therapeutic situation in which the patient is engaged in efforts at pathological projective identification, to which the therapist is responding with efforts at metabolism and cognitive interpretation, though it seems evident that he is unable to maintain this level of functioning and ultimately responds with unconscious pathological projective identifications of his own. As a result, the therapeutic situation appears stalemated and disturbed.

The patient's initial associations allude not only to his own difficulties in communicating meaningfully, but to the nature of the therapist's interventions as well (a point confirmed, in part, by the therapist's own subjective awareness). The patient's recollection of the previous hour was filled with distortions to the point where the therapist felt attacked, angry, crazy, and under pressure to see himself as bad. The shift in the patient's associations to the sister and brother-in-law provided a moment of relief for the therapist, but he nonetheless intervened in an effort to process the material in terms of the interactional pressures that seemed to prevail. Much of the intervention, however, is stated in terms of manifest contents, and to some extent is an effort to blame the patient for distorting everything the therapist says and for feeling attacked when the therapist has no such intention.

A more adequate intervention might well have been derived if the therapist had continued to process the patient's projective identifications in terms of efforts to destroy his grasp on reality, attack him, and drive him crazy—a transversal communication that unconsciously alludes to both patient and therapist, and that has some representation in the cognitive material. This intervention could have been related to the adaptive context of the therapist's specific interventions in the previous session, which although unreported here, did indeed have qualities of attacking the patient, disturbing his grasp of reality, and driving him crazy.

We can see then that this material is part of a spiraling exchange of pathological projective identifications between patient and therapist. Any intervention that would adequately process this material would have to allude to this spiraling interaction, to the patient's experiences of the therapist's interventions, and to the patient's attempts to place these disturbances back into the therapist. It would have to be stated in transversal form, alluding to patient and therapist, reality and fantasy, nontransference and transference, and noncountertransference and countertransference.

Such an intervention should not be offered to the patient until silently validated in the cognitive material. The associations to the sister and brother-in-law provide indirect validation to some degree, but it is wise to wait for the patient's associations to form a new bridge back to the therapeutic interaction. There is a danger here of intervening prematurely in a way that would constitute a further unconscious attack on the patient and a further projective identification of disruptive defenses and contents into him. Granted this bridge, however, the therapist could have pointed out that the patient seems to be experiencing the therapeutic interaction in a manner not unlike what had happened with his sister and brother-in-law: there is a sort of spiraling interaction without relief in which both himself and the therapist are being seen as attacking, blaming, and accusatory. The patient is experiencing the therapist as provocative and destructive, and as placing crazy and destructive contents into him, and he responds in kind by overreacting, distorting as had the brother-in-law, and by attempting to disturb the therapist in turn.

Such a transversal intervention, initiated in terms of a specific adaptive context, draws mainly upon Type Two derivatives. It is an attempt to understand the nature of the unconscious interactional mechanisms as they exist in this bipersonal field, and in both patient and therapist. The therapist might add, if the material permitted, that the patient seems to feel he is being cast in the role of someone who is sick and crazy, someone to be demeaned, and that in turn he attempts to have the therapist feel and behave similarly. To the extent that this interpretive processing is valid, the patient would respond cognitively with new material and, quite likely, with important genetic links; interactionally, there would be a positive introjective identification based on the therapist's valid containing and metabolizing functions, and his ability to interpret this unconscious exchange of pathological interactional projections.

In response to the rather mixed intervention that actually was offered, the patient describes an accusatory relationship between himself and his mother, one that it seems is unconsciously being repeated in the therapeutic interaction, rather than interpreted. The patient then alludes to fantasies of projectively identifying and discharging his bad inner stuff into the therapist. In the adaptive context of the antecedent intervention, this is an acknowledgment of some of the inappropriate qualities of the therapy, as it is being misused by both participants, though this is conveyed largely on a manifest level. It also contains, as Type Two derivatives along the me/not-me interface, an unconscious perception of the therapist who is using his own interventions as a means of attempting to get rid of the bad stuff within himself. In a sense, too, the patient's comments appear to convey a refusal to contain the therapist's badness and an effort unconsciously to interpret the therapist's unconscious projective identifications.

The therapist's final intervention is a direct self-revelation which has no place in the techniques being described here. His attempt to use subjective experiences and to hold the patient responsible for them reveals no effort to understand their basis. As is true of all such noninterpretive interventions, his comments serve as a confession of his own disorganization and as an effort to further attack the patient to engender guilt, and to blame him for the therapist's pathology. The therapist presents himself as a victim of the persecutions of the patient, in a form that now makes the patient a victim of the therapist's persecutions. The patient's responsive expression of his own fears of being crazy and his need to think of others as nuts, organized as Type Two derivatives in the adaptive context of this intervention, presents a compelling introject of this therapist's unconscious communications.

Mr. C was in once-weekly psychotherapy at a point when the therapist had brought up the possibility of termination. He had apparently decompensated during an earlier period in his life, and now had secured powerful barriers against this psychotic part of his personality. In the session to be described, he reported a dream of a man who seemed to be chasing him out of his own apartment. There was the danger of rape, but the patient then found himself in an empty vault with the door closed, safe and protected.

In associating, Mr. C spoke of mistrusting his banker, and conveyed thoughts of changing his bank because he no longer felt appreciated as a customer; still, he put the matter out of his mind.

When conflicted, he makes his mind a blank and feels relief. The therapist pointed out that the patient has a tendency to seal himself off from dangers and to seek safety in voids, and suggested that this is reflected not only in his dream, but in the way in which he was communicating in the session. In response, the patient recalled childhood fears of bombs and explosions, and recent fantasies of attacking his boss for firing a friend whom the patient very much liked. He wondered if this had anything to do with the recent sion of the termination of his therapy, and recognized that he felt much better and that perhaps it was time to think about it after all.

In this brief excerpt, the therapist attempted to offer a playback of derivatives which alluded to several metaphors of the patient's use of Type C barriers. While he did not identify a specific intervention context since it was not clearly available in the material, the metaphors are somewhat organized around the missing context of the pending termination The intervention was then confirmed through Type Two derivatives through which the patient expressed his need for vaults and blankness as a protection against inner disintegration. On another level, validation is reflected in the recollection of the fantasies of attacking the boss who had fired a friend. This derivative led the patient directly to termination, and to continued working through of his anxieties and reactions to the therapist's proposal in this regard.

We may conclude with a highly condensed vignette designed to illustrate a relatively sound application of the principles involved in developing a valid adaptive context interpretation. Mr. D was a young man in twice-weekly psychotherapy with Dr. Y—a woman—for episodes of depression, and difficulties both in his relationships with women and on his job in respect to achieving at a level commensurate with his abilities. He was being seen in a clinic, and at a point some months into the treatment, the therapist was delayed fifteen minutes at the start of one session. Because of her tight schedule, she had simply apologized and indicated that it would not be possible for her to make up the time. During that abbreviated session, the patient had spoken of feeling exploited by others and used, and the therapist had linked this to his feelings about her lateness. No effort was made, however, to adjust the fee for that session, which the patient had paid in advance.

In the session that followed, the patient began by noticing that the therapist was dressed in black, and commenting that he felt blue and black. He had been told that he looked like a cat burglar and the therapist looked even more so. He detailed factors that had nearly led to his lateness and said that there was something he wanted to bring up from last session, but he couldn't remember it. He asked the therapist if she did, and when she was silent, he went on to describe how he had taken a woman from work back to his sister's apartment (the sister worked at another branch of this clinic) and that he had quite reluctantly attempted to seduce her. After encouraging him, the woman had said that she was menstruating, and had refused intercourse. The trip home had felt dangerous.

He had a job interview pending, and it would mean an increase of twenty-five dollars a week in salary. He felt confused about what he wants, and felt too that he needed more comments from the therapist. If she could clarify things, he could work them over. He wasn't there to entertain her and he would welcome a couple of well-placed remarks. The therapist then intervened, pointing out that the patient wanted something more from her. He had seen her as a cat burglar, and this seemed to connect to his sense of rage and hostility. He was unable to recall the previous session, but she was able to do so. It involved a shortened session and their failure to have discussed a reduction in his fee because of the time that had been lost.

To analyze the session to this point, the *indicators* for this particular hour include the therapist's recent modifications in the frame through both her lateness to the previous session and her overcharging the patient—a deviation that as yet had not been rectified. There are also hints of resistance in the patient's having nearly arranged to be late. In addition, the therapist's intervention of the previous hour had been rather inadequate since it focused entirely on her lateness, and overlooked the implications of the fee situation. As a background indicator, the therapist has been alternately seductive and provocative with this patient, though she had been making efforts to bring this difficulty under control. In all, then, largely because of the frame issues and especially the unrectified fee problem, the material suggests a powerful need within the patient for an intervention.

Turning next to the communicative network, the intervention contexts overlap with the indicators in that they include the two frame issues—the lateness and the overcharge—as well as the therapist's incomplete intervention. Her provocativeness and seductiveness is a background context as well.

It seems likely that the best representation of the therapist's lateness is the patient's reference to how he himself had nearly been late for the session. The overcharge seems quite well represented in the allusion to the therapist as the cat burglar, and Dr. Y's alternation between seductiveness and hostility seem best portrayed in the reference to the woman from work who encouraged sexual relations only to forbid them because she was menstruating.

As for the central elements of the derivative complex, we may first organize this material around the adaptive context of the therapist's lateness. In this light, the patient's reference to feeling blue and black suggests his sense of being damaged by the shortened session, to which he is responding with a sense of anger. In this context, the incident with the woman reflects the patient's feelings of frustration in the light of the therapist's lateness, and a sense that the therapist offers something to him, only to take it away. The sexual idiom seems to reflect a transversal communication based on an interactional amalgam of the therapist's own unconscious seductiveness and the patient's sexualized responses to the therapist's hurt as a means of repairing his sense of damage. The job interview may allude to some thoughts of changing therapists, and the request for Dr. Y to speak appears to convey the patient's need for some clarification and repair.

In the adaptive context of the full charge for a shortened hour, the blue and black reference alludes to the damage that the patient is experiencing on this basis. The cat burglar rather dramatically conveys the patient's sense of having been robbed—a commentary that contains a considerable degree of truth and perceptiveness. The near lateness and anger can be viewed then as the patient's hostile response, as may Mr. D's reluctance to get involved with the woman at work. His efforts at seduction may be seen as an attempt to repair his sense of hurt, though in this context it also includes an unconscious perception of the therapist's seductiveness and hostility in expecting to be paid a full fee for partial hour. The reference to menstruation may well refer, then, to the patient's unconscious perception of the therapist as damaged and rejecting.

Continuing with Type Two derivatives in the context of the overcharge, the job interview suggests not only thoughts of leaving treatment for a better therapy, but again brings up the issue of money in terms of a model of an appropriate way to increase one's income—in contrast to what the therapist had done. The patient's sense of confusion seems both a response to the conflicting cues from the therapist and an introjection of her own uncertainties. The need for comment and clarification, and the patient's remark that he is not in treatment to entertain the therapist, convey his appeal for a much-needed interpretation and rectification of the frame, and his effort to suggest to the therapist that it is not his responsibility to inappropriately gratify her, but that there should be some other purpose to the therapeutic situation.

The material organizes in a similar manner around the background adaptive context of the therapist's alternation between seductiveness and provocativeness, much of which is expressed for the moment in her lateness and handling of the fee. There is, of course, a bridge back to the therapist at the point before she intervened, and, in all, we may summarize this situation as one in which there are powerful indicators and a richly meaningful communicative network. It seems clear too that for the moment the patient is expressing himself through the Type A mode, and there is evidence of analyzable communicative resistances in his failure to represent the adaptive context with a definitive link to the therapist. In this light, it might have been best initially to play back the derivative network around the unmentioned adaptive context of the charge for the full session, in the strong expectation that the patient would directly touch upon this missing adaptive context and add further confirmatory material.

In view of this evaluation, we can recognize immediately that the therapist attempted here to develop an interpretation, a step that required that she introduce impressions and details which the patient had not as yet alluded to either directly or indirectly with a sufficient lack of disguise. However, as an interpretation, the therapist attempted to deal with three indicators: the patient's resistances (referred to by Dr. Y in terms of his failure to recall the prior session), the shortened session, and the therapist's failure to rectify the fee. The latter also constituted the major adaptive context for the session. The interpretation alluded to this context and to selected derivative responses—the patient's wanting something from her, his view of her as a cat burglar, and his sense of rage and hostility. It fell short, however, of clearly defining the precipitant and the exact nature of the patient's reactions.

In terms of the criteria offered in this chapter, this is an effort at interpretation in which a particular adaptive context and derivative complex—communicative network—was utilized to explain and understand a group of indicators. There is a hint as well of intentions by the therapist to rectify the frame, another intervention which must be undertaken in light of the main therapeutic and adaptive context—the overcharge.

It is evident that there is a more intricate, convoluted derivative complex here, and that the therapist could have better shaped the available derivatives to clarify the patient's unconscious perceptions and fantasies in response to the transactions of the prior hour. Nonetheless, this particular intervention seems best appraised as an essentially valid, though somewhat incomplete interpretation, which includes, as well, certain elements introduced by the therapist. In supervision, Type Two derivative validation was anticipated, along with certain areas of nonvalidation and an unconcious response to the incorrect elements contained in the intervention—a countertransference aspect that is inevitable, though in varying degrees of intensity.

Returning to the session, the patient said that something had just popped into his mind: there has been a problem with the telephone bills at work because they changed the system, and are now keeping track of all calls. He had received a one dollar charge and thought that he had called an uncle, but then realized that he hadn't. He responded to the charge by saying that he would be damned if he would pay for someone else's call. He then remembered that he had found someone in his office using his telephone one day. He was an intruder, and it was not unlike the therapist finding someone else in her office, even though her office is not situated out in the open as is his. He was obnoxious to this fellow, insinuating that he would not pay for the man's time on his telephone, and that the man would have to pay.

The therapist responded that this was much like how the situation had been left at the end of the previous hour: he would be paying for someone else's time with her. She now proposed that he should not be penalized and that he should actually pay only two-thirds of the usual fee for that session. The patient responded that that is only a small amount of money, a dollar and a half, but then again, so was the cost of the phone call. Perhaps that was why he was in a hurry to be on time for his session today: he had had a short hour last time. He is worried that he is becoming too dependent on the therapist in telling her everything that comes to his mind.

We can see that the therapist's initial intervention did indeed obtain Type Two derivative validation through the recollection of an incident at work which portrayed in the form of thinly disguised, close derivatives the patient's unconscious perceptions of the inequity of his overcharge, his resentment toward the intruder who took the therapist's time from him, and the need for rectification—one should pay only for services rendered to oneself, and not to someone else. His response after the second intervention provides a small degree of additional Type Two derivative validation, but in the main constitutes a rather common reaction when the therapist has secured a damaged aspect of the framework: a dread of free associations and what they may contain, and of the need for the therapist—in all likelihood, based on a fear of the exposure of the patient's own inner mental disturbance. Nonetheless, this vignette illustrates the positive introjective identification derived from a sound interpretation—the allusions to the patient's ability to stand up for his own rights—and the cognitive insights, represented in a unique and unanticipated form, that also will emerge. Of course, the genetic implications of this experience and material are lacking, but clinical experience indicates that quite often, such links will emerge in the following session or two. This would then be an aspect of the further working through and analysis of this particular interlude.

Finally, it would seem that in this particular session, this patient both expressed himself and received the therapist's interventions in a Type A communicative mode. As a result, he appears to have understood in a meaningful manner his previously unconscious perceptions of the therapist and an aspect of his own responses to situations in which he is exploited. We can see too that it is quite likely that the further extensions of this material, which would probably move toward aspects of the patient's own psychopathology and the genetic basis for it, have created a new set of resistances and anxieties to which the patient has, for the moment, responded with some degree of defensiveness. It is an open question as to how he would proceed in the following session: he might erect Type C barriers against the possibility of a further unfolding of his inner disturbance, or he might continue to express himself in the Type A mode and remain open to further interpretive work.

CONCLUDING REMARKS

There is, I believe, a great deal to absorb and work through in the present volume and in those which preceded it. Nonetheless, I want to conclude this work with a look toward the future. It is my impression that the communicative approach has enabled us to answer many previously puzzling and unresolved questions about patients, therapists, and the therapeutic interaction, and especially about previously confusing stalemates and regressions in either participant. The communicative approach has explanatory powers that extend far beyond present classical thinking. Nonetheless, it is humbling to realize that this approach, like all others, has distinct limitations in regard to its potential as a curative process. There is little doubt that some limitations will prevail despite continued investigation and enhancement of the pertinent therapeutic procedures. It seems likely that such limitations obtain for any therapeutic process based on a relationship between two individuals which is created with the insightful symptom alleviation of one of the participants as a central goal. Still, the communicative approach also provides avenues of research and necessary tools of investigation to further enhance the therapeutic process in our continued search for the best possible available means of psychotherapeutic treatment.

Another indication of the great potential and current value of the communicative approach involves the many new questions raised by observations developed from this particular vantage point. While I have touched upon most of these in my writings up until this point, I will identify some of the more pressing issues with which communicative therapists are already concerned. There is the question of how to best analyze and resolve the difficulties faced by both patient and therapist alike in the presence of a Type B–C communicative mode—whether used by the patient or in the therapist. There is also the problem of developing analytic techniques that assist patients to resolve the extended pathological use of the Type C communicative mode, and the need to carry out clinical investigations which would clarify the apparently necessary and ultimately therapeutic qualities of a period during which a patient has a need to make use of this particular communicative modality as part of a self-curative process. Initial clinical observations suggest that some Type C patients do require a period of therapeutic autism, to use the term coined by Searles (1973), in the presence of a therapist capable of creating a sound holding environment. As a rule, these patients generate a series of lie-barrier systems in the guise of insight which are entirely divorced from the ongoing therapeutic interaction, and which nonetheless serve as flexible and adaptive derivative and nonderivative defensive formations in some cases. It was observations such as these that led to the concept of adaptive and maladaptive Type C barriers, a concept which now requires further investigation.

We must also investigate ways in which patients who are terrified of a secure holding environment can be helped to remain in therapy through techniques which do not compromise the therapeutic situation and outcome. Among such patients, the Type B–C communicator is especially prone to become engaged in violent efforts to modify the framework and to destroy meaning and meaningful relatedness, and failing that, to take flight from treatment entirely. While we already have considerable insight into the underlying dread and fears of annihilation involved, and the need for pathological symbiotic relatedness, we are in need of further understanding and additional technical tools. We must continue to explore the influence of conscious compromises in the ground rules and in basic therapeutic techniques as possible means for enabling these patients to remain in treatment under modified conditions. The argument is made that without such deviations—e.g., the signing of an insurance form, selected self-revelations by the therapist, direct reassurance, and other so-called supportive measures—these patients will leave treatment. My own initial observations indicate that, to the contrary, many of these patients can indeed be helped to remain in therapy by maintaining the optimal holding environment and interpreting the basis of their often massive and intensely disruptive resistances in terms of the specific elements of the intervention contexts related to the therapist's efforts to maintain a secure framework. Many of these patients benefit greatly from the therapist's containing and holding capacities, which are greatly strained by the patient's efforts to modify the frame and the therapeutic process. In addition, they learn a great deal about themselves and their dread of therapy, as well as their problems in their everyday lives, from the interpretive work which is usually feasible under these circumstances—even with a patient prone to Type B–C communication. I have also found that without exception any compromise in the ideal therapeutic environment has either subtle or blatant destructive effects, some of which are relatively unmodifiable and tend in general to produce a strikingly split image of the therapist with intensely negative components, whatever the positive elements may be, based on the more constructive aspects of his work. There is a strong tendency among therapists to inappropriately rationalize or justify deviations because of conscious and unconscious countertransference-based needs, some of them related to such practical issues as the fear of losing a patient and the need to maintain an income. I refer here not so much to therapists who evoke such deviations without subsequently applying the full listening process to the responses which follow from the patient, but therapists capable of such listening who nonetheless attempt to blunt the implications of the material, despite having conceptualized to some degree its evident meaning.

In this connection, we may also ask what measures are needed to increase the number of available truth therapists, and truth patients as well. Such efforts will undoubtedly involve a clarification of the dangers of truth therapy and the factors which create such enormous pressures within all of us toward the use of lie-barrier systems and lie therapy in general.

Another area worthy of extended research involves the remarkable extent to which patients universally show unconscious perceptiveness, complex modes of adaptive functioning, and unconscious curative endeavors in their relationships with their therapists. These tendencies speak for powerful capabilities and areas of functioning which lie beyond conscious awareness in all human beings, resources well worth both investigating and learning to tap so we may make them available consciously to the patient to the greatest extent possible. A related resource is the degree to which patients seem unconsciously aware of their therapeutic needs and the extent to which therapists satisfy them or depart from attending to these requisites. This is another important and fascinating phenomenon we must learn more about.

Related to many of these considerations is the striking dangers experienced by both patients and therapists alike in developing conscious realizations organized around activated adaptive contexts within the therapeutic interaction. While this type of listening, formulating, and intervening is inherently creative for anyone capable of applying it, it is also remarkably threatening despite its rewards in respect to adaptation and insight.

In keeping with these observations, there is the important finding that no human being can sustain extended periods of Type A communication for very long. There is a natural tendency to shift to the Type C communicative mode once acute internal and object related disequilibria have been interpretively resolved to the point where new adaptive resources have been developed. It is quite common for patients to enter psychotherapy using the Type A and Type A–B communicative modes, to show strong tendencies to seek framework deviation cures through a variety of attacks on the basic therapeutic environment, and to intensely work through for a period of some months the dynamically activated issues which lend themselves to holding, containing, and analytic resolution. In time, the patient comes to accept the therapist's framework, and enters the phase of Type C communicative working-through described above, a period during which most patients develop relatively flexible and useful lie-barrier systems much of it on the basis of Type One derivative self-interpretations. If the treatment experience moves along well, the patient will eventually introduce the issue of termination—usually indirectly at first—and hopefully set a termination date and work over the relevant fantasy and perception constellations through a return for a time to the Type A communicative mode which tends to alternate with Type C communication until treatment has ended.

Required here are, of course, fresh empirical studies of the varieties of ultimately sound therapeutic experiences and sequences. Preliminary observations already raise questions as to the optimal frequency of therapy and suggest a need to study the extent to which intensive treatment, such as psychoanalysis four or five times per week, actually offers a more adequate, lasting, and adaptive form of treatment. It may well be that the analytic setting provides patients with a far more intensive and useful sequence in which the therapeutic work during periods of Type A communication, and the self-analytic efforts which take place during extended periods of Type C communication fully justify the time and cost involved. On the other hand, present therapeutic practice is so biased toward deviations and insecure therapeutic environments, and relatively noninterpretive efforts, that it remains to be seen just how lasting and effective sound communicative psychotherapy on a once- or twice-weekly basis will prove to be.

Finally, we must now more carefully study the relationship between communication and psychopathology. We must learn more about how the pathological segments of the patient's personality and object relationships are expressed and defended against. We must study the interplay between communicative style and emotional problems. There is a need to investigate the communicative medium through which neuroses are expressed and interpretively resolved. It is here that symptoms must be explored in terms of their communicative implications, a much neglected dimension. For example, it is clear that patients suffering from schizophrenic syndromes are capable for long periods of time of adaptively utilizing the Type A communicative mode in their sessions. During such interludes, there is no immediate evidence of communicative disturbance, though there may be manifest signs of sickness. Nonetheless, the communicative capabilities of these patients during such interludes speaks strongly for their ability to benefit from the sound holding environment and interpretive work by the therapist. It appears as well that such patients are also prone to violent use of the Type B communicative mode, and that they tend more often than neurotic patients to express themselves in the quite difficult Type B–C communicative mode, including major assaults on the therapist's framework.

There is also much to be learned from the study of clinical phenomena which have been especially highlighted through the communicative approach: neurotic hallucinations and neurotic delusions. The latter, which are especially common, go almost unnoticed, but a patient or therapist who otherwise shows virtually no impairment in reality testing and in his object relationships, responds in a manner which reflects a usually latent or subtle disturbance in either of these two spheres to the point where his relationship with reality is momentarily disrupted and dominated by his own inner mental world and needs. Of special importance in this respect are indications that this type of disturbance is not uncommon among psychotherapists and psychoanalysts, and is reflected in important segments of the literature on the psychoanalytic situation and its techniques. Many of these neurotic delusions are unconsciously shared, supported, and sanctioned. These considerations may serve as well as a more general reminder that many of the areas of investigation discussed here will require a careful and meticulous investigation of processes and tendencies within therapists and analysts. It is, of course, one of the unique requisites of clinical psychotherapeutic research that it requires of the investigator an excruciating degree of self-awareness and insight into his own functioning.

Appendix A

THE BASIC COMPONENTS OF THE LISTENING-VALIDATING PROCESSES

The key to listening is the adaptive context, the disturbing or sometimes gratifying stimuli of importance to the patient psychologically, and especially to his neurosis. While these precipitants exist both outside and within the therapeutic situation, it has been found empirically that almost all significant adaptive contexts arise within the therapeutic interaction and are constituted by the therapist's interventions. These contexts lie in the area of his creation and management of the therapeutic environment and framework, and in his affective, verbal-nonverbal interventions. Modeled on the relationship between the day residue and the dream, adaptive contexts must be understood not only in terms of their manifest contents, implications, and intentions, but also in respect to their unconscious meanings and functions. The patient is especially perceptive of unconscious communications, and likely to introject and work over their implications.

The patient's material may be organized on three levels: *manifest content*, the surface of his associations and behaviors; *Type One derivatives*, inferences drawn from the material in isolation and based on psychoanalytic theory, knowledge of the patient, understanding of symbolism, and the like; and *Type Two* derivatives, meanings and functions generated entirely in light of the prevailing adaptive context. Type Two derivatives are most relevant to the expression of the patient's neurosis, and are communicated in disguised form in associations and behaviors as meaningful responses to the prevailing adaptive contexts. These derivative responses reflect unconscious fantasy and perception constellations, and are constituted by disguised expressions which may either be relatively flat and repetitive or complex and variable; the latter may constitute a set of *coalescing* (or coalescible) *derivatives*. Derivatives organized around an adaptive context form a *derivative complex*, while the total constellation of the adaptive context and derivative response is termed a *communicative network*.

Listening in the psychotherapeutic situation is keyed around the adaptive context and the patient's derivative responses. Two basic styles of communicating may be identified in patients and therapists, and two related communicative bipersonal fields. The first entails the *Type A* mode of expression. Here, the patient either represents directly or in easily detectable form the prevailing adaptive context, and then communicates a meaningful and coalescing derivative response. The Type A therapist is able to identify the adaptive context and derivative complex, and to respond accordingly with appropriate management of the framework and interpretations. In essence, this is symbolic communication, and the bipersonal field has a sense of illusion and is a play space in which the patient's derivative expression predominates, and sound interventions are generated by the therapist.

The *Type C* communicative mode is characterized by patients who either fail to meaningfully represent the prevailing adaptive context, or fail to generate a meaningful and coalescible derivative complex in light of an identified and represented precipitant. The purpose is to destroy meaning and relatedness, and to effect impenetrable barriers against underlying chaotic truths. Type C therapists characteristically intervene without coordinating the adaptive context and derivative complex, thereby generating clichés, false genetic reconstructions and dynamic formulations.

There is an intermediary communicative style, *Type B*, which is evacuatory, constituted by action-discharge, and based primarily on projective identification. There are two forms of Type B communicators, B–A and B–C. The B–A patient engages in interactional projection as a means of simultaneously ridding himself of accretions of psychic tension and discovering pertinent meanings. In the course of dumping, such patients will represent the adaptive context and generate a meaningful derivative complex. The B–C patient engages in interactional projection as a means of ridding himself of inner tension and dumping into the therapist, without any wish to understand and comprehend. There is an absence of a meaningful derivative network and a clear effort to destroy both meaning and relatedness.

In terms of the basic listening process, which centers around the detection of major adaptive contexts, their conscious and especially unconscious implications, and the patient's derivative responses, material from the patient consistently points to the need to maintain a secure frame and to resecure any deliberate or inadvertent deviations. Further, the optimal verbal response to such material is an interpretation-reconstruction. The patient will respond to interventions with *Type Two derivative validation,* modification of repressive barriers, and sudden realizations of unexpected material which shed entirely new light and affords unexpected meaning to previously disparate communications. Such realizations have been termed *selected facts* by Bion (1977), constant conjunctions which unify and give new meaning to previously unrelated elements.

Appendix B

A CLASSIFICATION OF
RESISTANCES AND
COUNTERRESISTANCES

I. Gross Behavioral Resistances
   A. Through action
      1. Absence and lateness
      2. Silence
      3. Other breaks in the frame
      4. Premature termination of therapy
      5. Acting out
   B. Within the patient's free associations
      1. Avoidance of significant material
      2. Gross rumination and repetitiveness

II. Communicative Resistances
   A. In respect to the representation of *indicators*, failure to allude to:
      (*Listed in hierarchical order of importance*)
      1. Therapist's errors in intervening and in managing the framework
      2. Patient's modifications of the frame
      3. All forms of gross behavioral communicative resistance
      4. Symptomatic responses within the patient

     5. Problems in the patient's life and in his relationship with outside figures

     6. The therapist's correct interventions

  B. In respect to the failure to clearly represent the activated adaptive contexts

  C. In respect to a lack of meaning, little divergency and coalescibility, and restrictions in the scope of the implications of the derivative complex—unconscious perceptions and fantasies

III. Counterresistances

  A. In the therapist's behaviors

     1. Absence, primarily if unplanned

     2. Lateness

     3. Inappropriate physical contact with the patient

     4. Terminating the patient prematurely

     5. Acting out

  B. Within the framework of his usual interventions and framework management responses

     1. Self-revelations and other violations of anonymity

     2. Nonneutral interventions

     3. Deviations in the fixed and other aspects of the framework

     4. Incorrect interpretations

     5. All other forms of irrelevant and inappropriate comments to the patient

  C. Communicative counterresistances

     1. All failures to interpret in terms of the prevailing indicators, the activated intervention context, and the most meaningful elements in the derivative complex

     2. All conscious and unconscious implications of the therapist's intervention which are not derived from the patient's material

     3. All inappropriate responses to the adaptive context of the patient's ongoing material

     4. All efforts to effect sectors of misalliance and bastions

Appendix C

THE BASIC COMPONENTS OF AN INTERVENTION

I. The Primary Sphere of the Intervention
   A. Management of the ground rules and boundaries—the framework
   B. All efforts at verbal intervention, with full cognizance of the nonverbal and affective qualities so contained
   C. All other nonverbal communications and behaviors, including the therapist's basic attitude toward the patient

II. The Formal Definition of the Intervention
   A. Silence
   B. Questions
   C. Clarifications
   D. Confrontations
   E. Interpretations
   F. Reconstructions
   G. All other, essentially noninterpretive interventions (e.g., so-called direct support, advice, manipulations, personal opinions, self-revelations, directives, counterresponses to the patient's inputs, etc.)

III. The level of Listening Reflected in the Intervention
   A. Manifest content: the intervention addresses the surface of the patient's associations and behaviors
   B. Type One derivative: the intervention uses evident inferences derived from the surface of the material without any consideration of an adaptive context
   C. Type Two derivative: the intervention defines the most important conscious and unconscious communications and expressions to be found in each activated adaptive context, and defines the meanings of the derivative complex response accordingly. All inferences are based on an understanding of the implications of the context at hand

IV. The Communicative Qualities of an Intervention
   A. Based on studies of Type Two derivative validation, interventions are restricted to silences, interpretations-reconstructions (and the playback of selected derivatives organized around a missing adaptive context, usually one that pertains to the fixed frame), and managements of the ground rules and framework (virtually always in the direction of securing or maintaining the frame)
   B. The communicative properties of an interpretation or reconstruction
      1. Uses the clearest representations of the most critical indicators or therapeutic contexts within the patient's material
      2. Alludes to the most pertinent, activated adaptive context in terms of their clearest representation:
         a. A direct reference to the context (usually made in passing)
         b. A disguised representation through an allusion to some other aspect of therapy and the therapeutic relationship
         c. A disguised representation through manifest contents which refer to transactions outside of therapy
         d. The absence of any significant representation
      3. A statement of the present and genetic implications of the derivative complex as a reflection of the patient's efforts to cope with and adapt to the communicative

implications of the adaptive context to which the complex is a response

4. The application of the integrated meanings and functions of the adaptive context-derivative complex interplay as it illuminates the unconscious basis for, and implications of, the major indicators in the session

V. The Properties, Conscious and Unconscious, of an Intervention

A. Clarity or confusion

B. Uses only the material from the patient or introduces elements and associations from the therapist

C. Is relatively concise or extended

D. Alludes to the therapist and treatment or fails to do so

E. Appears correct or incorrect

F. Shows evidence of preponderant countertransference or of minimal, inevitable countertransference

G. Reveals tact, sensitive timing, appropriate concern, and other necessarily human qualities in the therapist as inherent characteristics of the intervention, or fails to do so in one or more areas

H. Appears most meaningful on the manifest level, or in terms of its latent, derivative implications

I. Has the qualities of a projective identification, pathological or nonpathological, or appears to be essentially cognitive-affective

J. Implies efforts by the therapist to fuse or merge with the patient or tolerates an appropriate sense of distance

K. Appears to be an effort to effect interpersonal and defensive barriers in the relationship with the patient or maintains an appropriate sense of distance

L. Appears to reflect pathological parasitic or symbiotic needs or gratifies the appropriate therapeutic needs of the patient and the therapeutic functioning of the therapist

M. Appears to be designed for the defensive or pathologically gratifying needs of the therapist or serves the therapeutic needs of the patient

N. Appears to state the truth within the therapeutic interaction or to function instead as a lie barrier

VI. The Content or Nature of an Interpretation
  A. Attempts to illuminate the unconscious basis for resistance and defenses
  B. Attempts to explore key dynamic issues, core conflicts, and basic unconscious fantasy and perception constellations
  C. Constitutes an effort to interpret the implications of a frame issue generated by either the patient or therapist
  D. Deals with an adaptive context within treatment and with issues within the therapeutic interaction, to which outside problems are related, or deals exclusively with outside relationships (the last constituting a technical error according to the findings of the communicative approach)
  E. Attempts to interpret some aspect of the therapeutic relationship, transference or nontransference—distorted fantasies or valid unconscious perceptions
  F. Provides insight to the genetic links to the activated expressions of the patient's neurosis

VII. The Communicative Mode of the Therapist
  A. *The Type A mode*—the therapist has either secured the framework or rectifies the frame at the behest of the patient's material. In addition, there is an offer of an intervention which meets all of the criteria of an interpretation, and which therefore has as its nodal point the activated truths within the ongoing spiraling communicative interaction between the patient and therapist
  B. *The Type B mode*—the intervention, correct or incorrect, has the force of an interactional projection of either pathological or constructive contents and mechanisms. The Type B–A mode implies the therapist's genuine interest in understanding, though his efforts to do so are somewhat pressured. The Type B–C mode implies the use of projective identifications as a means of getting rid of countertransference-based tensions with virtually no interest in understanding the implications of these transactions
  C. *The Type C mode*—virtually all deviations in the framework and interventions which do not meet the criteria of a complete interpretation function in part to destroy

meaning and relatedness between the patient and therapist within the bipersonal field. The central feature is the failure to intervene on the basis of the most compelling implications of the adaptive context of the therapist's interventions, and to instead seal off and create barriers to the chaotic aspects of the unconscious communicative interaction and to offer the patient instead of the truth, a particular type of lie-barrier system

VIII. The Validation of Interventions. The criterion of Type Two derivative validation: the emergence of a selected fact, a truly new segment of material which provides in some indirect way a means of synthesizing and understanding previously disparate aspects of the material

GLOSSARY

Abstracting-Particularizing Process, the. That aspect of the listening process in which first-order, manifest themes are used to derive more general or abstract themes, from which second-order specific themes are generated. The latter are often monitored in terms of the therapeutic relationship and the me/not-me interface.

Adaptational-Interactional Viewpoint, the. A clinical-metapsychological approach to the patient and therapeutic interaction which takes into account both intrapsychic and interactional processes, conscious and unconscious in both spheres.

Adaptive Context, the. The specific reality that evokes in intrapsychic response. *Direct* or *nonneurotic* adaptive contexts are those stimuli which evoke linear intrapsychic reactions and nonneurotic communicative responses; in essence, they are unrelated to psychopathological reactions and mechanisms. *Indirect* or *neurotic* adaptive contexts are those precipitants that evoke convoluted, derivative intrapsychic responses that contain pathological unconscious fantasies, memories, and introjects; they are related to psychopathology and to neurosis. Often an adaptive context outside of the therapeutic relationship will have a direct context within its manifest content, and an indirect context in its latent content. The latter is, as a rule, a derivative of a significant adaptive context within the therapeutic situation itself, communicated in disguised form. On the whole, the major indirect and neurotic adaptive contexts derive from the therapeutic interaction. The term *primary adaptive task* is a synonym for adaptive context.

Adaptive Context, Form of Representation. The manner in which the patient portrays the manifest and latent contents of the adaptive context, and its links to the therapist, in the course of his behaviors and associations. A key factor in determining the possibility of interpretive and reconstructive interventions by the therapist, it is best conveyed via a passing manifest allusion to an intervention by the therapist.

Adaptive Context, Primary. A term used to specify the need to ultimately identify those adaptive stimuli which arise within the therapeutic interaction from the therapist and to which the patient responds, consciously and unconsciously. The word *primary* alludes here to the central and ultimately critical role of the interventions and behaviors of the therapist in the derivative responses of the patient.

Adaptive Context, Secondary. A term reserved for adaptive stimuli generated by individuals other than the therapist and by the patient himself—within or outside of therapy—to which he responds in both conscious and unconscious form. The term is of importance in that it stresses the more peripheral nature of such contexts. It points to the need to ultimately link such a constellation of stimulus and response to a prior or additional adaptive context derived from the therapist. Secondary adaptive contexts may occur in the patient's outside life or within treatment, the latter illustrated by a patient's lateness, absence, or other notable segment of behavior to which the patient himself then responds. These latter, however, are better termed *therapeutic contexts*.

Alliance Sector. A term virtually synonymous with *therapeutic alliance,* it is intended to emphasize the alliance as an aspect of the total relationship between patient and therapist, rather than as an entity in itself. The attributes of this sector are identical to those of the therapeutic alliance and are defined under the latter term. See also *Therapeutic Alliance, Working Alliance.*

Associational Matrix. See *Communicative Network.*

Bastion. A term first used by Baranger and Baranger (1966) to allude to a split-off part of the bipersonal field which is under interactional repression and denial, so that the contents involved are avoided by both patient and therapist or analyst.

Bipersonal Field, the. A term first used by Baranger and Baranger (1966) as a metaphor for the therapeutic situation. It stresses the interactional qualities of the field, and postulates that every experience and communication within the field receives vectors from both patient and therapist or analyst. The metaphor requires the concept of an *interface* along which communication occurs between the two members of the therapeutic dyad, and points to the need to conceptualize the presence, role, and function of a framework for the field.

Bridge to the Therapist. A manifest allusion to the therapist or therapy occurring in the patient's associations toward the latter part of a session. Its importance lies in facilitating both interpretive interventions and the playing back of selected derivatives that pertain to an unmentioned adaptive context related to the treatment situation.

Commentary. A term used to describe the patient's responses to interventions from the therapist (including managements of the framework). These associations and behaviors contain validating and nonvalidating communications, and they are to be viewed as a mixture of fantasy and reality, accurate perceptiveness and distortion. Often, commentaries take the form of *transversal communications*; unconsciously, they convey the patient's evaluation of the intervention.

Communication, Convoluted. An image used to describe the presence of derivatives and the indirect expression of pathological unconscious fantasies, memories, introjects, and interactional contents and mechanisms. It is one of the hallmarks of neurotic communication. See *Neurotic Communication.*

Communication, Linear. A sequence evoked by an adaptive context in which the intrapsychic response is relatively logical, readily apparent or easily inferred, directly responsive, and relatively undisguised. It is a form of reaction that characterizes the direct adaptive context and nonneurotic communication. See *Nonneurotic Communication.*

Communicative Field. The amalgam from patient and therapist that characterizes the dominant mode of communicative interaction in a given bipersonal field. See *Bipersonal Field, Type A Field, Type B Field, Type C Field.*

Communicative Interaction, Unconscious and Conscious, Spiraling. A term used to describe the central transactions between patient and therapist within the bipersonal field. It alludes to the conscious but, more especially, the unconscious exchanges between the two participants to therapy, as these exchanges take place as part of a to and fro interactional process.

Communicative Network. That aspect of the material from the patient which contains conscious and especially unconscious meaning. It comprises the adaptive context, the derivative complex, and the bridge back to the therapist or analyst. As a rule, analysis of the unconscious implications of the communicative network will reveal the implications of the therapeutic context or indicator. The term is synonymous with *associational matrix.*

Communicative Space. A metaphor for the interior of the bipersonal field and for the realm in which communication occurs between patient and therapist or analyst. The image suggests that there are a number of possible communicative spaces, each with a set of defining attributes. It allows, too, for the recognition that patient and therapist may be in separate communicative spaces, rather than sharing the same mode.

Communicative Style or Mode. The form of communicative expression that characterizes the interactional thrusts and form of relatedness of the patient and therapist or analyst. See *Type A Field and Mode, Type B Field and Mode, Type C Field and Mode.*

Communicative Therapeutic Alliance. See *Therapeutic Alliance, Communicative.*

Conception. A term first used by Bion (1962) to describe the outcome when a preconception mates with appropriate sense impressions. More broadly, the term may be used to describe the saturation of a preconception through a realization that satisfies its inherent expectations.

Confirmation, Primary. A term used to describe the patient's initial response to an intervention, often in the form of direct affirmation or negation. In general, direct agreement has little bearing on the validity of the intervention, while negation often suggest nonvalidation, though, in exceptional circumstances, it will constitute a defensive response that emerges prior to secondary confirmation.

Confirmation, Secondary. The extended response to the therapist's interventions (including managements of the frame) which contain selected facts, uniquely original and previously unknown communications from the patient that extend the intervention, especially in the form of Type Two derivatives. Psychoanalytic confirmation of an intervention requires the presence of truly unexpected Type Two derivatives. In general, their absence constitutes nonconfirmation. A synonym is Type Two derivative validation.

Contained, the. A metaphor first used by Bion (1962) to allude to the contents and psychic mechanisms that are projectively identified by an infant into his mother, and by a patient into his analyst. More broadly, they allude to the contents and functions of a projective identification emanating from a subject toward an object.

Container, the. A metaphor first used by Bion (1962) for the recipient of a projective identification. The container may be open to containing such projective identifications, or may be refractory. The metaphor also implies the processing or metabolizing of the introjected contents and functions. An adequate container is seen as being in a state of *reverie.*

Containing and Containing Function. A metaphor used to describe the taking in and processing of projective identifications. An adequate containing function has been described by Bion (1962) as a state of *reverie* in the mother or analyst, and may also apply to the therapist or patient. Containing function alludes to the receptiveness to projective identifications, and to an ability to metabolize and detoxify pathological *interactional projections,* returning them to the subject in appropriately modified form. For the therapist or analyst, this process implies the metabolizing of a projective identification to conscious insight, imparted to the patient through a valid interpretation and through the maintenance of a secure framework and hold.

Counterresistances. Applied to that aspect of the therapist's *countertransference* which creates obstacles to the progress of therapeutic work, counterresistances may appear in the therapist's gross behaviors—e.g., forgetting a session, lateness, touching the patient—or as part of his efforts to manage the framework and to intervene verbally. Verbal interventions constitute communicative counterresistances, and include interpretive errors, self-revelations, and mismanagements of the framework which reveal unconscious countertransference fantasies and pathological symbiotic and parasitic needs. In principle, all countertransference expressions will contribute to disturbances in treatment and function as counterresistances. The term is best reserved for inappropriate silences and interventions which are most disruptive to the therapeutic process and which significantly intensify the resistances within the patient.

Countertransference. A term used in this volume to allude to all inappropriate and pathological responses of the therapist to his patient. These reactions are founded on pathological unconscious fantasies, memories, introjects, and interactional mechanisms.

Countertransference, Inevitable. A term which implies not only the inescapability of countertransference expressions in the therapist's work, but also its existence as some small element of every attitude, silence, and intervention. This minimal quota of countertransference is a reflection of the ever-present unresolved, though relatively controlled, psychopathology of the therapist.

Countertransference, Preponderant. Inappropriate silences, interventions, and mismanagements of the framework which constitute major errors and reflect significant and relatively uncontrolled psychopathology within the therapist. While these may sometimes be reflected in the therapist's personality and basic attitudes, they more often take the form of acute errors which may be detected in the subsequent subjective reactions of the therapist, the absence of validation from the patient, and the patient's unconscious recognition and therapeutic work with the introjected conscious and unconscious qualities of the therapist's error.

Day Residue. A term first used by Freud (1900) to allude to the reality stimulus for the dream. More broadly, it may be seen as the external stimulus, filled with latent and unconscious meaning, that evokes any intrapsychic response. In that sense, it is virtually synonymous with the *adaptive context*.

Defense. A term which applies to all psychological efforts, conscious and unconscious, by an individual which are designed to protect him from danger situations, anxiety and other unpleasant affects, unbearable conflict, disruptive introjects, and disturbing conscious realizations. Defenses therefore constitute intrapsychically founded, protective, psychological mechanisms utilized by the ego in an effort to cope with disturbing external and internal realities, and conscious and unconscious fantasy and perception constellations which pose any degree of threat. Defenses may be pathological or nonpathological depending on their adaptive aspects and the extent to which they disturb the functioning of the user.

Defenses, nonresistant. Those intrapsychic and behavioral efforts by the patient to protect himself from psychic pain and conflict or from disturbances in his relationship with the therapist which do not at the same time foster gross behavioral or communicative obstacles to therapy. Such defenses tend to be adaptive.

Defenses, resistant. Behavioral and intrapsychic mechanisms which the patient uses to protect himself from pain and conflict, both intrapsychic and in his relationship with the therapist. These protective mechanisms may be reflected in the gross behaviors or communications of the patient. In essence, then, those defenses which are used in the service of resistances are termed resistant defenses.

Delusion, Neurotic. A false belief, usually held unconsciously and expressed largely through derivative communication, which would be readily modified and corrected if called to the attention of the patient or therapist who has conveyed it. See also *Hallucination, Neurotic.*

Denudation. A term used by Bion (1962) to metaphorically represent one type of effect that the contained may have on the container, and the reverse: the generation of a disruptive and destructive experience and set of affects, leading to some form of inner disturbance that often is characterized by the destruction of function and meaning.

Derivative Complex. A term used for the material from the patient as it is organized around a specific adaptive context in order to reveal unconscious implications, Type Two derivative meaning. This is one of the four elements involved in the basic formulation of each session.

Derivative Complex, Convoluted. See *Derivatives, Coalescing.*

Derivative Complex, Linear. A simplistic group of derivatives, related to a particular adaptive context, which tend to flatly repeat a single theme or function, without complexity or depth. See also *Communication, Linear.*

Derivative, Indirect Interactional. A manifest association which yields hidden and disguised meaning in light of an activated intervention context. The term is synonymous with *Type Two Derivative.*

Derivative, Inference. A manifest content element which is decoded for hidden meaning based on isolated implications derived from psychoanalytic theory or a general knowledge of the patient. Implications for the therapeutic interaction, and meanings organized by a particular adaptive context, are not included. The term is synonymous with *Type One Derivative* and *Translation Derivative.*

Derivative, Translation. See *Derivative, Inference.*

Derivatives. Manifest communications, verbal and nonverbal, which contain in some disguised form expressions of unconscious fantasies, memories, introjects, and perceptions. These are, then, the communicative expressions of neuroses, and the basis on which they are maintained. See *Type One Derivatives, Type Two Derivatives.*

Derivatives, Close. Associations from the patient which contain disguised representations of unconscious processes and contents in a form that is readily detectable, minimally defensive, and easily understood as a manifestation of the underlying qualities.

Derivatives, Coalescing. A Derivative complex which, when organized around a specific adaptive context, indirectly and quite unconsciously reveals a wide range of divergent, underlying meanings and functions in relationship to that context. Such a group of derivatives may include unconscious fantasies and unconscious perceptions, and reflect as well a variety of unconscious dynamics and genetics. They may also include the patient's unconscious interpretations and other speculations pertaining to both the therapist and himself. Together, they form a divergent but organizable entity which reveals a multiplicity of meanings pertaining to the relevant adaptive context. See also *Communication, Convoluted.*

Derivatives, Distant. Those aspects of the patient's associations which represent unconscious processes and contents with considerable disguise, barely detectable meaning, and great defensiveness and resistance.

Derivatives, Embedded. A representation of an unconscious fantasy, memory, introject, or perception that is communicated as a seemingly irrelevant component of a sequence of manifest contents, in a form that seems peripheral to the main conscious intention and to the major first-order and general themes.

Derivatives, Playing Back. An intervention offered in the presence of a strong indicator and a meaningful derivative complex, but in the absence of any clear representation of the adaptive context with an evident link to the therapist. It is designed to create a state of tension and need—a preconception—which can be transformed into a condition of fulfillment—a conception—only through the direct recall and clear representation of the adaptive context—a step that is essential to further interpretive work.

Designated Patient. The party to the therapeutic situation who is seeking help, and who is likely to be paying the fee and free associating. He is usually symptomatic, and is the recipient of the manifest interventions of the designated therapist. See also *Functional Patient.*

Designated Therapist. The party to the therapeutic situation who represents himself as capable of alleviating the emotional difficulties of those who seek his help—designated patients. He is likely to be the person who makes use of free-floating attention, shapes the conditions of treatment, receives the fee, and intervenes intermittently to the designated patient. See also *Functional Therapist.*

Detoxification. A term used a describe the metabolism of a projective identification so that its relatively primitive and destructive qualities are altered through some appropriate means, usually through cognitive understanding directed toward insight. This process is an essential quality of *reverie.*

Deviations, Grades One, Two, and Three. A classification of modifications in the ideal framework of the therapeutic situation. Grade One deviations are primarily interpretive-reconstructive errors; Grade two deviations entail nonneutral, noninterpretive verbal-affective interventions; and Grade Three deviations involve modifications in the fixed and stable aspects of the therapeutic framework.

Empathy. A form of emotional knowing and noncognitive sharing in, and comprehending, the psychological and affective state of another person. Empathy involves both affect and cognition, and is based on a relatively nonconflicted interplay of introjective and projective mechanisms, and a variety of forms of unconscious sharing. It is a temporary form of immediate engagement and understanding, which must then be processed and validated. It must include a sensing of the patient's derivative as well as manifest communications.

Faith. A term used by Bion (1962) to describe a form of passive listening or intuiting by the therapist or analyst that is founded upon entering each session without desire, memory, or understanding. It implies a fundamental belief that the patient will put into the therapist or analyst in derivative form all that he needs for his own cure, and all that the latter requires for his interventions. It also implies an appreciation of the principle that each session should be its own creation, and that, unconsciously, the patient will provide the therapeutic situation with all that is necessary for his cure, except for the therapist's or analyst's interpretive interventions and management of the framework, which are themselves based on the ingredients provided by the patient.

First-Order Themes. See *Themes, First-Order.*

Frame. A metaphor for the implicit and explicit ground rules of psychotherapy or psychoanalysis. The image implies that the ground rules create a basic hold for the therapeutic interaction, and, for both patient and therapist, that they create a distinctive set of conditions within the frame that differentiate it in actuality and functionally from the conditions outside the frame. The metaphor requires, however, an appreciation of the human qualities of the frame and should not be used to develop an inanimate or overly rigid conception.

Frame, Fixed, Stable, or Steady. The relatively unchangeable or easily set ground rules such as the fee, time and length of sessions, the physical setting, and total confidentiality and privacy.

Frame, Variable or Fluid. Those aspects of the ground rules which will inevitably vary based on the presence of some degree of humanness and residual countertransference reflected in the on-going work of the therapist. While the therapist strives to maintain these aspects of the framework at an optimal level, variations are bound to occur. Included here are the ground rules related to the therapist's relative anonymity and neutrality, the rule of abstinence, and, for the patient, the fundamental rule of free association and the need to analyze all major decisions.

Framework. A term used synonymously with *frame*, usually as a means of referring to the ground rules of the bipersonal field.

Framework Cures. The maladaptive alleviation of symptoms through an inappropriate modification in the frame.

Framework Deviation Cure. Previously termed *framework cure*, this concept covers the maladaptive alleviation of symptoms through inappropriate modification of the framework by either patient or therapist.

Framework Rectification Cure. The adaptive symptom alleviation occurs through the establishment, securing, and maintenance of the ground rules of psychotherapy or psychoanalysis. Though unaccompanied by cognitive insight, such relief derives from unconscious positive introjects of the therapist, in terms of his constructive management of the framework, and from the inherently supportive holding and containing functions that are expressed when the framework is rectified and then maintained in a stable manner.

Functional Capacity or Meaning. A term used to indicate that associations never exist as isolated mental products, and that among their most essential dynamic implications are the unconscious communications contained within the material as they pertain to the therapeutic relationship and interaction. In essence, it is a concept that stresses that all associations have some dynamic relevance to the prevailing primary adaptive context.

Functional Patient. The member of the therapeutic dyad who, in light of the prevailing adaptive contexts from either the designated patient or the designated therapist, is expressing himself consciously or unconsciously as in need of help with emotional symptoms and conflicts. This individual expresses himself to the other member of the communicative dyad in a manner that reflects underlying psychopathology, doing so either through representations that state directly, or imply in some relatively disguised manner, a need for therapeutic help. Thus, the *functional capacity* of such communications is to express illness. Within the treatment situation, the designated patient and/or the designated therapist may express themselves simultaneously or alternately as the functional patient. See also *Designated Patient*.

Functional Therapist. The member of the therapeutic dyad who expresses himself directly and consciously, or indirectly and through derivatives, in a manner designed to cure the other participant and, at times, himself. This individual, in light of the prevailing adaptive contexts contained in the patient's material and the therapist's interventions, responds with communications designed to be insightful and curative. It is crucial that when the designated therapist wishes to serve as the functional therapist he must do so on a conscious level, through valid interpretations and managements of the framework. On the other hand, it has frequently been observed that designated patients who shift to the role of functional therapist do so on an unconscious level, basing their therapeutic efforts largely upon valid unconscious perceptions of the therapist (and sometimes of themselves), as well as the consequent pathological introjects. Such work therefore is expressed primarily through derivatives and entails unconscious interpretive, confronting, and framework management types of interventions. See also *Designated Therapist*.

Ground Rules. The implicit and explicit components of the analytic or therapeutic situation which establish the conditions for treatment and the means through which it shall be undertaken.

Hallucination, Neurotic. A false image or perception, usually experienced in some unconscious and derivative way, which would be readily modified and corrected if brought to the attention of the patient or therapist who has experienced it. See also *Delusion, Neurotic*.

Holding. A term used to describe the therapist's or analyst's establishment and maintenance of a secure and safe therapeutic situation. The result is a holding environment that is created through the implicit and explicit delineation of the ground rules, explicated through their maintenance, and significantly elaborated through valid interpretive efforts. The holding capacity of the therapist or analyst may be likened to his containing capacity, although the former is a more general concept, while the latter specifically refers to the taking in of interactional projections.

Identification. An intrapsychic process through which the self-representations and other aspects of the subject's internal mental world and defenses are unconsciously modified in keeping with a model derived from an external object.

Indicators. A clinical term that refers to all communications from the patient which point toward a need on his part for an intervention from the therapist. See *Therapeutic Context*.

Interactional Defenses. Intrapsychic protective mechanisms which are formed through vectors from both patient and therapist. This type of defense may exist in either participant to the therapeutic dyad, and has both intrapsychic and interactional (external) sources.

Interactional Projection. A synonym for projective identification (Langs 1976a).

Interactional Resistances. Any impediment to the progress of therapy that receives vectors, usually on an unconscious level, from both patient and therapist.

Interactional Symptoms. An emotional disturbance in either participant to the therapeutic dyad with significant sources from both participants.

Interactional Syndrome. Clusters of interactional symptoms.

Interface, Me/Not-Me. See *Me/Not-Me Interface.*

Interface of the Bipersonal Field. A metaphor used to describe a hypothetical line along which the communications between patient and therapist take place within the bipersonal field. It implies that vectors which determine this interface are derived from both patient and therapist, and that these may be contained in relatively fixed intermixtures or may vary considerably. Among the determinants of the qualities and location of the interface, pathological inputs from both patient and therapist are especially significant.

Interpretation. An attempt through verbal communication by the therapist to render unconscious meanings and functions conscious for the patient. Properly executed, this intervention alludes to an adaptive context, and to the relevant derivative complex in terms of unconscious perceptions and fantasies to which genetic implications are appended. Proper execution requires also that the intervention be stated in terms of the prevailing unconscious communicative interaction between the patient and the therapist, and its extension into the present and past from that nodal point, and that it illuminate the prevailing therapeutic contexts.

Interpretation, Definitive. An intervention which identifies an activated adaptive context and a reactive derivative complex as a way of understanding the unconscious basis for an indicator or therapeutic context, and which does so almost entirely in terms of a single dimension of the therapeutic relationship—transference or non-transference, reality or fantasy, patient or therapist. This type of intervention is to be contrasted with *transversal interpretations*, which tend to incorporate significant aspects of both extremes of these dualities. While all interpretations have minor transversal qualities, those which emphasize one dimension far more than its opposite are to be termed definitive interpretations.

Intervention, Manifest. An intervention, usually verbal, offered by the therapist to the patient, designed to meet the therapeutic needs of the latter. The major interventions include silence, establishment and management of the framework, and comments designed to impart cognitive understanding, either through interpretation or reconstruction, or through the playing back of selected derivatives around an unmentioned adaptive context.

Intervention, Silent. A tentatively formulated intervention constructed as the therapist listens to the patient and subjected to silent validation before being presented.

Introject. An intrapsychic precipitate which stems from the process of introjective identification. Its specific qualities are determined by the extent to which it is transient or becomes structuralized, the degree to which it is incorporated into the self-image and self-representations or maintained as separate from them, the extent to which it is pathological or nonpathological, and the degree to which it is constructive or benign rather than destructive or malignant. In addition, these internal representations of conscious and unconscious traits and interactions have a variety of specific qualities in keeping with the nature of the object, the subject, their relationship, and the qualities of their separate and shared experiences. See *Unconscious Introject.*

Introjective Identification. The interactional process through which introjects are formed. As a rule, it is evoked by a projective identification from the object, although it may also entail active incorporative efforts by the subject. The process is influenced both by the nature of the object, the contents and processes that are being taken in, and the inner state of the subject.

Intuition. An immediate form of knowing, understanding, or learning developed without the conscious use of reasoning and knowledge.

Latent Content. The hidden dimension of the patient's associations contained in disguised form within the surface of that material. The term is usually used to refer to readily available inferences from the manifest content—disguised specific unconscious fantasies, memories, introjects, and perceptions.

Lie. A term used nonmorally to refer to manifest, but more commonly latent and unconscious, falsifications as these arise in the free associations of the patient and the interventions of the therapist. By and large, such misrepresentations are designed to falsify the truth as it pertains to the patient's neurosis, to that of the therapist, and to the therapeutic interaction. The effort here, which is largely unconscious, is to offer some substitute of the truth, to deny its presence, and to erect either derivative defenses or impervious barriers against its realization. Empirically, a therapist's unconscious lie is constituted by any intervention in which the framework is mismanaged or the therapist intervenes without organizing his response interpretively around the prevailing adaptive context and derivative complex. A patient's unconscious lie is expressed either by his failure to meaningfully represent the activated adaptive context or to generate a meaningful, coalescing derivative complex. See also *Truth.*

Lie, Derivative. A falsification or misrepresentation, conscious or unconscious, which contains in some disguised form expressions of the underlying and chaotic truths it is designed to cover over.

Lie, Nonderivative. A falsification or misrepresentation which in no way reflects, and is therefore impervious to, the underlying chaotic truths it is designed to seal off.

Lie-Barrier, Derivative and Nonderivative. The type of defensive system seen in lie therapy, and in lie patients and lie therapists. Derivative lie barriers are seen in the Type A communicative field in which the patient's efforts at falsification reveal in disguised form the underlying truths. On the part of the therapist, derivative lie interventions, while erroneous, contain in some disguised form expressions of the truth of the therapeutic situation and of the patient's material. However, interventions of this kind are insufficient to generate conscious insight within the patient, though they may be part of an interchange in which such realizations are ultimately fulfilled. On the other hand, nonderivative lie-systems are relatively impervious barriers designed to seal off underlying chaotic truths without expressing in any disguised form the nature of the underlying disturbance. Lie patients and lie therapists tend to communicate in the Type C mode. The latter intervene erroneously in a manner unrelated to the true nature of the disturbance within the bipersonal field.

Lie Systems or Lie-Barrier Systems. Complex defensive formations generated by either patient or therapist which are designed to seal off underlying chaotic truths as they pertain to the activated pathology of the patient, and secondarily to that of the therapist and within the therapeutic interaction. There are many types of lie-barrier systems, and these include false genetic reconstructions, false statements of dynamics, and blatant misrepresentations. The patient and therapist may share and reinforce each other's lie-barrier systems, may make use of different lie-barrier systems, or may find themselves within an interaction in which one of the two participants utilizes a lie-barrier system while the other uses the single available truth system applicable to a particular segment of the therapeutic interaction. Lie systems may be derivative and reveal in disguised form the nature of the underlying and chaotic truth, or nonderivative, serving as impenetrable barriers against such truth.

Lie Therapy. Any form of therapy designed to bypass or falsify the true basis, conscious and unconscious, of the patient's neurosis. In this type of therapy, even evident statements of fact are used *functionally* to deny and falsify the most active expressions of the patient's neurosis within the ongoing communicative interaction. See also *Truth Therapy*.

Link to Therapist. A term used when investigating the manner in which the patient represents the adaptive context in the material of a given session. When this representation includes some allusion to the therapist or therapy, the link to the therapist is present. By contrast, when the adaptive context is represented through some outside relationship, the link to the therapist is absent. This distinction proves critical in that by and large the presence of the link fosters the use of interpretations, while its absence suggests a need to intervene through the playing back of selected derivatives around the unmentioned or poorly represented adaptive context.

Listening Process, the. A term used in the broadest possible psychoanalytic sense to refer to all conscious and unconscious intaking and organizing processes within both patient and therapist. For the therapist, the term includes all available cognitive and interactional sources of information about the patient, verbal and nonverbal, and his own use of sensory and nonsensory, conscious and unconscious, sensitivities. Included too are efforts at synthesizing and formulating cognitive material, the experience of role pressures and image evocations, and the metabolism of projective identifications. The process culminates in conscious understanding or insight, in proper holding and containing, and in the formulation of a valid intervention. Similar processes take place within the patient, although, as a rule, much of it on an unconscious level.

Manifest Content. The surface of the patient's associations and the therapist's interventions. The term refers to the direct and explicit meanings so contained. See also *Relatedness, Manifest Content.*

Maturational Relationship Sphere. That dimension of the therapeutic relationship which involves the mode of relatedness between patient and therapist designed to effect instinctual drive and other satisfactions for one or both participants in a way that is geared toward (or against) growth, relatively autonomous functioning, and separateness and individuation. Maturational relationships may be autistic, healthy or pathologically symbiotic, parasitic or commensal. The extent to which the therapeutic relationship is designed for the maturation and development of the patient (and secondarily, the therapist) is one of the basic dimensions of the object relationship between the two participants to therapy and of the therapeutic interaction itself. A synonym for this term is that of *developmental relationship sphere*.

Me/Not-Me Interface. An imaginary interface of the patient's communications so designed that every aspect refers on one level to the patient himself, while on another level to the therapist or analyst. The me/not-me is stated from the patient's vantage point and indicates that every communication contains allusions to both himself and the therapist or analyst.

Metabolism, or the Metabolism of Projective Identifications. A term first used by R. Fliess (1942) to describe the processing by the analyst of temporary trial identifications with the patient. The concept is used more broadly to refer to all efforts to work over sensory and nonsensory inputs from the patient, and in another specific sense to refer to the introjective identification and containing of a projective identification from the patient, ultimately processed toward cognitive understanding and insight. This last sense of the term may also be applied to the patient's efforts to introjectively identify and contain projective identifications from the therapist, so long as efforts are made toward understanding.

Mini-Psychotic Act. Actions by a patient or therapist, otherwise intact and in contact with reality, which indicate a usually brief, momentary break with reality and impairment in reality testing. This may be seen when a patient, for example, throws his keys away and tries to open the door to his apartment with a scrap of paper. These behaviors are on a par with neurotic hallucinations and neurotic delusions. (See *delusions, neurotic* and *hallucinations, neurotic*.)

Misalliance. A quality of the basic relationship between patient and therapist, or of a sector of that relationship, which is consciously or unconsciously designed to bypass adaptive insight in favor of either some other maladaptive form of symptom alleviation or the destruction of effective therapeutic work.

Mode of Relatedness, Autistic. A relationship between two participants in which one or both remain essentially unrelated to the other. There is a failure here to meaningfully experience and relate to the other person, and a type of withdrawal which precludes the development of meaningful internal representations of the other person (the object). In its essence, an autistic mode is one in which meaning and relatedness have been destroyed.

Mode of Relatedness, Commensal. A form of object relationship in which each participant satisfies the healthy needs of the other, and receives in turn a full measure of appropriate satisfaction of his own. While a symbiotic relationship is skewed toward the gratification of one of the members of the relationship dyad, a commensal relationship provides roughly equal satisfactions for both participants. By and large this is a healthy mode of relatedness and ideal for most dyads outside of therapy. However, within psychotherapy, because of the patient's neurosis, the optimal therapeutic relationship is a *healthy symbiosis*.

Mode of Relatedness, Healthy Symbiotic. A relationship between two individuals (in this book, primarily patient and therapist) in which the needs of one (the object, or symbiotic receiver or recipient) are largely gratified, while the needs of the other (the subject, or the symbiotic donor or provider) are satisfied to a lesser degree. A healthy symbiosis is designed for the growth and ultimate separation and individuation of the object—as well as for the subject, though less so—and involves those gratifications appropriate to the therapeutic relationship and which are needed for its sustenance and eventual dissolution. For the patient, this implies being held and contained through the establishment and maintenance of clearly defined ground rules and boundaries in the therapeutic relationship and setting, as well as the patient listening and appropriate interpretations of the therapist. For the therapist, this entails the satisfaction of listening to and working interpretively with the patient, maintaining a sound therapeutic environment, receiving a fee, and seeing the patient eventually resolve his neurosis. Contained within these manifest satisfactions are a number of growth-promoting instinctual drive gratifications which are well modulated (sublimated) and essentially nonpathological.

Mode of Relatedness, Parasitic. A form of relationship in which the inputs of one or both participants exploit, misuse, and abuse the other person (the object) with essentially no concern for his appropriate needs. A parasitic mode of relatedness is essentially self-gratifying for the subject at the expense and destruction of the object.

Mode of Relatedness, Pathological Symbiotic. A mode of relatedness in which the object (or symbiotic recipient) obtains major satisfactions from the subject (or symbiotic provider) of a kind which are essentially pathological, and which are therefore designed to gratify inappropriate instinctual drive needs as well as to maintain a stultifying sense of fusion or merger between the two participants. A pathological symbiosis is designed for a variety of inappropriate immediate gratifications, and does not serve as a basis for ultimate separation, individuation, and relative autonomy. For the patient, such satisfactions are derived from modifications in the ground rules and boundaries of the therapeutic relationship, and from the satisfactions of noninterpretive responses from the therapist. For the therapist, these arise from his own noninterpretive interventions, mismanagements of the framework, erroneous interpretations, and from any other inappropriate use of the patient beyond working with him toward insightful symptom alleviation. In a pathological symbiosis, usually both participants achieve inappropriate satisfactions, though they tend to accrue more to one member of the dyad, either patient or therapist.

Negative Projective Identification. A term used to describe an empty or voidlike interactional projection designed to destroy meanings within the bipersonal field and to disrupt the mental capacities of the object or recipient of the interactional projection.

Neuroses. A term used in a special sense to allude to all forms of psychopathology, ranging from symptomatic disturbances to character disorders, from neurotic disturbances to borderline syndromes and narcissistic disorders to psychoses, and from psychosomatic disorders to addictions, perversions, and other emotionally founded syndromes. In essence, then, the term refers to all types of syndromes based on intrapsychic and interactional emotional disturbances and dysfunctions.

Neurotic Communication. That form of behaving and conveying meanings that is related to the neuroses, and which is characterized by the use of derivative and convoluted sequences, related ultimately to pathological unconscious fantasies, memories, introjects, and perceptions.

Nonconfirmation. See *Nonvalidation.*

Noncountertransference. The essentially nonconflicted sphere of the therapist's or analyst's functioning expressed in his appropriate capacity to relate to the patient, listen, intervene, manage the framework, and the like.

Nonneurotic Communication. A means of conveying conscious and unconscious meaning that is essentially unrelated to neuroses. It is characterized by manifest messages, readily available inferences, and linear causal sequences.

Nontransference. The essentially nonconflicted areas of the patient's valid functioning within the therapeutic relationship. It is exemplified by validatable conscious and unconscious perceptions and reactions to the therapist, and by other spheres of adequate functioning and interaction. See also *Unconscious Nontransference Constellation.*

Nonvalidation. A response to an intervention by the therapist or analyst (management of the framework or verbal) that is flat, lacking in unique contents or a selected fact, repetitious, linear, and without surprise. It is an indication that the intervention has been erroneous, and falls largely into the sphere of secondary confirmation—here constituting secondary nonconfirmation.

Parameter. A term coined by Eissler (1953) to refer to those alterations in standard psychoanalytic technique that are required quite specifically because of a patient's ego dysfunctions or impairments. The concept is based on the thesis that certain patients with severe psychopathology require a modified therapeutic situation. It properly includes the idea that these modifications should be kept to a minimum, should be rectified as quickly as possible, and that the entire experience—deviation and rectification—should be subjected to analysis. It was also noted that parameters can be utilized in the service of the therapist's countertransferences and as an inappropriate replacement for interpretive technique. In addition, the effects of parameters may not be resolvable through verbal analytic work, and may result in unanalyzable restrictions in therapeutic outcome. The thesis that parameters are necessary in the psychotherapy and psychoanalysis of severely disturbed patients has been questioned by a number of analysts.

Precipitant or Reality Precipitant. A synonym for *day residue,* and a term synonymous with *adaptive context* when used to refer to the evocation of an intrapsychic response.

Preconception. A term first used by Bion (1962) to represent a state of expectation and more broadly a state of need, a quality in need of fulfillment or closure—an unsaturated state which once saturated would generate a *conception.*

Predictive Clinical Methodology. A mode of psychoanalytically oriented therapy founded on the validating process, and especially on efforts at prediction so designed that validation takes the form of Type Two derivatives.

Primary Adaptive Task. A synonym for *adaptive context.*

Projective Counteridentification. A term coined by Grinberg (1962) to allude to all countertransference-based responses within the analyst to the patient's projective identifications. The term implies a failure to metabolize the relevant interactional projections and the reprojection into the patient of nondetoxified contents and mechanisms.

Projective Identification. An interactional effort by a subject to place into the object aspects of his own inner mental state, inner contents, and unconscious defenses. The term *identification* is used here in the sense of remaining identified with the externalized contents and wishing to evoke in the object an identification with the subject.

Proxy, Evocation of a. A form of projective identification described by Wangh (1962) which stresses an interactional effort to place into the object areas of malfunctioning and disturbance, largely as a means of evoking adequate responses which can then be introjected.

Psychoanalytically Oriented Psychotherapy, or Insight Psychotherapy. A form of psychotherapy which takes place within a well-defined bipersonal field and which is designed to provide the patient symptom relief based on cognitive insights and the inevitable positive introjective identifications that derive from the therapist's capacity to hold the patient, contain and metabolize his projective identifications, establish and manage the framework, and interpret the neurotic communications and expressions from the patient.

Psychoanalytic Cliché. An intervention based on psychoanalytic theory and on the material from the patient at a point at which it is communicated in a nonneurotic form. It is a statement of apparent psychoanalytic meaning or truth which is essentially and functionally false in light of the prevailing adaptive contexts—sources of inner anxiety and turmoil, conflict and disturbance within the patient and/or the therapist. It is therefore unconsciously designed to serve as a barrier to the underlying catastrophic truths and as a means of disrupting the meaningful relationship links between patient and therapist.

Real Relationship. A term used by some analysts to refer to the reality-oriented, undistorted relationship between patient and therapist or analyst (Greenson 1967). More broadly, the term has sometimes been used to refer to the actualities of both patient and therapist, and of the therapeutic setting. However, in light of the usual use of the term in a sense that implies that the real relationship is one of several relationships between patient and therapist, of which the transference relationship is another, the term is of limited or questionable value. It seems preferable to speak of the realistic aspects of the therapeutic relationship and to include these qualities under the concept of nontransference and noncountertransference.

Reconstruction. An attempt by the therapist, through a verbal intervention, to indicate to the patient important events and fantasies from the past, most often in his childhood, of which he has no conscious recall. Such an intervention would begin with the adaptive context and the derivative complex, would be linked to a therapeutic context, and would on this basis derive implications in regard to past actualities; it would always be rooted in the current communicative interaction, and would extend into the past from there.

Regression, Nontherapeutic. A shift toward more primitive communication and expression of derivatives of unconscious fantasies, memories, introjects, and perceptions that take place under conditions of unneeded modifications in the framework and in response to other errors in technique by the therapist or analyst. The impairments in the framework render such regressions difficult to analyze and resolve, and the restoration of the frame is essential to a shift from a nontherapeutic to a *therapeutic regression.*

Regression, Therapeutic. An adaptive form of regression that takes place within a secure bipersonal field and is a means of describing the constructive emergence of unconscious fantasies, memories, introjects, and perceptions related to the patient's neurosis as mobilized by the therapeutic interaction and based on earlier genetic experiences and traumas. This emergence of relatively primitive material occurs in a form and under conditions that render the neurotic components analyzable and modifiable through insight.

Relatedness, Manifest Content. A form of relationship and interaction initiated by either patient or therapist in which the communicative transactions take place in terms of the surface of both the patient's associations and the therapist's interventions. The therapist listens, formulates, intervenes, and "validates" in terms of the manifest content of the patient's material. The patient attempts to evoke direct comments and interventions from the therapist. Functionally, this type of relatedness is designed to exclude the derivative implications of the patient's material to the extent that they convey disguised expressions of his underlying unconscious fantasy and perception constellations. For the therapist, this mode of relatedness constitutes an effort to exclude the unconscious implications of his attitudes and interventions, and to adhere only to their manifest meanings and functions. This mode of relatedness is a pathologically symbiotic, superficial, and often naive form of lie therapy in which nonderivative lie-barriers are common. See also *Manifest Content.*

Relatedness, Mode of. The nature of an object relationship, in this book applied primarily to the patient and therapist. The mode of relatedness includes, for both participants, self- and object representations, and efforts to obtain actual satisfactions or their renunciation. Among the important dimensions of the object relationship between the patient and therapist is the extent to which merger or fusion needs are satisfied, and these may be pathological or healthy and appropriate. There is also the extent to which the relationship satisfies healthy or pathological instinctual drive needs and superego pressures, as well as meeting the requirements of the ego-ideal in each participant. Also pertinent is relative autonomy and individuation. Another quality of this relatedness involves the extent to which the overall needs of each participant are given due consideration and satisfaction by the partner, as compared to exploitation, harm, or other misuse. Five types of object relationships have been identified between patients and therapists: *Autistic, Parasitic, Healthy Symbiosis, Pathological Symbiosis,* and *Commensal.* See under *Mode of Relatedness.*

Relatedness, Type One Derivative. A mode of relating and interacting which may be initiated by either patient or therapist, and which is founded on speculations regarding the implications of the patient's material without any connection to an adaptive context. The therapist makes use of readily available inferences derived from the manifest content of the patient's associations, doing so based on his general knowledge of the patient, his understanding of psychoanalytic theory, and his broad sensitivity to implicit meanings and functions. The patient who participates in this mode of relatedness offers similar speculations. In general, this type of interaction is designed to exclude an understanding of the patient's derivative responses to specific adaptive contexts, and thereby to deny the pathological (and more rarely nonpathological) elements implicitly contained in the therapist's erroneous interventions—i.e., to deny the expressions and consequences of his countertransferences. This mode of relatedness is a form of pathological symbiosis and lie therapy in that it excludes the most immediate expressions of the patient's psychopathology (and secondarily the therapist's) as these are mobilized within the interaction. Derivative lie-barriers, elaborate fictions, clichés, and false genetic reconstructions abound. Formulations in terms of transference and fantasy are characteristic, and, functionally, they often serve to exclude the patient's valid unconscious perceptions and introjects of the therapist. See also *Type One Derivatives*.

Relatedness, Type Two Derivative. A mode of relating and interacting which may be initiated by either patient or therapist in which the material from the patient is formulated and interpreted in terms of significant prevailing adaptive contexts derived from the therapist's interventions. These interventions are understood in terms of their manifest and latent contents and functions, and full attention is accorded the unconscious communicative interaction. The therapist maintains a secure therapeutic environment and framework, and confines himself to interpretive-reconstructive interventions and sound management of the ground rules and setting. All such interventions are generated in light of adaptive contexts generated by the therapist. The patient's responses are in the Type A communicative mode; the adaptive context is clearly represented and there is a strong and meaningful derivative complex. It is this type of relatedness that characterizes truth therapy and permits access to the most meaningful derivative expressions of the patient's neurosis—mobilized unconscious fantasy and perception constellations, and their dynamic and genetic components. Also implicit in this type of relatedness is a healthy symbiosis and the full recognition of the unconscious ramifications of the therapist's interventions. See also *Type Two Derivatives.*

Relationship Sphere, Developmental. See *Maturational Relationship Sphere.*

Relationship Sphere, Maturational. See *Maturational Relationship Sphere.*

Resistance. A term used to describe any impediment within the patient to the work of therapy or analysis. It is a conception based on a subjective evaluation by the therapist or analyst. In its narrow clinical sense, these obstacles are founded on defenses against intrapsychic conflict and anxiety, as they are expressed within the therapeutic relationship. Within the therapeutic interaction itself, these impediments are often based on contributions from both patient and therapist. Resistance may be distinguished from defense in the finding that the former may be relatively absent on a communicative level in the presence of continued defensive operations within the patient which disguise his communications even at a point when they are easily understood and interpreted. See *Interactional Resistances.*

Resistances, Communicative. Obstacles to the work of therapy or analysis that are discovered through an analysis of the communicative network. Most common among these are the failure to represent the adaptive context with the link to the therapist, and the development of a fragmented or noncoalescing derivative complex. The evaluation of communicative resistances is subjective for the therapist and is open to countertransference-based influences. In addition, the presence of all such resistances may receive unconscious contributions from the inappropriate interventions of the therapist, including misinterpretations and mismanagements of the framework. The analysis of all types of resistance requires the rectification of the therapist's contribution and interpretations in which both unconscious perceptions and/or introjections and distorted unconscious fantasies and/or projections are considered.

Resistances, Gross Behavioral. Impediments to the work of psychotherapy or psychoanalysis that appear in the direct behaviors and associations of the patient. While all such evaluations by the therapist are subjective and must be checked for possible counter-transference contributions, these obstacles to therapeutic progress tend to be readily recognized. They include silences, gross disruptions of the session, thoughts about or efforts directed toward premature termination, absences, direct but inappropriate opposition to the therapist and repudiation of his interventions, and the like. As manifest phenomena their unconscious meanings and functions must be determined by an identification of the prevailing adaptive context and the relevant derivative complex—the associative network.

Resistances, nontransference. A term used to describe those obstacles to treatment, reflected in the behaviors and communications from the patient, to which the therapist has contributed more than the patient. These difficulties derive primarily from the patient's valid unconscious perceptions of countertransference interventions from the therapist. Technically, their recognition is especially important, in that they require not only an interpretation of the unconscious basis within the patient for the resistance, but also a recognition of the unconscious contribution from the therapist and the *rectification* of these inputs as well.

Resistances, relationship. A term which alludes to all obstacles to treatment which are expressed behaviorally or communicatively by the patient and which are based on some aspect of his relationship with the therapist. Similar to *interactional resistance*, in that it implies the presence of inputs to the resistance from both the patient and therapist, relationship resistance is preferred to the terms *transference resistance* and *nontransference resistance* when obstructive behaviors and impaired communications of the patient have obtained significant contributions from both participants to treatment.

Resistances, transference. A term reserved for those obstacles to treatment reflected in the patient's behaviors and communications, which are based on pathological unconscious fantasy constellations involving the therapist. The latter's input in respect to these resistances is minimal, while the patient's contribution is maximal. Transference resistances appear only when the therapist has secured the ground rules and framework of the therapeutic situation, and is working with sound and validated interpretations.

Reverie. A term used by Bion (1962) to describe the state of the mother, therapist, or analyst who is capable of receiving the projective identifications from the infant or patient, appropriately metabolizing them, and returning them to the subject in a relatively detoxified form. In a psychotherapeutic situation, this implies a correct interpretation and appropriate management of the framework.

Second-Order Themes. See *Themes, Second-Order.*

Selected Fact, the. A term used by Bion (1962), borrowed from Poincaré, to describe a newly discovered formulation, finding, or fact that introduces order and new meaning into, and unites into a whole, previously disparate elements. It is the realization, then, that links together elements not previously seen to be connected.

Silent Hypothesis. A formulation derived from the various avenues of the intaking aspect of the listening process, developed, as a rule, around a specific adaptive context. Its development relies too on the abstracting-particularizing process, monitoring material around the therapeutic interaction, and utilizing the me/not-me interface, as well as all other means available to the therapist or analyst for generating dynamic, adaptive conceptions of the most pertinent unconscious meanings of the patient's material. In its most complete form, it will entail the identification of the most active unconscious fantasies, memories, introjects, and perceptions within the patient, and will include links to his psychopathology. While these hypotheses may be developed at any point in a session, they are especially common in the opening segments of each hour, and are maintained by the therapist without intervening. In principle, they should be subjected to *silent validation* before the therapist or analyst intervenes, doing so most often at a point when there is a relevant bridge between the silent hypothesis itself and the communications from the patient.

Silent Intervention. See *Intervention, Silent.*

Silent Question. An issue that arises within the mind of the therapist as he listens to the patient, leading him to raise it subjectively while not directing it to the patient. When pertinent, such queries will, as a rule, be answered in some derivative form by the patient's ongoing associations. In principle, silent questions are to be preferred to direct queries of the patient, which tend to serve a variety of defensive and countertransference needs within the therapist or analyst, and to impair the patient's use of indirect, derivative communication.

Silent Validation. An aspect of the evaluation of the material from the patient that follows the development of a silent hypothesis. When subsequent material further coalesces with the initial hypothesis, and supports it through the communication of Type Two derivatives, the silent hypothesis is seen as confirmed. See also *Validation.*

Supervisory Introject. A partly conscious, but primarily unconscious, incorporative precipitate within the supervisee based on his work with his supervisor. This introject derives from the conscious and unconscious communications of the supervisor, and may be positive or negative, constructive or destructive, in various intermixtures. The term *supervisory introject* implies the incorporation of mental processes within the supervisor and his transactions with the supervisee, while the related term *supervisor introject* would stress incorporation of dimensions of the supervisor himself— attitudes, mental contents, and the like.

Symbiotic Provider or Donor. That member of the symbiosis who offers to the other person the major share of gratification. The symbiotic provider therefore obtains a smaller measure of satisfaction than his partner, the *Symbiotic Receiver or Recipient.*

Symbiotic Receiver or Recipient. The member of a symbiotic dyad who obtains the larger measure of satisfaction or gratification.

Termination, Forced. The premature cessation of a therapeutic situation caused, as a rule, by some circumstance external to the direct therapeutic interaction. Among the most common causes are clinic policies, the move of therapist or patient, and a major change in life circumstance or health in either one. A termination of this kind modifies the standard tenet that psychotherapy should be undertaken until the point of insightful symptom resolution within the patient.

Themes, First-Order. The general contents and specific subject matter that can be derived from an examination of the manifest content of the patient's material.

Themes, Second-Order. Derivative contents developed through the use of the abstracting-particularizing process. First-order manifest themes are identified and general thematic trends are then formulated; inferences derived on that basis are considered second-order themes. As a rule, such themes are developed in terms of the ongoing therapeutic relationship and interaction, and take on specific form and meaning when related to pertinent adaptive contexts within that relationship.

Therapeutic Alliance. The conscious and unconscious conjoint efforts of patient and therapist to join forces in effecting symptom alleviation and characterological change for the former through development of cognitive and affective adaptive insight. This is the cooperative sphere of the relationship between patient and therapist, and requires of the patient trust and a variety of cognitive capacities and nonconflicted spheres of functioning, as well as an ability to communicate, both consciously and through interpretable derivatives. Of the therapist, a sound therapeutic alliance requires a capacity to establish and maintain a secure therapeutic environment, and to offer well-timed and sensitive interpretations and reconstructions. The therapeutic alliance has a variety of surface attributes, which include the patient's free associating, evident cooperation, and attention to the therapist's interventions, as well as the therapist's sensitive listening and sound therapeutic work. However, it also entails aspects of the therapeutic relationship which are part of the unconscious communicative interaction. On this level, it requires of the patient the Type A Communicative mode, and of the therapist sound management of the framework and interpretations consistently organized around the adaptive contexts of his interventions. There is thus a manifest and a latent alliance, each with conscious and unconscious attributes. See *Alliance Sector, Working Alliance.*

Therapeutic Alliance, Communicative. A term which applies primarily to the unconscious communicative interaction between patient and therapist. A sound communicative alliance is one in which the patient is expressing himself in the Type A communicative mode, and the therapist has secured the therapeutic environment and is responding interpretively to the patient's material —i.e., in terms of adaptive contexts and derivative complexes. Impairments in the communicative alliance are reflected in communicative resistances, primarily as failures to adequately represent the prevailing adaptive context and, at times, as failures by the patient to generate a meaningful derivative complex. Mismanagements of the framework, interpretive failures, and other types of errors form the basis for impairments in the communicative alliance stimulated by the therapist. These problems fall into the realm of his countertransference responses, and are based on failures to adequately comprehend and respond to the associations and behaviors of the patient. It is possible to have an impaired communicative alliance in the presence of a seemingly sound manifest alliance. See *Therapeutic Alliance, Manifest; Therapeutic Alliance;* and *Working Alliance.*

Therapeutic Alliance, Manifest or Surface. A term virtually synonymous with the working alliance, the direct and surface cooperation between patient and therapist. The state of the manifest alliance may correspond to, or differ from, the state of the communicative alliance. Thus there may be manifest cooperation but communicative dissidence, or there may be evident surface disruptions in the cooperative sphere at a point when the patient is expressing himself meaningfully through derivative expressions. An additional dimension of the state of the communicative alliance is the extent to which the patient's derivative associations as organized around prevailing adaptive contexts serve to illuminate current indicators.

Therapeutic Context. A term synonymous with *indicator,* and a component of the listening process. It refers to any communication from the patient that suggests a need for understanding, resolution, and intervention from the therapist. Such communications serve as important second-order organizers of the patient's material. His associations and behaviors are first organized in terms of the communicative network—the adaptive context, its representation, the derivative complex, and the bridge back to the therapist—to provide Type Two derivative meaning in terms of unconscious processes, fantasies, perceptions, and introjects. Once these unconscious meanings and functions are identified, the material is then reorganized around the therapeutic context and the revealed derivative meanings as they pertain to the unconscious implications of the indicator. Therapeutic contexts may be divided into those involving life crises and symptoms within the patient (e.g., homicidal and suicidal concerns and impulses, acute regressions, acting out) and those involving disturbed aspects of the therapeutic interaction (e.g., alterations in the framework by therapist or patient, errors by the therapist, ruptures in the therapeutic alliance, and major and minor resistances).

Therapeutic Interaction. A term used to describe the conscious and unconscious communicative interplays between the patient and therapist or analyst.

Therapeutic Misalliance. An attempt to achieve symptom alleviation through some means other than insight and the related positive introjective identifications with the therapist. See *Misalliance,* an essentially synonymous term.

Therapeutic Relationship. A term that embraces all components, conscious and unconscious, pathological and nonpathological, of the interaction between patient and therapist. For the patient, the therapeutic relationship involves both transference and nontransference components, while for the therapist it involves countertransference and noncountertransference elements. The term is strongly preferred to "transference" when describing the patient's relationship with the therapist, and equally preferred to "countertransference" when describing the therapist's or analyst's relationship to the patient. See *Transference, Nontransference, Countertransference,* and *Noncountertransference.*

Therapy, Lie. Any form of, or interlude in, psychotherapy or psychoanalysis in which the actual unconscious basis for the patient's symptoms, resistances, and the like are either not sought after or are sealed off. It entails both efforts at avoidance and attention to levels of meaning that in the therapeutic interaction serve primarily to create barriers and falsifications, to destroy more pertinent meaning, and thereby to seal off underlying chaotic truths.

Therapy, Truth. A form of therapy or analysis designed to foster the emergence and discovery, within the therapeutic interaction, of the unconscious processes, fantasies, memories, introjects, and transactions which are the basis for the patient's neurosis.

Transference. The pathological component of the patient's relationship to the therapist. Based on pathological unconscious fantasies, memories, and introjects, transference includes all distorted and inappropriate responses and perceptions of the therapist derived from these disruptive inner mental contents and the related mechanisms and defenses. These distortions may be based on displacements from past genetic figures, as well as on pathological interactional mechanisms. Unconscious transference fantasies and mechanisms are always communicated in some derivative form, while the manifest communication may allude to either the therapeutic relationship itself (disguised, however, in regard to the latent content) or to outside relationships. Transference responses are always maladaptive and can only be understood in terms of specific, indirect adaptive contexts. See also *Unconscious Transference Constellation.*

Transversal Communication. Associations from the patient that bridge, and therefore simultaneously express, both fantasy and reality, transference and nontransference; unconscious perception and distortion, truth and falsehood, self and object. Such communications are, on one level, entirely valid, while on another level, essentially distorted.

Transversal Intervention. A particular type of communication from the therapist or analyst to the patient which is shaped in keeping with the presence of a transversal communication. In essence, such interventions, usually in the form of interpretations, although sometimes developed through the playback of derivatives related to an unidentified adaptive context, take into account the dual qualities of transversal communications, and are stated in a manner that is open to the contradictory elements contained in the patient's associations.

Trial Identification. An aspect of the listening process especially developed by R. Fliess (1942) as an important means of empathizing with and cognitively understanding the communications from the patient. It entails a temporary merger with, or incorporation of, the patient and his material in the presence of distinct self-object boundaries in most other respects. It is a temporary form of being and feeling with the patient, and the cognitive-affective yield from such experiences must then be processed toward insightful understanding and subjected to the validating process.

Truth. A term used to describe the actualities, manifest and latent, conscious and unconscious, of the ongoing communicative interaction between patient and therapist, especially as it pertains to the neurosis of the patient and, secondarily, of the therapist. Truth within the therapeutic experience pertains to the underlying basis of the patient's neurosis as activated and mobilized by the adaptive contexts of the therapist's interventions, and secondarily by intrapsychic factors within the patient. While such truths can be the subject of conscious realizations, they are most commonly expressed in derivative form by the patient and therefore require interpretive realizations from the therapist. See also *Lie*.

Truth Therapy. That form of psychotherapy or psychoanalysis which is designed to arrive at the actual conscious and unconscious basis for the patient's neurosis, as mobilized by events within the ongoing, spiraling communicative interaction. See also *Lie Therapy.*

Type A Field, the, and Type A Communicative Mode, the. A bipersonal field and communicative style in which symbolism and illusion play a central role. Such a field is characterized by the development of a play space or transitional space within which the patient communicates analyzable derivatives of his unconscious fantasies, memories, introjects, and perceptions, ultimately in the form of Type Two derivatives. Such a field requires a secure framework, and a therapist or analyst who is capable of processing the material from the patient toward cognitive insights which are then imparted through valid interpretations. Such endeavors represent the therapist's capacity for symbolic communication. The Type A communicative mode is essentially symbolic, transitional, illusory, and geared toward insight.

Type B Field, the, and Type B Communicative Mode, the. A bipersonal field characterized by major efforts at projective identification and action-discharge. The mode is not essentially designed for insight but instead facilitates the riddance of accretions of disturbing internal stimuli. It can, however, despite the interactional pressures it generates, be used in a manner open to interpretation.

Type C Field, the, and Type C Communicative Mode, the. A field in which the essential links between patient and therapist are broken and ruptured, and in which verbalization and apparent efforts at communication are actually designed to destroy meaning, generate falsifications, and to create impenetrable barriers to underlying catastrophic truths. The Type C communicative mode is designed for falsification, the destruction of links between subject and object, and for the erection of barriers designed to seal off inner and interactional chaos.

Type C Narrator, the. A patient who utilizes the Type C communicative mode through the report of extensive dream material or the detailed description of events and experiences within his life or in regard to the therapeutic interaction. Such material is characterized by the absence of a meaningful adaptive context, the lack of analyzable derivatives, and the use of these communications essentially for the generation of nonmeaning and the breaking of relationship links. It is not uncommon for the Type C narrator to interact with a therapist or analyst who makes extensive use of psychoanalytic clichés, generating a therapeutic interaction falsely identified as viable analytic work, while its primarily dynamic function falls within the Type C communicative mode.

Type One Derivatives. Readily available inferences derived from the manifest content of the patient's associations, without the use of an adaptive context. These inferences constitute one level of the latent content, arrived at in isolation and without reference to the dynamic state of the therapeutic interaction and to the adaptive-dynamic function of the material at hand. See also *Relatedness, Type One Derivative.*

Type Two Derivatives. Inferences from the manifest content of the patient's material that are arrived at through the abstracting-particularizing process when it is organized around a specific adaptive context. These disguised contents accrue specific dynamic-adaptive meaning when so organized, and are the main medium for the therapist's or analyst's interpretations, primarily in terms of the therapeutic interaction. See also *Relatedness, Type Two Derivative.*

Unconscious Fantasy. The working over in displaced form of a particular adaptive context. The relative contents are outside the patient's awareness and are expressed in derivative form in the manifest content of his associations. This is a type of daydreaming without direct awareness of the essential theme, and may be either pathological or nonpathological. The derivatives of unconscious fantasies are an essential medium of interpretive work and have important genetic antecedents. Among the most crucial unconscious fantasies are those related to the therapist, and when they are distorted they fall into the realm of transference, while those that are nondistorted belong to nontransference. These daydreams include representations from the id, ego, superego, self, and from every aspect of the patient's inner mental world, life, and psychic mechanisms.

Unconscious Fantasy Constellation. A term used to embrace intermixtures of unconscious fantasies (in the narrow sense), unconscious introjects, and unconscious memories. Together these constitute a major underlying basis for symptom formation and neuroses. When the emphasis is on unconscious perceptions and valid introjects, the term *unconscious perception constellation* is to be preferred.

Unconscious Interpretation. A communication usually from patient to therapist, expressed in disguised and derivative form, and unconsciously designed to help the therapist understand the underlying basis for a countertransference-based intervention. These interpretations can be recognized by taking the therapist's intervention as the adaptive context for the material from the patient that follows; hypothesizing the nature of the therapist's errors; and accepting the patient's material as reflecting an introjection of the error, and an effort to heal the disturbing aspects of that introject. Put in other terms, the patient's responses are viewed as a *commentary* on the therapist's intervention, and are found to contain unconscious efforts to assist the therapist in gaining insight in regard to the sources of his errors.

Unconscious Introject. A network of intrapsychic precipitants derived from interactions between the subject and object, in the past and present. They are derived from the process of introjective identification, and depend on the nature of the contents and mechanisms involved, as well as qualities within both subject and object. Introjects may be short-lived or relatively stable, pathological, incorporated into the self-image and self-representations or isolated from them, and may involve any of the structures of the mind, id, ego, and superego. In psychotherapy, an especially important form of introjection occurs in response to the therapist's projective identifications, either helpful or traumatic, nonpathological or pathological, which generate alterations in the inner mental world of the patient. Such a process is continuous with the therapeutic interaction and may, in addition, occur within the therapist as a result of projective identifications from the patient. See also *Introjects*.

Unconscious Memory. Derivative precipitates of past experiences—mixtures of actuality and distortion—expressed through indirect communication and inner representations of which the subject is unaware. Such reminiscences without awareness may be pathological or nonpathological, and the former are an important aspect of the genetic basis of the patient's psychopathology.

Unconscious Nontransference Constellation. The unconscious basis for the patient's valid functioning in his relationship with the therapist or analyst. This constellation is constituted by the patient's valid unconscious perceptions and introjects of the therapist, and includes both earlier genetic counterparts and present dynamic implications. See also *Nontransference*.

Unconscious Perception. A term used to describe evidence of valid perceptiveness of another person's (an object's) communications and cues of which the subject is unaware. These may be identified through a correct appraisal of the nature of an adaptive context, including an accurate understanding of the object's unconscious communications. While outside the subject's awareness, his derivative communications demonstrate an essentially veridical perception in terms of the prevailing underlying realities. When the adaptive context is known, unconscious perceptions are reflected in Type Two derivatives. They are the basis for nondistorted introjects.

Unconscious Perception Constellation. A term used to include both current unconscious perceptions and those derived from important genetic experiences with significant early figures. Such a constellation includes valid introjects and pertinent unconscious memories in which the veridical core is central.

Unconscious Transference Constellation. A core component of transference, constituting its underlying basis. The unconscious transference constellation includes all unconscious fantasy constellations which pertain to the therapist or analyst. Within the therapeutic situation, it is these constellations which are actively mobilized by a valid therapeutic experience—sound interventions and a secure setting—and which then form the focus of interpretive work. See also *Transference*.

Validated Hypothesis. A silent hypothesis that has been confirmed via Type Two derivatives, and especially an interpretation or management of the frame that has been communicated to the patient and which is affirmed through the development of Type Two derivatives and the appearance of a *selected fact*.

Validating Process, the. A term used to describe conscious and unconscious efforts within either patient or therapist to affirm, support, and substantiate conscious or unconscious formulations and hypotheses. It is a crucial component of the listening process, receives its ultimate test in the patient's responses to the therapist's interpretations and management of the framework, and must take the form of confirmation via Type Two derivatives and the development of a *selected fact*.

Validation, Indirect. See *Validation via Type Two Derivatives*, with which it is essentially synonymous.

Validation via Type Two Derivatives. A form of confirmation that is synonymous with the development of a *selected fact*, and with the modification of repressive barriers. This type of indirect, derivative validation is the essential proof of the truth of a psychoanalytic clinical formulation and intervention. Every clinical psychoanalytic hypothesis can be accepted as a general truth only if it has been subjected to this type of validation.

Vested Interest Deviation. A modification in the standard framework regarding which the therapist has a special investment. Examples are his having his office in his home and the signing of insurance forms in order to enable him to receive his fee. The concept draws its importance from the finding that deviations in which the therapist has an inordinate investment tend to generate silent sectors of misalliance with the patient. The responses of the latter tend to be highly disguised, and often appear in the form of embedded derivatives. As a result, the material related to such a deviation tends to be difficult to recognize and interpret. Often the therapist has a significant blind spot in this area, rendering the bastion and misalliance so generated difficult to identify and even more difficult to modify.

Working Alliance. A term used by some analysts to refer to that segment of therapeutic relatedness that is based on the patient's rational, noneurotic wish to get well and on his surface efforts in this direction, and on the analyst's rational, nonneurotic offer of assistance and his own capacity to cooperate with the patient in the therapeutic effort. The term stresses manifest cooperation, as well as mutual respect and trust, mature object relatedness, and sound ego capacities. Because unconscious factors tend to be neglected, in respect both to the definition of this type of alliance and to the factors seen to influence its course, the term is of limited value. See also *Alliance Sector, Therapeutic Alliance.*

REFERENCES

*

Adler, G., and Myerson, P. (1973). *Confrontation in Psychotherapy.* New York: Jason Aronson.

Arlow, J. (1963). Conflict, regression and symptom formation. *International Journal of Psycho-Analysis* 44:12–22.

Baranger, W., and Baranger, M. (1966). Insight in the analytic situation. In *Psychoanalysis in the Americas,* ed. R. Litman, pp. 56–72. New York: International Universities Press.

Barchilon, J. (1958). On countertransference "cures." *Journal of the American Psychoanalytic Association* 6:222–236.

Bibring, E. (1954). Psychoanalysis and the dynamic therapies. *Journal of the American Psychoanalytic Association* 2:745–770.

Bion, W. (1962). *Learning from Experience.* In W. Bion, *Seven Servants.* New York: Jason Aronson.

—— (1970). *Attention and Interpretation.* In W. Bion, *Seven Servants.* New York: Jason Aronson.

—— (1977). *Seven Servants.* New York: Jason Aronson.

Bird, B. (1972). Notes on transference: universal phenomenon and hardest part of analysis. *Journal of the American Psychoanalytic Association* 20:267–301

Blanck, G., and Blanck, R. (1974). *Ego Psychology: Theory and Practice.* New York: Columbia University Press.

—— (1979). *Ego Psychology II. Psychoanalytic Developmental Psychology.* New York: Columbia University Press.

Brenner, C. (1969). Some comments on technical precepts in psychoanalysis. *Journal of the American Psychoanalytic Association* 17:333–352.

—— (1976). *Psychoanalytic Technique and Psychic Conflict.* New York: International Universities Press.

Breuer, J., and Freud, S. (1893–1895). Studies on hysteria. *Standard Edition* 2:255–305.

Calef, V. (1971). Concluding remarks [to the panel on the transference neurosis]. *Journal of the American Psychoanalytic Association* 19:89–97.

Daniels, R. S. (1969). Some early manifestations of transference: their implications for the first phase of psychoanalysis. *Journal of the American Psychoanalytic Association* 17:995–1014.

Dewald, P. (1972). *The Psychoanalytic Process: A Case Illustration.* New York: Basic Books.

—— (1976). Transference regression and real experience in the psychoanalytic process. *Psychoanalytic Quarterly* 45:213–230.

Fenichel, O. (1941). *Problems of Psychoanalytic Technique.* New York: Psychoanalytic Quarterly.

Freud, A. (1936). *The Ego and Mechanisms of Defense.* New York: International Universities Press.

Freud, S. (1900). The interpretation of dreams. *Standard Edition* 4 and 5.

—— (1905). Fragment of an analysis of a case of hysteria. *Standard Edition* 7:3–122.

—— (1909). Notes upon a case of obsessional neurosis. *Standard Edition* 10:153–320.

—— (1910). The future prospects of psychoanalytic therapy. *Standard Edition* 11:139–152.

—— (1912). The dynamics of transference. *Standard Edition* 12:97–108.

—— On beginning the treatment (further recommendations on the technique of psychoanalysis III). *Standard Edition* 12:121–144.

—— (1914). Remembering, repeating, and working through (further recommendations on the technique of psycho-analysis, II). *Standard Edition* 12:145–156.

—— (1915). Observations on transference love (further recommendations on the technique of psycho-analysis III). *Standard Edition* 12:157–171.

—— (1918). From the history of an infantile neurosis. *Standard Edition* 17:3–122.

—— (1926). Inhibitions, symptoms and anxiety. *Standard Edition* 20:77–175.

—— (1937a). Analysis terminable and interminable. *Standard Edition* 23:209–254.

—— (1937b). Constructions in analysis. *Standard Edition* 23:255–269.

Gill, M. (1979). The analysis of the transference. *Journal of the American Psychoanalytic Association* 27(Supplement):263–288.

Gill, M., and Muslin, H. (1976). Early interpretation of transference. *Journal of the American Psychoanalytic Association* 24:779–794.

Glover, E. (1955). *The Technique of Psycho-Analysis.* New York: International Universities Press.

Greenson, R. (1967). *The Technique and Practice of Psychoanalysis* Vol. I. New York: International Universities Press.

—— (1968). The use of dream sequences in detecting errors of technique. In *Explorations in Psychoanalysis,* pp. 313–332. New York: International Universities Press, 1978.

—— (1978). *Explorations in Psychoanalysis.* New York: International Universities Press.

Grotstein, J. (1977a). The psychoanalytic concept of schizophrenia: I. The dilemma. *International Journal of Psycho-Analysis* 58:403–426.

—— (1977b). The psychoanalytic concept of schizophrenia II. Reconciliation. *International Journal of Psycho-Analysis* 58:427–452.

Halpert, E. (1972). The effect of insurance on psychoanalytic treatment. *Journal of the American Psychoanalytic Association* 20:122–133.

Hatcher, R. (1973). Insight and self-observation. *Journal of the American Psychoanalytic Association* 21:377–398.

Kernberg, O. (1975). *Borderline Conditions and Pathological Narcissism.* New York: Jason Aronson.

—— (1976). *Object Relations Theory and Clinical Psychoanalysis.* New York: Jason Aronson.

Klauber, J. (1968). The psychoanalyst as a person. *British Journal of Medical Psychology* 41:315–322.

Klein, M. (1952). The origins of transference. *International Journal of Psycho-Analysis* 33:433–438.

Kohut, H. (1971). *The Analysis of the Self.* New York: International Universities Press.

—— (1977). *The Restoration of the Self.* New York: International Universities Press.

Langs, R. (1973). *The Technique of Psychoanalytic Psychotherapy.* Vol. 1. New York: Jason Aronson.

—— (1974). *The Technique of Psychoanalytic Psychotherapy.* Vol. 2. New York: Jason Aronson.

—— (1975a). Therapeutic misalliances. *International Journal of Psychoanalytic Psychotherapy* 4:77–105.

—— (1975b). The therapeutic relationship and deviations in technique. *International Journal of Psychoanalytic Psychotherapy* 4:106–141.

—— (1976a). On becoming a psychiatrist: Discussion of "Empathy and intuition on becoming a psychiatrist: A case study" by Ronald J. Blank. *International Journal of Psychoanalytic Psychotherapy* 5:255–280.

—— (1976b). *The Bipersonal Field.* New York: Jason Aronson.

—— (1976c). *The Therapeutic Interaction.* 2 vols. New York: Jason Aronson.

—— (1978a) *The Listening Process.* New York: Jason Aronson.

—— (1978b). The adaptational-interactional dimension of countertransference. In *Technique in Transition,* pp. 537–588. New York: Jason Aronson.

—— (1978c). Interventions in the bipersonal field. In *Technique in Transition.* pp. 627–674. New York: Jason Aronson.

—— (1978d). Validation and the framework of the therapeutic situation. *Contemporary Psychoanalysis* 14:98–124.

—— (1979). *The Therapeutic Environment.* New York: Jason Aronson.

—— (1980a). *Interactions: The Realm of Transference and Countertransference.* New York: Jason Aronson.

—— (1980b). On the properties of an interpretation. *Contemporary Psychoanalysis* 16:460–478.

—— (1980c). Modes of "cure" in psychoanalysis and psychoanalytic psychotherapy. *International Journal of Psycho-Analysis,* in press.

—— (1980d). Interactional and communicative aspects of resistance. *Contemporary Psychoanalysis* 16:16–52.

Leites, N. (1977). Transference interpretations only? *International Journal of Psycho-Analysis* 58:275–288.

—— (1979). *Interpreting Transference.* New York: W. W. Norton.

Lipton, S. (1977). Clinical observations on resistance to the transference. *International Journal of Psycho-Analysis* 58:463–472.

Little, M. (1951). Countertransference and the patient's response to it. *International Journal of Psycho-Analysis* 58:255–274.

Loewald, H. (1960). The therapeutic action of psycho-analysis. *International Journal of Psycho-Analysis* 41:16–33.

Loewenstein, R. (1954). Some remarks on defenses, autonomous ego and psychoanalytic technique. *International Journal of Psycho-Analysis* 35:188–193.

Racker, G. de (1961). On the formulation of the interpretation. *International Journal of Psycho-Analysis* 42:49–54.

Racker, H. (1957). The meaning and uses of countertransference. *Psychoanalytic Quarterly* 26:303–357.

Reich, W. (1928). On character analysis. In *The Psychoanalytic Reader,* ed. R. Fleiss, pp. 129–147. New York: International Universities Press, 1948.

—— (1929). The genital character and the neurotic character. In *The Psychoanalytic Reader,* ed. R. Fleiss, pp. 148–169. New York: International Universities Press, 1948.

—— (1933 [1949]). *Character Analysis.* New York: Noonday Press.

Sandler, J. (1976). Countertransference and role-responsiveness. *International Review of Psycho-Analysis* 3:43–47.

Sandler, J., Dare, C., and Holder, A. (1973). *The Patient and the Analyst: The Basis of the Psychoanalytic Process.* New York: International Universities Press.

Sandler, J. and Joffe, W. (1969). Toward a basic psychoanalytic model. *International Journal of Psycho-Analysis* 50:79–90.

Sandler, J. and Sandler, A. (1978). On the development of object relationships and affects. *International Journal of Psycho-Analysis* 49:285–296.

Searles, H. (1965). *Collected Papers on Schizophrenia and Related Subjects.* New York: International Universities Press.

—— (1973). Concerning therapeutic symbiosis. *Annual of Psychoanalysis* 1:247–262.

—— (1975). The patient as therapist to his analyst. In *Tactics and Techniques in Psychoanalytic Therapy. Vol. II: Countertransference,* ed. P. Giovacchini, pp. 95–151. New York: Jason Aronson.

Stone, L. (1973). On resistance to the psychoanalytic process: some thoughts on its nature and motivations. In *Psychoanalysis and Contemporary Science. Vol. 2,* ed. B. Rubinstein. New York: Macmillan, pp. 42–73.

Weinchel, E. (1979). Some observations on not telling the truth. *Journal of the American Psychoanalytic Association* 27:503–532.

Index

Abreaction, 602
Abstracting-particularizing process,
  719
Acting in, 120
Acting out, 426–427, 440, 466
  Freud's concept of, 468–469
  interactional, 206–207, 212
  modification of frame as, 574
  by therapist, 213
Active interventions, 244, 254–255
Adaptational-interactional viewpoint,
  719
Adaptation-evoking context, 10
  responses to, 48, 154–155
Adaptive context, 19, 42, 155, 707,
  719–720
  background, 697
  change in framework as, 204
  clarity of representation of, 44
  communicative resistance and,
    147–148
  forced termination as, 171–172, 175
  ideal representation of, 130
  as identical with indicator, 67
  implications of, 208–209
  and indicators, 212, 635
  layering of, 252
  link to, 317
  manifest allusion to, 264, 582–583
  multiple, 180–181, 183, 531–532, 654
  need of, 329, 331
  primary, 212, 720
  representation of, 441, 442, 720
  repressed, 582–583
  resistances and, 529–533
  secondary, 212, 318, 720
    patient's break in frame as, 246
  supervision as, 4–5

synonyms for, 10–11, 43n
tape recording as, 58–59
Adaptive context interpretations,
  674–675
Adler, G., 642
Alliance sector, 720–721
  see also therapeutic alliance
Analyst, idealized image of, 137
Anonymity, modification of, 109
Anxiety
  castration, 57
  evoked by insight, 376–377
  primitive, 545–546
  separation, 32, 102
Arlow, J., 482
Associational matrix, see
  communication network
Associations, functional capacity of, 63
Autism, therapeutic, 701
Autistic relationship, 29, 161
Avoidance, 149, 160–61
  mutual, 358

Baranger, M., 220, 544, 721
Baranger, W., 220, 544, 721
Barchilon, J., 387
Barriers
  tape recording as, 11
  Type C, 92, 217, 575
  see also lie-barrier systems
Bastions, 342, 360, 544, 721
  indicators of, 369
  patient's commentary on, 366–367
  shared lie-barrier system as, 375
Bibring, E., 14, 602, 603
Bion, W.R., 6, 29, 52–53, 384, 531, 552,
  609, 627, 629, 639, 666, 673, 689,
  709, 726, 729, 742, 749